CHARTERS OF NORTHERN HOUSES

ANGLO-SAXON CHARTERS

1 CHARTERS OF ROCHESTER, edited by A. Campbell (1973)
2 CHARTERS OF BURTON ABBEY, edited by P. H. Sawyer (1979)
3 CHARTERS OF SHERBORNE, edited by M. A. O'Donovan (1988)
4 CHARTERS OF ST AUGUSTINE'S ABBEY, CANTERBURY, AND MINSTER-IN-THANET, edited by S. E. Kelly (1995)
5 CHARTERS OF SHAFTESBURY ABBEY, edited by S. E. Kelly (1996)
6 CHARTERS OF SELSEY, edited by S. E. Kelly (1998)
7 CHARTERS OF ABINGDON ABBEY 1, edited by S. E. Kelly (2000)
8 CHARTERS OF ABINGDON ABBEY 2, edited by S. E. Kelly (2001)
9 CHARTERS OF THE NEW MINSTER, WINCHESTER, edited by S. Miller (2001)
10 CHARTERS OF ST PAUL'S, LONDON, edited by S. E. Kelly (2004)
11 CHARTERS OF MALMESBURY ABBEY, edited by S. E. Kelly (2005)
12 CHARTERS OF ST ALBANS, edited by Julia Crick (2007)
13 CHARTERS OF BATH AND WELLS, edited by S. E. Kelly (2007)
14 CHARTERS OF PETERBOROUGH ABBEY, edited by S. E. Kelly (2009)
15 CHARTERS OF GLASTONBURY ABBEY, edited by S. E. Kelly (2012)
16 CHARTERS OF NORTHERN HOUSES, edited by D. A. Woodman (2012)

Supplementary volumes

1 FACSIMILES OF ANGLO-SAXON CHARTERS, edited by Simon Keynes (1991)

ANGLO-SAXON CHARTERS · 16

CHARTERS OF NORTHERN HOUSES

EDITED BY

D. A. WOODMAN

Published for THE BRITISH ACADEMY
by OXFORD UNIVERSITY PRESS

Oxford University Press, Great Clarendon Street, Oxford OX2 6DP

First edition published in 2012

British Library Cataloguing in Publication Data
Data available

Library of Congress Cataloging in Publication Data
Data available

Typeset by 4word Ltd, Bristol
Printed and bound by CPI Group (UK) Ltd, Croydon, CR0 4YY

ISBN 978-0-19-726529-1

TO MY MOTHER AND FATHER

FOREWORD

Dr David Woodman's edition of the extant pre-Conquest charters from northern English houses takes this series for the first time north of the river Humber. Despite Northumbria's huge contribution, both politically and culturally, to the development of English identity in the Early Middle Ages, its violent military history has unfortunately ensured that early medieval documentary records have been very much more sparsely preserved in the north than in midland, southern or eastern archives. In making all the earliest extant charters from the north available in a single superb critical edition, Dr Woodman has therefore made a huge contribution to the political, ecclesiastical and economic history of the region, especially in the tenth and eleventh centuries, and to northern archival, cultural and linguistic history over the whole medieval period. The twenty-one charters edited here come from four different ecclesiastical houses: York, Durham, Ripon and Beverley, while a single document comes from the archive of the Marquess of Lowther. The contrasts between the practices of record-keeping in different northern centres have much to tell us of their variant ecclesiastical fortunes throughout the Middle Ages, while the inclusion of the single writ of Gospatric extends the geographical range of this volume uniquely into Cumberland and also shows how the writ form was being used by lay lords in the eleventh century to make public pronouncements about their landed and fiscal rights; it serves to emphasise what a huge quantity of pre-Conquest lay vernacular documents have been lost to us because the archives of the late Anglo-Saxon aristocracy have not survived.

This is the sixteenth volume in the series organised under the auspices of the research project on Anglo-Saxon Charters set up jointly by the British Academy and the Royal Historical Society to provide a critical edition of all the surviving pre-Conquest charters. It is particularly welcome in introducing a new scholar into the select fellowship of those who have succeeded in bringing these complex interdisciplinary editions to completion. The organisation of editions in this series, archive by archive, posed the project committee from the start with the problem of how best to cope with the archives which had too few charters to comprise a single volume on their own. This is therefore the first of the 'portmanteau' volumes, which will gather the charters from several small archives in related areas together to form viable volumes editing documents from specific regions.

The project committee was therefore delighted when Dr Woodman's doctoral studies were devoted to the charters from the archives of both York and Durham, but it owes him a much greater debt for his willingness, despite modern pressures on academics for speedy publication, to include within this volume all the early extant charters from the whole of northern England and to increase from two to five the archives whose history over the last thirteen hundred or so years he has had to master. Thereby he has created a volume which is a triumph of comparative scholarship and which will become a fundamental resource for northern historians, geographers and philologists who have early medieval interests. In this work Dr Woodman has had extensive assistance from several members of the research project's Committee: especially from its Director and Honorary Treasurer (and his research supervisor), Professor Simon Keynes, from the co-ordinating editor, Dr Susan Kelly, whose knowledge of the whole corpus and expertise in bringing volumes to publication is unrivalled, and Mrs Joy Jenkyns, whose Langscape project has helped him to make sense of some very corrupt boundary clauses. Several other members of the Committee (currently comprising in addition Professor John Blair, Dr Julia Crick, Professor Sarah Foot, Dr Rosalind Love, Dr David Parsons, Dr Rebecca Rushforth, Professor Richard Sharpe, Professor Eric Stanley and myself, as Chairman) have given advice on specific points or at earlier stages of the enterprise. This edition is therefore a welcome further example of the benefits of this project's ability to make progress through generous collaboration. It is a huge privilege to chair its proceedings and to welcome this new addition to the series.

NICHOLAS BROOKS

CONTENTS

BEVERLEY

RIPON

DURHAM

ILLUSTRATIONS

PLATES

MAPS

ACKNOWLEDGEMENTS

My foremost debt is to my undergraduate teacher and doctoral supervisor, Professor Simon Keynes. It was singular good fortune which first delivered me into his guidance as an undergraduate student and I have profited from his inspirational scholarship ever since. Given his own interests, it was a natural progression for me to work, as a graduate, on Anglo-Saxon charters, and this book has benefited at every turn from Professor Keynes' advice. I owe a similar debt of gratitude to Professor Nicholas Brooks (who examined the PhD thesis that lies at the core of this volume) and Dr Susan Kelly. They have been unfailingly patient, not only in reading many draft versions of the whole work, but also in answering numerous queries. My work has been much improved by their learned advice. In a feat of great generosity, Dr Lesley Abrams read, and commented, on a copy of the entire volume and I am singularly grateful to her for her numerous suggested improvements. All of the research that has gone into this book was conducted while I was a member of the Department of Anglo-Saxon, Norse and Celtic in the University of Cambridge. Dr Rosalind Love, who also examined my PhD thesis, has offered support beyond what could be expected of a friend and colleague, for which I cannot adequately express my gratitude. Other members of the same Department have given advice: I am indebted to Dr Richard Dance, Dr Fiona Edmonds, Dr Helen Foxhall Forbes, Dr Rory Naismith, Mr Levi Roach and Dr Peter Stokes, who have instructed me respectively on issues of Old and Middle English, the history of the north west of England, on matters to do with the Anglo-Saxon church, on the coinage of Anglo-Saxon England, on continental charters and on various palaeographical problems. For any errors that remain in the volume I must take the responsibility.

My PhD dissertation, which comprised an edition of the charters preserved in York Minster and Durham Cathedral, was written while I was a student at Trinity College, Cambridge, with the aid of an award from the Arts and Humanities Research Council. I am extremely grateful to both institutions for their support. The simultaneous awards of a British Academy Postdoctoral Research Fellowship and a Research Fellowship at Robinson College, Cambridge, provided me with the invaluable opportunity of adding to the volume the charters preserved in the archives of Beverley and Ripon Minsters and a rare surviving writ from Lowther. My time at Robinson College, among the Warden and Fellows, has proved inspiring: in particular, Dr Martin Brett has been consistently kind in discussing and answering many queries about manifold aspects of medieval history.

Anyone who works on a volume for the Anglo-Saxon Charters series benefits from the expert advice of the Charters committee, from Professor John Blair, Dr Julia Crick, Dr David Parsons, Dr Rebecca Rushforth and Professor Richard Sharpe, and I am certainly no exception to this. Work on the northern archives, in particular on the York archive, has involved the interpretation of Old English boundary clauses and name-forms that are highly corrupt: here I was extremely fortunate to receive advice from Mrs Joy Jenkyns and Professor Eric Stanley, and, as will be clear from the edited texts, my interpretations of the boundary clauses in the York charters have relied heavily on the work done for the LangScape project (http://www.langscape.org.uk/index.html) by Mrs Joy Jenkyns, to whom I am most grateful for making this available to me. The palaeographical issues provided by the document edited below as **21** were equally complicated and I am thankful for the expert guidance given to me by Dr Julia Crick and Dr Teresa Webber. In similar fashion, Dr Stephen Baxter made various suggestions about the interpretation of evidence from Domesday Book, and other matters, which have served only to improve this book. My research into the northern archives involved many visits to different libraries around the country, during which Mr Julian Harrison of the British Library brought to my attention a York cartulary which contains previously unknown copies of **1** and **8**, Mr Peter Young helped me with the York Minster archives and Mr Alan Piper and Dr Michael Stansfield, of Durham University Library, advised me and guided me through the Durham collections. I am similarly grateful to Mr Peter Kidd who, very close to the end of my work on the northern charters, alerted me to a copy of **12** in a manuscript in the Schøyen collection, which was about to be put up for sale.

In addition to all those people who have helped and encouraged me with my academic studies, during my time in Cambridge, and afterwards, I have been fortunate enough to have some quite exceptional friends. No little thanks are due to Ashley Bown, Jordana Burdon Bailey, Will Catton, Catherine Craig, Grace Cullen, Alan Doyle, Dan Gammon, Dan Holland, Dan Jane, Anthony Leyton-Thomas, Richard Loke, Camille Naish, Chris Pedder, Christophe Salvat, Peter Smye, Stuart Schofield and Alex Wilshaw. My brother, John, has been steadfastly supportive.

Having grown up in the shadow of Durham Cathedral, it seems inevitable that my interests have always been focused on the Northumbrian church and in particular on St Cuthbert's community. Were it not for my parents and their constant support and encouragement, I would never have started, let alone finished, this research. This book is dedicated to them.

ABBREVIATIONS

BL	London, British Library
Bodleian	Oxford, Bodleian Library
CACC	Cumbria Archive Centre, Carlisle
CCCC	Cambridge, Corpus Christi College
D. & C.	Dean and Chapter
GDB	Great Domesday Book
Mag. Reg. Alb.	*Magnum Registrum Album*
ON	Old Norse
s.	*saeculo*
TNA: PRO	London, The National Archives, Public Record Office
TRE	*Tempore Regis Eadwardi*
TRW	*Tempore Regis Willelmi*

BIBLIOGRAPHICAL ABBREVIATIONS

AA	*Archaeologia Aeliana*
Abing	For 'Kelly, *Abingdon*' in citations of charters
Abrams 2000	L. Abrams, 'Conversion and Assimilation' in Hadley and Richards, *Cultures in Contact*, pp. 135–53
Abrams 2001	L. Abrams, 'The Conversion of the Danelaw', *Vikings and the Danelaw: Select Papers from the Proceedings of the Thirteenth Viking Congress, Nottingham and York, 21–30 August 1997*, ed. J. Graham-Campbell, R. Hall, J. Jesch and D.N. Parsons (Oxford, 2001), pp. 31–44
Abrams 2008	L. Abrams, 'King Edgar and the Men of the Danelaw' in Scragg, *Edgar,* pp. 171–91
Abrams and Parsons 2004	L. Abrams and D.N. Parsons, 'Place-Names and the History of Scandinavian Settlement in England', in Hines *et al.*, *Land, Sea and Home*, pp. 379–431
Aird, *St Cuthbert*	W.M. Aird, *St Cuthbert and the Normans: the Church of Durham, 1071–1153* (Woodbridge, 1998)

Aird 1992	W.M. Aird, 'The Making of a Medieval Miracle Collection: the *Liber de translationibus et miraculis sancti Cuthberti*', *NH* xxviii (1992), pp. 1–24
Alcuin, *Ep.*	*Epistolae Alcuini*, ed. E. Dümmler, MGH Epp. IV, Epistolae Karolini Aeui II, (Berlin, 1895)
Alcuin, *Versus*	Alcuin, *Versus de Patribus Regibus et Sanctis Euboricensis Ecclesiae*
Allott, *Alcuin*	*Alcuin of York*, ed. S. Allott (York, 1974; repr. 1987)
AND	*Anglo-Norman Durham 1093–1193*, ed. D.W. Rollason, M. Harvey and M. Prestwich (Woodbridge, 1994)
Angenendt 2004	A. Angenendt, 'How was a Confraternity Made? The Evidence of Charters', in Rollason *et al.*, *The Durham*, pp. 207–19
Armstrong *et al.*, *Excavations*	*Excavations at Lurk Lane Beverley, 1979–82*, ed. P. Armstrong, D. Tomlinson and D.H. Evans, Sheffield Excavation Reports i (Sheffield, 1991)
Arnold, *Sym. Op.*	*Symeonis Monachi Opera Omnia*, ed. T. Arnold, RS lxxv, 2 vols (London, 1882–5)
ASC	*Anglo-Saxon Chronicle*
ASE	*Anglo-Saxon England*
Aylmer and Cant, *History*	*A History of York Minster*, ed. G.E. Aylmer and R. Cant (Oxford, 1977)
Bailey 1991	R.N. Bailey, 'St Wilfrid: Ripon and Hexham', *Studies in Insular Art and Archaeology*, ed. C. Karkov and R. Farrell, American Early Medieval Studies i (1991), pp. 3–25
BAR	British Archaeological Reports
Barker 1977	E.E. Barker, 'Two Lost Documents of King Athelstan', *ASE* vi (1977), pp. 137–43
Barker, *York Gospels*	*The York Gospels*, ed. N. Barker, The Roxburghe Club (London, 1986)
Barlow, *English Church*	F. Barlow, *The English Church 1000–1066: a History of the Later Anglo-Saxon Church*, 2nd edn (London, 1979)
Barr 1977	C.B.L. Barr, 'The Minster Library', in Aylmer and Cant, *History*, pp. 487–539
Barr 1986	C.B.L. Barr, 'The History of the Volume', in Barker, *York Gospels*, pp. 101–17
Barrow 1994	J. Barrow, 'English Cathedral Communities and Reform in the Late Tenth and Eleventh Centuries', in *AND*, pp. 25–39
Barrow 2000	J. Barrow, 'Survival and Mutation: Ecclesiastical Institutions in the Danelaw in the Ninth and Tenth Centuries', in Hadley and Richards, *Cultures in Contact*, pp. 155–76
Barrow 2004	J. Barrow, 'Oscytel', in *ODNB*, vol. xlii, ed. H.C.G. Matthew and B. Harrison (Oxford, 2004), pp. 41–2
Bates, *RRAN: William I*	*Regesta Regum Anglo-Normannorum: the Acta of William I (1066–1087)*, ed. D. Bates (Oxford, 1998)

Bath	For 'Kelly, *Bath and Wells*' in citations of charters
Battiscombe, *Relics*	*The Relics of St Cuthbert*, ed. C.F. Battiscombe (Oxford, 1956)
Baxter 2004	S. Baxter, 'Archbishop Wulfstan and the Administration of God's Property', in Townend, *Wulfstan*, pp. 161–205
BCS	For 'Birch' in citations of charters
Bede, *Epistola*	Bede, *Epistola ad Ecgbertum*, in Plummer, *Bede* I, pp. 405–23
Bede, *HE*	Bede, *Historia Ecclesiastica*
Bede, *VCP*	Bede, *Vita sancti Cuthberti prosaica auctore Beda*, in Colgrave, *Two Lives*, pp. 142–307
Birch	W. de G. Birch, *Cartularium Saxonicum*, 3 vols (London, 1885–93)
Bishop 1981	M.W. Bishop, 'Multiple Estates in Late Anglo-Saxon Nottinghamshire', *Trans of Thoroton Soc.* lxxxv (1981), pp. 37–47
Blackburn 2004	M. Blackburn, 'The Coinage of Scandinavian York', in Hall (R.A.) *et al.*, *Aspects*, pp. 325–49
Blackwell	*The Blackwell Encyclopedia of Anglo-Saxon England*, ed. M. Lapidge, J. Blair, S. Keynes and D. Scragg (Oxford, 1999)
Blair, *Church*	J. Blair, *The Church in Anglo-Saxon Society* (Oxford, 2005)
Blair 1991	J. Blair, 'The Early Churches at Lindisfarne', *AA*^{5} xix (1991), pp. 47–53
Blair 1992	J. Blair, 'Anglo-Saxon Minsters: a Topographical Review', *Pastoral Care Before the Parish*, ed. J. Blair and R. Sharpe (London, 1992), pp. 226–66
Blair 2001	J. Blair, 'Beverley, *Inderauuda* and St John: A Neglected Reference', *NH* xxxviii (2001), pp. 315–16.
Blair (P.H.) 1949	P.H. Blair, 'The Boundary between Bernicia and Deira', *AA*^{4} xxvii (1949), pp. 46–59 (repr. in his *Anglo-Saxon Northumbria*, ed. M. Lapidge and Pauline H. Blair [London, 1984], no. V)
Blair (P.H.) 1963	P.H. Blair, 'Some Observations on the *Historia Regum* Attributed to Symeon of Durham', *Celt and Saxon: Studies in the Early British Border*, ed. N.K. Chadwick (Cambridge, 1963), pp. 63–118 (repr. in his *Anglo-Saxon Northumbria*, ed. M. Lapidge and Pauline H. Blair [London, 1984], no. IX)
BNJ	*British Numismatic Journal*
Boffey and Edwards, *Index*	J. Boffey and A.S.G. Edwards, *A New Index of Middle English Verse* (London, 2005)
Bolton, *Cnut*	T. Bolton, *The Empire of Cnut the Great: Conquest and the Consolidation of Power in Northern Europe in the Early Eleventh Century*, The Northern World (Leiden and Boston, 2009)

Bonner 1989	G. Bonner, 'St Cuthbert at Chester-le-Street', in *St Cuthbert*, pp. 387–96
Breeze 1992	A. Breeze, 'Old English *Wassenas* 'Retainers' in Gospatrick's Writ', *Notes and Queries* xxxix (1992), pp. 272–5
Briggs 2004	E. Briggs, 'Nothing but Names: the Original Core of the Durham *Liber Vitae*' in Rollason *et al.*, *The Durham*, pp. 63–85
Brooks, *Church of Canterbury*	N. Brooks, *The Early History of the Church of Canterbury: Christ Church from 597 to 1066* (Leicester, 1984)
Brooks 2000	N. Brooks, 'Anglo-Saxon Charters: A Review of Work 1953–73; with a Postscript on the Period 1973–98' in his *Anglo-Saxon Myths: State and Church 400–1066* (London, 2000), pp. 181–215
Brooks and Kelly, *Christ Church, Canterbury*	*Charters of Christ Church, Canterbury*, ed. N. Brooks and S.E. Kelly, Anglo-Saxon Charters (Oxford, forthcoming)
Brooks and Cubitt, *St Oswald*	*St Oswald of Worcester: Life and Influence*, ed. N. Brooks and C.R.E. Cubitt (London and New York, 1996)
Brooks, Gelling and Johnson 1984	N. Brooks, M. Gelling and D. Johnson, 'A New Charter of King Edgar', *ASE* xiii (1984), pp. 137–55
Broun 2004	D. Broun, 'The Welsh Identity of the Kingdom of Strathclyde *c.* 900–*c.* 1200', *The Innes Review* lv (2004), pp. 111–180
Brown *et al.*, *Index*	*The Index of Middle English Verse*, ed. C. Brown and R.H. Robbins (New York, 1943)
Brown, *Durham Ritual*	T.J. Brown, *The Durham Ritual: A Southern English Collectar of the Tenth Century with Northumbrian Additions: Durham Cathedral Library A.IV.19*, Early English Manuscripts in Facsimile xvi (Copenhagen, 1969)
Bullough, *Alcuin*	D.A. Bullough, *Alcuin: Achievement and Reputation, Being Part of the Ford Lectures Delivered in Oxford in Hilary Term 1980* (Brill, 2004)
Bullough 1983	D.A. Bullough, 'Burial, Community and Belief in the Early Medieval West', *Ideal and Reality in Frankish and Anglo-Saxon Society: Studies Presented to J.M. Wallace-Hadrill*, ed. P. Wormald with D.A. Bullough and R. Collins (Oxford, 1983), pp. 177–201
Burt	For 'Sawyer, *Burton*' in citations of charters
Byrhtferth, *VSO*	Byrhtferth, *Vita sancti Oswaldi*, ed. M. Lapidge in *Byrhtferth of Ramsey: The Lives of St Oswald and St Ecgwine*, Oxford Medieval Texts (Oxford, 2008), pp. 2–203
Cambridge 1984	E. Cambridge, 'The Early Church in County Durham: a Reassessment', *Journal of the British Archaeological Association* cxxxvii (1984), pp. 65–85
Cambridge 1989	E. Cambridge, 'Why did the Community of St Cuthbert Settle at Chester-le-Street?', in *St Cuthbert*, pp. 367–86
CamDEPN	*The Cambridge Dictionary of English Place-Names*, ed. V. Watts (Cambridge, 2004)

Campbell 1989 — J. Campbell, 'Elements in the Background to the Life of St Cuthbert and his Early Cult', in *St Cuthbert*, pp. 3–20

CantCC — For 'Brooks and Kelly, *Christ Church, Canterbury*' in citations of charters

CantStA — For 'Kelly, *St Augustine's*' in citations of charters

CB — *Continuatio Bedae*, in Colgrave and Mynors, *Bede's Ecclesiastical History*, pp. 572–6

Chaplais 1962 — P. Chaplais, 'The Original Charters of Herbert and Gervase Abbots of Westminster (1121–1157)', *A Medieval Miscellany for Doris Mary Stenton*, ed. P.M. Barnes and C.F. Slade (Pipe Roll Society, New Series XXXVI, London, 1962), pp. 89–110 (repr. in his *Essays in Medieval Diplomacy and Administration* [London, 1981], no. XVIII)

Chaplais 1965 — P. Chaplais, 'The Origin and Authenticity of the Royal Anglo-Saxon Diploma', *JSA* iii.2 (1965), pp. 48–61 (repr. in Ranger, *Prisca Munimenta*, pp. 28–42)

Chaplais 1966 — P. Chaplais, 'The Anglo-Saxon Chancery: from the Diploma to the Writ', *JSA* iii.4 (1966), pp. 160–76 (repr. in Ranger, *Prisca Munimenta*, pp. 43–62)

Chaplais 1969 — P. Chaplais, 'Who Introduced Charters into England? The Case for Augustine', *JSA* iii.10 (1969), pp. 526–42 (repr. in Ranger, *Prisca Munimenta*, pp. 88–107)

Chaplais 1985 — P. Chaplais, 'The Royal Anglo-Saxon "Chancery" of the Tenth Century Revisited', *Studies in Medieval History presented to R.H.C. Davies*, ed. H. Mayr-Harting and R.I. Moore (London, 1985), pp. 41–51

Charles-Edwards, *Ireland* — T.M. Charles-Edwards, *Early Christian Ireland* (Cambridge, 2000)

Cheney and Jones, *Handbook* — *A Handbook of Dates: for Students of British History*, Royal Historical Society Guides and Handbooks iv, ed. C.R. Cheney and rev. M. Jones, rev. edn (London, 2000; repr. Cambridge, 2004)

Chronicle of the Archbishops of York — *Chronicle of the Archbishops of York*, ed. Raine, *HCY* II, pp. 312–87

Chronicon Æthelweardi — *Chronicon Æthelweardi*, ed. A. Campbell (London, 1962)

Clay, *YMF* — C.T. Clay, *York Minster Fasti; being Notes on the Dignitaries, Archdeacons and Prebendaries in the Church of York prior to the Year 1307*, The Yorkshire Archaeological Society, Record Series CXXIII–CXXIV, 2 vols (Wakefield, 1958–9)

CMD — *Cronica monasterii Dunelmensis*, reconstructed in Craster 1925*a*, pp. 523–29, to which references relate

Coates 2002 — Coates, 'Beverley: A Beaver's Lodge Place', *Journal of the English Place-Name Society* xxxiv (2002), pp. 17–22

Coatsworth, *Corpus* — E. Coatsworth, *Corpus of Anglo-Saxon Stone Sculpture, VIII: Western Yorkshire* (Oxford, 2008)

Colgrave, *Life of Wilfrid*	*The Life of Bishop Wilfrid by Eddius Stephanus*, ed. B. Colgrave (Cambridge, 1927)
Colgrave, *Two Lives*	B. Colgrave, *Two Lives of Saint Cuthbert* (Cambridge, 1940)
Colgrave 1950	B. Colgrave, 'The Post-Bedan Miracles and Translations of St Cuthbert', *The Early Cultures of North-West Europe: H.M. Chadwick Memorial Studies*, ed. C. Fox and B. Dickins (Cambridge, 1950), pp. 307–32
Colgrave 1958	B. Colgrave, 'The Earliest Saints' Lives Written in England', *Proceedings of the British Academy* xliv (1958), pp. 35–60
Colgrave and Mynors, *Bede's Ecclesiastical History*	*Bede's Ecclesiastical History of the English People*, ed. B. Colgrave and R.A.B. Mynors, Oxford Medieval Texts (Oxford, 1969; rev. edn 1991)
Cooper, *Archbishops of York*	J. Cooper, *The Last Four Anglo-Saxon Archbishops of York*, Borthwick Paper no. 38, University of York (York, 1970)
Cooper 1968	J. Cooper, 'The Dates of the Bishops of Durham in the First Half of the Eleventh Century', *Durham University Journal* lx (1968), pp. 131–7
Cooper 1969	J. Cooper, 'The List of Ælfric's Festermen in the York Gospels', *YAJ* xlii.3 (1969), pp. 328–32
Councils and Synods	*Councils & Synods with other Documents Relating to the English Church, I: A.D. 871–1204*, ed. D. Whitelock, M. Brett and C.N.L. Brooke, 2 pts (Oxford, 1981)
Cramp, *Anglian and Viking York*	R.J. Cramp, *Anglian and Viking York*, Borthwick Paper no. 33, University of York (York, 1967)
Cramp, *Corpus*	R.J. Cramp, *Corpus of Anglo-Saxon Stone Sculpture, i (Parts 1 and 2): Co. Durham and Northumberland* (Oxford, 1984)
Cramp 1970	R.J. Cramp, 'The Position of the Otley Crosses in English Sculpture of the Eighth to Ninth Centuries', *Kolloquium Über Spätantike und Frühmittelalterliche Skulptur* ii (1970), pp. 55–63
Craster 1925*a*	E. Craster, 'The Red Book of Durham', *EHR* xl (1925), pp. 504–32
Craster 1925*b*	E. Craster, 'Some Anglo-Saxon Records of the See of Durham', *AA*^{4} i (1925), pp. 189–98
Craster 1954	E. Craster, 'The Patrimony of St Cuthbert', *EHR* lxix (1954), pp. 177–99
Craster 1957	E. Craster, 'The Peace of St Cuthbert', *JEH* viii (1957), pp. 93–5
Crick, *St Albans*	*Charters of St Albans*, ed. J. Crick, Anglo-Saxon Charters xii (Oxford, 2007)
Cubitt, *Councils*	C.R.E. Cubitt, *Anglo-Saxon Church Councils* c. *650*– c. *850* (London, 1995)
Cubitt 1989	C.R.E. Cubitt, 'Wilfrid's "Usurping Bishops": Episcopal Elections in Anglo-Saxon England *c.* 600–*c.* 800', *NH* xxv (1989), pp. 18–38

Davies (G.T.) 1983 — G.T. Davies, 'The Anglo-Saxon Boundaries of Sutton and Scrooby, Nottinghamshire', *Trans of Thoroton Soc.* lxxxvii (1983), pp. 13–22

Davies (J.C.) 1951–2 — J.C. Davies, 'The Muniments of the Dean and Chapter of Durham', *Durham University Journal* xliv (1951–2), pp. 77–87

Davis, *Cartularies* — G.R.C. Davis, *Medieval Cartularies of Great Britain: a Short Catalogue* (London, 1958)

Davis, *Cartularies* (rev. edn) — G.R.C. Davis, *Medieval Cartularies of Great Britain and Ireland*, revised by C. Breay, J. Harrison and D.M. Smith (London, 2010)

Davis 1905 — H.W.C. Davis, 'Cumberland Before the Norman Conquest', *EHR* xx (1905), pp. 61–5

DEPN — E. Ekwall, *The Concise Oxford Dictionary of English Place-Names*, 4th edn (Oxford, 1960)

Dickens 1961 — A.G. Dickens, 'York before the Norman Conquest', *A History of Yorkshire: The City of York*, ed. P.M. Tillott, The Victoria County History of the Counties of England (Oxford, 1961), pp. 2–24

Dixon, Owen and Stocker 2001 — P. Dixon, O. Owen and D. Stocker, 'The Southwell Lintel, its Style and Significance', *Vikings and the Danelaw: Select Papers from the Proceedings of the Thirteenth Viking Congress, Nottingham and York, 21–30 August 1997*, ed. J. Graham-Campbell, R. Hall, J. Jesch and D.N. Parsons (Oxford, 2001), pp. 245–68

DMLBS — *Dictionary of Medieval Latin from British Sources*, ed. R.E. Latham and D.R. Howlett (London, 1975–)

Dolley 1978 — R.H.M. Dolley, 'The Anglo-Danish and Anglo-Norse Coinages of York', in Hall (R.A.), *Viking Age York*, pp. 26–31

Downham, *Viking Kings* — C. Downham, *Viking Kings of Britain and Ireland: The Dynasty of Ívarr to A.D. 1014* (Edinburgh, 2007)

Doyle 1992 — S. Doyle, 'The Barrington Manuscripts: from Durham to the Inner Temple', *The Law Librarian* xxiii, no. 2 (1992), pp. 66–74

Drögereit 1935 — R. Drögereit, 'Gab es eine Angelsächsische Königskanzlei?', *Archiv für Urkundenforschung* xiii (1935), pp. 335–436

Dugdale, *St Paul's* — W. Dugdale, *The History of St Paul's Cathedral in London, from its Foundation*. Appendix: *An Historical Account of the Northern Cathedrals, and Chief Collegiate Churches in the Province of York*, 2nd edn with author's corrections and additions (London, 1716)

Dumville, *Wessex and England* — D.N. Dumville, *Wessex and England from Alfred to Edgar: Six Essays in Political, Cultural and Ecclesiastical Revival* (Woodbridge, 1992)

Dumville 2004	D.N. Dumville, 'Old Dubliners and New Dubliners in Ireland and Britain: a Viking-Age Story', *Medieval Dublin* vi (2004), pp. 78–93
Earle, *Hand-Book*	J. Earle, *A Hand-Book to the Land-Charters, and other Saxonic Documents* (Oxford, 1888)
Edmonds 2009	F. Edmonds, 'Personal Names and the Cult of Patrick in Eleventh-Century Strathclyde and Northumbria', *Saints' Cults in the Celtic World*, ed. S. Boardman, J.R. Davies and E. Williamson, Studies in Celtic History xxv (Woodbridge, 2009), pp. 41–65
EHR	*English Historical Review*
Ekwall, *Scandinavians*	E. Ekwall, *Scandinavians and Celts in the North-West of England* (Lund, 1918)
EPNS	English Place-Name Society
Faith, *English Peasantry*	R. Faith, *The English Peasantry and The Growth of Lordship* (London, 1997)
Farmer 1974	D.H. Farmer, 'Saint Wilfrid', in Kirby, *Saint Wilfrid*, pp. 35–59
Farrer, *EYC*	*Early Yorkshire Charters*, vol. I, ed. W. Farrer (Edinburgh, 1914)
Faull and Moorhouse, *West Yorkshire*	*West Yorkshire: an Archaeological Survey to A.D. 1500*, 3 vols, ed. M.L. Faull and S.A. Moorhouse (West Yorkshire, 1981)
Fellows-Jensen, *SPNLY*	G. Fellows-Jensen, *Scandinavian Personal Names in Lincolnshire and Yorkshire*, Navnestudier 7 (Copenhagen, 1968)
Fellows-Jensen, *SSNEM*	G. Fellows-Jensen, *Scandinavian Settlement Names in the East Midlands*, Navnestudier 16 (Copenhagen, 1978)
Fellows-Jensen, *SSNNW*	G. Fellows-Jensen, *Scandinavian Settlement Names in the North-West*, Navnestudier 25 (Copenhagen, 1985)
Fellows-Jensen 1977	G. Fellows-Jensen, 'Place-Names and Settlement History: a Review', *NH* xiii (1977), pp. 1–26
Fellows-Jensen 1990	G. Fellows-Jensen, '*Amounderness* and *Holderness*', *Namn och Bygd* lxxviii (1990), pp. 23–30
Fellows-Jensen 1998	G. Fellows-Jensen, 'The Origin and Development of the Name of York', in Rollason *et al.*, *Sources*, pp. 226–37
Fellows-Jensen 2004	G. Fellows-Jensen, 'The Anglo-Scandinavian Street-Names of York', in Hall (R.A.) *et al.*, *Aspects*, pp. 357–71
Finberg, *Agrarian History*	H. P. R. Finberg, 'Anglo-Saxon England to 1042', *The Agrarian History of England and Wales I.ii, A.D. 43–1042* (Cambridge, 1972), pp. 383–525
Finberg, *ECW*	H.P.R. Finberg, *The Early Charters of Wessex* (Leicester, 1964)
Fleming 1985	R. Fleming, 'Monastic Lands and England's Defence in the Viking Age', *EHR* c (1985), pp. 247–65
Fletcher, *Bloodfeud*	R. Fletcher, *Bloodfeud: Murder and Revenge in Anglo-Saxon England* (London, 2002)

Foot, *Æthelstan* — S. Foot, *Æthelstan, the First King of England* (New Haven and London, 2011)

Foot, *Monastic Life* — S. Foot, *Monastic Life in Anglo-Saxon England* c. *600–900* (Cambridge, 2006)

Fowler, *Extracts* — *Extracts from the Account Rolls of the Abbey of Durham* II, ed. J.T. Fowler, SS c (Durham, 1899)

Fowler, *MCPW* — *Memorials of the Church of SS. Peter and Wilfrid, Ripon*, 4 vols, ed. J.T. Fowler, SS lxxiv, lxxviii, lxxxi and cxv (Durham 1882–1908)

Fowler, *Rites* — *Rites of Durham Being a Description or Brief Declaration of All the Ancient Monuments, Rites, and Customs Belonging or Being Within the Monastical Church of Durham Before the Suppression. Written 1593*, ed. J.T. Fowler, SS cvii (Durham, 1903)

Gelling and Cole, *LPN* — M. Gelling and A. Cole, *The Landscape of Place-Names* (Stamford, 2000)

Gent, *Rippon* — T. Gent, *The Antient and Modern History of the Loyal Town of Rippon* (York, 1733)

Gerchow 2004 — J. Gerchow, 'The Origins of the Durham *Liber Vitae*' in Rollason *et al.*, *The Durham*, pp. 45–61

Giandrea, *Episcopal Culture* — M.F. Giandrea, *Episcopal Culture in Late Anglo-Saxon England*, Anglo-Saxon Studies 7 (Woodbridge, 2007)

Gneuss, *Handlist* — H. Gneuss, *Handlist of Anglo-Saxon Manuscripts: a List of Manuscripts and Manuscript Fragments Written and Owned in England up to 1100*, Medieval and Renaissance Texts and Studies ccxli (Tempe, Arizona, 2001)

Gneuss 1985 — H. Gneuss, 'Liturgical Books in Anglo-Saxon England and their Old English Terminology', *Learning and Literature in Anglo-Saxon England: Studies Presented to Peter Clemoes on the Occasion of his Sixty-Fifth Birthday*, ed. M. Lapidge and H. Gneuss (Cambridge, 1985), pp. 91–141

Godman, *Alcuin* — *Alcuin: The Bishops, Kings, and Saints of York*, ed. P. Godman, Oxford Medieval Texts (Oxford, 1982)

Greenwell 1904 — W. Greenwell, 'The House of Gospatric', *A History of Northumberland, VII: the Parish of Edlingham, the Parish of Felton, the Chapelry or Parish of Brinkburn*, ed. J.C. Hodgson (Newcastle and London, 1904), pp. 14–106

Grierson and Blackburn, *MEC I* — P. Grierson and M. Blackburn, *Medieval European Coinage, with a Catalogue of the Coins in the Fitzwilliam Museum, Cambridge*, I, *The Early Middle Ages (Fifth to Tenth Centuries)* (Cambridge, 1986)

Griffiths 1995 — J. Griffiths, 'Manuscripts in The Schøyen Collection Copied or Owned in the British Isles before 1700', *English Manuscript Studies 1100–1700*, ed. P. Beal and J. Griffiths, vol. v (1995), pp. 36–42

GP	*William of Malmesbury: Gesta Pontificum*, ed. R.M. Thomson and M. Winterbottom, Oxford Medieval Texts, 2 vols (Oxford, 2007)
GR	*William of Malmesbury: Gesta Regum Anglorum*, ed. R.A.B. Mynors, R.M. Thomson and M. Winterbottom, Oxford Medieval Texts, 2 vols (Oxford, 1998–9)
Haddan and Stubbs	*Councils and Ecclesiastical Documents Relating to Great Britain and Ireland*, ed. A.W. Haddan and W. Stubbs, 3 vols (Oxford, 1869–78)
Hadley, *Northern*	D.M. Hadley, *The Northern Danelaw: Its Social Structure,* c. *800–1100* (Leicester, 2000)
Hadley, *Vikings*	D.M. Hadley, *The Vikings in England: Settlement, Society and Culture* (Manchester, 2006)
Hadley and Richards, *Cultures in Contact*	*Cultures in Contact: Scandinavian Settlement in England in the Ninth and Tenth Centuries*, ed. D. Hadley and J.D. Richards (Turnhout, 2000)
Hall (D.) 1984	D. Hall, 'The Community of St Cuthbert – Its Properties, Rights and Claims from the Ninth Century to the Twelfth' (unpubl. DPhil. Dissertation, Oxford 1984)
Hall (D.) 1989	D. Hall, 'The Sanctuary of St Cuthbert', in *St Cuthbert*, pp. 425–36
Hall (I.) 1982	I. Hall, 'The Minster', in Miller *et al.*, *Beverley*, pp. 7–16
Hall (R.A.) *et al.*, *Aspects*	*Aspects of Anglo-Scandinavian York*, ed. R.A. Hall *et al.*, The Archaeology of York, 8/4 (York Archaeological Trust, 2004)
Hall (R.A.), *Viking Age York*	*Viking Age York and the North*, ed. R.A. Hall, Council for British Archaeology, Research Report xxvii (London, 1978)
Hall (R.A.) 1978	R.A. Hall, 'The Topography of Anglo-Scandinavian York', in Hall (R.A.), *Viking Age York*, pp. 31–6
Hall (R.A.) 1987	R.A. Hall, 'Ripon Yarns 2: Return to the Hill', *Interim* 12.3 (1987), pp. 15–22
Hall (R.A.) 1988	R.A. Hall, 'York 700–1050', *The Rebirth of Towns in the West A.D. 700–1050*, ed. R. Hodges and B. Hobley, Council for British Archaeology, Research Report lxviii (London, 1988), pp. 125–32
Hall (R.A.) 1995	R.A. Hall, 'Antiquaries and Archaeology in and around Ripon Minster', *Yorkshire Monasticism: Archaeology, Art and Architecture from the 7th to 16th Centuries*, ed. L. Hoey, British Archaeological Association Conference Transactions xvi (Leeds, 1995), pp. 12–30
Hall (R.A.) 1999	R.A. Hall, 'York', in *Blackwell*, pp. 497–9
Hall (R.A.) 2000	R.A. Hall, 'Anglo-Scandinavian Attitudes: Archaeological Ambiguities in Late Ninth- to Mid-Eleventh-Century York', in Hadley and Richards, *Cultures in Contact*, pp. 311–24

Hall (R.A.) 2004	R.A. Hall, 'The Topography of Anglo-Scandinavian York' in Hall (R.A.) *et al.*, *Aspects*, pp. 488–97
Hall and Whyman 1996	R.A. Hall and M. Whyman, 'Settlement and Monasticism at Ripon, North Yorkshire, from the Seventh to Eleventh Centuries A.D.', *Medieval Archaeology* xl (1996), pp. 62–150
Harding 1945–55	F.J.W. Harding, 'Mickleton and Spearman Manuscripts', *The Durham Philobiblon* i (1945–55), pp. 40–4
Harmer, *Writs*	F.E. Harmer, *Anglo-Saxon Writs* (Manchester, 1952)
Harrison 1959–62	K. Harrison, 'The Pre-Conquest Churches of York with an Appendix on Eighth-Century Northumbrian Annals', *YAJ* xl (1959–62), pp. 232–49
Harrison 1973	K. Harrison, 'The *Annus Domini* in Some Early Charters', *JSA* iv.7 (1973), pp. 551–7
Hart, *Danelaw*	C.R. Hart, *The Danelaw* (London and Rio Grande, 1992)
Hart, *ECNE*	C.R. Hart, *The Early Charters of Northern England and the North Midlands* (Leicester, 1975)
Harvey 1966	J.H. Harvey, 'The Fire of York in 1137', *YAJ* xli (1966), pp. 365–7
Heywood and James 1995	B. Heywood and E. James, 'York in the Roman and Early Medieval Periods: a Context for the Excavations' in Phillips and Heywood, *Excavations*, pp. 1–15
Hill and Brooke 1977	R.M.T. Hill and C.N.L. Brooke, 'From 627 Until the Early Thirteenth Century' in Aylmer and Cant, *History*, pp. 1–41
Hinckley 1935	H.B. Hinckley, 'The Riddle of *The Ormulum*', *Philological Quarterly* xiv, no. 2 (1935), pp. 193–216
Hines *et al.*, *Land, Sea and Home*	*Land, Sea and Home*, ed. J. Hines, A. Lane and M. Redknap, The Society for Medieval Archaeology Monograph 20 (Leeds, 2004)
Horrox, *Beverley*	*Beverley Minster: An Illustrated History*, ed. R. Horrox (Cambridge, 2000)
HR	*Historia regum*, in Arnold, *Sym. Op.* II, pp. 3–283, composite text cited here in the form *HR* (1–9) together with the relevant page number in Arnold, *Sym. Op.* II and also *sub anno* where appropriate. First five sections attributed to Byrhtferth of Ramsey.
HR (1)	The Kentish Legends (pp. 3–13)
HR (2)	Early Northumbrian Kings (pp. 13–15)
HR (3)	Material derived from Bede, particularly from the *Historia abbatum* (pp. 15–30)
HR (4)	A chronicle from 732 to 802, also known as *York Annals* (pp. 30–68)
HR (5)	A chronicle from 849 to 887, derived mainly from Asser (pp. 69–91)
HR (6)	A chronicle from 888 to 957 (pp. 91–5)
HR (7)	Extracts from William of Malmesbury (pp. 95–8)

HR (8)	A chronicle from 848 to 1118, derived mainly from John of Worcester (pp. 98–253)
HR (9)	A chronicle from 1119 to 1129 (pp. 253–83)
HRH	*The Heads of Religious Houses, England and Wales 940–1216*, ed. D. Knowles, C.N.L. Brooke and V.C.M. London (Cambridge, 1972; rev. edn, 2001)
HSC	*Historia de Sancto Cuthberto: a History of St Cuthbert and a Record of his Patrimony*, ed. T. Johnson South (Woodbridge, 2002)
Hughes 1971	K. Hughes, 'Evidence for Contacts between the Churches of the Irish and the English', *England Before the Conquest: Studies in Primary Sources Presented to Dorothy Whitelock*, ed. P. Clemoes and K. Hughes (Cambridge, 1971), pp. 49–67
Hugh the Chanter	*Hugh the Chanter: The History of the Church of York, 1066–1127*, ed. C. Johnson, revised by M. Brett, C.N.L. Brooke and M. Winterbottom, Oxford Medieval Texts (Oxford, 1990)
JEH	*Journal of Ecclesiastical History*
John 1970	E. John, 'The Social and Political Problems of the Early English Church', *Agricultural History Review* xviii (1970), *Essays Presented to Professor H.P.R. Finberg*, pp. 39–63
John of Worcester II	*The Chronicle of John of Worcester, vol. II: the Annals from 450 to 1066*, ed. R.R. Darlington and P. McGurk, Oxford Medieval Texts (Oxford, 1995)
Johnson South 1996	T. Johnson South, 'Changing Images of Sainthood: St Cuthbert in the *Historia de Sancto Cuthberto*', *Saints: Studies in Hagiography*, ed. S. Sticca, Medieval and Renaissance Texts and Studies Volume 141 (New York, 1996), pp. 81–94
Jolliffe 1926	J.E.A. Jolliffe, 'Northumbrian Institutions', *EHR* xli (1926), pp. 1–42
Jones 1961	G.R.J. Jones, 'Basic Patterns of Settlement Distribution in Northern England', *Advancement of Science* lxxii (1961), pp. 192–200
Jones 1975	G.R.J. Jones, 'Early Territorial Organisation in Gwynedd and Elmet', *NH* x (1975), pp. 3–27
Jones 1995	G.R.J. Jones, 'Some Donations to Bishop Wilfrid in Northern England', *NH* xxxi (1995), pp. 22–38
Jones 2000	G.R.J. Jones, 'The Ripon Estate: Landscape into Townscape', *NH* xxxvii (2000), pp. 13–30
JSA	*Journal of the Society of Archivists*
Kapelle, *Norman*	W.E. Kapelle, *The Norman Conquest of the North: the Region and its Transformation, 1000–1135* (London, 1979)

KCD	For 'Kemble' in citations of charters
Kelly, *Abingdon*	*Charters of Abingdon Abbey*, ed. S.E. Kelly, Anglo-Saxon Charters vii–viii (Oxford, 2000–1)
Kelly, *Bath and Wells*	*Charters of Bath and Wells*, ed. S.E. Kelly, Anglo-Saxon Charters 13 (Oxford, 2007)
Kelly, *Malmesbury*	*Charters of Malmesbury Abbey*, ed. S.E. Kelly, Anglo-Saxon Charters xi (Oxford, 2005)
Kelly, *Peterborough*	*Charters of Peterborough Abbey*, ed. S.E. Kelly, Anglo-Saxon Charters 14 (Oxford, 2009)
Kelly, *St Augustine's*	*Charters of St Augustine's Abbey, Canterbury, and Minster-in-Thanet*, ed. S.E. Kelly, Anglo-Saxon Charters iv (Oxford, 1995)
Kelly, *St Paul's*	*Charters of St Paul's, London*, ed. S.E. Kelly, Anglo-Saxon Charters x (Oxford, 2004)
Kelly, *Selsey*	*Charters of Selsey*, ed. S.E. Kelly, Anglo-Saxon Charters vi (Oxford, 1998)
Kelly, *Shaftesbury*	*Charters of Shaftesbury Abbey*, ed. S.E. Kelly, Anglo-Saxon Charters v (Oxford, 1996)
Kelly 1990	S.E. Kelly, 'Anglo-Saxon Lay Society and the Written Word', *The Uses of Literacy in Early Mediaeval Europe*, ed. R. McKitterick (Cambridge, 1990; repr. 1995, 1998), pp. 36–62
Kemble	J.M. Kemble, *Codex Diplomaticus Aevi Saxonici*, 6 vols (London, 1839–48)
Kennedy 1995	A. Kennedy, 'Law and Litigation in the *Libellus Æthelwoldi Episcopi*', *ASE* xxiv (1995), pp. 131–83
Ker, *Catalogue*	N.R. Ker, *Catalogue of Manuscripts Containing Anglo-Saxon* (Oxford, 1957; repr. with addenda, 1990)
Ker 1971	N.R. Ker, 'The Handwriting of Archbishop Wulfstan', *England Before the Conquest: Studies in Primary Sources Presented to Dorothy Whitelock*, ed. P. Clemoes and K. Hughes (Cambridge, 1971), pp. 315–31
Keynes, *Atlas*	S. Keynes, *An Atlas of Attestations in Anglo-Saxon Charters, c. 670–1066*, Department of Anglo-Saxon, Norse and Celtic, University of Cambridge (2002)
Keynes, *Diplomas*	S. Keynes, *The Diplomas of King Æthelred 'the Unready' 978–1016: a Study in their Use as Historical Evidence* (Cambridge, 1980)
Keynes 1985	S. Keynes, 'King Athelstan's Books', *Learning and Literature in Anglo-Saxon England: Studies Presented to Peter Clemoes on the Occasion of his Sixty-Fifth Birthday*, ed. M. Lapidge and H. Gneuss (Cambridge, 1985), pp. 143–201
Keynes 1986	S. Keynes, 'The Additions in Old English', in Barker, *York Gospels*, pp. 81–99
Keynes 1988	S. Keynes, 'Regenbald the Chancellor (*sic*)', *Anglo-Norman Studies* x (1988), pp. 185–222

Keynes 1990	S. Keynes, 'Royal Government and the Written Word in Late Anglo-Saxon England', *The Uses of Literacy in Early Mediaeval Europe*, ed. R. McKitterick (Cambridge, 1990; repr. 1995, 1998), pp. 226–57
Keynes 1994	S. Keynes, 'Cnut's Earls', *The Reign of Cnut, King of England, Denmark and Norway*, ed. A.R. Rumble (London, 1994), pp. 43–88
Keynes 1997	S. Keynes, 'Giso, Bishop of Wells (1061–88)', *Anglo-Norman Studies* xix (1997), pp. 203–71
Keynes 1999*a*	S. Keynes, 'The Vikings in England', *The Oxford Illustrated History of the Vikings*, ed. P. Sawyer (Oxford, 1999), pp. 48–82
Keynes 1999*b*	S. Keynes, 'Wulfstan I', in *Blackwell*, pp. 492–3
Keynes 2008	S. Keynes, 'Edgar, *rex admirabilis*', in Scragg, *Edgar*, pp. 3–58
Kirby, *Saint Wilfrid*	*Saint Wilfrid at Hexham*, ed. D.P. Kirby (Newcastle upon Tyne, 1974)
Kirby 1962	D.P. Kirby, 'Strathclyde and Cumbria: a Survey of Historical Development to 1092', *TCWAAS*, New Series lxii (1962), pp. 77–94
Kirby 1974	D.P. Kirby, 'Northumbria in the Time of Wilfrid', in Kirby, *Saint Wilfrid*, pp. 1–34
Kirby 1983	D.P. Kirby, 'Bede, Eddius Stephanus and the "Life of Wilfrid"', *EHR* xcviii (1983), pp. 101–14
Kirby 1995	D.P. Kirby, 'The Genesis of a Cult: Cuthbert of Farne and Ecclesiastical Politics in Northumbria in the Late Seventh and Early Eighth Centuries', *JEH* xlvi (1995), pp. 383–97
Knowles, *Monastic Order*	D. Knowles, *The Monastic Order in England*, 2nd edn (Cambridge, 1963)
Lambert 2009	T.B. Lambert, 'Spiritual Protection and Secular Power: The Evolution of Sanctuary and Legal Privilege in Ripon and Beverley, 900–1300', *Peace and Protection in the Middle Ages*, ed. T.B. Lambert and D.W. Rollason, Durham Medieval and Renaissance Monographs and Essays I (Durham, 2009), pp. 122–40
Lang, *Corpus*	J.T. Lang, *Corpus of Anglo-Saxon Stone Sculpture, iii: York and Eastern Yorkshire* (Oxford, 1991)
Lapidge, *ALL* 1	M. Lapidge, *Anglo-Latin Literature 600–899* (London, 1996)
Lapidge, *ALL* 2	M. Lapidge, *Anglo-Latin Literature 900–1066* (London, 1993)
Lapidge, *AS Library*	M. Lapidge, *The Anglo-Saxon Library* (Oxford, 2006)
Lapidge 1985	M. Lapidge, 'Surviving Booklists from Anglo-Saxon England', *Learning and Literature in Anglo-Saxon England: Studies Presented to Peter Clemoes on the Occasion of his Sixty-Fifth Birthday*, ed. M. Lapidge and H. Gneuss (Cambridge, 1985), pp. 33–89

Lapidge 1989	M. Lapidge, 'Bede's Metrical *Vita S. Cuthberti*', in *St Cuthbert*, pp. 77–93
Lawson, *Cnut*	M.K. Lawson, *Cnut: The Danes in England in the Early Eleventh Century* (London and New York, 1993)
Leach, *Memorials*	*Memorials of Beverley Minster: The Chapter Act Book of the Collegiate Church of S. John of Beverley A.D. 1286–1347*, 2 vols, ed. A.F. Leach, SS xcviii and cviii (Durham, 1898–1903)
Leach, *Visitations*	*Visitations and Memorials of Southwell Minster*, ed. A.F. Leach, Camden Society, New Series xlviii (Westminster, 1891)
Leland, *Collectanea*	*Joannis Lelandi Antiquarii De Rebus Britannicis Collectanea cum Thomae Hearnii Praefatione Notis et Indice ad Editionem Primam* (London, 1770; 2nd edn 1774)
Le Patourel, Long and Pickles, *Yorkshire Boundaries*	*Yorkshire Boundaries*, ed. H.E.J. Le Patourel, M.H. Long and M.F. Pickles (Leeds, 1993)
Le Patourel 1993	H.E.J. Le Patourel, 'Amounderness', in Le Patourel, Long and Pickles, *Yorkshire Boundaries*, pp. 113–16
Levison, *England and the Continent*	W. Levison, *England and the Continent in the Eighth Century* (Oxford, 1946)
Liebermann, *Gesetze*	F. Liebermann, *Die Gesetze der Angelsachsen*, 3 vols (Halle, 1903–16)
Liebermann 1903	F. Liebermann, 'Drei nordhumbrische Urkunden um 1100', *Archiv für das Studium der Neueren Sprachen und Literaturen* (1903), pp. 275–84
LondStP	For 'Kelly, *St Paul's*' in citations of charters
Long 1993	M.H. Long, 'Sherburn', in Le Patourel, Long and Pickles, *Yorkshire Boundaries*, pp. 117–24
Long and Pickles 1993*a*	M.H. Long and M.F. Pickles, 'Newbald', in Le Patourel, Long and Pickles, *Yorkshire Boundaries*, pp. 135–41
Long and Pickles 1993*b*	M.H. Long and M.F. Pickles, 'Patrington', in Le Patourel, Long and Pickles, *Yorkshire Boundaries*, pp. 143–50
Longley 1976	K.M. Longley, 'Towards a History of Archive-Keeping in the Church of York: I. The Archbishop's Muniments', *Borthwick Institute Bulletin*, vol. 1, no. 2 (1976), pp. 49–74
Longley 1977	K.M. Longley, 'Towards a History of Archive-Keeping in the Church of York: II. The Capitular Muniments', *Borthwick Institute Bulletin*, vol. 1, no. 3 (1977), pp. 103–118
Loyn, *Wulfstan Manuscript*	H.R. Loyn, *A Wulfstan Manuscript Containing Institutes, Laws and Homilies: British Museum Cotton Nero A.I.*, Early English Manuscripts in Facsimile xvii (Copenhagen, 1971)

LVD	*The Durham* Liber Vitae, *London, British Library, MS Cotton Domitian A. VII, Volume I: Introductory Essays, Edition, Commentary on the Edition and Indexes*, ed. D.W. Rollason and L. Rollason (London, 2007)
Lyth 1982	P. Lyth, 'The Southwell Charter of 956 A.D.: an Exploration of its Boundaries', *Trans of Thoroton Soc.* lxxxvi (1982), pp. 49–61
Lyth and Davies 1992	P. Lyth and G. Davies, 'The Southwell Charter of A.D. 956: a New Appraisal of the Boundaries', *Trans of Thoroton Soc.* xcvi (1992), pp. 125–9
Magilton, *Church of St Helen-on-the-Walls*	J.R. Magilton, *The Church of St Helen-on-the-Walls, Aldwark*, The Archaeology of York, 10/1 (London, 1980)
Malm	For 'Kelly, *Malmesbury*' in citations of charters
McDermid, *Beverley Minster Fasti*	R.T.W. McDermid, *Beverley Minster Fasti*, Yorkshire Archaeological Society, Record Series cxlix (Huddersfield, 1993)
McIntosh *et al.*, *Linguistic Atlas*	*A Linguistic Atlas of Late Medieval English*, ed. A. McIntosh, M.L. Samuels and M. Benskin, 4 vols (Aberdeen, 1986)
Meehan 1975	B. Meehan, 'Outsiders, Insiders, and Property in Durham around 1100', *Studies in Church History* xii (1975), pp. 45–58
Meehan 1976	B. Meehan, 'The Siege of Durham, the Battle of Carham and the Cession of Lothian', *Scottish Historical Review* lv (1976), pp. 1–19
Meehan 1994	B. Meehan, 'Durham Twelfth-Century Manuscripts in Cistercian Houses', in *AND*, pp. 439–49
MGH	Monumenta Germaniae Historica
Miller *et al.*, *Beverley*	K. Miller, J. Robinson, B. English and I. Hall, *Beverley: An Archaeological and Architectural Study*, Royal Commission on Historical Monuments in England, Supplementary Series: 4 (London, 1982)
Miller, *New Minster, Winchester*	*Charters of the New Minster, Winchester*, ed. S. Miller, Anglo-Saxon Charters ix (Oxford, 2001)
Mon. Angl.	R. Dodsworth and W. Dugdale, *Monasticon Anglicanum*, 3 vols (London, 1655–73)
Mon. Angl. (rev. edn)	W. Dugdale, *Monasticon Anglicanum*, ed. J. Caley, H. Ellis and B. Bandinel, 6 vols in 8 (London, 1817–30)
Morris 1977	C.D. Morris, 'Northumbria and the Viking Settlement: The Evidence for Land-holding', *AA*^{5} v (1977), pp. 83–103
Morris 1978	C.D. Morris, 'Aycliffe and its Pre-Norman Sculpture', *Anglo-Saxon and Viking Age Sculpture and its Context: Papers from the Collingwood Symposium on Insular Sculpture from 800 to 1066*, ed. J.T. Lang, BAR British Series xlix (1978), pp. 97–137

Morris 1981 — C.D. Morris, 'Viking and Native in Northern England: A Case-Study', *Proceedings of the Eighth Viking Congress: Århus 24–31 August 1977*, ed. H. Bekker-Nielsen, P. Foote and O. Olsen (Odense, 1981), pp. 223–44

Morris, 1984 — C.D. Morris, 'Aspects of Scandinavian Settlement in Northern England: A Review', *NH* xx (1984), pp. 1–22

Morris (C.J.), *Marriage* — C.J. Morris, *Marriage and Murder in Eleventh-Century Northumbria: a Study of the 'De Obsessione Dunelmi'*, Borthwick Paper no. 82, University of York (York, 1992)

Morris (R.K.), *Churches in the Landscape* — R.K. Morris, *Churches in the Landscape* (London, 1989)

Morris (R.K.) 1986 — R.K. Morris, 'Alcuin, York and the *Alma Sophia*', *The Anglo-Saxon Church: Papers on History, Architecture, and Archaeology in Honour of Dr. H.M. Taylor*, ed. L.A.S. Butler and R.K. Morris, Council for British Archaeology, Research Report lx (London, 1986), pp. 80–9

Morris (R.K.) 1988 — R.K. Morris, 'Churches in York and its Hinterland: Building Patterns and Stone Sources in the 11th and 12th Centuries', *Minsters and Parish Churches: The Local Church in Transition 950–1200*, ed. J. Blair (Oxford, 1988), pp. 191–9

Morris and Cambridge 1989 — R.K. Morris and E. Cambridge, 'Beverley Minster Before the Early Thirteenth Century', *Medieval Art and Architecture in the East Riding of Yorkshire*, ed. C. Wilson, The British Archaeological Association Conference Transactions for the year 1983 (Leeds, 1989), pp. 9–32

Mynors, *Durham Cathedral* — R.A.B. Mynors, *Durham Cathedral Manuscripts to the End of the Twelfth Century* (Oxford, 1939)

NH — *Northern History*

North, *EHC I* — J.J. North, *English Hammered Coinage Volume I: Early Anglo-Saxon to Henry III* c. *600–1272*, 3rd edn (London, 1994)

Norton 1998*a* — C. Norton, 'History, Wisdom and Illumination', in Rollason, *Symeon: Historian*, pp. 61–105

Norton 1998*b* — C. Norton, 'The Anglo-Saxon Cathedral at York and the Topography of the Anglian City', *Journal of the British Archaeological Association* cli (1998), pp. 1–42

Norton 2004 — C. Norton, 'York Minster in the Time of Wulfstan', in Townend, *Wulfstan,* pp. 207–34

ODNB — *Oxford Dictionary of National Biography: from the Earliest Times to the Year 2000*, ed. H.C.G. Matthew and B. Harrison, 60 vols (Oxford, 2004)

O'Donovan, *Sherborne* — *Charters of Sherborne*, ed. M.A. O'Donovan, Anglo-Saxon Charters iii (Oxford, 1988)

Offler, *De Iniusta* — *De Iniusta Vexacione Willelmi Episcopi Primi per Willelmum Regem Filium Willelmi Magni Regis*, ed. H.S. Offler, rev. A.J. Piper and A.I. Doyle, Camden Miscellany xxxiv, Camden Fifth Series x (Cambridge, 1997), pp. 49–104

Offler, *Durham Episcopal* — *Durham Episcopal Charters 1071–1152*, ed. H.S. Offler, SS clxxix (Gateshead, 1968)

Offler, *Medieval Historians* — H.S. Offler, *Medieval Historians of Durham* (Durham, 1958) (repr. Offler, *North of the Tees*, no. I)

Offler, *North of the Tees* — H.S. Offler, *North of the Tees: Studies in Medieval British History*, ed. A.J. Piper and A.I. Doyle (Collected Studies; Aldershot, 1996)

Offler 1951 — H.S. Offler, 'The Tractate *De Iniusta Vexacione Willelmi Episcopi Primi*', *EHR* lxvi (1951), pp. 321–41 (repr. Offler, *North of the Tees*, no. VI)

Okasha, *Hand-List* — E. Okasha, *Hand-List of Anglo-Saxon Non-Runic Inscriptions* (Cambridge, 1971)

Oliver, *Beverley* — G. Oliver, *The History and Antiquities of the Town and Minster of Beverley* (Beverley, 1829)

O'Sullivan 2001 — D. O'Sullivan, 'Space, Silence and Shortages on Lindisfarne. The Archaeology of Asceticism', *Image and Power in the Archaeology of Early Medieval Britain: Essays in Honour of Rosemary Cramp*, ed. H. Hamerow and A. MacGregor (Oxford, 2001), pp. 33–52

Palliser 1984 — D.M. Palliser, 'York's West Bank: Medieval Suburb or Urban Nucleus?', *Archaeological Papers from York presented to M.W. Barley*, ed. P.V. Addyman and V.E. Black, York Archaeological Trust (York, 1984), pp. 101–08

Palliser 1992 — D.M. Palliser, 'An Introduction to the Yorkshire Domesday', *The Yorkshire Domesday*, Alecto Historical Editions (London, 1992), pp. 1–38

Palliser 1993 — D.M. Palliser, 'Domesday Book and the "Harrying of the North"', *NH* xxix (1993), pp. 1–23

Palliser 2000 — D.M. Palliser, 'The Early Medieval Minster', in Horrox, *Beverley*, pp. 23–35

Pantin 1933 — W.A. Pantin, 'English Monastic Letter-Books', *Historical Essays in Honour of James Tait*, ed. J.G. Edwards, V.H. Galbraith and E.F. Jacob (Manchester, 1933), pp. 201–22

Parsons 2004 — D. Parsons, 'The Inscriptions of Viking-Age York', in Hall (R.A.) *et al.*, *Aspects*, pp. 350–6

Pet — For 'Kelly, *Peterborough*' in citations of charters

Phillips and Heywood, *Excavations* — D. Phillips and B. Heywood, ed. M.O.H. Carver, *Excavations at York Minster I: From Roman Fortress to Norman Cathedral*, Royal Commission on the Historical Monuments of England, 2 parts (London, 1995)

Philpott 1994	M. Philpott, 'The *De iniusta uexacione Willelmi episcopi primi* and Canon Law in Anglo-Norman Durham', in *AND*, pp. 125–37
Phythian-Adams, *Land of the Cumbrians*	C. Phythian-Adams, *Land of the Cumbrians: A Study in British Provincial Origins, A.D. 400–1120* (Aldershot, 1996)
Pierquin, *Recueil*	H. Pierquin, *Recueil général des chartes anglo-saxonnes: les Saxons en Angleterre, 640–1061* (Paris, 1912)
Plummer, *Bede*	*Venerablis Baedae Opera Historica*, 2 vols (Oxford, 1896)
Plummer, *Chronicles*	C. Plummer, *Two of the Saxon Chronicles Parallel*, 2 vols (Oxford, 1892–6)
PN Cumb. I	A.M. Armstrong, A. Mawer, F.M. Stenton and B. Dickins, *The Place-Names of Cumberland: Part I Eskdale, Cumberland and Leath Wards*, EPNS xx (Cambridge, 1950)
PN Cumb. III	A.M. Armstrong, A. Mawer, F.M. Stenton and B. Dickins, *The Place-Names of Cumberland: Part III*, EPNS xxii (Cambridge, 1952)
PN Notts.	J.E.B. Gover, A. Mawer and F.M. Stenton, *The Place-Names of Nottinghamshire*, EPNS xvii (Cambridge, 1940)
PN YorksER	A.H. Smith, *The Place-Names of the East Riding of Yorkshire and York*, EPNS xiv (Cambridge, 1937)
PN YorksWR	A.H. Smith, *The Place-Names of the West Riding of Yorkshire*, 8 parts, EPNS xxx–xxxvii (Cambridge, 1961–3)
Poulson, *Beverlac*	G. Poulson, *Beverlac; or, The Antiquities and History of the Town of Beverley*, vol. I (London, 1829)
Ragg 1903	F.W. Ragg, 'A Charter of Gospatrik', *The Ancestor* vii (1903), pp. 244–7
Ragg 1905	F.W. Ragg, 'Gospatrik's Charter', *TCWAAS*, New Series v (1905), pp. 71–84
Ragg 1917	F.W. Ragg, 'Five Strathclyde and Galloway Charters – Four Concerning Cardew, and one the Westmorland Newbigging', *TCWAAS*, New Series xvii (1917), pp. 198–234
Raine, *Fabric Rolls*	*The Fabric Rolls of York Minster, with an Appendix of Illustrative Documents*, ed. J. Raine, SS xxxv (Durham and London, 1859)
Raine, *HCY*	*The Historians of the Church of York and its Archbishops*, ed. J. Raine, RS lxxi, 3 vols (London, 1879–94)
Raine, *SDSB*	*Sanctuarium Dunelmense et Sanctuarium Beverlacense*, ed. J. Raine, SS v (London, 1837)
Ranger, *Prisca Munimenta*	*Prisca Munimenta: Studies in Archival and Administrative History Presented to Dr A.E.J. Hollaender*, ed. F. Ranger (London, 1973)

Regesta I	H.W.C. Davis, *Regesta Regum Anglo-Normannorum 1066–1154, I: Willelmi Conquestoris et Willelmi Rufi 1066–1100* (London, 1913)
Regesta II	C. Johnson and H.A. Cronne, *Regesta Regum Anglo-Normannorum 1066–1154, II: Henrici Primi 1100–1135* (Oxford, 1956)
Regesta III	H.A. Cronne and R.H.C. Davis, *Regesta Regum Anglo-Normannorum 1066–1154, III: Regesta Regis Stephani ac Mathildis Imperatricis ac Gaufridi et Henrici Ducum Normannorum 1135–1154* (Oxford, 1968)
Robertson, *Charters*	*Anglo-Saxon Charters*, ed. A.J. Robertson, 2nd edn (Cambridge, 1956)
Rollason, *Cuthbert*	D.W. Rollsaon, ed., *Cuthbert: Saint and Patron* (Durham, 1987)
Rollason, *Northumbria*	D.W. Rollason, *Northumbria, 500–1100: Creation and Destruction of a Kingdom* (Cambridge, 2003)
Rollason, *Symeon: Historian*	*Symeon of Durham: Historian of Durham and the North*, ed. D.W. Rollason (Stamford, 1998)
Rollason, *Symeon: Libellus*	*Symeon of Durham: Libellus de Exordio atque Procursu istius hoc est Dunhelmensis Ecclesie: Tract on the Origins and Progress of this the Church of Durham*, ed. D.W. Rollason, Oxford Medieval Texts (Oxford, 2000)
Rollason *et al.*, *Sources*	*Sources for York History to AD 1100*, ed. D.W. Rollason, D. Gore and G. Fellows-Jensen, The Archaeology of York, 1 (York Archaeological Trust, 1998)
Rollason *et al.*, *The Durham*	*The Durham* Liber Vitae *and its Context*, ed. D.W. Rollason, A.J. Piper, M. Harvey and L. Rollason (Woodbridge, 2004)
Rollason 1978	D.W. Rollason, 'Lists of Saints' Resting-Places in Anglo-Saxon England', *ASE* vii (1978), pp. 61–93
Rollason 1987	D.W. Rollason, 'The Wanderings of St Cuthbert', in Rollason, *Cuthbert*, pp. 45–59
Rollason 1989	D.W. Rollason, 'St Cuthbert and Wessex: the Evidence of Cambridge, Corpus Christi College MS 183', in *St Cuthbert*, pp. 413–24
Rollason 1992	D.W. Rollason, 'Symeon of Durham and the Community of Durham in the Eleventh Century', *England in the Eleventh Century*, ed. C. Hicks (Stamford, 1992), pp. 183–98
Rollason 1995	D.W. Rollason, '995: The Beginnings of the Diocese of Durham', *Friends of Durham Cathedral Annual Report*, vol. lxii (Durham, 1995), pp. 23–34
Rollason 1996	D.W. Rollason, 'Hagiography and Politics in Eighth-Century Northumbria', *Holy Men and Holy Women: Old English Prose Saints' Lives and their Contexts*, ed. P. Szarmach, SUNY Series in Medieval Studies (New York, 1996), pp. 95–114

Rollason 1998	D.W. Rollason, 'The Making of the *Libellus de Exordio*: the Evidence of Erasures and Alterations in the Two Earliest Manuscripts', in Rollason, *Symeon: Historian*, pp. 140–56
Rollason 1999*a*	D.W. Rollason, 'Monasteries and Society in Early Medieval Northumbria', *Monasteries and Society in Medieval Britain: Proceedings of the 1994 Harlaxton Symposium*, ed. B. Thompson (Stamford, 1999), pp. 59–74
Rollason 1999*b*	D.W. Rollason, 'Historical Evidence for Anglian York', in Tweddle *et al.*, *Anglian York*, pp. 117–40
Rollason 2004	D.W. Rollason, 'Anglo-Scandinavian York: The Evidence of Historical Sources', in Hall (R.A.) *et al.*, *Aspects*, pp. 305–24
Roper 1974	M. Roper, 'Wilfrid's Landholdings in Northumbria', in Kirby, *Saint Wilfrid*, pp. 61–79
RS	Rolls Series
St Alb	For 'Crick, *St Albans*' in citations of charters
St Aug's	For 'Kelly, *St Augustine's*' in citations of charters
St Cuthbert	*St Cuthbert: his Cult and Community to A.D. 1200*, ed. G. Bonner, D.W. Rollason and C. Stancliffe (Woodbridge, 1989)
Sawyer	P.H. Sawyer, *Anglo-Saxon Charters: an Annotated List and Bibliography*, Royal Historical Society Guides and Handbooks viii (London, 1968) (new edn with additions, ed. S.E. Kelly *et al.*, forthcoming; see meanwhile http://www.esawyer.org.uk)
Sawyer, *Burton*	*Charters of Burton Abbey*, ed. P.H. Sawyer, Anglo-Saxon Charters ii (Oxford, 1979)
Sawyer 1995	P.H. Sawyer, 'The Last Viking Kings of York', *NH* xxxi (1995), pp. 39–44
Scragg, *Edgar*	*Edgar, King of the English, 959–975*, ed. D. Scragg (Woodbridge, 2008)
Sel	For 'Kelly, *Selsey*' in citations of charters
Shaft	For 'Kelly, *Shaftesbury*' in citations of charters
Sharpe, *Handlist*	R. Sharpe, *A Handlist of the Latin Writers of Great Britain and Ireland before 1540* (Turnhout, 1997)
Sharpe, *Norman Rule*	R. Sharpe, *Norman Rule in Cumbria, 1092–1136: A Lecture Delivered to Cumberland and Westmorland Antiquarian and Archaeological Society on 9th April 2005 at Carlisle*, Cumberland and Westmorland Antiquarian and Archaeological Society Tract Series xxi (Kendal, 2006)
Sharpe 1998	R. Sharpe, 'Symeon as Pamphleteer', in Rollason, *Symeon: Historian*, pp. 214–29
Sharpe 2003	R. Sharpe, 'The Use of Writs in the Eleventh Century', *ASE* xxxii (2003), pp. 247–91
Sherb	For 'O'Donovan, *Sherborne*' in citations of charters

Simpson 1989	L. Simpson, 'The King Alfred/St Cuthbert Episode in the *Historia de Sancto Cuthberto*: its Significance for Mid-tenth-century English History', in *St Cuthbert*, pp. 397–411
Sims-Williams 1988	P. Sims-Williams, 'St Wilfrid and Two Charters Dated A.D. 676 and 680', *JEH* xxxix (1988), pp. 163–83
Smith, *Bede*	*Historia Ecclesiastica Gentis Anglorum*, ed. J. Smith (Cambridge, 1722)
Smith, *EPNE*	A.H. Smith, *English Place-Name Elements*, 2 vols, EPNS xxv–xxvi (Cambridge, 1956)
Smyth, *Scandinavian*	A.P. Smyth, *Scandinavian York and Dublin: The History and Archaeology of Two Related Viking Kingdoms*, 2 vols (Dublin, 1975–9)
SS	Surtees Society
Stancliffe 1989	C. Stancliffe, 'Cuthbert and the Polarity between Pastor and Solitary', in *St Cuthbert*, pp. 21–44
Stancliffe, *Bede, Wilfrid and the Irish*	C. Stancliffe, *Bede, Wilfrid and the Irish*, Jarrow Lecture 2003 (Jarrow, 2003)
Stenton, *ASE*	F.M. Stenton, *Anglo-Saxon England*, 3rd edn (Oxford, 1971)
Stenton, *Feudalism*	F.M. Stenton, *The First Century of English Feudalism 1066–1166* (Oxford, 1932; repr. 1961)
Stenton, *Latin Charters*	F.M. Stenton, *The Latin Charters of the Anglo-Saxon Period* (Oxford, 1955)
Stenton, *Preparatory to ASE*	*Preparatory to Anglo-Saxon England, being the Collected Papers of Frank Merry Stenton*, ed. D.M. Stenton (Oxford, 1970)
Stenton, *Types*	F.M. Stenton, *Types of Manorial Structure in the Northern Danelaw*, Oxford Studies in Social and Legald History ii, ed. P. Vinogradoff (Oxford, 1910)
Stevenson, *Lib. Vit.*	*Liber Vitae Ecclesiae Dunelmensis*, ed. J. Stevenson, SS xiii (Durham, 1841)
Stevenson 1912	W.H. Stevenson, 'Yorkshire Surveys and Other Eleventh-Century Documents in the York Gospels', *EHR* xxvii (1912), pp. 1–25
Stocker 2000	D. Stocker, 'Monuments and Merchants: Irregularities in the Distribution of Stone Sculpture in Lincolnshire and Yorkshire in the Tenth Century', in Hadley and Richards, *Cultures in Contact*, pp. 179–212
Story, *Carolingian Connections*	J. Story, *Carolingian Connections: Anglo-Saxon England and Carolingian Francia, c. 750–870* (Ashgate, 2003)
Story 1998	J.E. Story, 'Symeon as Annalist', in Rollason, *Symeon: Historian*, pp. 202–13
Summ. Cat.	*A Summary Catalogue of Western Manuscripts in the Bodleian Library at Oxford*, 7 vols (Oxford, 1895–1953)

Symeon, *LDE*	Symeon of Durham, *Libellus de Exordio atque Procursu istius hoc est Dunhelmensis Ecclesie*
Taylor and Taylor, *Anglo-Saxon Architecture*	H.M. Taylor and J. Taylor, *Anglo-Saxon Architecture*, 3 vols (Cambridge, 1965–78)
TCWAAS	*Transactions of the Cumberland and Westmorland Antiquarian and Archaeological Society*
Thacker 1989	A.T. Thacker, 'Lindisfarne and the Origins of the Cult of St Cuthbert', in *St Cuthbert*, pp. 103–24
Thomas, *Survey of Worcester*	W. Thomas, *A Survey of the Cathedral Church of Worcester; also an Appendix of many Original Papers and Records* (London, 1737)
Thompson, *Lib. Vit.*	*Liver Vitae Ecclesiae Dunelmensis: a Collotype Facsimile of the Original Manuscript. Vol. I: Facsimile and General Introduction*, ed. A.H. Thompson, SS cxxxvi (Durham and London, 1923)
Thorpe, *Diplomatarium*	B. Thorpe, *Diplomatarium Anglicum Ævi Saxonici* (London, 1865)
Tinti, *Sustaining Belief*	F. Tinti, *Sustaining Belief: The Church of Worcester from* c. *870 to* c. *1100* (Farnham, 2010)
Townend, *Wulfstan*	*Wulfstan, Archbishop of York: The Proceedings of the Second Alcuin Conference*, ed. M. Townend (Turnhout, 2004)
Trans of Thoroton Soc.	*Transactions of the Thoroton Society*
Tweddle *et al.*, *Anglian York*	*Anglian York: A Survey of the Evidence*, ed. D. Tweddle, J. Moulden and E. Logan, The Archaeology of York, 7/2 (York Archaeological Trust, 1999)
VCA	*Vita Sancti Cuthberti auctore anonymo*, in Colgrave, *Two Lives*, pp. 60–139
VCH	*Victoria County History*
VCH Cumb. ii	*The Victoria History of the County of Cumberland, ii*, ed. J. Wilson (London, 1905; repr. 1968)
VCH Dur.	*The Victoria History of the County of Durham*, ed. W. Page (London, 1968)
VCH Notts. i	*The Victoria History of the Counties of England: A History of Nottinghamshire, i*, ed. W. Page (London, 1906)
VCH Yorks. iii	*The Victoria History of the Counties of England: A History of Yorkshire, iii*, ed. W. Page (London, 1913)
VW	Stephanus, *Vita Wilfridi*
Wainwright 1975	F.T. Wainwright, 'The Battles at Corbridge', *Scandinavian England: Collected Papers by F.T. Wainwright*, ed. H.P.R. Finberg (Chichester, 1975), pp. 163–79
Wallace-Hadrill (J.M.), *Bede*	J.M. Wallace-Hadrill, *Bede's Ecclesiastical History of the English People: a Historical Commentary*, Oxford Medieval Texts (Oxford, 1988; repr. 1991)
Wareham 1996	A.F. Wareham, 'Saint Oswald's Family and Kin', in Brooks and Cubitt, *St Oswald*, pp. 46–63

Watson 2011	R. Watson, 'Viking-Age Amounderness: A Reconsideration', *Place-Names, Language and the Anglo-Saxon Landscape*, ed. N.J. Higham and M.J. Ryan, Publications of the Manchester Centre for Anglo-Saxon Studies Volume 10 (Woodbridge, 2011), pp. 125–41
Wells	For 'Kelly, *Bath and Wells*' in citations of charters
Whitelock, *EHD*	*English Historical Documents c. 500–1042*, ed. D. Whitelock, English Historical Documents i, 2nd edn (London, 1979)
Whitelock 1959	D. Whitelock, 'The Dealings of the Kings of England with Northumbria in the Tenth and Eleventh Centuries', *The Anglo-Saxons*, ed. P. Clemoes (London, 1959), pp. 70–88 (repr. in *History, Law and Literature in 10th–11th Century England*, ed. D. Whitelock [London, 1981], no. III)
Whitelock 1965	D. Whitelock, 'Wulfstan at York', *Medieval and Linguistic Studies in Honor of Francis Peabody Magoun, Jr.*, ed. J.B. Bessinger Jr. and R.P. Creed (London, 1965), pp. 214–31
William of Malmesbury, *Vita Wulfstani*	William of Malmesbury, *Vita Wulfstani*, in William of Malmesbury, *Saints' Lives: Lives of SS. Wulsftan, Dunstan, Patrick, Benignus and Indract*, ed. and trans. M. Winterbottom and R.M. Thomson, Oxford Medieval Texts (Oxford, 2002), pp. 1–155
Williams 2005	A. Williams, 'The Cunning of the Dove: Wulfstan and the Politics of Accommodation', *St Wulfstan and His World*, ed. J. Barrow and N. Brooks (Ashgate, 2005), pp. 23–38
Wilson, *St Bees*	J. Wilson, *The Register of the Priory of St Bees*, SS cxxvi (Durham and London, 1915)
Wilson 1904	J. Wilson, 'An English Letter of Gospatric', *Scottish Historical Review* i (1904), pp. 62–9
Wilson 1966	P.A. Wilson, 'On the Use of the Terms "Strathclyde" and "Cumbria"', *TCWAAS* lxvi (1966), pp. 57–92
WinchNM	For 'Miller, *New Minster, Winchester*' in citations of charters
Witty 1921	J.R. Witty, 'The Rhyming Charter of Beverley', *Transactions of the Yorkshire Dialect Society* xxii (1921), pp. 36–44
Wood 1987	I.N. Wood, 'Anglo-Saxon Otley: an Archiepiscopal Estate and its Crosses in a Northumbrian Context', *NH* xxiii (1987), pp. 20–38
Wood 2008	I.N. Wood, 'Monasteries and the Geography of Power in the Age of Bede', *NH* xlv (2008), pp. 11–25
Wood 2010	I.N. Wood, 'The Gifts of Wearmouth and Jarrow', *The Language of Gift in the Early Middle Ages*, ed. W. Davies and P. Fouracre (Cambridge, 2010), pp. 89–115
Wood, *Proprietary Church*	S. Wood, *The Proprietary Church in the Medieval West* (Oxford, 2006)

Woodman 2012	D.A. Woodman, 'The Forging of the Anglo-Saxon Past in Fourteenth-Century Beverley', *English Manucripts before 1400*, ed. A.S.G. Edwards and O. Da Rold, *English Manuscript Studies: 1100–1700*, Vol. xvii (London, 2012), pp. 26–42.
Woodman, forthcoming	D.A. Woodman, '"Æthelstan A" and the Rhetoric of Rule' (forthcoming in *ASE* xlii)
Woolf, *Pictland*	A. Woolf, *From Pictland to Alba 789–1070*, The New Edinburgh History of Scotland Volume 2 (Edinburgh, 2007; repr. 2008)
Wormald, *Bede and the Conversion*	P. Wormald, *Bede and the Conversion of England: the Charter Evidence*, Jarrow Lecture 1984 (Jarrow, 1985)
Wormald, *Law I*	P. Wormald, *The Making of English Law: King Alfred to the Twelfth Century: Vol. I, Legislation and its Limits* (Oxford, 1999)
Wormald 1991	P. Wormald, 'In Search of King Offa's 'Law-Code'', *People and Places in Northern Europe 500–1600. Essays in Honour of Peter Hayes Sawyer*, ed. I.N. Wood and N. Lund (Woodbridge, 1991), pp. 25–45
YAJ	*Yorkshire Archaeological Journal*
Yorke, *Kings and Kingdoms*	B. Yorke, *Kings and Kingdoms of Early Anglo-Saxon England* (London and New York, 1990; repr. 1992, 1997, 2000 and 2002)

GENERAL INTRODUCTION

This book comprises an edition of all genuine and forged Anglo-Saxon charters from the Minster archives of York, Beverley and Ripon and also of Durham Cathedral and Lowther Castle. Whilst this edition provides individual historical accounts of the four northern churches (and a more general introduction of the north west for Lowther Castle), it also invites comparisons between them, their experiences, and above all the types of charter preserved in their archives.[1] Such comparisons aid an understanding of the ecclesiastical and political make-up of Northumbria.

1. THE SURVIVAL OF CHARTERS FROM ANGLO-SAXON NORTHUMBRIA

One striking feature of the northern archives is the paucity of Anglo-Saxon documentation to have survived: eleven charters from York, three from Beverley, two from Ripon, four from Durham and one from Lowther Castle.[2] When we consider that the archive of Christ Church, Canterbury, the southern archbishopric, has preserved some 180 charters, then the low numbers of charters from the northern archives become all the more arresting. It is remarkable that York, the northern archbishopric (from 735), can yield only eleven such documents.

In fact, the situation is more serious still. The present edition takes into account the archives of four Northumbrian churches and also a rare surviving

[1] In citing Anglo-Saxon charters I follow the methodology given by S. Keynes in 'A Conspectus of the Charters of King Edgar, 957–75', in Scragg, *Edgar*, pp. 60–80 (at pp. 60–2). Thus Anglo-Saxon charters are cited first by their number in 'Sawyer', abbreviated to 'S' and a relevant number. Where a charter has been edited in the British Academy series, 'Anglo-Saxon Charters', its relevant number is cited in brackets using an abbreviation for the name of the archive (following those used by Keynes) and its number in that archive of texts. For example, S 418 (*WinchNM* 10) refers to Miller, *New Minster, Winchester*, no. 10 (pp. 54–9). Where there is no British Academy edition yet available, pre-975 charters are cited from 'Birch' (abbreviated to BCS) and post-975 charters are cited from 'Kemble' (abbreviated to KCD).

[2] For an investigation about what early Northumbrian narrative sources, such as Bede's *Historia abbatum*, can tell us about gift-giving and charters in Northumbria, see Wormald, *Bede and the Conversion* and Wood 2010.

writ from Lowther Castle;[3] but it is clear from other evidence—narrative sources, archaeology, surviving sculpture, place-names and Domesday Book—that a very great number of churches and monasteries existed in Anglo-Saxon Northumbria.[4] These churches, even if they were staffed by just one priest, would have required an endowment to survive, which would have involved the accumulation of land and presumably also of charters.[5]

Various early eighth-century narrative sources make it clear that charters were in relatively frequent use in early Northumbria. Perhaps most famously, Stephanus' *Vita Wilfridi* includes a passage which seems to rely in part on charter diplomatic, and Bede's *Epistola ad Ecgbertum* discusses the use of charters.[6] In this letter, Bede laments what he saw as the various failings of the Northumbrian church around him. He depicts, for example, the existence of 'innumerable places, as we all know, allowed the name of monasteries by a most foolish manner of speaking, but having nothing at all of a monastic way of life';[7] and, as part of an attempt to rid Northumbria of these establishments, Bede calls for Ecgberht and King Ceolwulf to 'annul the irreligious and unjust acts and writings of our predecessors, and to provide for those things which may be useful to our province, whether in

[3] For the Lowther archive, see below, pp. 366–7.

[4] Some famous examples of Northumbrian churches include Hexham, Monkwearmouth-Jarrow, Gateshead, Crayke (for which see **18**), Escomb (for which see **19**) and Gilling. The list of religious houses existing in the pre-1066 period in D. Knowles and R.N. Hadcock, *Medieval Religious Houses: England and Wales* (London, 1953; 2nd edn 1971), pp. 463–87, suggests a further thirty-four churches from Anglo-Saxon Northumbria. But this is still too few. The evidence of sculpture, place-names and Domesday Book suggests a much larger number. Morris (R.K.), *Churches in the Landscape*, p. 141, states: 'In Yorkshire, out of a medieval total of perhaps 550 churches, about 390 (71 per cent) retain either fabric or a font of the period before 1150, or pre-Conquest sculpture equatable with the presence of an ecclesiastical site, or both'; for the evidence of sculpture in this regard see pp. 153–4 and for place-names, pp. 154–61; see also Morris (R.K.) 1988, p. 191, for an overview of the possible number of pre-Conquest churches in Yorkshire and Palliser 1992, pp. 21–3, for further discussion. For the use of sculpture in suggesting the site of a church, see Cambridge 1984, p. 68. For the Northumbrian church in general in the Anglo-Saxon period, see, for example, Hall (D.) 1984; Hadley, *Northern*, esp. pp. 216–97; Rollason, *Northumbria*; Blair, *Church*; Foot, *Monastic Life* and the unpublished 2006 Oxford DPhil thesis, 'The Church in Anglo-Saxon Yorkshire: Minsters in the Danelaw, *c.* 600–1200', by Dr T. Pickles, to whom I am most grateful for sending me a copy. For a recent assessment of 'clusters' of monastic sites in Northumbria, and conversely of those monasteries that were in competition with each other, see Wood 2008.

[5] This is not to suggest that charters would have constituted the only means of guaranteeing a sale of land and, as is discussed further below in the general introduction, there may have been grants made orally which required nothing more than the presence of certain witnesses.

[6] See *VW*, c. XVII (discussed in detail below, pp. 234–5) and Bede, *Epistola*, esp. pp. 413–17; see also Wormald, *Bede and the Conversion* (at pp. 19–21, for Bede's *Epistola*). For the presence of a leaden papal bull at Whitby, see Levison, *England and the Continent*, p. 17, n. 2.

[7] Bede, *Epistola*, § 10: '…sunt loca innumera, ut nouimus omnes, stilo stultissimo in monasteriorum ascripta uocabulum, sed nichil prorsus monasticae conuersationis habentia…', translated in Whitelock, *EHD*, no. 170 (p. 804).

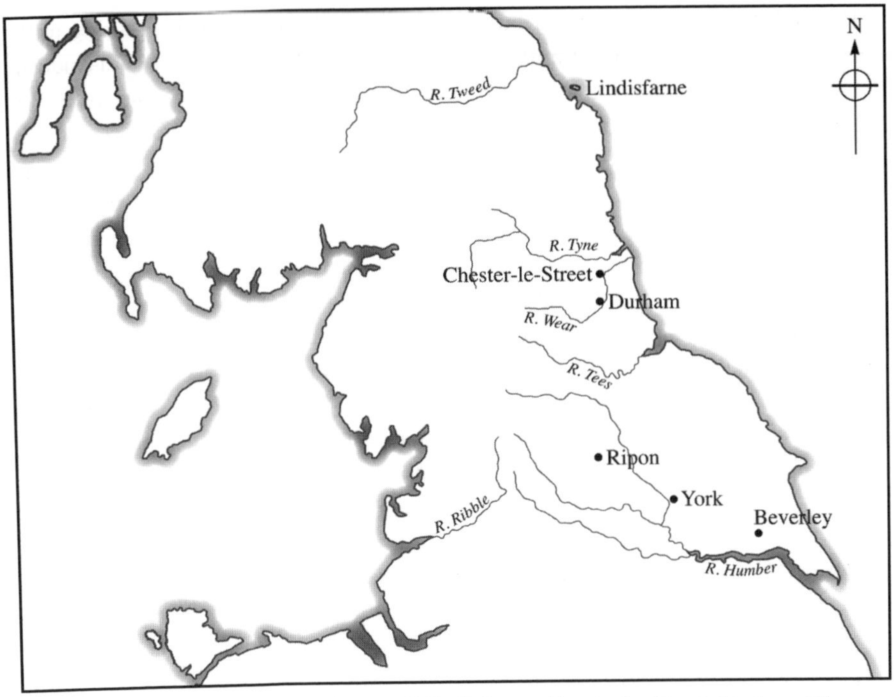

Map 1. Location, and nearby rivers, of Lindisfarne, Chester-le-Street, Durham, Ripon, York and Beverley

matters of Church or state',[8] where it seems certain that the reference to 'writings' (*scripta*) is to charters. In the next passage of the letter, Bede continues with much the same theme and describes how certain laymen manage to buy estates with the ostensible purpose of founding a religious establishment but in fact go on to use the property for their own 'lust' (*libidini*). It is with a sense of despair that Bede notes that laymen caused these estates to be given to them 'in hereditary right by royal edicts (i.e. charters), and even get those same documents of their privileges confirmed, as if in truth worthy of God, by the subscription of bishops, abbots and secular persons'.[9] These extracts from Bede's *Epistola* demonstrate that already by the early eighth century the royal charter had assumed importance in Northumbria, so much so that it was susceptible to being abused by unscrupulous laymen.

[8] Bede, *Epistola*, § 11: '...iniqua priorum gesta atque scripta conuellere, et ea quae prouinciae nostrae, siue secundum Deum, siue secundum seculum sint utilia, prospicere...', translated in Whitelock, *EHD*, no. 170 (p. 805).

[9] Bede, *Epistola*, § 12: '...in ius sibi haereditarium regalibus edictis faciunt asscribi, ipsas quoque litteras priuilegiorum suorum quasi ueraciter Deo dignas, pontificum, abbatum, et potestatum seculi obtinent subscriptione confirmari', translated in Whitelock, *EHD*, no. 170 (p. 805); for the causes of Bede's despair, and of his dislike of charters, see Wormald, *Bede and the Conversion*, pp. 20–4.

Beyond these references in narrative sources, it is difficult to say anything more about Northumbrian charters until the early tenth century when **1** was issued in the name of King Æthelstan and subsequently preserved in the York archive. But Story has recently drawn attention to a letter written by George, bishop of Ostia and Amiens (753–98), to Pope Hadrian following the visit of papal legates to Northumbria and Mercia in 786.[10] The letter describes how George proceeded northwards from Kent, was received at the Mercian court of King Offa,[11] and then journeyed onwards to Northumbria to visit King Ælfwald (d. 788) and Archbishop Eanbald I of York (d. 796).[12] At the meeting of a council which included all of the important ecclesiastical and secular Northumbrian figures, a set of religious reforms was announced and the resulting twenty canons are preserved in the text of the letter itself.[13] What is of interest for our present purposes is that the letter concludes with a description of how the canons had been read out publicly at a meeting of the king and his councillors; and it recounts how those present 'set down the sign of the holy cross on the charter of this page with a careful pen', some details of which are reminiscent of the kind of ceremony regularly enacted by Anglo-Saxon kings at meetings where charters were produced.[14] In George's

[10] Story, *Carolingian Connections*, pp. 55–78 (at pp. 64–78); this discussion of George's letter is indebted to the work of Story. For more about the report of the 786 legatine mission, see Wormald 1991, pp. 28–45 and Cubitt, *Councils*, pp. 153–90, who stresses the Northumbrian background to the mission. For further information about George see, for example, Levison, *England and the Continent*, pp. 127–9 and 154–5.

[11] The text of the letter is edited by Dümmler in Alcuin, *Ep*., no. 3 (pp. 19–29); Story, *Carolingian Connections*, p. 58 (and n. 12), notes that the only extant copy of the letter was made *c*. 1000 and survives in the Wolfenbüttel library as Wolfenbüttel, Herzog-August-Bibliothek, MS Helmstadt 454; see also Wormald 1991, p. 40, n. 37.

[12] See George, *Epistola ad Hadrianum*, in Alcuin, *Ep*., no. 3 (pp. 20–1) and Story, *Carolingian Connections*, pp. 58–9. For Archbishop Eanbald I, see below, pp. 38–40.

[13] For these twenty canons, see George, *Epistola ad Hadrianum*, in Alcuin, *Ep*., no. 3 (pp. 21–7). Wormald 1991, proposes that these canons may actually be synonymous with Offa's law-code. Cubitt, *Councils*, pp. 164–85, discusses the possibility of Alcuin's influence in the drafting of these legatine canons.

[14] George, *Epistola ad Hadrianum*, in Alcuin, *Ep*., no. 3 (p. 27): '...stilo diligenti in charta huius paginae exarauerunt signum sanctae crucis...', cited also by Story, *Carolingian Connections*, p. 68, where she notes that the unique manuscript copy of George's letter provides at this point a depiction of the type of cross used by the Northumbrian witnesses in signing the document (the attestations of the first three witnesses, King Ælfwald, Bishop Tilberht (of Hexham) and Archbishop Eanbald all have crosses following their subscriptions); as Story states, the use of such autograph crosses is not a usual feature of Anglo-Saxon diplomatic. The crosses supplied in a late tenth century charter of King Æthelred from the Abingdon archive, S 876 (*Abing* 124), may be an exception to this; see Keynes, *Diplomas*, p. 101, n. 54, Kelly, *Abingdon* 1, p. cxiv and Kelly, *Abingdon* 2, pp. 477–83 (at p. 483). For meetings of the king and his councillors, see, for example, J.R. Maddicott, *The Origins of the English Parliament 924–1327. The Ford Lectures delivered in the University of Oxford in Hilary Term 2004* (Oxford, 2010; repr. 2011), pp. 1–56.

letter the document signed by the Northumbrians is explicitly identified as a 'charter' (*charta*), and what then follows this statement is a list of witnesses, who attest with just the type of subscription formula common to Anglo-Saxon charters.[15] Following the list of twelve witnesses at this Northumbrian council, George's letter resumes its narrative, describing how the legates then went back to Mercia and there King Offa, together with Archbishop Jænberht, convened a second council. Again the twenty canons were read out, which those present promised to uphold, and then the document (described as a *chartulam*) was attested by the Mercian dignitaries, who once more are listed using forms of subscription found in Anglo-Saxon diplomatic.[16]

It is likely that the twenty canons and two witness-lists originally existed as a discrete document separate from George's letter to Pope Hadrian.[17] The document itself is not a traditional charter in the sense of granting lands or privileges. And its overall form, and perhaps also its subject matter, seems in fact to suggest closer parallels with Frankish legal documents, in particular an early kind of capitulary.[18] But it is undeniable that it preserves traces of Anglo-Saxon diplomatic, and, since it may originally have been composed in Northumbria, it is of great value as further evidence of Northumbrian diplomatic in the eighth century.[19]

So it is apparent that the northern archives, as they are preserved today, are relatively deficient in their holdings and one can only speculate as to the reasons why. Charters may have been accidentally lost or deliberately destroyed. Particularly violent events in Northumbria's history, such as the arrival and

[15] For example, King Ælfwald and Bishop Tilberht attest with these formulae in the first person: 'Ego Aelfuualdus, Transhymbrane gentis rex, consentiens signo sanctae crucis subscripsi; Ego Tilberthus, Agustadensis ecclesiae presul, gaudens signo sanctae crucis subscripsi'; see George, *Epistola ad Hadrianum*, in Alcuin, *Ep.*, no. 3 (p. 27).

[16] See George, *Epistola ad Hadrianum*, in Alcuin, *Ep.*, no. 3 (pp. 28–9).

[17] Wormald 1991, pp. 40–1, suggests that the original document would have been different in form from that included in George's letter; see also Story, *Carolingian Connections*, p. 75 (and pp. 76–7, for some very interesting observations about how the unique manuscript copy of George's letter, despite being made *c.* 1000, may, in places, be mimicking the original lay-out of an Anglo-Saxon charter. For example, she notes that the 'lesser names (*Alchardus episcopus* to *Edihard* (sic) *abbas*) in the list of Mercian attestations were copied into the manuscript two to a line, suggesting that they were copied from a list written in two columns. Again this structure is commonplace in Anglo-Saxon charters' (p. 76)).

[18] For the similarities of the document with its twenty canons to early Carolingian capitularies, perhaps especially Charlemagne's *Admonitio generalis* of 789, see Wormald 1991, pp. 34 and 42–3, Cubitt, *Councils*, pp. 160–4 and Story, *Carolingian Connections*, pp. 78–92. Story, *ibid.*, p. 91, concludes, 'The decrees were written down as a capitulary but were attested like a charter and presented in synodal diplomatic form'.

[19] For a much more detailed discussion of the diplomatic form of this document, see Story, *ibid.*, pp. 64–78 (at p. 77, for the suggestion that the document was originally made in Northumbria).

settlement of a Scandinavian population,[20] the razing of Ripon Minster by King Eadred or the 'harrying of the north' by William the Conqueror,[21] may have meant that everyday legal documents stood little chance of survival.[22]

2. THE EVIDENCE FOR ORAL TRANSACTIONS IN NORTHUMBRIA

If it is impossible to know the precise reasons why there are now so few Northumbrian documents, it is nonetheless clear that written documentation was not the only means of guaranteeing and proving land ownership. Allowance seems also to have been made for the oral transfer of land and rights, where the production of a written diploma was perhaps not expected (or necessary).[23] Evidence for this practice survives in two forms, both of which are connected with the York archive. On f. 161v of the York Gospels (York, Minster Library, Add. 1), a list of some seventy or eighty names has been preserved; the list is a copy of an earlier document, made in a hand of the late eleventh century, which has the title: *Ðis sindan þa festermen Elfricas*, 'These are the festermen of Ælfric'.[24] The word

[20] The question of the impact of vikings and Scandinavian settlers on the Church has been much discussed; see, for example, P. Wormald, 'Viking Studies: Whence and Whither?', *The Vikings*, ed. R.T. Farrell (London, 1982), pp. 128–53; Morris 1984; Dumville, *Wessex and England*, pp. 29–54; Hadley, *Northern*, pp. 289–97; Hadley and Richards, *Cultures in Contact*; Abrams and Parsons 2004; Blair, *Church*, pp. 291–341 and Hadley, *Vikings*, pp. 192–236.

[21] For an assessment of the severity of the so-called 'harrying of the north', see Palliser 1992 and Palliser 1993. For Hugh the Chanter's statement about the effects of the harrying for York Minster and its archives, see below, p. 68.

[22] Even major Anglo-Latin compositions struggled to survive; H. Gneuss, 'Anglo-Saxon Libraries from the Conversion to the Benedictine Reform', *Settimane* xxxii (1986), pp. 643–88 (repr. in his *Books and Libraries in Early England* (Aldershot, 1996), no. II) notes that as a result of viking raids, 'texts that are known to have been available in the great northern libraries…including writings by Anglo-Latin authors, were no longer to be found in England and had to be imported from the Continent, especially when the tenth-century reformers began to stock the new monastic libraries' (at p. 676).

[23] Of course Anglo-Saxon charters themselves seem to have been the products of some kind of oral conveyance ceremony witnessed by a gathering of the king and his councillors (for the production of Anglo-Saxon charters, see Keynes, *Diplomas*, pp. 28–39 (esp. pp. 35–7, for the use of charters in ceremonies of conveyance); for the importance of the written word in Anglo-Saxon society, and also of the various functions of Anglo-Saxon charters, see Kelly 1990 and Keynes 1990). The difference in these instances in Northumbria, as will be seen, is that there seems to have been no resultant written documentation, giving details of the nature and terms of the land transfer. The notes in the Durham archive, edited here as **18–20**, may be representative of some kind of ceremony carried out orally at the altar of St Cuthbert's church; for discussion of this practice, see below, pp. 13–14.

[24] This list of *festermen* is edited as Appendix 2. For the date of this list, see Stevenson 1912, pp. 11–12 and Ker, *Catalogue*, p. 469. For the difficulties involved in determining how many people are listed,

festerman derives from the Old Norse *festu-maðr*, meaning 'a bail, surety'; its use was restricted to eastern and northern England.[25] *Festermen*, or men standing as surety, could be required for various situations. The *Law of the Northumbrian Priests*, a work influenced by Archbishop Wulfstan but perhaps compiled a generation later, states as item 2.3: 'And each priest is to provide himself with 12 sureties (*festermen*), that he will rightly observe the priests' law'.[26] In this instance a *festerman* was someone who was willing to guarantee the behaviour of a priest.

A much longer and more detailed set of memoranda involving sureties survives in the Peterborough archive, S 1448a (*Pet* 30). Here the word *festermen* is used synonymously with the Old English *borhhanda*, meaning 'pledge-holders'.[27] In this document the *festermen* are explicitly those who at a public meeting were prepared to stand as guarantors for a vendor in some kind of oral land transaction.[28] The preponderance of Scandinavian personal names in the Peterborough document and the use of Scandinavian terms such as *wepentac* ('wapentake') or *oxangang* ('oxgang') suggests that the Peterborough area had been heavily influenced by Scandinavians.[29] It is striking that in no part of the Peterborough memoranda is there any suggestion that written title-deeds were used or that the new owners would seek to have the transaction guaranteed by the production of a charter.[30] Kennedy has shown that the *Libellus Æthelwoldi* provides a similar description of land transactions made in the Danelaw where charters were not necessarily the preferred means of conducting a transfer of land (or of defending land during litigation);[31] and Kelly suggests that with the Peterborough memoranda 'we may catch a glimpse of a Danelaw society where landholding operated on a different

---

see Cooper 1969, pp. 328–32 and Keynes 1986, pp. 98–9. On the identity of 'Ælfric', see Farrer, *EYC*, p. 28, Cooper 1969, p. 332 and, for a contrary view suggesting the likelihood that 'Ælfric' is the same as Ælfric Puttoc, archbishop of York (1023–51), see Keynes 1986, p. 99. For the York Gospels, see below, pp. 76–7.

[25] See Robertson, *Charters*, p. 330.

[26] For a text and translation of the *Law of the Northumbrian Priests*, see *Councils and Synods*, Part I, pp. 452–68, at p. 453. For a recent re-dating, see Wormald, *Law I*, pp. 208–10 and 396–7 (at p. 397, n. 613, for one of Wulfstan's successors at York, either Archbishop Ælfric or Archbishop Cynesige, as being the most likely author of the *Law of the Northumbrian Priests*; for Ælfric and Cynesige, see below, pp. 64–5).

[27] In the corpus of Anglo-Saxon laws, *borhhanda* were sureties used for a variety of purposes; see Keynes 1986, p. 98.

[28] The Peterborough document can be explicit about where the meeting took place and who was involved; see Kelly, *Peterborough*, p. 335.

[29] Kelly, *ibid.*, pp. 336–7.

[30] Kelly, *ibid.*, p. 335.

[31] Kennedy 1995, pp. 131–83 (at pp. 167–9, for instances of the Ely monastery's preference for oral proof when defending its endowment, despite its apparent possession of the necessary documentation; and pp. 172–3, for the role of the charter in the 'wider complex of oral procedures' where litigation was concerned).

basis, relying on oral witness and not requiring written title-deeds; there is indeed little sign of any royal involvement, although ealdormen are more visible'.[32]

By analogy with the Peterborough memoranda and the evidence of the *Libellus Æthelwoldi*, it seems likely that Ælfric's sureties, listed in the York Gospels, had been recruited as a means of guaranteeing a sale of land.[33] The very large number of men listed might suggest that the transaction was a particularly important one. Or, since the record in its current form is a copy of an earlier document, it may be that the original document included more detail about the sureties, and about the transaction(s) for which they were providing surety, but that this was subsequently omitted by the copyist. This copyist, who was a near-contemporary of the original sale of land(s), perhaps considered it unnecessary to note this extra detail and so only recorded the names of the *festermen*. Unfortunately the exact circumstances and indeed the identities of the men listed, many of whom have Scandinavian names, cannot be known for sure.[34]

A further intriguing piece of evidence from York Minster, the so-called 'horn of Ulf', may also be representative of some kind of oral land transaction. The horn is traditionally associated with a pre-Conquest grant of land by a man named Ulf, son of Thorald, who is supposed to have given land to the York church just after the death of King Cnut, in about the year 1036.[35] Problems abound in accepting this story, however, not least in the dating of the horn itself.[36] Recent research

[32] Kelly, *Peterborough*, p. 335, where she likewise draws attention to the work of Kennedy.

[33] It seems rather less probable that the list of *festermen* was made to guarantee Ælfric's good behaviour; see Cooper 1969, p. 330 and Keynes 1986, p. 99.

[34] Some of the sureties listed, *Ulfcetel*, *Farðain*, *Forna*, and *Rauan*, might be identical with the *Ulfkytel*, *Farþegn*, *Forna* and *Rafen* in **8**, but it is impossible to be sure; see Keynes 1986, p. 99. These names, spelled here in the form in which they are given in the list of *festermen* and in **8**, may ultimately derive from Old Norse, 'Ulfketill', 'Farþegn', 'Forni' and 'Rafn', for which see the relevant entries in Fellows-Jensen, *SPNLY*.

[35] The horn had silver mounts attached to it by Henry Lord Fairfax in 1675. The silver mount had a Latin inscription written on it which reads: 'cornu hoc Ulphus, in occidentali parte Deirae princeps una cum omnibus terris et redditibus suis olim donavit: amissum vel abreptum. Henricus de Fairfax demum restituit, dec. et cap. de novo ornavit An. dom. 1675'. A much earlier mount and chain had been fitted to the horn in the late fourteenth or early fifteenth century by the Treasurer, John de Neweton; see Raine, *HCY* III, p. 386. The horn is made from an elephant's ivory; carvings on the horn suggest that it was made in the south of Italy, perhaps Salerno in particular; see H. Swarzenski, 'Two Oliphants in the Museum', *Bulletin of the Museum of Fine Arts, Boston* lx (1962), pp. 27–45 (at pp. 37 and 43–4). For the supposed date of the grant see, for example, S. Gale, 'An historical dissertation upon the antient Danish horn, kept in the Cathedral Church of York', *Archaeologia* i (1770), pp. 168–82, at pp. 172–3 and T.D. Kendrick, 'The Horn of Ulph', *Antiquity* xi (1937), pp. 278–82, at p. 280.

[36] Another problem is the identity of Ulf; for the tentative suggestion that 'Ulf' could be synonymous with Archbishop Wulfstan, see Barr 1986, p. 105, n. 7, which also has useful bibliographical citations concerning Ulf's horn. For more about Wulfstan, who had a major hand in **6** and **7**, see below, pp. 61–4.

into the decoration of Ulf's horn has suggested that a date in the first half of the eleventh century is impossible and, on the basis that the horn's ornamentation bears a strong resemblance to the Salerno panels, a date in the 1080s has been proposed as more likely.[37] There is therefore difficulty in accepting a pre-Conquest date for the horn. But even if a date just after the Conquest is more appropriate, it is still striking that the gift of a horn of tenure was considered a fitting method for guaranteeing a land grant.[38] Whether or not this had been a long-established, and widely used, Northumbrian Anglo-Saxon practice, the details of which are now unknown, is a good question.[39]

3. NORTHUMBRIAN DIPLOMATIC

If one characteristic of the northern archives is the low number of documents to have survived, another is the particular range and type of document on display. Analysis of the diplomatic formulation of the charters and writs surviving in the archives presented here, especially of those preserved in the York and Durham archives,[40] can provide invaluable information about the political situation in Northumbria at various points in the Anglo-Saxon period. What becomes clear is that the old division of Northumbria between Deira to the south of the River Tees and Bernicia to the north died hard.[41]

The sequence of charters from the York archive begins in the early tenth century with a famous document drafted by the scribe known as 'Æthelstan A' and issued

[37] See R.P. Bergman, *The Salerno Ivories:* Ars sacra *from Medieval Amalfi* (Cambridge, MA, 1980), p. 90, citing the 1979 Harvard PhD thesis by D. Ebitz, 'Two Schools of Ivory Carving in Italy and the Mediterranean Context of the Eleventh and Twelfth Centuries', for the argument redating Ulf's horn to the 1080s. For more on the artwork of Ulf's horn, see D. Tweddle, 'Art in Pre-Conquest York', in Hall (R.A.) *et al.*, *Aspects*, pp. 446–58 (at pp. 457–8).

[38] The horn was evidently important enough to the York church that they had it carved into the very fabric of their minster (see S. Brown, *'Our Magnificent Fabrick': York Minster, An Architectural History c. 1220–1500* (Swindon, 2003), p. 125); when the church's lands were divided into prebends after the Conquest, one prebend became known as the *terra Ulfi*. The Pusey horn was believed in the fifteenth century to have represented a land grant by King Cnut to the Pusey family; on horns of tenure in general, see J. Cherry, 'Symbolism and Survival: Medieval Horns of Tenure', *The Antiquaries Journal* lxix (1989), pp. 111–18, at p. 114, for the Pusey horn.

[39] For the much better documented situation in eastern England, where it is clear that a range of different kinds of transaction took place, see Kennedy 1995.

[40] The nature of those few documents preserved in the Beverley and Ripon archives, makes them rather less useful for the present discussion.

[41] For the River Tees as the most likely boundary between these two kingdoms, see Blair (P.H.) 1949, p. 58 and Yorke, *Kings and Kingdoms*, p. 74. For Northumbria in the Anglo-Saxon period, see, for example, P.H. Blair, *Anglo-Saxon Northumbria*, ed. M. Lapidge and Pauline H. Blair (London, 1984); N.J. Higham, *The Kingdom of Northumbria AD 350–1100* (Frome, 1993) and Rollason, *Northumbria*.

by King Æthelstan at a meeting of 7 June 934 at Nottingham.[42] In the years 928 to 935, 'Æthelstan A' was entrusted with a monopoly over charter production; he seems to have travelled around the country and drawn up charters in time for the meeting of the king and his councillors. These charters are remarkable because not only do they display several modifications to the existing diplomatic form of an Anglo-Saxon charter, but they are also written in a highly ornate and learned Latin style. It seems to be no coincidence that these documents appear in the year following Æthelstan's significant success in bringing the Northumbrian kingdom within his dominion.[43]

At this moment in the 930s, the York church, having recently been in close alliance with a series of Scandinavian kings,[44] was prepared to recognise the authority of Æthelstan, a southern English king. The preservation of **1** in the York archive, a product of Æthelstan's chancery, is emblematic of York's new stance. And **1** is of further significance since some of its diplomatic peculiarities may actually be indicative of 'Æthelstan A's' attempts to deal with an area of the country that was relatively unknown to the southern court.[45]

On the same journey northwards, Æthelstan stopped off at St Cuthbert's community at Chester-le-Street, to the north of the River Tees; again the king made gifts of land and of other items. However, no 'Æthelstan A' charter has been preserved as a witness to this grant. Instead it was the Cuthbertine community itself which took note of Æthelstan's presence by using its own, idiosyncratic method. Although St Cuthbert's community recognised the authority of this southern king, the responsibility for the record seems to have been that of the religious community. The Durham *Liber Vitae* (hereafter *LVD*), a precious book closely linked to the history, identity and prosperity of the Cuthbertine community, provided the context in which Æthelstan's visit was recorded.[46] His eminence is acknowledged by the insertion of his name at the head, and thus out of chronological order, of the list of names of Northumbrian *regum vel*

[42] For more about 'Æthelstan A', including relevant bibliographical material, see the commentary to **1**.

[43] For Æthelstan's conquest of Northumbria, see *ASC D*, s.a. 926 (*recte* 927). In this assessment of the charters of 'Æthelstan A', I have benefited greatly from the lectures of Professor Simon Keynes which I attended as an undergraduate; on the style of the 'Æthelstan A' charters, see further Woodman, forthcoming.

[44] For the sequence of Scandinavian kings at York from the late ninth to the mid-tenth century, see below, pp. 42–7.

[45] See the commentary to **1** for a full discussion of its various diplomatic oddities, perhaps most notably its boundary clause.

[46] For the Durham *Liber Vitae*, see Stevenson, *Lib. Vit.*; Rollason *et al.*, *The Durham* and the new edition, *LVD*; see also below, pp. 318–20.

ducum;[47] but the very nature of this record and the manuscript into which it was inserted suggest that Æthelstan was involved in an arrangement which was quite different from the one he had earlier effected with York.[48] Once he had stepped beyond the River Tees, Æthelstan entered an area in which the influence of St Cuthbert's community was paramount and operations seem to have been carried out according to terms dictated by them.[49]

These differing dealings of the York and Cuthbertine communities with King Æthelstan prefigure a clearer diplomatic distinction seen later in the tenth and eleventh centuries between the style of document preserved in the York archive (**1–5** and **8–11**) and those preserved at Durham (**18–20**). After the last Scandinavian ruler left York in 954, southern kings of Anglo-Saxon England took steps to draw the York see into their jurisdiction and this is reflected by the type of charter preserved in the York archive. As will be seen, charters **1–5** and **8–10** are documents which fit clearly into the southern diplomatic mainstream of the day. They indicate that the York archbishopric was willing to accommodate itself to southern hegemony and that the southern kings were able to exert increased influence on this northern church. The benefit for the York archbishopric was that initially the southern kings of England were able to offer some sort of stability after the turbulent viking era; **2** and **3**, which grant lands in Nottinghamshire, show Kings Eadwig and Edgar aiding the York church to claim estates in the heart of Scandinavian territory. And the southern kings had every reason to draw York further into their control: not only had Archbishop Wulfstan I (931–56) demonstrated his willingness to side with Scandinavian rulers earlier in the tenth century,[50] but there was also the possibility of the re-establishment of the nexus between the viking kingdoms of York and Dublin.[51] This led to subsequent archbishops being carefully selected by the southern regime. And the process was intensified when, from the time of Archbishop Oswald (970/1–92), York was at times held in plurality with the bishopric of Worcester.[52]

The situation was entirely different further to the north, in Bernicia. In its earliest days the religious community founded at Lindisfarne was intended to

47 Æthelstan's name is recorded immediately after the title *nomina regum vel ducum* on f. 15r of the *LVD*.

48 Some names of Æthelstan's retinue may also have been noted in the *LVD*: see below, pp. 319–20; some twelfth-century entries of Anglo-Saxon names may ultimately derive from two lost diplomas in the name of Æthelstan (although the second group of names is prehaps more likely to derive from a record made into a gospel book): see Barker 1977.

49 Details of Æthelstan's visit to St Cuthbert's community, and the gifts he bestowed while there, are also given in *HSC*, c. 26 (discussed below, pp. 299–302).

50 For Wulfstan's political machinations, see below, pp. 53–5.

51 See below, pp. 51–2.

52 For all of this, see below, p. 59.

be the base from which the Celtic Christianizing mission to Northumbria could be implemented. But the unfolding of events, in particular the decision at a 664 council in Whitby for the Northumbrian church to follow Roman forms of Christianity, represented a very serious threat to Lindisfarne.[53] And matters became worse when Wilfrid, the prime opponent of Celtic Christianity and of Lindisfarne, managed to gain actual control of the Lindisfarne see on Cuthbert's death in 687. The community reacted by memorialising Cuthbert, who had been one of its most eminent members, in order to emphasise its identity. His cult was promoted and considerable hagiographical material, produced for the first time in Northumbria, was published as propaganda for the community.[54]

It was this sense of identity which enabled the religious community not only to weather various turbulent political times but even to establish itself as a 'corporate' strength within the kingdom of Northumbria. Unlike the situation at York in the late ninth century, St Cuthbert's community did not suffer a protracted settlement of vikings within its sphere of influence and land holdings. The evidence of place-names and cultural artefacts suggests that vikings accomplished no significant settlement further north than the River Tees and in the Bernician area.[55] This enabled Cuthbert's community to expand its area of control and jurisdiction. Part of this process involved a physical relocation. In *c.* 875 the Cuthbertines embarked on a period of wandering which saw them eventually move from their marginal position on Lindisfarne to Chester-le-Street. During this period they were accompanied by Cuthbert's body and relics, which provided a symbol of continuity with their former times on Lindisfarne and thus helped to validate their rights to hold any land which had been given to St Cuthbert.[56] Although our sources depict this as a time of uncertainty forced upon the community by the arrival of vikings, it seems reasonable to suggest that the community made the

[53] See below, pp. 274–5.

[54] For overviews of the politics of this time see, for example, Kirby 1974, Kirby 1995 and Cubitt 1989. For the hagiographical output, see Colgrave 1958 and W. Goffart, *The Narrators of Barbarian History (A.D. 550–800): Jordanes, Gregory of Tours, Bede, and Paul the Deacon* (Princeton, 1988; repr. 2009), pp. 235–328.

[55] See, for example, R.N. Bailey, *Viking Age Sculpture in Northern England* (London, 1980), p. 34 and Rollason, *Northumbria*, p. 213. To the north of Bernicia and in the modern-day Scottish borderlands there is ample evidence for Scandinavian place-names and Scandinavian settlement, particularly in the south-west of Scotland, as one would expect; see W.F.H. Nicolaisen, *Scottish Place-Names: Their Study and Significance* (London, 1976), pp. 84–120 and the collection of essays, *Scandinavian Settlement in Northern Britain. Thirteen Studies of Place-Names in their Historical Context*, ed. B.E. Crawford (London and New York, 1995). There are, however, pockets of Scandinavian place-names in Durham, notably near Gainford. Morris 1977, p. 101, suggests that these were generated by 'persons of more lowly status who did the day-to-day running of the estate, and who could possibly be seen as "in-filling" certain areas alongside the native peoples'.

[56] See also the comments of Rollason 1987, pp. 46–7.

most of their situation by strengthening ties with their traditional outposts. And, as they moved southwards, the Cuthbertines sought to absorb the jurisdiction and territory of those communities at Monkwearmouth-Jarrow and Hexham which had ceased to exist.[57]

The close association of Cuthbert's followers with their local saint meant that they became a kind of 'saintly corporation', the *populus sancti Cuthberti*, as they are described in the *Historia de Sancto Cuthberto*.[58] This latter description found expression in Old English as *haliwerfolc* ('the people of the holy man'), which seems to have referred to the people of the lands which belonged to St Cuthbert; and in later centuries inhabitants of Durham were still called by this name.[59] It is symptomatic of this close association between saint and people that documents **18–20**, which are very brief notes and which take the form of 'charters' as employed by Cuthbert's community, describe the grants of land as being made to St Cuthbert himself;[60] the association with the saint is further underlined because the note is recorded within a precious manuscript intimately connected to the growth and development of Cuthbert's church. This was a deliberate strategy. Any grantor of land, or indeed any would-be defrauder of the community's possessions, would have been fully aware that if he contravened the terms of the grant he would have to deal with the powerful saint himself rather than a mere temporal institution.[61] In such circumstances the re-invention of Cuthbert's image—from that of a pious saint in the eighth-century *Vitae* to that seen in the mid-eleventh-century text called the *Historia de Sancto Cuthberto* (hereafter *HSC*)—becomes more intelligible.[62] The *HSC* not only depicts the saint as the recipient of land,[63] but also shows what can happen if the saint is defrauded:

> Nam abstulit ab eo Billingham, et Illeclif, et Wigeclif, et Creca. Et ideo ira Dei et sancti confessoris accensa est super eum...sed mox ira Dei et sancti confessoris perterritus, ceso exercitu fugit et corruit, uitamque et regnum perdidit...Iccirco

[57] For the wanderings of St Cuthbert's community, see Rollason 1987 and Blair, *Church*, p. 312; for the absorption of the jurisdiction and territory of Monkwearmouth-Jarrow and Hexham, see below, pp. 293–4.

[58] *HSC*, cc. 16 and 20.

[59] On the terms *populus sancti Cuthberti* and *haliwerfolc*, see Rollason 1987, p. 56; Johnson South 1996, p. 92 and Rollason, *Symeon: Libellus*, p. 114, n. 66.

[60] For the suggestion that a gift of land made directly to a saint is symptomatic of Celtic charters, see Wormald, *Bede and the Conversion*, p. 17; see also Rollason 1987, pp. 54–5.

[61] See also the comments of Meehan 1975, pp. 48–9.

[62] For the *HSC*, see Craster 1954 and the edition by Johnson South, *HSC*; for its place in the Durham archive, see below, pp. 324–6.

[63] See *HSC*, c. 5, 'And King Ecgfrith and Archbishop Theodore gave to St Cuthbert...all the land that lies from...', and *HSC*, c. 9, 'Afterwards the same holy bishop Ecgred built a church in the village that is called Gainford and gave it to St Cuthbert with whatever pertains to it' (trans. Johnson South).

> caueant reges et principes ne mentiantur et ne quid auferant sancto Cuthberto, nec consentiant auferentibus.[64]

In the *HSC*, posthumous miracles involving Cuthbert now show a ruthless saint who would punish and avenge wrong-doers, especially those attempting to deprive the community of its land.[65]

The evidence of **18–20** suggests that St Cuthbert's community sought to guarantee any potential transaction by means of a ceremony involving St Cuthbert himself.[66] The *LVD*, which is the manuscript into which **18–20** have been written, is known to have been kept on the high altar at Durham. It is probable that the grantor of the land to St Cuthbert's church stood at the altar and witnessed his name being inserted into one of the community's most revered manuscripts; such a ceremony would impress upon that man the need to uphold his half of the arrangement. Records of later land transactions carried out at Durham indicate that this is exactly how St Cuthbert's community operated. For example, when restoring monastic lands in 1128, Bishop Ranulf Flambard (1099–1128) placed his ring on the high altar of St Cuthbert's Church and the document which records this deed, Durham, Dean and Chapter, 2.1.Pont.1, notes that the estates were given 'sancto Cuthberto et monachis eius super altare per unum anulum spontanea uoluntate'.[67] It is no wonder, then, that in the *HSC* the saint takes on a new and vengeful image: the intention was to make it clear to individuals who had had some dealing with the community what would happen to them should they be caught misappropriating property from Cuthbert's community.

[64] *HSC*, c. 10, 'For he [King Ælle] stole from him Billingham and Cliffe and Wycliffe and Crayke. And this ignited the wrath of God and of the holy confessor against him...terrified by the wrath of God and St Cuthbert, his [Ælle's] army having been struck down, he fled, and fell, and lost life and kingdom...Therefore let kings and princes beware lest they lie and lest they take anything from St Cuthbert' (trans. Johnson South).

[65] For this image of Cuthbert in the *HSC*, see Rollason 1987, pp. 54–6; Johnson South 1996 and Johnson South in *HSC*, pp. 77–9.

[66] As noted above (p. 6, n. 23), it is possible that mainstream diplomas, such as **1–5** and **8**, were also sometimes granted after a symbolic ceremony of conveyance whereby the charter or a sod of earth was placed on an altar and so endowed with divine authority. But the difference with the notes in the Durham archive is that they are made directly over to the saint of the community and into one of the community's precious manuscripts: this was a body of religious men that revolved around the image of their saint. For more on the ceremony used in the conveyance of charters and how the diplomatic formulae in charters is sometimes closely linked to liturgical terms, see Angenendt 2004; for a recent discussion of the ritual characteristics of charters, see L. Roach, 'Public Rites and Public Wrongs: Ritual Aspects of Diplomas in Tenth- and Eleventh-Century England', *Early Medieval Europe* xix (2011), pp. 182–203.

[67] This document is printed in Offler, *Durham Episcopal*, no. 24. There is also a remarkable knife preserved at Durham which symbolises Stephen of Bulmer's agreement in the late twelfth century with the monks of Lindisfarne about the chapel of Lowick. For more on this, see M.T. Clanchy, *From Memory to Written Record: England 1066–1307* (Blackwell, 1979; repr. 1993), pp. 258–9.

Although Cuthbert's community clearly did cultivate relations with southern English kings, especially from the early tenth century,[68] it nevertheless seems to have operated according to its own rules and its own prescribed form of diplomatic document; and this is indicative of the independence it had come to enjoy, an independence which had proved to be the only sure means for its continued existence in the politically turbulent Northumbrian kingdom.[69] Later in the tenth century, as part of an anti-monastic reaction triggered by the death of King Edgar in 975, an earl by the name of Thored robbed the York church of a portion of its lands and granted some Yorkshire estates to St Cuthbert's community, presumably as part of an attempt to win the favour of that powerful Northumbrian church. This donation was duly noted by the Cuthbertine house, again in the form of a grant made directly to St Cuthbert himself and inserted into the *LVD*: it is **18** in the Durham archive. It is important to remember the contemporary means by which the York archbishopric came to possess land. **5** is a grant of the Newbald estate to Earl Gunner; it was later acquired for the York church by Archbishop Oscytel some time in the period *c*. 963 to 971. It was not necessary for a fresh document to be written in order to prove that the land was being transferred from the earl's possession into that of the York church: ownership of the original charter granted to Earl Gunner was considered sufficient documentation. Thus, at the very same time as York was involved with documents which belonged to the southern diplomatic mainstream of the day, Cuthbert's community can be found continuing to assert its own methods for the guarantee of its possessions and dealing with Thored exactly as it had dealt with King Æthelstan.[70]

The evidence just discussed suggests that St Cuthbert's community had developed its own methods of recording and proving its land ownership. But the Cuthbertines' independence of action raises important questions about how land transactions that did not involve them were carried out in the rest of northern Northumbria. Although there is almost a complete dearth of extant evidence, **21**, a writ of the mid- to late eleventh century, is a critical survival from the north-west of Northumbria. Issued in the name of a certain Gospatric,[71] who belonged to

[68] See below, pp. 299–305. Only slender evidence exists which might suggest that Cuthbert's community may also at one stage have possessed Anglo-Saxon charters; see below, pp. 316–18.

[69] Rollason 1987, pp. 56–8. Although Cuthbert's community seems to have been able to operate with documents produced outside of the southern diplomatic mainstream, this is not to suggest that it escaped the attentions of the southern English kings.

[70] A further indication of the special rights and laws that grew around the figure of Cuthbert is provided by the law known as the 'Peace of St Cuthbert', which aimed to guarantee safe passage to pilgrims who came to the September festival in the name of Cuthbert; see Craster 1957.

[71] For the difficulties in identifying which Gospatric this might be, and therefore also in dating **21**, see below, pp. 363–4.

the House of Bamburgh, **21** is of fundamental importance because its diplomatic form shows clear affiliations with writs produced in the name of contemporary southern English kings, albeit with slight changes which have seemingly been introduced on the basis of local practice. This conformance to English diplomatic documentation is all the more striking in the face of the distinctiveness of the Cuthbertine community's conventions and is emblematic of a complex political situation.

4. THE AUTHENTICITY OF THE NORTHERN CHARTERS

For the sake of convenience, it has seemed sensible to provide here an overview of the authenticity of the charters edited in this volume. Each archive is discussed in turn below.[72]

York

It is simplest to begin with those charters about whose authenticity or inauthenticity there seems to be no doubt. The exact similarity of **3** to S 674 (*Pet* 13) in the Peterborough archive implies that **3** is an authentic copy of a 958 charter of Edgar and a similar case can be put forward for **5** in that it is a typical 'Edgar A' charter. **6** is a genuine Old English memorandum in the name of Archbishop Oswald (975–92), composed in an attempt to understand the condition of the York church's estates. It has various later additions which are thought to be in the hand of Archbishop Wulfstan (1002–23) himself.[73] **7 (a–c)** is a genuine group of estate-surveys of the early eleventh century entered into the back of the York Gospels, again connected with Archbishop Wulfstan. **9** and **10** are both genuine copies (perhaps slightly modernised) of Old English writs in the name of King Edward the Confessor. **11**, however, is an extravagant forgery which claims to grant the entire Worcester bishopric to the York church.

The remaining charters, **1**, **2**, **4** and **8** are perhaps less straightforward. **1**, which grants Amounderness on the north-west coast to the York church, very clearly displays some later tampering with its dating-clause, which not only is incorrect for the actual date at which the charter was issued (7 June, 934) but is also identical to that found in S 428 (BCS 701) from the Worcester archive. Other diplomatic oddities include a boundary clause in Latin, rather than the more

[72] For much more detailed discussions of each northern charter, see the relevant commentaries to the documents themselves.

[73] For more information, see the commentary to **6**.

usual Old English, and various features of the dispositive section are perhaps suspicious. But it should be remembered that S 428 (BCS 701) exists as a copy in a Worcester cartulary drawn up in the eleventh century at a time when York and Worcester were held in plurality; so it is possible that S 428 (BCS 701) was forged by reference to **1**. It is also important to recognise that **1** was issued at a moment when the southern king, Æthelstan, was finally able to exert influence in the north following a generation of Scandinavian settlement across Northumbria. It may be that the slight diplomatic oddities in **1** reflect this new political situation. And it is further encouraging that **1** bears a close resemblance to S 425 (*CantCC* 106), another 'Æthelstan A' charter issued only ten days prior to **1** and extant in its original form. Perhaps the strongest reason of all for accepting **1** as a broadly authentic copy is that in later years the York church did not lay claim to Amounderness and so there is no discernible motive for its having been forged.

2 is arguably less problematic. Its diplomatic formulae are all standard for a charter in the name of King Eadwig. The only slight issue arises with the dispositive section which, since it names only the central estate being granted and omits the dependencies (which themselves are only named in the boundary clause), might be taken as an indication that the vernacular boundary clauses have been added to an otherwise genuine diploma at some point after the composition of **2**. But **2** deals with a 'multiple estate', which was a kind of estate structure typical in the north of England. As such it had to adopt an innovative form and this may help also to explain the use of the phrase 'sake and soke'.

4, granted in the name of King Edgar, has in its dispositive section a problematic phrase ('ut in eternam meam domum in Sancte Trinitatis patrocinio quamdiu uiuat habeat') which makes no sense and which is perhaps suspicious. It seems likely that the first part of this phrase has occurred as a result of some corruption of an original reading which may have been: 'ut in eternam hereditatem meum donum in Sancte Trinitatis patrocinio quamdiu uiuat habeat'.[74] But the expression 'in Sancte Trinitatis patrocinio' is unparalleled elsewhere in Edgar's charters and may read as a later insertion into this part of the charter. This corrupt, and possibly rewritten, part of **4** seems to be the only problematic section in an otherwise genuine document.

Because **8**, issued in the name of King Cnut, borrows diplomatic formulae from other charters in the York archive, namely **3** and **4**, it is correct to be suspicious of its authenticity. But the production of charters during Cnut's reign seems, to a greater extent than before, to have been delegated to regional scriptoria. This means that it is not unusual to find a charter of Cnut which contains forms

[74] See further the commentary to **4**.

borrowed from earlier documents in the same archive and so its authenticity should not be discounted on this basis.[75]

Beverley

Charters in the Beverley archive are relatively straightforward. **13** can be accepted as a copy of a genuine Old English writ of King Edward the Confessor, while **14** is most likely a post-Conquest Latin translation of an authentic Old English writ. **12** is an elaborate Middle English rhyming charter in the name of King Æthelstan, clearly a forgery.

Ripon

Both **15** and **16** are obvious forgeries used as part of the Ripon chapter's defence of its rights in a 1228 trial held at the Ripon chapter house. **15** takes the form of a Latin writ whilst **16** is a Middle English rhyming charter, quite possibly modelled on some earlier form of the Beverley version, **12**.

Durham

The Durham archive is unproblematic. Whilst **17** is a clear twelfth-century forgery, **18–20** are genuine notices of land grants copied into the *LVD*; these notices are idiosyncratic in form and strikingly different to the charters preserved in the York archive.[76]

Lowther Castle

21 survives in only one copy, a non-contemporary single-sheet which could have been made at any point between the thirteenth and seventeenth centuries.[77] Although the document is fundamentally authentic, various corrupt passages indicate that it has suffered in transmission and parts of it may well have been rewritten or updated at some point after its original issue.

[75] For more detail, see the commentary to **8**.

[76] For more about the type of document preserved in the Durham archive, see below, pp. 316–23.

[77] See below, p. 372.

LIST OF NORTHERN CHARTERS

YORK

1. King Æthelstan grants land at Amounderness, Lancashire, to the church of St Peter at York. A.D. 930 [for 934] (7 June)

2. King Eadwig grants twenty hides of land at Southwell, Nottinghamshire, with dependencies at Normanton, Upton, Fiskerton, Farnsfield, Kirklington, Morton, Gibsmere, Bleasby, Goverton, Halloughton and Halam to [Arch]bishop Oscytel. A.D. 958 [for 956]

3. King Edgar grants ten hides at Sutton, Nottinghamshire, to [Arch]bishop Oscytel. A.D. 958

4. King Edgar grants twenty hides at Sherburn-in-Elmet, Yorkshire, to Æslac. A.D. 963

5. King Edgar grants thirty hides at Newbald, Yorkshire, to Gunner, *dux*. A.D. 963

6. Memorandum by Archbishop Oswald concerning the estates belonging to the archbishopric of York. [A.D. 975 × 992]

7. Survey of the estates at (**a**) Sherburn-in-Elmet, (**b**) Otley and (**c**) Ripon, belonging to the York Archbishopric. [*c*. A.D. 1020–3]

8. King Cnut grants forty-three hides at Patrington, Yorkshire, to Ælfric, archbishop of York. A.D. 1033

9. King Edward declares that he has granted to Archbishop Ealdred judicial and financial rights over his lands and over all his men. [A.D. 1060 × 1066]

10. King Edward announces that he has granted to Ealdred, the 'deacon' of Archbishop Ealdred, the minster at Axminster, Devon, as a pious benefaction for St Peter's minster at York. [A.D. 1060 × 1066]

11. King Edward grants the see of Worcester to Archbishop Ealdred. A.D. 1065 (31 December)

BEVERLEY

12. King Æthelstan grants privileges to St John's, Beverley. [A.D. 927 × 939]

13. King Edward declares that Archbishop Ealdred has his permission to draw up a *priuilegium* for all the lands pertaining to St John's Minster at Beverley;

and that the Minster and its property shall be as free as any other minster. [A.D. 1060 × 1065]

14. King Edward declares that he has granted to Archbishop Ealdred judicial and financial rights over his men within the king's own soke as fully and as completely as the archbishop has them in his own lands. [A.D. 1060 × 1065]

RIPON

15. King Æthelstan confirms the Ripon Church and Chapter's rights to its peace, all its liberties and rights, a court in which to hear quarrels, its judgment through *frodmortele* and that all its lands and men are to be believed *per suum ya et per suum na*. [A.D. 927 × 939]

16. King Æthelstan grants privileges to the Church and Chapter of Ripon. [A.D. 927 × 939]

DURHAM

17. King Ecgfrith grants land at Crayke, North Yorkshire, and at *Lugubalia* (Carlisle) to Cuthbert. A.D. 685

18. Note of a grant of land at Smeaton, Crayke and Sutton-on-the-Forest, Yorkshire, from Earl Thored to St Cuthbert's Community. [Late tenth century]

19. Note of a grant of land at Escomb, Durham, from Earl Northman to St Cuthbert's Community. [Early eleventh century]

20. Note of a grant of land at Norton, County Durham, from Ulfketel, son of Osulf, to St Cuthbert's Community. [Early eleventh century]

LOWTHER CASTLE

21. Gospatric declares that Thorfynn mac Thore be free with regards to all things that are Gospatric's in Allerdale; and that those men dwelling with Thorfynn at Cardew and Cumdivock be as free, along with him, as Melmor and Thore and Sigulf were; and Thorfynn is also to have jurisdictional rights over all the lands in Cardew and Cumdivock that were given to Thore in the days of Moryn, free from the obligation of providing messengers and witnesses. s. xi$^{\text{mid-ex}}$

CONCORDANCE

	Sawyer	Kemble	Birch	Farrer, *EYC*	Robertson, *Charters*	Harmer, *Writs*	Hart, *ECNE*
1	407	352	703, 1344	1			119
2	659	472	1029, 1348	2			114
3	679		1044, 1349	3			115
4	712	500	1112, 1352	6			123
5	716	504	1113, 1353	5			124
6	1453		1278, 1279		54		125
7	1461a			7	84		
8	968	749		8			133
9	1159	893		10		118	136
10	1161					120	
11	1037a	815					
12	451	359	644, 645, 1339				120a
13	1067	1343		87		7	137
14	1160			11		119	118
15	456	358	646, 858			Appendix I (p. 537)	
16	457	360	647, 859	114			
17	66	25	66				146
18	1660		1255		60		126
19	1659	925	1255		68		127
20	1661	925	1256		68		128
21	1243					121	134

YORK

INTRODUCTION

1. THE HISTORY AND ENDOWMENT OF YORK MINSTER

Before 1086 and the Domesday survey, it is very difficult to trace the process by which the York church acquired its landed endowment in the Anglo-Saxon period. We may be sure that York, like other religious communities in Anglo-Saxon England, benefited at times from gifts of land made by kings and by local nobles; and also that some of those bishops and archbishops in charge of the York see used their personal resources in order to purchase lands on behalf of the York church. But the details of these transactions have been lost to us and one can only reflect on the numbers of charters, writs and wills which must have once belonged to the York archive and have since somehow perished. For the period before 934, the date of the earliest grant of land to be preserved in the York archive (**1**), only incidental information remains regarding the accumulation of land by the York church. There is more documentary evidence for the tenth and eleventh centuries but still not nearly as much information as, for example, at the southern archbishopric in Canterbury. The following historical account allows those documents we do possess to be set in their proper historical context, but it also helps to discern those periods when the York church was thriving and those when it may have been under pressure.[1]

a. *Uncertain Beginnings (627–732): The First Bishops of Anglian York*

From the very earliest years of the Christian mission to Anglo-Saxon England, it was Pope Gregory the Great's intention that London and York were to become archiepiscopal sees upon which twenty-four other bishoprics were dependent, twelve for each archbishopric.[2] Although Gregory's plans as a whole were

[1] For the history of York Minster, and York in general, see, for example, Dickens 1961; Cramp, *Anglian and Viking York*; Hill and Brooke 1977; Tweddle *et al.*, *Anglian York*; Norton 2004; Rollason 2004; Rollason *et al.*, *Sources*; Hall (R.A.) *et al.*, *Aspects* and Blair, *Church* (especially pp. 66–8 and 313–14); for the later Anglo-Saxon period, see Cooper, *Archbishops of York*; for a study of the archaeology of York Minster, see Phillips and Heywood, *Excavations*.

[2] Bede, *HE*, i.29; see M. Gibbs, 'The Decrees of Agatho and the Gregorian Plan for York', *Speculum* xlvii (1973), pp. 213–46. For the political background to these years (627–732), see Kirby 1974 and Rollason 1999*b*.

ultimately unrealistic,[3] some of these aspirations were later realised when the first Anglo-Saxon church at York was 'hastily built of wood' so that Edwin could be baptised there in 627.[4] But this was only the beginning of the intended project, as Edwin 'very soon after his baptism...set about building a greater and more magnificent church of stone, under the instructions of Paulinus, in the midst of which the chapel which he had first built was to be enclosed'.[5] Although no archaeological trace of these early buildings has been found,[6] this stone church is believed to have been situated in the ruins of the Roman legionary fortress,[7] on the opposite side of the River Ouse to the old Roman walled civilian town (*colonia*).[8]

[3] The fact that Gregory suggested London, rather than Canterbury, as the location for the southern metropolitan bishop, suggests that he was unaware of the reality of the situation in Anglo-Saxon England (see Cramp, *Anglian and Viking York*, p. 4, Colgrave and Mynors, *Bede's Ecclesiastical History*, p. 104, n. 3 and Blair, *Church*, pp. 8–9). Gregory's plans for the structure of the Anglo-Saxon church did not come to fruition. Theodore, the reforming archbishop of Canterbury (669–90), managed to increase the number of dioceses (and in so doing broke up the large Northumbrian diocese controlled by Wilfrid, below pp. 236–8) but never to the level that Gregory had intended. For more, see Blair, *Church*, pp. 79–80.

[4] Bede, *HE*, ii.14. Bishop Finan's church at Lindisfarne was another example of an early Northumbrian church made from wood (Bede, *HE*, iii.25). For instances of re-use of pre-historic or Roman sites in the establishment of early Anglo-Saxon churches, see Blair, *Church*, pp. 183–91.

[5] Bede, *HE*, ii.14. For the building of wooden churches, which were often later replaced by stone churches, see Foot, *Monastic Life*, pp. 110–17 (at p. 114 for York).

[6] For late seventh- or early eighth-century stele fragments surviving from the Minster, see Lang, *Corpus*, pp. 60–7.

[7] Many attempts have been made to identify the site of the Anglo-Saxon cathedral. Norton 1998*b*, pp. 11–12 (at p. 6 for a diagram), on the basis of available topographical evidence, has suggested that a square enclosure to the north-west of the current Minster preserves the location of the Anglo-Saxon cathedral and therefore that the Anglo-Saxon cathedral had been situated outside of the Roman *principia*. Hall (R.A.) 2004, p. 493, suggests that the pre-Norman cathedral stood either to the south or the north of the current Minster but he also denies the possibility that it was situated within the Roman *principia*. But the discovery of a pre-Conquest cemetery underneath the south arm of the transept of the present Minster has suggested to Blair that Edwin's church was situated in the ruins of the Roman *principia* (Blair, *Church*, p. 66, n. 224, where he questions Norton's conclusions). Palliser 1984, suggests that a Roman and Anglian episcopal church was originally situated on the west bank of the River Ouse but that this later shifted to the east bank of the Ouse within the legionary fortress. For the cemetery, see Phillips and Heywood, *Excavations*, pp. 75–92, Morris (R.K.) 1986, p. 81 and Blair, *Church*, p. 66, n. 224. For a useful summary of the archaeological situation, see Norton 2004. For the possibility that, by the end of the eighth century, the topography of Anglo-Saxon York was arranged so as to create a bi-polar 'holy city', see below, p. 37, n. 76.

[8] For an approximate topographical map of York, see p. 29. The walled civilian town (*colonia*) on the west of the River Ouse and the legionary fortress (containing the *principia*) on the east of the Ouse, with their defended enclosures and well-defined entrances, were the most enduring legacy of Roman York: Hall (R.A.) 2004, pp. 489–90. One of the name-forms to be applied to York, in the period *c.* 895–*c.* 1150, was *Eoforwicceaster*, reflecting the presence of the Roman fortification there with the Old English element *ceaster*, 'old (Roman) fortification'; for this information, see *CamDEPN*, p. 711. York was also known as *Eoforwic*, the *-wic* element suggesting that York was an urban settlement; see Fellows-Jensen 1998 and *PN YorksER*, pp. 277–80. See below, p. 42, for the development to *Jórvík*.

Construction of this second, stone, church was interrupted in 633 by the Battle of Hatfield when a joint force of Cadwallon, king of Gwynedd, and Penda, heathen ruler of Mercia, defeated and killed Edwin, whose head was later placed in the side-chapel (*porticus*) of Pope Gregory in St Peter's church at York.[9] The confusion caused by the defeat of Edwin led Paulinus to take Queen Æthelburh, Edwin's wife, back to Kent. Thus any plan that may have involved the realisation of Pope Gregory's original intention to make York an archbishopric was interrupted; and the *pallium* sent from Rome for this purpose was taken by Paulinus to his new see at Rochester.[10] York was not to become an archbishopric for another century.[11] Conditions at York in the period 633 to 664 are unclear.[12] Following the departure of Paulinus (together with the *pallium*) for Rochester, some stability may have been restored to the York church when it came under the control of James the Deacon. Bede praises James for his pastoral work and describes him as a man much skilled in church music, able to teach people how to sing in a Roman and Kentish manner.[13] Perhaps, then, it was to York's benefit that James 'remained for a long time in the church' (...*multo exhinc tempore in ecclesia manens*...),[14] and whose life overlapped with Bede's (*c*. 673–735).[15] Nevertheless, the accession of King Oswald in 634 surely signalled a difficult time for the York church. Although Oswald was responsible for completing the building of Edwin's second church at York,[16] his sympathies lay ultimately with the Ionan mission and the Lindisfarne church.[17] It was during this time that the episcopal see for Northumbria was transferred from York to Lindisfarne, with the result that the Lindisfarne bishops gained responsibility for the York church.[18] Since we learn that later bishops of York were

[9] Bede, *HE*, ii.20; but note also Bede, *ibid*., ii.24, where he says that Edwin was buried at Whitby and does not mention the possibility that Edwin's head was missing (see Colgrave and Mynors, *Bede's Ecclesiastical History*, p. 204, n. 2). See also Dickens 1961, pp. 4–5. On the division of Oswald's body and the spread of his cult, see A. Thacker, '*Membra Disjecta*: the Division of the Body and the Diffusion of the Cult', in *Oswald: Northumbrian King to European Saint*, ed. C. Stancliffe and E. Cambridge (Stamford, 1995), pp. 97–127. Bede, *ibid*., ii.14, states that Edwin's children, Æthelhun and Æthelthryth, were buried in the York church.

[10] Bede, *HE*, ii.20.

[11] For more about these events, see Hill and Brooke 1977, pp. 4–5.

[12] On the death of Edwin in 633, Northumbria may have reverted to paganism: Rollason 1999*b*, p. 125.

[13] Bede, *HE*, ii.20.

[14] James also spent a lot of time in a village near Catterick: Bede, *HE*, ii.20.

[15] Bede, *HE*, ii.16.

[16] Bede, *HE*, ii.20.

[17] King Oswald (634–42) was a strong supporter of the mission from Iona and Lindisfarne; it was Oswald who sponsored the work of the missionary Aidan in converting the Northumbrians. For a useful summary, see R. Sharpe, 'Iona' in *Blackwell*, pp. 254–5. For Oswald, Aidan and Lindisfarne, see below, pp. 270–3.

[18] The Lindisfarne bishops at this time were Aidan (635–51), Finan (651–61) and Colman (661–4).

obliged to restore the York church, we may be permitted to conjecture that, in the intervening time, the Lindisfarne leaders had taken little active interest in upholding York's fortunes.[19] York was also threatened by the actions of Penda and his Welsh allies since between *c*. 641 and the battle of the *Winwæd* in 654/5, Deira was beset two or three times by these forces.[20] Unfortunately our sources give no impression of the effect such raids may have had on the York church and its assets.

In 664 the council of Whitby brought together, and into debate, those advocates of the Irish church and those of the Roman church. The crucial issue over which they argued was the correct method for calculating the date of Easter. This was a most public display of the ideological divide in the Northumbrian church.[21] Wilfrid, who was later to become bishop of York, put forward the case for the Roman side and scored a notable victory.[22] The immediate consequence of Wilfrid's success was that the York church was restored as the episcopal see for the Northumbrian kingdom.[23] Wilfrid was appointed as bishop of York and travelled to Gaul in order to be consecrated; but during his absence, Chad was uncanonically put forward in his place.[24] Five years later, in 669, Chad was removed from office owing to his irregular consecration and became bishop of the Mercians with his base at Lichfield;[25] Wilfrid was re-appointed to York in his place.[26]

[19] Cramp, *Anglian and Viking York*, pp. 4–5, Hill and Brooke 1977, p. 6 and Rollason 1999*b*, pp. 126–7.

[20] See Hill and Brooke 1977, p. 6. At one stage Penda's raiding reached as far north as Bamburgh, the very heart of the Bernician kingdom; Bede, *HE*, iii.16. For the Battle near the River *Winwæd*, see Bede, *HE*, iii.24.

[21] For much fuller discussions of the council of Whitby and the Easter controversy, see, for example, Charles-Edwards, *Ireland*, pp. 391–415 and W.K. North, 'History, Tradition, and Authority in Bede's Interpretation of the Council of Whitby, 664', *Anglo-Saxon* i (2007), pp. 1–53.

[22] Colman, who had argued on behalf of Lindisfarne and the Celtic side, withdrew to Ireland after being defeated; Bede, *HE*, iii.25.

[23] After the council of Whitby, Bishop Tuda was selected by King Oswiu to replace Colman at Lindisfarne; the Northumbrian see was later moved from Lindisfarne to York. John 1970, p. 49, argues that Gregory the Great's initial intention that York be the see for all of Northumbria must have been discussed at the meeting at Whitby and he therefore suggests that it was always King Oswiu's intention that Tuda should move the see to, and be bishop from, York ('one of the consequences of the synod was an acceptance of Gregory's original wishes for the siting of the principal northern see', at p. 49). But Wallace-Hadrill (J.M.), *Bede*, p. 129, says that he cannot accept this view that Tuda was always meant to be bishop of York.

[24] *VW*, c. XIV. Chad was sponsored by King Oswiu (642–70) because of Oswiu's argument with his son, Alhfrith (sub-king of Deira, *c*. 655–64), who had been Wilfrid's champion (on Alhfrith's support of Wilfrid, see below, p. 231). See Colgrave and Mynors, *Bede's Ecclesiastical History*, p. 316, n. 2 and Colgrave, *Life of Wilfrid*, p. 160. It was at this moment in the 660s that there was a vacancy in the Canterbury see which meant that Chad had to be consecrated by the West Saxon bishop, Wine, and two other British bishops (see Brooks, *Church of Canterbury*, pp. 68–9). This made Chad's consecration all the more irregular.

[25] Bede, *HE*, iv.3.

[26] For Theodore's role in the removal of Chad from York, see Charles-Edwards, *Ireland*, pp. 429–30.

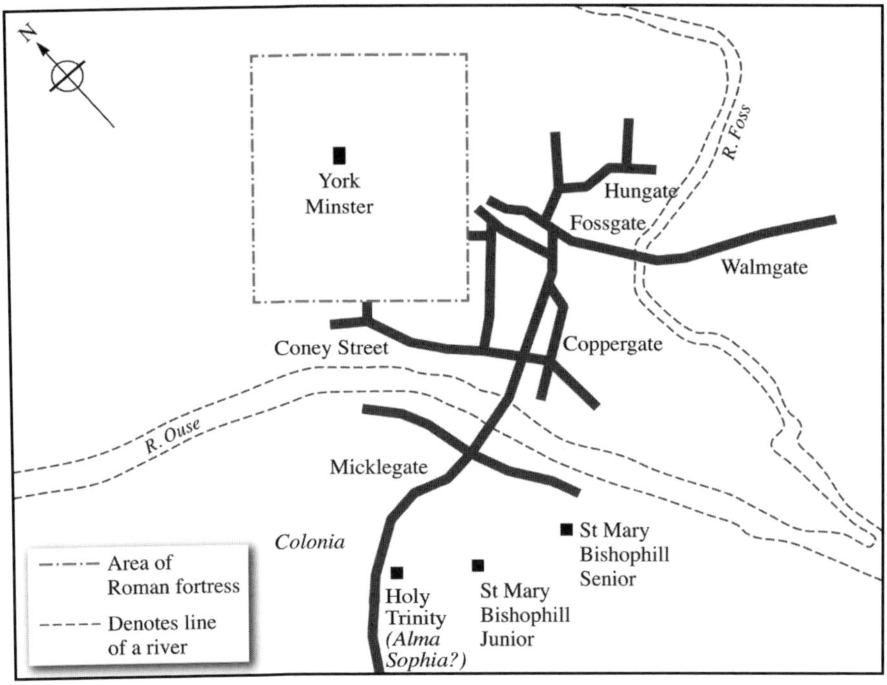

Map 2. York: location of the present Minister within the Roman fortress, facing a complex of churches on the opposite bank of the River Ouse, within the Roman *colonia*; including some of the principal streets (modified and simplified version of a map in Hall (R.A.) 1978, p. 33)

From this moment onwards it seems likely that the fate of the York church and its landed endowment would have been connected to the progress of Wilfrid's career. Wilfrid was to become an exceptionally powerful figure and one who owned a great deal of land; but, as we shall see, he was to fall in and out of favour with various Northumbrian kings. Because Wilfrid regarded the lands which belonged to his churches as his personal possessions,[27] York's fortunes must have changed according to whether or not Wilfrid was in political favour.

Wilfrid had found Edwin's church at York in a dire condition: 'But now the ridge of the roof owing to its age let the water through, the windows were unglazed and the birds flew in and out, building their nests, while the neglected walls were disgusting to behold owing to all the filth caused by the rain and the birds'.[28] One

[27] Wilfrid refers to the church of York being *propriam sedem* and *sua propria loca episcopatus sui*. See *VW*, cc. XV, XXIV, XLIII, and XLIV. For more on this, see Roper 1974, pp. 61–3, for the six main stages of Wilfrid's career.
[28] *VW*, c. XVI, quoted also in Hill and Brooke 1977, p. 6.

of his first acts as bishop was to restore this building: he renovated the broken roof and lined it with lead and put glass back into the windows. He then turned his attention to the building's interior, which he had whitewashed and filled with new furniture and ornaments.[29] In order to make sure that the job was done properly, Wilfrid employed masons and skilled workers, men whom he had brought with him from Gaul.[30] It is difficult to tell how much of this information should be thought of as exaggeration on the part of Wilfrid's biographer; and the fact that no physical remains of this early York church have been found makes it especially problematic to verify details. But we should bear in mind the stature of one of Wilfrid's other foundations, Hexham; although no traces of this church remain above ground, its famous crypt still exists and displays something of the grandeur and scale of his church at Hexham.[31]

From 669, when Archbishop Theodore restored Wilfrid to his see, until 678, Wilfrid was at the height of his power and influence.[32] This allowed him to invest heavily in those monasteries which he owned both in Mercia and in Northumbria, especially Ripon and his new foundation at Hexham, recently endowed by Queen Æthelthryth; and he also consolidated his position as the primary bishop in the Northumbrian church. Although Wilfrid's assumption of the episcopal see in 669 therefore signalled a period of prosperity for the York church, his own position later became threatened. In 678 he had a severe disagreement with King Ecgfrith which resulted in his exile from the Northumbrian kingdom to that of the South Saxons.[33] In order to try to regain his former position, Wilfrid journeyed to the Continent to plead his case with the pope and at a 679 synod in Rome he can be found claiming to be the ecclesiastical representative of the whole of northern Britain.[34]

It is unclear what exactly the consequences of Wilfrid's first exile must have been for the York church and whether this left the see's lands vulnerable

[29] *VW*, c. XVI.

[30] *VW*, c. XIV; see also the comments of Hill and Brooke 1977, p. 7. After he had completed this task, Wilfrid also secured a suitable landed endowment for the York church, which may have compensated for any earlier depredations at the hands of the Lindisfarne bishops.

[31] E. Gilbert, 'Saint Wilfrid's Church at Hexham', in Kirby, *Saint Wilfrid*, pp. 81–113. By comparing Stephanus' description of various Northumbrian churches (of Ripon and Hexham) with those given by Bede (of Wearmouth and Jarrow), Hill and Brooke 1977, p. 7, suggest what York may have looked like. For the crypt at Ripon, see below, p. 235, n. 34.

[32] See Cubitt 1989, p. 19. For the claims of Theodore and Wilfrid regarding the geographical extent of their metropolitan authority, see Charles-Edwards, *Ireland*, pp. 429–38.

[33] It was the joint intention of Archbishop Theodore and King Ecgfrith that Wilfrid's diocese be divided into three parts: that of York, Lindisfarne and Hexham. Wilfrid's refusal to accept this scheme led to his exile (see Farmer 1974). For Wilfrid's time in Sussex and his role in the dissemination of charter diplomatic, see below, p. 236.

[34] Haddan and Stubbs III, pp. 140–1. For discussion of this extensive claim, see Charles-Edwards, *Ireland*, pp. 432–6.

to exploitation. There are signs at least that the vigour of religious life at York did not diminish. Between 678 and 686 Bosa had replaced Wilfrid as bishop, and during his tenure of the see had organised a monastic community in York.[35] It may also be the case that, despite Wilfrid's dismissal, York retained some of its superior status in Northumbria even over the Lindisfarne community; for, in 685, Cuthbert came to York to be consecrated as bishop.[36] Bede states that this ceremony was carried out by seven bishops under the presidency of Archbishop Theodore. The initial intention was that he should be consecrated to the Hexham see but it seems this was against the wishes of Cuthbert, who exchanged with Eata the see of Hexham for that of Lindisfarne.[37]

In 685 the death of King Ecgfrith, one of Wilfrid's principal opponents, allowed Wilfrid to return to the Northumbrian scene, where he can be found by 686/7.[38] Archbishop Theodore encouraged a peaceful settlement and urged the new king, Aldfrith (686–705), to accept Wilfrid back into the Northumbrian church. Stephanus states that he regained some of his previous levels of influence by returning to his see at York and to his two monasteries at Ripon and Hexham; and, in 687, he even gained control of the Lindisfarne see, much to the latter's displeasure.[39] But not only are there indications that the situation was perhaps more complex than Stephanus allows (with the possibility that Bosa continued to be bishop at York),[40] but these seem also to have been temporary measures for

[35] Alcuin, *Versus*, ll. 857–70. This reference to Bosa's plans for a monastic community is arguably the first indication that a monastery separate to St Peter's church existed in early Anglo-Saxon York. For more about this separate monastic building, its location and also about the *Alma Sophia*, see below, pp. 35–8 and Morris (R.K.) 1986. For the suggestion that this refers to a monastic community in the cathedral church of St Peter itself, rather than a separate monastery, see Rollason *et al.*, *Sources*, pp. 153–4.

[36] Bede, *HE*, iv.28. The *HSC*, c. 5, records that it was also on this occasion that King Ecgfrith and Archbishop Theodore gave to St Cuthbert, 'in the city of York all the land that lies from the wall of the church of St Peter as far as the great gate towards the west, and from the wall of the church of St Peter as far as the city wall towards the south'. For discussion of the various possible locations of this land grant, see Palliser 1984, p. 104, Morris (R.K.), *Churches in the Landscape*, p. 218, Rollason *et al.*, *Sources*, pp. 140–1, Norton 1998*b*, pp. 17–18 and the commentary by Johnson South in *HSC*, pp. 80–1. Norton 1998*b*, p. 18 (and Appendix, pp. 28–35) suggests a very different reading of this event, that in fact Cuthbert was here being made bishop of York and that this grant of land was made as recognition of Cuthbert's superiority over the York church. But this interpretation is full of difficulties.

[37] Bede, *HE*, iv.28.

[38] *VW*, c. XLIV and Cubitt 1989, p. 20.

[39] *VW*, c. XLIV. For the Lindisfarne reaction to these events, see below, pp. 275–82; Cubitt 1989, p. 20, suggests that Wilfrid had driven Cuthbert from his see.

[40] It is difficult to know what happened to Bosa (who had previously been appointed bishop of York) on Wilfrid's return in 686/7. One view is to suggest that Bosa was expelled from York in 686/7, only to be restored when Wilfrid was exiled a second time in 691/2 and to continue ruling there until his death in 706 (see Hill and Brooke 1977, p. 8, A. Thacker, 'Bosa' in *ODNB* and M. Lapidge, 'Bosa' in *Blackwell*, p. 71). Cubitt 1989, pp. 20 and 25, takes a different view: that the account of Stephanus is

in 688 both Lindisfarne and Hexham had new superiors (Eadberht at Lindisfarne and John of Beverley at Hexham).

In 691–2 Wilfrid's situation worsened once more; he became embroiled in a dispute with King Aldfrith over whether or not Ripon should be the seat of a bishopric. The argument could not be resolved and the outcome was a second period of exile in Mercia where Wilfrid sought aid and protection from King Æthelred (674/5–704). If Wilfrid had succeeded in regaining the York church after his first exile in the years following 686/7,[41] this second exile meant that he was never again to be in charge of the York see, which was now certainly governed by Bosa. In 702–3 it seemed as if the exclusion of Wilfrid from Northumbrian religious life in general had been made permanent: an ecclesiastical council was convened at *Ouestraefelda*, under the leadership of Archbishop Berhtwald of Canterbury, at which it was decided that Wilfrid should be stripped of all of his possessions, except for the Ripon monastery, and of his episcopal status.[42] After more, relatively unsuccessful, petitions to Rome, Wilfrid's fortunes finally revived when his chief opponent, King Aldfrith, died in 705. In a rather strange turn, Wilfrid became the guardian of Aldfrith's son and heir, Osred, which allowed for Wilfrid's return for a second time. With the death of Bosa of York in 706, John of Beverley, then bishop of Hexham, was translated to fill the vacancy in the York see, which left Hexham to be once more in the hands of Wilfrid.[43]

Although Wilfrid had been central to the restoration and expansion of the York church, his tumultuous political life must have had both a positive and a negative effect on the York bishopric and its assets. It may, therefore, have been with some relief that York's incumbents saw Wilfrid occupy the church of Hexham after his return from exile in 705/06, rather than their own.

The next three bishops to be in charge of the York see had all been trained as monks at Whitby under the direction of Abbess Hild. As already noted, John of Beverley was Bosa's immediate successor (consecrated 706, retired sometime before 721);[44] Bede commends John as an active bishop, a man who specifically sought out those in need of aid and who was particularly able in the curing of the

not credible and that there is no 'other evidence to suggest that Bosa's rule at York was interrupted'. Bede, *HE*, v.19, states that, in 686/7, Wilfrid was 'restored to his episcopal seat and his bishopric' (... *sedem suam et episcopatum...recepit*).

[41] For the possibility that Bosa continued to be bishop of York during this time, see above, p. 31, n. 40.

[42] *VW*, cc. XLVI–IX. It is noticeable that Bede, in his *HE*, makes no mention of this synod at *Ouestraefelda*, which suggests that it must have been a very controversial meeting. See Colgrave and Mynors, *Bede's Ecclesiastical History*, p. 525, n. 2. Stephanus' account of the synod is inevitably unreliable; see Brooks, *Church of Canterbury*, p. 79.

[43] Bede, *HE*, v.3.

[44] For the difficulty in determining when John retired as bishop of York, see below, p. 33, n. 47.

sick.[45] He can be found dedicating the churches of two *gesiths*, Puch and Addi, but unfortunately not much more is known of John's time at York.[46] Bede tells us that old age caused him to relinquish his episcopal duties and he therefore retired to his monastery at Beverley, where he remained until his death there in 721.[47]

On his retirement from York, John consecrated his priest (*presbyter*) Wilfrid (consecrated sometime before 721, deposed 732) as his replacement.[48] Alcuin narrates that Wilfrid II did much to enrich the York church,[49] and although there is no way to verify this information, Alcuin's intimate knowledge of the York community perhaps suggests that his testimony should not be discounted.[50] The *Continuatio Bedae* states that Wilfrid II was deposed in 732 and died later on 29 April 744 or 745.[51]

b. *From Bishopric to Archbishopric: Ecgberht and Ælberht*

Ecgberht acceded to the bishopric in 732/3; his episcopacy witnessed some significant happenings at York.[52] One of the foremost developments was that

45 Bede, *HE*, v.2–6.
46 For more about John of Beverley and Puch and Addi, see below, pp. 176–8.
47 Bede, *HE*, v.6. For 714 as the likely date for John's retirement from York, see D.M. Palliser, 'John of Beverley' in *ODNB*; for 718 as an alternative possibility, see Hill and Brooke 1977, p. 8. For more about John and Beverley Minster, see below, pp. 174–5.
48 It is difficult to know the exact date when Wilfrid II took over as bishop since he replaced John of Beverley when John could no longer carry out his duties (which Bede, *HE*, v.6, indicates was some time before his eventual death in 721, but is unfortunately no more specific). Wilfrid II is described by Alcuin as having been not only a priest in the York church but also 'bishop's deputy' (*vicedomnus*) and 'abbot' (*abbas*): Alcuin, *Versus*, ll. 1216–1218; this differentiation between the role of an abbot and that of a bishop may be further evidence for the existence of a monastery at York: see Morris (R.K.) 1986, p. 81 and below, pp. 35–6.
49 Alcuin, *Versus*, ll. 1222–7.
50 Alcuin, *Versus*, ll. 1228–9, suggests that Wilfrid II also adorned other churches in York with riches.
51 For Wilfrid II's death, see *ASC DE*, s.a. 744 and *HR* (4), pp. 38–9. Attached to the end of the earliest manuscript copy of Bede's *HE* are additional annals for the years 731–4; another group of (continental) manuscript copies of Bede's work have more annals covering the years 732 to 766; collectively these annals are known as the *Continuatio Bedae* (for this information, see Story, *Carolingian Connections*, pp. 11–12; see also Colgrave and Mynors, *Bede's Ecclesiastical History*, pp. lxvii–lxix and, for the text, pp. 572–6). As Story, *ibid.*, pp. 11–12 and 94–5, notes, the *Continuatio Bedae* is closely related to a chronicle known as the *York Annals*. The *York Annals* are preserved today as annals 732–802 in the twelfth-century northern compilation, the *Historia regum*. They have been termed the *York Annals* by Hunter-Blair because of their concentration on York and York events (Blair (P.H.) 1963, pp. 98–9). It is likely that a set of now-lost 'Northern Annals', compiled in Northumbria in the early ninth century, formed the basis of the *Continuatio Bedae*, the eighth-century *York Annals* and the northern recension of the *Anglo-Saxon Chronicle* for the same years; see Story, *Carolingian Connections*, pp. 11–12 and pp. 95–6, for a very clear description of the *York Annals* (also pp. 126–33, for Alcuin's role in the evolution of the *York Annals*).
52 The exact date of his accession is difficult to determine; Rollason *et al.*, *Sources*, pp. 57–8.

Ecgberht became the first resident of the York see, after Paulinus, to be recognised as an archbishop.[53] The standing of the York church was further increased when, in 738, three years after Ecgberht had received the *pallium*, his brother, Eadberht, acceded to the throne of Northumbria.[54] This coalition of brothers in two of the most powerful roles in Northumbria presumably provided a measure of security for the York community.[55] And Ecgberht, like Wilfrid II before him, is remembered by Alcuin as a patron of the York church: 'He adorned them with silver, gold and gems, hanging silken tapestries of foreign pattern'.[56] The security brought to York by the joint rule of brothers as king and archbishop is symbolised by the evidence of coins which bear both Eadberht's and Ecgberht's names. York was one of the first Anglo-Saxon mints to be established and it had produced a distinctive series of gold shillings in the mid-seventh century;[57] by the time of Ecgberht the coins of the York mint, now of silver, had taken on a rather striking appearance: Archbishop Ecgberht's name is printed on the reverse together with an image of a person bearing a cross and crozier or perhaps simply two crosses.[58] The church's endowment may well have grown alongside its elevation in status during Ecgberht's time.

Just before his death in 735, Bede had written a letter to Ecgberht, who had been one of his former students, suggesting the need for ecclesiastical and secular reforms and also advising Ecgberht on the duties expected of a bishop.[59] Ecgberht evidently took Bede's letter seriously since he subsequently wrote the *Dialogus*

[53] *ASC DE*, s.a. 735, *CB*, s.a. 735 and *HR* (4), p. 31 (s.a. 735). For the importance of this event, see Dickens 1961, p. 5. Story, *Carolingian Connections*, pp. 49–50, argues that York's elevation to archbishopric should be seen in the wider context of similar developments in the Frankish Church. The death of Tatwine, archbishop of Canterbury, in 734, perhaps made the creation of the northern archbishopric possible: Cubitt, *Councils*, p. 233. See also the comments in Cramp, *Anglian and Viking York*, p. 6. Lang, *Corpus*, p. 67 (no. 25), suggests that one extant part of a cross-shaft, with its particular forms of decoration, 'may reflect York's aspirations to metropolitan status in the English church'.

[54] *ASC C*, s.a. 738. On the influence of archbishops in this period, see Campbell 1989, p. 16.

[55] Alcuin, *Versus*, ll. 1277–1281, celebrates the rule of the two brothers. See also Rollason 1999*b*, p. 130.

[56] Alcuin, *Versus*, ll. 1267–8.

[57] P. Grierson, 'The Authenticity of the York "Thrymsas"', *BNJ* xxxi (1962), pp. 8–10 and J. Moulden and D. Tweddle, 'The 7th Century Gold Coins from York', in Tweddle *et al.*, *Anglian York*, pp. 226–30.

[58] J. Booth, 'Sceattas in Northumbria', in *Sceattas in England and on the Continent: the Seventh Oxford Symposium on Coinage and Monetary History*, ed. D. Hill and D.M. Metcalf (BAR British Ser. 128; Oxford, 1984), pp. 71–112, at pp. 72–3, for the notion that these coins were a response to the debasement of contemporary coins that had been manufactured in Mercia, East Anglia and Kent. Grierson and Blackburn, *MEC I*, p. 173, state that this coinage 'established a precedent for the archiepiscopal coinages that were to follow at York until the Viking conquest in 867 and at Canterbury until 923'.

[59] For the *Epistola ad Ecgbertum*, see Plummer, *Bede* I, pp. 405–23. In chapter nine of his letter (Plummer, *Bede* I, pp. 412–13), Bede calls for Ecgberht to increase the number of bishops in Northumbria to twelve, in line with Pope Gregory's initial plans (above, pp. 25–6). Any creation of new sees, which would have divided York's archdiocese, had the potential to diminish the size of

Ecclesiasticae Institutionis.[60] Constructed in dialogue form, it is designed to advise a religious community in its dealings with secular society; not only does this constitute evidence for the administrative and legal interest Ecgberht took in his archdiocese, but it is representative of the recent coalition of the religious and secular worlds in York, encapsulated by Ecgberht as archbishop and his brother, Eadberht, as king.[61]

In 741, the *Anglo-Saxon Chronicle* records that the city of York in general burnt down; but the *Historia regum*, which at this point derives its information from a lost set of northern annals, specifies that it was the *monasterium* of York itself which was destroyed.[62] There has been debate over the actual identity of the *monasterium* in question and some have argued that the *Historia regum* is here describing a religious establishment that was entirely separate from St Peter's church.[63] The possibility that there was a *monasterium*, perhaps in this instance referring very literally to some form of monastic community,[64] in York distinct from St Peter's is conceivably implied by Alcuin at several points in his *Versus de Patribus Regibus et Sanctis Euboricensis Ecclesie*.[65] If it is correct to suggest

---

York's own endowment. But there is no evidence that Ecgberht created any new dioceses (Cubitt, *Councils*, p. 114).

60 Haddan and Stubbs III, pp. 403–13.

61 The ideals set out in the *Dialogus Ecclesiasticae Institutionis* could only have held force with royal support; see H. Mayr-Harting, 'Ecgberht' in *ODNB*. For more about Ecgberht, see M. Lapidge, 'Anglo-Latin Literature', in *A New Critical History of Old English Literature*, ed. S.B. Greenfield and D.G. Calder (New York and London), pp. 5–37, reprinted in Lapidge, *ALL* 1, pp. 1–35 (at pp. 20–1 for Ecgberht). It may be that Ecgberht took an interest in more scholarly matters too as, in a letter dated to between 746 and 747, Boniface thanks Ecgberht for the books he had sent; see Whitelock, *EHD*, no. 179; it is given in M. Tangl, *Die Briefe des heiligen Bonifatius und Lullus*, MGH, Epistolae Selectae 1 (Berlin, 1916), pp. 156–8 (no. 75).

62 *ASC DE*, s.a. 741 and *HR* (4), p. 38 (s.a. 741). For the *York Annals*, embedded in the *Historia regum* in the years 732–802, which themselves are based on a lost set of northern annals, see above, p. 33, n. 51.

63 See Morris (R.K.) 1986 and Heywood and James 1995, p. 10. For a summary of these different arguments, see Rollason *et al.*, *Sources*, p. 59 and p. 144 (at pp. 153–5, for the opposing argument that the *monasterium* mentioned in the annal for 741 in the *Historia regum* actually refers to St Peter's church itself).

64 Of course the term *monasterium* could be employed by early Anglo-Saxon authors to refer to a variety of different kinds of religious house; it does not necessarily imply a 'monastic' establishment. For discussion, see, for example, S. Foot, 'Anglo-Saxon Minsters: a Review of Terminology', in *Pastoral Care Before the Parish*, ed. J. Blair and R. Sharpe (Leicester, London and New York, 1992), pp. 212–25, J. Blair, 'Ecclesiastical Organization and Pastoral Care in Anglo-Saxon England', *Early Medieval Europe* iv (1995), pp. 193–212 and Foot, *Monastic Life*, pp. 283–336 (esp. p. 289).

65 For example, Alcuin describes Wilfrid II (d. 745) as having been both a 'bishop's deputy' (*vicedomnus*) and, crucially, an 'abbot' (*abbas*) before he became bishop; Alcuin, *Versus*, l. 1218 and above, p. 33, n. 48. Later on in his poem, Alcuin states that Ælberht had been in a *monasterium* in his youth (Alcuin, *Versus*, l. 1417). The evidence is discussed by Godman, *Alcuin*, pp. 95–7, under the note for line 1218 and by Morris (R.K.) 1986, p. 81. The same evidence is interpreted in a different fashion in Rollason *et al.*, *Sources*, pp. 153–5.

the existence of a separate *monasterium*,[66] it is nonetheless impossible to know where it had been situated.[67]

After the death of Ecgberht on 19 November 766, Ælberht (consecrated 24 April 766 or 767, died 8 November 779 or 780) took his place as archbishop of York.[68] St Peter's church now became the centre for a school whose most celebrated student was to be Alcuin.[69] Ælberht did a great deal to increase the prestige and stature of the York community. Alcuin describes Ælberht as his *magister* ('teacher') and one who adorned the York see: 'he also endowed the churches with ornaments of varied beauty, filled with zeal for the Faith'.[70] An indication of the prosperity of the York church during this period is provided by Alcuin's description of the York school as a significant place of learning:

> Illic invenies veterum vestigia patrum:
> quicquid habet per se Latio Romanus in orbe,
> Graecia vel quicquid transmisit clara Latinis,
> Hebraicus vel quod populus bibit imbre superno,
> Africa lucifluo vel quicquid lumine sparsit:
> quod pater Hieronymus, quod sensit Hilarius atque
> Ambrosius praesul, simul Augustinus et ipse
> sanctus Athanasius, quod Orosius edit acutus,
> quicquid Gregorius summus docet et Leo papa,
> Basilius quicquid Fulgentius atque coruscant,
> Cassiodorus item, Chrysostomus atque Iohannes.[71]

[66] For the possible organisation of a monastic community by Bosa, see above, p. 31, n. 35. Bullough, *Alcuin*, pp. 155–6, suggests that the *monasterium* is unlikely to be identified with St Peter's cathedral. Bullough 1983, p. 178, suggests that in eighth-century York there was a complex of churches and a letter of Alcuin, which refers to a *cella sancti Stephani*, may provide corroborative evidence of this; see also Bullough, *Alcuin*, p. 156 and Rollason *et al.*, *Sources*, p. 159. For pre-Conquest York churches, see Harrison 1959–62 and D. Tweddle, 'The Anglian City', in Tweddle *et al.*, *Anglian York*, pp. 151–212 (at pp. 177–88). The existence of multiple churches is, of course, a well known phenomenon; see, for example, below, p. 273, n. 26, and, more generally, Blair, *Church*, p. 199.

[67] Morris (R.K.) 1986, pp. 81–2, Heywood and James 1995, p. 10.

[68] For the death of Ecgberht, see *ASC DE*, s.a. 766 and *HR* (4), p. 43 (s.a. 766). Previously, in 758, his brother Eadberht had voluntarily relinquished the throne and taken the tonsure; *ASC DE*, s.a. 757 (*recte* 758) and *HR* (4), p. 41 (s.a. 758). Following Eadberht's resignation, Northumbria became a politically troubled place: Rollason 1999*b*, pp. 130–1. For Ælberht's consecration see *ASC DE*, s.a. 766 and *HR* (4), p. 43 (s.a. 767); for his death see *ASC DE*, s.a. 779 and *HR* (4), p. 47 (s.a. 780); Ælberht received the *pallium* from Pope Hadrian in 773: *HR* (4), p. 45 (s.a. 773). The evidence of Alcuin, *Versus*, l. 1565, suggests that Ælberht retired as archbishop two years before his death, in 778.

[69] Hill and Brooke 1977, pp. 9–10, trace the roots of the York school to the time of Wilfrid I. But Godman, *Alcuin*, pp. lx–lxii, shows that this is unlikely and suggests that the only firm evidence we have of a school at York dates to the reigns of Ecgberht and Ælberht. See also Lapidge, *ALL* 1, pp. 381–98.

[70] Alcuin, *Versus*, ll. 1488–9.

[71] Alcuin, *Versus*, ll. 1536–1546: 'There you will find the legacy of the ancient fathers: all the Roman possessed in the Latin world, whatever famous Greece has transmitted to the Latins, draughts of

Alcuin does not stop there but continues with a list of works which ranges from Aldhelm to Cominianus.[72] It is difficult to establish which of these texts were actually available in the library of eighth-century York. Even the vast majority of compositions by Alcuin himself were written after he had departed from York and arrived at Charlemagne's court in 781/2.[73] But Godman shows that Alcuin's poem about York, completed in the period 790 to 793, was one of the few written at York during a return visit by Alcuin to his homeland.[74] And, by compiling a list of those principal texts used by Alcuin in this poem, Godman reveals a well stocked, if not remarkable, library.[75]

Ælberht's contribution to the well-being of the York community was significant. One of his final, and most lasting, acts as archbishop was the construction of a new church, an accomplishment which itself demonstrates that York's financial situation and thus its landed endowment were in a stable condition. Alcuin himself and Eanbald, who was later to become archbishop, were heavily involved in the task. The church was completed just before Ælberht's death in 779/80 and in time for him to dedicate it to *Alma Sophia* ('Benevolent Wisdom').[76] Alcuin's description of the new church suggests that it was a remarkable one:

---

the Hebrew race from Heaven's showers, and what Africa has spread abroad in streams of light: the perceptions of father Jerome and of Hilary, of bishop Ambrose, Augustine, and of saint Athanasius, the writings of astute Orosius, the teachings of Gregory the Great and of pope Leo, the glowing words of Basil and Fulgentius, of Cassiodorus and John Chrysostom' (trans. Godman).

72 Alcuin, *Versus*, ll. 1547–1557.

73 For Alcuin's departure, see Godman, *Alcuin*, p. xxxvii. Lapidge, *ALL* 1, pp. 383–5, sets out those works of Alcuin completed at York.

74 Godman, *Alcuin*, pp. xliii and xlvi–xlvii; see also Lapidge, *ALL* 1, pp. 381–98.

75 Godman, *Alcuin*, pp. lxxiii–lxxiv, where he notes that this collection was nothing out of the ordinary when compared to contemporary European standards. When Alcuin was at Charlemagne's court he wrote a number of letters back to the community at York, letters which testify to continuing scholarly exploits there. Lapidge, *AS Library*, p. 41, suggests that the York library would have contained some one hundred volumes (see also Lapidge 1985, pp. 45–9). The *York Annals* (see above, p. 33, n. 51) have also, among other works, been attributed to York (see Blair (P.H.) 1963, pp. 86–99 and Lapidge, *ALL* 2, pp. 317–42). It may be that Aediluulf, the author of the poem known as *De abbatibus*, had been taught his skill in hexameter-composition by Hyglac, a former member of the York school. Aediluulf resided at the religious establishment at Crayke and he was perhaps able to compose his poem because he had access to the York library; see Lapidge, *ALL* 1, pp. 381–98.

76 There has been much debate about the possible location of the *Alma Sophia*. In 1986, Morris proposed that the Holy Trinity church (also known as Christ Church) situated to the west of the River Ouse in the area now known as 'Bishophill' preserved the site of the *Alma Sophia* (Morris (R.K.) 1986). If this can be accepted, then it would have significant ramifications for the Christian topography of York in the eighth century since it would create a kind of bi-polar 'holy city' with St Peter's, the principal church, situated within the Roman walls, and a complex of monastic buildings, one of which is the *Alma Sophia*, situated outside of these walls. This may have the further implication that York was imitating the topography of Canterbury (and thus of Rome); this view has been endorsed by Blair, *Church*, pp. 66–7 (at p. 66, n. 224 and p. 68, n. 225) and p. 126 and Rollason 1999*b*, p. 138. But Norton 1998*b*, pp. 14–15, stresses that there is no archaeological evidence to support this

> Haec nimis alta domus solidis suffulta columnis,
> supposite que stant curuatis arcubus, intus
> emicat egregiis laquearibus atque fenestris.[77]

It is questionable how far this poetical description can be regarded as a true depiction of Ælberht's church.[78] But there is one detail which encourages the view that this was intended to be a rather special building: its dedication to *Alma Sophia*, which can be paralleled only once elsewhere in Anglo-Saxon England.[79]

c. *A Time of Political Upheaval (780–837): From Eanbald I to Wulfhere*

In the period following Ælberht's death, the kingdom of Northumbria became an increasingly troubled place.[80] In 790 King Osred II was deposed from power and received the tonsure at York before being driven into exile.[81] This occurred whilst Eanbald I was archbishop (consecrated 779 or 780, died 10 August 796) and is suggestive of an increasing role of the York see in politics.[82] Kings and

---

suggestion regarding the location of the *Alma Sophia* and wonders whether the chapter-house situated near the present Minster preserves the location of the *Alma Sophia*. Bullough likewise questions this interpretation, preferring instead to suggest that the *Alma Sophia* would have been associated with the York school 'with the corollary...that it was close to wherever the cathedrals' schooling was conducted'; see Bullough, *Alcuin*, p. 326 (and p. 157, n. 86). Evidence for the existence of at least one church on the Bishophill site is provided by the survival of an eighth- or ninth-century inscription on a cross-head found at St Mary Bishophill Junior. The inscription reads: *Salue pro meritis pr(e)s(byter) alme tuis* ('Hail, holy priest, on behalf of your merits'). For the inscription, see Okasha, *Hand-List*, p. 132 (no. 148) and Bullough 1983, pp. 178–9 (and p. 179, n. 4). Morris (R.K.) 1988, p. 192, notes that pre-viking sculpture can also be linked to St Mary Bishophill Junior.

[77] Alcuin, *Versus*, ll. 1509–1511: 'This lofty building, supported by strong columns, themselves bolstering curving arches, gleams inside with fine inlaid ceilings and windows' (trans. Godman, p. 119).

[78] Morris (R.K.) 1986, p. 80, queries Alcuin's description not least because of verbal borrowings from the work of Paulinus of Nola. If Alcuin's description of the *Alma Sophia* having thirty altars can be believed, it must have been a large church: Alcuin, *Versus*, l. 1514 and Norton 1998*b*, p. 15.

[79] A twelfth-century Hexham interpolation in the *Historia regum* states that the same dedication was found as an inscription on an altar in the tomb of Acca. The inscription read: *Almae Trinitati, Agie Sophie, Sanctae Mariae* (*HR* (4), p. 33); for the interpolation, see Blair (P.H.) 1963, pp. 87–90. For a detailed discussion of the dedication, see Bullough, *Alcuin*, pp. 320–6 (at pp. 322–3, for the record of the consecration of York's *Alma Sophia* in a calendar copied at Prüm; at pp. 324–6, for the connection between the York church, the dedication of Ælberht's church and a mythical Roman female saint called Sophia).

[80] There is a marked deficiency in our historical sources for the early ninth century which makes it extremely difficult to trace the fortunes of St Peter's church.

[81] *HR* (4), p. 52 (s.a. 790). Osred II had become king in 788: *ASC DE*, s.a. 789 (*recte* 788) and *HR* (4), p. 52 (s.a. 788); he died in 792 and was buried at Tynemouth: *ASC DE*, s.a. 792 and *HR* (4), p. 54 (s.a. 792).

[82] For Eanbald I's accession, see *ASC DE*, s.a. 779 and *HR* (4), p. 47 (s.a. 780); the combined evidence of the annal for 779 in *ASC DE* and Alcuin, *Versus*, ll. 1518 and 1565, suggest that Eanbald I had been elected as Ælberht's successor before Ælberht's death and perhaps worked as an 'associate bishop'

powerful noblemen who found themselves threatened often sought out the church as a political safe haven. In 791 the *Historia regum* records:

> ...filii Elfwaldi regis ab Eboraca ciuitate ui abstracti, et de ecclesia principali per promissa fallacie abducti, miserabiliter sunt perempti ab Ethelredo rege in Wonwaldremere, quorum nomina Oelf et Oelfwine fuere.[83]

It seems reasonable to suggest that the *ecclesia principalis* referred to in this passage is St Peter's at York and the annal cited implies that St Peter's had developed rights of sanctuary which would, as a consequence, have drawn it more fully into the political world.[84] There are other instances of eminent political figures retiring to St Peter's church: in 794 the death of Earl Æthelheard is recorded, who was 'formerly an earl, then a priest';[85] then, in 796, the death of Earl Ælric is noted in similar fashion.[86] Clearly St Peter's was not unaccustomed to receiving men of high noble status into its community. Alcuin, writing from his continental viewpoint, disapproved of many of these happenings. He was particularly anxious lest the intrusions of nobles into religious life at York lead not to an increase in the church's assets but to the defrauding of church lands; he therefore urged the church of York to avoid any simoniacal practice.[87]

The increasing role of the York archbishopric in secular affairs may have been a decision forced upon the church by the fragility of the contemporary political scene;[88] it would have been much to the benefit of the York see and its archdiocese

(*socio...praesule*). For the death of Eanbald I, see *ASC DE*, s.a. 796 and *HR* (4), p. 58 (s.a. 796); the entry in *HR* adds the detail that Eanbald I had died in the monastery called *Ætlæte* and that his body was subsequently conveyed to St Peter's, which is where he was buried. A 795 letter of Alcuin suggests that Eanbald I had difficulty with his York clergy: Alcuin, *Ep.* 47 (Allott, *Alcuin* 4).

83 *HR* (4), p. 53 (s.a. 791). For a translation, see Whitelock, *EHD*, no. 3: 'The sons of King Ælfwald were taken by force from the city of York, being brought from the principal church by false promises, and were miserably killed by King Æthelred at *Wonwaldremere*; their names were Œlf and Œlfwine'.

84 The use of the adjective *principalis* strongly suggests that the *Historia regum* is referring to St Peter's at York rather than the church which had been dedicated to *Alma Sophia* (or indeed the *monasterium* which is mentioned in the annal for 741 in *HR* as having been burnt down; see above, pp. 35–6, Morris (R.K.) 1986, p. 82 and Rollason *et al.*, *Sources*, pp. 144–5). Other religious communities of the eighth century, such as Hexham, Beverley and Ripon, found themselves being used as havens for political exiles. Just such a phenomenon can be seen at various points in the history of St Cuthbert's community, as can the emergence of sanctuary rights around Cuthbert's tomb. For discussion of northern sanctuary, see Hall (D.) 1989, Lambert 2009 and below, pp. 181–3 and pp. 244–5. On the 'false promises' offered to Œlf and Œlfwine, see Cubitt, *Councils*, p. 183.

85 *HR* (4), p. 56 (s.a. 794): *quondam dux, tunc autem clericus*.

86 *HR* (4), p. 57 (s.a. 796): *quondam dux, tunc autem clericus*. For these entries, see also Dickens 1961, p. 6.

87 Alcuin, *Ep.* 104 (Allott, *Alcuin* 25).

88 The difficulties of the time are best exemplified by the fact that Osbald, having been chosen as king in 796, only managed to reign for twenty-seven days before he sought refuge at Lindisfarne; *HR* (4), p. 57 (s.a. 796).

to have a politically stable environment and one can imagine that the church therefore acted to ensure a measure of peace. A rather ingenious solution can perhaps be seen in St Peter's involvement in the consecration of King Eardwulf in 796. The *Historia regum* notes:

> ...et in Eboraca in ecclesia sancti Petri ad altare beati apostoli Pauli, ubi illa gens primum perceperat gratiam baptismi, consecratus est vii. kal. Iunii.[89]

The annal suggests that the setting provided by St Peter's church was central to some sort of ceremony involving a rite of anointment, and presumably intended to confer divine authority upon Eardwulf's reign.[90] As one scholar has put it, 'sophisticated clergy...faced with increasing instability, may have found in their Bibles a possible remedy for the sanguinary tendencies of their countrymen'.[91]

Eanbald I died on 10 August 796 and was buried in St Peter's church; his successor, Eanbald II (consecrated 14 August 796, still archbishop in 808, exact date of retirement/death unknown) was a priest from St Peter's and was appointed immediately in his stead.[92] Alcuin's letters show that Alcuin himself was initially delighted with the choice of Eanbald II as archbishop,[93] but they also demonstrate that Eanbald II had taken over at a particularly difficult moment in the political world of Northumbria, when King Æthelred I had recently been murdered.[94]

[89] *HR* (4), p. 58 (s.a. 796): '...and was consecrated on the seventh kalend of June in York in the church of St Peter at the altar of the blessed Apostle Paul, where that nation first received the grace of baptism'. Eardwulf ruled at least until 806, at which point *ASC DE* state that he was driven from his kingdom. But evidence from the *Royal Frankish Annals* suggests that Eardwulf was returned to power in 808–10 by Charlemagne and Pope Leo III; see Story, *Carolingian Connections*, pp. 145–56.
[90] Story, *Carolingian Connections*, pp. 156–60, discusses the significance of this event and suggests that the anointment may have been similar to the rite adopted by the Carolingian king, Pippin III in 751, perhaps as a means of legitimising Eardwulf's new regime (at p. 160). Story, *ibid*., pp. 145–64, describes the remarkable collusion between King Eardwulf and Charlemagne (at pp. 156–7, for the possibility that Eardwulf had married one of Charlemagne's daughters) and the longstanding connections between Northumbria and Francia.
[91] Cubitt, *Councils*, p. 186.
[92] *ASC DE*, s.a. 796 and *HR* (4), p. 58 (s.a. 796); Eanbald II received the *pallium* on 8 September 797: *ASC DE*, s.a. 797 and *HR* (4), p. 58 (s.a. 797).
[93] Alcuin, *Ep*. 114 (Allott, *Alcuin* 6). That Eanbald II was a conscientious bishop is perhaps corroborated by the fact that he convened a synod of the Northumbrian church at *Pincanheale*; see *HR* (4), p. 59 (s.a. 798) and Cubitt, *Councils*, pp. 291–2 (at p. 27 for the sites of Northumbrian synods). It may be that the high standards of learning witnessed earlier at York had not yet diminished. In a letter of 796, Alcuin asks Charlemagne that he may be allowed to send students to York to bring back books which were not available to him on the Continent. See Alcuin, *Ep*. 121 (Allott, *Alcuin* 8).
[94] Alcuin, *Ep*. 116 (Allott, *Alcuin* 7). The death of Æthelred I on 18 April 796 is recorded in *HR* (4), p. 57 (s.a. 796). In a letter of 797 to Pope Leo III, Alcuin entreats the pope to grant the *pallium* to Eanbald II so that his authority might be strengthened during these troubled times: Alcuin, *Ep*. 125 (Allott, *Alcuin* 18).

Although Alcuin realises that political developments were causing Eanbald II various problems, he also suggests that the behaviour of Eanbald II himself was not above reproach. In two letters of 801, he accuses Eanbald II of, among other things, stealing land and harbouring the enemies of the new king, Eardwulf.[95] Despite Eanbald II's actions, Alcuin still thought it appropriate to send him gifts, one of which was a hundred pounds of tin so that a belfry (*domuncula cloccarum*) could be properly roofed.[96] It is difficult to know which belfry was to be given a new roof (it may have been destined for a belfry connected to St Peter's or perhaps to Ælberht's most recent establishment dedicated to *Alma Sophia* or it may have been a freestanding belfry),[97] but the passage clearly demonstrates Alcuin's continuing concern for his old church.[98]

From this point onwards, historical sources contain even fewer details of the deeds of the archbishops and of St Peter's church: the episcopacies of Wulfsige (808 × ?–830 × 37), Wigmund (837–54) and Wulfhere (854–92/3 or 854–900) are poorly attested.[99] In a letter of the 830s written by Ecgred, bishop of Lindisfarne, to Archbishop Wulfsige, we learn that Wulfsige had taken pains to ensure that the Lindisfarne community was following the true catholic faith and that they had not succumbed to the ancient heresies of Nial and Pehtred.[100] We have preserved coins both of the styca type and a remarkable gold solidus (inscribed *munus diuinum*) which bear Wigmund's name.[101] And there may have been continued

[95] Alcuin, *Ep.* 232 and 233 (Allott, *Alcuin* 20 and 21). For comment on Eanbald II and his retinue of men, see Campbell 1989, p. 16 and Rollason, *Northumbria*, pp. 131–2; see also Story, *Carolingian Connections*, pp. 133 and 202.

[96] Alcuin, *Ep.* 226 (Allott, *Alcuin* 19).

[97] Norton 1998*b*, p. 8, suggests that Alcuin's letter here implies the existence of a freestanding bell tower which was perhaps the precursor of the medieval church of St Michael-le-Belfrey; Norton also suggests that this medieval church of St Michael-le-Belfrey is to be equated with a church of St Michael mentioned by Folcard (at p. 14).

[98] Alcuin, *Ep.* 114 (Allott, *Alcuin* 6), shows Alcuin urging Eanbald II to build a hospital in York.

[99] Because there are so few details about these bishops it is impossible to be precise about the dates of their accession and retirement/death, which can often only be surmised by reference to sources of the twelfth century. For the problems involved in these calculations, see Rollason *et al.*, *Sources*, pp. 58–9.

[100] Haddan and Stubbs III, pp. 615–16; it is translated in Whitelock, *EHD*, no. 214 and re-edited by her: D. Whitelock, 'Bishop Ecgred, Pehtred and Niall', in *Ireland in Early Mediaeval Europe: Studies in Memory of Kathleen Hughes*, ed. D. Whitelock, R. McKitterick and D. Dumville (Cambridge, 1982), pp. 47–68 (at pp. 48–9, for the edition of the letter).

[101] North, *EHC I*, p. 45. The gold solidus is an exceptional coin and it is difficult to know how to interpret it (see the comments of Grierson and Blackburn, *MEC I*, p. 330, who suggest that the solidus may have been an honorific coin struck in a south-eastern mint such as Canterbury). As for those more standard examples to do with the archbishops of York, such as the styca type of Wigmund, it seems likely that they were the product of a similar situation as that described in Æthelstan's II law-code (issued at Grately) which notes, as item 14.2, that one moneyer's die and the profits from it were

scholarly interest too. In the early 850s two letters were written by Lupus, abbot of Ferrières, and sent to the York community: they are vitally important because they form our last glimpse of learned activity at York before the arrival of vikings in the 860s. One is addressed to Archbishop Wigmund himself and entreats him to commemorate the abbey of Ferrières in his prayers and also to renew friendship through the exchange of letters.[102] The other is addressed to Ealdsige, abbot of York, whom Lupus knew to be a keen scholar; in it Lupus requests that Ealdsige send him copies of Jerome, Bede and Quintilian.[103] It seems that in the 850s desire for knowledge, and the facilities with which to study texts, had not been lost to those dwelling at St Peter's.[104]

d. *866/7–954: The Arrival of Vikings and a time of Intermittent Rule*

On 1 November 866, the 'Great Army' of vikings, which had been operating in East Anglia, shifted its attention to the north and captured York; one of its leaders was Ivar.[105] The viking army then continued its advance and reached as far as the River Tyne. But this allowed time for the two rival Northumbrian kings, Ælle and Osberht, to unite and to expel the vikings from York. A second attack was required and in March of 867 vikings again took control of York.[106] This seizure brought about widespread change at York. From this point in its history until 954, York (or *Jórvík* as it came to be known to Scandinavians)[107] was subject to the power of various rulers, both those of Scandinavian extraction, who were mostly the heirs of Ivar, and, at times, those drawn from the southern dynasty of English kings.[108]

assigned to the archbishop, just as most others were the prerogative of the king (see Whitelock, *EHD*, no. 35). I am grateful here to Dr R. Naismith for much useful advice about Northumbrian coinage.

[102] See E. Dümmler, ed., *Epistolae Karolini Aeui* IV, MGH (Berlin, 1925), p. 61 (no. 61) and Haddan and Stubbs III, pp. 634–5; for an English translation, see Whitelock, *EHD*, no. 215.

[103] See E. Dümmler, ed., *Epistolae Karolini Aeui* IV, MGH, p. 62 (no. 62); Haddan and Stubbs III, pp. 635–6; Whitelock, *EHD*, no. 216. It may be significant that Ealdsige is addressed as an 'abbot' which perhaps suggests the presence of some kind of monastic establishment at York; see above, pp. 35–6 and Morris (R.K.) 1986, p. 81, for this particular reference.

[104] Nevertheless, it seems as if York did not provide the requested copies of Jerome and Quintilian since Lupus can be found in 855–59 asking for copies of these same works from Pope Benedict III; see the introductory comments in Whitelock, *EHD*, no. 216.

[105] The *Chronicon Æthelweardi*, IV.2, names Ivar as leader; see also Stenton, *ASE*, p. 246 and Downham, *Viking Kings*, p. 63.

[106] Symeon, *LDE*, ii.6. *ASC C*, s.a. 868 (*recte* 867), notes the arrival of vikings at York but does not mention two attacks, as Symeon does.

[107] Fellows-Jensen 1998, pp. 232–36; see also the comments of Abrams and Parsons 2004, pp. 385 and 393.

[108] For an overview of this period, see Downham, *Viking Kings*, pp. 63–120. For the various forms of interaction between the Scandinavian incomers and those already living in Northumbria, see Hadley and Richards, *Cultures in Contact*.

These were turbulent years and the obscurity of the historical record bears witness to the attendant confusion. In fact, this period is so poorly attested that some of the Scandinavian kings at York are known only because we have extant coins minted in their name. Nevertheless, a sequence of kings based at York can be discerned, which it is useful to reproduce here.[109] The rule of Scandinavian kings begins most certainly with Halfdan,[110] a brother of Ivar, who was king of Northumbria in 875/6 until his death in Ireland in 877.[111] Unfortunately, there is almost a complete lack of written evidence for the 880s in Northumbria. Blackburn has pointed out that two coins minted in the mid-880s, which display stylistic links with coinage produced in the Five Boroughs,[112] bear the name Halfdan (ALFDENE RX).[113] Since Halfdan, the first Scandinavian king in Northumbria, had died in 877, this must be a reference to an otherwise unknown Scandinavian king.[114] Perhaps the only certain record of the next Scandinavian king of York, Guthfrith, concerns his death in 895;[115] no precise information about the date of his accession is known. It is likely that he is to be identified as being one and the same as that 'Guthred' whom the *Historia de Sancto Cuthberto* claims was brought to power by the otherworldly intercession of St Cuthbert and also by the joint actions of two northern religious leaders, Eadred, abbot of Carlisle and Eardwulf, bishop of Lindisfarne (and later of Chester-le-Street).[116]

[109] The following sequence of Scandinavian and English kings of York is intended only as a summary guide. It is often extremely difficult to be precise when it comes to matters of chronology for this period of Northumbrian history and, in the case of each king, readers will be referred to secondary literature which discusses these issues in more detail. This section has benefited in particular from the work of Downham, *Viking Kings*.

[110] It is unclear what happened immediately following the viking capture of York in 866/7 but it seems as if the vikings set up a subordinate English king, Egbert, who was succeeded by a man of similar standing, Ricsige: for discussion, see Rollason *et al.*, *Sources*, p. 63, Woolf, *Pictland*, pp. 73–5 and below, pp. 47–8.

[111] Halfdan can be found in England in the period 871 x 876. He may have been made king following the departure of his brother, Ivar, in 870: Downham, *Viking Kings*, pp. 68–71. It is not entirely clear that he was based at York: Rollason *et al.*, *Sources*, p. 63 and Rollason, *Northurmbria*, p. 216.

[112] Grierson and Blackburn, *MEC I*, p. 319.

[113] North, *EHC I*, p. 108 (nos. 481–2).

[114] Blackburn 2004, pp. 327–8. This Halfdan may have ruled in the Five Boroughs (as Blackburn 2004, p. 328 tentatively suggests) or he may be the same Halfdan who was king of York slightly later and whose death is recorded in 910 (for whom see below, p. 44). This latter possibility is suggested in Downham, *Viking Kings*, p. 72 and briefly considered in an earlier work of Grierson and Blackburn, *MEC I*, p. 319.

[115] *Chronicon Æthelweardi*, IV.3; he was buried in York Minster, for which see below, p. 48. A coin from the hoard deposited at Ashdon in Essex bearing the inscription 'GUDEF.RE' may have been minted in the name of this Guthfrith (North, *EHC I*, p. 109 and Grierson and Blackburn, *MEC I*, p. 319). It is probable that he was ruling in the 890s: Downham, *Viking Kings*, pp. 75–8; see also Dumville 2004, pp. 87–9.

[116] For this event, see *HSC*, c. 13 and Rollason, *Northumbria*, pp. 244–9; for further discussion, see below, pp. 291–2. It is particularly interesting to find here the abbot of a Cumbrian religious house

Following the death of Guthfrith in 895, written evidence once more disappears and it is now mainly coins that give details of York kings.[117] The first such is Sigeferth, probably king in York from *c.* 895 to *c.* 900, whose name is inscribed on coins in the form SIEFREDUS or SIEVERT.[118] His successor was named Cnut, who seems, on the basis of numismatic evidence, to have ruled in York *c.* 900–*c.* 905.[119] Because the names of Sigeferth and Cnut appear inscribed on some of the same coins, it may be that they shared a period of rule.[120] Some coins of the years 900–902 bear the name ALVVALDUS,[121] which supports the entry in the *Anglo-Saxon Chronicle* stating that *c.* 900 the atheling Æthelwold rebelled against his cousin King Edward the Elder, and was accepted as king in Northumbria.[122] From the end of Cnut's reign *c.* 905 until the accession of Rægnald *c.* 918, very little is known about the Scandinavian kings in Northumbria. The only information that survives can be found in the account of the Battle of Tettenhall in 910, in which the 'army of Northumbria' was defeated with the result that kings Eowils and Halfdan were killed;[123] the *Chronicon Æthelweardi* adds the detail that a further king, Ivar, was also killed.[124] Unfortunately, there is no more information about these three kings and no way of telling whether they had any base at

---

acting in combination with the bishop of Cuthbert's community; Aird, *St Cuthbert*, p. 38, suggests that Abbot Eadred may have been forced to flee from the north-west of the country into St Cuthbert's community in the face of Scandinavian settlement in the Cumbrian region; see also Woolf, *Pictland*, pp. 81–3, on Eadred's role and below, p. 289, n. 125.

[117] For the remarkable nature of this regal coinage, see Blackburn 2004, pp. 329–32. For a recent survey of historical material with a bearing on York in the early tenth century, see R. Hall, 'A Kingdom Too Far: York in the Early Tenth Century', in *Edward the Elder 899–924*, ed. N.J. Higham and D.H. Hill (London and New York, 2001), pp. 188–99.

[118] North, *EHC I*, pp. 110–12. Some of these coins are inscribed 'CSIEFREDUS REX', where the meaning of the initial 'C' is unclear but which may refer to a baptismal name. See Grierson and Blackburn, *MEC I*, p. 321, Blackburn 2004, p. 331 and Downham, *Viking Kings*, p. 79. He is likely to be that *Sigeferð piraticus de Northhimbriorum* who can be found harrying the English coast in 893: *Chronicon Æthelweardi*, IV.3. But see Rollason 2004, p. 309 and Downham, *ibid.*, p. 79, for the difficulties with his identification.

[119] Blackburn 2004, p. 329. Cnut is even more difficult to identify: Grierson and Blackburn, *MEC I*, p. 321, Rollason 2004, p. 309 and Downham, *Viking Kings*, pp. 79–80. That both Sigeferth and Cnut were kings based at York is implied by the fact that some of their coins are inscribed with the York mint name: North, *EHC I*, pp. 110–12.

[120] Grierson and Blackburn, *MEC I*, p. 321, Blackburn 2004, p. 329.

[121] North, *EHC I*, p. 111 (no. 505).

[122] *ASC CD*, s.a. 901 (*recte* 900). For the implications of Æthelwold's presence in Northumbria, see Downham, *Viking Kings*, pp. 81–2. Woolf, *Pictland*, p. 139, suggests that Æthelwold may have been accepted as king of the West Saxons in Northumbria, rather than as king of Northumbria.

[123] *ASC AB*, s.a. 910; *ASC CD*, s.a. 911. This Halfdan may be synonymous with the Halfdan whose name has been found inscribed on two mid-880s coins; see above, p. 43.

[124] *Chronicon Æthelweardi*, IV.4.

York;[125] their deaths marked the end of the Anglo-Danish dynasty that had begun in the 870s.[126]

After the Battle of Corbridge in 918,[127] a Gaelic-Scandinavian ruler named Rægnald took over as king of York in 919.[128] His successor, Sihtric 'Caoch' ('the One-Eyed'), arrived in York in 920 and perhaps deposed Rægnald, who died soon afterwards in 921.[129] Sihtric himself negotiated a marriage alliance with the English king, Æthelstan, and ruled in York until his death in 927.[130] Sihtric was succeeded by his brother, Guthfrith, who briefly tried to secure York in the same year but who was quickly driven out by King Æthelstan.[131] Æthelstan's conquest of Northumbria, which was followed by formal recognition of his status at Eamont, marked a significant achievement for the line of English kings.[132] By a combination of methods, he held Northumbria until his death in 939.[133]

Although Æthelstan's reign severely hampered the aspirations of Scandinavian kings in Northumbria,[134] it did not prevent Olaf Guthfrithson, the nephew of Sihtric 'Caoch', from once more taking control of York in 939.[135] But Olaf's reign was

[125] See Rollason *et al.*, *Sources*, p. 66. For the possibility that Æthelred of Mercia was overlord of Northumbria in 910, see Downham, *Viking Kings*, pp. 88–9.

[126] Woolf, *Pictland*, p. 139.

[127] The *Historia de Sancto Cuthberto* refers to two battles at Corbridge (*HSC*, cc. 22 and 24). Irish annals and 'The Chronicle of the Kings of Alba' suggest that there was in fact only one battle at Corbridge and that it took place in 918: see the commentary of Johnson South in *HSC*, pp. 105–7, Downham, *Viking Kings*, pp. 92–3 and Woolf, *Pictland*, pp. 143–4 (where he also suggests an alternative chronology for some major Northumbrian events in this period).

[128] The *Historia regum* reports Rægnald's capture of York in 919: *HR* (6), p. 93 (s.a. 919); the northern recension of the *Anglo-Saxon Chronicle* places the capture even later in 923 (*ASC D*, s.a. 923) but the most probable date, given previous happenings at Corbridge, is 919. Rægnald's coins are inscribed 'RAIENALT' or 'RACNOLDT'; they interrupted the remarkable series of St Peter's coins. For the St Peter's coins, see below, pp. 50–1. For Rægnald's coinage, see North, *EHC I*, p. 113, Grierson and Blackburn, *MEC I*, pp. 322–3 and Blackburn 2004, pp. 333–4. For Rægnald's actions in Ireland prior to his intervention in Northumbria, see Woolf, *Pictland*, pp. 140–2 (and p. 145, for useful remarks about the cultural impact of Rægnald's arrival in Northumbria).

[129] For this sequence of events, see Downham, *Viking Kings*, pp. 97–8; it seems likely that the Northumbrians under Rægnald briefly submitted to the rule of the English king Edward the Elder in 920 (Downham, *ibid.*, pp. 95–7 and Woolf, *Pictland*, pp. 146–7).

[130] *ASC D*, s.a. 926 (*recte* 927). Coins of Sihtric are inscribed 'SITRIC': North, *EHC I*, p. 113.

[131] *ASC E*, s.a. 927 and Woolf, *Pictland*, p. 151. No known coins of Guthfrith survive: Blackburn 2004, p. 335.

[132] *ASC D*, s.a. 926 (*recte* 927).

[133] For Æthelstan and Northumbria, see Whitelock 1959, p. 71 and Downham, *Viking Kings*, pp. 99–105. Æthelstan stopped the minting of Anglo-Scandinavian coins at York and instead introduced a new type of coinage which was made according to English standards; see Blackburn 2004, p. 335.

[134] Downham, *Viking Kings*, p. 105.

[135] Although the northern recension of the *Anglo-Saxon Chronicle* records Olaf's election as king under the year 941, it probably took place much sooner after Æthelstan's death since Irish annals report his departure from Dublin in 939: see *ASC D*, s.a. 941 and Downham, *Viking Kings*, p. 107.

short-lived and his death in 941 saw the succession of his cousin, Olaf Sihtricson ('Cuarán', meaning 'of the Sandal').[136] These were troubled times and in the years 940–3 the English king, Edmund, fought hard to suppress the northern kingdom.[137] The annal for 943 in the *Anglo-Saxon Chronicle* suggests the presence of another king of Northumbria (presumably from York), Rægnald Guthfrithson,[138] and coins in the name of an otherwise unknown King Sihtric imply the existence of three kings at York.[139] In 944 Olaf Sihtricson and Rægnald Guthfrithson were expelled from Northumbria by King Edmund.[140] Following the expulsion of both kings, King Edmund was able to take control of the kingdom of Northumbria and so began a second period of English rule over Scandinavian York. But the murder of Edmund soon afterwards in 946 meant that the next English king, Eadred, had to move quickly to establish his position in Northumbria. Although Wulfstan, then archbishop of York,[141] 'and all the councillors of the Northumbrians' swore, in 947, to side with Eadred, they were quickly false to their word and in 947 accepted a certain Eric as their new king.[142] Eric was overthrown by Eadred in 948,[143] who then held on to Northumbria until 950. The political tide was to turn again, however, as Olaf Sihtricson, the very same king who had been expelled by Edmund in 944, returned to Northumbria in 949 and seemingly ruled that kingdom until the Northumbrians themselves drove him out in 952, this time in favour of Eric again.[144] Eric ruled for a second period in Northumbria until he was driven out in 954 by the Northumbrians.[145] From this moment onwards, the

[136] Despite his short reign, Olaf Guthfrithson oversaw a campaign to remove English coinage from circulation in York whilst simultaneously introducing coins with a dramatic design of a viking raven and with the Old Norse inscription, 'ANLAF CVNVNC'; these coins may have continued under Olaf Sihtricson: Blackburn 2004, p. 336 and Dolley 1978, p. 28. On Olaf Guthfrithson's death, some Northumbrians may have chosen Edmund as their king instead of Olaf Sihtricsson: Downham, *Viking Kings*, p. 108.

[137] Edmund won back the 'Five Boroughs' (Leicester, Lincoln, Nottingham, Stamford and Derby) from the Scandinavians in 942: *ASC C*, s.a. 942.

[138] *ASC C*, s.a. 943.

[139] North, *EHC I*, p. 115 and Blackburn 2004, p. 336.

[140] *ASC C*, s.a. 944.

[141] See below, pp. 53–5.

[142] *ASC D*, s.a. 947 and s.a. 948.

[143] *ASC D*, s.a. 948.

[144] See *ASC E*, s.a. 949, for Olaf Sihtricson's return to Northumbria and *ASC E*, s.a. 952, for the expulsion of this Olaf in favour of Eric. In the period 944–48, Olaf Sihtricson had been campaigning for power in Dublin: Downham, *Viking Kings*, p. 113.

[145] For a different interpretation of the chronology of this period, which posits just one period of rule for Eric from 950–2/4 and a longer reign for Olaf, 947–50, see Sawyer 1995. For further discussion about the chronology of these events, see Rollason 2004, p. 310. The king named Eric is traditionally identified as 'Eric Bloodaxe'. But Downham, *Viking Kings*, pp. 119–20, questions this and suggests instead that Eric was, like so many of the other Scandinavian kings of York, a descendant of Ivar; for

Northumbrians finally relented to King Eadred and to the rule of subsequent kings of Anglo-Saxon England.[146]

This overview has shown that, in the period after the arrival of vikings in 866/7 until 954, there was a rapid turnover of Scandinavian and also of English kings of Northumbria, many of whom were based specifically at York.[147] The arrival of vikings may have been followed by the despoliation of various local landowners, including the church.[148] But there are strong indications that the York see managed to engineer its own survival and its place within this new society;[149] indeed the very first years after the viking invasion may have witnessed the archbishop retain some of his standing by siding with the invaders.[150] The evidence of Symeon, in his *Libellus de Exordio atque Procursu istius hoc est Dunhelmensis Ecclesie*, and also of the *Historia regum*, suggests that one of the initial deeds of the vikings was to set up an indigenous figure, Egbert, as king; Symeon further notes that he 'ruled only over those who lived to the north of the river Tyne'.[151] But in an uprising of 872, the Northumbrians managed to expel Egbert from the kingdom; since we learn that Archbishop Wulfhere was exiled at the same moment, it seems reasonable to suggest that the archbishop had chosen to ally himself and the York see to the viking cause.[152] In the following year, 873, the viking army is recorded as leaving London and making its way to Northumbria,[153] perhaps in

further discussion, see A. Woolf, 'Erik Bloodaxe Revisited', *NH* xxxiv (1998), pp. 189–93 and Woolf, *Pictland*, pp. 187–8.

146 *ASC D*, s.a. 954.

147 Although this quick succession of kings is indicative of a complex and turbulent political situation, Anglo-Scandinavian York did develop into a major urban centre; excavations in the Coppergate area, for example, have revealed that plots of land were laid out and developed in the period *c*. 900–*c*. 935 and also that York had extensive trading links. See Hall (R.A.) 1988, p. 130, Hall (R.A.) 1999, p. 499, Hall (R.A.) 2000, pp. 315–17 and Hall (R.A.) 2004, pp. 490 and 494, where he describes York as experiencing an 'economic boom' in these years. The city was expanding in these years too, as is revealed, for example, by Anglo-Scandinavian sculpture found south-west of the River Ouse in the Bishophill area: see the comments of Cramp, *Anglian and Viking York*, p. 17 and Palliser 1984. Norton 1998*b*, pp. 27–8, argues that the expansion of the city took place earlier than the Anglo-Scandinavian period; but see also the comments of R.A. Hall, '*Jórvík*: a Viking-Age City', in Hines *et al*., *Land, Sea and Home*, pp. 283–95 (at pp. 285–7).

148 For the possible effects of the viking arrival on landholding, see Dumville, *Wessex and England*, pp. 53–4, Barrow 2000, p. 169 and Abrams 2000, p. 142.

149 The survival of the York church during this period is widely accepted. See, for example, Barrow 2000, Blair, *Church*, pp. 313–14 and Hadley, *Vikings*, p. 45.

150 Wulfhere was archbishop at this time; he had received the *pallium* in 854: *HR* (5), p. 71 (s.a. 854) and *HR* (8), p. 101 (s.a. 854).

151 Symeon, *LDE*, ii.6 and *HR* (8), p. 106 (s.a. 867). It does not seem likely that Egbert's rule was only over territory to the north of the river Tyne, for which see Woolf, *Pictland*, pp. 73–5 (at p. 75).

152 *HR* (8), p. 110 (s.a. 872). See Stenton, *ASE*, p. 251, Hadley, *Vikings*, p. 11 and Hall (R.A.) 2000, p. 312.

153 *HR* (5), p. 81 (s.a. 873) and *HR* (8), p. 110 (s.a. 873).

an attempt to reinstate their candidate, Egbert. This ultimately failed and Egbert was replaced by another local man, Ricsige. On the accession of Ricsige in 873, Wulfhere was simultaneously restored to the archbishopric, perhaps indicating that the viking army had had at least some success in its journey from London to Northumbria.[154]

In 876 the presence of the Scandinavians seems to have become more permanent; the *Anglo-Saxon Chronicle* records that Halfdan 'shared out the land of the Northumbrians, and they proceeded to plough and to support themselves'.[155] The very few details we have which involve the York church seem to suggest that it had evolved to operate in collaboration with its viking rulers. The *Chronicon Æthelweardi* notes for the year 895:

> Transeunte etiam anni unius decursu obiit et Guthfrid, rex Northhymbriorum, in natalitia sancti Bartholomæi apostoli Christi; cuius mausoleatur Euoraca corpus in urbe in basilica summa.[156]

It is almost certain that this Guthfrith is the same king as that Guthred mentioned as being elevated to the throne by St Cuthbert's community.[157] That Guthfrith was buried in York may suggest that he was using that city as his base; and his entombment in St Peter's implies that he was on good terms with the religious community, perhaps even that he was a Christian.[158] It seems that the re-instated

[154] Hadley, *Vikings*, p. 11.

[155] *ASC C*, s.a. 877 (*recte* 876). For the profusion of Scandinavian place-names in Yorkshire see, for example, G. Fellows-Jensen, *Scandinavian Settlement Names in Yorkshire*, Navnestudier 11 (Copenhagen, 1972) and *eadem*, *The Vikings and their Victims: the Verdict of the Names*, The Dorothea Coke Memorial Lecture in Northern Studies delivered at University College London 21 February 1994 (London, 1995; repr. Birmingham, 1998), which also discusses the evidence of Scandinavian personal names; for an important recent discussion of the Scandinavian settlement in England, with particular reference to the evidence of place-names and the dates at which they may have appeared, and whether place-names can be used as an index for the density of Scandinavian settlement, see Abrams and Parsons 2004 (esp. pp. 392–4, for comments about how to use the evidence of place-names and pp. 395–404, for what *bȳ*-names can indicate about Scandinavian settlement in the Danelaw). The density of the Scandinavian settlement in York itself is indicated especially by the variety of Scandinavian street names that are preserved there: Fellows-Jensen 1977, pp. 4–8 and Fellows-Jensen 2004, pp. 359 and 367.

[156] *Chronicon Æthelweardi*, IV.3: 'When the course of one year had completed, Guthfrid, king of the Northumbrians, died on the day of St Bartholomew apostle of Christ; whose body is entombed in the city of York in the high basilica'.

[157] *HSC*, c. 13. For the role of St Cuthbert's community in this event, see below, pp. 291–2; see also the comments of Dumville 2004, pp. 87–8.

[158] Dumville 2004, p. 88. As Dumville points out, an extant coin inscribed with Guthfrith's name indicates 'a king who had assimilated to his surroundings'. For this coin, see Grierson and Blackburn, *MEC I*, p. 319. Lang, *Corpus*, p. 8, suggests that a lack of pagan graves in Yorkshire suggests that 'the colonial Scandinavian was quick to assimilate Christianity'; see also the comments of Stocker 2000, pp. 194–5. For a similar suggestion regarding coins, see Dolley 1978, Blackburn 2004 and Hadley,

Archbishop Wulfhere had managed, at the least, to strike a working relationship with these various viking leaders.[159]

The evidence of coinage is particularly interesting. The fundamental study of the viking coins of York is that of Blackburn, who distinguishes various stages of coin production.[160] The first identifiably Anglo-Scandinavian series dates to the period from *c.* 895 to 905. It is termed the 'York regal coinage' by Blackburn and is distinctive in form.[161] What is of immediate interest is that, although these were coins of the viking kings, they display a strong Christian theme and are especially remarkable for their use of liturgical phrases such as 'Dominus Deus Rex'. Blackburn states that this 'regal coinage' was designed to emphasise that 'the York kingdom had the credentials to be a respected member of the western Christian states'.[162] It seems almost certain that viking kings would have consulted the York archbishopric about the inclusion of these Christian elements on their coins and this is therefore further corroboration for the notion that Wulfhere had managed to secure the standing of the church.[163]

Following the death of Archbishop Wulfhere *c.* 900,[164] Æthelbald was consecrated to the York see in his stead.[165] It is striking that the *Chronicon Æthelweardi* states that his consecration was carried out to the south, in London,[166] not least because this was the same moment that the atheling Æthelwold was rebelling against the rule of the new English king, Edward the Elder, and receiving the support

---

Vikings, p. 45. For difficulties with the term pagan, see Abrams 2000, p. 135, n. 1 and, for problems in accepting that Guthfrith had become Christian, Abrams 2001, p. 37.

159 Smyth, *Scandinavian* I, pp. 41–2, emphasises the relative stability of the Scandinavian kingdom at York as opposed to the Scandinavian kingdom at Dublin in the period 877–914, leading him to suggest that this was a stable environment for the York church. Other churches in the Danelaw did not engineer their own survival and in the later ninth century and early tenth century the York church perhaps took over the episcopal role for Lindsey; see P. Sawyer, *Anglo-Saxon Lincolnshire*, History of Lincolnshire III (Lincoln, 1988), p. 144 and pp. 149–54.

160 Blackburn 2004.

161 Blackburn 2004, pp. 329–30, notes that there was no uniform design and there were no moneyers' names on the coins although the mint name does appear. Blackburn states that these coins do not rely on Anglo-Saxon or Carolingian precedents but rather display their own, idiosyncratic designs.

162 Blackburn 2004, p. 332; see also Hadley, *Vikings*, p. 45.

163 If it is correct to assign a role for the York church in the design of these coins, then this would suggest that intellectual activity at York had not vanished entirely. Blackburn 2004, p. 332, stresses how different this 'regal coinage' was from what had gone before and he attributes this to a group of people of no little intellectual ability. For Smyth, *Scandinavian* I, p. 53, the coins of Sigeferth and Cnut (who succeeded Guthfrith at York and who are known principally because their names appear on York coinage) 'provide further evidence for the continuing close relationship between the archbishops of York and the Scandinavian invaders'.

164 For the possible date of Wulfhere's death, see Rollason *et al.*, *Sources*, p. 59.

165 *HR* (6), p. 92 (s.a. 900) and *HR* (8), p. 121 (s.a. 900).

166 *Chronicon Æthelweardi*, IV.4, relating to the year 900.

of the Northumbrians.[167] It may be that Æthelbald was promoted as archbishop by Æthelwold and his supporters; or perhaps Edward the Elder was trying to impose his own choice of candidate on the Northumbrian church and thereby to achieve some political leverage in York.[168] Although it may seem strange that the Scandinavian party in York would be willing to accept a candidate who perhaps had been approved by an English king,[169] the Scandinavians were arguably motivated to accept religion, and the leaders of the church, in an attempt to wield political power more effectively. The evidence of coins has already suggested a certain amount of collaboration and this impression is reinforced by the late ninth- and early tenth-century Anglo-Scandinavian grave slabs found in excavations of a pre-Conquest cemetery under the south transept of the current Minster.[170]

For the period from *c.* 905 to 927, coins are again our main source of information. But they have now taken on a wholly different form. Apart from a brief interruption in *c.* 919 to 921 when coins of the Gaelic-Scandinavian King Rægnald appeared, the name of the king is no longer displayed and is replaced by the legend, 'SCI PETRI MO', on one side and the name of the city on the other.[171] Study of the 'St Peter's coins' has resulted in debate as to who was in charge of their production. The lack of the king's name and the use of the inscription 'St Peter's', the name of the principal York church, have led Rollason to suggest that these were coins produced by the archbishops of York; and this has subsequently led him to believe that the York church was the effective ruler of the city at this time.[172] But this has come under considerable attack from Blackburn, who concludes that 'it would be without precedent in Europe for control of all minting to be granted away by

[167] For Æthelwold's rebellion, see above, p. 44 and the *ASC D*, s.a. 901 (*recte* 900).

[168] Downham, *Viking Kings*, p. 82.

[169] See the comments of Abrams 2000, p. 143.

[170] See Lang, *Corpus*, pp. 26–7, 39–40 and the York Minster stones, nos. 30–1, 34 and 39. The creation of various proprietary churches later in the tenth century (*c.* 950–*c.* 1000), including St Mary Bishophill Senior and St Mary Castlegate, which may have had Scandinavian patrons or founders, perhaps implies that such collaboration continued; see Barrow 2000, pp. 168–9 and Stocker 2000, pp. 203–7. For Anglo-Scandinavian sculpture surviving from St Mary Bishophill Senior, see Lang, *Corpus*, pp. 88–95, especially nos. 3, 4, 5, 7, 14 (part of a hogback), 16, 17 and 22. For Anglo-Scandinavian sculpture from St Mary Castlegate, including the tenth- or eleventh-century dedication stone inscribed with the Old Norse names 'Grim' and 'Æse', see Lang, *ibid.*, pp. 96–9 (nos. 2–4). Excavations at Aldwark have revealed the location of the church of St Helen-on-the-Walls, which may have had its origins in the late tenth century; see Magilton, *Church of St Helen-on-the-Walls*, pp. 18 and 42. No Scandinavian sculpture was found there: Stocker 2000, p. 205, n. 14. For other pre-Conquest churches in York, see Hall 1988 and Hall 2004, pp. 496–7, for a list of these churches.

[171] By 919, Rægnald was in charge of the Dublin and the York kingdom and his coinage was designed to promote these Scandinavian successes; see Blackburn 2004, p. 333. The second series of 'St Peter's Coins', which occur after 921, are characterised by the added appearance of a sword on them.

[172] Rollason 2004, p. 313.

a state'.[173] Even if we deny the possibility that the archbishopric was in control of the York mint, the strong Christian element and the use of the inscription 'St Peter', suggest the very real likelihood that the York church was influencing the production of coins, and therefore secular policy, in this period.[174]

In 927 fiery portents heralded the succession of a southern king, Æthelstan, rather than a Scandinavian ruler 'to the kingdom of the Northumbrians; and he brought under his rule all the kings who were in this island'.[175] Manuscript witness 'E' of the *Anglo-Saxon Chronicle* adds the detail that King Æthelstan had driven out the Scandinavian King Guthfrith. Æthelstan interrupted the issue of 'St Peter's coins' and, in an attempt to bring York and the surrounding territory into line with the rest of England,[176] introduced coins which had designs of a church or reliquary inscribed onto them. Æthelstan soon afterwards introduced the 'Circumscription Cross' type and the 'Bust Crowned' type.[177] If the later testimony of William of Malmesbury can be believed Æthelstan was even able to use York as a base at which to receive envoys sent by Harold Fairhair, king of Norway.[178]

Although Æthelstan did effect some changes at York, it does not seem probable that he had incorporated it fully into his control.[179] **1** sees Æthelstan granting land in the north-west of the country, known as Amounderness, to St Peter's church; it was made on 7 June 934, at a meeting of the *witan* at Nottingham. The name of the territory being granted, which may derive ultimately from the Scandinavian personal name *Agmundr* or *Ǫgmundr*,[180] perhaps suggests that this area of land had previously been in Scandinavian hands.[181] **1** represents a

[173] Blackburn 2004, p. 333. But see also Smyth, *Scandinavian* I, p. 55, who also suggests that the archbishopric had taken control over the minting of coins in this period.

[174] The archbishop at this time was a man called Hrothweard (904x928–31); very little is known about him, barely even the dates of his archiepiscopate, which are inferred on the basis of his attestations to charters; for a discussion of this, see Rollason *et al.*, *Sources*, p. 70. Downham, *Viking Kings*, p. 102, suggests that Hrothweard was promoted to the archbishopric only after Æthelstan had taken control of York in 927.

[175] *ASC D*, s.a. 926 (*recte* 927).

[176] For an assessment of Æthelstan's coinage across England in these years, see Foot, *Æthelstan*, pp. 151–7.

[177] Blackburn 2004, pp. 335–6.

[178] *GR*, ii.135.1.

[179] See Rollason, *Northumbria*, p. 263 and Hadley, *Vikings*, pp. 64–5.

[180] *DEPN*, p. 9, Fellows-Jensen, *SSNNW*, p. 99, Fellows-Jensen 1990 and Hadley, *Vikings*, p. 62.

[181] Fellows-Jensen further suggests that the final element of the place-name 'Amounderness' is derived from Old English *hērness*, meaning a 'district in subjection to secular or ecclesiastical authority', implying that this was an old administrative district belonging to *Agmundr* (*Ǫgmundr*); see Fellows-Jensen 1990 (at pp. 28–9) and G. Fellows-Jensen, *The Vikings and their Victims: the Verdict of the Names*, p. 18. For the Scandinavian settlement of the north-west of the country in the early tenth century, see, for example, G. Fellows-Jensen, 'Scandinavian Place-Names of the Irish Sea Province', *Viking Treasure from the North-West: the Cuerdale Hoard in its Context*, ed. J. Graham-Campbell

shrewd attempt by Æthelstan to secure his position in Northumbria. As we have seen, there is evidence to suggest that previous York archbishops had chosen to ally themselves to the viking kings at York in order to secure their own standing. **1** shows Æthelstan trying to break the York church's viking alliance;[182] it is a grant made directly to St Peter's church and indirectly to Archbishop Wulfstan. The amount of land granted would have demonstrated to the York church that this southern king could be generous. But, perhaps more importantly, the area covered in **1** represented one region which vikings arriving from Dublin would have had to traverse in order to reach York.[183] Not only was Æthelstan trying to buy the support of the York archbishop (Wulfstan), but he was sending a message to would-be invaders: the York church now supported Æthelstan and could be shown to possess a swathe of the country which blocked their approach.[184]

The fragility of any southern dominance over York and the York archbishopric is highlighted by the events which accompanied Æthelstan's death.[185] In 937 Æthelstan had defeated Olaf Guthfrithson, viking King of Dublin (934–41), at the famous Battle of *Brunanburh*; Olaf then retreated to Dublin in 938.[186] But

(Liverpool, 1992), pp. 31–42; Rollason, *Northumbria*, pp. 249–55; D. Griffiths, 'Settlement and Acculturation in the Irish Sea Region', in Hines *et al.*, *Land, Sea and Home*, pp. 125–38, N.J. Higham, 'Viking-Age Settlement in the North-Western Countryside: Lifting the Veil?', in *ibid.*, pp. 297–311, Hadley, *Vikings*, pp. 61–3 and Woolf, *Pictland*, pp. 131–3. For the suggestion that the settlement of vikings in Amounderness in general was not as dense as previously thought, see Watson 2011.

[182] From the York church's point of view, it may have been continuing a policy of siding with whichever figure was ruler of York.

[183] For Æthelstan's attempt to create a defensive 'buffer zone' in this area of the north-west, see Hadley, *Vikings*, p. 63 and Rollason, *Northumbria*, p. 263. For more about the political background to this grant, see the commentary to **1**; see also Barrow 2000, p. 160, Downham, *Viking Kings*, pp. 102–3 and Woolf, *Pictland*, pp. 158–68 (esp. p. 163, for the suggestion that the succession crisis following the death of Guthfrith, king of Dublin, in 934, enabled Æthelstan to purchase Amounderness for himself from a contender for the Dublin throne who needed that English king's money).

[184] It is very difficult to know whether the York church would have been able to control the whole of Amounderness as it lay in an area which had been settled by Scandinavians. Perhaps the most important aspect of **1** was that it represented a political manoeuvre on the part of Æthelstan in an attempt to win over the York church to his cause.

[185] Foot, *Æthelstan*, p. 90, notes the possibility that, a few years before his death, Æthelstan held a council at York in 936 (on the basis of evidence provided by Flodoard of Rheims and Richer of Rheims). If this can be accepted as true, it may have been the insecurity of his hold over Northumbria which had caused Æthelstan's presence at York.

[186] For the Battle of *Brunanburh*, see *ASC ABCD*, s.a. 937; for Olaf Guthfrithson's return to Dublin, see *Annals of Ulster*, ed. S. Mac Airt and G. Mac Niocaill (Dublin, 1983), s.a. 938, 'Amlaib son of Gothfrith in Ath Cliath again'. For a discussion of various possible sites for the *Brunanburh* encounter, with the suggestion that Bromborough on the Wirral has much to recommend it, see Foot, *Æthelstan*, pp. 172–9 (at pp. 178–9).

when Æthelstan died in 939, Olaf returned almost immediately and took power in York.[187]

Throughout these uncertain and tumultuous political times, it must have been an immensely difficult task for the archbishop of York to sustain his, and St Peter's, status: the career of Archbishop Wulfstan (931–56) perhaps demonstrates this better than anything else. He had achieved quite a high standing at the court of King Æthelstan and from 931 until 935 he attests charters in second place behind Æthelhelm, archbishop of Canterbury.[188] But from 936 to 941 he disappears from Æthelstan's charters and is not mentioned in any other historical source. When he reappears in 943 he has shifted his allegiances: he can now be found on the side of vikings and in opposition to southern powers. The *Anglo-Saxon Chronicle* states: 'Here King Edmund besieged King Olaf and Archbishop Wulfstan in Leicester, and he might have controlled them had they not escaped from the stronghold in the night'.[189] It seems certain that, following the death of Æthelstan in 939 and the subsequent arrival of Olaf Guthfrithson, Wulfstan found it necessary to side with the new viking power in the region.[190]

Wulfstan continued to be politically involved and a remarkable sequence of annals in the *Anglo-Saxon Chronicle* details his behaviour. By 946, King Eadred had succeeded to the Anglo-Saxon kingdom; in 947 he 'came to Tanshelf, and there Archbishop Wulfstan and all the councillors of the Northumbrians pledged themselves to the king, and within a short space they were false to it all, both pledge and oaths as well'.[191] The Northumbrians then accepted a certain Eric

[187] *ASC D*, s.a. 941, 'In this year the Northumbrians were false to their pledges, and chose Olaf from Ireland as their king'. Despite the date of the annal in 'D', this probably took place earlier, in 940; see also *HR* (6), p. 93 (s.a. 939). For more about the political situation at this moment, see, for example, Woolf, *Pictland*, pp. 174–5.

[188] Keynes, *Atlas*, table XXXVII.

[189] *ASC D*, s.a. 943.

[190] See Keynes 1999*b*, for a full analysis of Wulfstan's allegiances during this time; see also Downham, *Viking Kings*, pp. 110–15, for a similar assessment of Wulfstan's behaviour; Downham points out that 'Wulfstan appears to support the viking-kings of York whenever he felt safe to do so' (at p. 110). The coins produced during this period seem to confirm the notion that Olaf and Wulfstan had become allies. Olaf used coinage to announce his political achievements; he abandoned the coins used during Æthelstan's period of rule at York and, employing a classic pagan symbol, inscribed the coins with ravens. But Blackburn 2004, p. 336, notes that these pagan symbols were also readily identifiable within a Christian context and he suggests that they were emblematic of the 'apparent alliance with Olaf Guthfrithsson'. Smyth, *Scandinavian* II, pp. 92–3, states that this annal (i.e. for 943) in the *Anglo-Saxon Chronicle* proves not that Wulfstan had merely found it necessary to side with the vikings, but that this was a deliberate ploy by the York church so that its own interests could be furthered.

[191] *ASC D*, s.a. 947. It is striking that following this incident, Wulfstan is absent from meetings of Eadred's *witan* in the years 947–8: Keynes 1999*b*; but note also the comments of Downham, *Viking Kings*, p. 114.

as their king (in 948);[192] this angered Eadred so greatly that he marched swiftly northwards and ravaged the Ripon minster.[193] But when King Eadred was marching back to the south, 'the army [which] was in York overtook the king's army at Castleford, and they made a great slaughter there. Then the king became so angry that he wished to march back into the land and destroy it utterly. When the councillors of the Northumbrians understood that, they deserted Eric and paid to King Eadred compensation for their act'.[194] That the *Anglo-Saxon Chronicle* explicitly names Wulfstan at the beginning of this sequence suggests that he was heavily involved in, and perhaps even influenced, the changing of allegiances enacted by the Northumbrians.[195] It is no wonder that, when King Eadred had the chance in 952, he 'ordered Archbishop Wulfstan to be taken into the fortress of *Iudanbyrig*, because accusations had often been made to the king against him' and had him imprisoned.[196] The outline of events delivered by the northern recension of the *Anglo-Saxon Chronicle* suggests that Eadred's capture of Wulfstan may have been the key to his eventual accession to the kingdom of Northumbria. It is noticeable that, in the very same annal which records Eadred's assumption of the northern kingdom, 'Wulfstan received a bishopric again, in Dorchester':[197] it was only after he had secured the northern part of his kingdom that Eadred felt it possible to release the rebellious and powerful Wulfstan from captivity; but this time Wulfstan did not resume his role as archbishop and instead was given a bishopric which was very far from the traditional centre of his power at York.[198] Although Wulfstan was removed from Northumbria because of his

[192] On the identity of this Eric, see above, p. 46, n. 145.

[193] For this event, see below, pp. 245–6.

[194] *ASC D*, s.a. 948.

[195] For Archbishop Wulfstan's close alliance with Eric, see Smyth, *Scandinavian* II, pp. 180–2.

[196] *ASC D*, s.a. 952. It would be interesting to know exactly which place is meant by *Iudanbyrig*; Hart, *ECNE*, p. 377, says this is 'probably Castle Gotha in Cornwall'; but Plummer, *Chronicles* II, pp. 148–9, suggests that, whilst the common view is that *Iudanbyrig* is Jedburgh, it is perhaps more likely that it should be identified with 'Bede's *Ythancaestir*, on the Pant *or* Blackwater in Essex... certainly the mention of Thetford immediately afterwards suggests that it may have been somewhere in the Eastern Counties'. If *Iudanbyrig* were located in Cornwall then this would indicate Eadred's desire to imprison Wulfstan in an area far removed from his natural power base in the north; if it were located in Jedburgh then it would be testimony for how far north Eadred's jurisdiction in Northumbria stretched in the early 950s.

[197] *ASC D*, s.a. 954.

[198] The meaning of the entry in *ASC D*, s.a. 954: 'Wulfstan received a bishopric again, in Dorchester', is not entirely clear and two possible interpretations are apparent: either that Wulfstan received back the York bishopric when at Dorchester (perhaps during a ceremony); or that Wulfstan was removed from the York see and given instead the bishopric of Dorchester. Plummer, *Chronicles* II, pp. ix and 149, suggests that the latter explanation is more probable. The *ASC BC*, s.a. 971, reads: 'In this year died Archbishop Oscytel, who was first consecrated as a diocesan bishop, of Dorchester, and afterwards consecrated archbishop of York by the consent of King Eadred and of all his councillors'.

political duplicity,[199] it seems clear that he had been acting in the best interests of the York church, at a time when it would have been impossible to tell whether southern kings or their Gaelic-Scandinavian rivals would establish control of the northern kingdom.[200]

e. *York and English Kings from the South*

The process of endowment was intensified with the accession of Oscytel as head of the York church in the period 954–5.[201] The promotion of Oscytel from bishop of Dorchester was a politically astute move. Wulfstan had come to reject the rule of Northumbria by an English dynasty of southern origin, so we may deduce that his placement as bishop at Dorchester upon his release from prison in 954 was an attempt by King Eadred to establish him where he could be more closely monitored and his influence limited. Though the diocese of Dorchester extended over much of the Scandinavian-dominated East Midlands, the see itself lay in the Upper Thames valley, where the dynasty descended from Egbert, Æthelwulf and Alfred had deep roots and much of its landed wealth. The bishopric there seems always to have been controlled by the English kings, and Oscytel is likely to have risen in their service. He was a shrewd choice as archbishop. The name Oscytel is an English adaptation of a Scandinavian name, which suggests the strong possibility that Oscytel was of Scandinavian descent.[202] If Oscytel was of Scandinavian extraction, his election would have helped to appease those Scandinavians still settled at York; but at the same time the southern dynasty of English kings could be confident that he was less likely to rebel against its rule than the previous York incumbent, Wulfstan.

Oscytel had succeeded to the York archbishopric during a period of intense uncertainty in Northumbria. Oscytel's attestations to charters of this period

---

Since this annal suggests that Oscytel had become Archbishop of York during the reign of King Eadred (949–55), then this further implies that Wulfstan, who died on 16 December 956 (*ASC D*, s.a. 957 (*recte* 956); he was buried at Oundle, which was in the diocese of Dorchester), had been given Dorchester upon his release from prison in 954, rather than York which was then in the hands of Oscytel. Whitelock 1959, p. 73, also favours this interpretation, as does Keynes 1999*b*. But, for a different view, see Barrow 2004. For further discussion, see the commentary to **2**.

199 Another possibility is that Wulfstan's health was now failing and therefore that Oscytel had to take over his archiepiscopal role. For both possibilities, see Keynes 1999*b* and Hadley, *Vikings*, p. 51.

200 Downham, *Viking Kings*, p. 114, who also suggests that Wulfstan was acting in the interests of Northumbrian independence as a whole; for a similar view, see Hadley, *Vikings*, p. 50.

201 Barrow 2004, pp. 41–2, at p. 41, has recently questioned the date at which Oscytel became archbishop. She suggests that Oscytel's promotion to the archbishopric should be delayed until 958/9 and that there was a vacancy at York in the intervening time. But this seems incorrect; for further discussion, see the commentary to **2**.

202 Stenton, *Preparatory to ASE*, p. 367 and Hart, *ECNE*, pp. 353–4.

seem to suggest that he retained his see at Dorchester at the same time as being metropolitan.[203] Whitelock suggests that such a set-up, where Oscytel would have been able to benefit financially from his attachment to Dorchester, was deliberately engineered by the English kings so that Oscytel would be less inclined to be rebellious in the same way that Wulfstan had been.[204] It seems only natural that after the threat posed by the settlement of the Scandinavians in and around York, and the York church's compliance with these settlers, the English kings desired to create a situation which sought to guarantee the loyalty of the York church. Thus Oscytel's holding of York and Dorchester in plurality was a striking forerunner to the later and better attested holding of Worcester and York at the same time by Oswald, Ealdwulf and Wulfstan II.

An indication of the favourable regard in which Oscytel was held by the English king, Eadwig, is provided by **2**; it is a 956 royal grant of the estate of Southwell and its dependencies to Oscytel. Stenton has drawn attention to the significance of this transaction. In 956 it was by no means clear that Eadwig, or any subsequent English king, would be able to bring the Northumbrian kingdom within his control. And the region in the immediate vicinity of York had been heavily settled by Scandinavians. **2** represents a concerted effort to endow the York church with lands in the heart of Anglo-Scandinavian territory, in the centre of Nottinghamshire; it was designed to enable the York church to regain some of its status and independence.[205]

Interest in the York see did not cease after **2**. By 957, the Anglo-Saxon kingdom had been split between King Eadwig and his brother Edgar; Eadwig had dominion over Wessex and Edgar over Mercia, Northumbria and East Anglia.[206] **3** is a grant of Sutton, which was situated in the north of Nottinghamshire, by Edgar to Oscytel. Edgar may have intended this grant to be an extension of that already

[203] Oscytel was appointed to the archbishopric while Wulfstan was still alive. Wulfstan continued to attest charters as 'archbishop' (see S 563 and S 582, both dated 955) even after his exchange of sees with Oscytel but it seems unlikely that he would have been allowed to return to Northumbria, where he had the potential to cause more trouble for the English kings.

[204] See Whitelock 1959, pp. 73–5. Whitelock also shows (at pp. 74–5) that Leofwine may have shared the episcopal role at Dorchester with Oscytel, presumably after the death of Wulfstan in 956. See also Smyth, *Scandinavian* II, pp. 173–4.

[205] See Stenton, *Preparatory to ASE*, p. 365, for comments about **2**.

[206] *ASC C*, s.a. 957. Before the division of the kingdom Oscytel can be found attesting Eadwig's charters as 'bishop'; see, for example, the 957 charters S 574 (BCS 987), S 641 (*WinchNM* 20), S 643 (*Bath* 11), S 1291 (*Sel* 20), S 645 (BCS 994), S 649 (BCS 1003) and S 646 (BCS 999 and 1347). But from 958, and after the division of the kingdom, Oscytel then attests those charters granted by Edgar, as king of the Mercians (see S 674 [*Pet* 13], **3**, S 677 [*Wells* 31], S 675 [BCS 1042], S 678 [*Abing* 82], S 676 [BCS 1037], S 676a and S 681 [*Pet* 14]), reflecting the fact that York lay within the half of the kingdom ruled by Edgar; see Keynes, *Atlas*, table LII. For more detail about Oscytel's attestations during these years, see **2**; for attestations in general in charters of this period, see Abrams 2008.

given in **2**, which would have helped the York archbishopric to secure its fortunes in the Danelaw.[207]

2 and **3** show Oscytel to have been actively involved in the acquisition of land for his archbishopric. This receives confirmation from a later document composed in the period 975–992 when Oswald was archbishop of York. It is known as Oswald's *Memorandum* and it states:[208]

> þis syndan þa land þe Oscytel yrcebiscop begeat on Norþhymbralande mid his feo and him mon geald for unrihtan hæmede.[209]

This passage declares that Oscytel himself had bought lands in Northumbria; it also notes that there were lands forfeited to him because of an illegal marriage. This second piece of information is very interesting indeed, since it seems to imply not only that Oscytel had been able to establish ecclesiastical law in Northumbria, but also that he was able to effect punishment for any contravention of that law.[210] The precarious position of Oscytel's predecessor, Wulfstan, may have meant that it was impossible for him to have imposed such control. If we can accept the statement made by Oswald's *Memorandum* (**6**), then this is an indication that Oscytel, as the first archbishop of York during the time of more certain southern dominion, had managed to enhance significantly the standing of the York church and to establish some sort of ecclesiastical stability in Northumbria.[211] The York archbishopric was now emerging from the depredations caused by the era of viking settlement in the north; and the process had been initiated by an archbishop who was installed by English kings, Oscytel.

In 959 Eadwig died and Edgar succeeded to the whole of the Anglo-Saxon kingdom, including Wessex, Mercia and Northumbria.[212] **4** and **5** are grants of land made by Edgar while he was king of this recently united kingdom; they both date to 963. **4** and **5** differ from **1**, **2** and **3** because they are not made directly to

[207] The term 'Danelaw' first appears in the early eleventh century in legal texts associated with Archbishop Wulfstan of York. There is no agreed territorial definition; for discussion, see, for example, K. Holman, 'Defining the Danelaw', *Vikings and the Danelaw: Select Papers from the Proceedings of the Thirteenth Viking Congress, Nottingham and York, 21–30 August 1997*, ed. J. Graham-Campbell, R. Hall, J. Jesch and D.N. Parsons (Oxford, 2001), pp. 1–11, at pp. 4–7 for the difficulties in defining the territorial limits of the Danelaw, and L. Abrams, 'Edward the Elder's Danelaw', *Edward the Elder, 899–924*, ed. N.J. Higham and D.H. Hill (London and New York, 2001), pp. 128–43, at pp. 128–33.

[208] Oswald's *Memorandum* is preserved in the manuscript British Library, Harley 55, f.4v; it is **6** below.

[209] 'These are the lands which Archbishop Oscytel acquired in the land of the Northumbrians with his money and [which] were rendered to him for unlawful marriage'.

[210] Stenton, *Preparatory to ASE*, p. 367, discusses the importance of this evidence.

[211] Stenton, *Preparatory to ASE*, p. 367, suggests that Oscytel's actions should place him 'among the greatest churchmen who ever held the see of York'.

[212] *ASC C*, s.a. 959.

the York church; instead they are grants to secular figures and later came into the archbishopric's possession. It is quite probable that Oscytel should again be credited with both of these purchases.

4 is a grant of the Sherburn estate made over to a certain 'Æslac', who is most probably to be identified with Earl Oslac, a powerful Northumbrian magnate.[213] Our sources suggest that the Northumbrian kingdom was at this time divided, perhaps along the line of the River Tees.[214] Oslac was entrusted with rule over the York area of Northumbria while a certain Eadulf *Yvelcild* ruled to the north.[215] But the fact that Edgar made Oslac alone responsible for enforcing his law-code IV in Northumbria suggests that he was considered the principal Northumbrian earl by the English king.[216] The initial grant of **4** was made in 963. Oswald's *Memorandum* (**6**), which postdates **4**, talks of those areas of Sherburn as being *lost* to the archbishop and therefore shows that **4** came into the possession of the York see at some point between 963 and the date of the composition of the *Memorandum* (975–992). As we shall see, **5** was an estate bought by Oscytel and this may suggest that we should think of **4** as another of his acquisitions.

5 is a grant of the Newbald estate by King Edgar to an earl known as Gunner.[217] The governmental arrangements of Northumbria at this time were complicated. It was not a simple matter of the English king possessing outright rule, or of the English king delegating control to one or two earls. In fact many earls, who must have been subordinate figures in charge of designated districts, appear in charter witness-lists and are not otherwise noted in the historical record.[218] Many of these figures were native Northumbrians and Gunner is an example. Although Gunner's first certain attestation of a charter dates to 949, it is possible that he is the very same Gunner who attests a charter of King Æthelstan's reign in 931.[219] He cannot be found attesting any charters after 963. **5** may be further evidence of the aggressive policy of estate acquisition adopted by Archbishop Oscytel.

[213] Oslac is the anglicized version of Old Norse 'Áslákr/Ásleikr', for which see Fellows-Jensen, *SPNLY*, pp. 33–4; see further the commentary to **4**.

[214] Whitelock 1959, pp. 77–9, where she also discusses those sources which suggest the River Tyne may have formed the boundary (at p. 78, n. 1).

[215] See also Rollason, *Northumbria*, p. 267.

[216] The *De primo adventu Saxonum* contains a list of Northumbrian earls which preserves these details about Oslac and Eadulf *Yvelcild*; the text of this list is given in Arnold, *Sym. Op.*, II, p. 382. Edgar IV is given in Liebermann, *Gesetze* I, pp. 206–15; it is translated in Whitelock, *EHD*, no. 41. See Whitelock 1959, pp. 76–9, for much more detail about the division of the Northumbrian kingdom and the relative influence of these earls.

[217] The name Gunner derives ultimately from Old Norse, 'Gunnarr'; see Fellows-Jensen, *SPNLY*, pp. 113–14.

[218] Whitelock 1959, pp. 78–9 and Rollason, *Northumbria*, pp. 266–9.

[219] Whitelock 1959, p. 78. The charter of Æthelstan is S 416 (BCS 677); that of 949 is S 550 (BCS 882).

Oswald's *Memorandum* (**6**) states that Oscytel 'bought the estate at Newbold for 120 mancuses of red gold from King Edgar'.[220] Since **5** is dated 963 and Oscytel died in 971 it must have been during this time-frame that Oscytel bought Newbald for the York archbishopric.[221]

Oscytel was succeeded at York in 971 by a kinsman, namely Oswald who, prior to his elevation as archbishop, had been bishop of Worcester for some ten years.[222] Oswald is best known as the youngest of the saintly trinity of celebrated tenth-century monastic reformers, alongside St Dunstan and St Æthelwold.[223] In a move which was to be repeated in later years by future York archbishops, Oswald was permitted to retain the Worcester see at the same time as gaining the archbishopric; he subsequently held the two sees in plurality until his death in 992.[224] The exact motive behind this situation is unknown. It may be that Edgar, the king at the time, sought to draw the northern archbishopric more fully into the orbit of southern power and, by that means, to eliminate the possibility of being confronted by a rebellious archbishop such as Wulfstan had been. But the explanation could be a simpler one. It may be that Oscytel's acquisition of various estates and lands for the York see had not done enough to guarantee its well-being: the combination of the rule of York and Worcester under one figure would have meant that Oswald was in a position to supplement the revenue of one by reference to the other.[225]

A remarkable series of leases made by Oswald at Worcester show him to be a man with a keen administrative mind and one who possessed the ability to generate revenue for his church.[226] Although Oswald was heavily involved

220 See **6**: 'þæt land æt Neoweboldan he gebohte mid hundtwelftigun [ge]mancsun reades goldes æt Eadgare cyn[ing]eþ'. For more about the initial grant of **5** to Gunner, see Bolton, *Cnut*, p. 111.

221 For Oscytel's death, see *ASC BC*, s.a. 971.

222 Oswald was appointed bishop of Worcester in 961. For biographical details of Oswald, see Hart, *ECNE*, p. 356. Oswald's life and career is more thoroughly discussed by Wareham 1996; Wareham notes that Oswald '(was) a well-connected aristocrat of Danish descent from the southern Danelaw' (at p. 49); Wareham also suggests that the powerful kinship ties and his great wealth, allowed Oswald to run his diocese efficiently (at p. 62). One northern source, Symeon's *Letter on the Archbishops of York*, notes the brief archiepiscopacy of a certain 'Edwaldus' in 970/1, before Oswald, but who resigned immediately because he preferred a quieter life (*...quietiorem vitam diligeret*); the text of this letter is given in Arnold, *Sym. Mon. Op.* I, pp. 222–28 (at p. 226).

223 For more about Oswald, see Brooks and Cubitt, *St Oswald* and Tinti, *Sustaining Belief*, pp. 20–38.

224 Tinti, *Sustaining Belief*, p. 20 and p. 25, n. 65.

225 On the use of Worcester revenues for the benefit of the northern church, see Barlow, *English Church*, p. 228 and also Hill and Brooke 1977, pp. 14–15.

226 The extant Oswald leases are preserved in the Worcester archive. They begin in 962 with S 1298 (KCD 496) and end in 991 with S 1366 (KCD 676) and number some seventy-four documents. For the shrewd estate management practised by Oswald, see Wareham 1996 and Tinti, *Sustaining Belief*, pp. 20–38.

in both the administration of the Worcester see and the progress of the tenth-century reformation, he also found time to investigate the fortunes of the York see.[227] As has already been noted, some time in the years 975 to 992 he drew up a *Memorandum* (**6**) relating to the estates of the York church. Although **6** does demonstrate Oswald's interest in the see's affairs, the details it contains show that York's prosperity was being threatened. It describes three principal matters: those villages taken from Otley, Ripon and Sherburn; those lands bought by Archbishop Oscytel; those lands 'stolen' from St Peter's by Earl Thored.[228]

6 highlights the fragility of the York see by alluding to events of the mid-970s involving Thored, which are worth brief scrutiny here.[229] King Edgar, with the help of the prelates Oswald, Dunstan and Æthelwold, had vigorously promoted the progress of monastic reformation in the tenth century. His death in 975, as the *Anglo-Saxon Chronicle* narrates, sparked a fierce anti-monastic reaction led by Ealdorman Ælfhere of Mercia.[230] We are also told that in the same year Earl Oslac was 'driven from the country'. It must be remembered that Oslac had risen to become one of the most powerful figures in Northumbria; the fact that King Edgar entrusted the enforcing of his law-code IV to Oslac testifies not only to Oslac's standing but also to the close co-operation that existed between the earl and the king. It was therefore a natural consequence of Edgar's death that an anti-Edgar faction took the opportunity to oust one of his most powerful supporters from the scene. Subsequent events suggest very strongly that the agent of this coup was Earl Thored. We find Thored, immediately after his rise to power, robbing the York church of some estates.[231] The question that must be asked is: why did Thored choose to deprive York? There are three possible answers: firstly that York was targeted simply because it was the seat for Oswald, one of the principal figures of the tenth-century reform. Another possibility is that the York archbishopric had actively supported one of Edgar's chief northern personages, Oslac. It is notable

[227] For Oswald's visitation of Ripon, by now an impoverished place, see below, pp. 247–8.

[228] For these details, see **6** and its commentary.

[229] Rollason 2004, p. 317, suggests that the poor condition of the York church at this moment meant that it could not be a base for a monastic reform of the northern church under the guidance of Oswald. Nevertheless, Oswald may well have attempted to introduce monks to Ripon, for which see below, pp. 247–8.

[230] *ASC C*, s.a. 975; manuscripts *DEF* of the *ASC* for the same year supply the information that Ealdorman Ælfhere (of Mercia) was the leader in the destruction of the monasteries.

[231] Thored may well have become earl with the death of King Edgar and the banishment of Earl Oslac in 975, although he does not attest a charter as *dux* until 979; see Whitelock 1959, p. 79. **6** seems to state that the York church was deprived of estates upon Thored's promotion as earl. Unfortunately, Thored's name in **6** occurs in a part of the manuscript that is difficult to read and some of the letters are illegible. A sixteenth-century copy of this document, BL Harley 6841, f. 128rv, supplies the reading *þerað*, which Whitelock suggests may have been copied from an original reading of *þorað*; see Whitelock *ibid.*, p. 79, Whitelock, *EHD*, p. 565, n. 8 and below, pp. 138–9 (commentary to **6**).

that **4**, which was originally a grant of land to Oslac by Edgar, came into the possession of the York church in obscure circumstances; it may be that this was a gift by Oslac to the religious community for its support of his, and therefore of Edgar's, cause. A third possibility rests on the tentative identification of Thored as being the same man as that Thored, Gunner's son, who ravaged Westmorland in 966.[232] Since **5** describes a gift of the Newbald estate to Earl Gunner and since **6** describes the loss of Newbald from the York church's possession because of Thored, it may be that Thored's actions were motivated by a desire to recapture lands previously in his father's possession.[233] Whatever the reason, it is very striking that Thored directly targeted the assets of the York church and then granted some of those assets to York's principal rival in the religious world of Northumbria, St Cuthbert's community.[234] Thored's intention must have been to demonstrate that he would not tolerate any threat to his rule.

In 992 Oswald died and Ealdwulf, who had been the abbot of Peterborough, succeeded Oswald at York and at Worcester.[235] Although Peterborough traditions remember Ealdwulf as an effective administrator,[236] very little is known about his time as archbishop; he died in 1002.[237]

In stark contrast to the obscurity which surrounds Ealdwulf, we know a great deal about Wulfstan the homilist, who was archbishop of York from 1002 to 1023 and who also held the see of Worcester in plurality from 1002 until 1016.[238] This Wulfstan is perhaps best known for his vernacular sermon entitled, *Sermo Lupi ad Anglos*.[239] In his role as bishop of Worcester, Wulfstan was actively involved

232 *ASC D*, s.a. 966.

233 For the difficulty in identifying Thored, see Whitelock 1959, p. 79 (and p. 79, n. 6, for a similar explanation regarding the cause of Thored's discontent).

234 **18** records Thored's grant of Yorkshire estates to St Cuthbert's community.

235 *ASC CDE*, s.a. 992. Relics of Wilfrid and the five Ripon abbots found by Oswald (see below, p. 247, n. 110) were later discovered in the high altar at Peterborough and it may have been Ealdwulf's Peterborough connections which caused this situation (see Brooks, 'Oswald', in *ODNB*). See also Kelly, *Peterborough*, p. 57 (and n. 179 and literature cited therein, where she discusses the possibility that Oswald made gifts of relics from Ripon to both Ramsey and Peterborough).

236 Kelly, *Peterborough*, pp. 113–15; and for his involvement in the augmentation of Peterborough's endowment, see S 1448a (*Pet* 30).

237 *ASC CDE*, s.a. 1002. A lease preserved in the Worcester archive, S 1381 (KCD 695), and made in Ealdwulf's name, perhaps indicates that he was not unaccustomed to administrative affairs. For more about Ealdwulf, see Tinti, *Sustaining Belief*, p. 124.

238 Even though Wulfstan resigned his Worcester bishopric in 1016, there is evidence to suggest that he continued to control some of its endowment. This may explain the low regard in which he is noted by Worcester sources: see Baxter 2004, p. 163 and Tinti, *Sustaining Belief*, p. 41, n. 124.

239 For the text and introduction to this sermon, see Whitelock, *Sermo Lupi ad Anglos*, rev. edn (Exeter, 1976; repr. 1989). There is a great deal of secondary literature about Wulfstan. See, for example, D. Whitelock, 'Archbishop Wulfstan, Homilist and Statesman', in her *History, Law, and Literature*, XI, P. Wormald, 'Archbishop Wulfstan: Eleventh-Century State-Builder', in Townend, *Wulfstan*,

in pursuing those estates and renders which were due to his see.[240] In order to help him in this task, Wulfstan provided the impetus for the composition of England's earliest extant cartulary, British Library, Cotton Tiberius A.xiii. Ker discovered that this manuscript actually contained two cartularies, the first now known as *Liber Wigorniensis* and the second as 'Hemming's cartulary'.[241] The *Liber Wigorniensis* was probably written shortly after Wulfstan became bishop of Worcester in 1002 and the personal interest Wulfstan took in the manuscript is shown by the appearance of his annotating hand in the manuscript.[242] Baxter's recent study of the leases which were entered into the *Liber Wigorniensis* demonstrates this cartulary's function. Baxter points out that the details written in to the manuscript often include the name of the estate being leased, the primary beneficiary and then any subsequent lessee. He suggests that these leases acquired their annotations because this part of the cartulary was intended to be a 'working register', a document which enabled the community to keep a record of what was happening to its estates and its tenants.[243]

Wulfstan's care and attention for the management of his southern church's estates extended also to the York archbishopric.[244] Wulfstan can be found taking an interest in the work on estates carried out by the archbishopric's previous incumbents: thus his annotating hand can be seen in the Old English *Memorandum* drawn up by Archbishop Oswald (**6**), to which reference has already been made. Wulfstan added to the document the title *Đis swutelunge gedihte Oswald arcebiscop and awritan het* ('Archbishop Oswald proclaimed these declarations

pp. 9–27 and S. Keynes, 'An Abbot, an Archbishop, and the Viking Raids of 1006–7 and 1009–12', *ASE* xxxvi (2007), pp. 151–220. A legal text of great interest for Northumbrian history, known as 'The Northumbrian Priests' Law', was once thought to be the work of Wulfstan himself (it survives in only one copy, CCCC 201, a compilation of Wulfstan laws and homilies); for a convenient translation, see Whitelock, *EHD*, no. 52. But Wormald, *Law I*, pp. 208–09 and 396–7, argues that while this text displays some of Wulfstan's concerns and mannerisms, it is more likely to have been composed by one of his two immediate successors at York.

240 Nevertheless, there is still difficulty in reconstructing Wulfstan's activities at Worcester; see the remarks in Tinti, *Sustaining Belief*, pp. 40–1.

241 See N.R. Ker, 'Hemming's Cartulary', in *Studies in Medieval History Presented to F.M. Powicke*, ed. R.W. Hunt, W.A. Pantin and R.W. Southern (Oxford, 1948), pp. 49–75. For more about the structure, contents and purpose of Hemming's cartulary, see, for example, F. Tinti, 'From Episcopal Conception to Monastic Compilation: Hemming's Cartulary in Context', *Early Medieval Europe* xi (2002), pp. 233–61.

242 This hand was identified by Ker 1971. For the involvement of Wulfstan in the commissioning of *Liber Wigorniensis*, and possibly also of Ealdwulf, see Tinti, *Sustaining Belief*, pp. 123–4 (with a hypothetical arrangement of the original cartulary on pp. 122–3).

243 See Baxter 2004, pp. 172–3. Baxter also points to several marginal entries in the manuscript which were augmented and added to by different hands and he suggests therefore that the details of the leases were updated as and when new tenants acquired their estates.

244 Whitelock 1965, pp. 214–26, discusses those manuscripts connected to Wulfstan and perhaps also to his time at York. For an overview of Wulfstan's career, see Tinti, *Sustaining Belief*, pp. 40–2.

and had them written'), the references to Oswald and the concluding words, *wrece God swa he wille* ('may God avenge it as he will').

A group of Old English texts, the constituents of which are all somehow tied to Archbishop Wulfstan, has been added at the back of the York Gospels. One of these texts takes the form of a survey of the archiepiscopal estates of Otley, Ripon and Sherburn, written *c.* 1020–3 and edited below as **7**.[245] In addition to **7**, there are three homilies by Archbishop Wulfstan (the *Sermo Lupi*, *Be hæðendome* and *Be cristendome*) and Cnut's letter to the English people which is, in its closing sections, written in Wulfstan's style.[246] Wulfstan's own hand can even be found annotating the three homilies.[247] Since Wulfstan was the author of the homilies and of parts of Cnut's letter, and since the surveys (**7**) were written in the York Gospels in the early 1020s, it seems more than likely that Wulfstan had a defining role in the production of **7** as well.[248]

The combined evidence of **6** and **7** suggests the very real likelihood that the York archbishopric was prospering and gaining from the work carried out by Wulfstan. Not only was he investigating the condition of the York see's estates (shown by his annotations to **6**), but his commissioning of **7** in the York Gospels demonstrates his desire both to reclaim lost possessions and to keep an up-to-date record of the church's estates, much as he had done at Worcester in the *Liber Wigorniensis*.[249] Whereas Oswald's *Memorandum* (**6**) recorded the loss of various dependent vills of the estates of Otley, Ripon and Sherburn, the surveys (**7**) document those vills which belonged to the three estates.[250] This suggests that any vill noted in both Oswald's *Memorandum* (**6**) and in the surveys (**7**) was one that had been restored to the archbishopric's possession during Wulfstan's archiepiscopacy.[251] The surveys also enable a comparison between the details of

245 For discussion, see Stevenson 1912, Keynes 1986 and Baxter 2004.

246 For the additions made to Cnut's letter by Wulfstan, see Keynes 1986, pp. 95–6. Further Old English additions to the York Gospels include a list of church treasures (edited as Appendix 1), some bidding prayers and a list of Ælfric's *festermen* (edited as Appendix 2 and discussed in the General Introduction).

247 Ker 1971, pp. 330–1.

248 Keynes 1986, p. 84 and Baxter 2004, p. 179.

249 See also the comments of Cooper, *Archbishops of York*, p. 10.

250 See Baxter 2004, p. 179 and the commentaries to **6** and **7**. As Keynes 1986, pp. 84–6 notes, an interesting question is why it was that the estates of Otley, Ripon and Sherburn in particular were chosen to be surveyed. It may be that these three estates were the most valuable to the archbishopric and the evidence of Domesday Book certainly shows that they were important assets. But it may also be that Archbishop Wulfstan had been investigating the losses to these estates as recorded in Archbishop Oswald's *Memorandum* (**6**) and sought to keep a record of the gains that had been made.

251 Although Baxter 2004, pp. 179–82, warns that the surveys in the York Gospels (**7**) could be statements of aspiration rather than of reality, he concludes that it is difficult not to see these as additions to the landed possessions of the York church made by Wulfstan.

the size of the Sherburn estate as it was granted in 963 (**4**) and then as it appears in the surveys of *c.* 1020–3 (**7**). The result of such a comparison is that we find that the Sherburn estate has increased considerably in size in the intervening years: it again seems likely that the enlargement of Sherburn should be credited to the activities of Wulfstan.[252]

In 1023 Ælfric, a monk of Winchester, succeeded Wulfstan in the archbishopric at York and in 1026 he journeyed to Rome where he received the *pallium* from Pope John XIX; he was the first archbishop of York since Wulfstan I in the first half of the tenth century not to have been translated from another bishopric.[253] Ælfric can be found performing an elaborate translation of the remains of St John at Beverley and also buying land with his own money on behalf of the Beverley church.[254] The evidence provided by **8** suggests also the personal interest Ælfric may have taken in acquiring estates and lands for the York church. In **8**, Patrington is granted directly to Ælfric himself and the particular diplomatic formulae employed in the charter suggest strongly that the archbishop may have had a role in the way the document was drawn up.[255] Ælfric died at Southwell in 1051 and was buried in Peterborough Abbey.[256]

Ælfric's successor was a man drawn from the Danelaw, Cynesige (1051–60).[257] Cynesige, like Ælfric before him, invested in Beverley and built a stone tower there; he also gave bells to Beverley, and to Southwell and Stow.[258] But he seems to have lacked the political prominence which some of his predecessors

[252] See Baxter 2004, p. 186. For a table depicting these details, see the commentary to **7**.
[253] *John of Worcester II*, s.a. 1023, states that Ælfric had been prior of Winchester. Because of Ælfric's background at Winchester, a house with which Cnut was intimately connected, Bolton has suggested the possibility that Ælfric was made archbishop as a result of the favour of Cnut; see Bolton, *Cnut*, p. 84. For Ælfric's journey to Rome, see *ASC D*, s.a. 1026. It may be that in 1040–1 Ælfric briefly acquired the see of Worcester following the accusation that the bishop there, Lyfing, had been implicated in the murder of the *atheling* Alfred; see *John of Worcester II*, s.a. 1040. For a much fuller account about Archbishop Ælfric, see Cooper, *Archbishops of York*, pp. 14–18.
[254] *Chronicle of the Archbishops of York*, pp. 342–3 and below, p. 183.
[255] For more about this, and the suggestion that **8** was originally granted just to Ælfric, see the commentary to this charter. For the possibility that **8** was a politically-charged grant by Cnut intended to increase the authority of the York church in an area controlled by Thurbrand, see Bolton, *Cnut*, pp. 132–4. Worcester historical traditions seem to have regarded Ælfric in dubious terms. Thus John of Worcester in his *Chronicon* (see *John of Worcester II*, s.a. 1023) is the first to allot Ælfric the derogatory nickname 'Puttoc' which means 'Kite', a bird of prey. It is possible that the Worcester see was by now resentful of those York archbishops who held the two sees in plurality and that this explains such traditions. But it may also have been the case that Ælfric in particular was threatening the Worcester church. For more about these matters, see Cooper, *Archbishops of York*, pp. 17–18.
[256] *John of Worcester II*, s.a. 1051. Peterborough traditions remember Ælfric as a patron of their community: see Kelly, *Peterborough*, p. 57.
[257] Cooper, *Archbishops of York*, pp. 18–23.
[258] *Chronicle of the Archbishops of York*, pp. 343–4.

at York had possessed. Although he had a notable role in 1059 when, along with Bishop Æthelwine of Durham and Earl Tostig, he led the Scottish king, Malcolm, into England in order to meet King Edward the Confessor, he seems otherwise to have been mostly withdrawn from the political scene.[259] And Cynesige's archiepiscopacy overlapped with that of Stigand, who was archbishop of Canterbury and a notorious pluralist. Stigand's position in the age of the Reform Papacy was by no means a secure one; in 1053 he is described as being 'bishop of Canterbury' and although he was to receive a *pallium* in 1058, this had been sent by the anti-Reform Tusculan pope, Benedict X, who was himself deposed after holding power in Rome for less than a year. Though in England Stigand was styled 'archbishop' thereafter, his authority as metropolitan remained in question.[260] We might have expected Cynesige to take full advantage of the weakness of Canterbury's position in order to thrust the York archbishopric into the role of being the primary see in Anglo-Saxon England.[261] But Cynesige was evidently not politically inclined; he died on 22 December 1060 and, like Ælfric before him, was buried at Peterborough.[262]

The next archbishop of York, Ealdred (1060–9), was heavily involved in the political world.[263] Even before he acquired the archiepiscopal see he was evidently a man of quite some standing.[264] In 1046 he had become bishop of Worcester and from 1056 until 1060, he was also bishop of Hereford.[265] Thus by 1060, when Cynesige died and Ealdred was appointed as archbishop of York in his place, Ealdred had already risen to a position of eminence in the Anglo-Saxon political world. In order to confirm his new position in the archbishopric, Ealdred travelled

[259] *HR* (8), p. 174 (s.a. 1059). This particular sentence in the *Historia regum* was added at the foot of the page, in a hand different, but contemporary to that of the main text; see the comments of Arnold, *Sym. Op.* II, p. 174, n. 1.

[260] See *ASC C*, s.a. 1053 and *ASC D*, s.a. 1058 and Brooks, *Church of Canterbury*, pp. 306–7.

[261] Cooper, *Archbishops of York*, p. 23.

[262] *ASC DE*, s.a. 1060. *John of Worcester II*, s.a. 1060, adds the detail that Cynesige died at York and was then transferred to Peterborough, a community which he may have patronised: Kelly, *Peterborough*, p. 58.

[263] Cooper, *Archbishops of York*, pp. 23–9.

[264] It may be that Ealdred was somehow allied to the all-powerful Earl Godwine. The *ASC D*, s.a. 1052 (*recte* 1051), narrates that Edward the Confessor had sent Ealdred from London with a force in order to intercept the recently outlawed Godwine; but, in a suggestive remark, the annalist notes that Ealdred and his men 'could not—or would not' and so implies that the bishop had sided with Godwine.

[265] *ASC D*, s.a. 1047 (*recte* 1046). *John of Worcester II*, s.a. 1046, adds the detail that Ealdred had first been a monk of Winchester and was afterwards abbot of Tavistock. Cooper, *Archbishops of York*, p. 23, notes that Ealdred's career seems to have been closely linked to that of Bishop Lyfing. For Ealdred as bishop of Worcester, see V.J. King, 'Ealdred of York: The Worcester Years', *Anglo-Norman Studies* xiii (1996), pp. 123–37 and Tinti, *Sustaining Belief*, pp. 53–8.

to Rome in 1061 to receive the *pallium* from Pope Nicholas. But this may not have been a straightforward mission. Although the *Anglo-Saxon Chronicle* and John of Worcester's *Chronicle* provide no details, the *Vita Wulfstani* by William of Malmesbury notes that the Pope refused to grant Ealdred the *pallium* until he had relinquished control of the see of Worcester, and the *Gesta Pontificum* (also by William of Malmesbury) narrates that the Pope behaved severely towards Ealdred and stripped him of all his honours because he was guilty of simony.[266] On the return homewards, Ealdred and Earl Tostig, who had accompanied him to Rome, were attacked by bandits who robbed them of all their money. Ealdred and Tostig returned to Rome, which afforded Ealdred the opportunity of asking for the *pallium* once more. This time he seems to have been successful, partly because Tostig intervened with some harsh words directed towards the Pope and threatened that the King of England would refuse to pay the tax known as St Peter's pence to Nicholas when he heard of this disgrace.[267]

During the first few years of his archiepiscopacy, less mention is made of Ealdred in the historical record. He reappears in 1066 and the *Anglo-Saxon Chronicle* notes that Ealdred first supported, along with the people of London, the claim of Edgar *Cild* after the Battle of Hastings. But he changed his allegiance soon afterwards and on Christmas day of 1066 Ealdred himself consecrated William as king at Westminster.[268]

The York church benefited from Ealdred's time as archbishop; his elevated political profile placed him in a position to ensure that the church was always well provided for.[269] The mid-twelfth-century *Chronicle of the Archbishops of*

[266] William of Malmesbury, *Vita Wulfstani*, i.10.1–3 and *GP*, iii.115.14–18; see also Cooper, *Archbishops of York*, p. 26.

[267] *GP*, iii.115.14–18. It seems clear that Ealdred had expected to be allowed to retain Worcester, just as many of his archiepiscopal predecessors had. But the Pope's decision that he was not permitted to rule over two sees at once does *not* seem to have deterred Ealdred from continuing to exact financial benefit from Worcester. Ealdred deliberately promoted the election of Wulfstan, then prior of Worcester, over Æthelwig, then abbot of Evesham, as bishop of Worcester. As A. Williams, 'The Cunning of the Dove: Wulfstan and the Politics of Accommodation', in *St Wulfstan and His World*, ed. J. Barrow and N. Brooks (Ashgate, 2005), pp. 23–38, at pp. 25–6, points out, Ealdred had good reason to do so for the *Vita Wulfstani* describes Æthelwig as being skilled in secular business. If Ealdred wanted to continue with his involvement at Worcester then the removal of Æthelwig was important. Indeed Williams notes that 'even when Wulfstan took charge of his bishopric, it was only with difficulty that he persuaded the archbishop to release control of Worcester's estates, and Ealdred seems to have kept the episcopal, as opposed to the monastic, manors until his death' (at p. 26). For more about Ealdred and his attempts to keep control over his Worcester episcopal estates, see Barlow, *English Church*, p. 88, n. 5; for a more positive view of Ealdred at Worcester, see Tinti, *Sustaining Belief*, pp. 54–5.

[268] *ASC D*, s.a. 1066. *John of Worcester II*, s.a. 1066, states that earlier in the year Ealdred had consecrated Harold as king, which was in accordance with the wishes of Edward the Confessor.

[269] See Barlow, *English Church*, p. 88, for Ealdred's skill as an administrator.

York credits Ealdred as being a more generous benefactor towards the houses of secular canons in York than any of his predecessors; in particular Ealdred is described as buying many lands with his own money and adding them to his churches.[270] He also carried out refurbishments: he had new refectories built at Southwell and York, and at Beverley he completed the building of a refectory and dormitory which had been begun by his forebears in the archbishopric, Ælfric and Cynesige. Ealdred also built a new presbytery right next to the old church at Beverley and had it dedicated to John the Evangelist and he ensured that the whole Beverley church was ornamented with sculptures and paintings and with a new pulpit which was made of bronze, gold and silver.[271] Two writs issued by King Edward to Ealdred indicate the freedom with which the archbishop was able to operate in York and the revenue he was able to generate as he possessed 'sake and soke over his lands and over all his men, to toll and to team, within town and without'.[272]

Ealdred also did his utmost to protect the rights of the York church: when a royal sheriff carried off the archbishop's goods from his servants, Ealdred reacted immediately and confronted the official. When this man responded in an insolent fashion, Ealdred journeyed at once to London in order to address the king in person. The *Chronicle of the Archbishops of York* describes a lengthy speech made by Ealdred to King William which, although clearly embellished,[273] does suggest that Ealdred was remembered at York for his defence of their possessions.[274]

Ealdred did not neglect his pastoral or intellectual duties as archbishop. When he was in Cologne as an ambassador to the emperor, he heard and saw many things which pertained to the rigour of ecclesiastical discipline and which, after he had returned to England, he sought to institute in his churches.[275] And Ealdred was also a patron of learning. Folcard, in his *Life* of St John of Beverley, refers to the very great friendship he had with the archbishop and the very numerous gifts he had received from him; Folcard also states that it was at the request of Ealdred himself that he had written the *Life* of St John.[276] Ealdred's time as archbishop at York had been fruitful; upon his death in 1069, the northern recension of the *Anglo-Saxon Chronicle* notes that he was buried in the cathedral city of York itself and that he

270 See also Cooper, *Archbishops of York*, p. 27.

271 *Chronicle of the Archbishops of York*, pp. 353–4 and below, pp. 184–6.

272 See **9** and **14** below; the quotation is taken from **14**.

273 Barlow, *English Church*, p. 89.

274 *Chronicle of the Archbishops of York*, pp. 351–3. Cooper, *Archbishops of York*, p. 28, notes two other instances where Ealdred can be found defending the church's rights.

275 *Chronicle of the Archbishops of York*, p. 345. Ealdred's ownership of a copy of a Romano-German Pontifical shows his desire for liturgical and ceremonial reform: Lapidge, *ALL* 2, pp. 453–67.

276 For Folcard's work, see Raine, *HCY* I, pp. 239–41. It has been argued that Ealdred was the inspiration behind the compilation of the 'D' version of the *ASC*; see *The Anglo-Saxon Chronicle: A Collaborative Edition, vol. 6, MS D*, ed. G.P. Cubbin (Cambridge, 1996), pp. lxxviii–lxxxi.

had occupied the see 'with great honour for ten years all but fifteen weeks'.[277] And by 1086, Domesday Book records that the York archbishopric owned lands in Gloucestershire, Nottinghamshire, Yorkshire, Lincolnshire and Leicestershire; this made it, according to Giandrea, the fifth most valuable episcopal see, behind Canterbury, Winchester, Sherborne and London.[278]

2. THE HISTORY OF THE YORK ARCHIVE

a. *The Anglo-Saxon Documents in the York Archive*

The vicissitudes which afflicted St Peter's Minster during the Anglo-Saxon and Anglo-Norman periods suggest that we are very fortunate to possess any Anglo-Saxon charters from York at all. In 1068 local men from Durham murdered Robert Cumin who had been installed as Earl of Northumbria by William the Conqueror. The king's response was to march northwards and engage some of those involved in the crime in an encounter at York; the city was damaged and we are told that St Peter's Minster was made 'an object of scorn' (*to bysmere macede*).[279] Whether or not the York archives were affected on this occasion, events of the following year were still more serious. As part of a campaign known as the 'harrying of the north', designed to subdue the rebellious Northumbrian kingdom, King William ravaged Yorkshire, and those Normans already stationed in York 'thoroughly destroyed and burnt the holy minster of St Peter' (*halie mynster scs Petrus eall for hergod and forbærned*).[280] Hugh the Chanter specifies the effect this devastation had on St Peter's muniments:

> Incensa quoque et Beati Petri metropolis ecclesia, et ornamenta illius, carte et priuilegia combusta uel perdita fuerunt.[281]

Thus historical accounts suggest that the burning of St Peter's by the Normans caused almost wholesale destruction of its archives. If it is remembered that the

[277] *ASC D*, s.a. 1069 (where the annal for 1069 is not marked in the 'D' manuscript and so is part of the preceding annal for 1068).

[278] See Giandrea, *Episcopal Culture*, pp. 125–6 (at p. 126 for a table of episcopal endowments in Domesday Book). In any assessment of York's Domesday endowment, the omissions and inadequacies of the Yorkshire Domesday record must be remembered; see Palliser 1992, pp. 9–10 and 18 (also p. 31, for a table of the thirty largest fiefs in Yorkshire, in which the York archbishop is ranked fourth).

[279] *ASC D*, s.a. 1068.

[280] *ASC D*, s.a. 1069.

[281] *Hugh the Chanter*, pp. 2–3: 'The metropolitan church of St Peter was also burned, and its ornaments, charters and privileges were consumed or destroyed'.

Anglo-Saxon library at York has also almost entirely disappeared, then such statements should be taken seriously.[282]

Nevertheless, a total of eleven Anglo-Saxon documents have survived from the York archive, two of which are preserved as pre-Conquest copies.[283] **6** is an Old English *Memorandum* compiled by Archbishop Oswald in the period 975 to 992. It is preserved as a copy in a composite manuscript now in the British Library, Harley MS 55, where it is written in a hand of the early eleventh century; it also has annotations in the hand of Archbishop Wulfstan (1002–23) himself.[284] Ker demonstrates that some additional glosses in the so-called 'tremulous hand' mean that the manuscript was presumably at Worcester by the early thirteenth century.[285] Indeed Norton questions whether **6** ever belonged to the York church;[286] but its very nature, as a survey of the condition of the York church's estates, makes it highly likely that **6** was originally drawn up in the north in the interests of the archbishopric.

7 (a–c) constitutes a group of surveys of the York church's estates which was entered into the back of the York Gospels *c.* 1020–3, as part of a series of Old English additions, all of which are somehow connected to Archbishop Wulfstan.[287] The text of St John's Gospel finishes on f. 156r and the first survey, which concerns the Sherburn-in-Elmet estate, follows immediately on f. 156v. Surveys of the estates of Otley and Ripon are written on f. 157r. The remaining additions are not surveys but constitute different kinds of texts. On ff. 158r–160v, three homiletic tracts by Wulfstan and Cnut's first Letter to the English people have been copied into the manuscript. These texts have been written by a single scribe and the homilies contain annotations in the hand of Wulfstan himself. At the top of f. 161r a list of church goods at Sherburn-in-Elmet has been added to the manuscript and the rest of the page has been left blank; this list of goods is edited in Appendix 1. The verso of f. 161 has been used for the entry of a set of bidding prayers and below this is a list of Ælfric's *festermen*; the list of *festermen* is given in Appendix 2.[288]

282 Lapidge, *AS Library*, pp. 40–2: '...leaving these conjectures aside, the library at York has vanished' (at p. 42).

283 **11** is an audacious forgery in the name of Edward the Confessor.

284 For the date of the hand and the contents of the manuscript, see Ker, *Catalogue*, no. 225 and below, pp. 75–6. For the Wulfstan annotations, see the commentary to **6**.

285 Ker, *ibid.*, p. 302. For the work of this thirteenth-century Worcester scribe, see C. Franken, *The Tremulous Hand of Worcester. A Study of Old English in the Thirteenth Century* (Oxford, 1991), pp. 5–28 (at pp. 29n. and 74, for the glosses in BL Harley 55).

286 Norton 2004, p. 211.

287 Stevenson 1912, Keynes 1986 and Baxter 2004.

288 Another item to be considered alongside the documents concerned with the estates of the York archbishopric, is Ulf's horn, for which, see above, pp. 8–9.

Apart from **6** and **7**, the remaining York charters (**1–5** and **8–11**) survive as copies in manuscripts from the post-Conquest period. Two of these copies, of **1** and **8**, have only recently been identified in a York cartulary which is in the British Library under the classmark, Cotton Claudius B.iii and which dates to the end of the thirteenth century.[289] The copy of **8** comes first in the cartulary and has been made on ff. 68v–69r. The copy of **1** has been made immediately afterwards, on f. 69rv. The textual features of these copies of **1** and **8** are almost exactly identical to those copies of **1** and **8** in Part II of another York cartulary, the *Magnum Registrum Album*. This suggests that the copies in the second York cartulary may have been made directly from those found in the earlier York cartulary, Cotton Claudius B.iii.[290] A marginal note next to the copy of **8** in the Cotton Claudius B.iii cartulary may suggest that the scribe making the copy had a single-sheet document in front of him: we learn that his exemplar had been *in coffino* ('in a chest'), which was often how single-sheet documents were stored, and there is also a rough sketch of a chrismon, which may indicate that the single-sheet document he was looking at had a chrismon at the beginning of its text.

Copies of the majority of York charters, of **1–5** and **8–11**, can be found in a mid-fourteenth-century register (mentioned above) which has been known from medieval times as the *Magnum Registrum Album* and which is divided into four main parts.[291] The first item in Part I of the *Magnum Registrum Album* is Hugh the Chanter's *The History of the Church of York* which occupies ff. 1–32;[292] the work of Hugh is followed without a break in the manuscript by a Continuation. The cartulary itself begins on f. 34 and nine pre-Conquest texts, which have all been copied by the same scribe, occupy ff. 56v–62v: in the cartulary the charters are not copied in chronological order, which is the order adopted in this edition. The first two (numbered **4** and **5** in this edition) are charters of King Edgar which date to 963 and in which he grants land to prominent Northumbrian secular figures. **4** is a record, transcribed on ff. 56v–57v, of a grant of twenty hides at Sherburn-in-Elmet to 'Æslac' who is probably to be identified as Earl Oslac. **5** is another 963 grant by King Edgar of Newbald but this time to a certain Gunner; it is transcribed on f. 57rv.

[289] Davis, *Cartularies* (rev. edn), no. 1086. I am very grateful to Julian Harrison of the British Library for bringing these copies to my attention.

[290] Clay, *YMF* 2, p. 157, suggests that many of the texts in the *Magnum Registrum Album* were based on those in Cotton Claudius B.iii. For the possible existence of yet another York cartulary which is no longer extant but which seems also to have had copies of Anglo-Saxon charters, see below, pp. 72–3.

[291] This manuscript is York, Minster Library and Archives, L2/1; it is also known as the *Liber Albus*. It is listed in Davis, *Cartularies* (rev. edn.), no. 1087; see also N. Vincent, 'Medieval Cartularies: Additions and Corrections', *Monastic Research Bulletin* iii (1997), pp. 7–38, at p. 32.

[292] A description of the contents of the *Magnum Registrum Album* can be found below, pp. 79–80.

The next two charters copied into the *Magnum Registrum Album* are both grants made directly to Archbishop Oscytel. **3** is transcribed on ff. 57v–58r; it gives details of King Edgar's gift of ten hides at Sutton, Nottinghamshire, to Oscytel in 958. **2** is transcribed on ff. 58r–59r; it is a grant of land at Southwell in Nottinghamshire (with dependencies at Normanton, Upton, Fiskerton, Farnsfield, Kirklington, Morton, Gibsmere, Bleasby, Goverton, Halloughton and Halam) to Archbishop Oscytel. **2** was issued by King Eadwig and is dated in its text to 958, which is an error for 956.[293] The fifth Anglo-Saxon charter, **1**, is transcribed on f. 59rv. It is perhaps the most remarkable charter to have been preserved in the York archive and is a grant of an unusually large amount of land at Amounderness in Lancashire to Archbishop Wulfstan I (931–56). There has been some evident tampering with the dating-clause: the correct date of its issue, 7 June 934, has been changed to '930'.[294] **8** is transcribed on ff. 59v–60v; it is a 1033 grant by King Cnut to Archbishop Ælfric of land at Patrington in Yorkshire. **11**, which is preserved on ff. 60v–61r, is a spurious grant of the Worcester diocese by King Edward the Confessor to Archbishop Ealdred, although it may take some of its form from authentic documents. The two remaining Anglo-Saxon documents in the *Magnum Registrum Album* are both writs of King Edward the Confessor and are both transcribed on f. 61v. The first, **10**, tells of the king's announcement that he has granted to a certain Ealdred, the 'deacon' of Archbishop Ealdred, the minster at Axminster. The second, **9**, announces that King Edward has granted judicial and financial rights over his lands and over his men to Archbishop Ealdred; **9** has been copied twice into the *Magnum Registrum Album*, once on f. 61v and once on f. 62v. Two of the Anglo-Saxon charters in the *Magnum Registrum Album* have been copied again in Part II of that manuscript, and are seemingly by the same scribe who made the copies in Part I: thus **8** is found in Part II on f. 78rv and **1** occurs in Part II, ff. 78v–79v.

b. *The Later History of the Archive*

The chances of survival for any document composed before 1069 and stored in the York archive were very slim indeed; and any document that had survived also had to endure a fire in 1137 which seems to have affected York's muniments in particular.[295] It is therefore a remarkable stroke of luck that any Anglo-Saxon charters withstood the Norman punitive expeditions to York, as well as later disasters, to be copied into cartularies of the late thirteenth and mid-fourteenth

293 For an explanation of this error in the dating-clause, see the commentary to **2**.

294 For this alteration in **1** and connections with S 428 (BCS 701), see the commentary to **1**.

295 See Harvey 1966; for the severity of the fire, see Palliser 1984, p. 106. For a very full and interesting history of the York Minster Library, see Barr 1977.

centuries. It is equally fortunate that the York Gospels, which are still used during the enthronement of an Archbishop, also weathered this period and bear a series of Old English additions made at various points in the eleventh century.

In fact the earliest surviving document in its original form in the York archive is a grant by Archbishop Murdac dated *c.* 1148–50.[296] An interest in the maintenance and organisation of the archive did not emerge until the late fourteenth century when a volume known as the *Chapter Act Book* was composed. This composition takes the form of an inventory of some eighty documents which were housed in three chests and subdivided into *pixides* ('boxes'), *cophini* ('chests') and a *hanoperia* ('hamper').[297] Most of these documents were later copied into the York cartularies such as the *Magnum Registrum Album* or the Minster *Doomsday Book*.[298] The marginal note in the copy of **8** in the cartulary now in British Library, Cotton Claudius B.iii, suggests that the single-sheet exemplar for this copy had been stored in one of these *cophini*.

In the early sixteenth century Thomas Water, who was then chapter clerk, attempted to catalogue all of the York church's muniments. He compiled a list of those containers used to store documents: he found twelve chests and a great box with three trays containing documents concerning the archbishopric. Water then composed two initial inventories (catalogued in the York archives as M2/2a and M2/2b) as part of a preparatory process for his most substantial catalogue of those documents which concerned the rights and possessions of the York church, the *Repertorium et Extenta Prebendarum* (M2/2c).[299] The first forty-two folios of the *Repertorium et Extenta Prebendarum* constitute a classified finding list of documents which existed both in their original form and also as copies in the York church's registers, such as the Minster *Doomsday Book*, the *Magnum Registrum Album* and in a separate manuscript known as the 'old white register' which no longer survives. On ff. 17r–18v, entitled 'de archiepiscopatu Ebor.', are entries detailing some, but not all, of the Anglo-Saxon charters extant today in the York archive.

There is a third inventory, catalogued today as M2/2p and extant as two paper gatherings, which is probably in the hand of one of Thomas Water's clerks and dates *c.* 1520. It is of interest because it is an index to a now missing cartulary known as 'Register B'. Longley suggests that this 'Register B' is identical to the 'old white register' mentioned several times by Water in his *Repertorium* (for

[296] Longley 1976, p. 59; this section, on the later history of the York archive, is indebted to the work by Longley.

[297] Longley 1976, p. 59.

[298] For the Minster *Doomsday Book*, see Davis, *Cartularies* (rev. edn), no. 1088.

[299] Longley 1976, p. 60. For the inventories M2/2a, M2/2b and M2/2c, see Davis, *Cartularies* (rev. edn), nos. 1091, 1090 and 1092 respectively.

example, on f. 14r), and which was clearly distinct from the *Magnum Registrum Album*.[300] On p. 24, the last of the first paper gathering, is a reference to two charters of an unnamed king concerning the Patrington estate, both of which apparently appeared on f. 81 of the now missing cartulary. The titles of these charters read, 'Carta regis super Patrinton archiepiscopo concessa' and 'Alia carta regis super terra archiepiscopo concessa quae vix potest legi secundum modernos'. It seems likely that these were further copies of **8** and therefore that there were copies of at least one Anglo-Saxon charter in 'Register B'.

Two major national movements, first of the mid-sixteenth century, and then of the mid-seventeenth century, shaped the medieval holdings of the York archive. The Reformation of the English Church saw numerous volumes removed from York's custody. 1547 seems to have been a particularly disastrous year for the York archive.[301] Up until this point, royal articles had been issued for a general ecclesiastical visitation of the whole country. But 1547 saw the publication of injunctions which dealt specifically with cathedrals and their treasures. A survey of those precious texts housed in the Minster treasury, which was conducted shortly before the despoliation of 1547, records the presence of eleven manuscripts which had been decorated with expensive materials such as gold and silver and which had bindings resplendent with jewels. Of particular interest among this collection was a two-volume gospel book given by Wilfrid to the Minster.[302] Out of all of these precious manuscripts, only the York Gospels have survived to this day.[303] Some manuscripts which were not richly decorated managed to survive the Reformation: several reached Sir Robert Cotton's Library and it may have been at this time that the York cartulary of the late thirteenth century, which contains copies of **1** and **8** (British Library, Cotton Claudius B.iii), came into Cotton's possession.

The second upheaval, and a renewed threat from looters, came during the period of Civil War from 1642 to 1651. But it appears that York did not suffer as much as other ecclesiastical institutions in the country. Barr shows that this was due to the concerted efforts of a few individuals, in particular two successive

[300] Longley does not discuss this index to 'Register B' in her 1976 article; but, owing to the help of the current York archivist Mr. Peter Young, I was able to gain access to Longley's own notes about this index (which are kept alongside the index in the York archives). The index is listed in Davis, *Cartularies* (rev. edn), no. 1096.2 (p. 223); the so-called 'Register B' is listed as 'untraced' in Davis, *ibid.*, no. 1096.1 (p. 223).

[301] For these later events, see especially Barr 1986.

[302] For the entry concerning the gospel book given by Wilfrid to York Minster, which is described, among other things, as having been decorated in gold and silver, see J. Raine, ed., *The Fabric Rolls of York Minster with an Appendix of Illustrative Documents*, SS xxxv (Durham, 1859), p. 223.

[303] An indication of the severity of this royal visitation at York is provided by the fact that after 1547 the office of treasurer at York was no longer regarded necessary as there were no treasures left to be maintained; see Barr 1986, p. 109.

barons of Fairfax, Ferdinando and Thomas. These men wanted to protect their family library which had been housed at York Minster and so published notices which advertised punishments for soldiers who looted the church and which also offered rewards for those soldiers who recovered missing documents. Ferdinando and Thomas also ensured that someone was employed as a keeper of the Minster Library during these tumultuous times.[304] It was also during the Civil War that some documents passed into the hands of individuals who ensured that they were kept safely until the restoration of the Church and Crown. One such man was a canon by the name of George Stanhope who, by the time of his death in 1644, possessed documents which belonged to the Dean and Chapter of York.[305] It seems to have been during this period that the York Gospels passed temporarily out of the custody of the Minster authorities. Unfortunately nothing is known about when this manuscript first left its home at York; and it is also unclear whether an official body took responsibility for the York Gospels or whether one individual in particular took it upon himself to protect the manuscript. But what is known is that on 1 August 1678 the Gospels were returned to the Minster by the executors of the will of Henry King, the recently deceased bishop of Chichester, and this event is recorded in the *Chapter Acts* of York Minster.[306]

From this moment onwards interest continued to be taken in the deeds stored at York. In the late seventeenth and early eighteenth centuries, Archbishop Sharp (1691–1714) was the remarkable figure who carried out a thorough investigation of all of those privileges and possessions of the entire York diocese and every church therein. One of the more serious problems confronting York archivists of this time was the conditions in which the documents were being stored; this became more urgent still from the beginning of the nineteenth century and was intensified by a fire at the Minster in 1829 which threatened documents stored in the 'Will Office'. After another fire in May 1840, which endangered the new location of the registry, the church's documents were removed from the Old Library and the Chapter clerk was now positioned in the Zouche Chapel in the Minster. But storage conditions remained far from ideal and William Bruce, with the aid of Charles Dickens, carried out an examination of the condition of some of the ecclesiastical registries in England.[307] In 1850 Charles Dickens himself commented on the York registry:

[304] See Barr 1986, p. 111.

[305] See Longley 1977, p. 103.

[306] See Raine, *The Fabric Rolls of York Minster*, p. 357. Barr 1986, pp. 112–14, speculates as to how the York Gospels had come into King's possession. See also Barr 1977, pp. 489–90 and 505.

[307] For all of these details concerning the York archive, see Longley 1976, pp. 62–72. For another discussion of the York archive, see J. Purvis, 'The Archives of York', in *The Noble City of York*, ed. A. Stacpoole *et al.*, (York, 1972), pp. 717–36.

> [The registry is] a kind of shed – such as is usually called a lean-to – squeezing itself, as if it were (with very good reason) ashamed, into the south-west corner of the cross, which the ground-plan of the cathedral forms, and sticking to it like a dirty little pimple. ...a confined den within, which would have made an indifferent chandler's shop, with a pestilent little chimney in it, filling it with smoke like a Lapland hut, was the "Searching Office".[308]

3. THE MANUSCRIPTS

a. *BL Harley 55* [C]

C is a composite manuscript. Together with numerous unfoliated modern paper flyleaves, are two parts which contain Anglo-Saxon material. The first part is foliated 1– 4v and consists of four half-sheets, perhaps originally from the end of a manuscript.[309] It is written in a hand dating to the beginning of the eleventh century and contains:

1. ff. 1–3: Medical Recipes.
2. ff. 3v–4v: Laws of King Edgar (extracts from II and III Edgar).
3. f. 4v: Archbishop Oswald's *Memorandum* on the church of York's lands at Otley, Ripon and Sherburn-in-Elmet (**6**).[310]

6 is written in a narrow and pointed Anglo-Saxon minuscule hand and has large initials in brown ink (the Medical Recipes and Laws of King Edgar are written in two different hands). Various additions to **6**, which are in the hand of Archbishop Wulfstan,[311] indicate that this manuscript was intimately connected to that metropolitan. The very presence of **6** might be taken to imply that the manuscript was once at York. But there are also glosses on ff. 3v and 4 which have been written by the so-called 'tremulous' hand and which therefore demonstrate that the manuscript was certainly kept at Worcester in the early thirteenth century.[312] The manuscript was later owned by John Selden (d. 1654) and then by Sir Simonds d'Ewes (d. 1650) and by his grandson, also called Sir Simonds d'Ewes (d. 1722). It was acquired by Harley in 1705.[313]

[308] The quotation from Charles Dickens is found in Longley 1976, p. 67; it was originally printed in H. Stone, *The Uncollected Writings of Charles Dickens: Household Words, 1850–59*, i (London, 1969), pp. 173–81.

[309] Ker, *Catalogue*, no. 225.

[310] As Ker, *Catalogue*, no. 225 notes, the fourth folio is rubbed, as if from exposure.

[311] See the commentary to **6**.

[312] See also above, p. 69.

[313] For this information regarding the later ownership of C, see Ker, *ibid*. It is listed also in Gneuss, *Handlist*, no. 412.

The second part containing Anglo-Saxon material is foliated 5–13; these nine folios were probably also originally from the end of a manuscript. It is written in a script of the middle of the twelfth century and contains some of King Cnut's laws. It has three large initials in red and some small initials in brown. The first letter of a sentence is decorated with red. It, too, was owned by Selden and d'Ewes.[314]

b. *York, Minster Library, Add. 1 (the York Gospels)* [D]

D is the magnificent York Gospels.[315] After various oaths and other preliminary material on ff. 1–9, which were added in the thirteenth century, the main text of the Gospels themselves starts on f. 10 and extends to f. 156r. This main text was written and illuminated in the period *c.* 990–1000.[316] The principal scribe wrote ff. 15v–156r (except for f. 23v and for the Canon Table numerals on ff. 15v–19r) in a Caroline hand which also has square minuscule features. A second scribe, who was perhaps a contemporary of the main scribe working in the same scriptorium, was responsible for the preliminary folios, ff. 10–14; his hand has been described as a 'vigorous square minuscule'.[317] Perhaps two further scribes contributed to work on the Canon Tables on f. 15v and f. 16 and the hand of Eadwig Basan, a monk and scribe of Christ Church, Canterbury, has been identified on f. 23v.[318]

It is difficult to locate the origin of the York Gospels. McGurk suggests that the combined use of square minuscule script and Caroline script, and also the similarity of the square minuscule to that of other square minuscule manuscripts from St Augustine's, might indicate that St Augustine's, Canterbury, is a possible place of origin. He also points out that Eadwig Basan's contribution to f. 23v is most easily explicable if it is understood that the manuscript was at that scribe's scriptorium at Christ Church, Canterbury. McGurk also highlights the links between Christ Church, Canterbury, and the Glastonbury scriptorium and so in the end the origin of the York Gospels could equally well be either of the Canterbury houses or Glastonbury.[319]

[314] See Ker, *Catalogue*, no. 226.

[315] For a facsimile edition of the York Gospels, complete with introductory essays, see Barker, *York Gospels*.

[316] For the illumination in the manuscript, see J.J.G. Alexander, 'The Illumination of the Gospels' in Barker, *York Gospels*, pp. 65–79.

[317] All of this palaeographical information about the York Gospels is taken from P. McGurk, 'Palaeography' in Barker, *York Gospels*, pp. 37–42 (at p. 40 for the quotation). See also J.P. Gilson, *Description of the Saxon Manuscript of the Four Gospels in the Library of York Minster* (York, 1925).

[318] Eadwig Basan, working in the early decades of the eleventh century, wrote a very distinctive Anglo-Caroline script, which can be identified in various gospel books, psalters and charters; for a useful biographical overview, see the entry for Eadwig by R. Gameson in *ODNB*.

[319] See McGurk, *ibid.*, pp. 41–2.

At various points in the eleventh century, additions in Old English were made into the York Gospels and it is these additions which are of primary interest for this present edition. The additions were made onto the last six leaves of the Gospels, after the end of the Gospel of St John; they occupy ff. 156v–161v. Below is a list of the contents of the additions and the dates at which they were added to the York Gospels:[320]

1. ff. 156v–7r: Three surveys of the York church's estates (**7**), which may be in three different, although contemporary hands dating to *c.* 1020 and include:[321]
   (a) f. 156v: survey of Sherburn-in-Elmet.
   (b) f. 157r: survey of Otley.
   (c) f. 157r: survey of Ripon.
2. ff. 158r–9v (f. 157v is blank): Three homilies by Archbishop Wulfstan. All three are written by a single scribe working *c.* 1020–3.[322] The homilies include:
   (a) f. 158rv: the *Sermo Lupi*.
   (b) f. 159r: *Be hæðendome*.
   (c) f. 159v: *Be cristendome*.
3. f. 160rv: King Cnut's letter to the people of England, which is written by the same scribe as that of the three homilies listed above and can therefore be dated *c.* 1020–3. (The letter itself belongs historically to the year 1019 or 1020.)
4. f. 161r: A list of church treasures to be found at Sherburn-in-Elmet (edited below as Appendix 1). This list is clearly written in a different hand to items 1–3 listed above, which Ker dates to the middle of the eleventh century.[323]
5. f. 161v: Bidding prayers, written probably in the second quarter of the eleventh century.[324]
6. f. 161v: the list of Ælfric's *festermen* (edited below as Appendix 2). The script of this list is clearly later than that of the other Old English items and is dated to the second half of the eleventh century by Ker.[325]

[320] For discussions of these Old English additions, see Stevenson 1912 and Keynes 1986.
[321] See Ker, *Catalogue*, no. 402, and Keynes 1986, pp. 83–91 (at p. 82 for the suggestion that the scribe of the Ripon survey might be the same as the scribe of lines 13–18 of the Sherburn survey); for more detail, see below, the commentary to **7**.
[322] For the date, see Keynes 1986, p. 83.
[323] Ker, *Catalogue*, no. 402d.
[324] For the date, see Keynes 1986, p. 83.
[325] Ker, *Catalogue*, no. 402f.

c. *BL Cotton Claudius B. iii* [E]

E is the earliest extant York cartulary, dating *c.* 1280, with additions to the fourteenth century.[326] E is a general cartulary, with red rubrics and which comprises:[327]

1. ff. 3–134: the cartulary opens with some royal charters. The title, 'Hic incipiunt carte, ordinaciones, confirmaciones, resignaciones et quieteclamaciones ac alia scripta Decanatui Ebor. spectancia', occurs on f. 6v.
2. ff. 134–165: miscellaneous additions.
3. ff. 166–197: a separate compilation with details about terriers and rentals of the prebends.
4. ff. 198–207: miscellaneous additions.
5. ff. 208–213: a contemporary table which classifies the material according to the dignitaries it concerns.

E does not contain copies of all of the York charters, merely those of **1** and **8**, which are both copied in the first section comprising royal charters. **8** is copied first on ff. 68v–69r and **1** occurs immediately afterwards on f. 69rv; both are in the same hand. Rubrics to both charters are written in red. The script of these copies is idiosyncratic in its tendency to give the letter **d** an ascender that is heavily thickened with black ink. Other letters can also have these thickened ascenders, such as initial **h** and **b**; the suspension bar which signals an abbreviation can also be similarly thickened. Although the Old English names copied in the witness-lists of these two versions of **1** and **8** are corrupt, the scribe has at least attempted in places to copy the Old English letter-forms, wynn and thorn. A marginal addition next to the copy of **8** may indicate that the scribe of E was working, in the late thirteenth century, from a single-sheet copy of the charter.[328] These versions of **1** and **8** were later recopied and entered into part II of F, which is described below. As noted by Clay, a signature on f. 160 suggests that E was later owned by a certain William Redman, who is not to be equated with the William Redman who was bishop of Norwich and who died in 1602.[329] By whatever means, E then came into Sir Robert Cotton's collection and appears in a 1621 catalogue of Cotton's collection.[330]

[326] It is listed in Davis, *Cartularies* (rev. edn), as item 1086; for a very useful description of E, together with a detailed list of its contents, see Clay, *YMF* 2, pp. 155–64 (Appendix C). For the previous existence of another York cartulary which is now lost, see above, pp. 72–3.

[327] This list of contents is taken from Davis, *Cartularies* (rev. edn), no. 1086.

[328] See above, p. 70.

[329] Clay, *YMF* 2, p. 157, n. 5.

[330] For these details, see Clay, *YMF* 2, p. 157.

d. *York, Minster Library and Archives, L 2/1 (the 'Liber Albus' or 'Magnum Registrum Album')* [F]

F is a truly vast York cartulary and the main source of the York charters, as it contains copies of **1–5** and **8–11**.[331] It is written mainly in a hand (or hands) of the mid-fourteenth century. Rubrics to the charters are written in red ink.[332] It is bound in wooden boards and the boards have a brown leather covering which has a 'stamped design of the seventeenth century'.[333] As noted by previous scholars, F contains:[334]

1. ff. i–iv: modern blank leaves.
2. pp. 1–4: originally blank (apart from the title *Magnum Registrum Album* on p. 1) but later filled with notes about eighteenth- and nineteenth-century litigation in which the manuscript was used.
3. pp. 5–10: alphabetical list of contents made by Thomas Water.[335]
4. pp. 11–12: blank.
5. pp. 13–29: fourteenth-century list of contents (p. 27 has historical memoranda).
6. p. 30: blank.
7. p. 31: letters of Archbishop John Thoresby, dated 1357.
8. p. 32: further copy of the historical memoranda found on p. 27.

There is now a new pagination:

9. pp. 1–24: extracts from the Domesday survey for Yorkshire.

Now the main register begins, which is divided into four parts, and has fourteenth-century foliation:

10. ff. 1–74: Part I:
    ff. 1–32: Hugh the Chanter's *History of the Church of York*, followed by the continuation to that work which is based on John of Hexham and ends on f. 33v.[336]
    ff. 34–74v: charters (including copies of **1–5** and **8–11**).
11. ff. 1–100: Part II. This part contains further copies of **1** and **8**.
12. ff. 1–100: Part III.
13. ff. 1–118v: Part IV: here the original register ends on f. 108v and the remaining folios are filled with additions.

331 For comments about the enormous size of the volume, see Davis, *Cartularies* (rev. edn.), p. xv (it is listed in that same work as item number 1087).

332 There is a very detailed description of F in *Hugh the Chanter*, pp. lv–lxi, to which this section is greatly indebted.

333 See *Hugh the Chanter*, p. lv (and n. 2, for the possible existence of an earlier white-leather covering, from which the volume probably took its name).

334 This list of contents is taken from *Hugh the Chanter*, pp. lv–lvi.

335 For Thomas Water, see above, pp. 72–3.

336 This is the only manuscript to preserve a complete version of Hugh's work.

Inasmuch as any guiding principle can be discerned, the latest dated documents are found in Part IV, up to 1344.[337] The evidence of early headings on the first folio of each part (called 'Part the First', 'Part the Second' and so on), the contemporary foliation, and the fourteenth century contents list (item 5 in the list above), all suggest that the division of the *Magnum Registrum Album* into four parts was an early development.[338] Duplicated copies of various documents can be found in the four different parts; and so second copies of **1** and **8** are found in Part II.

In Part I of the cartulary the Anglo-Saxon charters are all copied by the same scribe on ff. 56v–62v in a hand of the mid-fourteenth century; they are not arranged in any particular chronological or geographical order.[339] (**9** has been copied twice into Part I of F on f. 61v and f. 62v.) The copyist's hand is very difficult to read and some letter-forms, in particular **c** and **t**, are almost indistinguishable from each other. The poor quality of the copying is nowhere more apparent than with the Old English boundary clauses and also name-forms. The boundary clauses are practically incomprehensible in their extant form (the copies in Part I of F are the only ones to preserve the Old English boundary clauses for the York charters). The scribe makes routine copying errors (which may actually belong to his exemplar), the most common of which is the miscopying of **g** as **s**. There are also errors which demonstrate that the copyist did not understand or recognise Old English letter-forms: thus wynn and thorn are rendered with a **y** and **Đ** is copied as **D**.[340] If these obviously miscopied letters are corrected, then the boundary clauses become vaguely intelligible. But there are many instances where it is far from clear what the original Old English reading had been.[341]

The duplicated copies of **1** and **8** (referred to above) occur on ff. 78r–79v of F's Part II. They are seemingly written by the same scribe of the mid-fourteenth century who was responsible for the Anglo-Saxon charters in Part I. These versions of **1** and **8** are copies of **1** and **8** found in the earlier York cartulary, manuscript E.

e. *Copies by antiquaries* [G, H, I, J]

i. *BL Harley 6841* (G): s. xvi. f. 128rv has a later Latin translation of Archbishop Oswald's Old English Memorandum, **6**; f. 129rv is a later copy of the Old English **6**.

[337] *Hugh the Chanter*, p. lvi.

[338] See *Hugh the Chanter*, p. lvi.

[339] For the order in which the charters are copied, see above, pp. 70–1.

[340] These miscopied Old English letter-forms may already have been in the copyist's exemplar. For the variety of letter-forms that are routinely miscopied, see pp. 83–4.

[341] A note in manuscript E's copy of **8** shows how difficult it was for these cartulary scribes of the late thirteenth century and mid-fourteenth century to decipher Old English. It reads: 'qui quidem termini scribuntur Anglice qui uix secundum linguam modernam legi possent'.

ii. *Bodleian, Dodsworth 9* (H): s. xvii. This Dodsworth manuscript contains copies of several northern charters, not just those from the York archive.[342] A copy of **1** occurs on ff. 4v–5r and lacks witnesses; a copy of **3** occurs on f. 3v, which lacks witnesses and bounds; a copy of **4** occurs on f. 1rv and lacks bounds and witnesses; a copy of **5** occurs on f. 2v, which lacks bounds, witnesses and a dating-clause; the copy of **8** on f. 6rv also lacks bounds, witnesses and dating-clause. These copies of York charters derive ultimately from Part I of the *Magnum Registrum Album* (MS F). This manuscript also has copies of **12** from the Beverley archive and **17** from the Durham archive.[343]

iii. *Bodleian, Dodsworth 10* (I): s. xvii. This Dodsworth manuscript, a first draft of the *Monasticon Anglicanum*,[344] has copies of three northern charters, only one of which is from the York archive. On ff. 42r–43r is a copy of **1**, made ultimately from Part I of the *Magnum Registrum Album* (MS F); this copy ends with the name 'Wlmer minister' on f. 43r and so misses out sixteen of the witnesses. There are also copies of **12** from the Beverley archive and **17** from the Durham archive.

iv. *Bodleian, Dodsworth 125* (J): s. xvii. This Dodsworth manuscript has a copy of **4** on ff. 75r–76r, a copy of **5** on f. 76rv, a copy of **3** on f. 77rv, a copy of **1** on ff. 78r–79r, a copy of **8** on ff. 79r–80r and of **9** on f. 80r; all of these copies derive from Part I of the *Magnum Registrum Album*.[345]

342 It is indexed in *Summ. Cat.*, no. 4151.
343 For these copies, see below pp. 202 and 343.
344 See *Summ. Cat.*, no. 4152.
345 *Summ. Cat.*, no. 5066.

SIGLA

Note. In this series the siglum A is reserved for original documents and the siglum B for non-contemporary copies on single-sheets; the York archive has neither type of document.

C. BL Harley 55 (s. xi^{in})
D. York, Minster Library, Add. 1 (s. xi^{in})
E. BL Cotton Claudius B. iii (s. xiii^{ex})
F. York, Minster Library and Archives, L2/1 (*Magnum Registrum Album*), pt. I (s. xiv^{med})
F. York, Minster Library and Archives, L2/1 (*Magnum Registrum Album*), pt. II (s. xiv^{med})
G. BL Harley 6841 (s. xvi)
H. Bodleian, Dodsworth 9 (s. xvii)
I. Bodleian, Dodsworth 10 (s. xvii)
J. Bodleian, Dodsworth 125 (s. xvii)

NOTE ON THE METHOD OF EDITING

It is the principle of this edition to provide texts which are as close as possible to the original versions. Since it is impossible to be certain about the author's orthography, the most reasonable reading has been chosen from the manuscript witnesses. Where evident corruptions and misreadings in the text have been corrected, the manuscript reading is always given in the apparatus. In order to avoid over-burdening the critical apparatus, only the significant variants are given for the texts. Where an emendation is suggested in the critical apparatus, it is prefaced by the word *For*. Standard abbreviations have been expanded silently. The Latin charters in the York archive are preserved in (1) British Library, Cotton Claudius B.iii (Manuscript E); (2) York, Dean and Chapter, *Magnum Registrum Album*, part I (Manuscript F); and (3) York, Dean and Chapter, *Magnum Registrum Album*, part II (Manuscript F). Since the texts given in part II of F are direct copies of E, I have not supplied their manuscript readings. Similarly, the two other manuscript witnesses of the Latin York charters are from the antiquary Dodsworth's collection in the Bodleian Library; they are direct copies of the versions in Manuscript F and therefore I have not used them when compiling the text. Punctuation is editorial and follows modern practice. Proper nouns have been capitalised. Where Classical Latin requires '*ae*', the manuscript witnesses often contain simply '*e*' or *e*-caudata. This is normal practice in manuscripts from the late eleventh century onwards and I have retained it in my text.

The texts of the Old English boundary clauses in charters **2–5** and **8** are preserved only in part I of F; they are enormously corrupt. It is clear that the scribe of F routinely miscopies certain letters: **g** is often copied as **s**, **s** can be copied as **r** (occasionally **s** is copied as **l**), **e** can be copied as **f**, **Ð** is copied as **D**, **ð** is copied as **d** and the letters wynn, thorn and **y** are all identical (apart from the scribe's occasional use of **ẏ**). It is the practice of this edition to emend these miscopied letters in the edited text of each charter. The scribe's most common miscopyings, such as **s** for **g** or **d** for **ð**, are silently corrected; where the error is a less common one, such as **e** being miscopied as **f**, the manuscript reading is always given in the apparatus. Emendations and interpretations are necessarily tentative and where there is any doubt, I have always given the manuscript reading in the apparatus.

There are similar high levels of corruption with the Old English name-forms in **1–5**, **8** and **11**, preserved in E and F. Name-forms are treated in exactly the same fashion as the Old English boundary clauses and obviously miscopied letters have been emended. Thus the manuscript's form, 'Cynelige', is given in the edited text as 'Cynesige'. The practice of emending miscopied letters most often results in a name-form that is recognisable to the modern reader. So where the manuscript has 'Ayeline', the edited text will have 'Aþeline'. Although this is ultimately a version of the name 'Æþelƿine', I have not given this form in the edited text, since this departs too far from the manuscript version; this suggested 'original' form is given as a note in the apparatus. Names can also be found in their original form (like 'Æþelƿine') in Index I, together with the various spellings of each name. Where name-forms are completely incomprehensible, even after emendation of letters that are clearly miscopied, I have supplied the suggested 'original' form in the apparatus; this has been particularly necessary for charter **2**. Where the name-forms survive in both E and F, the oldest available spelling has been selected, thus **þ** in preference to **th**, or **ƿ** in preference to **w**. One common error in the copies of York charters in F is the omission of the letter **u** following initial **W**- in name-forms. Thus **1** has 'Wllaf', 'Wlfhelm' and 'Wlfbold'. In these instances, no editorial intervention or explanation has been deemed necessary. In more complicated examples, such as 'Wlmer' or 'Wlnoð', also from **1**, a note in the apparatus supplies the suggested 'original' forms, 'Wulfmær' and 'Wulfnoð', as a guide to readers. Such suggestions are not intended as definitive.

THE CHARTERS OF YORK

1

King Æthelstan grants land (tellus) *at Amounderness, Lancashire, to the church of St Peter at York*. A.D. 930 [for 934] (7 June)

E. BL Cotton Claudius B. iii, 69rv: copy, s. xiii[ex]
Rubric: Alia carta regis super terra archiepiscopo concessa que vix potest legi secundum modernos.
F1. York, Minster Library and Archives, L 2/1 (*Mag. Reg. Alb.*), pt. I, 59rv: copy, s. xiv[med]
Rubric: Collacio terre non modice in Eborum facta beato Petro per Ailstanum regem tempore domini Wlstani de Eborum archiepiscopo.
F2. York, Minster Library and Archives, L 2/1 (*Mag. Reg. Alb.*), pt. II, 78v–79v: copy of E, s. xiv[med]
Rubric: Alia carta regis super terra archiepiscopo concessa que vix potest legi secundum modernos.
H. Bodleian, Dodsworth 9, 4v–5r: copy of F1, s. xvii [no witnesses]
I. Bodleian, Dodsworth 10, 42r–43r: copy, s. xvii
J. Bodleian, Dodsworth 125, 78r–79r: copy of F1, s. xvii
Ed.: a. *Mon. Angl.*, iii. 129–30, from F1
b. *Mon. Angl.* (rev. edn.), vi, pt. 3, p. 1176 (no. 5)
c. Kemble 352, from F1 and F2
d. Birch 703, from Kemble
e. Birch 1344, from F1
f. Farrer, *EYC*, no. 1, from F1 and F2
Translated: Whitelock, *EHD*, pp. 548–51 (no. 104)
Listed: Sawyer 407; Hart, *ECNE*, no. 119
Edited from E and F1

Fortuna fallentis seculi procax[a] non lacteo immarcessibilium[b] liliorum candore amabilis sed fellita eiulande[c] corrupcionis amaritudine odibilis, fetentis filios ualle in lacrimarum carnis rictibus debacchando[d] uenenosis mordaciter dilacerat; que[e] quamuis arridendo sit infelicibus attractabilis Acherontici ad ima Cociti[f] ni satus alti subueniat boantis, impudenter est decurribilis;[g] et ideo quia ipsa ruinosa deficiendo tanaliter dilabitur, summopere festinandum est[h] ad amoena indicibilis letitie arua, ubi angelica ymnidice iubilationis organa, mellifluaque uernantium[i] rosarum odoramina[j] a bonis beatisque naribus inestimabiliter dulcia capiuntur, sineque calce[k] auribus cliuipparum suauia audiuntur. Cuius amore felicitatis[l] illectus fastidiunt iam infima, dulcescunt superna, eisque pro percipiendis semperque specie indefectiua fruendis, ego Eþelstanus[m] rex Anglorum per omnipatrantis[n] dexteram, que Christus est, totius Britannie regni solio sublimatus, quandam non modicam telluris particulam Deo omnipotenti et beato Petro apostolo, ad ecclesiam suam in ciuitate Eborum tempore quo Wulfstanum[o] archiepiscopum illuc constitui, in loco quem solicole Agmundesness[p] uocitant, sub Dei timore libenter attribuo; ut ille episcopus ea sine iugo exose seruitutis, cum pratis, pascuis, siluis, riuulis, omnibusque ad eam utilitatibus rite pertinentibus, quamdiu aura naribus spirabili,[q] ocellorumque conuolatu cernibili utatur, ac sacris[r] heredibus post se[s] semper illius ecclesie in eternam hereditatem derelinquat. Hanc prefatam donationem propria et non modica emi pecunia; non solum illam, quin potius cuncta illius pretitulate[t] predia basilice, uidelicet sancti Petri principis apostolorum obrizo[u] empta auro, perpetualiter donaui. Si autem, quod absit, aliquis typo[v] supercilii turgens hanc mee compositionis ac confirmationis breuiculam elidere uel infringere temptauerit, sciat se nouissima ac tremenda concionis die classica archangeli[w] clangente bucina[x] somatibus tetra postponentibus poliandria,[y] cum Iuda impie proditionis compilatore, infaustis quoque Iudeis Christum ore sacrilego ara in crucis blasphemantibus, eterna confusione, edacibus fauillantium tormentorum ignibus [z]sine fine[z] poenaliter arsurum. Huius namque a Deo Dominoque Iesu Christo [a2]inspirante atque uiuente[a2] uoluntatis scedula anno incarnationis dominice .dcccc. .xxx. regni uero mihi commissi .vi. indiccione .vii. epacta .iii. concurrente .ii. septimis Iunii idibus luna .xxi.[b2] in ciuitate omnibus notissima que Snotingham dicitur, tota optimatum generalitate sub alis[c2] regie dapsilitatis ouante prescripta est. Cuius etiam inconcusse firmitatis auctoritas hiis testibus roborata constat, quorum nomina subtus grammulis[d2] depicta annotantur.

Sed prius decurrant termini hiisque decursis promissa constipulatorum[e2] promulgentur nomina.[f2] Primitus autem a mari sursum [g2]in Cocur usque[g2] ad fontem[h2] illius fluminis, ab illo fonte[i2] directe in alium fontem[j2] qui dicitur Saxonice Duleshope[k2] sic per descensum riuuli in Hodder ipso dirigamine in Ribbel[l2] et sic in illo flumine per dimidium alueum iterum recursus in mare. Nunc ut predixi heroicorum[m2] constipulationes ne obliuioni tradantur cartulariis[n2] apicibus inserende uidentur:

Ego Eþelstanus[o2] singularis priuilegii ierarchia preditus rex huius acumen indiculi[p2] cum signo sancte semperque adorande crucis corroboraui et subscripsi

Ego Ƿulfhelmus[q2] Dorobernensis ecclesie archiepiscopus consensi et subscripsi [*Canterbury*]

Ego Wlstanus[r2] Eboracensis ecclesie archiepiscopus [s2]consensi et subscripsi[s2] [*York*]

Ego Hoƿel[t2] subregulus consensi et subscripsi[u2]
Ego Morcant subregulus consensi [v2]et subscripsi[v2]
Ego Judƿald[w2] subregulus consensi [x2]et subscripsi[x2]
Ego Alfwynus[y2] episcopus consensi et subscripsi[z2] [*Lichfield*]
[a3]Ego Eadwlf[b3] episcopus consensi et subscripsi [*Crediton*]
Ego Cenƿald[c3] episcopus consensi et subscripsi [*Worcester*]
Ego Beornstan[d3] episcopus consensi et subscripsi[a3] [*Winchester*]
Ego Þeodred[e3] episcopus consensi et subscripsi [*London*]
Ego Ƿulfun[f3] episcopus consensi et subscripsi [*Selsey*]
Ego Ƿinsige[g3] episcopus consensi et subscripsi [*Dorchester*]
Ego Alfheah[h3] episcopus consensi et subscripsi [*Wells*]

Ego Oda episcopus consensi et subscripsi [*Ramsbury*]
Ego Alfred[i3] episcopus consensi et subscripsi [*Sherborne*]
Ego Tidhelm[j3] episcopus consensi et subscripsi [*Hereford*]
Ego Burhric[k3] episcopus consensi et subscripsi [*Rochester*]
Ego Alfred[l3] episcopus consensi et subscripsi [*Unknown see*]
Ego Conan episcopus consensi et subscripsi [*Cornwall*]
Ego Cynsi[m3] episcopus consensi et subscripsi [*Unknown see*]
Ego Ƿulfhelm[n3] episcopus consensi et subscripsi [*Unknown see*]
Ego Ƿired[o3] episcopus consensi et subscripsi [*Chester-le-Street*]
Ego Elfƿald[p3] dux consensi et subscripsi
Ego Osferð[q3] dux consensi et subscripsi
Ego Ethelstan[r3] dux consensi et subscripsi
Ego Osulf dux consensi et subscripsi
Ego Uhtredus[s3] dux consensi et subscripsi
Ego Elfstan[t3] dux consensi et subscripsi
Ego Uhtred dux consensi et subscripsi
Ego Regnƿald[u3] dux consensi et subscripsi
Ego Inƿaer[v3] dux consensi et subscripsi
Ego Hadd[w3] dux consensi et subscripsi
Ego Scule dux consensi et subscripsi
Ego Þurferð[x3] dux consensi et subscripsi
Ego Haelfden[y3] dux consensi et subscripsi
[z3]Odda minister
Walgar[a4] minister
Alfehah minister
Aðelstan minister
Aðelmund minister
Aðelnoð minister
Alfsig[b4] minister
Wlmer[c4] minister
Helmstan minister
Wllaf minister
Wlfhelm minister
Wlnoð[d4]
Wlfbold
Alfere
Aþewold[e4]
Eadric
Winsi[f4]
Sigered

Aþelward
Alfere
Eadric
Aþelsi[g4]
Alfric
Aþelferð

[a] prodax FI [b] in marcissibilium E [c] eiulanda E; eius FI [d] debachando E, FI
[e] qua E [f] chochiti FI (*with marginal note,* ima cochyti) [g] incurribilis E (*supra lineam* de)
[h] *Omitted* FI [i] uternancium E [j] adoramina FI [k] auribus calce E; calice FI
[l] suauitatis FI [m] Athelstanus E [n] omnipotentis E [o] Wlstanum FI
[p] Ahemundesnes FI [q] spiritali E, FI [r] sacius FI [s] se E (*supra lineam*)
[t] pretitulare FI [u] obrixo E, FI [v] typho E [w] angeli FI [x] *Omitted* FI
[y] postulandria FI [z...z] fine sine E [a2...a2] inspirante atque annuente FI; *for* inspirate atque inuente (*compare S 425, S 426*) [b2] .xxxi. FI [c2] sobolis E [d2] gammulis E
[e2] stipulatorum FI [f2] nomina *omitted* FI [g2...g2] in quo curusque E [h2] pontem E
[i2] ponte E [j2] pontem E; spontem FI [k2] duleshoppe E [l2] ribbes FI [m2] hero quorum E
[n2] *Possibly for* caracteribus (*compare S 425*) [o2] Ayelstanus FI [p2] indiluculi FI
[q2] Wlfhelmus FI [r2] Thulfstanus E [s2...s2] *Omitted* FI [t2] Hoyael FI
[u2] subscripsi *omitted* FI [v2...v2] *Omitted* FI [w2] Judhald E [x2...x2] *Omitted* FI
[y2] Elfine E; *from this point onwards, witnesses are set out in two columns in* E
[z2] *From this point onwards, verbs of attestation are not given in* FI [a3...a3] *These three subscriptions appear after that of* Ƿired *at the end of the episcopal subscriptions* FI
[b3] Eepulf E [c3] Cenyald FI [d3] Beorstanus FI [e3] Yeodred FI [f3] Wlfinus FI
[g3] Ƿinsige *omitted* FI [h3] Elfeah E [i3] Elfred E [j3] Trohelmus FI [k3] Burkir E
[l3] Elfred E [m3] Ƿinsige E; *for* Cynesige [n3] Wlfelmus FI [o3] Wiredus FI
[p3] Alfwald FI [q3] Oseferd E [r3] Adelstan FI [s3] Utþred E [t3] Alstan FI
[u3] Reinwald FI [v3] Imper E [w3] Hadder FI [x3] Yurberd FI [y3] Hehalfden E
[z3] Et plures alii milites qui inseruntur in eadem carta consenserunt et subscripserunt E, *which stops here* [a4] *For* Wulfgar [b4] Alfsis FI; *for* Ælfsige [c4] *Perhaps for* Wulfmær
[d4] *For* Wulfnoð [e4] *For* Æþelwold [f4] *For* Winsige [g4] *For* Æþelsige

1 is a 934 grant of a large amount of land in the north-west of England by King Æthelstan to the York church. In its received form it has one diplomatic formula which demonstrates clearly that its text has been altered at some later stage. Nevertheless, there is reason to believe, as we shall see, that the document is fundamentally authentic and that other diplomatically peculiar features may actually have arisen as a result of this being an early example of a grant by an English king in the recently conquered Northumbrian kingdom.

The first task in an examination of **1** is to establish its text as the two copies of the witness-list as preserved in E and FI contain variations in the order in which certain individuals attest. The witness-list in E has been arranged in two columns and the *ministri* as given in FI are not present in E. A note in E shows that the scribe of that copy did see the *ministri* but chose not to copy them; it reads, 'Et plures alii milites qui inseruntur in eadem carta consenserunt et subscripserunt'. It is probably the case that the scribe of E omitted the *ministri* because there was not room on his page into which to copy all four columns of his exemplar. It is simple enough to correct this omission by providing those *ministri* in the order in which they are listed in FI.

The main discrepancy between the two copies concerns the bishops Eadwulf, Cenwald and Beornstan: in both manuscript versions Eadwulf, Cenwald and Beornstan attest as a group, and in the same order, but in E they are placed at the head of the list of bishops while in F1 they occur at the foot. A comparison with witness-lists of other contemporary Æthelstan charters suggests which order is correct. It is a unique feature of the early charters of Æthelstan's reign that the bishop of Lichfield is made to attest near to the top of the list of bishops (for which see Keynes, *Atlas*, table XXXVII; the high regard with which the bishopric of Lichfield was held is reflective of the Mercian roots of Æthelstan's power). We should therefore expect Eadwulf, Cenwald and Beornstan to attest immediately after the bishop of Lichfield, who is indeed the first bishop to attest in both manuscripts. This is the same as the order seen in E and not in F1. S 425 (*CantCC* 106), an extant original charter granting land to the *minister* Ælfwald in the Christ Church Canterbury archive, is particularly relevant here. In many ways it is identical to **1**. It too is an 'Æthelstan A' charter beginning with the same 'Fortuna fallentis' proem. It was granted on 28 May 934, that is, only ten days before **1** was made on 7 June 934. The almost exact similarity in charter diplomatic (S 425 [*CantCC* 106] and **1** were drawn up by the same draftsman) and the fact that they are records of events which happened within a short time of each other suggest that we should expect the retinue of men in attendance on the king to be virtually the same. And the position of Eadwulf, Cenwald and Beornstan in E agrees exactly with S 425 (*CantCC* 106). The only significant difference which remains between the copies in E and in F1 probably arose due to simple miscopying. Thus in F1, between the names Wulfhun and Ælfheah, the scribe has forgotten to insert the name Wynsige; this is probably an example of 'eye-skip' (parablepsy).

Stevenson's opinion regarding **1** was that it could 'hardly be anything but a later forgery' (the various comments made by Stevenson about this charter seem to have been personal communications to Farrer; thus when I refer to Stevenson in this context it is to his views as they are printed in Farrer, *EYC*; for this particular opinion of Stevenson, see p. 4). Whilst **1** does contain some oddities, its diplomatic features as a whole fit very well indeed with that remarkable series produced, between 928 and 935, by the scribe known as 'Æthelstan A' (the term 'Æthelstan A' was first used in Drögereit 1935, pp. 345–8; see also Chaplais 1965, pp. 59–60 and Keynes, *Diplomas*, pp. 42–4). The proem of the 'Fortuna fallentis' type is readily paralleled in other 'Æthelstan A' charters such as S 425 (*CantCC* 106), S 426 (BCS 704) and S 458 (BCS 745). In **1** Æthelstan is styled as 'rex Anglorum per omnipotentis dexteram, quae Christus est, totius Britannie regni solio sublimatus', which is either identical with, or very similar to, Æthelstan's royal style in S 403 (*Sel* 17), S 412 (BCS 674), S 413 (*Abing* 23), S 416 (BCS 677), S 417 (BCS 689), S 418 (*WinchNM* 10), S 418a, S 419 (*Shaft* 8) and S 425 (*CantCC* 106). The sequence of clauses which first specify the territory being granted ('in loco quem solicole...uocitant') and then the rights to the land the beneficiary was receiving ('ut ille...ea sine iugo exose seruitutis, cum pratis, pascuis, siluis, riuulis, omnibusque ad eam utilitatibus rite pertinentibus, quamdiu aura naribus spirabili, ocellorumque conuolatu cernibili utatur...') are again standard formulae of 'Æthelstan A' charters and can be found, for example, in S 417 (BCS 689), S 418a, S 425 (*CantCC* 106) and S 458 (BCS 745). 'Æthelstan A' is renowned for his ability to create charters which contain an elaborate Latin style. The sanction was one part of a charter which allowed 'Æthelstan A' the freedom to experiment. As such it is difficult to find the exact same formula as seen in **1** but it is very close to other sanctions in 'Æthelstan A' charters such as S 417 (BCS 689), S 425 (*CantCC* 106) and S 426 (BCS

704). An interesting variation of the phrase which introduces the sanction ('Si autem, quod absit, aliquis typo supercilii turgens hanc mee compositionis ac confirmationis breuiculam elidere uel infringere temptauerit') can be found in S 1044 (KCD 769), a much later charter of 1042x1044, where King Edward grants land in Kent to Æthelred. The style of the very detailed dating-clause which specifies the indiction, epact, day of the month and age of the moon and which begins with *huius namque...uiuente* and ends with a note about witnesses who will sign at the end of the document ('Cuius etiam inconcusse firmitatis auctoritas hiis testibus roborata constat...annotantur') is instantly reminiscent of other 'Æthelstan A' charters, for example, S 425 (*CantCC* 106) and S 426 (BCS 704) (although for more on the dating-clause of **1** see further below in the commentary). The most pressing reason for believing that **1** is fundamentally authentic is its very close similarity to S 425 (*CantCC* 106), in which King Æthelstan grants land to his *minister* Ælfwald. As we have seen, a very significant detail about S 425 (*CantCC* 106) is that it was issued after a meeting of the king's *witan* only ten days prior to the granting of **1**. It is therefore very encouraging that both S 425 (*CantCC* 106) and **1** make use of almost identical diplomatic formulae and that the principal witnesses in both charters are the same. S 425 (*CantCC* 106) and **1** provide a very real glimpse at the king's *witan* conducting business in different areas of the country and making use of the scribe, 'Æthelstan A'.

Despite the authentic basis of **1**, there are indications that this charter has suffered at least some later tampering to its text. The most obvious instance of this occurs in the dating-clause, where a date of 930 is given despite the fact that most details in the charter point to a 934 date as being correct. As we have already seen, the style of the dating-clause, which contains highly elaborate and specific dating criteria, is typical of 'Æthelstan A' productions. Because 'Æthelstan A' took such care to be specific about the date and place of issue, it is in itself striking that the incarnational date of 930, as given in **1**, cannot be correct for the charter. The date 930 does agree with the subsequent detail in **1** that it is the sixth year of Æthelstan's reign (Æthelstan acceded to the Mercian throne in 924, was consecrated later in 925 at Kingston-upon-Thames and became king of the English in 927; the regnal year in **1** has been reckoned from the time when Æthelstan was king of Mercia), but the detail of the indiction, epact, and concurrence all require that the year should be 934 (and it is this error which condemned **1** as a forgery in the eyes of Stevenson; see Farrer, *EYC*, p. 4). Also, some of the names of the witnesses could only belong to 934 and could not be seen to be attesting in 930. For example, among the bishops who attest, Beornstan was not ordained bishop until 931 and therefore could not have subscribed as a bishop as early as 930 (see *ASC A*, s.a. 931; Stevenson in Farrer, *EYC*, p. 5, makes the additional note that Burhric had only been appointed as bishop of Rochester in 934). Another striking feature of this dating clause is that it is identical, in all respects, to one found in a patently spurious diploma, drafted in the name of Æthelstan, which belongs to the Worcester archive, S 428 (BCS 701) (Dumville, *Wessex and England*, p. 168, n. 182, points out that S 428 [BCS 701] is probably a forgery based on **1** and S 406 [BCS 700]; see also J.A. Robinson, *St Oswald and the Church of Worcester*, British Academy Supplementary Papers v [London, 1919], pp. 3–51, at pp. 32–3). Stevenson suggests (in Farrer, *EYC*, p. 4) that this similarity indicates that each draftsman (of **1** and of S 428) was relying on the same genuine exemplar (now lost) in an attempt to create his own forgery.

Although there is an error in the dating clause, this is not reason enough to regard the whole document as a forgery. As Whitelock points out, this spurious charter from the

Worcester archive should not be taken to have a bearing on the authenticity of **1**, since S 428 (BCS 701) is preserved in an eleventh-century cartulary drawn up when York and Worcester were held in plurality and thus the Worcester cartularist could simply have been using **1** as an exemplar for his forgery (see Whitelock, *EHD*, no. 104). It seems reasonable to suggest, as Whitelock does, that the date of 930 in the text of **1** is probably due to later tampering in an attempt to make the date closer in line with the charter's statement that it was made at the time of the appointment of Wulfstan as archbishop in 931 (he was archbishop until 956; see Whitelock, *EHD*, no. 104).

There are other diplomatic oddities. **1** states that the grant is made over to God and to St Peter; such references to non-specific beneficiaries are immediately suspicious in an Anglo-Saxon diplomatic context. But it is important to note that this reference is followed in the very next instance not only by a statement which says that the grant took place when Wulfstan was archbishop but also by an *ut*-clause which effectively makes Wulfstan a beneficiary of the grant as well. Whitelock regarded the reference to Wulfstan's election as being a genuine element of **1** and, as we have seen, it is possible that the dating-clause in **1** was modified so that it agrees more closely with this statement about Wulfstan. Of course one could disagree with Whitelock and suggest that the phrase which notes Wulfstan's recent election was added at the same time as the dating-clause and this would mean that **1** originally was granted simply to God and to St Peter. If this were the case, then the addition of a reference to Wulfstan would have served to sharpen the connection to the York church. But it is also important to stress that it is perhaps not an odd feature that **1** is made over to God and St Peter. The evidence provided by coins of York for the early tenth century suggests that York and the York church had come to rely on its association with St Peter. The most remarkable testimony to this is provided by the series of so-called 'St Peter's coins' produced between *c.* 905 and 927 and which had the legend 'SCI PETRI MO' inscribed onto them (see above, pp. 50–1). It is possible that, in an era of viking depredations, the York church had come to require that gifts were associated with the patron saint of their church, in an attempt to make them less vulnerable to would-be defrauders.

Another diplomatic oddity is that, in addition to making a grant of Amounderness, the charter attempts to confirm estates which St Peter's church already possessed: '...I have granted in perpetuity not only it, but rather all the estates of that aforementioned church, namely of St Peter, Prince of the Apostles, bought with refined gold'. The normal practice of Anglo-Saxon charters is to specify just one estate or territory in any grant. Therefore to have a statement which adds 'all the estates of that aforementioned church' raises suspicion. It is difficult to make any firm resolution about this clause. It could be the result of later tampering with the charter, perhaps inserted at a time when York's estates were under threat and when it was desirable to possess a document which claimed ownership to the estates in question. But it is also very important to be aware of the unique historical situation to which **1** bears witness (on which see further below). Before Æthelstan conquered Northumbria in 927 (*ASC D*, s.a. 927), York and its surrounding territory had been heavily settled by vikings and the York church's assets were likely to have suffered as a result. Given their precarious situation, it is probable that the York church wanted to gain as much reassurance as possible from Æthelstan regarding their estates. And since beneficiaries of grants often had some input into the terms denoted, it may be that this clause should not be regarded as surprising.

Bounds of Amounderness

Stevenson also found the boundary clause of **1** questionable, perhaps primarily because it is written in Latin and not (as was usually the case) in Old English. But it should be remarked in this connection that although the bounds are in Latin, they have a format (*Primitus... recursus in mare*) which exactly parallels that of a standard Old English boundary clause (*Ærest...þanon eft on sæ*).

The bounds in **1** have been thoroughly discussed by Le Patourel 1993; they are notoriously vague, using only rivers as boundaries and therefore offer difficulties in interpretation.

1. *First from the sea* (mare) *up on the Cocker* ('crooked river'; see *DEPN*, p. 114) *as far as the spring/source* (fons) *of that river* (flumen). The bounds start at their northern-most point on the north-west coast near the Irish Sea and follow the line of the River Cocker to its source.

2. *From that spring/source straight to the other spring/source, which is called in English Dunshop*. As Le Patourel notes, this portion of the bounds provides particular difficulty as there is a gap of quite some distance between the River Cocker and the River Dunshop for which no details are given in **1**. It may be that the River Wyre, which became the boundary for the later hundred of Amounderness, provided the route **1**'s bounds took as they made their way towards the River Dunshop (Le Patourel 1993, p. 113, where it is noted that M. Gelling observed that the place-name 'Marshaw' (SD 591535) may have the meaning 'boundary shaw' which would lend authority to the notion that the River Wyre was the boundary at this point). As the River Wyre proceeds towards the River Dunshop, which is the next stage in **1**'s boundary clause, it flows past the modern-day town of Tower Lodge (SD 603539), and reaches an area to the north-west of the River Dunshop called Threaphaw Fell (SD 6254). If it is from here that **1**'s bounds flow 'into a spring called Duleshope' ('in...fontem qui dicitur...Duleshope') then the most obvious boundary marker for this section would be the Brennand River which meets Threaphaw Fell at SD 631547 and flows in a south-easterly direction to join the more major River Dunsop at SD 653533 (Le Patourel 1993, p. 115, makes the important observation that the reading of **1** as 'ab illo fonte directe in alium fontem qui dicitur Saxonice Duleshope' could equally well be 'ab illo *p*onte directe in alium *p*ontem qui dicitur Saxonice Duleshope' [my italics] as is suggested by Manuscript E's readings. If this is correct then the bounds may not have followed the River Brennand into the River Dunshop but may have deviated just after the town of Tower Lodge at SD 612539 and followed the Trough of Bowland instead which, as Le Patourel notes, is a 'very obvious feature'. The Trough of Bowland runs in a south-easterly direction and connects with the town of Dunsop Bridge at SD 658501).

3. *So, down the stream* (riuulus) *to the Hodder* ('pleasant stream'; see *DEPN*, p. 243) *? straight on to the Ribble* (if this place-name is English it might be derived from the adjective *ripel*, meaning 'tearing'; for more see *DEPN*, pp. 385–6; *CamDEPN*, p. 498, suggests that no reasonable solution has been proposed) *and so on that river* (flumen) *by way of half of the river-bed/channel* (alueus) *and back again to the sea* (mare). The remainder of the bounds in **1** seem to be clear enough. From Dunshop (which could either be the River Dunshop or the town Dunsop Bridge, depending on which manuscript reading is preferred), they follow the River Hodder southwards until they meet the River Ribble at SD 709371; from here the bounds turn westwards and follow the course of the River Ribble until it reaches the sea at SD 3526.

This relatively non-detailed tracing of the bounds of Amounderness represents the outline of a huge Anglo-Saxon grant which measures some fifteen miles from north to south and twenty-five miles from east to west; included within its bounds are the modern towns of Fleetwood, Blackpool, Lytham St Annes, Preston (on the Ribble) and the inland settlements of Garstang, Poulton-le-Fylde and Longridge (for a more detailed discussion, see Le Patourel 1993). This is an extremely large and unprecedented area being granted (Hart, *ECNE*, p. 117, believes this is the largest of all Anglo-Saxon grants). It is possible that these could be interpreted as a suspicious features in the diploma, perhaps later insertions by a draftsman seeking to extend the boundaries of the original grant.

There are, however, other possible explanations for the boundary clause of **1** being in Latin and lacking detail. It could be that the scribe of **1** entered a Latin summary of the Old English boundary clause which he found in his exemplar. This can be the case with later copies of charters preserved in cartularies. If this is true here, then it would explain both the problem of the boundary clause being in Latin and, because it is a summary, the fact that it lacks detail. It may be objected to this hypothesis that the other documents in the same York cartulary do not contain Latin summaries but rather preserve the Old English. But it should also be stressed that the Old English which is preserved in these other documents is extremely corrupted and the scribe of the cartulary copies evidently struggled to interpret his exemplars. It is impossible to know how many stages of copying had been carried out before **1** was recorded as we have it today, and it may be that, at some earlier interval than those copies which formed the basis of E and F1, the Old English boundary clause was removed. But it may be that a seemingly odd feature of **1**, the large amount of territory being granted, is actually the cause of the peculiar form of **1**'s boundary clause: perhaps it was impossible for those drawing up the limits of the territory, or for those providing the details of the area (who were quite likely to be the beneficiaries of the grant), to be precise about the landmarks involved. Æthelstan himself was the first southern king to grant land to the York archbishopric after a period of viking intrusion and settlement and those entrusted with the composition of the bounds in **1** may have been quite unfamiliar with the estate structure of the north and the methods that had been adopted there for granting land (an absence of shire organisation in the north, which was the normal situation in the south, may have confused those men employed to draw up the limits of the grant in **1**. Faced with this predicament, the draftsmen reverted to an older mode of boundary description and abandoned the use of Old English in favour of Latin; as a whole, estate structure in the north was vastly different, often involving so-called 'multiple estates'; there is extensive literature about such matters for which see Hadley, *Northern*, pp. 94–164). If so, it is not surprising that specific vills are not granted and that the bounds of the estate seem large. And this interpretation makes sense in the context of the archive. Later York charters, of King Eadwig (**2**) and of King Edgar (**4**), show new levels of understanding of northern estate structure. And this is accounted for by the introduction of new phrases and diplomatic innovations (see the commentaries to **2** and **4**). But perhaps the most pressing reason of all for accepting the basic details as supplied by **1**, is that, in the event, the large estate in question was not claimed as a possession by the York church in later years and therefore there is no ostensible motive for its having been forged. (It seems more than likely that on Æthelstan's death in 939, and with the return of viking rulers to York, Amounderness would have been removed from the York church's possession; but York may well have retained **1** in the hope that Amounderness could later be reclaimed.)

Historical Background

The wording of **1** carefully implies a role for the archbishop rather than assigning ownership to the York community as a whole: this was perhaps meant as an incentive to him to act, in a sense, as a West Saxon ambassador (for a full discussion of the remarkable Latin of the 'Æthelstan A' charters, see Woodman, forthcoming). The archbishop at this time was Wulfstan I who, having been chosen as head of the see in 931, appears to have played a major role in Northumbrian life and politics until his death in 956 (Whitelock 1959, pp. 71–5 and Keynes 1999*b*). Much of what can be learned about his early career comes from his attestations in charters and from the northern recension of the *ASC*. From the start of his archiepiscopate he attests (in second place behind Æthelhelm, archbishop of Canterbury) all of Æthelstan's charters until 935 (Keynes, *Atlas*, table XXXVII), perhaps suggesting that Æthelstan, if not the sponsor of Wulfstan's election, was at least in favour of his holding the position (see Keynes 1999*b*). There then follows a period (from 936 to 941) when Wulfstan no longer attests and seems to be absent from the king's court. Unfortunately, there is no mention of Wulfstan's activities during this period in either the *ASC* or any other (northern) source and so it is impossible to tell whether Wulfstan had actively rebelled against Æthelstan's rule, whether he had fallen from favour at the southern court, or whether he was simply absent for some unknown reason. When Wulfstan reappears in the historical record in 943, however, it is on the side of the Scandinavians and in opposition to English hegemony ('Here King Edmund besieged King Olaf and Archbishop Wulfstan in Leicester, and he might have controlled them had they not escaped from the stronghold in the night'; *ASC D*, s.a. 943). It is clear, then, that Wulfstan's (and thus York's) support was not guaranteed (for more, see above, pp. 53–5). The history of Wulfstan's relations with the subsequent kings of Anglo-Saxon England, Edmund (939–46) and Eadred (946–55), is equally turbulent and indicative of a northern polity which was, for southern powers, intensely difficult to control (Wulfstan's actions were so clearly rebellious that King Eadred had him imprisoned in 952; *ASC D*, s.a. 952; for a summary of the various dealings of this time, see A. Campbell, 'Two Notes on the Norse Kingdoms in Northumbria', *EHR* lvii [1942], pp. 85–97 and Sawyer 1995). Of course Wulfstan's changing of allegiance should be judged from a northern point of view as well. It is quite possibly the case that this support for first one king and then another made perfect sense for the York archbishopric which would have been equally aware of the power (both potential and real) of both Wessex and the rulers of the Dublin Scandinavians (for the continual presence and rule of Dublin Scandinavian figures in York, see Smyth, *Scandinavian* II, pp. 90–4 and 155–90 and Downham, *Viking Kings*, pp. 63–135).

In the context of these political quicksands, the area represented by the grant of land in **1** becomes very important since, although there were a variety of routeways across the Pennines to York, the Amounderness territory did block one approach for any Dublin Norse who landed in this part of England and wanted to proceed to York. But the north-western part of the country was not just a landing ground for those Scandinavians who desired to make their way to York. In fact, by the time Æthelstan came to grant **1**, there had already been Scandinavian settlement in this area. Although Anglo-Saxon sources, most notably the *ASC*, make no mention of Scandinavian expansion in a north-westerly direction, Wainwright has shown that an Irish source known as the *The Fragmentary Annals* contains a story about the invasion and settlement of Scandinavians headed by a certain Ingimund which has a definite claim to represent genuine events (see F.T. Wainwright, 'Ingimund's Invasion', *EHR* lxiii [1948], pp. 145–69; see further Smyth,

Scandinavian I, p. 62). And the work of various scholars on the Scandinavian place-names in north-western England can be used to support the view of Scandinavian settlement there, although recently the scale of this settlement has been questioned; see Ekwall, *Scandinavians*, p. 95, Fellows-Jensen 1990 and G. Fellows-Jensen, *The Vikings and their Victims: the Verdict of the Names*, The Dorothea Coke Memorial Lecture in Northern Studies delivered at University College London 21 February 1994 (London, 1995; repr. Birmingham, 1998), pp. 18–19; for the suggestion that the idea of a mass Scandinavian migration into the north-west, and into Amounderness, is inappropriate, see N.J. Higham, 'Viking-Age Settlement in North-Western Countryside: Lifting the Veil', in Hines *et al.*, *Land, Sea and Home*, pp. 297–311 and Watson 2011 respectively. Since **1** needs to be seen against this background of Scandinavian settlement, it is with considerable interest that **1** preserves the statement that Æthelstan himself bought the land in question for the York archbishopric (*propria et non modica emi pecunia*). This is highly unusual: normally the recipient of the grant would be responsible for its purchase. Clearly something entirely extraordinary is represented by **1** (we must remember the fact that **1** is the first recorded grant by a southern king to the York church). It may be that Æthelstan, with his growing political superiority, was the only one capable of carrying out such a deal with the settled Scandinavians. Amounderness is itself a Scandinavian territorial name (the first element is formed of the personal name *Agmundr* or *Ǫgmundr*, while the second element may derive from Old English *hērness*, which means 'a district in subjection to secular or ecclesiastical authority'; see *DEPN*, p. 9, Fellows-Jensen, *SSNNW*, p. 99 and Fellows-Jensen 1990), perhaps suggesting that it had belonged to a Scandinavian just before Æthelstan bought it. Certainly it represented a considerable investment by Æthelstan.

And **1** was perhaps also a politically important grant which satisfied the mutual interests of Æthelstan and the York church. It allowed King Æthelstan not only to cultivate ties with the York see (and in this way to guarantee its loyalty) but it also indicated that perhaps he expected them to hold the coastal area against the arrival of Scandinavians or, at the least, to be less receptive to viking intrusion at York. And, from the York church's point of view, they now possessed a document which gave them rights to an area of land which had previously been densely settled by Scandinavians.

1 tells that the king's *witan* had gathered at Nottingham and that it was there that this grant was drawn up (the 'Æthelstan A' charters are the first to be so precise about the date of their transaction and the place of issue; Keynes, *Diplomas*, p. 35). It seems likely that Æthelstan broke his journey at Nottingham (Nottingham was situated in a disputed zone of influence between southern kings and northern kings and so formed a symbolic place for the *witan* to congregate), in 934, as he was making his way north on an expedition to Scotland. **1** thus affords a remarkable glimpse of the type of retinue that Æthelstan would have taken with him on such a military foray, including as it does various Welsh sub-kings and Scandinavian earls. The ealdormen Osferth and Ælfstan, and the earls Regenwold, Thurferth, Hadd, Inhwær and Halfdene all cease to attest any further charters of King Æthelstan and it is just possible, as Hart suggests (Hart, *ECNE*, p. 118), that these men had been killed whilst campaigning in Scotland (although with the disappearance of 'Æthelstan A' in 934/5, charters no longer preserve such detailed records of major national assemblies and so it may not be surprising that the northern earls no longer attest).

The Domesday folios for Yorkshire show that Amounderness later became an area of waste and devastation (Lancashire, the county in which Amounderness is today situated, did not exist in 1086; see GDB, f. 301v, for the assessment of Amounderness). Owing to a lack of documentation, it is impossible to discover who had possession of the district at subsequent periods but, by the time of the Domesday survey, it had passed away from royal control and into the hands of the then earl of Northumbria, Tostig. Clearly Amounderness had been an area over which different peoples and powers had tried to gain influence. The toponymy of the region, and the evidence afforded by the coins found in the Cuerdale hoard (for the hoard, see J.A. Graham-Campbell, 'The Cuerdale Hoard: a Viking and Victorian Treasure', in *Viking Treasure from the North West: the Cuerdale Hoard in its Context: Selected Papers from the Vikings of the Irish Sea Conference, Liverpool, 18–20 May 1990*, ed. J.A. Graham-Campbell (Liverpool, 1992), pp. 1–14), suggest that no one political power had managed to exert itself and rather that Amounderness remained an area over which rival authorities could attempt to win control.

2

King Eadwig grants [Arch]bishop Oscytel twenty hides (mansas) *of land at Southwell, Nottinghamshire, with dependencies at Normanton, Upton, Fiskerton, Farnsfield, Kirklington, Morton, Gibsmere, Bleasby, Goverton, Halloughton and Halam*. A.D. 958 [for 956]

F. York, Minster Library and Archives, L 2/1 (*Mag. Reg. Alb.*), pt. I, 58r–59r: copy, s. xiv[med]
Rubric: Donatio facta per regem Eadwy eidem Echetello episcopo de possessionibus quibusdam in Suthwell.
Ed.: a. *Mon. Angl.*, iii. 129, from F
b. *Mon. Angl.* (rev. edn.), vi, pt. 3, p. 1176 (no. 3)
c. Kemble 472 (without bounds), from F
d. Birch 1029 and Birch 1348 (bounds only), from F
e. Pierquin, *Recueil*, pt. 2, no. 113
f. Farrer, *EYC*, no. 2, from F
Translated: Whitelock, *EHD*, pp. 556–7 (no. 108)
Listed: Sawyer 659; Hart, *ECNE*, no. 114
Edited from F

Domino nostro Iesu Christo imperpetuum regnante. Uisibilia et inuisibilia, temporalia et eternalia, ab ipso erunt discernenda. Et ideo ego Eadwy rex Anglorum, pro amore Domini nostri Iesu Christi,[a] cuidam meo desiderabili episcopo Oscytello concedo partem mee telluris ubi dicitur [b]7 Sudpellan[b] .xx. mansas in hereditatem cum pascuis, pratis, siluis et omnibus ad se rite maioris minorisue pertinentibus. Quamdiu uixerit eam utiliter possideat et post illius transitum cuicumque sibi uidetur, siue notis siue ignotis, derelinquat. Sit autem hec donacio regis predicta ab omni obstaculo mundiali preter hiis tribus: pontis, expeditione et arcis constructione [c]et hostilitate.[c] Si quis uero catholicorum aut ortodoxorum hanc donacionem regis augere uoluerit, augeat illi Deus temporalia bona; si uero minuere aut uiolare, sciat se cum apostatis inferno inferiori demersum esse, nisi in hac mortali uita ante obitum emendauerit quod inique gessit. Acta est prefata donacio anno dominice incarnacionis .dcccc.luiii. indiccione .xiiii. Istis terminis circumcincta uidetur terra esse.[d]

Ðis sinda ðam landgemare into Sudƿellan:[e] of ðam forda 7lang[f] Greotan sƿa[g] se ealda stream[h] sceot[i] beeastan 7 besuðan ðam egete;[j] þon gerihte ðurħ niƿa[k] tunes broc sceot[l] on Greotan[m] up be broce besuðan sunninsale[n] holme; ꝥ[o] on bradan lege[p] ƿeasteƿearde;[q] þanon to cottan; of cottan 7lang strāt on holan broc; 7lang broces ꝥ[o] up be þan hlince;[r] an furlang ƿiðinnan þane graf;[s] ꝥ[o] ut on þa ac; of þere[t] ac a be þan heafdan[u] on þone norðran þorn; of þam þorne on Greotan;[v] 7lang Greotan ꝥ[w] eft[x] on þone ford.

Ðis sint þa longemaere to Normantune: of Greotan[v] to þere dil halle; andlang þas[y] hagan[z] on þaene broc; andlang broces ꝥ[o] on þa dene; 7lang dene a be þan heafidan on ðam len broc; of þan on hise; a be þare hicse[a2] on þa ealdarn treot; 7lang straet ꝥ[o] eft[x] on Greotan.[b2]

Ðis sind ðan landgemare to[c2] Uptune: of[d2] Greotan[m] 7lang þare ealdan strat[e2] benorðan hocer ƿuda; of þære[f2] strat ofer þaene mor to dreng[g2] haga[h2] norðeƿeardan; þanen up to ðare aeppel treou;[i2] of þiere appels treou[i2] ongerihte ofer mid þaene miclan beorh[j2] inon þaene mor on þ[k2] fule fleot; 7lang fleotes[l2] ꝥ[o] eft[x] on Greotan.[m]

Ðis sint þa landgemare to Fiscetune:[m2] 7lang Greotan[m] on Traentan on hasele[n2] forð; of ðam forda andlang streot[o2] to cƿeorn[p2] dune; of cƿeorn[q2] dune ongerihtoñ on niƿan[r2] tunes[s2] broc; 7lang broces[t2] ꝥ[o] eaft[u2] on Greotan.[m]

Ðis sint ðam tunes[v2] ðe birað into Sudƿellan[e] mid sacce 7 mid sacne: Fearnefelð, Cyrlingtune,[w2] Nordmantune, Uptune, Mortune, Fiscertune,[x2] Gypesmere,[y2] Blisetune, Gofertune,[z2] Healhtune, Healum.

On Fearnesfelda[a3] gebyrað tƿega[b3] manna hlot landes[c3] into Sudƿellan;[e] on Healun [d3]a se[d3] seoxta[e3] acer 7 ðreom[f3] manna hlot; on Normantune a se ðridda acer;[g3] on Fiscertune[h3] dam tƿegen[i3] dales 7 feoƿer manna hlot ealles ðaes[j3] landes. Ego Eadwi rex cum consensu episcoporum et doctorum meorum sancto sygillo expressi[k3]

Ego Odo archiepiscopus confirmaui	[*Canterbury*]
Ego Eadgar[l3] frater Regis subscripsi	
Ego Oscytel archiepiscopus corroboraui	[*Dorchester/York*]
Alsi[m3] episcopus	[*Winchester*]
Brihtelmus episcopus	[*London*]
Daniel episcopus	[*Cornwall*]
Eleƿaldus[n3] episcopus	[*Crediton*]
Wlsi[o3] episcopus	[*Sherborne*]
Aðulf episcopus	[*Elmham*]
Eadmund dux	
Aðelstan dux	

Gunnere dux
Aðelsi[p3] dux
Aðelmund dux
Urm dux
Alfere dux
Aðelpad[q3] dux
Leot dux
Uhred[r3] dux
Anfred dux
Elfeh[s3] minister
Wlfric minister
Alfsi[m3] minister
Alfric minister
Alsi[m3] minister
Eadric minister
Eadwald minister
Alfwald minister
Alfsi[m3] minister
Osulf minister
Ospard minister
Alfwine minister
Oswy minister
Wlfric minister
Byrnric minister
Alðelsi[p3] minister

[a] Southwell *has been written in the margin next to* Christi F [b...b] *For* æt Sudpellan [c...c] et hostilitate *perhaps a later interpolation in* F (*compare S 594*) [d] *The Old English boundary clause is highly corrupt; see the note on editorial method, pp. 83–4* [e] Sudyellan F [f] *Where* F *has an ampersand in the boundary clause, a Tironian et has been used* [g] sia F [h] rtrean F [i] poeot F [j] esete F [k] niya F [l] sofot F [m] Sreotan F [n] *Perhaps for* sunningale *(see commentary)* [o] y F [p] lese F [q] yeasteẏfarde F [r] hlinee F [s] sraf F [t] yfre F [u] hfafdan F [v] Streotan F [w] ħ F [x] est F [y] yar F [z] hasan F [a2] *Perhaps a form of* hecge *(see commentary)* [b2] Steotan F [c2] F *has incorrectly written* to *twice here* [d2] os F [e2] scrat F [f2] yefre F [g2] drens F [h2] hasa F [i2] treon F [j2] veorh F [k2] y F; *possibly for* þam [l2] fleocer F [m2] Fircetune F [n2] harele F [o2] *Perhaps for* Greot *or possibly a corruption of* stræt *(see commentary)* [p2] oyeorn F [q2] cẏ forn F [r2] niyan F [s2] tuner F [t2] brocer F [u2] east F [v2] tuner F [w2] Cyrlinstune F [x2] Fircertune F [y2] Sypermere F [z2] Sofertune F [a3] Fearnerfelda F [b3] tyesa F [c3] lander F [d3...d3] are F [e3] reoxta F [f3] dreon F [g3] arer F [h3] Fircertune F [i3] tyesen F [j3] dans F [k3] expresse F*; the witnesses are copied across the page* F [l3] Eagelr F [m3] *For* Ælfsige [n3] Eleyaldus F*; for* Ælfpold [o3] *For* Wulfsige [p3] *For* Æðelsige [q3] Adelyad F*; for* Æðelpold [r3] *For* Uhtred [s3] *For* Ælfheah

2 is a grant of the Southwell estate in Nottinghamshire, together with various dependencies. As Stenton suggested, it 'certainly seems to be founded upon a tenth-century original' (Stenton, *Types*, p. 79), but it does contain some unusual diplomatic elements which require explanation.

Most of the diplomatic formulae used in **2** are conventional; it begins with a verbal invocation which is of a type readily found in other charters of Eadwig, for example S 598 (BCS 976), S 603 (*Abing* 61), S 604 (BCS 979) and so on. The proem is rather short: 'Uisibilia et inuisibilia, temporalia et eternalia, ab ipso erunt discernenda'. But this is not an unusual feature. Although some proems of King Eadwig's charters are quite long and also concern some rather 'exotic' themes, there are also those which are short and to the point (the year 956, when **2** was composed, witnessed the production of an abnormally large number of diplomas, which may have resulted in greater variety in the styles of proem; Kelly, *Selsey*, pp. 83–4). For example, an extant original, S 649 (BCS 1003), which sees King Eadwig granting land to his *minister* Wulfstan displays an equally perfunctory proem, which suggests that we should not question that in **2**. The remainder of diplomatic formulae in **2** can be paralleled in other diplomas issued by King Eadwig. Eadwig's royal style in **2** is simple (*rex Anglorum*); although this does not equate with some of the elaborate claims of other genuine contemporary diplomas (for example, S 649 [BCS 1003]), it is certainly found in other charters of Eadwig (for example, S 589 [BCS 938] or S 642 [BCS 992]). The clauses which specify the rights to the land conferred to Oscytel ('quamdiu uixerit eam utiliter possideat et post illius transitum cuicumque sibi uidetur, siue notis siue ignotis, derelinquat') are standard formulae for mid-tenth-century charters. It is possible that a later copyist has inserted the words *et hostilitate* at the end of the clause concerning the three common burdens, since these words are not normally found in this position in charters of Eadwig: compare S 594 (*Abing* 54). The sentence which introduces the boundary clause in **2** ('Istis terminis circumcincta uidetur terra esse') is found in S 581 (*Abing* 53), a 956 charter of Eadwig. Eadwig's attestation, which refers to 'cum consensu episcoporum et doctorum meorum sancto sygillo expressi', is of particular interest. This use of 'doctorum' is only found in three other charters in the mid-tenth century: S 646 (BCS 999 and 1347), an extant original of 957 in which King Eadwig grants land to Archbishop Oda (probably from the Ely archive and written by a royal scribe; Keynes, *Diplomas*, p. 67); and S 772 (BCS 1229) and S 773 (BCS 1234), both 969 grants by King Edgar to his *minister* Ælfwold and both preserved in the Worcester archive (Dumville, *English Caroline Script and Monastic History: Studies in Benedictinism, A.D. 950–1030* [Woodbridge, 1992], pp. 70–3, argues that S 772 [BCS 1229] may have been forged on the basis of S 773 [BCS 1234]). The combination and order of these clauses within **2** are also mirrored elsewhere in the corpus of Eadwig's charters. S 657 (*Abing* 81) is a genuine diploma of Eadwig in favour of his *minister* Wulfric, dated 958. Although the diplomatic formulae used in S 657 (*Abing* 81) are not identical, the themes they describe are similar to those in **2**; and the order in which these elements occur is the same, the only real difference being that the dating-clause follows the witness-list of S 657 (*Abing* 81) whereas in **2** it precedes it. There is one error in the main text of **2**, which involves the dating-clause. The indiction points to a date of 956 whereas the incarnational date is given as 958. The indiction date of 956 should be preferred, for, in 958, Eadwig was no longer king of this part of England, as his brother, Edgar, had been chosen in his place (see **3** and *ASC BC*, s.a. 957). This error is no great cause for concern. At the point in the text of **2** at which the incarnational date occurs, there is a cluster of 'i's both in the Roman numeral itself and in the beginning of the following word, 'indiccione', which raises the possibility that a simple error of miscopying has taken place.

Perhaps a more suspicious feature of **2** concerns the details of the estate being conveyed: the dispositive clause of **2** notes that twenty hides of land at Southwell have been granted to Oscytel and it is only in the vernacular boundary clause that the precise identities of the estates granted is revealed. Such a format is untypical of Anglo-Saxon diplomatic and leaves the possibility that the vernacular boundary clauses have been added to an otherwise genuine diploma at some point after the original composition of **2**. But it may also be the case that the draftsman of the charter felt it inappropriate to list in the dispositive section all of the details of the estates being granted and instead left it to the boundary clause to provide the bulk of the necessary information. There are extant Anglo-Saxon charters which display similar diplomatic features and which have therefore been judged to be spurious in their received form: see, for example, S 630 (*Shaft* 21). But these examples should not have a bearing on our judgment of **2**, since it is concerned with a grant of land in the Danelaw. As such **2** deals with a type of 'multiple estate' that is distinctively characteristic of northern England in which a central manor, Southwell, is surrounded by vills dependent on it, Normanton, Upton, Fiskerton, Farnsfield, Kirklington, Morton, Gibsmere, Bleasby, Goverton, Halloughton and Halam (Jones 1975 has shown the very great similarity between this system in the north of England and that in Wales; see also Jones 1961, p. 200). The problem for the draftsman of **2**, who was compiling his document according to the diplomatic standards of King Eadwig's time, was knowing how to incorporate the details of such a grant within his charter template. The use of the dispositive section to name the central manor and the number of hides being granted and then the boundary clause for the extended details of the dependencies and their bounds seems an entirely reasonable solution. It may be that another unusual feature of **2**, its use of the expression 'sake and soke' in the boundary clause, also occurred as part of an attempt to deal with this 'multiple estate'. Although this expression is hitherto unprecedented in Anglo-Saxon diplomatic history, it appears in an undisputed charter of 959, S 681 (*Pet* 14), and Stenton regarded it as genuine: he suggested that the use of 'manlot' in the same passage is one which suggests some antiquity; 'manlot' is a word of Scandinavian origin and may have been used to apply to a portion of land which was granted to one of the Scandinavian soldiers who settled in the area (for 'sake and soke', see Stenton, *Types*, p. 79 and, for a more precise definition, Hadley, *Northern*, pp. 167–72; for 'manlot', see Stenton, *ASE*, pp. 514–15 and Faith, *English Peasantry*, p. 147; for more about estate structure in the north at this time, see K.M. Hall, 'Pre-Conquest Estates in Yorkshire', in Le Patourel, Long and Pickles, *Yorkshire Boundaries*, pp. 25–38). The expression 'sake and soke' can be used to denote, among other privileges, the jurisdictional rights enjoyed by certain major lords over estates within a territory (see further Hadley, *Northern*, pp. 168–70). In **2**, 'sake and soke' is used to detail the relationship of various vills that were somehow dependent on the central manor, Southwell. If we can accept, as Stenton does, that 'sake and soke' is a genuine element of **2**, then this seems to be good reason to suggest that the vernacular boundary clause in its extant form was inserted at the time of the original compilation of **2** (for Southwell as a major soke centre in Nottinghamshire, see Hart, *Danelaw*, pp. 246–8 and Hadley, *Northern*, p. 123). It may even be the case, as we shall see, that the expressions seen in **2** such as 'sake and soke', which in part define the jurisdictional terms of the grant, are to be connected to the cares and actions of the recipient of **2**, Oscytel.

The very large number of diplomas issued in 956 alone allows for unique comparative opportunities. On the basis of witness-lists, Keynes has identified four principal groupings of charters, each of which represents the output of a single meeting of the king's *witan* (Keynes, *Diplomas*, pp. 48–68). **2** is one of the few charters whose witness-list falls outside of these groupings. The most likely cause of the discrepancy in **2** is that it is concerned with a grant of land in the north of England. We therefore encounter persons hitherto unknown and not usually present at a meeting of the southern English king's council: ealdormen such as Gunner, Urm and Leot. These are men with Scandinavian names and it is likely that they were figures who were closely associated with, and formed their careers in, the Danelaw; they were individuals who had some standing in the localities in the north and east but did not retain such influence elsewhere in the country (for more about such individuals, see Abrams 2008). And this seems to be confirmed by the evidence of their attestations in charters of a later date. Gunner is present in S 674 (*Pet* 13), S 679 (**3**), S 712 (**4**), S 712a and S 716 (**5**): three of these are charters preserved in the York archive, S 674 is in the Peterborough archive, and, although it is unknown which archive S 712a originally belonged to, it is concerned with a grant of land in Derbyshire (for the possibility that Gunner can be found attesting a charter of 949, S 550 [BCS 882], and of 956, S 633 [BCS 937], see Brooks, Gelling and Johnson 1984, p. 144, n. 31). It is surely significant, then, that these are all charters which deal with estates in the north and the east of England, are preserved in archives from the same region, and are therefore firmly associated with the area of the Danelaw. These connections are corroborated by the attestations of Urm, who appears in S 674 (*Pet* 13) and S 679 (**3**); and also of Leot, who appears in S 679 (**3**) and S 681 (*Pet* 14). **2** therefore provides invaluable witness to the composition of Danelaw society in the year 956 (for more detailed discussion of these issues, see Abrams 2008).

The recipient of **2** is Archbishop Oscytel. Until recently, an ambiguous annal for 954 in the *ASC* has been thought to imply that after Archbishop Wulfstan I's release from prison, he was made bishop of Dorchester rather than being permitted to return to his see at York and that Oscytel therefore exchanged sees with Wulfstan I and became archbishop of York in his stead (Whitelock 1959, pp. 73–5 and above, p. 54, n. 198, for the interpretation of the 954 annal). This position was strengthened by the annal for 971 in the *ASC* which, when recording Oscytel's death, states: 'who was first consecrated as a diocesan bishop, of Dorchester, and afterwards consecrated archbishop of York by the consent of King Eadred and of all his councillors' (*ASC BC*, s.a. 971). Since Eadred died in 955, this was taken as confirmation that Oscytel had indeed been made archbishop of York already before 955. But, in a recent article, Barrow has questioned this sequence of events (Barrow 2004). She stresses that for the years 957–8 Oscytel attests as *episcopus* rather than *archiepiscopus* and she also doubts the testimony of the 971 annal in the *ASC*, describing it as 'garbled'. For Barrow, Oscytel did not become archbishop until 958/9 and she thinks there was therefore a vacancy at York in the intervening period.

This is an important suggestion because, if Barrow's reasoning is accepted, **2** and **3** would have to be viewed as grants to Oscytel while he was bishop of Dorchester rather than archbishop of York and therefore that the Dorchester diocese included parts of Nottinghamshire at this time. However, there are fundamental difficulties with this revised interpretation. The first problem lies with Barrow's suggestion that the annal for 971 in *ASC BC* is 'garbled'. Since the exemplar of *ASC BC* was written within a generation of 971 (see Simon Taylor, *The Anglo-Saxon Chronicle, A Collaborative Edition: 4: MS B* (Cambridge, 1983), pp. xxiii–xxiv), it is unlikely that its details are incorrect. It would also be strange that an annalist writing at the end of Edgar's reign might think that Oscytel had been consecrated to York in Eadred's reign if in fact that had been one of Edgar's promotions. Secondly, it seems unproblematic that Oscytel, after 954/5 and until 959, continues to attest as *episcopus* even though he has now replaced Wulfstan as archbishop of York. This may rather be a reflection of the fact that Oscytel had been uncanonically translated from Dorchester to York and that Wulfstan I was alive until 956. Until the division of the kingdom in 957, Oscytel attests all of Eadwig's diplomas as *episcopus* usually after Ælfsige, bishop of Winchester; but it is interesting to note that in S 615 (*Abing* 62), S 581 (*Abing* 53), S 630 (*Shaft* 19) and S 616 (*Sel* 19), all dated 956, and in S 574 (BCS 987) dated 957, Oscytel takes precedence over Ælfsige and the most likely explanation is that he was at this moment archbishop of York. After the division of the kingdom in 957, Oscytel continues to attest Edgar's charters of the north and the midlands as *episcopus* and most usually at the head of the episcopal attestations: see S 674 (*Pet* 13), S 675 (BCS 1042), S 678 (*Abing* 82), S 676 (BCS 1037) and S 676a; once again, this elevated status suggests that Oscytel is already considered archbishop of York. Oscytel first attests as *archiepiscopus* from 959 (see, for example, S 673 [*Abing* 84], S 680 [BCS 1051], S 681 [*Pet* 14], S 682 [*Abing* 85] etc.) and, since Brooks has highlighted a story in the *Chronicon abbatiae Rameseiensis* showing that Oscytel travelled to Rome in 958/9 to collect the *pallium*, this suggests a reason why Oscytel continued to attest as *episcopus* in the years 956 (the death of Wulfstan I) to 959. Indeed, for Brooks, tenth-century archbishops went to Rome 'for their pall if they had been uncanonically translated to their metropolitan church from another see' (see N. Brooks, 'Oswald', in *ODNB*). Barrow questions this story in the *Chronicon abbatiae Rameseiensis* on the basis that no other source documents the trip (Barrow 2004); but since there is very little extant information in general about journeys to collect the *pallium*, this alone does not discount the testimony of the Ramsey *Chronicon*. In summary, it seems likely that, following Wulfstan I's release from prison in 954, Oscytel was promoted to be archbishop of York while Wulfstan I was given Oscytel's old see at Dorchester. Upon Wulfstan I's death in 956, Oscytel wanted to secure the *pallium* to confirm his position as archbishop but, for some unknown reason, his journey to Rome was delayed until 958/9. Oscytel was also permitted to keep his old see of Dorchester while in charge of the York church (for this practice, see Whitelock 1959, pp. 73–5 and above, pp. 55–6). **2** and **3** should be regarded as grants of land to Oscytel as archbishop of York (I am most grateful to Prof. N. Brooks for his generous advice about Oscytel).

It may be that the election of Oscytel as archbishop, whose name contains Scandinavian elements, was part of a policy of King Eadwig which sought to incorporate those potentially rebellious Scandinavian-settled areas into his kingdom. Oscytel owned lands in Leicestershire and indeed most of the archbishops appointed to the York see after Wulfstan I (d. 956) seem to have had links to eastern counties: this may have been a deliberate ploy, as these men, already familiar with an Anglo-Scandinavian society, would have adapted to the situation at York well (see Whitelock 1959, pp. 73–4 and Wareham 1996, pp. 48–9). It seems likely that the presence of vikings at York had negative effects for the landholding of the archbishopric and **2** therefore represents a significant attempt at the strengthening of the archbishopric's assets in the Danelaw region. Oscytel emerges as a man concerned to augment the landed resources of the York archbishopric: he is the direct recipient of **2** and **3** and Archbishop Oswald's *Memorandum* (**6**) tells us that it was Oscytel who bought the estate in **5** for the York archbishopric: it may therefore be the case that he should be credited with the acquisition of **4** as well. Oswald's *Memorandum* (**6**) also supplies the statement that Oscytel received some estates which had been forfeited to him due to 'unlawful marriage' (*unrihtan hæmede*). This raises the possibility that Oscytel, during his time as archbishop, had managed to implement a system of law in the York area the rules of which were subsequently adhered to (see also above, p. 57). Although this is a remarkable achievement in itself, it is perhaps also important in any consideration of the details given in **2**. It has already been noted that **2** is unusual for its use of the jurisdictional expression 'sake and soke'. Since **6** suggests that Oscytel may have been concerned with the implementation of a legal infrastructure, it may be that it was his involvement in particular which led to the development and use of the expression 'sake and soke'. As Oscytel was the first archbishop to be appointed after the time of viking rule at York, it seems entirely likely that he wanted to be able to define exactly on what terms the archbishopric held its estates in an area which was heavily settled by Scandinavians. Perhaps it was Oscytel himself who had pursued the adoption of the legal expression 'sake and soke' and who therefore influenced the form of the boundary clause seen in **2**.

It is unclear whether there was already a church at Southwell by the time **2** was granted to Oscytel. An entry in the *Secgan be þam Godes sanctum þe on Engla lande ærost reston* states that the relics of a certain Eadburh were buried at Southwell (see Rollason 1978, p. 89) and since this part of the *Secgan* seems to have been derived from a ninth-century list, then this suggests the presence of at least some kind of religious centre in the pre-Viking period (but see also the comments of Dixon, Owen and Stocker 2001, p. 255, who suggest that the first record of a church at Southwell occurs in the early eleventh century); perhaps **2** was intended as a grant to revitalise a Southwell church that had experienced particularly difficult times during the viking settlement. Hadley has tentatively suggested an identification for Eadburh as the early eighth-century abbess of Repton and, if this can be accepted, she further wonders whether there had once been a nunnery at Southwell which was in some way associated with Repton (Hadley, *Northern*, pp. 231–2; for the location of the Anglo-Saxon minster in relation to the present-day Southwell church, see Dixon, Owen and Stocker, *ibid.*, pp. 256–7). Southwell may also have been a sometime residence for the archbishops of York as, in 1051, Archbishop Ælfric is said to have died there (*John of Worcester II*, s.a. 1051). Archbishop Cynesige, Ælfric's successor, favoured the community at Southwell by providing it with a gift of bells (*Chronicle of the Archbishops of York*, pp. 343–4). Ealdred, the last Anglo-Saxon archbishop of York, is noted in our sources as being the most generous of the archbishops towards Southwell; not only did he endow Southwell with lands bought from his own money but he also built a refectory there, and this may be an indication of that archbishop's desire to establish a *vita communis* for the Southwell community, just as he did at Beverley (see *Chronicle of the Archbishops of York*, pp. 353–4 and below, pp. 184–5).

Although it is impossible to be certain, the evidence preserved from the Domesday survey, which notes that there were twelve berewicks attached to Southwell, suggests that the original formation of the estate, as seen in **2**, was one that endured from the mid-tenth century to the end of the eleventh century (GDB, f. 283r). The only difference is that, by the time of Domesday, there appears to be one more berewick attached to Southwell; either one of the existing berewicks of Southwell was divided to create a new one or another vill had subsequently been annexed to the manor (Farrer, *EYC*, p. 9). It is also interesting to note that the twenty hides at which Southwell and its dependencies were judged in 956 are exactly equal to the 22.5 carucates at which the same estate was judged by the time of Domesday (Farrer, *EYC*, pp. 9–10; Stenton, in *VCH Notts*. i, pp. 209–10, shows that the wapentake of Thurgarton, which included Southwell in its boundaries, had developed a unique method for calculation of taxation, a method which seems to be based on a unit of 9 bovates. Stenton shows that this differentiates the assessment of this district from the rest of the shire. Stenton, *Types*, p. 78, demonstrates that the sum of 22.5 carucates represents exactly 20 of those 9-bovate units upon which the assessment of this part of Nottingham was based).

Bounds of Southwell

The bounds of the estates granted in **2** have been thoroughly investigated in Lyth 1982. The charter begins with a description of the boundaries of Southwell and then continues, in a clockwise direction, with the bounds of three other manors, Normanton, Upton and Fiskerton. Lyth has attempted to identify the boundaries of the estates listed in **2** and he concludes on the basis of field observations that, with the exception of Bleasby, they in large part coincide with present-day parish boundaries (Lyth 1982, p. 59; he later redefines the boundaries in Lyth and Davies 1992, pp. 125–8). The bounds are also discussed by Stevenson in Farrer, *EYC*, pp. 7–8.

1. *These are the estate-boundaries of Southwell: from the ford* (ford) *along (the river) Greet as the old stream* (eald + stream) *flows to the east and to the south of the ? eaves/eyot* (egete). The place-name 'Southwell' means 'South spring'; 'Greet' is a derivative of OE *greot*, 'gravel': *PN Notts*., p. 175 and pp. 4–5 respectively. The starting-point, the ford, is today situated at the north-east corner of Southwell parish at the point at which Easthorpe Road (the A 612) crosses the River Greet (SK 711541), which is the same juncture where Potwell Dyke meets the Greet (today Greet Bridge stands here and on the other side of Greet Bridge a road continues in a north-westerly direction to Normanton and in an easterly direction to Upton; Lyth 1982, p. 51). **2**'s bounds then follow the line of the River Greet on a south-easterly course. At this point Lyth and Davies have reconsidered the boundary that Lyth alone originally proposed in 1982; instead of following the River Greet to a Roman Road, Lyth and Davies now suggest that the bounds turn southwards and thus away from the course of the River Greet and through Easthorpe Car Dyke to meet Beck Dyke somewhere near SK 7152 (Halloughton Dumble becomes Beck Dyke at SK 7152). Kitson suggests that the manuscript reading *esete* could be a corruption of *efes*, meaning 'eaves, an edge or border (esp. of a wood)' (the forthcoming work of Kitson was communicated to me by Dr S.E. Kelly). Jenkyns has suggested two alternative interpretations: that *esete* is a miscopying of *egete* which means 'eyot' or that an initial 'g-' has been omitted in copying and that the reading was once *gesete*, meaning 'habitation, stable or fold' (see the relevant entry in 'LangScape'; for the latter suggestion, see also Lyth and Davies 1992, p. 126).

2. *Thence straight until new farm's brook* (niwe + tun + broc) *flows into (the) Greet*. Here the bounds flow along Beck Dyke ('new farm's brook' is today the Halloughton Dumble/Beck Dyke; see Lyth and Davies 1992, p. 126) eastwards until they meet the River Greet again at SK 729524.

3. *Up by (the) brook* (broc) *on the south of* 'sunninsale' *holm* (holmr). At this point the bounds turn to the west and travel up by the brook on the south of *sunninsale* creek/water-meadow and Lyth and Davies 1992, p. 126, suggest that the approximate location of **2**'s bounds at this moment is near present-day Weldon Farm (SK 708518). It is unclear what landmark is intended by *sunninsale*, but it may be a corruption of *sunningale*. *Holmr* is an Old Norse place-name element, meaning 'holm, isle, small island, or water-meadow'; see Smith, *EPNE* I, pp. 258–9.

4. *Thence to a broad clearing* (brad + leah) *westwards* (westeweard). The course of **2** has now left the line of the Halloughton Dumble (which itself later becomes Beck Dyke) just as today's parish boundary does (see Lyth 1982, pp. 53–4, and Lyth and Davies 1992, p. 126, for this section of the bounds). **2** continues westwards past a broad clearing which must be the area where today's parish boundary comes close to Halloughton (SK 6951). Stevenson (in Farrer, *EYC*, p. 8, n. g), suggests that an alternative reading of *bradan lege* could be *Hradan-lege*, 'a possible older form of Radley, in Southwell'.

5. *Thence to the cottages* (cot)*; from the cottages along the street* (stræt) *into hollow brook* (holan + broc). **2** now advances to the cottages (*cot*; for which see Smith, *EPNE* I, pp. 108–10) and from the cottages along a street to the 'hollow brook'. As Lyth and Davies 1992, p. 126, point out, **2**'s bounds must here be travelling to the north of Halloughton (SK 6851) and of Halloughton Wood (SK 6751), perhaps along the line of the present-day Cotmoor Lane (SK 6652) until they arrive at Holbeck (SK 6552). For the place-name Holbeck and its relationship to the *holan broc* of **2**, see Farrer, *EYC*, p. 8, n. i and Fellows-Jensen, *SSNEM*, p. 226.

6. *Along the brook* (broc) *thence up by the bank/terrace* (hlinc)*; one furlong within the copse* (graf). The direction which takes us along the brook in **2** must be the area just to the north of present-day Holbeck Farm (SK 656526) which lies near a branch of Halam beck. The bounds of **2** are said to follow this brook, which at this point runs roughly parallel to Oxton Road (SK 6652) and into a copse, which 'implies coppicing, an early method of woodland management' (Lyth 1982, p. 55). Stevenson suggests that the 'furlong' measurement may have been a marginal annotation which found its way into the text (see Farrer, *EYC*, p. 8, n. j).

7. *Thence out to the oak-tree* (ac). This part of **2** must be somewhere to the south-east of Halam (SK 6754) but north-west of Westhorpe (SK 6953). Lyth points out that it may be significant that even quite recently this point in the modern-day parish boundary between Halam and Westhorpe was marked by an 'Elm Tree' and he locates this feature just to the south-west of Norwood Hill (SK 683542) (Lyth, *ibid.*, p. 55).

8. *From the oak-tree* (ac) *always by the headlands* (heafod) *to the more northerly thorn tree* (norðran þorn). Thus from Holbeck Farm (SK 656526) to Norwood Hill (SK 683542), **2**'s bounds have been following the north-westerly course of today's parish boundary. They now travel from the oak-tree by the headland to the more northerly thorn tree. Lyth points out that the 'headland' must be a reference to an open field over Norwood Hill whilst Gover, Mawer and Stenton note that 'the more northerly thorn tree' should be equated with modern-day Maythorn (SK 6955) (see Lyth 1982, p. 55. and *PN Notts.*, p. 176; today we can find Maythorn Orchard [SK 692551], Maythorn Cottages [SK 693552], Maythorne Farm [SK 697556] and Maythorn Mill [SK 698556]).

9. *From the thorn tree to (the) Greet; along (the) Greet until back to the ford.* Southwell's bounds then advance from the thorn tree to the River Greet and, as Lyth notes, the phrase 'from the thorn (tree) to the Greet' implies that the 'thorn (tree)' was not actually situated on the River Greet and it may therefore be the case that the Maythorn of **2** (described in **2** as *þone norðran þorn*) should be equated with the area covered by Maythorn Orchard (SK 692551) and Maythorn Cottages (SK 693552) which are not situated on the River Greet rather than the more northerly Maythorne Farm (SK 697556) and Maythorn Mill (SK 698556) which are both located on the River Greet. The very final section of Southwell's bounds, which describes the route along the River Greet and back to our starting point, the ford, is easy enough to decipher as the River Greet here flows to the north-east of

Southwell and joins with the ford at SK 711541 (i.e. the point where Potwell Dyke meets the River Greet).

Bounds of Normanton

1. *These are the estate-boundaries of Normanton: from (the) Greet to the dill hollow/ nook* (dile + healh). The place-name 'Normanton' means 'farm of the Northmen': *Northmanna tun* (*PN Notts.*, pp. xx, 78–9 and 176; see also Fellows-Jensen, *SSNEM*, pp. 262–4). Normanton (SK 7054) lies slightly north-east of Southwell. **2** begins these bounds by travelling along the Greet to the 'dill hollow'. Lyth 1982, p. 55, points out that the bounds of Normanton are not said to begin at a ford and he therefore proposes that the starting-point intended by the draftsman for Normanton's bounds is at Maythorn, the last and northernmost corner of Southwell's bounds. If one travels north along the River Greet from Maythorn, the Greet naturally becomes the modern-day parish boundary between Normanton and Kirklington (SK 6757) at SK 692561, with Kirklington located to the north-west of Normanton. The boundary then leaves the line of the River Greet and continues northwards to Corkhill (SK 6956) and the 'dill hollow' of **2**, which has been identified by Lyth (*ibid.*, p. 55), can be seen at SK 695566, slightly to the east of modern-day Meadow Farm (SK 693567) and north of Corkhill Lane. For the place-name element *healh*, and its various possible meanings, see Gelling and Cole, *LPN*, pp. 123–33.

2. *Along the hedge/enclosure* (haga) *to the brook* (broc). Lyth 1982, p. 55, suggests that the 'hedge/enclosure' was probably a 'fenced enclosure in the woodland of Corkhill, which is now Far Corkhill Farm', situated at SK 695566 (for *haga*, see Smith, *EPNE* I, p. 221). The 'brook' is a reference to Hockerton Dumble and the point at which the present-day boundary of Normanton meets Hockerton Dumble forms the north-westernmost corner of Normanton's bounds at SK 698571 and is presumably exactly the place referred to in **2**.

3. *Along (the) brook* (broc) *until into the valley* (denu). Here the bounds turn to the east and travel slightly southwards and if we follow the course of Hockerton Dumble (which is to the south of Hockerton itself) it does indeed enter a valley (Lyth 1982, p. 56). For *denu*, see Smith, *EPNE* I, p. 130 and Gelling and Cole, *LPN*, pp. 113–23.

4. *Along (the) valley* (denu) *always by the headlands* (heafod) *to the* len *brook* (*obscure* + broc)*; from that to the hedge* (hege). Lyth, together with Davies, has rethought his original ideas about this part of **2**'s boundary. Lyth and Davies now suggest that, rather than continuing to follow the line of Hockerton Dumble (i.e. the *broc* of **2**), **2**'s bounds take a sharp turn southwards (just as the modern parish boundary does at SK 707567) and this fulfils the requirement set out by **2** that the bounds should travel 'always by the headlands' (Lyth and Davies 1992, p. 128). The *len broc* of **2** would therefore be an off-shoot of the Hockerton Dumble, which Lyth and Davies place at SK 715557. Jenkyns, in her entry for 'Normanton' in 'LangScape', wonders whether the 'Len' of this part of the bounds is another example of the name of the River Leen, found elsewhere in Nottinghamshire (and see also the comments of Lyth 1982, p. 56). The word for 'hedge' in the manuscript is written *hise*, a very corrupt form; it is written *hicse* in the next section of the bounds, number 5.

5. *Always by the hedge* (hecge) *to the old street* (eald + stræt)*; along (the) street* (stræt) *until back to (the) Greet*. This part of Normanton's bounds has proved difficult to identify with certainty (see Lyth 1982, p. 56 and also Lyth and Davies 1992, p. 128). The final

part of Normanton's bounds travel along the 'old *stræt*' until they arrive back at the River Greet. Since Normanton's bounds have to finish back at the ford on the River Greet (see further below), Lyth and Davies, in their reappraisal, suggest that the 'old *stræt*' must have followed the line of the street which can today be found coming from Easthorpe (as the A 612), over Greet Bridge and then continuing northwards along the same route as Normanton's modern-day parish boundary. But whereas today's parish boundary then branches to the east so that it can include Hockerwood (SK 719552) within its bounds, Lyth and Davies suggest that the 'old *stræt*' must have followed the present-day western boundary of Hockerwood (SK 7155) until it joins the north-east boundary of Normanton (Lyth and Davies 1992, p. 128). And from here it runs back to the ford which provided the starting-point for Southwell's bounds described above (i.e. at the point where Potwell Dyke and the Greet Bridge meet the River Greet, SK 711541).

Bounds of Upton

1. *These are the estate-boundaries at Upton: from (the) Greet along the old street* (eald + stræt) *on the north of hillock wood (Hockerwood)* (hocer + wuda). 'Upton' means 'Higher farm' (*uppe*, *tun*); it suggests the centre of the village is on the summit of a low hill; *PN Notts*., p. 179. The 'hillock wood', comprised of the elements *hocer* + *wuda*, survives as the place-name 'Hockerwood'; see *DEPN*, p. 243. The starting-point on the River Greet must again be the ford (SK 711541). From here Upton's bounds follow the old *stræte* which has been shown to be along the line of the common boundary of Normanton and Hockerwood, and thus to the west of Hockerwood (Lyth and Davies 1992, p. 128). If we follow this course then **2**'s bounds do indeed travel 'by the north of Hockerwood' at SK 7155.

2. *From the street* (stræt) *over the moor* (mor) *to warrior enclosure* (dreng + haga) *northwards* (norþeweard). Lyth suggests that the moor must be in the vicinity of Cliff and Gorse Hill and also that the *dreng* enclosure would have been near present-day Lodge Farm (SK 729558) (Lyth 1982, p. 56).

3. *Thence up to the apple-tree* (æppel treow)*; from the apple-tree straight on over the middle of the great barrow (Micklebarrow)* (micel + beorg) *on to the moor* (mor) *to the foul creek* (ful + fleot); *along (the) creek until back to (the) Greet*. The elements *micel* + *beorg*/*berg*, 'great barrow', survive today in the place-name, Micklebarrow (Hill), which could be of Norse or English origin; *PN Notts*., p. 181 (s.v. 'Mickelborough Hill'). The apple-tree is the northernmost point of Upton's boundary (see the map in Lyth 1982, p. 50). Upton's northern parish boundary today touches the southern edge of Cheveral Wood (at SK 732563) and it is likely that in Anglo-Saxon times a distinctive apple tree at the southern edge of Cheveral Wood formed the boundary marker here referred to in **2** (Lyth 1982, p. 56). From the appletree, **2**'s bounds continue directly over the middle of Micklebarrow. Today's parish boundary follows exactly this course straight from Cheveral Wood, past Gorse Hill (SK 735560) and Spring Wood (SK 741556) until it arrives at the top and centre of Micklebarrow Hill (at a height of 56m and a position of SK 745554); this boundary divides Upton (SK 7354) from Averham (SK 7654). Upton's bounds in **2** now move onto the moor and to the foul creek; the moor must be just to the south of Micklebarrow Hill at SK 7454 and it seems likely that the foul creek is near the point at which Car Dyke becomes Pingley Dyke at SK 7454 (see Lyth 1982, pp. 57–8). From here, **2** directs us along the creek and back to the River Greet. Thus **2**'s bounds follow the line of Car Dyke upstream and to the south of Upton until they meet with the River Greet and

flow back to the starting-point of Southwell's bounds at SK 711541. Today this area forms the parish boundary between Upton and Rolleston (Lyth, *ibid.*, pp. 57–8).

Bounds of Fiskerton

1. *These are the estate-boundaries at Fiskerton: along (the) Greet to (the) Trent to hazel ford (Hazelford)* (hæsel + ford). 'Fiskerton' means 'farm of the fishermen'; *PN Notts.*, p. xvii and p. 164 and also Fellows-Jensen, *SSNEM*, p. 183. The 'hazel ford', *hæsel + ford*, survives as the modern place-name, Hazelford; *PN Notts.*, p. 156 (s.v. 'Hazelford Ferry'). As Lyth 1982, p. 58, points out, for this first section of Fiskerton's bounds to make sense, one needs to begin from where Upton's bounds finished. From here the River Greet is followed as it winds in a south-easterly direction and connects with the River Trent at SK 743515 (near today's Fiskerton Road), a point which is situated right between Fiskerton (SK 7351) and Rolleston (SK 7452). **2**'s bounds then follow the River Trent upstream until they reach Hazelford, probably at a point near modern-day Hazelford Ferry (SK 7249), which is opposite 'The Nabbs Island' (SK 7349); see Lyth, *ibid.*, p. 58.

2. *From the ford* (ford) *along (the) Greet (or perhaps 'street') to quern/mill hill* (cweorn + dun). It is the proximity here to Nabbs Island which makes the next part of **2**'s bounds understandable since, as Lyth *ibid.*, p. 58, notes, the position of Nabbs Island makes the River Trent fordable near Hazelford and it seems very likely that this is therefore the landmark referred to in **2**. However, the next part of the circuit in **2** is not so certain, not least because of corruption in the text. The manuscript reads *streot* (which I have retained in the charter's text owing to the difficulties of interpretation), which could either be a corrupted form of 'Greet', with the scribe's usual confusion of **s** and **g** and the accidental addition of an extra **t**; or it could be a corrupt form of *stræt*. Stevenson (in Farrer, *EYC*, p. 7), prefers the reading *stræt*, while Jenkyns (in her entry for Fiskerton in 'LangScape') opts for 'Greet' as the correct interpretation. Lyth 1982, p. 58 and Lyth and Davies 1992, p. 128, both suggest that **2** should read *stræt* at this point and, in the revised 1992 work, they suggest that this feature must join the River Trent at a point 'directly opposite the present Fiskerton/Bleasby boundary'. But the problem with the new interpretation of Lyth and Davies, which is based on more examinations of Hazelford, is that it then becomes less obvious how to reach the next landmark in **2**, the 'quern/mill hill'. They suggest that this is most likely to be a reference to 'Quernhill', which today can be equated with High Cross Hill (SK 7050). However, as Lyth and Davies note, if their new interpretation of the line of the *stræte* is correct (i.e. further to the north and not running through Bleasby) then High Cross Hill lies somewhat out-of-the-way and further to the west of the present-day border; unfortunately, Lyth and Davies cannot resolve this issue (Lyth and Davies 1992, p. 128).

3. *From quern/mill hill straight on to new farm's brook* (niwe + tun + broc)*; along (the) brook* (broc) *until back in (the) Greet*. Again it is likely that 'new farm's brook' should be equated with the Halloughton Dumble (SK 7051) and the route from *cweorn dune* to Halloughton Dumble probably joined at a point just after Rudsey Farm at SK 708516 (Lyth 1982, p. 59). **2**'s bounds now follow Halloughton Dumble eastwards, as it becomes Beck Dyke (SK 7152) and then joins back up with the River Greet at either SK 729523 or SK 739522, and thus completes **2**'s circuit.

Once the bounds of Southwell, Normanton, Upton and Fiskerton have been detailed, **2** concludes with a list of those towns (including Normanton, Upton and Fiskerton), which are part of the jurisdiction of Southwell. Thus we find that *Fearnefelð, Cyrlingtune, Mortune, Gypesmere,*

Blisetune, Gofertune, Healhtune and *Healum* are all somehow connected to Southwell too. These places are known today as Farnsfield (SK 6456; see *PN Notts.*, p. 163), Kirklington (SK 6757; see *PN Notts.*, p. 170), Gibsmere (SK 7148; see *PN Notts.*, p. 155), Bleasby (SK 7149; see *PN Notts.*, p. 155), Goverton (SK 7050; see *PN Notts.*, p. 155), Halloughton (SK 6851; see *PN Notts.*, p. 168) and Halam (SK 6754; see *PN Notts.*, p. 167) respectively.

The final sentence in the boundary clause of **2** demonstrates the procedures that were in use in the north of England for the measurement, and subsequently the division, of land between various parties. Translated this sentence reads, 'In Farnsfield the lands of two *manna hlot* (lit. men's shares/lots) pertain to Southwell; in Halam every sixth acre and three *manna hlot*; in Normanton every third acre; in Fiskerton the two shares and four *manna hlot* of all the land' (see Faith, *English Peasantry*, p. 44 and Hadley, *Northern*, p. 120). Systems for the assessment of land were different in the Anglo-Saxon north. Whereas hides, themselves subdivided into four yardlands, were the standard form of assessment in the south, in the north hides were being replaced by division into ploughlands, each of which was composed of eight oxgangs; and it is likely, as the word ploughland suggests, that this alternative form of assessment was influenced by Scandinavian incomers (Stenton, *ASE*, p. 514). Stenton demonstrated the interest of the word *manna hlot*, again of Scandinavian origin; he suggested that the area of land intended by the *manna hlot* was roughly equal to an oxgang and he further thought that it may have referred to that area of land apportioned to a normal Danish soldier who had come to settle in the Danelaw (Stenton, *ibid.*, pp. 514–15; see also Faith, *English Peasantry*, p. 147 and Hadley, *Northern*, p. 120, n. 86). Therefore **2** provides crucial evidence for how this area of Nottingham was divided and the systems of governance that were in place. Whilst the term *mid sacce and mid sacne* was a legal innovation which sought to define how the various estates mentioned in **2** were bound to the main manor, Southwell, so too *manna hlot* is highly distinctive and represents the limits of the grant on the ground. It is significant to note also that these legal terms, which display Scandinavian origins, are here accompanied in **2** by place-names which themselves demonstrate Scandinavian influence (in particular Normanton and Bleasby).

3

King Edgar grants ten hides (casati) *at Sutton, Nottinghamshire, to Oscytel, [Arch]bishop of York.* A.D. 958

F. York, Minster Library and Archives, L 2/1 (*Mag. Reg. Alb.*), pt. I, 57v–58r : copy, s. xiv[med]
Rubric: Donatio facta per eundem regem cuidam Ochitel episcopo de possessionibus et rebus aliis.
H. Bodleian, Dodsworth 9, 3v: copy of F, s. xvii [no bounds or witnesses]
J. Bodleian, Dodsworth 125, 77rv: copy of F, s. xvii
Ed.: a. Birch 1044 and Birch 1349 (bounds only), from F
b. Farrer, *EYC*, no. 3, from F
c. Davies 1983, p. 21
Listed: Sawyer 679; Hart, *ECNE*, no. 115
Edited from F

Regnante imperpetuum Domino nostro Iesu Christo. Omnibus prudentibus qui Deifice contemplationis beatitudinem in mentis sue hospicio cernere cupiunt manifestissimis signis constat, quod quisque potens est transitoriis uiis alta celestia sine fine mansura capescere. Iccirco ego Eadgarus industrius Anglorum rex ceterarumque gentium persistentium gubernator et rector .ii°. anno imperii mei literatoriis apicibus roboraui quod cum consensu heroicorum uirorum cuidam meo dilectissimo pontifici uocitato nomine Oscytel, id est .x. casatos generaliter, eternaliter tradendo concessi ubi turbarum collatione iamdudum nomen illatum hoc adesse profertur et[a] Suttune, ut terram iam prefatam meo scilicet ouante concessu[b] tramitibus sue possideat uite; deinceps namque sibi succedenti cui uoluerit heredi derelinquat, seu predixi, illam terram hereditatem. Maneat igitur meum hoc immobile donum [c]eterna libertate[c] iocundum cum omnibus que ipsum locum pertinere dinoscuntur, tam in magnis quam in modicis rebus, campis, pascuis, pratis, siluis, excepto communi labore, expeditione pontis, arcisue coedificatione. Si qui denique michi non optanti hanc libertatis cartam liuore depressi uiolare satagerint, agminibus [d]tetre caliginis[d] lapsi, uocem audiant examinationis die arbitris sibi dicentis[e] 'Discedite a me maledicti',[1] ubi cum demonibus ferreis sartaginibus[f] crudeli torqueantur in pena, si non ante mortem digna hoc emendauerint penitentia.[g] Istis terminis ambitur predicta tellus:[h]

Đis sint ða landgemara to Scroppenþorpe[i] ⁊[j] Þuresby:[k] of langan forda dic, ⁊lang dices ꝥ[l] on þa miclan dic; ⁊lang dices on Blidan et celfa geƿeade;[m] ⁊lang Blidan on beo lege[n] suðeƿearde; ꝥ[l] up ða miclan strat; ⁊lang strat[o] ut þurħ beo leage[p] norð ut þone felð; ꝥ[l] adun on Blidan; up be Blidan on Iddil; up be Iddel on þone fulan broc; ⁊lang brocci eft[q] on langan forð.

Đis sint ða landgemarei to Suttune: of fulan forda ⁊lang stret[r] to þam grafe; þon geriht mid þone graf on þone broc; ⁊lang broces[s] on langan forð; ongerihte[t] on[u] Scirƿuda[v] middeƿeardne on Iddel at brodan fleote; ꝥ[l] up a be Iddel eft[q] on fulan forð. Donne is[w] Sigotes[x] land binnan ðisum[y] gemaret.

Acta est prefata donacio anno dominice incarnacionis .dcccc.lviii. indiccione prima.

Ego Eadgarus rex Anglorum indeclinabiliter concessi	
Ego Oscytel episcopus cum signo sancte crucis roboraui	[*Dorchester/York*]
Ego Dunstan episcopus consignaui	[? *London or Worcester*]
Ego Cynesige episcopus confirmaui	[*Lichfield*]
Ego Aðulf episcopus acquieui	[*Elmham*]
Ego Leofpine[z] episcopus coroboraui	[*Lindsey*]
Ego Aldred episcopus non renui	[*Chester-le-Street*]
Elfhere[a2] dux	
Urm dux	
Aðelstan dux	
Gunner dux[b2]	
Aðelmund dux	
Brihtnoð dux	

Uthred dux
Leod dux
Mirdach dux
Ascured dux
Halfden dux
Morcare dux

Aþered[c2] dux[d2]
Alfwine minister
Wlfhelm minister
Sigulf[e2] minister
Alfwine minister
Wlsi[f2] minister
Wlnoð[g2] minister
Aðelstan minister
Aðelward minister

Aðelwod[h2] minister[i2]
Sigered minister
Elfred minister
Alfwold minister
Ðurkitel[j2] minister
Ðurmod minister
Alfere minister
Alfsi[k2] minister
Alfnoð minister

Ulfketel minister[l2]
Hrowald minister
Ðurstan minister
Sumerled minister
Arkitel minister
Ðor minister
Ourde minister
Soca minister
Cytelbearn minister
Forno[m2] minister
Dunstan minister

[a] *For Old English* æt [b] concensu F; *compare S 465, S 674* [c..c] eternalitate F; *compare S 465, S 674* [d..d] terre caliginibus F; *compare S 465, S 674* [e] ducentis F [f] sataginibus F; *compare S 465, S 674* [g] potentia F; *compare S 465, S 674* [h] *The Old English boundary*

clause is highly corrupt; see the note on editorial method, pp. 83–4 [i] Scroppen yorpe F [j] *Where* F *has an ampersand in the boundary clause, a Tironian et has been used* [k] Yuresby F [l] y F [m] seyeade F [n] lese F [o] ytrat F [p] Beolease F [q] ert F [r] siret F [s] brocer F [t] ongerilite F [u] of F [v] Sciryuda F [w] ir F [x] sisotef F [y] diyum F [z] Leolfyine F [a2] Elferf F [b2] *At this point in* F *the witness-list is no longer written across the page as it had been for the first ten witnesses and instead is arranged in columns* [c2] Ayered F [d2] *This is the first name of column two* F [e2] Silulf F [f2] *For* Wulfsige [g2] *For* Wulfnoð [h2] *For* Æðelwold [i2] *This is the first name of column three* F [j2] Dulkitel F [k2] *For* Ælfsige [l2] *This is the first name of column four* F [m2] Fforno F

[1] Matt. 25:41

3 is a document which was produced in the name of King Edgar when he was monarch of Mercia, East Anglia and Northumbria only and not of all Anglo-Saxon England (see Keynes 2008, pp. 7–9, for more about the division of the kingdom); it can be accepted as a copy of an authentic charter (that Edgar attests as 'rex Anglorum' and is styled in the same way in the body of the charter is perhaps a problem in a charter issued when Edgar was king only in Mercia, East Anglia and Northumbria; but, as is the case with S 674 (*Pet* 13), it may be that the regnal style was taken over from an earlier exemplar without considering that it needed to be adapted; see Keynes, *Diplomas*, p. 69, n. 135). Much of **3**'s formulation is standard for a charter of the mid-tenth century. But the most pressing reason for considering **3** as a genuine document is provided by its exact similarity to S 674 (*Pet* 13), another 958 charter in which Edgar grants five hides of land at Orton, Huntingdonshire, to Ælfheah his *minister*. The only differences between **3** and S 674 (*Pet* 13) are the names of the beneficiaries and the land involved in the grant. The identical diplomatic of the two charters suggests that they should be thought of as the work of one and the same draftsman: one scholar has suggested that the diplomatic features of **3** and S 674 (*Pet* 13) indicate that they were the products of a 'central agency' or chancery (Keynes, *Diplomas*, pp. 69–79), under the direction of Edgar while he was king of Mercia, East Anglia and Northumbria, which would have met to deal with the business of land transactions and other matters. The principal witnesses of **3** and S 674 (*Pet* 13) are identical, and indeed the lists as a whole are extremely similar, which, in combination with the fact that the body of the two charters is identical, suggests that they represent the products of the same meeting of the king's *witan* in 958. The subsequent preservation of **3** and S 674 (*Pet* 13) in disparate archives makes it highly unlikely that they could be independent forgeries and thus the two would seem to authenticate each other (Keynes, *Diplomas*, p. 69, points to two other documents which are suggestive of 'centralised' production and which represent a second meeting of the *witan* in 958. S 676 (BCS 1037) is a grant of land in Essex by King Edgar while he was still king only of Mercia, East Anglia and Northumbria and it displays the same formulation and witness-list as S 678 (*Abing* 82), a grant of land in Oxfordshire by Edgar, again whilst Edgar was king only of Mercia, East Anglia and Northumbria).

The evidence provided by the witness-lists of charters for the years 957 to 959 suggests that the division of the kingdom in 957 (*ASC BC*, s.a. 957) between Eadwig, who retained Wessex, and Edgar, who received Mercia, East Anglia and Northumbria, was both planned and ordered. Thus those bishops whose sees were located in Eadwig's part of the kingdom (such as the bishoprics of Ramsbury, Crediton, Wells and Cornwall) remained in attendance on Eadwig and those in the more northerly part of the kingdom (such as York, Elmham, Lichfield and Chester-le-Street) naturally became members of Edgar's court. Exactly the same pattern is seen with those ealdormen who attest charters during this period, and this further suggests that the division in 957 was not the outcome of any rebellion but rather an event which was carefully organised (Keynes, *Atlas*, table LII). In 959, when Eadwig died, the two divisions of the kingdom reunited under King Edgar and the attestations in charters after this point, of those bishops and ealdormen who had previously been associated with two separate courts, suggest that the two were joined into a single body of men under the leadership of the new king (for discussion of the evidence of attestations in the period 957–9, see Keynes, *Diplomas*, pp. 69–70 and pp. 75–6 and Keynes 2008, pp. 7–9).

As we have seen, **3** is a grant of land made by Edgar in 958 while he was king only of Mercia, East Anglia and Northumbria: since the division of the kingdom in 957 saw an ordered reorganisation of the king's council between those who attended Eadwig south of the Thames and those who attended Edgar to the north of the Thames, **3** offers a possible insight into those men who formed the core of Edgar's support in the north (for the Thames as the boundary between the two kingdoms, see *John of Worcester II*, s.a. 957). It is necessary to investigate those charters granted by Edgar, both while he was king of Mercia, East Anglia and Northumbria in 957–959, and afterwards when he was king of Wessex as well, to see whether or not certain individuals emerge as having a greater role in the north than elsewhere (for an invaluable guide to all of the charters issued by Edgar, see S. Keynes, 'A Conspectus of the Charters of King Edgar, 957–75', in Scragg, *Edgar*, pp. 60–80).

During his reign as king to the north of the Thames, the majority of charters issued by Edgar contain witness-lists attested by thegns who have Old English names only; for example, S 667 (BCS 1041 and 1888), S 675 (BCS 1042), S 676 (BCS 1037), S 676a, S 677 (*Wells* 31) and S 678 (*Abing* 82). But there are three charters which contain Scandinavian names and which may provide evidence for the existence at Edgar's northern court of a group of men who had their roots in the Danelaw: S 674 (*Pet* 13) is a 958 grant of land by King Edgar to Ælfheah, his *minister*, at Orton and preserved in the Peterborough archive; S 679 (**3**) is also dated to 958 and grants land at Sutton to Archbishop Oscytel; and finally S 681 (*Pet* 14), a 959 grant by Edgar to Quen, his faithful *matrona*, of land at Howden and Old Drax and preserved in the Peterborough archive (the interest of these attestations is demonstrated and fully explored in Abrams 2008, from which this present section has greatly benefited). Among those who attest S 674 (*Pet* 13), two out of eight of the ealdormen, Urm and Gunner, have Scandinavian names, as do four out of the nineteen thegns who attest, Sigulf, Thurkytel, Thurmod and Ufa (which may be an abbreviated version of Ulfcytel). Among the thirteen ealdormen who attest **3** the Scandinavians Urm and Gunner recur, but this time they are accompanied by others with Scandinavian names, Leod, Mirdach, Ascured, Halfden and Morcar (Brooks, Gelling and Johnson 1984, p. 144, note that the name 'Mirdach is an English spelling of Old Irish Muiredach (cf. modern Scots Murdoch), and it is possible that he was an earl among the Hiberno-Norse (or perhaps Scotto-Norse) settlers of north-western England'); among the twenty-eight thegns in **3** a large proportion have Scandinavian names, Sigulf, Thurkytel, Thurmod, Ulfketel, Hrowald, Sumerled, Arkitel, Thor, Ourde, Soca, Cytelbearn and Forno. Among the six ealdormen who attest S 681 (*Pet* 14), Leot and Oskytel have Scandinavian names, as do six of the twelve thegns, Ulfkytel, Rold, Dragmel, Sigeferð, Thurferð and Thurkytel.

It is an important question whether the attestations of these Scandinavian figures are limited to these three charters (S 674 [*Pet* 13], **3** and S 681 [*Pet* 14]) and to the time when Edgar was king of Mercia, East Anglia and Northumbria or whether they occur elsewhere in the corpus of Edgar's charters and after Edgar had acceded to the rule of Wessex as well as territory to the north of the Thames. An investigation into the witness-list of **3** shows that half of the Scandinavian names found there are unique, one-off attestations. And those Scandinavians who do attest elsewhere are found in charters concerned only with Danelaw estates and Danelaw archives. Thus the ealdormen Gunner and Mirdach attest S 712a, a charter which grants land in Derbyshire; Gunner alone attests S 712 (**4**) and S 716 (**5**), both of which are in the York archive; and finally the thegns Thurkytel, Ulfketel, Hrowald and Forno attest S 779 (BCS 1266), a charter preserved in the Ely archive (for more about these Scandinavian figures, see Abrams 2008).

The evidence cited suggests very strongly that those Scandinavian names in **3** are representative of a group of men whose power and influence did not extend beyond the Danelaw. After Edgar acceded to the rule of the whole kingdom in 959, he no longer required the presence of these men at his court and thus most of these Scandinavian figures cease to attest the king's charters. And those few Scandinavians that do attest at a date after the unification of the kingdom only appear in charters which are associated with the Danelaw region. Abrams 2008 shows that this pattern with regard to the Scandinavian names in **3** holds true for the two other charters with Scandinavian witnesses composed during Edgar's time as king to the north of the Thames, S 674 (*Pet* 13) and S 681 (*Pet* 14), both from the Peterborough archive.

Thus **3** provides a glimpse at those men who came to form a band of support for Edgar which was crucial in the Danelaw region and who helped to ensure both that the division of the kingdom was effected properly and also that Edgar could assert his own authority in Mercia, East Anglia and Northumbria with a minimum of resistance (for the importance of such local men, see Abrams 2008). And, if we remember that as recently as 954 Eric Bloodaxe, a viking ruler, had been established at York (see above, p. 46, n. 145, for questions about Eric's identity), then the incorporation of these Scandinavian men may have been a part of Edgar's policies which was vital for the successful implementation of his rule in the north.

The estate granted in **3** is Sutton, which is situated in Nottinghamshire. Since **2** was also a grant of land in Nottinghamshire, but one made by King Eadwig before the division of the kingdom, the details of **2** and **3** together provide more evidence for the ordered nature of the division of the kingdom. It is reasonable to suggest that with **2** King Eadwig had initiated a policy designed to reclaim certain areas of the Nottinghamshire Danelaw for the York archbishopric in the period immediately following viking settlement of the late ninth and early tenth centuries; the fact that **3** is also concerned with the Nottinghamshire area suggests that Edgar, as king of Mercia, East Anglia and Northumbria, was continuing his brother's intentions (see further Hart, *Danelaw*, p. 248). Keynes thought **3** to be the product of a form of Mercian chancery in operation under King Edgar and, if true, this fact alone would suggest a level of organisation and efficiency achieved by the king in his new role. But we also find that the core of those Scandinavians who had been involved with King Eadwig's grant of **2** (men such as Urm, Gunner, Uhtred and Leod) are again listed in **3** and thus had been incorporated into Edgar's Mercian court. Therefore **3** is the endorsement of an earlier policy of Eadwig by Edgar who had acceded to the kingdom north of the Thames in 957. **2** and **3** represent not only an attempt by the West Saxon house to revitalise the York archbishopric in a time after significant depredations, but also an effort on the part of the kings Eadwig and Edgar to extend their authority via the church through those areas recently settled by Scandinavians. (Barrow 2004, suggests that **2** and **3** were grants made to Oscytel while he was bishop of Dorchester, rather than archbishop of York; for a contrary view, see the commentary to **2**.

Details of the later history of the Sutton estate are provided in Domesday Book, by which time the manor of Sutton and its berewicks still belonged to the archbishop of York. However, the rating of Sutton, Scrooby and Lound in Domesday Book at one carucate and six bovates falls a long way short of the assessment of the same area in **3** which totalled ten *casati* (GDB, f. 283r). Farrer suggested that the substantial amount of sokeland, that is land which was dependent on a manorial centre (see Hadley, *Northern*, pp. 167–72, for a definition of 'sokeland'), which belonged to the manor of Sutton in 1086 should be added to the figures (Farrer, *EYC*, pp. 11–12), which would raise the total to seven carucates and five and a half bovates. As the combined details of **4**, **6** and **7** show, land could quickly be lost from, or added to, estates in the north of England; these three documents also show how land that once belonged to a central manor outright as so-called *agenland* (meaning literally 'ownland') could also be converted into sokeland and vice versa (for more about these issues, see the commentary to **7**). So it is not at all surprising to see that the original grant of land totalling ten *casati* in **3** in 958 had undergone various changes by the time of the Domesday survey (Davies 1983, p. 14, has a different interpretation of the Domesday evidence).

Bounds of 'Scroppenþorpe' (? Scrooby) and 'Thuresby'

Just south of Bawtry, the River Idle divides in two, the main stream of which continues to the south-east, whilst a tributary, the River Blyth (Ryton), branches to the south-west (at SK 658 921). It is between these two rivers that the estates of Sutton and Scrooby lie, with Scrooby being the more northerly and westerly of the two (for the relationship between 'Scroppenþorpe' and Scrooby, see below).

1. *These are the estate-boundaries of 'Scroppenþorpe' and 'Thuresby': from long ford* (lang + ford) *ditch/dyke* (dic)*, along the ditch/dyke until to the great ditch/dyke* (miclan + dic)*; along the (great) ditch/dyke to (the river) Blyth at calves' ford* (cealf + ? [ge]wæd). The place *Scroppenþorpe* is a lost vill, which has sometimes been identified as 'Scrooby' (see Farrer, *EYC*, p. 12). But, as Fellows-Jensen points out, the only certainty is that modern-day 'Scrooby' is situated in the bounds of *Scroppenþorpe* as described in **3** (see Fellows-Jensen, *SSNEM*, p. 67). As noted in *CamDEPN*, p. 533, *Scroppenþorpe* perhaps means, 'Skroppa's outlying farm', comprising the Old Norse female name *Skroppa* + 'thorp' (for other possibilities, and further discussion, see *PN Notts*., pp. 96–7 and Fellows-Jensen, *SSNEM*, p. 116; for the 'thorp' element, and the significance of this instance for the survival of a group of Danelaw 'thorps' dating to the second half of the tenth century, see P. Cullen, R. Jones and D.N. Parsons, *Thorps in a Changing Landscape*, Explorations in Local and Regional History Volume 4 (Hatfield, 2011), p. 57). *Thuresby*, another lost vill, is a combination of the personal name 'Þurir (ON Þórir)' and the suffix '-by'; see *DEPN*, p. 466, Fellows-Jensen, *SSNEM*, p. 74 and *CamDEPN*, p. 609. *Scroppenþorpe* and *Thuresby* form part of a dense group of Scandinavian place-names in the vicinity of the Rivers Maun and Idle, which bear witness to Scandinavian settlement there. The bounds are described as beginning at 'long ford ditch/dyke' and then ending at 'long ford', Point 1 on Davies' map (Davies 1983, p. 14). This very same ford is referred to in both the boundary clause of *Scroppenþorpe* and that of Sutton (Davies *ibid*., pp. 14 and 16). From the starting point of the 'long ford', two channels flow in a southerly direction and the boundary of Scrooby (SK 6590) follows the course of the western channel (referred to in **3**

as a dyke, *dic*) and past Ranskill (SK 6588) until it reaches a great dyke (*miclan dic*) which runs east-west just after Barnby Moor (SK 6684). The boundary proceeds along this great dyke until it meets the River Blyth (Ryton) at the 'calves' ford', presumably a point near SK 6383 (Davies *ibid*., p. 17, notes that this is the line of the present parish boundary).

2. *Along (the river) Blyth to the southern part of bee wood* (beo + leah)*; thence up the great street* (micel + stræt)*; along the street* (stræt) *out through bee wood*. An alternative translation of the first part of this clause is, 'Along (the river) Blyth to bee wood southwards'. The interpretation of *beo lege* being derived from Old English *beo* ('bee') and *leah* ('wood') is that of Jenkyns (see the online entry in 'LangScape'). The River Blyth is now known as the River Ryton. For the possible location of this part of **3**'s bounds, see Davies 1983, p. 17.

3. *North out of the open land/field* (feld)*; thence down into (the river) Blyth; up by (the river) Blyth to (the river) Idle; up by (the river) Idle to the foul brook* (ful + broc)*; along the brook* (broc) *back again to long ford*. The River Idle (*Iddil/Iddel*) may derive its name from Old English *idel*, meaning 'idle, empty, lazy'; see *PN Notts*., p. 5. Once at the 'great street' (mentioned in part 2 of the clause above), the boundary follows the direction of the street northwards until it reaches a 'field/open land'. Davies equates this 'great street' with what is now known as 'Roman Bank Lane' and which forms the natural eastern border of Serlby (from SK 6387 to SK 6489). Davies also suggests that the 'field/open space' was situated near modern-day Bishopfield Farm (SK 648887) (Davies 1983, pp. 17–18). From the field/open land (Bishopfield Farm), it turns west and meets the River Blyth (Ryton) (*Blidan*), presumably at SK 643898, and follows this northwards until it reaches the confluence with the River Idle (*on Iddil*) at SK 658921. From this point the boundary turns southwards, first along the River Idle and then it leaves this waterway and continues along the line of the foul brook (*fulan broc*) until it arrives back at its origin, the long ford.

Bounds of Sutton

1. *These are the estate-boundaries of Sutton: from foul ford* (ful + ford) *along the street* (stræt) *to the wood/copse* (graf). 'Sutton' means literally, 'South farm/settlement'; *PN Notts*., p. 100 and *CamDEPN*, pp. 590–1. The foul ford has been located at the south-east corner of the territory at the point where the southern boundary of Sutton and the River Idle meet (SK 703843); it is close to modern-day Tiln (Davies 1983, pp. 14 and 18). From here, the bounds run to the west along a street, which is still a path today, until they reach a wood/copse, which is probably Sutton Wood (Davies, *ibid*., p. 19).

2. *Then straight through the middle of the wood/copse* (graf) *to the brook* (broc)*; along the brook to long ford* (lang + ford). When it reaches the brook, the boundary turns northwards and follows the line of the brook until it arrives again at the long ford, which was the starting point of the bounds of Scrooby.

3. *Straight on to the middle part of Sherwood to (the river) Idle at broad creek* (brad + fleot)*; thence up continuously along (the river) Idle back to foul ford* (ful + ford). 'Sherwood' means 'wood belonging to the shire'; see *PN Notts*., p. 10 and *CamDEPN*, p. 544. The boundary now turns to the east and advances directly out of the middle of Sherwood forest and follows the boundary between Lound to the south and Mattersey to the north at SK 6987 (it is still a bridleway today) until it reaches the River Idle at that point which is called 'broad creek' at SK 7187 (Davies 1983, pp. 19–20). From 'broad creek', along the old main course of the River Idle, the Old Ea (the 'Old Ea' today forms the western boundary of Clayworth, SK 7388), until it connects with the stream at the

south of the boundary and continues along the line of this stream until finally reaching the 'foul ford'; the boundary that has been traced for Sutton roughly equates with the present boundary of Sutton-cum-Lound: Davies, *ibid.*, p. 20.

4. *Then is Sigot's land within this boundary* ([ge]mære). A person named Sigot seems to have had some land within the Sutton circuit.

4

King Edgar grants twenty hides (casati) *at Sherburn-in-Elmet, Yorkshire, to Æslac.* A.D. 963

F. York, Minster Library and Archives, L 2/1 (*Mag. Reg. Alb.*), pt. I, 56v–57r: copy, s. xiv^{med}
Rubric: Collacio domini Edgari Regis facta de Shirburn
H. Bodleian, Dodsworth 9, 1rv: copy of F, s. xvii [no bounds or witnesses]
J. Bodleian, Dodsworth 125, 75r–76r: copy of F, s. xvii
Ed.: a. *Mon. Angl.*, iii. 128, from F
b. *Mon. Angl.* (rev. edn.), vi, pt. 3, pp. 1175–6 (no. 2)
c. Kemble 500 (without bounds), from F
d. Birch 1112 and Birch 1352 (bounds only), from F
e. Farrer, *EYC*, no. 6, from F
Listed: Sawyer 712; Hart, *ECNE*, no. 123
Edited from F

In nomine Dei et Domini nostri Iesu Christi ueri redemptoris mundi. Anno uero dominice incarnacionis .dcccclxiii., indiccione .xiiii. Ego Eadgarus, omnicreantis disponente clementia Angligenarum omniumque gentium undique secus habitantium rex, diuino ductus amore ab eodem Deo et Domino nostro populis et tribubus preordinatus in regem anno imperii mei .vi. non inmemor fui quomodo et quam mirabiliter omnia supernus rector firme rationis serie gubernat atque custodit seu omnibus sapientibus notum ac manifestum constat quod quosquam nutu mirifico interdum exaltat quosdam iterum seu 'stipulam uento raptam'[1] fortunali euentu illico depellit. Iccirco minime in obliuione habui mee regalis dignitatis quod quoddam regni mei rus meorum episcoporum testimonio principum turmis heroicorum[a] uirorum astipulatione uenerabili Æslac nomine aliquam telluris porcionem id est .xx. casatos tota mentis auiditate[b] perpetualiter impertio penes illum locum ubi antiquorum Anglorum relatu dicitur Sireburnan [c]ut in eternam <hereditatem> meum donum in Sancte Trinitatis patrocinio[c] quamdiu uiuat habeat, gaudens gaudeat, possidensque possideat per secula sospes cum omnibus que ad eundem locum pertinere noscuntur tam in magnis quam in modicis rebus campis, pascuis, pratis, siluis, ut perhenniter ab omni iugo secularis uiolencie ac[d] liberaliter semper sit meum donum immune preter arcem construendam atque pontem componendum agonisque militiam. Nunc igitur dum uitale spiramen suum fouerit corpus animo iocundo nostra dapsili redditione perfruatur, decurso scilicet sue curriculo uite heredi cui uoluerit impendat imperpetuum karisma. Si quis autem hanc nostram donationem amplificare aut augere decreuerit, augeatur ei hoc in seculo felicitas et prosperitas et in futuro cetibus angelicis iungi mereatur in euum ut uocem Christi ualeat audire ita fantis: uenite benedicti patris mei; nunc cum pace pia sacrum percipite <a>[e] principio mundi regnum uobis quod rite paratum est.[2] Si autem, quod absit, quis filius perditionis hoc nostrum decretum infringere aut inmutare conatus fuerit, sit ipse Acherontis cuius turbidus gurges ceno ac uasta uoragine estuare asseritur, nisi prius hic ad satisfaccionem peruenerit et digna penitentia emendare maluerit.[f]

Ðys synt ðara .xx. hida Landgemara to Sciretburnan [g]ð · Et[g] inlandes: arest on suðeƿeardan;[h] ƿest[i] 7lang[j] brotty on ðone hereƿoð;[k] norð 7lang ƿeges[l] to scearpan brycge. East[m] ðanan 7lang sledes þt[n] hit cimð[o] on ðone ƿeg.[p] 7 healfe hide on Hibaldes tofte, 7 ane hide on Fryþetune,[q] on Hillum tƿegra[r] oxenagang, 7 on[s] Lundby tƿegra[t] oxenagang 7 ðriddehealfe hyrde on Mylenforda[u] 7 on Stiuetune 7 on Miclanfelda .ii. hyda landes[v] 7 eal[w] Luttringtun butan anre hide, 7 oðer healf hyde on Fentune, 7 oðre healf hyde on Kaƿuda,[x] 7 eal ꝥ[y] lid[z] ðe ðerto gebireð,[a2] 7lang Usan betƿeonan[b2] Ƿeorf[c2] 7 [d2]ða cy[d2] on ƿuda[e2] 7 on ƿæter[f2] 7 on felda.

Predicta siquidem tellus hiis terminis circumcincta clarescit. Hec uidelicet donacio facta est anno dominice incarnacionis .dcccc.lxiii. et nostri imperii .ui^o^. cunctis meis consentientibus optimatibus et precipue hiis quorum nomina subnotata recensentur.

Ego Eadgarus gratia Dei totius Britannie telluris dominus meum donum proprio sigillo confirmaui

Ego Dunstanus archiepiscopus regie roborator donacionis agie crucis triumphale signaculum depinxi [*Canterbury*]

Ego Oscytel archiepiscopus Eboracensis ecclesie signo salutifero hanc legalem largicionem prenotaui [*York*]

Ego Oswald episcopus ciuitatis heroice hanc regiam stabilitatis donacionem signo prepollenti prefixi [*Worcester*]

Ego Cynesige[g2] episcopus Lichefeldensis ecclesie hanc regis munificenciam gabulo glorioso prepinxi [*Lichfield*]

Ego Aðulf episcopus Elmhamnensis ecclesie hanc cartulam dictitans[h2] rege suisque precipientibus perscribere iussi [*Elmham*]

Ego Osulf episcopus confirmaui [*Ramsbury*]

Ego Brihthelm episcopus consensi [*Wells*]

Ego Aðelƿold episcopus confirmaui [*Winchester*]

Ego Eadelm episcopus consensi [*Selsey*]

Ego Alfhere dux

Ego Alfheah[i2] dux

Ego Aðelstan dux
Ego Eðelpne[j2] dux
Ego Byrhtnoð dux
Ego Eadmund dux
Ego Gunar dux
Ego Durre dux
Ego Alfwold minister
Eanulf minister
Alfhere minister
Þulstan minister
Þinsige minister
Aðelferð minister
Þulfheah minister
Þulfsige minister
Osmund minister

[a] hereticorum F [b] auididitate F [c...c] ut in eternam meam domum in Sancte Trinitatis patrocinio F [d] ab F [e] *Word omitted* F [f] *The Old English boundary clause is highly corrupt; see the note on editorial method, pp. 83–4* [g...g] *Possibly for* ðæs [h] sudeyfardan F [i] yert F [j] *Where* F *has an ampersand in the boundary clause, a Tironian et has been used* [k] hereyoð F [l] yeses F [m] Rast F [n] h\i/ F [o] cinð F [p] yes F [q] Fryyetune F [r] tyssra F [s] F *has incorrectly written* on *twice here* [t] tyesra F [u] Mysenforda F [v] landfy F [w] lal F [x] Kayuda F [y] ħ F [z] *Probably for* land [a2] sebired F [b2] getyfonan F [c2] Yeorf F [d2...d2] *Possibly for* ða eg*; see commentary* [e2] puda F [f2] yster F [g2] Cynelige F [h2] dictitatis F [i2] Alfheal F [j2] Edelyne F; *for* Æðelpine

[1] Isaiah 41:2
[2] cf. Matt. 25:34

4 is a 963 grant of Sherburn to a certain 'Æslac' (for whom see further below), an estate that became very important for the York church. Although **4** seems to be fundamentally authentic, in its received form it may betray some later rewriting of part of its dispositive section, which perhaps also caused some corrupted text.

The suspicious clause in question reads: 'ut in eternam meam domum in Sancte Trinitatis patrocinio quamdiu uiuat habeat'. It is reasonable to suggest that the first part of this clause has occurred as a result of some corruption in the text. There are various possible solutions to this problem. It may be that *in eternam* should read *in eternum*, an idiom which can be found in early charters such as S 103a (dated 716 × 745) and also in later charters such as S 597 (*Abing* 55) (a charter of King Eadwig dated 956); and whose meaning is most readily paralleled in other Anglo-Saxon charters by the words *perpetualiter* (for example, S 691 [*Abing* 90] and S 705 [*Abing* 94]) or *eternaliter* (for example, S 674 [*Pet* 13] and **3**): this would be a mistake explicable by attraction to the feminine *meam domum*. Yet *meam domum* is itself an expression unparalleled in other charters and one which makes no sense here. I therefore suggest that *meam domum* is a corruption of *meum donum*, which can be found throughout the corpus of Anglo-Saxon charters (see, for example, S 26

[*CantStA* 48], S 126 [BCS 233], S 721 [BCS 1104], S 761 [*Abing* 107], S 853 [*Burt* 24], S 902 [*Abing* 131] etc.), and that *hereditatem*, commonly found in this position in Anglo-Saxon charters, has been mistakenly omitted; the phrase *eternam hereditatem* occurs, for example, in S 512 (BCS 780). The clause will now read: 'ut in eternam hereditatem meum donum in Sancte Trinitatis patrocinio quamdiu uiuat habeat'.

The second part of the clause, 'in Sancte Trinitatis patrocinio' ('under the patronage/protection of [the] Holy Trinity'), is unparalleled and arguably reads as a later interpolation into an otherwise standard statement of powers. If it is the work of a later copyist (and it could have been inserted at any point up until the mid-fourteenth century, the time when this copy of **4** was made in F), its purpose may simply have been to stress that the gift was hereditary, held under ecclesiastical protection (*patrocinio*). And it may be that the first part of the clause became corrupted as a result of this later revision (I am very grateful to Prof. N. Brooks and Dr S.E. Kelly for much helpful discussion about this clause).

Two, more straightforward, textual difficulties remain. The formula with which Bishop Æthulf attests is problematic since the use of *dictitatis* makes no sense. Almost identical wording in seven other charters (S 730 [*Shaft* 25], S 755 [BCS 1197], S 774 [BCS 1228 and 1264], S 931b, S 936, S 937 [*Abing* 129] and S 983) suggests that *dictitans* is the correct reading. The only other difficulty with the text of **4** concerns the dating clause: the indiction should be six and not fourteen if the grant is to be dated to 963 as the incarnational date says it should be. The regnal year given (six) is also incorrect if it is reckoned from the time when Edgar became king of the Mercians rather than of the whole of Anglo-Saxon England. Two 'Mercian' charters of 963, S 712a and S 723 [BCS 1119], have the seventh regnal year which must be correct. These dating errors in **4** may be due to some simple copying error.

Apart from the corrupt, and possibly rewritten, clause in the dispositive section of **4**, the diplomatic formulae used in the main body of the charter are relatively standard. It seems to have been this draftsman's practice not to adhere to the diplomatic fashion of his immediate time but to hark back to diplomatic conventions of the 940s and 950s. Thus the combination of verbal invocation, royal style and exposition found in **4** can be seen in charters of the 940s of King Edmund such as S 490 (*Shaft* 14) and S 512 (BCS 780) and also of the 950s of King Eadwig such as S 575 (BCS 902), S 585 (BCS 948), S 645 (BCS 994) and S 650 (*Abing* 78). *Iccirco minime in obliuione habui* is also found in S 490 (*Shaft* 14) and the statement of powers which begins 'nunc igitur dum uitale spiramen suum fouerit' and ends 'decurso scilicet sue curriculo uite heredi cui uoluerit impendat imperpetuum karisma' is paralleled in charters of Eadwig such as S 634 (*Abing* 69) and also in an extant original of King Eadwig, S 624 (*Abing* 65). The style of the sanction in **4**, along with its description, 'Acherontis cuius turbidus gurges ceno ac vasta voragine estuare…', takes inspiration from charters which were composed in an era earlier than the reigns of Eadwig and Edmund, a time when the most distinctive draftsman of King Æthelstan's time, 'Æthelstan A', was responsible for the majority of documents being produced (the practice of looking back to the style of previous draftsmen was not uncommon and can be seen in other charters of Edgar, for example S 725 [*Abing* 101]). Interestingly, this particular form of sanction in **4** recurs later on in the year 965 in an extant original of King Edgar, S 736 (BCS 1165), which grants land in Dorset to Wulfheard. We are further encouraged to accept the authenticity of **4** by the fact that the witnesses who attest seem acceptable for the charter's date of 963; it is particularly reassuring that the recent promotion of Bishop Æthelwold, from the abbacy at Abingdon, to the bishopric of Winchester, is recognised

(*ASC AE*, s.a. 963). Furthermore, the estates in question in **4** are known to have belonged to the see of York by the early eleventh century (see **6** for these details) and in any case it seems unlikely that the York church would forge a charter granting an estate to a layman. It is therefore reasonable to suggest that **4** represents the occasion of the initial grant of Sherburn-in-Elmet to a certain 'Æslac'.

The diplomatic formulae used in **4** make it a fascinating document. The years 960–3 witnessed a high level of diplomatic regularity when the production of charters tended to be entrusted to the draftsman known as 'Edgar A'; such charters are immediately recognisable as they often have the same immunity clause, sanction (which refers to the '... eternis baratri incendiis lugubris...'), dating-clause, and wording of subscriptions (Keynes, *Diplomas*, pp. 75–6, suggests that King Edgar had established a centralised agency for the production of charters while he was king of the Mercians and that whoever was responsible for the 'Edgar A' diplomas had therefore started his career in Mercia. Kelly, *Abingdon* 1, pp. lxxxiv–xcii, suggests a contrary view which associates 'Edgar A' with Abingdon and Æthelwold). **4**, composed in 963, is clearly a document which was produced outside that diplomatic mainstream and it perhaps offers an opportunity to see the charters of the time of 'Edgar A' being produced in unusual circumstances. There are seventeen extant charters of the year 963, and four of these (**4**, **5**, S 714 and 722 (*Abing* 98, 99)), are attested by Æthelwold as bishop of Winchester and must therefore be dated after his consecration on 29 November 963 (*ASC E*, s.a. 963 and Keynes 2008, p. 15). It therefore seems likely that all four were produced during a single meeting of the king's *witan* in December 963, perhaps near Christmas. As Keynes notes, it is interesting to find that, of these four documents, **4** is the only one which was not produced by the draftsman 'Edgar A'. Perhaps **4** therefore indicates that there was more than one draftsman utilised in the drafting of royal diplomas and that, during times of increased productivity, the composition of some charters had to be delegated away from 'Edgar A' (see Keynes, *ibid.*, pp. 15–16). The tendency of **4** to use formulas from earlier reigns may also indicate that its scribe/draftsman was consciously avoiding the 'Edgar A' model (for more about the possible agencies at work in the production of Edgar's charters, see Keynes 2008, pp. 14–23). It should also be noted that the sanction used in **4** appears later on in Edgar's reign in S 736 (BCS 1165), an extant original in the name of King Edgar which grants land in Dorset to Wulfheard: could it be that this is a trace of the very same scribe of **4** in operation again in 965? Another idiosyncratic feature of **4** is its use of *impertio* as its dispositive verb. Most of Edgar's charters employ some derivative of the verb, *largior*, or of the verb, *concedo*, in the dispositive clause. The only other Edgar charter to use the same verb as found in **4** is S 725 (*Abing* 101), which has *impertitus sum*. S 725 (*Abing* 101) is a charter which has also been produced outside of the diplomatic mainstream and Kelly suggests that the draftsman who made S 725 (*Abing* 101) was aware of the diplomatic conventions of the day but was perhaps 'not regularly involved in their production' (see Kelly, *Abingdon* 2, p. 405). Is this therefore another trace of this scribe?

Another interesting diplomatic feature of **4**, which is again not typical of regular 'Edgar A' charters, is the form of attestation of the archbishops and some of the bishops, who are made to attest in a very mannered style. For example, Dunstan signs 'agie crucis triumphale signaculum depinxi' and Cynesige signs 'gabulo glorioso prepinxi' (for more about these elaborate styles of attestation, see Keynes 2008, p. 18, n. 74). Similarly elaborate attestation formulas are found in S 690 (*Abing* 87), an original charter of 961, whose main text and boundary clause were written by 'Edgar A', but whose dating-clause and witnesses were added after the document was horizontally folded by a scribe with a different, Style I Anglo-Caroline script (see Kelly, *Abingdon* 2, pp. 357–8). This suggests the possibility that the writing of the dating-clause and witness-list had been assigned to a contemporary of 'Edgar A', to be completed at some point after 'Edgar A' had finished the main body of the charter (for this, see Keynes 2008, p. 18). And it may be that this second scribe was also responsible for the drafting of **4** which has similarly mannered forms of attestation.

As **4** stands so clearly apart from the normal diplomatic practice associated with King Edgar's charters in the years 960–3, it is interesting to find that Æthulf, the bishop of Elmham in 963, attests **4** with the following phrase, 'hanc cartulam dictitans rege suisque precipientibus perscribere iussi'. Apparently Æthulf, after drafting this charter on the orders of the king and his men, has ordered it to be written out. Such a procedure could explain why **4**'s formulation is distinct from that associated with 'Edgar A'. The king may have assigned Bishop Æthulf to draft **4**, rather than his principal draughtsman, and one of Æthulf's staff may then have served as scribe. Moreover it is noteworthy that the identical attestation formula recurs in other Edgar charters (for further discussion of this particular formula, see Keynes 2008, p. 18, n. 74). It is ascribed to Æthulf himself in S 1213 (BCS 1084), a dubious diploma of the year 962 in the name of Wulfstan of Dalham rather than of the king, which concerns land in Suffolk (i.e. within Æthulf's own diocese) but which might derive its formulas from a royal diploma of that date. It recurs in a royal diploma of 964 preserved at Shaftesbury in the attestation of Bishop Æthelwold of Winchester (S 730 [*Shaft* 25]) and in a grant of 967 from Exeter for the witness of Bishop Wulfsige of Cornwall (S 755 [BCS 1197]). Scholars have been uncertain how far to trust tenth-century attestation formulas wherein particular bishops or abbots are said to have 'composed', 'drafted' or to 'have ordered the writing' of the grant (Chaplais 1966, pp. 163–5; Chaplais 1985, pp. 44–6; Keynes, *Diplomas*, pp. 26–8; Brooks 2000, pp. 208–10), but Keynes has emphasised those which attribute the initiative in charter production to bishops and is willing to allow that such special arrangements for their drafting and writing may on occasions have needed to be made. It remains possible that **4** was produced by Bishop Æthulf in accordance with Edgar's wish.

The beneficiary of the grant is named in the manuscript as being a certain 'Æslac'. As Keynes 1986, p. 87, points out, 'Oslac' is an anglicised form of the Scandinavian name, 'Áslákr' (see also Fellows-Jensen, *SPNLY*, p. 33 and Keynes 2008, p. 16). It is therefore plausible to suggest that the 'Æslac' of **4** is synonymous with the powerful northern ealdorman, 'Oslac' (for Oslac, see Whitelock 1959, pp. 77–9). Whitelock noted a problem with regard to Oslac's status: on the grounds that he was described as being an ealdorman (*dux*) in one charter of 963 (**5**) and two in 965 (S 732 [*Abing* 103] and S 733 [*Abing* 104]) she argued that this therefore contradicted the evidence provided by the northern recension of the *ASC* which recorded Oslac's promotion to the ealdormanry as occurring later in 966 (see *ASC DEF*, s.a. 966 and Whitelock 1959, p. 78). Whitelock then noted that a charter of 966, S 738 (BCS 1176), listed Thored as *dux* and Oslac as *minister*, which she took as supporting the statement in the *ASC* that Oslac did not become an ealdorman until 966; this therefore led her to question the authenticity of the charter of 963 (**5**) which gave Oslac's status as an ealdorman. But what should be stressed is that these terms used to describe the differing stations of men seem to have been used rather loosely with regard to Northumbrian figures. Thus Oslac himself is described in three different ways in charters of 963: he is not *dux* in S 712a but rather *dominus*; and here, in **4**, he is nowhere referred to as *dux*. It is only as a witness to **5** that Oslac occurs as *dux* and it may be that 'Edgar A', the draftsman of **5**, included Oslac among those who attest as *dux* because he was unsure of Oslac's precise status and thus of how to categorise this northern figure (see further Keynes 2008, p. 16, n. 65). If we accept that these terms were not rigid and absolute for men from Northumbria, then this removes any problem with the suggestion that **5** is an authentic document. Subsequently, Oslac himself became an especially powerful individual in Northumbria, to the extent that Edgar entrusted him alone with the duty of ensuring the observance of the king's law in Northumbria (Edgar IV). Thus the statement in the *ASC* which notes Olac's succession to the ealdormanry is perhaps one designed to reflect some new elevation in the authority and status that Oslac had acquired (Keynes 1986, p. 87, nn. 35 and 37, notes that the chronology of the *ASC* is generally unreliable for the 960s and suggests that there is nothing suspicious about the fact that Oslac is not styled *dux* in **4**).

The name of the estate being granted in **4**, Sherburn, often has a suffix, 'in Elmet', added to it (for example, in the relevant entry in GDB); there is therefore reason to believe that the estate lay in, and had something to do with, the old British kingdom of Elmet (Sherburn itself was an estate of high status, demonstrated by the find of a golden ring of Queen Æthelswith near it; for information about Sherburn's relationship to the kingdom of Elmet and the golden ring, see Long 1993, p. 118. An inventory of church treasures at Sherburn-in-Elmet written into the York Gospels on f. 161r may suggest that the York Gospels themselves had once been at Sherburn: see Keynes 1986, pp. 96–7 and Appendix 1). Not a lot is known about this kingdom but it seems to have developed in the immediately post-Roman period and is mentioned by Bede as being a Christianised place (*HE*, ii.14; for further comment, see Charles-Edwards, *Ireland*, p. 313). **4**'s boundary clause describes the limits of the 'twenty hides of the "inland" at Sherburn' (*xx hida…to Scireburnan ðæs inlandes*). The term 'inland' is a technical one common to many documents relating to regions of the Danelaw. It refers to an estate over which a lord had actual possession rather than one from which he merely received dues and rents: the 'inland' came with associated demesne (for 'inland' see Faith, *English Peasantry*, pp. 15–55 and pp. 56–88, at pp. 43–4, for the 'inland' of Sherburn in particular). The 'inland' in **4** is Sherburn, and ten vills are described as being somehow subordinate to, or dependent on, this central manor: these vills may have been detached parcels of demesne, perhaps early 'berewicks' (see Faith, *English Peasantry*, pp. 43–4 and Stenton, *Types*, p. 70, n. 3, for the date at which the term 'berewick' came into use; the relationship of such dependent estates was defined in **2** by the phrase 'sake and soke'; although no such expression is used in **4**, we may be fairly sure that a similar jurisdictional relationship existed between Sherburn and its dependent vills as the later evidence of **6** and **7** explicitly refer to such a system at Sherburn; see also Hadley, *Northern*, pp. 121–2). Nine of the ten vills have been identified and it has been suggested that seven of these can be located on a limestone ridge which formed the eastern border of Elmet (Long 1993, p. 118; Sherburn forms a 'multiple estate', for which see Jones 1975).

Although **4** is a grant to Earl Oslac, the Sherburn estate eventually came into the possession of the York see. Since Oswald's *Memorandum* (**6**) talks of those areas of Sherburn lost to the archbishopric, the implication is that, sometime in the period between 963 (the original granting of Sherburn in **4**) and 975 × 992 (the dates of **6**), Sherburn had come to be property of the York see. The suggestion (Stenton, *Types*, p. 86) that Edgar granted **4** to Oslac with an implicit understanding that he would pass it on to the archbishop seems unnecessary (see also Keynes 1986, p. 87). It is more probable that Oslac donated the land and charter to the church at some later time or that it passed to the archbishopric after Oslac was banished from the kingdom in 975 and deprived of his lands (*ASC ABC*, s.a. 975).

Documents compiled at a later date suggest that parts of the Sherburn estate did not remain in the church's endowment for very long (see also Keynes 1986, p. 88). Two documents in particular give us details of the subsequent history of the Sherburn estate. The first is the *Memorandum* written by Archbishop Oswald (**6**), a document which was later annotated by Archbishop Wulfstan (for these details, see the commentary to **6**). The *Memorandum* states what was removed from Sherburn: 'half of *Ceoredesholm* and half of Cawood – and *Gisferþesdæll* has always belonged to Sherburn – and half the soke which belongs to Sherburn'. The wording of this passage suggests that *Ceoredesholm* and Cawood were not considered part of the soke of Sherburn and that therefore they represented an actual loss of land. And the loss of half of Sherburn's soke would also have been a substantial blow, considering all the rights and dues that accompanied such jurisdiction (see Keynes 1986, p. 88).

It was perhaps the re-claiming of various vills attached to Otley, Ripon and Sherburn-in-Elmet that caused a group of surveys to be entered into the back of the York Gospels. These surveys (**7**), which form our second document to do with the history of the Sherburn estate, include a detailed description of the soke of Sherburn and were probably written *c.* 1020–23 (for more details, see the commentary to **7**). The soke of Sherburn given in **7** included all of those places mentioned in the boundary clause of **4** but also added a significant number of new vills, including Wistow, Upper Selby, two oxgangs in Flaxley, half of Barlow, all of Brayton except half a ploughland, all of Burn, all of Burton except half a ploughland, Gateforth, all of the two Thorpes, all of the two Hirsts, all of the two Haddleseys, five oxgangs in the third Haddlesey, half of Birkin, all of Sutton, all of Byram, all of Burton, all of Brotherton, all of Fairburn except two and a half ploughlands, two ploughlands in Ledsham, one ploughland in Newthorpe, five oxgangs in Barkston and *Hehferðe hegðe*. It seems, therefore, that between 963 and *c.* 1020–23 the size of the Sherburn estate had increased substantially and it may be that these gains should be accredited to Archbishop Wulfstan (Keynes 1986, p. 88 and Baxter 2004, p. 186).

Keynes shows that the same scribe of the survey, or perhaps someone working in collaboration with that scribe, returned at a later stage and added more details about the Sherburn estate (Keynes 1986, p. 88). We learn that (for the text and translation of this passage, see **7 (a)**):

> In Sherburn, in addition to the demesne land (*inland*), there are four hides of workland, and in Lotherton three hides, and in Barkston one hide and five oxgangs, and of the manor of Steeton three oxgangs.
>
> And in Wistow two oxgangs, and in Cawood two parts, of the land is *agenland* into Sherburn, and in Fenton is loan-land one and a half ploughlands.

It is not certain whether or not the demesne land (*inland*) cited here refers to the same Sherburn demesne land (*inland*) as originally given in **4** or whether it may have changed over the years (Keynes, *ibid.*, p. 88). The four hides of 'workland' clearly denoted lands which were separate from the demesne land (*inland*) and which perhaps owed some kind of labour to the owner of Sherburn (Keynes, *ibid.*, p. 88 and, for 'workland', see Robertson, *Charters*, p. 415). We are not told what the relationship of the land at Lotherton, Barkston and Steeton is to Sherburn but the statement that Wistow and Cawood form *agenland* (lit. 'ownland') to Sherburn presumably means that the owner of Sherburn owned these outright. The one and a half ploughlands at Fenton had been leased out by the York see (this second part to the survey may represent a correction to the details of the first part: Keynes 1986, pp. 88–9).

By 1086 Sherburn-in-Elmet, together with its berewicks, was rated at ninety-six carucates (GDB, f. 302v). At the time of Edward the Confessor it was worth £34 6s and this had not changed by William's time: it was therefore the most valuable estate the archbishop owned (Keynes, *ibid.*, p. 89). It is unfortunate, as Keynes points out, that the berewicks attached to Sherburn at the time of Domesday are not specified and it is therefore impossible to tell whether or not the estate had been restructured in the period between *c.* 1020–23 and 1086. Some of those places listed in **7** as being areas of soke to the Sherburn estate are detailed in Domesday as having left the jurisdiction of the archbishop but the fact that many cannot be found listed under different ownership suggests that the York see had secured its hold on the estate (Keynes *ibid.*, p. 89).

Bounds of Sherburn

1. *These are the estate-boundaries of the twenty hides* (hid) *at Sherburn of the inland. First on the south side: west along (the) brook* (brotty) *to the highway* (herepæð). The word *brotty* is most probably a miscopying of *broces* (see **3**(i) which has the form *brocci*). If so, the bounds here follow the line of the brook, which is probably Mill Dike (SE 4931), until they reach the highway (*herepæð*) (Long 1993, p. 120). *Herepæð* literally means 'army-road' and it is for this reason that Stevenson equated this part of **4** with the Roman road today known as the A 656, which meets Mill Dike at SE 4333 (Stevenson quoted by Farrer, *EYC*, p. 20). But Long 1993, p. 121, notes that, if the southern boundary followed the A 656, that would include Micklefield and Lotherton within the 'inland' of the Sherburn estate, whereas the boundary clause of **4** then goes on to list these two same vills among the ten places that were outside of Sherburn but dependent on it as the central manor. Long therefore suggests that a track running parallel to the A 656 at SE 455330 might be a better candidate for the *herepæð*.

2. *Northwards along (the) road* (weg) *to (the) steep/stony bridge* (scearp + brycg)*; eastward thence along (the) slade* (slæd) *until it comes to the road* (weg). **4**'s bounds now follow the line of this road northwards to the steep bridge (*scearpan brycge*) which Long suggests is to be found in the small Bragdale Valley at SE 453350 (Long 1993, p. 121); *scearp* literally means 'sharp' but here the meaning is that the bridge was 'rough' or 'stony' (I am very grateful to Professor E. Stanley for advice about this word and many others in the York boundary clauses). **4** then directs us eastwards from the steep bridge along the slade/valley until it comes to the 'road' and the most natural meeting point with the 'road' is at today's Coldhill Farm (SE 466354). Long 1993, p. 121, suggests a possible equation of **4**'s 'road' with Copley Lane.

3. *And half a hide* (hid) *in Hibald's homestead* (toft) *and one hide* (hid) *in [Monk] Fryston* (SE 5130), *in Hillam* (SE 5129) *two oxgangs* (oxenagang), *in Lumby* (SE 487303) *two oxgangs* (oxenagang), *and two and a half hides* (hid) *in Milford* (SE 4931) *and to Steeton* (SE 4831) *and Micklefield* (SE 4433) *two hides* (hid) *of land and all Lotherton* (SE 4536) *except one hide* (hid), *and one and a half hides* (hid) *in [Church] Fenton* (SE 5136) *and one and a half hides in Cawood* (hid) (SE 5737), *and all the land that belongs thereto along (the) Ouse between (the) Wharfe and the island* (? see commentary below), *in wood* (wuda) *and water* (wæter) *and field/open land* (feld). The bounds of **4** concludes with this

list of ten vills and the amount of land in these vills which was dependent on the central manor, Sherburn; only *Hibaldestofte* remains to be identified.

The recent investigation of these bounds in Long 1993, pp. 120–4, has suggested in general that the 'inland' of Sherburn appears to be smaller than previously thought, perhaps less than half the original area, and to the west of Sherburn itself (Stevenson's alternative views are given in Farrer, *EYC*, pp. 20–1). One of Long's most significant re-appraisals comes with the last part of **4**'s bounds and to the land described as being tributary to Sherburn and translated by Stevenson as being situated 'along the Ouse between the Wharfe and the Aire'. If Stevenson's translation is believed this would suggest that a large area of land, not specified in **4**, was tributary to Sherburn. But the word for 'Aire' in the manuscript is given as *dacy*. Long suggests that this is a mistranscription by the scribe of **4** for *ða eg* (or possibly *ða ea*) which would mean the 'island' or the 'river'. This implies that the last sentence in the boundary clause refers to only a small amount of land to do with the vill of Cawood itself (Long 1993, p. 122 and also *CamDEPN*, s.v. 'Aire').

5

King Edgar grants thirty hides (casati) *at Newbald, Yorkshire, to Gunner, his faithful* dux. A.D. 963

F. York, Minster Library and Archives, L 2/1 (*Mag. Reg. Alb.*), pt. I, 57 rv: copy, s. xiv[med]
Rubric: Collacio Domini Eadgari regis facta cuidam nobili et fideli super posicionibus et rebus aliis.
H. Bodleian, Dodsworth 9, 2v: copy of F, s. xvii [incomplete copy]
J. Bodleian, Dodsworth 125, 76rv: copy of F, s. xvii
Ed.: a. *Mon. Angl.*, iii. 129, from F
b. *Mon. Angl.* (rev. edn.), vi, pt. 3, p. 1176 (no. 4)
c. Kemble 504, from F
d. Birch 1113 and Birch 1353 (bounds only), from F
e. Farrer, *EYC*, no. 5, from F
Listed: Sawyer 716; Hart, *ECNE*, no. 124
Edited from F

Altitrono in eternum regnante. Universis sophie studium intento mentis conamine sedulo rimantibus liquido patescit quid huius uite periculis nimio [a]ingruentibus terrore recidiui terminus[a] cosmi apropinquare dinoscitur ut ueridica Christi promulgat sententia quibus dicit 'Surget gens contra gentem et regnum contra regnum'[1] et reliqua. Quamobrem ego Eadgarus totius Britannie basilius[b] quandam telluris particulam .xxx. uidelicet casatos, loco qui celebri et[c] Niubode nuncupatur uocabulo, cuidam duci mihi ualde fideli <qui>[d] ab huiusce patrie gnosticis nobili Gunnere appellatur uocabulo pro obsequio eius deuotissimo perpetua largitus sum hereditate ut ipse uita comite cum omnibus utensilibus,[e] pratis uidelicet pascuis,[f] uoti compos habeat et post uite sue terminum quibuscumque cleronomis inmunem derelinquat. Sit autem predictum rus omni terrene[g] seruitutis iugo liberum, tribus exceptis rata uidelicet expeditione, pontis arcisue restauratione.

Si quis igitur hanc[h] nostram donacionem in aliud quam constituimus transferre uoluerit, priuatus consortio sancte Dei ecclesie eternis baratri incendiis lugubris iugiter <cum>[i] Iuda Christi proditore eiusque complicibus puniatur, si non satisfaccione emendauerit congrua quod contra nostrum deliquid decretum. Hiis metis prefatum rus hinc inde giratur:[j]

Ðis sint þa[k] landgemaera to Niƿebotle:[l] aerest suðƿeard ƿeg[m] de gemaere to serirtre;[n] þonan[o] ƿest ƿid anes þornes;[p] þonan norð to þan broce,[q] ⁊[r] ilc oðer acra beeastan[s] hode; of þan broce ƿest to þan dice; ⁊lang dices to elfredes[t] bricge; þonne norð to ylemere; ⁊ þonan to saxferdes laƿe; of saxferdes[u] laƿa norð on þa dic; ⁊lang dices on þene sic;[v] ⁊lang sices[w] be þere acera anheafda on þa strete; of þere strete east onan up one ƿalde benorðan Faryisdal on þa ealdan dic; ⁊lang dices to brugun[x] laƿa; of rugun[y] laƿa ⁊lang þes[z] [a2]grene ƿeges[a2] þaet hit cynð to fif laƿan; ⁊ þonne suð ⁊lang ƿeges[b2] Deoppendala; suð andlang denes up to þan ƿege;[c2] andlang ƿeges[d2] to þing[e2] hougum;[f2] þon sƿa forð ⁊lang ƿeges[d2] ꝥ[g2] eft[h2] to saerirtre.[i2]

Anno dominice incarnacionis .dcccc.lxiii. scripta erat hec carta, hiis testibus consencientibus quorum inferius nomina subnotantur.

Ego Eadgarus rex Anglorum concessi
Ego Dunstanus archiepiscopus corroboraui [*Canterbury*]
Ego Oscytel archiepiscopus corroboraui [*York*]
Ego Osulf episcopus consolidaui [*Ramsbury*]
Ego Aþeƿold[j2] episcopus corroboraui [*Winchester*]
Ego Osƿold episcopus acquieui [*Worcester*]
Ego Aefere[k2] dux
Ego Aelfstan[l2] dux
Ego Astan[m2] dux
Ego Aþeline[n2] dux
Ego Oslac dux
Ego Cytelbearn dux
Ego Brihtferð
Ego Aelfƿne[o2] minister
Ego Ƿulfhelm minister
Ego Ƿulfstan minister
Ego Alfsige[p2] minister
Ego Alfƿold[q2] minister

[a..a] ingruente terrore redimini F; *the word* terminus *has fallen out here; compare S 700, S 702*
[b] *A spelling for* basileus [c] *For Old English* æt [d] *Omitted* F [e] utensibus F
[f] *The word* siluis *usually found in this position after* pascuis *may have fallen out here* F; *compare S 690* [g] tempore F [h] han F [i] *Omitted* F [j] *The Old English boundary clause is highly corrupt; see the note on editorial method, pp. 83–4* [k] p F [l] Nisebocle F

[m] yes F; *or possibly for* þes [n] serirtre *is very corrupt; see the discussion in the commentary* [o] bonan F [p] yorner F [q] broct F [r] *Where* F *has an ampersand in the boundary clause, a Tironian et has been used* [s] befastan F [t] Elfreder F [u] Saxferdeẏ F [v] ric F [w] sicer F [x] brusun F [y] rusun F [z] yer F [a2...a2] sreneẏeses F [b2] yeser F [c2] yese F [d2] yeser F [e2] yins F [f2] housum F [g2] y F [h2] est F [i2] saerirtre *is very corrupt; see commentary* [j2] Aẏeyold F; *for* Aþelpold [k2] *Perhaps for* Ælfhere [l2] Aelsstan F [m2] *For* Æðelstan [n2] Ayeline F; *for* Æþelpine [o2] Aelfyne F; *for* Ælfpine [p2] Alflige F [q2] Alfẏold F

[1] Mark 13:8; Luc. 21:10

We can be fairly certain that **5** is a copy of an authentic document. The witnesses who attest are correct for the date of the grant (963) and the diplomatic elements are readily identifiable as typical of charters belonging to King Edgar's reign. More specifically, the form of **5** matches the type of diploma drafted and compiled by the scribe known as 'Edgar A', who was responsible for a large number of charters produced between 960 and 963 (see Drögereit 1935, pp. 394–400, Keynes, *Diplomas*, pp. 70–9 and Kelly, *Abingdon* 1, pp. lxxxiv–xcii). The verbal invocation, the proem, the statement of powers, the immunity clause and the sanction (with its reference to '…eternis baratri incendiis lugubris…'), are all standard clauses of an 'Edgar A' charter. The charters produced by 'Edgar A' are renowned for a high level of diplomatic regularity, which means that **5** is almost identical to the charters S 700 (*Abing* 92), S 702 (BCS 1085), S 706 (BCS 1083), S 710 (*Shaft* 24), S 711 (*Bath* 16) and S 714 (*Abing* 98), all of which belong to the years 962 and 963 (S 767 [BCS 1216] has similar formulation but a later date of 968).The style of the subscriptions of the witnesses, who are made to sign with varying and alliterating attesting verbs, is also typical of 'Edgar A' charters. It has previously been suggested that the attestation of Oslac as *dux* in **5** casts doubt on its overall authenticity but these terms were not applied consistently to Northumbrians and we should not therefore question its use in this instance (see the commentary to **4** for more about these issues; for the suggestion that **5** is suspicious because of the attestation of Oslac, see Whitelock 1959, p. 78). As was discussed in the commentary to **4**, the attestation of Æthelwold as a bishop rather than an abbot in **5** makes it very likely that **5** belongs to a group of four charters (the other three being **4**, S 714 [*Abing* 98] and S 722 [*Abing* 99]) which were the product of the same meeting of the king's *witan* in December 963 (see Keynes 2008, p. 15).

Gunner, the beneficiary, was an ealdorman with lands in Yorkshire and can be found attesting a variety of charters from 931 until 963 and it is likely that he died soon after this date. In the annal for 966 in the *ASC*, Gunner's son, Thored, is mentioned as harrying the *Westmoringa land*, in an act which seems to have been one of personal violence rather than a deed ordered by King Edgar (Stenton, *Preparatory to ASE*, pp. 218–19). Although not all of the earls with Scandinavian names at this time should automatically be assigned to Northumbria, Whitelock favours the connection for Gunner and suggests that he was a subordinate earl (Whitelock 1959, p. 78). The name Gunner derives ultimately from Old Norse, 'Gunnarr'; see Fellows-Jensen, *SPNLY*, pp. 113–14.

The attestation of Brihtferð in **5** is of particular interest: he occurs between the list of ealdormen and thegns and is not afforded a title of *dux* or of *minister*. Brihtferð is also present in two other charters without a title: in S 684 (BCS 1056), an apparent original of 960 granting land in Cornwall, and in S 704, a 962 grant of land in Devon. That he attests elsewhere without a title suggests that this occurrence in **5** is not some kind of scribal blunder whereby the copyist failed to note Brihtferð's title. Instead it is a sign that there has been some difficulty for the draftsman when it came to classifying Brihtferð's exact status. S 684 (BCS 1056) aids in an understanding of why this may have occurred since it has the attestation of one Ælfgar, who also lacks a title. Since Ælfgar and Brihtferð both lack a title, there is the suggestion that they were considered to be of a similar status. And it emerges from other evidence that the two were brothers and were related to King Edgar himself; see the subscriptions of these two men in S 651 (*Abing* 79) and also *ASC A*, s.a. 962; this relationship is noted in Hart, *ECNE*, p. 301 and Keynes 2008, pp. 33–5, particularly p. 35, n. 155, who points out that not only Ælfgar and Brihtferð but also Æthelweard and Ælfwine were accorded special status among the king's councillors. Clearly Brihtferð was a man of no ordinary standing and, being a relative of the king, eluded regular classification here in **5**.

The estate conveyed in **5** is Newbald. Unlike those granted in previous charters, principally **2** and **4**, Newbald is not a 'multiple estate': no vills are described as being held as soke and there are no parcels of detached demesne. The Newbald region has evidence of very early settlement: there are archaeological sites present which range in date from the Roman period to Anglo-Saxon times (Long and Pickles 1993*a*, p. 135). An Anglo-Saxon royal centre at Goodmanham and a large cemetery at Sancton, both just to the north of Newbald, suggest that it was an important place (Long and Pickles *ibid.*, p. 135).

Although **5** is granted directly to Earl Gunner, the Newbald estate eventually came into the possession of the York church. The suggestion (Stenton, *Types*, p. 86 and Farrer, *EYC*, p. 16) that **5** was always intended for the York church seems unnecessary (see also the commentary to **4** for a similar situation). Archbishop Oswald's Old English *Memorandum* (**6**) provides detail about the later history of the Newbald estate which suggests that **5** did remain in the immediate possession of Gunner. It describes how Archbishop Oscytel had to buy 'the estate at Newbold for 120 mancuses of red gold from King Edgar'. It seems therefore that after Gunner, the beneficiary of **5**, had died, the estate passed back into the hands of the king only to be purchased with the charter to Gunner by Oscytel on behalf of the York see: since Gunner died *c.* 963 and Oscytel died in 971 it must have been during this time-frame that Newbald became the archbishop's property (for Oscytel's death, see *ASC BC*, s.a. 971). We can only guess at the subsequent history of the estate and whether or not it remained in the archbishopric's possession; but, as we will see, a small part of it (North Cave) became separated by the time of the Domesday survey, at which point both Newbald and North Cave were in the hands of Archbishop Thomas of York (Long and Pickles 1993*a*, p. 137, note that one of the properties given by Ulf son of Thorald to York Minster, and symbolised by Ulf's horn, was Newbald; for this horn of tenure, see above, pp. 8–9).

Bounds of Newbald

The York copyist of **5**, who is the same person responsible for all the copies of the charters in the *Magnum Registrum Album*, has again struggled with the Old English in the boundary clause. This has led to various differing interpretations of some of its elements (see Farrer, *EYC*, pp. 16–18, Hart, *ECNE*, pp. 121–3 (no. 124) and Long and Pickles 1993*a*). In the most recent analysis, Long and Pickles 1993*a*, p. 137, point out that the assessment of Newbald in **5** at thirty *casati* had dropped by the time of the Domesday survey to twenty-eight carucates and two bovates (GDB, f. 302v). Of course, changes in estate structure from the mid-tenth century to the late eleventh century are to be expected and so this might represent a natural evolution. But Long and Pickles 1993*a*, p. 137, further suggest that it is striking that, on the southern boundary of the Newbald estate, lies North Cave, which is rated, in 1086, at one carucate and six bovates (GDB, f. 302v): this accounts exactly for the difference between the rating given in **5** and that in Domesday Book (there were eight bovates to every carucate). North Cave was also held by the York see in 1086 and Long and Pickles therefore propose that it would originally have formed part of the estate granted in **5** and that at some point in the period 963 to 1086, it had become detached from Newbald (see also Farrer, *EYC*, p. 18). This understanding, in turn, suggests the general direction we should expect the bounds to travel in.

1. *These are the estate-boundaries of Newbald: first southwards [? along] the road* (weg) *by the boundary* (gemære) *to the street* (? stræt; but see commentary below)*; then west towards a thorn-tree* (þorn)*; then north to the brook* (broc). The opening to Newbald's bounds is very corrupt: *suðpeard peg de gemaere to serirtre*; only an approximate translation can be given above. The corrupted word *serirtre* causes particular difficulties of interpretation. Since Newbald's bounds end at a point described similarly as *saerirtre* (see bound 11 below), it is plausible that the word represents whatever was the starting- and end-point of the boundary clause. A typical feature of an Anglo-Saxon boundary clause is for it to start at some kind of landmark/feature, rather than the general prescription here of 'southwards [along?] the way'. As Dr S.E. Kelly has kindly pointed out to me (pers. comm.), this unusual opening clause in **5**, together with the corrupted word, *serirtre*, might suggest that the beginning of the circuit has somehow been tampered with, perhaps in an attempt to make sense of an unidentifiable landmark.

Despite these difficulties, Long and Pickles have attempted to trace **5**'s bounds in the landscape today. The bounds begin at a southerly point (SE 9234), proceed in a clockwise direction and cover an area which comprises the modern-day parishes of North and South Newbald (SE 9136 and SE 9135 respectively; see Hart, *ECNE*, p. 121). The boundaries of Newbald at first progress southwards along the way, which includes the detached portion of land in North Cave (Long and Pickles 1993*a*, p. 138), until they reach a boundary mark, the corrupt form *serirtre*, discussed above. Scholars have had different interpretations of what this could be. Farrer has followed the work of Stevenson and suggested that *serirtre* should be emended to *stræte*. Stevenson then suggests that, if this correction is acceptable, this is a reference to the Roman road from Brough to Market Weighton, the modern-day A 1034 (Stevenson's views are in Farrer, *EYC*, p. 16). Hart proposes a different interpretation. He would prefer that the northern dialect form of *tre* is accepted and that *serirtre* should be read as *seares tre*, 'withered tree' (Hart, *ECNE*, pp. 121–2). The topography of the region suggests that *stræte* is to be preferred as the bounds must have reached and crossed the line of the Roman road (somewhere near SE 914340) and then continued westwards until the point which was then marked by a thorn-tree (for this interpretation, see Long and Pickles 1993*a*, p. 138). At this thorn-tree the bounds take a turn northwards towards the brook, which has been identified as Newbald's Mill Beck (SE 906357; Mill Beck becomes Hotham Beck at SE 903356); see Long and Pickles 1993*a*, p. 138.

2. *And each second field* (æcer) *to the east of Hotham* (hode). It is likely that *hode* is an early form of the place-name, 'Hotham' which, in its earliest renderings, could either be in the dative singular, *hode*, or the dative plural, *hodum*, meaning 'at the shelters'. Another possibility is that this is a reference to the feature 'shelters', from which 'Hotham' took its name; for discussion, see Farrer, *EYC*, p. 17, *PN YorksER*, pp. 225–6 and *CamDEPN*,

pp. 318–19. This suggests a rather unusual situation whereby the territory of Newbald somehow overlaps with that of its neighbour to the south-west, Hotham. This has been explained by Long and Pickles since they note that this sharing obtained until modern times and that by this stage Newbald itself had divided into two parts, each of which possessed a detached parcel of land in Hotham (Long and Pickles 1993*a*, p. 138, with a useful map on p. 136; see also Finberg, *Agrarian History*, p. 491).

3. *From the brook* (broc) *west to the dyke/ditch* (dic)*; along (the) dyke/ditch* (dic) *to Ælfred's bridge* (brycg). Hart suggested two possible locations for Ælfred's bridge: either the point at which **5**'s bounds crossed Cliffe Road (SE 895366, a road which runs west–east from North and South Cliffe to North Newbald) or perhaps a location further north (SE 896371) 'where Ælfred's bridge would perhaps have carried a Roman road (now vanished) across the beck' (Hart, *ECNE*, p. 122; for a slightly different interpretation, see Long and Pickles 1993*a*, p. 139).

4. *Then north to* yle *pond* (? igil, *'hedgehog', but perhaps here 'leech'*, + mere)*; and then to Seaxferth's burial mound/tumulus* (hlæw). For *igil*, see Smith, *EPNE* I, p. 280, who discusses the regular combination with *mere* and suggests an alternative, 'leech'. The *ylemere* was identified as a pond located at SE 895377 by Hart (in *ECNE*, p. 122); but Long and Pickles suggest that it is not possible to be so specific since the nature of the landscape at this point means that any one of a number of ponds could be meant (Long and Pickles 1993*a*, p. 139). Then the bounds reach Saxferth's hill/burial-mound, which has not been identified (although Hart, *ECNE*, p. 122, conjectures that Saxferth's burial mound was located at SE 895385).

5. *From Seaxferth's burial mound/tumulus* (hlæw) *north to the dyke/ditch* (dic)*; along (the) dyke/ditch* (dic) *to the small stream* (sic). The *sic* ('small stream') refers to Newbald Syke, an area which is represented today by the Syke House Farm (SE 907384); see Farrer, *EYC*, p. 17, Hart, *ECNE*, p. 122 and Long and Pickles 1993*a*, p. 139.

6. *Along (the) small stream* (sic) *by the headland* (andheafod) *of the fields* (æcer) *to the street* (stræt). Hart, *ECNE*, p. 122, suggests the street here is the Roman road running north to Sancton which is crossed by the small stream.

7. *From the street* (stræt) *east right on up to a forest* (wold) *on the north of 'Faryisdal' to the old dyke/ditch* (eald + dic). Long and Pickles 1993*a*, p. 139, note that the valley covered by the description 'up to a forest on the north of *Faryisdal* to the old dyke/ditch' is now called Longdale but that it was, until recently, known as Farysdale.

8. *Along (the) dyke/ditch* (dic) *to the rough* (ruh) *burial mound/tumulus* (hlæw). After following the line of the dyke/ditch, **5**'s bounds come to the *brugun lapa* which seems most likely to be a corruption of *hrugan hlape*, 'rough burial mound/tumulus' (see Stevenson in Farrer, *EYC*, p. 17; Long and Pickles 1993*a*, p. 140, identify this tumulus as being at SE 931395; for a very different interpretation, see Hart, *ECNE*, p. 123).

9. *From (the) rough* (ruh) *burial mound/tumulus along the greenway* (grene + weg) *until it comes to (the) five burial mounds/tumuli* (hlæw). This set of 'tumuli' marked the far north-eastern corner of **5**'s bounds (Long and Pickles 1993*a*, p. 140). Farrer, *EYC*, p. 17, n. h, suggests that this reference to five tumuli in a row could be to Cherry Burton; but Hart, *ECNE*, p. 123 and Long and Pickles 1993*a*, p. 140, state that these five tumuli cannot be identified with any precision.

10. *And then south along (the) way* (weg) *to deep valley (i.e. Deepdale)* (deop + dæl)*; south along (the) valley* (denu) *up to the way* (weg). 'Deepdale', a common name meaning 'deep valley', has survived and is situated at SE 9235; see *PN YorksER*, p. 227. Long and

Pickles 1993*a*, p. 140, note that the part of the boundary involving a southwards direction along the valley has to be an anomaly since the valleys are all running from west to east; they suggest an alternative reading of, 'south along the head of the valley and up to the way'.

11. *Along (the) road* (weg) *to assembly mounds* (þing + haugr)*; then so forth along (the) road* (weg) *until back to the (?) street* (? stræt). The 'assembly mounds' have most recently been equated with the tumuli in Howe Hill Field (SE 947359) (see Long and Pickles 1993*a*, which goes against the previous interpretation of Hart, *ECNE*, p. 123). The last turn of the bounds takes them back along the 'road' until they reach the starting point, the *saerirtre*, possibly 'street'; the 'road' may be the modern-day B 1230 or perhaps a different road running along the boundary of South Newbald (Long and Pickles 1993*a*, pp. 140–1). Hart, *ECNE*, p. 123, again suggests that we should read *særistre* ('withered tree') instead of *stræt* ('street'); Long and Pickles 1993*a*, pp. 140–1, suggest that the tree element may be correct but that the 'first element is more likely to be a Norse personal name than an adjective'.

6

Memorandum by Archbishop Oswald concerning the estates belonging to the archbishopric of York. [A.D. 975 × 992]

C. BL Harley 55, 4v: copy, s. xi[in]
G. BL Harley 6841, 129rv: copy of C, s. xvi [with Latin translation, 128rv]
Ed.: a. Birch 1278, 1279, from C
b. Robertson, *Charters*, no. LIV (pp. 110–13), with translation, from C
c. Loyn, *Wulfstan Manuscript*, appendix (facsimile)
Translated: Whitelock, *EHD*, p. 565
Listed: Sawyer 1453; Hart, *ECNE*, no. 125
Edited from C with variants from G

[a]Ðas sƿutelunge gedihte Osƿald arcebiscop 7 aƿritan het;[a]

Þis syndon þa tunas þe syndan adon of Ottanlege · an ys Haddincham · oþer ys Hyllicleg · þridde Mensinctun · feoþe healf Burhleg fifte Gislicleh sixfe[b] Scefinc · seofeþe Middeltun ehtaþe Dentun healf ix. Timmel[c] .x. Lindeleh .xi. Stanburne .xii. Becƿudu .xiii. Byllinctun healf ·

þas tunas sindan adon of Rypum .i. ys Heaƿic oþer Heaƿic .iii. Ansætleh .iiii. Stanleh an[d] hid .v. Helperby .vi. æt Myðtune[e] · Of Poƿeltune tƿa hida ·

þis is genumen of Scirebunnan · Ceoredesholm healf · 7 Caƿudu healf 7 Gisferþ<es>dæll[f] hyrðe[g] æfre into Scirebunnan · 7 healfe socne þe gebyreþ into Scireburnan·

þis syndan þa land þe Oscytel yrcebiscop begeat on Norþhymbralande mid his feo 7 him mon geald for unrihtan hæmede · an ys Æffeltune[h] he gebohte mid .xxiiii. pundun · æt Deor<ƿ>ulfe[i] · Yferingaham he gebohte mid feoƿer 7 feoƿertigun pundun æt fæge Osulfes fæder · 7 þ land æt Neoƿeboldan he gebohte mid hundtƿelftigun <ge>mancsun[j] reades goldes æt Eadgare cyn<ing>eþ[k] 7 æt Heolƿerbi him ƿæs gegolden for unrihtan hæmede ƿæron tƿegen gebroþra hæfdon an ƿif · 7 into Heolƿerby hyrð Mytun tƿa dæl 7 Ƿibustan socn · 7 Þurulfestun · 7 Ioletun · 7 Þorp · 7 æt Scyteby he gebohte mid .xx. pundun · 7 þreo hida æt Bracenan[l] he gebohte æt Eadgare cinge 7 he hit him gebocode into sancte Iohanne · [m]\7 Ic Osƿold arcebiscop sƿutelige ꝥ/[m] ealle þas land þe [n]\se/[n] yrcebiscop Oscytel begeat on Norþhymbralande 7 min hlaford forgeaf hi me [o]\into sancte Pe<tre>/[o] þa he[p] ƿæs æt Snotingaham · þas oþre land þe her elles onstandaþ þæt ealle ic hy [q]h<æfde> <o>ð þ<.>rað in com[q] þa ƿæs sancte Peter bereafod 7 ic syððan · [r]\ƿrece God sƿa he ƿille/·[r]

[a..a] *Title added by hand of Archbishop Wulfstan* C [b] sixte G [c] Tunmel G [d] ten G [e] Nyðtune G [f] -es- *in* Gisferþesdæll *faded in* C [g] dælhhyrde G [h] Æppeltune G [i] *A letter has been erased in* C; *reading supplied from* G [j] ge- *faded in* C; *reading supplied from* G [k] *Not legible in* C; cyn...eþ G [l] Dracenan G [m..m] *Written above the line by hand of Archbishop Wulfstan* C; i' Oswold arceb swuteligaþ G [n..n] *Written above the line by hand of Archbishop Wulfstan* C [o..o] *Written in margin by hand of Archbishop Wulfstan, with last three letters of* Petre *illegible* C [p] he *followed by erasure in* C; þa he...pæs G [q..q] *Only a few letters of this part are legible in* C *(see commentary for further discussion)*; hæf oð þerað in com G [r..r] *Added by hand of Archbishop Wulfstan* C; G *has* bereafod *followed by an illegible word of three letters, then* syððan sece god spa he pille

Translation[a]

Archbishop Oswald composed this declaration and had it written.

These are the townships which have been taken from Otley: the first is Addingham, the second Ilkley, the third Menston, the fourth half of Burley, the fifth Guiseley, the sixth Chevin, the seventh Middleton, the eighth half of Denton, the ninth Timble, the tenth Lindley, the eleventh Stainburn, the twelfth Beckwith, the thirteenth half of *Byllinctun*.

These townships have been taken from Ripon: the first is Hewick, the second Hewick, the third *Ansætleh*, the fourth one hide at Stainley, the fifth Helperby, the sixth at Myton. Two hides from Poppleton.

This has been taken from Sherburn: half of *Ceoredesholm* and half of Cawood – and *Gisferþesdæll* has always belonged to Sherburn – and half the soke which belongs to Sherburn.

These are the lands which Archbishop Oscytel obtained in Northumbria with his money and which were given to him in compensation for illegal marriage: one is Appleton, which he bought for 24 pounds from Deorwulf. He bought Everingham for 44 pounds from Osulf's father, when he was at point of death, and he bought the estate at Newbold for 120 mancuses of red gold from King Edgar; and Helperby was given to him in compensation for illicit cohabitation

– there were two brothers who had one wife – and to Helperby belong two parts of Myton and the soke of Wide Open and Tholthorpe and Youlton and Thorpe. And he bought Skidby for 20 pounds, and three hides at Bracken he bought from King Edgar, and he granted it to him by charter for St John's. \I, Archbishop Oswald, declare that/ all these lands which \the/ Archbishop Oscytel obtained in Northumbria – and my lord granted them to me \for St Peter's/ when he was at Nottingham – [and] these other lands which are entered here besides, I had them all until [Thored?] ascended. Then St Peter was afterwards robbed [of them]. \ May God avenge it as he will/.

[a] *Translation taken from Whitelock,* EHD, *p. 565 (with slight modifications)*

As described by Ker, *Catalogue*, no. 225, p. 302, the copy of **6** in C is written in a narrow, pointed hand of the beginning of the eleventh century, with an **s** that is distinctively long or round, but not low. C itself is a composite manuscript: among various modern, unfoliated paper flyleaves are two parts containing Anglo-Saxon material. The first part is foliated 1–4v and contains, in addition to **6** on f. 4v, copies of medical recipes and extracts from the law-codes II and III Edgar (see above, pp. 75–6). In its current form, C's copy of **6** is faded and difficult to read in many parts perhaps, as Ker suggests, because it once formed the end of a different manuscript and so had been exposed (Ker, *Catalogue*, no. 225, p. 302). As noted in the edited text of **6**, Archbishop Wulfstan has made several additions to this copy, including both the title ('Archbishop Oswald composed this declaration and had it written') and its ending ('May God avenge it as he will'); for the identification of Wulfstan's hand, see Ker 1971, p. 327 and Ker, *Catalogue*, no. 225. G has a sixteenth-century copy of C, preceded by a Latin translation.

6, a memorandum about the York church's estates, was originally composed by Archbishop Oswald in the period 975 × 992. The dating limits for its composition are provided by the reference to Thored, who may have been appointed earl in 975, and by the death of Archbishop Oswald in 992 (as Whitelock 1959, p. 79, notes, Thored was perhaps made earl immediately following the banishment of Earl Oslac in 975, but he does not attest any charters in this position until 979; see also Keynes 1986, p. 84 and above, pp. 60–1). As we know from the large series of leases in Oswald's name in the Worcester archive, he was very active in administrative affairs and **6** is therefore entirely in keeping with Oswald's concerns for estate management (for Oswald's control of landed interests, see Wareham 1996 and above, pp. 59–60). **6** gives details about those estates lost from Otley, Ripon and Sherburn (see further the commentary to **7** below), but also those gains made by Archbishop Oscytel and finally those lands stolen from the York church by Earl Thored. **6** thus demonstrates just how vulnerable the northern church was to encroachment from external figures.

6 first details what townships, or parts of townships, were taken from Otley (for discussion of the early history of the Otley estate, see **7**); *Byllinctun* has not been certainly identified but it has been suggested that Bilton near Harrogate is a likely location (Whitelock, *EHD*, p. 521, n. 1 and Hart, *ECNE*, p. 123; but see also *PN YorksWR* V, p. 105); the other twelve places have been identified (see the relevant entries in *PN YorksWR* and *CamDEPN*). In the description of these losses, **6** gives no indication of the relationship between these townships and Otley: hence it is not clear whether they were part of the so-called *agenland*

(*agenland*, literally 'ownland', defines land that was owned outright; for more, see **7**) and therefore an outright possession or whether they were not outright possessions but rather formed part of Otley's soke (Keynes 1986, p. 89). **7**, a survey probably compiled at the request of Archbishop Wulfstan *c*. 1020–3, gives details of those townships that belonged to Otley; thus it is possible to tell which places were recovered 50 years later. **7** is even more useful as it provides information about the relationship of these townships to Otley. If it is permissible to work backwards, then **7** can aid a judgement about the type of losses represented by **6** (see Keynes 1986, pp. 89–90). We find that parts of Ilkley, Menston, Burley, Chevin, Middleton and Lindley were all recovered by *c*. 1020–3 and, at that time, were sokelands of the Otley manor (for the exact details, see **7 (b)**). It is possible, therefore, that they were also soke when **6** was compiled and that they were not owned outright by the York church. Timble and Denton were also recovered by *c*. 1020–3, by which time one and a half ploughlands at Timble formed an outright possession of the Otley estate and two ploughlands at Denton were *agenland* while another two ploughlands were sokeland. Perhaps these were therefore more substantial losses to the Otley estate as noted by **6**. The townships of Addingham, Guiseley, Stainburn, Beckwith and *Byllinctun* are not mentioned in **7**, which suggests that they had not been restored after the initial loss in the late tenth century (Keynes 1986, p. 90; Addingham seems to have been an archiepiscopal estate at least since 867 when Archbishop Wulfhere fled there; see the discussion of the Otley estate in the commentary to **7**; for tenth-century sculptural remains from Guiseley, see Coatsworth, *Corpus*, pp. 159–61). By the time of Domesday Book, Addingham, Stainburn and Beckwith were still lost from Otley; and, whereas Guiseley seems to have been recovered, Chevin had evidently been lost at some point after *c*. 1020–3 when it is recorded in **7** (see GDB, f. 303v). Unfortunately, Domesday Book gives no information about the composition of the Otley estate so we are unable to decipher which lands were held outright and which were held as part of sokeland (for further discussion of the Domesday evidence, see Keynes 1986, p. 90). The Otley estate had plunged in value from being worth £10 TRE to being worth £3 TRW.

Of the seven townships, or parts of townships, mentioned as lost from Ripon in **6**, only three seem to have been recovered by the time **7** was composed: the two Hewicks and Stainley (for the early history of the Ripon estate, see **7**). Helperby, Myton, Poppleton and *Ansætleh* remained lost (OE *ansetl*, 'a hermitage', may constitute an element in the unidentified place-name *Ansætleh*; Smith, *EPNE* I, p. 12; but see also, *The Vocabulary of English Place-Names (Á–BOX)*, ed. D. Parsons and T. Styles, with C. Hough (Nottingham, 1997), s.v. 'ansetl', where it is noted that '*ansætleh*...might be related to OE *ge-sete* 'seat, habitation, house' and northern dialect *onset* 'group of farm-buildings, farmstead'' (at p. 18)). Keynes suggests that the location of these townships to the east and south of Ripon meant that they were more likely to be given up as permanently lost (Keynes 1986, pp. 90–1). **7** states that Hewick was held as sokeland and that Stainley was both part of Ripon's soke and also part of the estate which helped to maintain the priests (*preosta land*); perhaps these were not such major losses for Ripon. By the time of Domesday Book, the Ripon estate had changed quite dramatically. Some townships had been added and some lost; some townships that were held in soke by Ripon in **7** were converted into outright possessions by 1086 and vice versa (for more details about the evolution of the estate, see the commentary to **7** and Keynes 1986, p. 91). By 1086 Ripon owned the berewicks of Littlethorpe, "Estuinc" [in Newby, near Ripon], Westwick, Bishop Monkton, Nidd, Killinghall, Bishop Thornton,

Sawley, Eavestone, Wilsill, 'Knayser' [in Skelding], Grantley, 'How' [in Markington] [and] Markington and Aldfield. The Ripon estate also possessed soke in "Estanlai" [in North Stainley], in Sutton Grange, another Studley [Studley Roger], North Stainley, Sleningford and "Sutheuuic" (GDB, f. 303v). Most of these places are described as being 'waste' which perhaps explains the vast drop in the value of Ripon from £32 TRE to £7 10s TRW.

Two places named in **6** in connection with the Sherburn estate can no longer be identified: *Ceoredesholm* and *Gisferþesdæll* (Keynes 1986, p. 88, suggests the meanings 'Ceolred's water-meadow' and 'Gislfrith's dell' respectively, for these two place-names; the Sherburn estate had been granted by King Edgar to Earl 'Æslac', probably 'Oslac', earlier in 963 in **4**). The list of places taken from Sherburn is far less detailed than for Otley and Ripon. Cawood is mentioned, which was reclaimed by Sherburn (both as *agenland* and sokeland) in **7**. But the compiler of **6** has been content simply to conclude that 'half the soke which belongs to Sherburn' had been removed. Since the majority of places named in **7** belonged to Sherburn as sokeland (including all, or part of, the following places: Cawood, Wistow, Upper Selby, Flaxley, Barlow, Brayton, Burn, Burton, Gateforth, the two Thorpes, the two Hirsts, the three Haddleseys, Birkin, Sutton, Burn, Brayton, Brotherton, Fairburn, Ledsham, Newthorpe, Micklefield, Hillam, Fryston, Lumby, Steeton, Milford, Fenton, Barkston, Lotherton, *Hehferðe hegðe* and Huddleston), it seems reasonable to conclude that this would have been a major loss to Sherburn and to the archbishopric. Domesday Book shows that the Sherburn estate was a very large and valuable one for the York church as it consisted of 96 carucates of land; it is striking that whereas Otley and Ripon had depreciated in value from Edward the Confessor's reign to William the Conqueror's time, Sherburn retained its worth at £34 6s (GDB, f. 302v). Domesday Book does not state, however, how many berewicks the Sherburn estate had or what kind of possessions they were, either *agenland* or sokeland.

The last section of **6** is arguably the most interesting: its incidental information affords an insight into conditions of life in Northumbria and at the vulnerability of those people or institutions who owned estates. The section begins by listing those lands bought by Archbishop Oscytel (d. 971) and also those lands which reverted to him because of illegal marriage (for which see further below), all of which passed into the possession of the York see. As was noted in the introduction (above, pp. 55–9), Oscytel did a great deal to revive and then to enhance the fortunes of the northern archbishopric. **6** states that Oscytel bought various estates 'with his money' which implies that the archbishop took a personal interest in augmenting York's assets; this receives corroboration from **2** and **3** in the York archive, both of which are charters granted directly to Oscytel (the first by King Eadwig, the second by King Edgar). Indeed it is quite likely that we should also credit York's possession of **4** and **5** to Oscytel (above, pp. 58–9).

But perhaps the most remarkable statement in the whole document occurs when describing how Oscytel acquired other estates:

> Þis syndan þa land þe Oscytel yrcebiscop begeat on Norþhymbralande mid his feo and him mon geald for unrihtan hæmede.

This passage seems to imply not only that Oscytel had managed to implement some system of ecclesiastical law in Northumbria but also that he was subsequently able to impose penalties under that law involving the confiscation of property and its acquisition by his church (see Stenton, *Preparatory to ASE*, p. 367). Since the archiepiscopacy of Oscytel's predecessor, Wulfstan, had been extremely turbulent, the establishment of proper penalties for ecclesiastical offences was no doubt a considerable success on Oscytel's part (see also above, p. 57).

Oscytel used his own money to buy Appleton from Deorwulf, Everingham from Osulf's father and also Newbald from King Edgar. Domesday Book shows that Everingham and Newbald remained in the possession of the archbishopric (Everingham was worth £14 TRE and £6 TRW; Newbald was worth £24 TRE and £10 TRW; see GDB, f. 302v) but it seems as if Appleton had passed out of the control of the archbishopric (GDB, f. 310v). **5** states that the Newbald estate had originally been granted by King Edgar to Earl Gunner. Since **6** states that Oscytel had to buy back the estate from King Edgar for 120 mancuses of red gold, it seems as if, on the death of Gunner, Newbald had reverted into the possession of the king. Gunner died *c.* 963 and Oscytel died in 971 so it must have been during this period that Newbald became the archbishop's property.

The Helperby estate was forfeited to Oscytel because of an illegal marriage (two brothers had the same wife). **6** suggests that two parts of Myton also belonged outright to the Helperby estate as did the soke of Wide Open, Tholthorpe, Youlton and Thorpe. By 1086 Helperby had largely maintained this structure but Myton was now held as soke rather than owned outright. Most of the estate is described as being 'waste' in 1086; it was worth 10s TRE and this dropped to 6s TRW (GDB, f. 303rv).

The next part of **6** states that Oscytel purchased Skidby for 20 pounds and also three hides at Bracken from King Edgar, 'and he granted it to him by charter for St John's'. The meaning of this clause seems to be that Edgar was booking the land for Oscytel to St John's of Beverley. This suggests the possible existence of a charter now lost from the Beverley archive (see below, p. 188). Bracken was in secular hands by the time of Domesday Book but Skidby still belonged to Beverley as a berewick (see GDB, f. 381v and f. 304r respectively).

Towards the end of the document, **6** states: '*I, Archbishop Oswald, declare that* all these lands which *the* Archbishop Oscytel obtained in Northumbria – and my lord granted them to me *for St Peter's* when he was at Nottingham – [and] these other lands which are entered here besides...'; those parts italicised have been added to **6** by Archbishop Wulfstan (see Ker, *Catalogue*, p. 302). This sentence seems to imply that the lands originally acquired by Archbishop Oscytel were subsequently granted to Archbishop Oswald for St Peter's by 'my lord'; as Keynes 1986, p. 84, n. 20, points out, it is unclear whether the lord referred to is King Edgar (d. 975), Edward the Martyr (d. 978) or Æthelred the Unready (d. 1016). The royal grant of these lands to Oswald took place at Nottingham, the same location for the grant of the earliest charter in the York archive, **1**. Nottingham, an area over which both southern and northern kings at times claimed jurisdiction (see, for example, *ASC C*, s.a. 942), would have formed a symbolic place for the meeting of the *witan* and the granting of land by a southern English king to the northern church. Wulfstan's annotations to this section were presumably entered during the course of his investigation about the York church's estates, which resulted in the composition of **7**, a survey concerned with just those three estates (Otley, Ripon and Sherburn) documented at the beginning of **6**.

Part of the closing lines of **6**, translated above as 'I had them all until [Thored?] ascended', is very difficult to read in C, with some letters that are entirely illegible. Ker, *Catalogue*, p. 302, suggests a reconstructed original reading of, *ealle ic hy h[æfde o]ð þ[.]rað in com*, which has been adopted in the edited text above. The sixteenth-century Harleian copy (manuscript G) has *ealle ic hy hæf oð þerað in com*, which seems to corroborate Ker's reconstruction. Whitelock suggests the original may have had the name-form *þorað*, from Old Norse *þórðr*; see Whitelock, *EHD*, p. 565, n. 8 and Whitelock 1959, p. 79, n. 6; and, for more about Thored, above, pp. 60–1.

7

Survey of the Estates at (*a*) *Sherburn-in-Elmet,* (*b*) *Otley and* (*c*) *Ripon, belonging to the York Archbishopric.* [*c.* A.D. 1020–3]

D. York, Minster Library, Add. 1, 156v–157r: memorandum, s. xi[in]
Ed.: a. Stevenson 1912, pp. 15–19, with translation
b. Farrer, *EYC*, no. 7, with translation, from Stevenson
c. Robertson, *Charters*, no. LXXXIV (pp. 164–9), with translation, from D
Listed: Sawyer 1461a; Ker, *Catalogue*, no. 402a

(**a**) Ðis is seo socn into Scyreburna mid folcrihte: ƿa dæl of Cauda · 7 Ƿicstow eal · 7 ufer Seleby eal · 7 ƿa oxna gang on Fleaxlege · 7 healf Bernlege · 7 eal Breiðetun butan healf ploges land · 7 eall Byrne · 7 eall Burhtun butan healf ploges land · 7 eall Gæiteford · 7 eall ƿegen Þorpas · 7 ƿa Hyrst eal · 7 ƿa Haðelsæ eall · 7 fif oxna gang on þriddan Haðelsæ · 7 healf Byrcene · 7 eall Suðtun · 7 eall Byrum 7 Breiðetun eal · 7 Broðertun eall · 7 eall Farenburne · butan healf þridde ploges land · 7 ƿa ploges land on Ledesham · 7 an on Niƿan þorp · 7 eall Miclafeld · 7 eall Hyllum · 7 eall Fristun · 7 eall Lundby · 7 eall Styfetun · 7 eall Myleford · 7 eall Fenntun · butan healf ploges land · 7 ƿa ploges land 7 fif oxna gang on Barcestune · 7 eall Luteringtun · 7 eal Hehferðe hegðe · 7 eall Hudelestun;;

On Scireburnan toecan þam inlande syndan .iiii. hida ƿeorclandes · 7 on Luteringatune .iii. hida 7 on Barcestune .i. hid · 7 fif oxna gang · 7 of Styfingtune tune þreora oxna gang.

7 on Ƿicstoƿe ƿegea oxnagang · 7 on Caƿuda ƿa dæl þæs landes is agen land into Scireburnan · 7 Fentun is læn oðer healf ploges land;

(**b**) Into Ottanleage .iiii. ploga land · 7 on Bægeltune .ii. On Hafecesƿeorðe .ii. On oðeran Hafecesƿeorðe .ii. On Dentune .ii. On Timbel oðer healf ploges land. On Ectune healf ploges land · þis is unbesacen agenland; 7 þærto eacan hyrað þas socn land. Into Ottanleage. On Ottanleage .ii. ploh · 7 on Bældune .ii. 7 on Hafecesƿeorðe .ii. 7 on \o/ðeran[a] Hafecesƿeorðe .ii. On Scefinge .i. On Mensingtune .iii. On Burhleage .vi. On Meðeltune .iii. On Yllicleage syx oxna gang. On Dentune .ii. ploh. On Cliftune .i. On Biceratune .iii. On Fearnleage .iiii. On Ectune oðer healf. On Pofle .iii. On Lindeleage .iii.

(c) Æt Rypum ærest mile gemet on ælce healfe · 7 Biscoptun is in on þam .ii. hida · 7 Carleƿic .v. hida · on healf Munecatun his agen land feorðe healf hide · 7 healf Mercingatun · þridde healf hide. On Herelesho healf hid. On Stodlege .iii. hida. On Suðtune oþer healf hide. On Nunneƿic .iii. hida. On Þorntune .ii. hida;

7 þis synd ƿeste land. An is Sallege. Oðer is Grantelege · þridde is Efestun · 7 feorðe is Ƿifeleshealh · 7 .v. is healf Cnearresƿeorð;

þon' syndan þis preosta land · on Ƿestƿic .iiii. hida. On Norð Stanlege .iiii. On Gyðingdale .i. hide. On Mercingtune · þreo oxna gang. On Munecatune þreo oxna gang. On Hotune .ii. oxna gang;

Ðis syndan socnland into Rypum. On Gyþingadeal .viii. hida · 7 ofer eall Munecatun .vii. hida · 7 on Eastƿic .ii. hida. On Mercingatune þridde healfe hide · 7 on Herelesho · þridde healf hide · 7 on Suðtune · oðer healf hide. On Nyrran Stanlege .v. hida · 7 on Norð Stanlege .i. hide · 7 on Nunneƿic .i. hide · 7 on Heaƿic .v. hida · 7 on Sleaningaforda .ii. hida;

[a] o- *inserted above the line in* D

Translation[a]

(a) This is the soke [pertaining] to Sherburn according to public law: two parts of Cawood, and all Wistow, and all Upper Selby, and two oxgangs in Flaxley, and half Barlow, and all Brayton except half a ploughland, and all Burn, and all Burton except half a ploughland, and all Gateforth, and all of the two Thorpes, and all of the two Hirsts, and all of the two Haddleseys, and five oxgangs in the third Haddlesey, and half Birkin, and all Sutton, and all Burn, and all Brayton, and all Brotherton, and all Fairburn except two and a half ploughlands, and two ploughlands in Ledsham and one in Newthorpe and all Micklefield, and all Hillam, and all Fryston, and all Lumby, and all Steeton, and all Milford and all Fenton except half a ploughland, and two ploughlands and five oxgangs in Barkston, and all Lotherton, and all *Hehferðe hegðe*, and all Huddleston.

In Sherburn, in addition to the demesne land, there are four hides of workland, and in Lotherton three hides, and in Barkston one hide and five oxgangs, and of the manor of Steeton three oxgangs.

And in Wistow two oxgangs, and in Cawood two parts, of the land is *agenland* into Sherburn, and in Fenton is loan-land one and a half ploughlands.

(b) To Otley [pertain] four ploughlands, and in Baildon two, and in Hawksworth two, in the second Hawksworth two, in Denton two, in Timble one and a half ploughlands, in *Ectune* half a ploughland; this is unquestionably *agenland*. And thereto in addition belong the sokelands [pertaining] to Otley: in Otley two ploughlands, and in Baildon two, and in Hawksworth two, and in the second Hawksworth two, in Chevin one, in Menston three, in Burley six, in Middleton three, in Ilkley six oxgangs, in Denton two ploughs, in Clifton one, in *Biceratune* three, in Farnley four, in *Ectune* one and a half, in Poole three, in Lindley three.

(c) At Ripon first the space of one mile on each side, and Bishopton is within that two hides, and *Carlewic* five hides, and half Monkton is *agenland* – three and a half hides – and half of Markington – two and a half hides – half a hide at How Hill, in Studley three hides, in Sutton one and a half hides, in Nunwick three hides, in Thornton two hides.

And these lands are waste: the first is Sawley, the second is Grantley, the third is Eavestone, and the fourth is Wilshill and the fifth is half of Knaresford.

And these are the priests' lands: in Westwick four hides, in North Stainley four, in Givendale one hide, in Markington three oxgangs, in Monkton three oxgangs, in Hutton two oxgangs.

These are the sokelands [pertaining] to Ripon: in Givendale eight hides, and over all Monkton seven hides, and in *Eastwic* two hides, in Markington two and a half hides, and in How Hill two and a half hides, and in Sutton one and a half hides, in the nearer Stainley five hides, and in North Stainley one hide, and in Nunwick one hide, and in Hewick five hides, and in Sleningford two hides.

[a] *Translation taken from those in Farrer,* EYC, *pp. 22–3 and Robertson,* Charters, *pp. 165–9*

7 (a–c) is a group of estate-surveys (of Sherburn, Otley and Ripon respectively) which has been entered into the back of the York Gospels on folios 156v–157r alongside other additions in Old English which were made at about the same time (Ker, *Catalogue*, no. 402; for discussion of these surveys, see Stevenson 1912 and Baxter 2004; see also Keynes 1986, to which this commentary is greatly indebted; for the York Gospels, see above, pp. 76–7). These other additions include: three Wulfstanian homilies with annotations in the hand of Wulfstan himself, the 1019/20 Letter from Cnut to the English people, an inventory of church treasures at Sherburn-in-Elmet (Appendix 1), some bidding prayers and also a list of 'festermen' (Appendix 2). Since Cnut's letter can be dated to 1019/20, and since the hand of Wulfstan has been identified as annotating the three Wulfstan homilies (see Ker, *Catalogue*, no. 402 and Ker 1971, pp. 330–1), it follows that **7 (a–c)** were written down between *c.* 1020 and the death of Wulfstan in 1023 (Keynes 1986, pp. 82–3, suggests that **7 (a–c)** probably belong to the earlier end of that dating range, to *c.* 1020). This makes it likely that Archbisop Wulfstan himself was responsible for **7 (a–c)** (see Keynes 1986, p. 84 and Baxter 2004, p. 179 and also pp. 187–9, for the significance of the fact that **7 (a–c)** were copied into the York Gospels themselves).

Map 3. Estates named in **7 (a–c)**, reproduced with kind permission of Professor Simon Keynes

All three of the estates surveyed in **7 (a–c)** belonged to the archbishopric of York and are located in the West Riding of Yorkshire (for a useful map of these estates and also of other places mentioned in **7**, see p. 142, reproduced with kind permission from Prof. S.D. Keynes; for an earlier version of this map, see Keynes 1986, p. 85); **6** deals with exactly these three estates as well and shows that various parts of them were lost from the York church's possession in the late tenth century. The surveys demonstrate the type of complex estate structure that existed in the north of England (for more about these kinds of estates, and 'multiple estates' that were common in the northern Danelaw, see the commentary to **2**). These estates could have different levels of ownership from outright possession (*agenland*, which literally means 'ownland') to jurisdictional rights, sokeland (for the complex nature of sokeland, see Hadley, *Northern*, esp. pp. 167–72). The 'inland' comprised the central manor together with any outlying townships that were attached to it. **7 (a–c)**, together with the earlier evidence provided by **4** and **6**, and also the later evidence of Domesday Book, provide the opportunity for studying the evolution of various estates (in particular that of Sherburn) which were in the York archbishopric's possession: so it is apparent, for example, that sokeland could be turned into *agenland* and vice versa and that townships could be added to a central manor or taken away (see Keynes 1986, p. 86). They also demonstrate that the English unit of land measurement, the hide, was in use alongside its Scandinavian equivalent, the ploughland, and its subdivision, the oxgang (these matters are discussed fully in Keynes 1986, p. 86). Each survey in **7** (labelled **a–c**) is discussed in turn below.

The Sherburn estate: 7 (a)

Of the seventeen-and-a-half lines that comprise **7 (a)**, there seems to be some distinction in script between the first twelve lines and lines 13–18, as noted by Keynes 1986, p. 82 (where he also describes the following distinctive letter-forms). In the upper section **s** is consistently tall and starts on the line (rather like a Caroline **s** would) whereas in lines 13–18 it is invariably low and perhaps more like an Insular **s**; its stem is also 'split' in some examples in the lower section; **x** is long and straight in lines 1–12 but is more curved in lines 14 and 15, finishing with a turned-over descender; **y** is rounded and dotted in lines 1–12 but, just as the **x** is finished with rather more of a flourish in the second portion (lines 13–18), so too the **y** in line 13 and line 15 displays a similar curve; the loop of **g** is consistently closed throughout **7 (a)** but is more rounded in lines 13–18; the characteristic serif which can be seen especially on the top of **d** and **ð** in lines 1–12 is not as pronounced in lines 13–18; 7 (abbreviation for *and*) is controlled and regular in lines 1–12 but, in lines 16 and 17, it is enlarged and seriffed and, particularly at the beginning of line 16, is intended as a capital. The **æ** is very distinctive as the **e** is tall and ascends well above the **a**; it has been suggested that this form should be linked with Wulfstan's circle as it can be found in the work of ten scribes associated directly with Worcester or York (see P.A. Stokes, *English Vernacular Script, ca 990 – ca 1035*, unpublished PhD dissertation, University of Cambridge 2006, p. 98). Since there is a distinction between letter-forms found in lines 1–12 and those in lines 13–18 (and lines 13–18 seem to be written in a darker ink), it is possible either that the same scribe was responsible for both productions but entered them at different times, or that two separate scribes were involved: for this, see Keynes 1986, p. 82.

7 (a) gives information about soke owed to the Sherburn estate (for the identification of all the place-names in **7 (a)**, see *PN YorksWR* IV and *CamDEPN*, under the relevant entries). Given the paucity of documents preserved in the York archive, it is very rare that we are provided with details about one estate in particular at different chronological intervals. But the York archive allows an examination of the history and evolution of the Sherburn estate. **4** is a grant of Sherburn by King Edgar to 'Æslac' (probably Earl Oslac) in 963; its boundary clause gives the limits of the 'twenty hides at Sherburn of the "inland"'. The 'inland' in **4** is Sherburn (for the definition of 'inland' see above, the commentary to **4** and Faith, *English Peasantry*, pp. 15–55) and ten townships are described as being somehow dependent upon this central manor. **6** (Oswald's *Memorandum*), composed 975 × 992, talks of those areas of Sherburn lost to the archbishopric and the implication is that at some point between 963 and 975 × 992 the Sherburn estate had passed out of the hands of Earl Oslac and into the control of the York see (for details of those areas of Sherburn lost see **6**). **7 (a)** then gives a detailed account of the soke of Sherburn, and what is immediately apparent is that **7 (a)** not only includes all of those places mentioned in **4** but also adds a good number of new townships (for a more detailed explanation of the history of the Sherburn estate, see the commentary to **4**, which is also summarised in tabular form below). **7 (a)** is of particular interest for the terms it employs to describe the relationships between the 'inland' of Sherburn and other areas. For example, 'At Sherburn in addition to the "inland" there are four hides of *workland*, and three hides at Lotherton, and one hide and five oxgangs at Barkston, and three oxgangs of the manor of Steeton. And two oxgangs in Wistow and two parts of the land at Cawood are *agenland* belonging to Sherburn, and one and a half ploughlands at Fenton are held on lease' (my italics). *Workland* presumably refers to land from which some kind of labour was owed to the lord of Sherburn (see Robertson, *Charters*, p. 415 and Keynes 1986, p. 88), whilst *agenland* seems to be a reference to the fact that the owner of Sherburn possessed these areas outright; no details of the relationships of Lotherton, Barkston or Steeton to Sherburn are given. By the time of the Domesday survey, Sherburn-in-Elmet was the most valuable estate belonging to the York archbishopric; in Edward's day it was worth £34 6s and this had not changed into William the Conqueror's reign (see GDB, f. 302v). Printed below is a table summarising which townships belonging to the Sherburn estate were granted in 963 (i.e. in **4**, represented by column 1), which townships were taken in 975 × 992 (i.e. in **6**, represented by column 2), and which townships belonged to the Sherburn estate in 1020 × 23 (i.e. in **7 (a)**, represented by column 3). Places underlined are those which feature both in **4** and in **7 (a)**; Cawood, in bold, features in **4**, **6** and **7 (a)**. (For a much more detailed tabulated analysis of all of the surveys of **7 (a–c)**, see Baxter 2004, pp. 183–4.)

The Otley estate: 7 (b)

7 (b) starts at the top of f. 157r: in the first example of **g**, the loop is closed but it is open in every other instance; **y** is dotted with a long descender and **x** has a similarly long descender; **s** stretches above and below the line (see *hafeces* on line 2) but sometimes only stretches below the line when it is at the end of words (*hafeces*, line 4); a similar **æ** can be found to that in **7 (a)**; and the abbreviation ⁊ (for *and*) is controlled except when it is used as a capital in line 3. **7 (b)** is the work of a different but contemporary scribe to **7 (a)**: Keynes 1986, p. 82.

The existence of an important ecclesiastical centre at Otley from at least the late eighth century is confirmed by the presence of fragments of two remarkable Anglo-Saxon stone

4 (963)	**6** (975 × 992)	**7 (a)** (1020 × 23)
Hibaldestofte	Ceoredesholm	Cauda
Fryþetune	**Cawood**	Wicstow
Hillum	Gisferþesdæll	Seleby
Lundby		Fleaxlege
Mylenford		Bernlege
Stiuetune		Breiðetun
Miclanfelda		Byrne
Luttringtun		Burhtun
Fentune		Gæiteford
Kawuda		Hyrst
		Haðelsæ
		Byrcene
		Suðtun
		Byrum
		Broðertun
		Farenburne
		Ledesham
		Niwanþorp
		Miclafeld
		Hyllum
		Fristun
		Lundby
		Styfetun
		Myleford
		Fenntun
		Barcestune
		Luteringtun
		Hehferðe hegðe
		Hudelestun
		Luteringatune
		Barcestune
		Styfingtune
		Wicstowe
		Cawuda

crosses there of that date (Cramp 1970, Wood 1987 and Coatsworth, *Corpus*, pp. 39–41, 69–71 and 215–28, where the signifcance of the design of the Otley crosses, in particular Otley 1, as an influence on other sculpture in the area is discussed; Otley also has sculpture surviving from the post-viking era, for which see Coatsworth, *ibid.*, pp. 221–8; for the identification of all those place-names given in **7 (b)**, see *PN YorksWR* IV–V and *CamDEPN*, under the relevant entries). Wood has suggested that the iconographical programme on these crosses makes it possible that they, and by extension the Otley estate, were already connected to the York church at this early date (Wood 1987, esp. pp. 35–6 and further Coatsworth, *Corpus*, p. 15; for the suggestion that chapter seventeen of Stephanus' *Vita Wilfridi*, in detailing the gift of an area of land around *Ingaedyne* (possibly 'Yeadon', a vill bordering the Otley estate), to Wilfrid's new foundation at Ripon, is describing a gift of properties that may have belonged to the Otley estate, see Faull and Moorhouse, *West Yorkshire* I, pp. 183 and 188–9 and Keynes 1986, p. 89; but Wood 1987 questions this interpretation; see also Jones 1995, pp. 30–6). In the late 860s Archbishop Wulfhere was able to take refuge from viking attack at Addingham in the valley called Wharfedale which is located 'super ripam fluminis Hwerf, inter Oteleiam et castellum de Scipetun' (Symeon, *Letter on the Archbishops of York*, in Arnold, *Sym. Op.* I, p. 225). Since **6** records that Addingham was one of those vills lost from the Otley estate in the late tenth century, it may be that Symeon's letter indicates that Addingham, and perhaps therefore also Otley (but see Wood 1987, p. 23 on this), had long been a possession of the York church (Keynes 1986, p. 89, Wood 1987, pp. 20–3 and Coatsworth, *Corpus*, p. 19; one cross-shaft dating from the late ninth or early tenth century survives from Addingham, for which see Coatsworth, *ibid.*, pp. 90–1).

The Otley estate suffered losses immediately after the appointment of Thored to the northern earldom (see above, pp. 135–6). Oswald's *Memorandum* (**6**) states that these townships, or parts of them, were taken from Otley: Addingham, Ilkley, Menston, Burley (half of it), Guiseley, Chevin, Middleton, Denton (half of it), Timble, Lindley, Stainburn, Beckwith and the unidentified *Byllinctun* (half of it); for the relevant passage, see **6** above and p. 135, for a suggested identification of *Byllinctun*. Unfortunately **6**, in describing these losses from the Otley estate, gives no indication of whether they represented the loss of land owned outright (*agenland*) or of sokeland (see further Keynes 1986, p. 89).

It was in the early eleventh century that many of those places mentioned by Oswald as being lost were restored to the Otley estate, perhaps as a result of the work of Archbishop Wulfstan; **7 (b)** constitutes a record both of this recovery and of the structure of the Otley estate. (*Ectune* remains unidentified, whilst *Biceratune* has been equated with Newhall, near Otley; see Farrer, *EYC*, p. 23 and Robertson, *Charters*, p. 415; for the relatively large amount of sculpture dating from the eighth to the tenth centuries to have survived at Ilkley, see Coatsworth, *Corpus*, pp. 167–77.) We learn that there were those places owned outright and without dispute by the York church (*unbesacen agenland*) but also those places where the archbishopric possessed sokeland instead (*socn land*). Keynes 1986, pp. 89–90, suggests that the structure of the estate as seen in **7 (b)** may have been the same before the losses recorded in **6**. If this suggestion is correct, then it follows that the major losses from the Otley estate were of soke (in Chevin, Burley, Middleton, Ilkley, Denton [two ploughs of soke] and Lindley) rather than actual land (at Timble). Meanwhile Addingham, Guiseley, Stainburn, Beckwith and *Byllinctun*, all of which were taken from the Otley estate in **6**, are not mentioned in **7 (b)** and were therefore presumably not recovered by the early eleventh century (see also Keynes 1986, p. 90). Domesday Book states that Addingham had not been recovered by the York church in 1086 (GDB, f. 301v, f. 326v and f. 380r); Guiseley was regained by the archbishopric as a berewick of Otley (GDB, f. 303v and f. 379r); Stainburn was lost to secular control (GDB, f. 301v and f. 380r), as was Beckwith (GDB, f. 326v). *Byllinctun* has been tentatively identified as Bilton near Harrogate (see Whitelock, *EHD*, p. 521, n. 1; Hart, *ECNE*, p. 123) and, if this is correct, it too had passed from the York church's control and into secular hands.

By the time of the Domesday survey, the Otley estate as a whole comprised 60 carucates and 6 bovates. Otley's berewicks are listed as being '"Stublham" [in Ilkley], Middleton [in Ilkley], Denton, Clifton [near Newall], "Bikerton" [in Newall with Clifton], Farnley [in Otley], Nether Timble, "Ectone" [in Lindley], Pool, Guiseley, Hawksworth, another

Hawksworth [Thorpe, in Hawksworth], Baildon, Menston, Burley in Wharfedale, Ilkley' (GDB, f. 303v). Since all of those places named in **7 (b)** (either as sokeland or as *agenland*), except Chevin and Lindley, are accounted for in the above list of berewicks, it seems as if the structure of the Otley estate remained fairly stable between *c.* 1020 and 1086 (Keynes 1986, p. 90, suggests that Chevin and Lindley were both 'probably assessed as part of Otley itself'). Furthermore, as Keynes 1986, p. 90, again notes, Domesday Book makes no distinction between land held outright by the archbishopric and land held in soke, which suggests that the archbishopric had come to possess all of the land as *agenland*. But by 1086, the value of Otley had dropped substantially from £10 to £3 and 'the greatest part of this manor is waste' (GDB, f. 303v).

The Ripon estate: 7 (c)

7 (c) begins directly underneath **7 (b)** on f. 157r with a relatively elaborate, enlarged Æ, which is followed by the characteristic **æ** seen in **7 (a)** and **7 (b)**; in line 9 the loop of **g** is open but for the rest of the time it is closed; **s** remains low throughout and tends to have a split stem; **y** is dotted, with a long, straight descender but there is a shortened and more curved version in line 18 (*Gyþinga*); **x** begins with a turned-up flourish at the start of a long stroke which runs from left to right (see also Keynes 1986, p. 82).

7 (c) gives details concerning the Ripon estate (for the identification of the place-names given in **7 (c)**, see *PN YorksWR* V and *CamDEPN*, under the relevant entries). The first notice of a gift of land at Ripon comes from Stephanus, who states that *c.* 660 King Alhfrith gave Wilfrid the monastery at Ripon (*Inhrypis*) along with thirty hides of land (see *VW*, c. VIII). Thus from the outset Ripon was an estate associated with the York see (since Wilfrid was to become bishop of York); for more about Ripon, see below, pp. 229–49. Damage to the Ripon estate is recorded by Archbishop Oswald's *Memorandum* (**6**), which states that these townships (or parts of them), were taken from Ripon: the two Hewicks, the unidentified *Ansætleh*, one hide at Stainley, Helperby, Myton and two hides from Poppleton. Unfortunately, **6** gives no indication of whether these places had belonged to the Ripon estate as outright possessions or whether they had represented sokeland (see also Keynes 1986, p. 90). Later on in **6** we find that Helperby and two parts of Myton (and also the soke of Wide Open, Tholthorpe, Youlton and Thorpe) had been very recent acquisitions as they had been confiscated by Archbishop Oscytel because of an illegal marriage arrangement (for the ramifications of this statement about ecclesiastical law, see above, p. 57; see also Keynes 1986, p. 90). **7 (c)** demonstrates that, of those estates lost in the late tenth century and recorded in **6**, only the soke of Stainley and Hewick were restored to Ripon, whilst Helperby, Myton and Poppleton were all still lost (*Ansætleh*, which was likewise not recovered, remains unidentified; for the possible elements in the name, see above, p. 136). Domesday Book suggests that at some point between *c.* 1020 and 1066 Helperby and Myton came back into the possession of the York church (see GDB, f. 303r and f. 381r). But Poppleton seems to have been permanently lost (GDB, f. 329r, f. 374r and f. 380r).

7 (c) is divided into four sections (see also Keynes 1986, p. 91, for these sections); the first deals with that property owned outright by the archbishop (on the basis of topography, Jones 2000, p. 18, suggests a new identification of *Carlewic* with Sharow; but the two are clearly not etymologically connected: see *CamDEPN*, p. 540); the second gives a list of those properties which were 'waste', perhaps as a consequence of events such as Eadred's raid in 948 (see below, pp. 245–6), and which seem also to have been owned by the archbishop; the third has details of estates which were used for the support of priests, again probably owned by the archbishop; and the fourth lists those estates which were held in soke by the archbishop. As Keynes highlights, it is of great interest where one estate occurs in these different parts of **7 (c)** (Keynes 1986, p. 91). Markington is a good example: half of this estate was owned outright by the archbishop, while the priests had three oxgangs and the archbishop also had jurisdictional rights over half of Markington.

Domesday Book begins its entry for Ripon by describing 'Wilfrid's league' around the church, which is also mentioned at the beginning of the survey in **7 (c)** (see GDB, f. 303v and *Æt Rypum ærest mile gemet on ælce healfe* in **7 (c)**; for more about this privileged area see below, pp. 244–5, Jones 2000 and Lambert 2009). Domesday Book gives the berewicks of Ripon as being, Littlethorpe, "Estuinc" [in Newby, near Ripon], Westwick, Bishop Monkton, Nidd, Killinghall, Bishop Thornton, Sawley, Eavestone, Wilsill, 'Knayser' [in Skelding], Grantley, 'How' [in Markington] [and] Markington and Aldfield. In total the value of the estate is given as 43 carucates and two bovates, and a further 21.5 carucates belonged to Ripon as sokeland (in "Estanlai" [in North Stainley], Sutton Grange, another Studley [Studley Roger], North Stainley, Sleningford [and] "Sutheuuic"). TRE the estate was worth £32 but this had plunged to £7 10s TRW, perhaps as a result of the harrying of the north in 1069 (but we should also remember that already in **7 (c)** there are those areas of Ripon mentioned as being waste). The structure of Ripon seen in Domesday Book shows that the estate had undergone a certain amount of reorganisation in the period *c.* 1020–1086: thus estates like Monkton or Markington became outright possessions of the archbishopric in the later period (whereas previously the archbishop had owned part as *agenland* and part as sokeland) and other estates, like Studley, were changed from being *agenland* to sokeland. There are also those vills which were added to the estate and those which were detached from the estate.

8

King Cnut grants forty-three hides (casati) *at Patrington, Yorkshire, to Ælfric, archbishop of York.* A.D. 1033

E. BL Cotton Claudius B. iii, 68v–69r: copy, s. xiii^{ex}
Rubric: Carta regis super Paterington archiepiscopo concessa.
F1. York, Minster Library and Archives, L 2/1 (*Mag. Reg. Alb.*), pt. I, 59v–60v: copy, s. xiv^{med}
Rubric: Concessio Cnut regis facta beato Petro tempore Elfrici archiepiscopi Eborum super .xliii. casatos in Patringtona.
F2. York, Minster Library and Archives, L 2/1 (*Mag. Reg. Alb.*), pt. II, 78rv: copy of E, s. xiv^{med}
Rubric: Carta regis super Paterington archiepiscopo concessa.
H. Bodleian, Dodsworth 9, 6rv: copy of F1, s. xvii [incomplete copy]
J. Bodleian, Dodsworth 125, 79r–80r: copy of F1, s. xvii
Ed.: a. *Mon. Angl.*, iii. 130, from F1
b. *Mon. Angl.* (rev. edn.), vi, pt. 3, pp. 1176–7 (no. 6)
c. Kemble 749 (without bounds), from F1 and F2
d. Pierquin, *Recueil*, pt. 6, no. 12
e. Farrer, *EYC*, no. 8, from F1 and F2
Listed: Sawyer 968; Hart, *ECNE*, no. 133
Edited from E and F1

In[a] nomine Dei uiui et ueri[b] Domini nostri Iesu Christi mundi redemptoris. Anno uero dominice incarnacionis millesimo xxxiii.[c] Ego Cnut[d] omnipotentis Dei disponente clementia Angligenarum[e] omniumque[f] gentium undique[g] secus habitantium rex, hanc scedulam[h] dictare[i] promisi, non inmemor quomodo et quam mirabiliter omnia supernus rector firme racionis serie gubernat atque custodit seu[j] omnibus sapientibus notum ac manifestum constat quod quosquam[k] nutu mirifico interdum exaltat quosdam iterum seu[j] 'stipulam uento raptam'[1] fortunali euentu illico[l] depellit. Et iccirco quoddam regni mei rus meorum optimatum testimonio cuidam uenerabili uiro meo archiepiscopo Alfrico[m] uidelicet Eborum ecclesie, id est .xliii. casatos loco qui celebri [n]et Pateringatuna[n] nuncupatur uocabulo pro redempcione anime mee patrisque mei omniumue[o] propinquitate mihi coniunctorum perpetua largitus sum hereditate atque omnibus suis successoribus ut terram iam prefatam meo scilicet ouante consensu tramitibus sue possideat uite; deinceps namque sibi succedenti digno heredi quemcumque Deus eligeret derelinquat ceu[p] predixi in eternam hereditatem. Maneat igitur meum hoc inmobile donum eterna libertate[q] iocundum cum omnibus que ad ipsum locum pertinere dinoscuntur tam in magnis quam in modicis rebus, campis, pascuis, pratis excepto communi labore, expedicione, pontis arcisue coedificacione. Si qui denique[r] mihi non optanti hanc libertatis cartam liuore depressi uiolare satagerint agminibus tetre caliginis lapsi uocem audiant examinacionis die arbitris sibi dicentis: 'Discedite a me maledicti in ignem eternum,'[2] ubi cum demonibus ferreis sartaginibus crudeli torqueantur in pena si non ante mortem digna hoc emendauerint[s] penitentia. Hiis[t] terminis circumdatur predicta tellus:[u]

Ðis sint ðam landgemare to Pateringatune:[v] Arest hit fehð[w] on ƿit; 7[x] sƿa andlang þer dic to þan stane; 7 þonan ofer þon meare to scare[y] scyƿne; 7 sƿa andlang þere dic beƿestan þorp on hole dic; 7 sia[z] to sealtan[a2] meare; 7 þonan sƿa[b2] man mage[c2] rihtest locian to scelle[d2] toft; 7 þonan to þaes dices east and; 7 sia[z] to earnes[e2] hoh; 7 sƿa[b2] onan to Humbran[f2] to earnes hoh ƿelle; 7 sƿa andlang Humbran[g2] to Pateringatune[h2] fleotes muðan; 7 sƿa[b2] andlang þaes fleotes up to cros fleotes; 7 ꝥ[i2] aefre mid[j2] þam fleote up oð hit cume tomiddes þare bricge betƿixe Pateringatune[k2] 7 Ƿinestede;[l2] 7 siððan þurh middenƿeard þaes[m2] fennes[n2] to bradan[o2] holm; 7 sƿa up mid þam sice aeft[p2] to pitte.

7 inland on Pateringtune[q2] .xxx. plogaland; 7 on Ƿinestode[r2] .viii.[s2] plogaland; 7 on Haliham þriddan healfes plogesland 7 healf an ofnan; 7 on Þorp[t2] .ii. plogagang[u2] landes 7 .i. oxangang 7 ealfes plogesland ou Sumeres[v2] mersc; 7 socne þaerto ofer eal Ƿifestade[w2] butan a<n>es[x2] plogesland;[y2] 7 ofer eal Halsaham; 7 .ii. plogaland on Þorp[t2] butan anes oxangang: þaet is[z2] ealles[a3] .x. plogaland socne landes. Nu syndon ealle þa land þe licgað butan þaere yrð merce Et Pateringatune[b3] mid þyssere boc sebelite[c3] eal sƿa ƿel[d3] sƿa rilnetun.

Hec uidelicet donacio facta est anno dominice incarnacionis millesimo .xxxiii.[e3] hiis testibus[f3] consencientibus quorum nomina subnotata recensentur.

Ego Cnut rex Anglorum hanc donacionem libenti animo dedi
Ego Elfgifu[g3] regina consensi
Ego Aþelnoð[h3] archiepiscopus confirmaui [*Canterbury*]
Ego Alfric[i3] archiepiscopus corroboraui [*York*]
Ego Alfwine[j3] episcopus [k3]consignaui [*Winchester*]
Ego Eþerik[l3] episcopus consolidaui [? *Selsey/Dorchester*]
Ego Brihtmer[m3] episcopus prenotaui [*Lichfield*]
Ego Aþelstan[n3] episcopus consensi[k3] [*Hereford*]
Ego Godþine[o3] dux
Ego Leofric[p3] dux
Ego Siward[q3] dux[r3]
Ego Alfwine[s3] dux
Ego Osgod[t3] Clapa
Ego Tovi[u3] Pruda
Ego Þurcyl[v3]
Ego Harald
Ego Þord
Ego Auti
Ego Halfden
Ego Godric
[w3]Ego Alfric[w3]
Ego Rold
Ego Swane[x3]
Ego Orm
Ego Ulfkytel[y3]
Ego Forna[z3]
Ego Godþine
Ego Farþegn[a4]
Ego Ketel
Ego Mergeat[b4]
Ego Gamal[c4]
Ego Asebearn[d4]
Ego Rafen[d4]
Ego Gamel[d4]
Ego Basingur[e4]
Ego Orm

[a] CNUT REX *has been written in the margin next to* In F1 [b] *An additional* et *is supplied after* ueri *in* E; *compare S 512 and* ***4*** [c] xiii E, *altered by erasure from* xxxiii *to* xiii F1 [d] Knut F1 [e] Anglinarum F1 [f] que *omitted* F1 [g] undique *omitted* F1; *compare S 490 and* ***4*** [h] sedulam F1 [i] ducitare F1 [j] sicut E; *compare* ***4*** [k] Patryngton *has been written in the margin next to* quosquam F1 [l] ilico E [m] Elphrico E [n...n] at Patringtune F1 [o] omniue F1 [p] ut E [q] liberalitate F1 [r] deinde E [s] emendauerit F1 [t] Istis E [u] qui quidem termini scribuntur Anglice qui uix secundum linguam modernam legi possent *added at this point in* E *which has no boundary clause; the Old English boundary clause in* F1 *is highly corrupt; see the note on editorial method, pp. 83–4* [v] Yaterinsatune F1 [w] fellid F1 [x] *Where* F1 *has an ampersand in the boundary clause, a Tironian et has been used* [y] *Perhaps for* þare [z] ria F1 [a2] realtan F1 [b2] rya F1 [c2] mase F1 [d2] rcelle F1 [e2] earearnes F1 [f2] F1 *has* Brumbran *with a letter* H *added above the initial* Br- *in a later hand* [g2] F1 *has* Bumbran *with a letter* H *added above the initial* B *in a later hand* [h2] Pateringstune F1 [i2] y F1 [j2] und F1 [k2] Paterinsatune F1 [l2] Yinestede F1 [m2] yaer F1 [n2] fannes F1 [o2] braean F1 [p2] aest F1 [q2] Paterinstune F1 [r2] Yinestode F1 [s2] Hide *has been written in the margin next to* .viii. F1 [t2] Yorp F1 [u2] plosasans F1 [v2] gangs *has been written in the margin next to* Sume- F1 [w2] Yifestade F1 [x2] aer F1 [y2] ploserland F1 [z2] ir F1 [a3] calles F1 [b3] Paterinsatune F1 [c3] *Perhaps for* gebohte [d3] yel F1 [e3] .xiii. E [f3] testibi F1 [g3] Aluiua F1 [h3] Eoþelnod E [i3] Elfrik E [j3] Elphine E [k3...k3] *For the last four episcopal subscriptions, the verbs of attestation are missing in* F1; *for the last three episcopal subscriptions,* Ego *is missing in* F1; episcopus *is also omitted after* Ayeric *in* F1*; see commentary* [l3] Ayeric F1 [m3] Birlicmer E [n3] Eþlstan E [o3] Godewine F1 [p3] Leopric E [q3] Silipard E [r3] *From this point to the end of the witness-list,* Ego *is omitted before each name in* F1 [s3] Elpine E, Afwine F1 [t3] Osegod E [u3] Thofi E [v3] Tþurcil E [w3...w3] *Omitted* E [x3] Spafa E [y3] Ulfkitel F1 [z3] Fforna E [a4] Ffarþegn E, Faryem F1 [b4] Merseat F1 [c4] Gamel E [d4] *Name omitted* F1 [e4] Basins F1

[1] Isaiah 41:2
[2] cf. Matt. 25:41

There are three main surviving manuscript copies of **8**, as listed above (E, F1 and F2); since F2 is probably a direct copy of E, its readings have not been supplied in the text edited here (for more on the relationship of these manuscript copies, see above, p. 70).

Diplomatic analysis of charters issued by King Cnut is a complicated affair. In general terms, the charters of Cnut's reign do not have the highly regularised diplomatic form which reached its zenith in the central decades of the tenth century and which made use of standard diplomatic formulae (from the reign of King Æthelred, especially from 993 onwards, charters display greater literary variation and elaboration: for discussion, see Keynes, *Diplomas*, pp. 95–126, where he analyses the implications for the production of charters in Æthelred's reign). This move away from standardisation reflects the fact that, during Cnut's reign, the drafting of charters took place 'under a greater variety of circumstances than had previously been the case, in a natural development of long-established procedures' (quotation from Keynes 1994, pp. 48–9; see also Keynes, *Diplomas*, p. 126, n. 136). As is common with the charters preserved in the York archive, confusion has occurred with the dating-clause. E, the earliest copy, has an incarnational date of 'millesimo xiii', while F1's original reading of 'millesimo xxxiii' has later been altered by erasure to 'millesimo xiii' (since F2 is a copy of E, it also has 'millesimo xiii' and it may be that F1 was altered to agree with this copy in the second part of the *Magnum*

Registrum Album). The reading of 'millesimo xxxiii' (1033) is to be preferred: Ælfric only became archbishop of York on receiving the *pallium* in 1026 and therefore could not have attested as archbishop in 1013 (*ASC D*, s.a. 1026); similarly, Ælfwine only became bishop of Winchester on the death of his predecessor, Ælfsige, in 1032 (*ASC EF*, s.a. 1032). We should therefore date **8** to the year 1033.

Despite the lack of standardisation in Cnut's charters, **8** does display diplomatic links with other contemporary documents. The verbal invocation ('In nomine Dei et uiui et ueri et domini nostri Iesu Christi mundi redemptoris') is followed by a dating-clause and then by Cnut's royal style; this opening to the charter is found elsewhere in S 973 (*Abing* 140), a 1034 charter in the Abingdon archive. And the style of sanction is similar, although not identical, to that in S 955 (*Shaft* 30), a 1019 charter of Cnut preserved in the Shaftesbury archive. The naming of the beneficiary in **8**, with the phrase *archiepiscopo Alfrico uidelicet Eborum ecclesie*, perhaps reads as a later interpolation where a copyist has sought to make it absolutely clear that **8** is a grant of land to the York church. But the most significant result of a diplomatic analysis of **8** is that one finds a number of diplomatic phrases which had been used in the compilation of two other charters preserved in the York archive, numbers **3** and **4**, both charters of King Edgar. It is therefore possible that the draftsman of **8** made use of these documents as his template. The verbal invocation of **8** is close to that in **4**; the royal style of **8**, although unparalleled elsewhere in the charters of Cnut, is exactly the same as in **4** and the proem in **8** is exactly similar to that in **4**. The main difference between **4** and **8** is that after the royal style **8** has an interesting insertion into an otherwise standard diplomatic formula which reads *hanc scedulam dictare promisi*. Expressions which convey a similar meaning to this one in **8** can be found elsewhere in Cnut's charters. Thus S 955 (*Shaft* 30) has *cedulamque istam illi adnotare mandavi* and S 956 (*WinchNM* 33), a charter from the New Minster archive, has an even more elaborate version: *hanc membranulam grammatum caracteribus canna sulcante precepi exarari*. The order of these initial elements in **8** also appears to follow that given in **4**, as they both begin with the verbal invocation, followed by the dating-clause, then by the royal style and then by the proem. At this point in **8**, **4** ceases to be its main model and **8** appears to draw inspiration instead from **3**. From *ut terram iam prefatam* until the end of the charter **8** now imitates **3** exactly, reproducing both the immunity clause and the sanction of **3** in their entirety. Such borrowing of forms from earlier charters, charters which are preserved in the same archive and cartulary, immediately arouses suspicion as to the authenticity of **8**. It could be the case that the compiler of the cartulary (or some earlier forger), seeking to augment the church's records, added a charter in the name of King Cnut and, in an attempt to make it seem like a genuine document, borrowed forms from two earlier records which were to hand in the archive. However, the procedures for the production of Cnut's charters which are seen elsewhere in Anglo-Saxon England suggest that it is not exceptional to find a charter of Cnut which contains forms borrowed from earlier documents in the same archive. As has already been mentioned, the rigorously controlled production of charters by a central body had begun to make way towards a more flexible system perhaps already under King Æthelred. This trend continued into the reign of Cnut and this Danish king's period of rule saw charters being produced under a wider variety of circumstances (Keynes 1994, pp. 48–9, where he also discusses the possibility that the diversity of diplomatic forms in charters of King Cnut might be due to a decline in the numbers of such documents issued each year, making it more unlikely that groups of charters produced by the same agency could be identified), perhaps sometimes by churchmen in different regions, for example S 975 (*Sher* 16), S 977 (KCD 736) and S

979 (KCD 1324), all possible regional productions (but see also the cautious comments in Keynes 1994, p. 52, n. 50, on S 975 and S 979). It seems to have been the case that in some areas of the country, when churchmen may have been responsible for drawing up charters, they sometimes looked to other charters in an archive to help them to create their new diploma (see Lawson, *Cnut*, pp. 237–9, where he cites evidence to suggest that areas such as Crediton, Cornwall and Sherborne were producing their own charters). So it is that S 964 and S 967, both Abingdon documents (*Abing* 138 and *Abing* 139 respectively), have parallel diplomatic elements and also use formulae which can be seen in other Abingdon charters (Lawson, *Cnut*, p. 239; for more detailed discussion of the diplomatic of these two charters, and of the related charter S 973 [*Abing* 140], see Kelly, *Abingdon* 2, pp. 542–8). Perhaps, then, it is not quite such an alarming feature that **8** relies on two earlier York documents for the majority of its wording. As **8** is a direct grant to the archbishop himself, it is possible that the archbishop had some hand in its compilation or perhaps some say in the way the document should be drawn up. The archbishop's involvement could also explain the desire of the draftsman to use charters already in the possession of the York church as his models (see also Keynes 1994, p. 51).

The witness-list of **8** seems entirely acceptable for its date of 1033. One of the bishops listed (given in E as *Eþerik* and in F1 as *Aþeric*), could either be Æthelric, bishop of Selsey, or it could refer to another Æthelric, bishop of Dorchester. It seems impossible to resolve this with certainty. At this moment in F1, the cartulary copyist has omitted the words *episcopus consolidaui Ego* after Æthelric's name, words which are found in E's copy. The final bishop to attest is Æthelstan, bishop of Hereford.

Four ealdormen also subscribe, Godwine, Leofric, Siward and Ælfwine (for the careers of Godwine and Ælfwine, see Keynes 1994, pp. 70–4 and 78, respectively). The list of thegns who attest includes a number of Scandinavian names. In fact **8**, as one would expect of a charter granted in the north and relating to land in the north, has the greatest number of attesting Scandinavian thegns of all of the charters granted by Cnut. Some of the Scandinavian thegns (for example, 'Rold' (ON Róaldr), 'Forna' (ON Forni), 'Farþegn', 'Ketel' (ON Ketill), 'Gamal' (ON Gamall), 'Basingur' (ON Basing) and 'Orm' (ON Ormr); for these Old Norse names, see Fellows-Jensen, *SPNLY*) do not attest any of Cnut's other diplomas and may have been local Scandinavian magnates whose power and influence was limited to the Danelaw in the north. Others (for example, 'Osgod Clapa' (ON Ásgautr), 'Tovi' (ON Tófi), 'Þurcyl' (ON Þorketill) and 'Harald' (ON Haraldr), who all attest towards the top of the witness-list in **8**) are witnesses in many of Cnut's charters, suggesting that they had been particularly successful in establishing themselves in Cnut's governmental machinery and were not just attesting **8** because of a local connection or eminence. Some of the names of those thegns listed in **8**, 'Ulfkytel' (ON Ulfketill), 'Forna' (ON Forni), 'Farþegn' and 'Rafen' (ON Rafn), also occur in the list of *festermen*, that is men who were trusted in the society of the north to act as sureties, which has been copied into the back of the York Gospels in the second half of the eleventh century on f.161v. Whilst the possibility exists that these might be a reference to the same men, the lack of comparative material makes it impossible to make this identification with any confidence (for more about these *festermen*, see above pp. 6–8, Appendix 2, Cooper 1969 and Keynes 1986, pp. 98–9).

Ælfric, beneficiary of the grant in **8**, had originally been a monk of Winchester and, in 1023, on the death of Archbishop Wulfstan, he became archbishop of York; in 1026 he travelled to Rome to receive the *pallium*, the traditional symbol of his archiepiscopal status, from the pope (see *ASC*, s.a. 1023 and 1026). Ælfric does not seem to have been as active politically as his predecessor, Wulfstan, during the time of King Cnut: he receives hardly any mention in the *ASC* at all and seems to have been more prominent in the reign of one of Cnut's successors, Harthacnut (for Ælfric's career, see Cooper, *Archbishops of York*, pp. 14–18; for the suggestion that Ælfric was made archbishop as a result of the support of Cnut, see Bolton, *Cnut*, p. 84). From the few facts there are it would appear that, in the time of Harthacnut, Ælfric was a controversial figure (*John of Worcester II*, s.a. 1023, is the first to record Ælfric as having the byname of 'Puttoc', a derogatory term meaning 'Kite'; Cooper, *Archbishops of York*, pp. 17–18, suggests that Ælfric acquired his nickname after his time at Worcester where he was not well received). William of Malmesbury's *GP* suggests that it was as a result of prompting from Ælfric that Harthacnut ordered the body of his predecessor, and half-brother, Harold Harefoot, to be mutilated (*GP*, iii.115.12 and *GR*, ii.188.4; see also *ASC CD*, s.a. 1040). After the removal of Bishop Lyfing from Worcester in 1040 (Lyfing had been implicated in the death of the atheling Alfred by Ælfric himself; see *John of Worcester II*, s.a. 1040), Ælfric received the bishopric of Worcester in his place and held it in plurality with York; his time as Bishop of Worcester also seems to have been problematical (Lyfing was restored to Worcester only a year later, in 1041). The *ASC* details how, in 1041, Harthacnut ordered that Worcestershire be raided and ravaged due to the fact that two of his 'housecarls' had been murdered when trying to collect tax from the area (*ASC CD*, s.a. 1041; *John of Worcester II*, s.a. 1041, names these officials as Feader and Thurstan). No mention is made in the *ASC* of Ælfric's role in the matter but the twelfth-century historians, whilst agreeing that the primary cause of the raid was the murder of the two housecarls, both imply that Ælfric had played some role in encouraging the king (Harthacnut) to carry out the deed (*GP*, iii.115 and *John of Worcester II*, s.a. 1041). Despite his dubious reputation, Ælfric does seem to have taken an interest in the welfare and maintenance of the churches over which he was in charge. In the York province, he continued work started by his predecessors and endowed houses of secular canons such as those at York, Beverley and Southwell. Cooper has also drawn attention to the fourteenth-century *Liber Monasterii de Hyda* which, after a note which tells of Ælfric's succession to York, has 'His primum quaeritur contra Dunelmium episcopum Edmundum, quo iure ipse Hangus...'. Unfortunately this is as much as is given and Cooper suggests that it is a reference to a dispute between the bishoprics of Durham and York over land at 'Hangus' which was 'in the valley of the River Ure and the south side of Swaledale, for this area comprised the old wapentake of Hang, a name which is first recorded in the form "Hangeschire" in 1157' (Cooper, *Archbishops of York*, p. 17). It appears, therefore, as if Ælfric had taken measures to protect and augment the landed possessions of the see of York and this fits in well with the evidence that can be gleaned from **8**, which is suggestive of the personal interest that Ælfric had in acquiring land for the church of St Peter's at York (see also Keynes 1994, p. 51). And it may be that **8** was simultaneously a grant of political importance on Cnut's part. Bolton has recently drawn attention both to the unusually large size of the Patrington estate and to the fact that it is situated to the east of York, and therefore away from other of the York church's landholdings, and in territory which was in the control of one Thurbrand, a powerful man in Northumbria. Bolton therefore suggests that 'this grant may represent an attempt by Cnut to extend the authority of his archbishop over that of some of the more independent aristocracy of southern Northumbria'; see Bolton, *Cnut*, pp. 132–4 (at p. 134).

Bounds of Patrington

8 grants, primarily, the estate of Patrington to Ælfric: it first details the 'inland' territory of Patrington and then suggests that detached portions of land at Winestead, Halsham, Thorpe and 'Sumeres Marsh' were included in the grant; the owner of Patrington also held soke over various areas. As with **2–5**, the Old English boundary clause in **8** is preserved in a corrupt form. This, coupled with the fact that the terrain covered in **8** may have been rather featureless, has made it difficult to locate the bounds in the landscape today (for a full discussion of **8**'s bounds, see Long and Pickles 1993*b*).

1. *These are the estate-boundaries of Patrington: first it commences at the pit* (pytt)*; and so along the dyke/ditch* (dic) *to the stone* (stan). These features are impossible to identify with certainty today: many of the field boundaries in the area are marked by ditches or dykes and there is no trace of a significant stone. But despite these difficulties, Long and Pickles 1993*b* suggest reasonably that **8**'s boundary begins at a north-eastern point somewhere near Bracken Hill (TA 326248) on the line of today's parish boundary.

2. *And thence over the pool (? or possibly 'boundary')* (mere *or possibly* mearc) *to the cattle-shed* (scypen). This part of **8** offers some difficulties of interpretation. The first feature mentioned is given as *meare* in the text: this could be a (corrupt) form either of *mere*, 'pond', *mearc*, 'boundary, boundary mark' or *(ge)mære*, 'boundary'. Jenkyns, in her work on this charter for 'LangScape', prefers that this should read *mere*, meaning 'pool'. Stevenson has made an additional suggestion, that the text's *meare* could be translated as a 'mark' and subsequently as a 'boundary' and Long and Pickles favour this interpretation (Stevenson in Farrer, *EYC*, p. 26). They note that 'mere' is frequently used, to this very day, to denote a boundary on either side of the Humber. They also highlight the presence of a 'Myers Lane', which is a track running to the south-east of Long Farm (TA 336243) in a parallel direction to Hollym Road towards Hollym; it seems possible that this leg of the bounds in **8** is coterminous with the present-day boundary (Long and Pickles 1993*b*, pp. 144–5). There is a further textual difficulty in this clause, with the words *scare scypne*. Jenkyns, again in 'LangScape', suggests two possible interpretations: either that *scare* is a corrupt form of *scearu*, meaning 'boundary', or that *scare* is simply a miscopying of *þare*, the definite article. Since Jenkyns thinks that the latter interpretation is more likely, it has been adopted in my translation above.

3. *And so along the dyke/ditch* (dic) *on the west of Thorpe (farm/secondary settlement)* (þorp) *to the hollow ditch* (hol + dic). The *þorp* of this part of the bounds may be identified as Welwick Thorpe (now Thorpe Hill), for which see *PN YorksER*, p. 23, s.v. 'Welwick Thorpe'. Today the township boundary passes to the west of Welwick Thorpe (TA 329217) which lies on Welwick Road, and Long and Pickles note that this stretch of **8**'s boundary can be clearly discerned in aerial photographs (Long and Pickles 1993*b*, p. 145).

4. *And so to salt pool (? or possibly 'Saltmarsh')* (sealt + mere)*; and thence in the straightest way that one can see to 'scelle'* (? scela; *see commentary*) *homestead* (toft)*; and thence to the east end* (ende) *of the dyke/ditch* (dic)*; and so to eagle's hill-spur/heel/projecting piece of land* (earn + hoh). The high level of corruption in the copy of this Old English boundary clause has caused two textual difficulties here. The first problem is with the 'salt pool', which is rendered in the text by the words *sealtan meare*. One interpretation is that *meare* is a corrupt form of *mere* meaning simply 'pool'; but Stevenson in Farrer, *EYC*, p. 25, n. b, preferred that *meare* was a miscopied form of *mersc* meaning 'marsh' and that this was therefore a reference to the place 'Saltmarsh' which lies to the west of

the township boundary above East Growths at TA 316208. If the 'Saltmarsh' interpretation can be accepted (Long and Pickles 1993*b*, p. 145, agree with this interpretation; but see *PN YorksER*, p. 254, s.v. 'Saltmarshe' where it does not seem to be accepted), then at this point in the bounds the landscape has been subject to a great amount of change due to the movements of the Humber. At first the area of land increased as a result of a large deposit of silt between the shore and the main channel of the estuary. That this was the case at Patrington is apparently highlighted by the reference in the next part of the clause to the boundary marker of *earnes hoh* which means 'hill-spur/heel/projecting piece of land of the eagle' (for all of this, see Long and Pickles 1993*b*, p. 145; for the possible meanings of *hoh*, see Smith, *EPNE* I, pp. 256–7). This trend was later reversed after a period of coastal erosion in the thirteenth century (Long and Pickles, *ibid*.). The second textual difficulty is with *scelle*: Long and Pickles suggest that this word may be derived from the Old English *scela* which means a temporary hut (Long and Pickels, *ibid*., pp. 145–7); but it could equally well be a miscopied form of *scelle*, meaning 'separation', of *sciell*, meaning 'shell', or of *stell*, meaning an 'enclosure' (all of these possibilities are suggested by Joy Jenkyns in 'LangScape'). The 'dyke' could be any of the early embankments in the area (Long and Pickles, *ibid*., p. 147).

5. *And so on to (the) Humber; to the spring* (well) *of eagle's hill-spur/heel/projecting piece of land* (earn + hoh)*; and so along (the) Humber to the mouth* (muða) *of Patrington creek* (fleot). It is uncertain what the 'spring of eagle's hill-spur/heel/projecting piece of land' refers to but the line of the Humber is obvious enough (Long and Pickles 1993*b*, pp. 145–7). For the difficulty in identifying the 'mouth of Patrington creek', see Long and Pickles, *ibid*., p. 147, where they also note that the general direction in which the bounds are now travelling is upstream and westwards.

6. *And so along the creek* (fleot) *to cross creek* (cros + fleot)*; and thence always by the creek* (fleot) *until it comes to the middle of the bridge* (brycg) *between Patrington and Winestead*. Just as 'Patrington creek' could not be identified, so too it is difficult to locate the 'cross creek', although an identification with the modern Winestead Drain might be possible: for discussion, see Long and Pickles 1993*b*, p. 147. Long and Pickles, *ibid*., pp. 147–8, further note that at this point in their recreation of the Anglo-Saxon bounds of Patrington there is a slight problem with a small area of land known as Patrington West Lands; this area lies to the west of Winestead Drain but cannot be brought into the bounds of **8**. They suggest the possibility that the 'half a ploughland on Sumeres marsh', noted later in **8** as a detached part of inland, may be a reference to these West Lands. If this is the case then **8**'s 'cross creek' must be that section of Winestead Drain which today takes a turn from its route westwards and instead heads northwards (at TA 285213; at this point there is a floodgate today). If we follow this section of Winestead Drain we eventually come to Winestead Bridge (TA 301235) which even today separates Patrington from Winestead and is presumably the same bridge as that one mentioned in **8**.

7. *And then through the middle of the fen* (fen) *to broad island* (brad + holmr)*; and so up with the small stream* (sic) *to the pit* (pytt). **8**'s boundary is here still following the line of Winestead Drain which now runs between Winestead Carrs to the north (TA 313239) and Patrington Carrs to the south (TA 315235): Long and Pickles 1993*b*, p. 148. The 'broad island' is not readily identifiable. The Old Norse word 'holmr' has the meaning of 'an island' especially one in a river or a creek (see Smith, *EPNE* I, pp. 258–9 and Gelling and Cole, *LPN*, pp. 55–7), and there are many such examples in the region of the Humber. Long and Pickles suggest that the 'broad island' referred to in **8** may be equated

with a patch of rising ground now known as 'Bracken Hill' which lies on the present-day boundary between Patrington and Hollym at TA 326248 (Long and Pickles 1993*b*, p. 148).

8. *And inland to Patrington thirty ploughlands; and in Winestead* (TA 299245) *eight ploughlands; and in Halsham* (TA 275270) *two and a half ploughlands and half an oxgang; and in Thorpe* (TA 330218) *two ploughlands and one oxgang and half a ploughland in 'Sumeres marsh'* (mersc)*; and the soke thereto over all Winestead except one ploughland; and over all Halsham; and two ploughlands in Thorpe except one oxgang: that is altogether ten ploughlands of sokeland. Now all the lands that lie outside the 'yrth'* (yrð) *mark/boundary* (mearc) *at Patrington are bought with this book/charter in the same manner as 'Rilnetune'.* **8** here gives the details of four detached portions of land belonging to the Patrington estate: those of Winestead, Halsham, Thorpe and 'Sumeres Marsh'. These are not to be included within the boundary clause just described and indeed **8** states that 'they lie outside the *yrð* mark (i.e. boundary) at Patrington'. Only 'Sumeres Marsh' remains unidentified. Later, at the time of the Domesday survey, Patrington continued to have four townships attached to it which were then termed 'berewicks' (GDB, f. 302r). Three of these were the same as those given in **8** (Winestead, Halsham and Thorpe) but the fourth is listed as being 'Thurlesthorp': Long and Pickles suggest that this may be the same as 'Sumeres Marsh' (Long and Pickles 1993*b*, p. 148). Long and Pickles also note the possibility of the existence of an earlier religious site at Patrington (suggested by the find of part of an eighth-century carved cross at Patrington; Long and Pickles, 1993*b*, p. 150, referring to Lang, *Corpus*, pp. 198–9) and it may therefore be the case that this grant of land in **8** was occasioned by the adding of those detached portions of lands that 'lie outside the *yrð* mark at Patrington' and which were 'bought with this book/charter in the same manner as *Rilnetune*'.

By the time of the Domesday survey, the size of the estate in **8** (including its berewicks), or simply the assessment of the estate, had decreased from forty-three *casati* to thirty–five and a half carucates, two bovates and two parts of one bovate (GDB, f. 302r). There are two striking differences: firstly, that the value of carucates of Patrington itself had halved from the thirty ploughlands in **8** to fifteen carucates and two bovates in 1086 (GDB, f. 382r); and secondly that the value of Halsham increased from two and a half ploughlands and half an oxgang in **8** to just over seven carucates in 1086 (GDB, f. 382r); for more about this, see Farrer, *EYC*, p. 27 and, for a different view, Long and Pickles 1993*b*, p. 150.

9

King Edward declares that he has granted to Archbishop Ealdred judicial and financial rights over his lands and over all his men. [A.D. 1060 × 1066]

F1. York, Minster Library and Archives, L 2/1 (*Mag. Reg. Alb.*), pt. I, 61v: s. xiv^med^

F2. York, Minster Library and Archives, L 2/1 (*Mag. Reg. Alb.*), pt. I, 62v: s. xiv^med^

J. Bodleian, Dodsworth 125, 80r: copy of F2, s. xvii

Ed.: a. Kemble 893, from F1 and F2

b. Farrer, *EYC*, no. 10, from F2

c. Harmer, *Writs*, no. 118, from F1

Listed: Sawyer 1159; Hart, *ECNE*, no. 136

Edited from F1 and F2

Eadpard[a] cynge gret mine b'es 7 mine eorlas and ealle myne[b] þegenas[c] on þam[d] sciran þaer Ealdred aerceb' haefð[e] land inne freondlice 7 ic cyðe[f] eop[g] [h]ꝥ ic pylle ꝥ[h] he beo his saca purðe[i] 7 his socna ofer his land 7 ofer [j]eallum his[j] mannum tolles and teames binnan porte 7 butan.

[a] –ward *omitted* F1 [b] mine F2 [c] yesenas F1, F2 [d] yam F1, yan F2 [e] haefd F1, F2
[f] cyde F1, F2 [g] eoy F1, me F2 [h..h] y ic y ylle y F1, y ic yille y F2
[i] *Omitted* F1, yurde F2 [j..j] *Omitted* F2

Translation[a]

King Edward sends friendly greetings to my bishops and my earls and all my thegns in the shires in which Archbishop Ealdred has land. And I inform you that my will is that he be entitled to his sake and his soke, over his lands and over all his people, to toll and to team, within town and without.

[a] *Translation taken from Harmer,* Writs, *p. 418*

9 seems entirely acceptable as a modernised copy of an authentic Anglo-Saxon writ; it is one of those writs which Harmer has classified by its use of the technical term *purðe* (Harmer, *Writs*, pp. 63–4 and pp. 412–13). The protocol is standard, with the use of the verb *gret* and the adverb *freondlice*, as is the declaration, *ic cyðe eop þæt ic pylle þæt*. Examples of writs with similar openings include S 1064, S 1068, S 1069, S 1072 and S 1074 and so on. But there are three writs in particular which bear a striking resemblance to **9**: S 1071, an extant original writ of King Edward from the Bury St Edmund's archive; S 1097, a writ of King Edward from the Cirencester archive; and S 1099, also a writ of King Edward but from the Coventry archive. All of these three writs have the same protocol and declaration as **9** and also the same, or similar, reference to the physical limit of the grant (**9** has *binnan porte 7 butan*; S 1071 has *binnan burh ge butan*; S 1097 has *binne buruh. ge buten*; and S 1099 has *bynnen borough 7 bouten*). **9** grants Archbishop Ealdred judicial and financial rights over his lands and all his men, as do S 1097 and S 1099 to their respective beneficiaries; S 1071 is not quite as extensive a grant as it only covers judicial rights. S 1097 and S 1099 are even more pertinent in that they too grant 'toll and team'. Harmer notes that possession of *toll* allows the owner of an estate to benefit from the sale of cattle or other goods on that estate; she also notes that *team* 'stands for the right to take profits, and perhaps to hold the procedure, in a case of "vouching to warranty", whereby a person accused of the unlawful possession of cattle or other goods could "vouch his warrantor", that is, pass on the charge to the person from whom he had acquired the disputed property' (Harmer, *Writs*, p. 76). It is noticeable that there is no prohibition or valediction in **9**.

This writ cannot be dated more closely than the limits provided by Ealdred's accession (1060) and King Edward's death (1066) (but see further below). It conforms to one of the most common types of Anglo-Saxon royal writ, of which examples survive from most of the major archives (see, for example, S 1068, S 1071, S 1095 and S 1111). It is likely that the purpose of such messages to the courts of the shires in which a bishop (or abbot) had lands was to let the courts know of the due appointment to the hitherto vacant see or abbey and to inform them that the new bishop or abbot should henceforth receive the financial and judicial dues that arose in the shire courts. There is no reason to think that this type of writ was ever a grant to the church in question of new rights *de nouo*. It is therefore likely that this writ was issued in 1060, that is at the start of Ealdred's tenure of York (I am most grateful to Professor N.P. Brooks for this information about the function and dating of **9**).

9 is granted to Archbishop Ealdred who, as we have already seen (above, pp. 65–8), was very powerful and seems to have done a good deal both to protect and to enhance the York church's standing. **9**, **10** and **14** are all grants of quite significant rights to Ealdred, which further adds to our impression of his high status.

10

King Edward announces that he has granted to Ealdred, the 'deacon' of Archbishop Ealdred, the minster at Axminster, Devon, as a pious benefaction for St Peter's minster at York. [A.D. 1060 × 1066]

F. York, Minster Library and Archives, L 2/1 (*Mag. Reg. Alb.*), pt. I, 61v: s. xiv[med]
Ed.: a. Harmer, *Writs*, no. 120, from F
b. *Councils and Synods*, pt. 1, no. 82, p. 559
Listed: Sawyer 1161
Edited from F

Eadƿard cynge gret Leofric biscop 7 Harold eorl 7 Ƿada 7 alle mine þegenas[a] on Defenascire freondlice 7 ic cyðe[b] eoƿ ꝥ[c] ic habbe geunnan Ealdrede þaes arcebiscopes dyacne Ealdredes[d] ꝥ[c] mynster at Axaminster 7 alc þaere þinge[e] þaes þe þaer mid rithe to gebyrað[f] mid saca[g] and mid socna ƿpa full 7 ƿpa forð[h] ƿpa hit aenig preost toforan him firmest haefide into Peteres mynster on Euerƿic to almesse.

[a] yesenas F [b] cyde F [c] y F [d] ? Ffaldredes F [e] yinse F [f] sebyrad F
[g] saca *altered from* sace F [h] ford F

Translation[a]

King Edward sends friendly greetings to Bishop Leofric and Earl Harold and Wada and all my thegns in Devonshire. And I inform you that I have granted to Ealdred, the deacon of Archbishop Ealdred, the minster at Axminster, and all the things lawfully pertaining thereto, with sake and with soke, as fully and as completely as ever any priest before him had it, as a pious benefaction for St Peter's minster at York.

[a] *Translation taken from Harmer,* Writs, *p. 419*

10 begins with a protocol and declaration that are entirely standard and much like those found in **9** (except with slightly different wording in the declaration; for examples of other writs with a similar opening, see the commentary to **9**).

10 is addressed to Leofric, who held the sees of Devon and Cornwall in plurality from 1046 (in 1050 he combined these two sees into one at Exeter) until his death in 1072; it is also addressed to Harold who, having been earl of East Anglia, later succeeded to the West Saxon earldom in 1053 (see *ASC C*, s.a. 1053); to Wada, whom we know from Domesday Book to have owned land in, for example, Modbury, 'Torridge', Bolberry, Shilston and Honicknowle (all in Devon; see GDB, ff. 105r–v; for other examples, see Harmer, *Writs*, p. 576) and who was thus an important man in the south-west of England; that Wada was named in person before the king's thegns in Devonshire are addressed, suggests that he was the shire-reeve of Devon.

10 announces that King Edward has granted to Ealdred the 'deacon' the minster at Axminster, presumably for Ealdred's own benefit but also for the communal good of residents at York ('...as a pious benefaction for St Peter's minster at York'); see also *Councils and Synods*, Part I, pp. 557–8. The existence of a church at Axminster by the late eighth century is confirmed by its mention in the famous annal of the *Anglo-Saxon Chronicle* regarding Cynewulf and Cyneheard (*ASC C*, s.a. 755 [*recte* 757]; see also Harmer, *Writs*, pp. 530–1 and *Councils and Synods*, Part I, p. 558). Evidence for the role of 'deacons' and 'archdeacons' can be found in the *Northumbrian Priests' Law* compiled in the generation following the death of Archbishop Wulfstan II in 1023 (see, for example, item 12 about wrongful ordination in Whitelock, *EHD*, pp. 472–3; Harmer, *Writs*, p. 530, suggests that the Ealdred 'deacon' addressed here was more likely to have been an 'archdeacon' and, if so, would have been the person responsible for the supervision of the diocesan finances; for more about archdeacons and some of their responsibilities, see Giandrea, *Episcopal Culture*, p. 122). The fact that Axminster is situated to the east of Devon near the River Axe, makes this a rather remarkable gift for the far-distant York church. But Archbishop Ealdred's links with the area provide a possible reason for the making of the grant. Not only had he been abbot of Tavistock in the period *c*. 1027–*c*. 1043 and succeeded Lyfing as bishop of Worcester in 1046 (see *ASC D*, s.a. 1047 [*recte* 1046], *John of Worcester II*, s.a. 1046 and *HRH*, p. 73; S 1004 [KCD 772], a charter of 1044, has Ealdred already attesting as 'bishop' which may suggest that he was by this stage helping the pluralist Lyfing with an episcopal role), but in 1066 he also owned other property in the Devon area, the estates of Denbury and Coffinswell (GDB, f. 103v), which are located about thirty-five miles south-west of Axminster (I am most grateful to Dr Stephen Baxter for pointing this out to me). And the link between Axminster and the York church seen in **10** continued beyond the Anglo-Saxon period, with the prebendaries of Warthill and Grindale of York Minster claiming a half hide of land in Prestaller in Axminster, the rectorial tithes of Axminster and the advowson there; for all of these details, see J. Davidson, *The History of Axminster Church in the County of Devon* (Exeter, 1835), pp. 8–9, Harmer, *Writs*, p. 417, Clay, *YMF* 2, pp. 153–5 and *Councils and Synods*, Part I, pp. 558–9. When Leland came to Axminster he noted: 'the church of Axminstre is famose by the sepultres of many noble Danes slain in King Athelstane's time at a batel on Brunesdown thereby, and by the sepultures likewise of sum Saxon lordes slain in the same feld' (quoted in J. Davidson, *The History of Axminster*, pp. 45–6).

Archbishop Ealdred took measures to introduce a communal ecclesiastical life at York and its daughter churches of Ripon, Beverley and Southwell (see above, pp. 66–7). One consequence of a communal life was that property was to be held in common by all. Although few contemporary records of the York canons' rights in the reign of Edward the Confessor have survived, Harmer has drawn attention to a confirmation in the name of Henry I which sets out the very great liberties thought to belong to the canons at the end of the Anglo-Saxon period (Harmer, *Writs*, p. 415). The confirmation states that the archbishop had no rights over the chapter and the canons' rights are specified as being extensive:

> Habebant canonici in domibus et in terris suis soccam et saccam, tol et team, intol et uttol, et infangantheof, et omnes easdem honoris et libertatis consuetudines quas ipse rex in terris suis habebat, et quas archiepiscopus de domino suo et de rege tenebat (see Raine, *HCY* III, p. 35).

The grant set out in **10** implies that Axminster's revenues were now divided between those taken by the deacon Ealdred on behalf of the York church and those left for the Axminster church itself (see Harmer, *Writs*, p. 416 and *Councils and Synods*, Part I, pp. 557–8). By the time of Domesday Book, there was land for forty ploughs at Axminster and the Axminster manor was owed various payments from other manors, payments which seem not to have been received. The manors of Deneworthy and Undercleave were also added to Axminster (for all of this information, see GDB, f. 100r–v).

11

King Edward grants the see of Worcester to Archbishop Ealdred.
A.D. 1065 (31 December)

F. York, Minster Library and Archives, L 2/1 (*Mag. Reg. Alb.*), pt. I, 60v–61r: copy, s. xiv[med]
Rubric: Concessio Eadwardi regis facta Eborum ecclesie de episcopatu Wirecestrie.
Ed.: a. *Mon. Angl.*, iii. 130–1, from F
b. Thomas, *Survey of Worcester*, Appendix No. 1, from *Mon. Angl.*
c. *Mon. Angl.* (rev. edn.), vi, pt. 3, p. 1177 (no. 7)
d. Kemble 815, from F
Listed: Sawyer 1037a
Edited from F

In nomine sancte et indiuidue trinitatis. Eadwardus diuina gratia largiente Anglorum rex. Quantum religiosi antecessores nostri dignitatem ecclesiarum clarissimam interdum fore perspexerunt terrenarum opulentia rerum, tantum que auctoritatis robur habere[a] quanta fulciebatur copia diuitiarum, digne tenuitatem[b] ecclesiasticam larga amplificare studuerunt manu tam in possessione praediorum quam ceteris redditibus legalium constitucionum. Etenim uero, cum ipsi fideles qui sumus in Christo ab apostolo uocemur et simus ecclesia quamprope quam ex numerosa multitudine gencium in unitate corporis sui ad ecclesiam Dei nuncupamus, sua Christus consecrauit gratia uidebimur adulterini et non filii, si in eius nos sedulos non exhibuerimus dilatanda gloria. Quapropter ego

Eadwardus, Christi pietate[c] rex Anglorum, dolens Eboracam metropolim nostro tempore deiectam ab antiqua celsitudine qua illustrabatur a piis regibus nostris predecessoribus in pristinum cupiens reparare dignitatis statum, nostro fideli domino[d] archiepiscopo eiusdem ecclesie metropolitano Eadwardo[e] [f]regali dono[f] nostro contulimus ad integrum, quicquid a pio patre nostro Aldredo[g] Anglorum rege eius antecessori Oswaldo predicte sedis pontifici est collatum, et post cum Rome peteret pallium a beato papa Formoso per privilegii descriptionem ei est traditum donum scilicet Wiricestris episcopii, per nostrum tamen consilium disponendum in archiepiscopatus dignitate exaltanda suplementum uicarium quod etiam idem Oswaldus et post eum Adulfus[h] et Wlstanus archipresules regio munere adepti sunt et tenuerunt quietum et solidum donec Anglia dirupta est et discissa inuasione Danorum et cum ceteris ornamentis ecclesiarum predicte ciuitatis illud pape Formosi privilegium constat esse incensum; hic autem carissimus noster Ealdradus episcopii curam suscipiens eiusdemque ecclesie iura requirens et sciens a beato papa Nicholao Rome pallio donatus, ad nos super ecclesie sibi commisse dignitate apostolica scripta signata detulit, quibus cum sua fidelitate commoniti iustam petitionem pape et suam nolumus refutare quod absit, presertim, cum super eadem re apostolicum presentauerit privilegium. Donauimus igitur consilio regine mee, et aliorum fidelium, ei eiusque posteris ordinationem Wiricestris episcopii, cum nostro tamen disponendam consilio, quatenus in exequenda episcopali cura eo specialius utatur uicario utque a beato papa Nicholao in eius scriptum habetur priuilegio. Quod si quis ex regibus posteris nostris infringere temptauerit, iram Dei incurrat et sit anathema secundum supradictum apostolici decretum, nisi resipiscat. Ut autem hec mee descriptionis priuilegium perpetuo inuiolatum seruetur, manus nostre signum sigillique auctoritas subter insignitur; item regie uxoris mee testimonio munitur; episcoporum quoque interminatio cum singulorum nomine et caractare exprimitur abbatum; et principum regni nostri contestificatione fulcitur.

Ego Eadwardus Dei gratia Anglorum rex hoc scriptum confirmaui

Ego Editha Dei pietate Anglorum regina iussu domini mei regis uoluntarie huic descriptioni faueo

Ego Stigandus archiepiscopus subscribo [*Canterbury*]

Ego Hermannus episcopus subscribo [*Ramsbury*]

Willelmus episcopus [*London*]

Leofricus episcopus [*Exeter*]

Robertus Stalre

Osbernus Capellanus

Raimboldus

Petrus

Haroldus Dei gratia dux

Tosti
Algarus dux
Girth dux
Leofwinus dux
Brihtric
Ulf
Suen
Alnod[i]
Walder subscripsi
Actum Wintonie in publica curia natalis Christi in die festiuitatis sancti Siluestri anno domini .mlxv. anno autem regni nostri .xxi. per omnia benedictus Deus Amen.
Ego Alfnoð abbas
Aselnodus[j] abbas
S. Leofricus abbas
Ego Aldridus subdiaconus scriptum recognoui

[a] *For* haberet [b] tenuiuitatem F [c] pietate pietate F [d] *Possibly for* domno [e] *For* Ealdrado [f..f] regali ḍṇọ dono F [g] *For* Æthelredo; *the manuscript has been altered at this point* [h] *For* Ealdwulf [i] *For* Æthelnoth [j] *For* Æthelnoth

The Latin of **11** is complex and its contents are irregular. The narrative is difficult to follow, repetitive and its meaning is often oblique. In it, King Edward is made to say that he is aggrieved by the lowering of the York church's status and wealth to the extent that he wanted to return it to its former glory (*in pristinum...statum*). **11** goes on to claim that Edward therefore restored whatever had been granted to York by his predecessor and that he also granted the bishopric of Worcester (*donauimus igitur consilio regine mee, et aliorum fidelium, ei eiusque posteris ordinationem Wiricestris episcopii*) to the church. **11** is clearly a spurious document; the very fact that it claims to grant the entire bishopric of Worcester to Archbishop Ealdred condemns it as a forgery, as does its textual content in various places. But this does not make it any less interesting, not least because some of its diplomatic formulae may be based on genuine Anglo-Saxon diplomatic practice and it seems likely, as will be seen, that the witness-list has been taken from an authentic diploma of Edward the Confessor's reign for the year 1064.

Since **11** is a forgery, it makes it very difficult to be sure whether errors present in our received text in Manuscript F were part of the original document or whether they are the result of later copying errors. But it does seem clear that in one sentence in **11** there have been some copying errors. Where the text reads 'nostro fideli domino archiepiscopo eiusdem ecclesie metropolitano Eadwardo', 'Eadwardo' is a mistake for 'Ealdrado'; this is explicable by attraction to 'ego Eadwardus' which came just before. Very shortly afterwards there is a reference to 'Aldredo' which, given the fact that **11** is here talking about the father of Edward the Confessor ('pio patre'), should be taken to mean King Æthelred (968–1016). This is most probably a simple copying error as 'Aldredo' is very close to 'Æðelredo'; or it may be that a later corrector at York, seeing that his exemplar was a charter granted to Archbishop Ealdred, thought that a reference to King Æthelred should actually be a reference to Archbishop Ealdred and thus changed it.

In general, authentic charters of Edward the Confessor's time tend to be more restrained than the more literary and extravagant forms that had been popularised at the end of the tenth century in Æthelred's reign. As such, many of Edward's charters hark back to the concise diplomatic fashion of the mid-tenth century. The verbal invocation with which **11** begins can be closely paralleled in four charters of King Eadwig's reign, S 606 (BCS 959), S 609 (BCS 958), S 624 (*Abing* 65) and S 635 (BCS 962), all of which are dated 956 and all of which seem to have been the products of one and the same meeting of the king's *witan* in February of that year (Keynes, *Diplomas*, pp. 55 and 61–5); whether one believes that the draftsman of **11** used an authentic mid-tenth-century charter to compose this part of his text is a matter of judgement, but the example in **11** is certainly not out of context in Anglo-Saxon diplomatic and indeed conforms to procedures in Edward's reign of looking back to the mid-tenth century diplomatic style. It can also be found in spurious charters of Edward the Confessor's reign (S 1002 [KCD 771], S 1039, S 1041 [KCD 825], S 1043 [KCD 824]) and in one charter, S 1061 (KCD 914), which is preserved in the Mont Saint-Michel archive and which is difficult to classify as spurious or authentic. The verbal invocation is followed by a royal style, 'Eadwardus diuina gratia largiente Anglorum rex'. The title itself 'Anglorum rex' is readily found elsewhere (e.g. S 1004) and the divine 'justification' for Edward's kingship given by 'diuina gratia largiente' is paralleled by similar, if not identical, versions: 'diuina mihi adridente gratia rex Anglorum' (S 1008 [KCD 781], an original charter of 1045; see also a 1049 original, S 1019 [KCD 787]) and 'dei indulgente clementia, Angul-Saxonum rex' (in S 1034 [*Bath* 22], a 1061 charter drafted by Bishop Giso of Wells). Although the contents of the royal style are not atypical themselves, it is the placement of this clause which is troubling. Most surviving original charters of Edward the Confessor's reign adopt the structure of verbal invocation, then proem, then exposition, and only then does the royal style occur: see S 1003, S 1004 (KCD 772), S 1005 (KCD 770), S 1008 (KCD 781), S 1010 (KCD 778), S 1019 (KCD 787) and S 1031. It is therefore surprising that the royal style arrives so early in **11**; this structure can be found elsewhere in S 1061 (KCD 914), the charter from the Mont Saint-Michel archive which is difficult to classify, but it is far from standard. That something is amiss at this point in **11** seems to be confirmed by the repetition of Edward's style further on in the diploma; indeed, as we shall see, repetition seems to be another feature of **11** which condemns it as a forgery.

The proem in **11** is problematic. (For the proem, Kemble had suggested a reading of '... tam quae auctoritatis robur habere quanta fulciebatur copia diuitiarum...' but expansion of the manuscript reading 'tm' to 'tantum' seems more appropriate; thus this phrase would mean '...so that it, i.e. the dignity of churches, would possess the strength of authority to the degree to which it was grounded in a great quantity of wealth...'; this would also require that 'habere' should be 'haberet'.) That the proem is unparalleled in the rest of Edward the Confessor's charters is not in itself suggestive of forgery: for although there was a tendency to conform to the concise standards set down by charters of Eadwig and Edgar's time, the extant originals of Edward's reign all display proems with a degree of variety and invention. Thus S 1003, S 1004 (KCD 772) and S 1005 (KCD 770) are all originals dated to 1044 and all exhibit differing proems. It seems to have been particularly desirable for draftsmen of this time to employ alliteration, *figura etymologica* and paronomasia in the proem, perhaps especially with the opening phrase, presumably a method designed to guarantee that a reader or listener would be impressed. S 1003 opens with '**Reg**is cunctorum

regum **reg**imine **reg**untur', S 1004 (KCD 772) begins '**P**os**t**quam **p**rot**o**p**l**as**ti** ser**p**en**ti**na suasione sedu**cti** s**t**ola immortalitatis perdita...' while a later example from 1042x44, S 1044 (KCD 769), has perhaps the most striking beginning of all: '**C**un**cti**tonan**tis** **c**lemen**tis**sima condito**ris** **clement**ia **clement**er **sacr**is **sacr**orum...'. Therefore variation and innovation are to be expected. But the proem in **11** seems uncharacteristic of pre-Conquest diplomatic. The basic function of an Anglo-Saxon proem is to announce the pious considerations that lie behind the making of the grant and they tend to encompass a limited range of themes such as the virtue of charity, the transitory nature of worldly things, the approaching end of the world or the frailty of human memory. Whilst the second sentence, beginnning 'Etenim uero' and ending 'dilatanda gloria', does fulfil this role, the first sentence, which describes how the religious predecessors (at York) 'recognised that the dignity of churches would be very notable at times (=might be increased?) by the opulence of earthly things, so that it (sc. the dignity of churches) would possess the strength of authority to the degree to which it was grounded in a great quantity of wealth' ('dignitatem ecclesiarum clarissimam interdum fore perspexerunt terrenarum opulentia rerum, tantum quae auctoritatis robur habere quanta fulciebatur copia diuitiarum') is rather unusual and perhaps suspicious. It suggests that the grant took place not only as a pious act but also because there was some worldly (literally 'terrenarum') and material benefit to be had: such sentiments are normally avoided in Anglo-Saxon diplomatic.

The exposition, which links the proem to the rest of the transaction ('Quapropter'), is entirely standard (see, for example, S 1005 [KCD 770]), as is the royal style which then follows. But then the draftsman of **11** once more demonstrates that this is not usual Anglo-Saxon diplomatic. We would expect the royal superscription to be followed by a dispositive clause granting the estate and land, naming the benificiary, giving the details of the estate and the terms on which the estate would be held (these extant originals of King Edward's reign, S 1003, S 1004 [KCD 772], S 1005 [KCD 770], S 1008 [KCD 781], S 1019 [KCD 787], S 1028 and S 1044 [KCD 769], all have this structure). Instead there is an insertion at this point in **11** which describes the deplorable state the archbishopric of York had fallen into ('dolens Eboracam metropolim nostro tempore deiectam ab antiqua celsitudine qua illustrabatur'). **11** then continues in an unusual fashion by again seeking to justify the grant being made ('in pristinum cupiens reparare dignitatis statum'). Between this point and the sanction the statements made in **11** are clearly the work of forgery and simply make no sense in Anglo-Saxon diplomatic. They describe the gift of the bishopric of Worcester (itself an impossible claim) and the draftsman again justifies this gift by describing how previous York archbishops (Ealdwulf and Wulfstan II) had had jurisdiction over Worcester. Again, this is not at all what one would expect to find in a charter. We are then confronted with several statements which have the cumulative force of suggesting that York's privileges ultimately stemmed from papal approval. Not only is this totally out of place in an Anglo-Saxon charter, but the careful mention of papal privileges perhaps suggests a reason why **11** was originally composed (see further below).

The sanction in **11** begins with 'Quod si' which, although rare in this position, is not unparalleled: it is found elsewhere in two rather irregular charters, S 1017 (*Burt* 38), a 1048 grant by King Edward to Tofig his *comes*, and in S 1028, a very unusual 1059 grant by King Edward of land in Oxfordshire to St Denis in Paris and preserved at St Denis. Various elements in the sanction suggest that it was composed at least with some care to imitate genuine Anglo-Saxon diplomatic conventions. Thus the use of '...infringere temptauerit' is common and found elsewhere in, for example, S 999 (*Abing* 142), S 1006

(KCD 774), S 1008 (KCD 781), S 1010 (KCD 778), S 1015, S 1031, S 1044 (KCD 769) and S 1050 (KCD 1344). Whilst the notion that a would-be defrauder would incur the wrath of God ('iram Dei incurrat') is commonly found, if not in these exact words, throughout the Anglo-Saxon charter corpus (including in S 1003 and S 1061 [KCD 914], two charters of King Edward the Confessor), the reference to 'sit anathema' is rather less common and found in S 1026 (KCD 801), a spurious 1055 charter from the Evesham archive. It is standard practice that Anglo-Saxon charter sanctions suggest that potential defrauders can avoid the punishments described in the charter by changing their minds or putting right their bad deeds and 'nisi resipiscat' fulfils this function in **11** and can be paralleled by 'nisi resipiscens' in S 999 (*Abing* 142). But this phrase is normally more fully developed and followed by the use of some derivative of the verb 'emendare' and it may be that **11** has therefore been shortened at this point. Thus, for example, S 999 (*Abing* 142) has 'nisi resipiscens digna satisfactione emendauerit' and S 1010 (KCD 778) has 'nisi prius digna satisfactione emendare uoluerit'. There are two elements of the sanction in **11** which arouse suspicion. The first is the phrase 'supradictum apostolici decretum' which refers the reader of the charter back to previous elements in the body of the diploma. Again this is a form of repetition and serves to emphasise the terms of the charter: it is reminiscent of the proem which, in a sentence which is uncharacteristic of Anglo-Saxon diplomatic, described why it was necessary for the grant to be made, a sentiment which is itself repeated later on in the charter. Such elements in **11** strongly suggest that at the forefront of the draftsman's mind was the need to justify the making of the grant and its terms: this desire for justification reads almost like special pleading and is highly suspicious. The second unusual element in the sanction of **11** is that which specifies that a potential defrauder could be a king: 'si quis ex regibus posteris nostris'. It is standard form for Anglo-Saxon diplomas to have simply 'Si quis' and not to specify the status of any future transgressor. Perhaps this is a clue that the forger of **11** was partly encouraged in his fabrication by a king who was trying to appropriate estates from the York church; or it may simply be a sign that kings in particular were feared as a threat to the church's estates.

After the sanction there is a clause which begins 'Ut autem' and ends 'contestificatione fulcitur': its function is to introduce the witness-list and to explain that the witness-list protects the details of the transaction for ever ('perpetuo'). Sometimes Anglo-Saxon charters do contain a sentence which introduces the witness-list and S 1044 (KCD 769), an extant original from the period 1042x44 in the Christ Church Canterbury archive, has just such an example: 'Et huius doni constipulatores extiterunt quorum inferius onomata caraxari cernuntur ueridica'. But it is unusual to find as developed a version as we see in **11**. Extant originals of the 1040s–60s tend to follow one of two patterns: either a dating-clause follows the sanction and then a boundary clause and then the list of witnesses, as in S 1003 and S 1019 (KCD 787), or the boundary clause follows the sanction and then the dating-clause and then the witnesses, as in S 1004 (KCD 772) and S 1008 (KCD 781). It is quite striking that another charter in the name of King Edward the Confessor, S 1041 (KCD 825), displays a similarly developed clause. S 1041 (KCD 825) claims to be a 1065 grant (made at Westminster on 28 December) to Westminster Abbey; in fact it is a forgery carried out by the notorious Osbert de Clare (prior of Westminster in the second quarter of the twelfth century) and is known as the 'Third' charter of Edward the Confessor for Westminster Abbey (a group of 'pre-Conquest' charters was identified by Chaplais as the work of Osbert; see Chaplais 1962. The so-called 'First' [S 1043], 'Second' [S 1011] and 'Third' [S 1041] charters of Edward the Confessor for Westminster Abbey were composed partly to promote the canonisation of King Edward). Following the sanction in S 1041 (KCD 825), the charter continues with: 'Ut ergo haec auctoritas nostris et futuris temporibus circa ipsum sanctum locum perenniter firma et inuiolata permaneat, uel per omnia tempora illaesa custodiatur atque conseruetur et ab omnibus optimatibus nostris et iudicibus publicis et priuatis melius ac certius credatur, manus nostrae superscriptionibus subter eam decreuimus roborare, et idoneos testes annotare, atque sigillo nostro iussimus sigillare'. Whilst there are no verbal similarities between the same clause in **11** and this equivalent in S 1041 (KCD 825), the very fact that they both serve the same function, a function which is hard to parallel elsewhere in Edward the Confessor's charters, suggests that there may be some sort of relationship between the two diplomas.

But the connections between **11** and S 1041, to which I will return further below, become more intriguing when one examines the witness-list. The witness-list in **11** is of considerable interest for the titles and status allotted to various individuals, titles which are not usually found in an Anglo-Saxon diplomatic document. Thus after the listed bishops we find 'Robertus *Stalre*' and 'Osbernus *Capellanus*'; such titles are suggestive of very specific offices within the king's household and an important question is whether or not they reflect accurate usage for Edward the Confessor's reign. Of course the main body of **11**, which describes the gift of the Worcester bishopric to Archbishop Ealdred, is a patent forgery; but when the witness-list of **11** is compared to others of the 1060s, it becomes apparent that the forger has compiled his document using a genuine witness-list or a memorandum which contained accurate information. First, all of the witnesses who attest **11** were alive at the purported time of the grant, '1065' (some scholars date the death of Earl Ælfgar to the period *c.* 1063 on the basis that Harold and Tostig, who in 1063 attacked Ælfgar's ally, Gruffudd ap Llywelyn, would not have done so without Ælfgar already being dead (see, for example, A. Williams, 'Ælfgar' in *ODNB* and S. Baxter, *The Earls of Mercia: Lordship and Power in Late Anglo-Saxon England* (Oxford, 2007), pp. 46–7); but the evidence of **11**'s witness-list together with its dating-clause, if they can be accepted as preserving genuine information, seem to contradict this date for Ælfgar's death (see also Keynes, *Atlas*, table LXXIV; I am most grateful to Dr S. Baxter for pointing out this issue to me); **11** states that it took place 'in die festiuitatis sancti Siluestri anno domini .mlxv. anno autem regni nostri .xxi.', 31 December '1065', which would actually mean 1064, if the year change was being reckoned (as Bede recommended and was common in late Anglo-Saxon practice) from 25 December; see Cheney and Jones, *Handbook*, p. 9. 31 December is evidently impossible, since Earl Tostig, who attests **11**, had been expelled from the country by 28 October 1065; see *ASC C*, s.a. 1065). Second, since these titles can be found in other charters which are wholly independent of **11**, it seems likely that they reflect genuine pre-Conquest usage (the interest of these titles is fully explained in Keynes 1988). 'Robertus Stalre', or Robert fitz Wimarc (a man of Breton or Norman origin), can be found attesting S 1033 (KCD 810) as *minister*, S 1034 (*Bath* 22) as *minister*, S 1002 (K 771) as *Stallere*, S 1036 (KCD 813) as *Regis Consanguineus*, S 1042 (*Wells* 40) as *procurator*, S 1043 (KCD 824) as *minister* and S 1041 (KCD 825) as *minister* (for a useful table of these titles, see Keynes 1988, p. 206). S 1002 (KCD 771), S 1030 (KCD 809), S 1043 (KCD 824) and S 1041 (KCD 825) are all the work of the forger Osbert de Clare but Keynes has shown that the witness-lists in these charters are based on genuine charters of Edward the Confessor (Keynes 1988, pp. 198–9); S 1034 (*Bath* 22) is considered genuine (see Keynes 1988, p. 204, n. 115 and p. 213, n. 170). Robert's style in S 1036 (KCD 813) (*Regis Consanguineus*) implies that he was related to King Edward, and that they were at least closely connected perhaps receives confirmation from an annal in the *ASC* which suggests that Robert aided Edward the Confessor's Norman allies when their position was threatened by the return of Earl Godwine (*ASC E*, s.a. 1052, records that 'the Frenchmen ... took horses and departed, some west to Pentecost's castle, and some north to Robert's castle'; K. Mack, 'The Stallers: Administrative Innovation in the Reign of Edward the Confessor', *Journal of Medieval History* xii [1986], pp. 123–34 (at p. 125), draws attention to this annal in the *ASC*). 'Staller' was a title first introduced in the reign of King Cnut. Mack has explored the role of the staller in the reign of King Edward the Confessor; she notes that the very great wealth of these men, and the specific configuration of their landed estates, set them apart from other thegns and indeed, as in **11**, they are often distinguished from normal thegns by their placement as a distinct group of attesters at the head of a witness-list. Mack shows that between 1053 and 1066 there was a decrease in the frequency of attesting thegns which was accompanied by an increase in the attestations of stallers and she therefore concludes that the role of the staller became more important as the reign progressed; she even suggests that Edward used his 'stallers' to carry out business which was of special concern to his own person, perhaps only within Westminster (K. Mack, 'The Stallers', pp. 130–2). That Robert had a role in the government of the country is suggested by the writ addressed to him, S 1128 (KCD 859). Thus the appearance of 'Robertus Stalre' immediately after the bishops in **11** accurately reflects the position of influence and power that 'stallers' had come to enjoy in the reign of the Confessor.

The 'Osbernus Capellanus' (also known as 'Esbern') of **11** was a cleric; he can be found attesting S 1036 (KCD 813) as *Regis Consanguineus* and S 1041 (KCD 825) as *Regis Capellanus*; he became Bishop of Exeter in April 1072. 'Raimboldus' (i.e. Regenbald) in **11** is variously styled *Regis Sigillarius* in S 1033 (KCD 810), *Cancellarius* in S 1030 (KCD 809), *Regis Cancellarius* in S 1036 (KCD 813), *Cancellarius* in S 1043 (KCD 824) and *Regis Cancellarius* in S 1041 (KCD 825). The very great interest posed by the career of Regenbald has been illustrated by Keynes who suggests that the corroborative evidence of charters and Domesday Book would make it 'perverse to doubt that Regenbald himself was known to his associates at Edward the Confessor's court as the king's *sigillarius* or *cancellarius*' (Keynes 1988, p. 209; the 'Petrus' of **11** should also be regarded as holding a special position at Edward's court as he is found in S 1041 [KCD 825] styled *Regis capellanus*). Thus the evidence provided by the styles of attesters suggests that we should accept the witness-list of **11** as being based on a genuine list of 1064. And the juxtaposition of the two comital brothers, Harold and Tostig, which is often how brothers were placed in Anglo-Saxon charters, only further strengthens the accurate impression delivered by the witness-list of **11**.

Keynes suggests that the use of these titles for officials at the Confessor's court, although hitherto unusual in the Anglo-Saxon world, is reflective of genuine practice in the mid- to late-eleventh century and Keynes also surmises that they may somehow be a response to contemporary continental practice (Keynes 1988, p. 208). Towards the end of the witness-list in **11**, but before the attestations of the abbots, there is a sentence ('Actum Wintonie in publica curia natalis Christi in die festiuitatis sancti Siluestri anno domini .mlxv. anno autem regni nostri .xxi. per omnia benedictus Deus Amen') which is wholly unusual for Anglo-Saxon diplomatic. But in the same way that the use of titles for those with specific roles at court became more usual at this later stage in Anglo-Saxon England, so too we must allow for the appearance of unexpected formulae, perhaps due to continental influence at the court of Edward the Confessor. Keynes draws attention to the fact that S 1036 (KCD

813), a 1062 grant to Waltham Abbey, ends with the subscription of Swithgar who claims to have written the charter himself ('Hec ego conscripsi ...'). Such claims of authorship are out of place in Anglo-Saxon charters and Keynes cites two other examples which are more explicit and which are both the work of the forger Osbert de Clare. The first comes from the 'First' charter for Westminster, S 1043 (KCD 824), and reads (both of these are formulae quoted in Keynes 1988, p. 209):

> Acta apud Westmonasterium .v. kalendas Ianuarii die sanctorum innocentiam anno dominice incarnationis .m.lxvi. indictione tertia, anno regni serenissimi Eaduuardi regis uigesimo quinto. Swiðgarus notarius ad uicem Reinbaldi regie dignitatis cancellarii hanc cartam scripsi et subscripsi in dei nomine foeliciter. Amen.

The second is from the 'Third' charter for Westminster, S 1041 (KCD 825):

> Stabilita apud Westmonasterium .v. kalendas Ianuarii die sanctorum innocentium . anno dominice incarnationis .M. LXVI. indictione tercia . anno regni EADWARDI nobilissimi et clementissimi regis . uigesimo .v. Ego Ælfgeatus notarius ad uicem Reinbaldi regie dignitatis cancellarii hoc priuilegium scripsi . et subscripsi . in dei nomine feliciter. Amen.

The difficulty here is in deciphering whether or not Osbert de Clare took this formula from the genuine charter of 1065 which constituted the basis for the authentic witness-lists of S 1043 (KCD 824) and S 1041 (KCD 825) or whether Osbert simply inserted this formula as part of his own fabricated creation. Keynes suggests that Swithgar's claim to authorship in S 1036, the grant to Waltham Abbey, and his appearance in a similar role in the first example cited above, S 1043 (KCD 824), might mean that Swithgar could indeed be a scribe in the service of Regenbald. And if this were so, then perhaps the 'Ælfgeatus' of S 1041 (KCD 825) should be thought of similarly (for these arguments, see Keynes 1988, p. 209). Keynes notes that just such a formula is known as the final protocol in Carolingian and Capetian charters and he concludes that the use of it in Edward the Confessor's charters may be due to the fact that 'one of the continental clerics in the Confessor's household... had thought that the usage was appropriate to a charter produced under the auspices of Regenbald' (Keynes 1988, p.210).

If we can follow Keynes in his conclusion that this formula found in S 1043 (KCD 824) and S 1041 (KCD 825) (the 'First' and 'Third' charters for Westminster forged by Osbert de Clare) is taken from a genuine charter of 1065, then it is interesting that an abbreviated version of the same formula can be found in **11** towards the end of the witness-list but before the attestations of the abbots (cited above). We should also note that Regenbald attests **11** and it may therefore be the case that this element in **11** should be regarded as based on a genuine charter of the 1060s (it is striking how many thematic links there are between S 1041 [KCD 825], the 'Third' charter for Westminster forged by Osbert, and **11**).

One does not need to search very far to find a motive on the part of the York community for the fabrication of a charter claiming to grant the bishopric of Worcester to York. From the time of Archbishop Oswald (971–92) and his two archiepiscopal successors, Ealdwulf (995–1002) and Wulfstan II (1002–23), Worcester was held in plurality with York; and there are hints that by the time Archbishop Ælfric occupied the see in the period 1023–51, the joint rule of Worcester and York by York archbishops was resented by those at Worcester (see Cooper, *Archbishops of York*, pp. 17–18). It may therefore be the case that part of the intention for the author of **11** was to justify once and for all York's involvement at Worcester: certainly this seems to be the aim of the diplomatically unusual clause 'quod etiam idem Oswaldus et post eum Adulfus (i.e. Ealdwulf) et Wlstanus (i.e. Wulfstan II) archipresules regio munere adepti sunt et tenuerunt quietum et solidum donec...'. **11** continues at this point by stating that the arrival of the Danes had two major effects: first that archbishops after the time of Wulfstan II no longer held Worcester in plurality; second, that previous privileges recording York's rights no longer existed ('...donec Anglia dirupta est et discissa inuasione Danorum et cum ceteris ornamentis ecclesiarum predicte ciuitatis illud pape Formosi priuilegium constat esse incensum'); such a statement is not to be expected in Anglo-Saxon diplomatic and is again an indication that, at the forefront of the forger's mind, was the need to justify the composition of **11**.

Throughout the main body of **11**, the draftsman takes care to make references to various popes and to suggest that certain privileges enjoyed by York were granted by the Papacy. An example is: 'post cum Rome peteret pallium a beato papa Formoso per priuilegii descriptionem ei est traditum donum scilicet Wiricestris episcopii' and

> noster Ealdredus...iura requirens et sciens a beato papa Nicholao Rome pallio donatus, ad nos super ecclesie sibi commisse dignitate apostolica scripta signata detulit, quibus cum sua fidelitate commoniti iustam petitionem pape et suam nolumus refutare quod absit, presertim, cum super eadem re apostolicum presentauerit priuilegium. Donauimus igitur...ordinationem Wiricestris episcopii, cum nostro tamen disponendam consilio, quatenus in exequenda episcopii cura eo specialius utatur uicario utque a beato papa Nicholao in eius scriptum habetur priuilegio.

Such claims of special privileges, derived ultimately from the Papacy, reinforce that **11** is a forgery. But these statements also suggest that one crisis in particular may have inspired the composition of **11**: the primacy debate between the archbishoprics of Canterbury and York (for an account of the primacy debate, see *Hugh the Chanter*, pp. xxx–xlv, Barlow, *English Church*, pp. 234–6 and M. Gibson, *Lanfranc of Bec* [Oxford, 1978], p. 119; for forgeries made at Canterbury in response to York's claims, see R.W. Southern, 'The Canterbury Forgeries', *EHR* lxxiii [1958], pp. 193–226. As well as the ability to prove that certain of its privileges had been granted by the Papacy, it was crucial for York to demonstrate that it had at least three suffragans, which were needed to consecrate a new archbishop, and so the claim to the Worcester bishopric was very important for the York church).

BEVERLEY

INTRODUCTION

1. THE HISTORY AND ENDOWMENT OF BEVERLEY MINSTER

After the time of Bede, there are very few contemporary sources which make any mention either of the history or of the endowment of Beverley Minster. Beverley sources from the early twelfth century and beyond suggest that the Minster suffered greatly at the hands of vikings in the 860s, only to be refounded and reformed by King Æthelstan in the 930s as a collegiate church. And the Minster's purported special connection with this king, whether based on fact or fabrication, can be attested today by various artefacts on display there. But it is important to question the validity of these late sources when used in any assessment of Beverley Minster in the Anglo-Saxon period. **6** in the York archive provides a brief glimpse of Beverley in the late tenth century and may suggest that Beverley had come to have an affiliation to the York archbishopric, perhaps as an archiepiscopal minster.[1] We are on more certain footing still in the mid- to late-eleventh century when we are given details about the careers of the last three York archbishops, all of whom seem to have been particularly generous towards Beverley. But it is only from the beginning of the twelfth century that numbers of sources increase; and by this stage Beverley had become a vibrant trading centre, specialising in cloth manufacture and the export of wool.

It is entirely likely that, during the Anglo-Saxon period, the Minster would have benefited from grants of land and privilege made by various kings and local nobles; and also from grants or purchases by its own bishops and abbots.

[1] Palliser 2000, p. 25, describes Beverley as a 'sub-cathedral'; Beverley, Ripon and Southwell are termed 'departmental cathedrals' in McDermid, *Beverley Minster Fasti*, p. xvii; Rollason, *Northumbria*, pp. 229–30, describes Beverley, Ripon and Southwell as 'subsidiary cathedrals', a role which (he suggests) may initially have been apportioned to them in the tenth century but which is better documented in the early twelfth century. For nineteenth-century histories of Beverley, see Oliver, *Beverley*, Poulson, *Beverlac* and C. Hiatt, *Beverley Minster – an Illustrated Account of its History and Fabric* (London, 1898). For modern accounts, see Hall (I.) 1982; Miller *et al.*, *Beverley*, Morris and Cambridge 1989; Palliser 2000; Horrox, *Beverley* and Blair 2001.

Today the Beverley archive contains only three documents: **12**, a patent forgery in the name of Æthelstan, and **13** and **14**, genuine writs of Edward the Confessor. Despite this paucity of documentation, slim even for the north of England, it is still possible to outline something of the growth and evolution of the Minster in Anglo-Saxon times and so to gain an impression of those times when Beverley was prosperous and those when it may have been under pressure.

a. *Beverley 'in the Wood': The Origins of Beverley Minster*

Later house traditions from Beverley Minster claim that it was founded by John who first was bishop of Hexham (687–706) and then later bishop of York (706–?714; d. 721) and who came to be known as John of Beverley. In his *Historia Ecclesiastica*, Bede connects John to a place called *Inderauuda* which Bede explains as meaning *In Silua Derorum*, 'in the wood of the Deirans'. It was to this monastery that John retired and saw out his last years.[2]

In the past there has been some doubt as to whether or not Bede's *Inderauuda* could be identified as being one and the same place as Beverley whose place-name is *Beferlic*.[3] But the name *Inderauuda* must originally have referred to a general, remote and unsettled area. *Beferlic* is a more precisely locative name which would have emerged as the monastery and associated settlement grew and became permanent. The fact that the place-name *Beferlic* refers to the topography of the site is a peculiarly English phenomenon.[4] Decisive proof for the equation of *Inderauuda* with *Beferlic* takes the form of an entry in a ninth-century liturgical calendar (Oxford, Bodleian Library, MS Digby 63, written in Northumbria in the period 844–92), to which Blair has recently drawn attention. Against 7 May (St John's feast-day) has been written: 'Sancte Iohannes on Beuerlic'. This conclusively demonstrates that St John's cult was present at

[2] Bede, *HE*, v.2 and v.6.

[3] The earliest extant Old English version of the place-name 'Beverley' has the form *Beferlic* and dates to the first half of the eleventh century; its most usual form is *Beverlac* or, in Latin, *Beverlacum*; Ekwall, *DEPN*, p. 40 and *CamDEPN*, p. 53, suggest that the place-name is made up of the Old English elements *beofor* + *licc*, meaning 'Beaver stream'. Coates 2002, p. 20, suggests a different interpretation: 'Beverley is therefore probably from early Brittonic **beßr-lïcc*, showing the impact of a place-name forming suffix, the whole meaning 'beaver-lodge place''. Large peat deposits in the area, the course of the River Hull a mile to the east of Beverley, with the River Humber just to the south, and marshes also to the east, all suggest the watery nature of Beverley and the reason for its name; Hall (I.) 1982, p. 7. Leach, *Memorials* I, pp. xv–xix suggested that, because of these two separate names with quite different meanings, *Inderauuda* and *Beverlac* should be thought of as two distinct places.

[4] See Blair, *Church*, p. 195. I am very grateful to Dr S.E. Kelly for her suggestions about *Inderauuda* and *Beferlic*.

Beverley in the mid- to late-ninth century.[5] Thus for Blair, 'the possibility that by the 880s St John's relics had been transferred from *Inderauuda* to the relatively obscure Beverley is so slight that it can virtually be discounted'.[6]

Bede states that John was buried in a *porticus* dedicated to St Peter ('sepultus est in porticu sancti Petri in monasterio suo'). While the word *porticus* was most often employed by Bede to refer to a separate side chapel, with an altar dedicated to a saint different from the main dedication of the church,[7] Cambridge has put forward various reasons for suggesting that the whole of the early Beverley church was dedicated to St Peter.[8] By the late eleventh century Beverley Minster was dedicated to St John the Evangelist, but this may have been an innovation of the late eleventh century when Archbishop Ealdred built a new high altar dedicated to that saint.[9]

Nothing much is known about the actual fabric of the early Beverley church.[10] In the late 1970s and early 1980s, excavations were carried out on a patch of ground just to the south of the present-day Minster, bordered by these streets: on the north by the Minster Yard South, to the west by Hall Garth and to the east by Lurk Lane. The excavations revealed a series of successive ditches 0.8m deep and between 2.5 and 3m wide with banks on their inner faces; they were made and reworked in the period from the early eighth- to the mid-ninth centuries.[11] The dimensions of the ditches suggest that they were intended as more than property boundaries and indeed they seem to form a curvilinear monastic enclosure of the type found elsewhere at minsters like Bampton or Brixworth.[12]

[5] This was clear to Folcard who, in his *Life* of John written in the eleventh century, silently replaces *Inderawuda* with Beverley.

[6] See Blair 2001, pp. 315–16. For the calendar entry itself, see F. Wormald, ed., *English Kalendars Before A.D. 1100*, Henry Bradshaw Society lxxii (London, 1934), p. 6. Morris and Cambridge 1989, p. 10, note the importance of the Old English *List of Saints' Resting-Places* (the *Secgan be þam Godes sanctum þe on Engla lande ærost reston*) in determining that John's body did indeed rest at Beverley before 900. This is a complicated source which, although it came into its present form *c.* 1031, is evidently made up of several different lists and also later interpolations. The section which contains an entry about Beverley seems to derive from an earlier list that concentrated on pre-viking resting places of saints and which used rivers as topographical markers. John's resting place is referred to in these terms: 'Đonne resteð sanctus Iohannes biscop on þare stowe Beferlic, neah þare ea Hul'; see Rollason 1978, pp. 62 and 87.

[7] See Colgrave and Mynors, *Bede's Ecclesiastical History*, p. 143, n. 3; St Augustine's, Canterbury, had altars dedicated to St Gregory and St Martin: see Bede, *HE*, ii.3 and ii.5 respectively.

[8] See Morris and Cambridge 1989, p. 18 and also Palliser 2000, p. 24.

[9] For developments in Ealdred's time, see below, pp. 184–7.

[10] Morris and Cambridge 1989, pp. 10–11 and p. 28, n. 14, speculate that the early Beverley church would have been made of stone.

[11] D.H. Evans in Armstrong *et al.*, *Excavations*, p. 246.

[12] Blair, *Church*, pp. 197–8 and Palliser 2000, p. 24. In the early ninth century, two tributary ditches were made which fed into a pre-existing main ditch and it may be that these formed a weir and fish trap; Armstrong *et al.*, *Excavations*, p. 5 and pp. 8–9.

Other than incidental fragments (see below), no parts of the Anglo-Saxon monastic buildings were found. Evans suggests that the original site is quite likely to be situated somewhere under the present Minster, perhaps even under the eastern end of the Minster if the altar had remained in the same place.[13] Nevertheless, the Lurk Lane excavations do demonstrate that in the eighth century, and continuing on into the first half of the ninth century, Beverley Minster and its surrounding area was thriving. This intensity of occupation is indicated in particular by the amount of food refuse (animal bone and oyster shells) found in ditches of this date; but also by domestic artefacts such as pottery. At the northern edge of the excavated site, evidence of a building was found within which various deposits indicate that it may well have been used for industrial manufacture, perhaps metalworking or smithing.[14]

Something of the ambition and quality of this early Beverley church may be suggested by the survival and recovery of two fragments of pale green window glass, which have been dated to the eighth century (and may perhaps be older than that). The style of these fragments demonstrates similarities with Anglo-Saxon glass from Monkwearmouth-Jarrow, perhaps suggesting that the fabric of the early Beverley church was of a similar quality.[15]

Contemporary details of the foundation and endowment of Beverley Minster in its earliest days are non-existent. Although Bede would presumably have had information about such matters, the nature and purpose of the *Historia Ecclesiastica* means that he is solely interested in those episodes which proved John as a holy man, many of which Bede learned from Abbot Berhthun of Beverley Minster.[16] One such miracle involved John healing the wife of a *gesith* named Puch who had asked John to dedicate a church for him.[17] The *Vita S. Johannis*, written in the 1060s by Folcard, gives the further information that this miracle took place

[13] D.H. Evans in Armstrong *et al.*, *Excavations*, p. 246.

[14] A cobbled path led to this building, which itself was located in strata of the excavation which date between the eighth and ninth centuries; see Armstrong *et al.*, *Excavations*, pp. 12–13 and 246–7.

[15] Armstrong *et al.*, *Excavations*, pp. 124 and 247. Morris and Cambridge 1989, p. 28, n. 20, make an important observation about the possible existence of a second church on the Beverley site: 'it is perhaps worth speculating that the church of St Martin formerly attached to the south-west corner of the present minster...perpetuates the site of a second pre-Conquest church'. They point out that the dedication to St Martin could indeed be early and Blair, *Church*, p. 199, shows that a religious community of any importance would have had two or more churches (as was the case at Lindisfarne, for which see below, p. 273, n. 26).

[16] See Bede, *HE*, v.2–6; Bede used information from Abbot Berhthun for four of the five miracles relating to John; he describes Berhthun (in *HE*, v.2) as 'diaconus quondam eius, nunc autem abbas monasterii quod uocatur Inderauuda'.

[17] Bede, *HE*, v.4.

at 'Australis Burtun', which Raine identified as Bishop Burton.[18] Leland, in his *Collectanea*, quotes extracts from another, later *Life* of John which does not now survive and whose author appears to have been unknown. Leland's extracts state that when Puch's daughter, Yolfrida, became a nun at Beverley, Puch used the occasion to give the manor of Walkington (*Walkington*) as a gift to Beverley.[19]

An almost identical sequence of events concerns a *gesith* named Addi whose attendant, Bede tells us, was cured by Bishop John (Addi had also asked John to dedicate a church for him).[20] Folcard mentions this miracle but adds no new information.[21] But in the extract from the anonymous later *Life* quoted by Leland, Addi makes the gift of Cherry Burton (*bor[ealem] Burton*) together with its church to Beverley Minster as a reward for John's help. Cherry Burton lies to the north of its sister estate, Bishop Burton, and both lie on the road from Beverley to York.[22]

There is the faint possibility that, underlying Bede, Folcard and the anonymous author of the later *Life*, are either lost charters, some kind of list of donations (perhaps a commemorative record of benefactors) or even an early collection of miracle stories. Hart has suggested that the extracts quoted in Leland represent authentic and early grants.[23] But it is impossible to verify these details and so it is better to remain sceptical as to whether or not they represent genuine early grants to Beverley Minster.[24]

In these two episodes involving the *gesiths* Puch and Addi, Bede notes that John had been present on each of their estates for the purpose of dedicating a church.

[18] Raine, *HCY* I, p. 249 and n. 1. See Ekwall, *DEPN*, s.n. Burton. For Folcard's *Life*, see below, p. 185.

[19] Leland, *Collectanea* IV, pp. 99–103. Leland describes the extracts as coming from 'ex libro incerti autoris de vita Sancti Joannis archiepiscope Ebor: sive de antiquitate Beverlacensi, quem in 3 divisit partes' (at p. 99). The extracts in Leland are conveniently collected in Leach, *Memorials* II, pp. 347–53. Walkington lies two miles south of Bishop Burton, which itself lies three miles to the west of Beverley; Hart, *ECNE*, no. 150b.

[20] Bede, *HE*, v.5.

[21] Raine, *HCY* I, pp. 250–1.

[22] For a summary of these gifts, see Hart, *ECNE*, no. 150b and no. 150c. For the identification of the estates involved and their location, see Raine, *HCY* I, p. 249 and Plummer, *Bede* II, p. 276; for further discussion, see H.R. Loyn, 'Gesiths and Thegns in Anglo-Saxon England from the Seventh to the Tenth Century', *EHR* lxx (1955), pp. 529–49 (at p. 536).

[23] The extracts quoted by Leland tell that Bishop John also bought lands 'in Midleton, in Welwik, in Bilton et Patrington' for Beverley; see Leach, *Memorials* II, p. 349 and Hart, *ECNE*, no. 150d.

[24] Bishop Burton, Cherry Burton, Middleton, Welwick and Bilton all belonged to Beverley by 1086: GDB, f. 304r; it may be the case that, in the post-Conquest period, when Beverley Minster owned these estates, it created a tradition which linked their acquisition with events in the pre-Conquest period. Nevertheless, in a separate study of Beverley's soke as preserved in GDB, Hart points out that Beverley itself had twenty-one berewicks spread through the three hundreds belonging to the wapentake of Holderness; he suggests that some of these will represent fragments of the early endowment of Beverley; Hart, *Danelaw*, pp. 257–9 (with a useful map on p. 258).

It is difficult to be precise about what kind of churches these would have been. Perhaps they were the private possessions of Puch and Addi; or alternatively they could have been satellite churches of Beverley Minster staffed with the Minster's clergy. As Blair points out, these two ideas are not necessarily mutually exclusive in that churches may well have been privately built and commissioned and yet still recognised a dominant regional mother church.[25] For C.D. Morris, these churches of Puch and Addi had purposefully been built at the *capites* of the *gesiths'* estates.[26]

If Bede himself is relatively reticent about Beverley, then details about the Minster's history after Bede's death are even less forthcoming. Indeed no contemporary source mentions Beverley again until the eleventh century. But a much later manuscript supposedly preserves the names of some eighth-century Beverley abbots (including that of Berhthun who was instrumental in giving information to Bede about John). The early sixteenth-century section of CCCC MS 298, which is divided into four parts,[27] lists the names of two other Beverley abbots, *Wynwaldus* (said to have died in 751) and *Ulfelth* (said to have died in 783). The same manuscript provides the information that in 742 a certain *Beata Polfrida* was honourably buried in the church at Beverley.[28] Leland also takes note of these Beverley abbots.[29] Unfortunately, it is impossible to know whether or not these sixteenth-century authors were relying on genuinely early documentation for their information about these Beverley abbots, abbots who are otherwise unrecorded.

b. *The 'Destruction' of Beverley and its 'Refoundation' by Æthelstan*

According to the *Anglo-Saxon Chronicle*, in 867 viking armies switched their attentions from East Anglia to Northumbria, taking advantage of civil strife

[25] Blair, *Church*, pp. 119–21 (at p. 120). Hadley, *Northern*, p. 240, sees no reason to suggest that these churches would have been dependent on the Beverley church and thinks instead that they were proprietary aristocratic churches.

[26] Morris 1977, p. 94.

[27] The information about Beverley abbots occurs in the second part of this manuscript, on ff. 151v–153v. This second part of the manuscript contains a collection of documents relating to the history and landholdings of Canterbury. The third part of the manuscript has an early fifteenth-century copy of the *Chronicle of the Archbishops of York*. This information can be found on the 'Parker Library on the Web' website: <http://parkerweb.stanford.edu/parker/actions/summary.do?ms_no=298>. For a transcription of all of the material relating to Beverley, see Leach, *Memorials* II, pp. 343–5.

[28] See Leach, *Memorials* II, p. 343. Polfrida was the daughter of the *gesith* Puch; see above, p. 177 (*Yolfrida*).

[29] For Leland's notes, see Leach, *Memorials* II, p. 349. Leland's information about these abbots is taken from the same three-part *Life* of John in which he found details of early land grants for Beverley Minster but which is now lost (see above, p. 177, n. 19); Leach suggested that the extract in CCCC 298 formed the basis of Leland's notes on the early history of Beverley (see Leach, *Memorials* II, p. 343, n.) even though Leland's notes clearly provide more material.

caused by the rival claims of Osberht and Ælle.[30] The arrival of vikings must have caused widespread disruption for Northumbrian churches, whose assets were vulnerable to being plundered.[31] At York a situation can be discerned whereby the archbishops reached a compromise with their new Scandinavian rulers, even if it did mean a loss to their resources and endowment.[32] Unfortunately, the evidence for events at Beverley is slight.[33] Later, twelfth-century records at Beverley itself preserve the tradition that the Minster was entirely destroyed and its inhabitants killed by vikings,[34] only to be 'refounded' as a college of seven secular canons by King Æthelstan. Those archaeologists working at Lurk Lane found a coin hoard which they understood as having been deposited *c.* 851 and which they suggest represents the end of occupation at Beverley, a situation which they think persisted into the early tenth century.[35]

There is difficulty in accepting this narrative of destruction and abandonment at Beverley Minster. The later Beverley traditions are hardly trustworthy since already by the late eleventh century such tales of viking atrocities had become part of an established rhetoric. And it may be that later residents at Beverley thought that the change in personnel from monks to secular clerks required justification and therefore fabricated a tradition whereby the religious community was abandoned in the viking period. In fact this mutation is part of a much wider secularisation of monasteries in the late eighth and ninth centuries, Inkberrow in Worcestershire being a well documented example.[36] And the coin hoard offers

[30] *ASC C*, s.a. 868 (*recte* 867).

[31] The lands of Northumbrian churches seem particularly to have been exploited: see Fleming 1985, p. 250 and Dumville, *Wessex and England*, p. 37.

[32] See above, pp. 47–55.

[33] There is a great deal of modern scholarship which discusses the fate of Danelaw churches in the face of Scandinavian settlement. There are those scholars who suggest a positive view of general survival and continuity (for example, Blair, *Church*, pp. 314–15, Hadley, *Northern*, pp. 239–41 and Hadley, *Vikings*, pp. 202–3; and the modified account by Barrow 2000, pp. 155–76, at pp. 166–7) and those who suggest a rather more chaotic scene in general: see especially Abrams 2000 and now Kelly, *Peterborough*, pp. 20–40 (at p. 30, for a useful summary of what types of evidence scholars look for in any assessment of continuity of religious site).

[34] See Leach, *Memorials* II, p. 344: '...qui uniuersos monachos, moniales et quosdam de presbiteris et clericis occiderunt, et quosdam diffugarunt, ecclesiam et locum combusserunt'. The Beverley Cartulary (BL Additional 61901, f. 82r, entitled 'Pro fabrica') also preserves this tradition of the abandonment of Beverley after the viking invasions; this particular section of the cartulary is quoted and discussed further below, p. 187–8.

[35] Armstrong *et al.*, *Excavations*, p. 7; in this volume (pp. 243–4), Evans also speculates that the Beverley religious community may have been forced to move on two separate occasions: once in 851, the first year that vikings were able to spend the winter in England (on Thanet), and then also in 867 when vikings turned their paths towards the north. There seems to be no good reason to uphold this view.

[36] See Blair, *Church*, p. 285 and Brooks, *Church of Canterbury*, pp. 175–206.

similar difficulties of interpretation. Whilst it may be indicative of a time of uncertainty, it does not follow that this implies wholesale abandonment by the religious community.[37]

In short, the extant evidence for the Beverley community in the late ninth century is so meagre that it would be hazardous to place too much trust in post-Conquest house traditions that emphasise the destruction of the community by vikings.[38] If the Minster did continue to function in some form, and there is evidence at least that St John's cult was active at Beverley at this moment,[39] excavations at Lurk Lane nevertheless suggest that the intensity of occupation declined in the late ninth century.[40]

It is likewise impossible to know what exact effect the Scandinavian settlement would have had on Beverley Minster's estates. On the basis of evidence provided by GDB, Hart shows that Beverley in the late eleventh century had twenty-one berewicks spread through the wapentake of Holderness. He suggests that 'when the area was settled by the Danes, the Beverley endowment and jurisdiction was given intact to one of the army leaders or 'holds' (whence 'Holderness') and became a soke'.[41] Some of Beverley's estates may have come into the possession of Scandinavian lords,[42] but it is impossible to be sure that the entire Beverley endowment was given away intact and as a single possession. **6** in the York archive shows the kind of piecemeal losses that occurred with the York church's estates. And

[37] R.A. Hall, in his review of Armstrong *et al.*, *Excavations*, suggests that the coin hoard cannot be used to demonstrate that the Beverley community abandoned its church in the mid-ninth century; see *YAJ* lxv (1993), pp. 182–3.

[38] The excavators at Lurk Lane, although favouring an interpretation of abandonment of the site in the face of vikings, also emphasise that there is 'no definite evidence for destruction in this part of the precinct' (D.H. Evans in Armstrong *et al.*, *Excavations*, p. 243). It would be difficult in the extreme to use archaeological evidence to demonstrate definitive abandonment of a particular site and this could only be done where the *whole* site had been excavated; see the comments of Dumville, *Wessex and England*, p. 36, n. 36.

[39] Blair 2001 and Blair, *Church*, p. 314 and above, pp. 174–5.

[40] Armstrong *et al.*, *Excavations*, p. 7 and pp. 243–4; see also Hadley, *Northern*, pp. 239–40 and Hadley, *Vikings*, pp. 202–3. Recent excavations on either side of Beverley Minster's nave have demonstrated that ecclesiastical life was certainly functioning in the last decade of the tenth century; see M. Johnson, 'Beverley Minster' and S. Allen, 'A Coffin from Beverley Minster', both of which are in *Yorkshire Archaeology Today* vi (2004), pp. 12 and 13 respectively.

[41] Hart, *Danelaw*, p. 259.

[42] The *HSC* provides evidence for just such a seizure of the property of St Cuthbert's community, for which see below, p. 298. The situation at *Medeshamstede* is better documented and Kelly suggests that between 870 and 970 there were profound changes in landholding patterns in the immediate surroundings of *Medeshamstede* as estates came into the possession of new Scandinavian landholders; she concludes that 'if some vestige of the *Medeshamstede* community did have a continuous existence through this difficult period, it seems likely that it would have lost much of its landed endowment, and that it would have found itself in an environment where some of its new neighbours were Scandinavian and, at least initially, pagan' (Kelly, *Peterborough*, pp. 33–4, at p. 34).

7 demonstrates that some, but not all, of these lost estates were later recaptured by the York see. The pattern of landholding was more complicated than Hart suggests.

As we have seen,[43] later Beverley traditions maintain that Æthelstan 'refounded' the Beverley church into a community staffed by seven secular canons.[44] The earliest extant written reference to a connection between Æthelstan and Beverley occurs in an 1136 charter of King Stephen.[45] Later Beverley accounts add further details to the extent that Æthelstan is credited with establishing Beverley's rights to thraves,[46] its right to sanctuary and with its position at the head of the whole East Riding of Yorkshire.[47] **12**, the elaborate rhyming Middle English charter in the name of King Æthelstan, was evidently an important legal tool for the Beverley community in which he is said to have granted a range of privileges to Beverley, but it is a complete fabrication.[48]

All of this information about Æthelstan and Beverley is derived from non-contemporary sources and therefore cannot be trusted.[49] It is possible that the

[43] Above, p. 179.

[44] The constitution of Beverley Minster is of peculiar interest. McDermid suggests that the Norman Conquest actually had little effect on the constitution of Beverley Minster (unlike at York Minster where prebends were created) and so the number of canons was limited to seven, reflecting its Anglo-Saxon constitution. For McDermid, the post-Conquest Beverley community preserves traces of a very ancient constitution: 'Thus, to a greater degree than perhaps any other comparable institution, the late medieval church of Beverley preserved within its constitution clear traces of its Anglo-Saxon origin. In broad outline the foundation attributed to Æthelstan survived changing fortunes and the reforming adjustments of archbishops to persist up to its final dissolution in the sixteenth century' (see his *Beverley Minster Fasti*, pp. xvii–xviii, at p. xviii). Palliser 2000, pp. 28–9, demonstrates that a very early system of pastoral care survived at Beverley into the post-Conquest period.

[45] See Farrer, *EYC*, no. 99. S.E. Wilson, 'King Æthelstan and St John of Beverley', *NH* xl (2003), pp. 5–23, discusses what the Beverley community had to gain from this association with Æthelstan. Wilson suggests that 'the composition of the legend may have been connected to the troubled reign of King Stephen' and to that king's claim over Scotland (at p. 20).

[46] A thrave is a render of grain. For the possible amount of grain belonging in a northern thrave, see the comments of McDermid, *Beverley Minster Fasti*, p. xvi, n. 9 and Palliser 2000, p. 29. Morris and Cambridge 1989, p. 12, stress the possible antiquity of Beverley's rights to thraves.

[47] Texts of the twelfth century, in particular the *Libertates ecclesiae sancti Johannis de Beuerlaco* attributed to Alfred of Beverley, printed in Raine, *SDSB*, pp. 97–108, credit various ancient rights as being the result of a gift of Æthelstan. Two collections of miracles about St John of Beverley, the first compiled by William Ketell in the first half of the twelfth century and the second an anonymous collection of *c.* 1180, discuss various gifts made by Æthelstan to Beverley; see Raine, *HCY* I, pp. 263–4 and 294–98 respectively. Later texts emanating from Beverley, such as the Beverley *Chapter Act Book*, which stretches from 1286 to 1347 and is printed in Leach, *Memorials* I–II, or the *Provost's Book*, extracts of which are printed in Leach, *Memorials* II, pp. 305–45, embellish upon this legend and shift the emphasis from John as founder of Beverley to Æthelstan; for more about this shift in emphasis, see Woodman 2012.

[48] For the importance of this forgery to the Beverley community, see the commentary to **12**.

[49] There exists a silver ring (which has this reconstructed inscription on the inside and outside of the hoop: 'IOHNSE BEVERLS ÆRCEB AĐELSTAN .R. GIFAN'; because of the difficulties involved

Beverley community may at least have had some dealings with Æthelstan since **1** in the York archive shows Æthelstan granting land to the York church and Æthelstan's presence at St Cuthbert's community is recorded by the insertion of his name into the community's *Liber vitae*.[50] But it is also probable, as Palliser points out, that Beverley sought to gain from its association with the first king who had united England and so it attributed the majority of its rights and possessions to the generosity of this figure.[51] It is much more likely that Beverley's accumulation of land and privileges was a gradual and fluctuating process, which took place across the reigns of various different kings.[52] Slender evidence for this process survives as one sentence in **6** in the York archive. This sentence seems to imply that Archbishop Oscytel (d. 971) had acquired the Skidby estate from King Edgar and that Edgar had granted the estate to Oscytel 'by charter for St John's'. Unfortunately this charter no longer survives but this part of **6** does demonstrate that archbishops

in recreating this inscription, its meaning is unclear — see the article cited below by Okasha) which provides further evidence for a purported link between Æthelstan and John. It is discussed by E. Okasha, 'A Rediscovered Medieval Inscribed Ring', *ASE* ii, pp. 167–71. Okasha wonders (at p. 170) whether this could be the ring that Leland referred to as being found in the coffin of St John on the occasion of his translation in 1037. But it is impossible to verify this identification. Okasha also notes (at p. 171) that the spelling and letter-forms actually suggest a post-Conquest date and concludes that 'the ring cannot be dated more closely than to the medieval period, while the texts are likely to have been inscribed in the early post-Conquest period'.

[50] For Æthelstan's dealings with St Cuthbert's community, see below, pp. 299–302. For the notion that Æthelstan was involved in a kind of contract with St Cuthbert's community, see pp. 301–2.

[51] Palliser 2000, pp. 24–5. The special association with Æthelstan was cherished throughout successive generations at Beverley: there exists a late-fourteenth-century drawing from the vicars' cartulary which depicts Æthelstan handing over a sealed charter (presumably intended to represent the fundamental rights and possessions of Beverley) to St John; two statues in the minster which depict Æthelstan and St John side-by-side in front of a screen; and a late-fifteenth-century panel which again shows Æthelstan giving St John a charter. For the cartulary drawing see Horrox, *Beverley*, p. 46; for the statues see p. 101; for the panel see p. ix (between pp. 136–7). For other instances in which Æthelstan's name is invoked (sometimes fraudulently) as a donor of certain rights, see Foot, *Æthelstan*, p. 125.

[52] For a detailed discussion of the sanctuary rights possessed by Beverley, which can be traced as far back as the late tenth century, see Lambert 2009. In later times, the Beverley 'frithstool', still extant today, conveyed the highest level of protection to anyone seeking sanctuary in the Minster (for the 'frithstool', see Lang, *Corpus*, p. 224). In the mid-twelfth century the sacrist of Beverley, Alfred (*Alvaredus*), suggests that Beverley's ability to offer sanctuary was originally a gift of King Æthelstan and that Æthelstan created a zone of privilege which extended for one league around Beverley Minster (see Raine, *SDSB*, pp. 97–108). Alfred also states that the outer boundaries of this zone were marked by the placement of stone crosses (known as *cruces Æthelstani*) at various points (Raine, *SDSB*, p. 99). Three of these crosses still survive, at Bishop Burton, at Walkington and at Bentley (for more about these crosses, see Miller *et al.*, *Beverley*, p. 34 and, for northern sanctuary in general, see Hall (D.) 1989). For similar rights to sanctuary at Ripon, see below, pp. 244–5.

of York were acquiring land for Beverley Minster in the mid-tenth century; and this may, in turn, indicate that by this stage Beverley was considered an archiepiscopal minster.[53]

c. *Beverley in the Eleventh Century*

Beverley re-emerges into historical records in the mid-eleventh century. By this point at the latest, Beverley seems to have developed stronger ties with the York archbishopric, in its position as a satellite house. The *Chronicle of the Archbishops of York*, written in the mid-twelfth century, records that the last three archbishops of York took a particular interest in the Minster's well-being.[54] We learn that Ælfric, who had become archbishop in 1023, had a casket of gold and silver and precious stones made (*...capsam auro et argento et lapidibus pretiosis opere incomparabili apud Beuerlacum fabricari fecit*) and then in 1037 had the remains of St John elevated and translated, and at the same time new relics were added to the tomb.[55] It may be that this reorganisation was designed to invigorate the cult of John of Beverley and so to enhance its status. Ælfric also took care to augment the landed possessions of Beverley as he bought land with his own money from a certain rich man named 'Forceo' and then gave it to Beverley.[56] The *Chronicle of the Archbishops of York* states that Ælfric also started to build a refectory and dormitory at Beverley, projects which were later completed by Archbishop Ealdred.[57] This kind of rebuilding is suggestive of an attempt to introduce a *vita communis* into eleventh-century Beverley.[58] Archbishop Cynesige (1051–60) continued this reorganisation by building a stone tower there and giving bells to Beverley (and also to Southwell and to Stow).[59] In fact, it seems as if there were concerted attempts by these successive northern archbishops to revamp the

53 At Ripon we find a connection with the next York archbishop, Oswald (971–92), who may have tried to introduce monks there as part of the Reform movement and who, finding Ripon in a dilapidated state, may have been attempting to revive the Minster's fortunes (Byrhtferth, *VSO*, v.9 and below, pp. 247–8). Barrow 2000, p. 161, notes that a connection between Oswald and Beverley is made possible by the survival of his chasuble there; for which see Raine, *HCY* II, p. 341.

54 For the date of the *Chronicle of the Archbishops of York*, see Morris and Cambridge 1989, p. 12 and Rollason *et al.*, *Sources*, p. 31.

55 *Chronicle of the Archbishops of York*, pp. 342–3. A description of the ceremony involved in this translation can be found in the Beverley Cartulary, BL Additional 61901, ff. 28r–29r.

56 The lands bought were: 'apud Milletune, et apud Holm, et quinque bouatas apud Fredeisthorp cum pecunia et hominibus qui errant in ea'; see *Chronicle of the Archbishops of York*, p. 343.

57 *Chronicle of the Archbishops of York*, pp. 353–4.

58 This was part of a national trend for reform, for which see Barrow 1994 and Giandrea, *Episcopal Culture*, pp. 71–82 (at pp. 78–9, for Beverley, Southwell and York).

59 *Chronicle of the Archbishops of York*, pp. 343–4; see also Armstrong *et al.*, *Excavations*, p. 247.

Beverley church both physically and financially. Whether or not this means that Beverley, by the early eleventh century, was therefore a place that was in need of regeneration and investment is a matter of speculation. It may simply be the case that these archbishops were motivated out of personal piety to enhance the appearance and status of a church connected to the archbishopric; or it may be that these changes were necessary so that a communal life could be introduced successfully at Beverley. Whatever the cause, Beverley's standing would have been increased and this was taken further during the time of the next York metropolitan.

There are two writs, **13** and **14**, both issued in the name of King Edward the Confessor, and both granted in the period 1060 × 1065, preserved in the Beverley archive. **13** records that Archbishop Ealdred had the right to draw up a *priuilegium* for those lands that belonged to Beverley. It also declares that the Minster is to be 'as free as any other minster is in all things' and that it was King Edward's will that 'minster-life and assembly shall be always maintained there as long as any man shall live'. **14** is a more general notice. King Edward here addresses Earl Tostig and all his thegns in Yorkshire and Nottinghamshire and makes it known that Archbishop Ealdred was to have sake and soke and toll and team over his men, even within areas in the king's jurisdiction; and it threatens anyone who seeks to remove these rights from Ealdred.[60]

The combined force of these documents suggests that Archbishop Ealdred was actively involved in the management of Beverley's lands and assets.[61] That Ealdred was given permission to draw up his own *priuilegium* suggests that he was trusted by the king; and we know from elsewhere that he was indeed an important figure (in political as well as ecclesiastical spheres) during Edward's reign.[62] Ealdred also continued the building work begun by his archiepiscopal

[60] **14** was edited and discussed by Harmer as if it belonged to the York archive; see Harmer, *Writs*, no. 119.

[61] The *Chronicle of the Archbishops of York*, p. 353, states that Ealdred bought some estates with his own money which he added to 'his churches' (*ecclesiis suis*) and from which he created prebends at Southwell Minster. The creation of prebends would have involved a reorganisation of Southwell's estates. In contrast, the Beverley constitution remained remarkably conservative and no new prebends were created until the late twelfth century; see Palliser 2000, p. 28 and McDermid, *Beverley Minster Fasti*, pp. xv–xviii.

[62] See above, pp. 65–8. Two writs preserved from William the Conqueror's reign suggest that Archbishop Ealdred's influence obtained beyond the time of Edward the Confessor. The first confirms Ealdred's rights, whilst the second, addressed to Earl Morcar and Gamel son of Osbern and all the thegns in Yorkshire, again grants Ealdred the right to draw up a *priuilegium* for the lands belonging to Beverley Minster (see Bates, *RRAN: William I*, nos. 31 and 32 respectively, where he notes that the text of the second writ, his no. 32, is based on an earlier writ in the Beverley archive, **13** in the present edition; see also Farrer, *EYC*, nos. 88 and 89). The second of these writs also suggests that Ealdred had acquired yet more land after the Conquest which he gave to Beverley

predecessors Ælfric and Cynesige, as he completed the refectory and dormitory at Beverley. Ealdred enlarged the Minster further by building a new presbytery, which he dedicated to St John the Evangelist; and he had a marvellously painted and decorated ceiling constructed, which stretched from the presbytery up to the tower which had been built by Cynesige.[63] This building programme, together with Ealdred's reform of the Beverley clergy's dress and way of life, were measures intended to consolidate a continental-style *vita communis* for the secular canons.[64] As part of an attempt to increase the Minster's renown, it was in the 1060s that Ealdred persuaded Folcard to write a *Life* of St John.[65] Ealdred's later establishment of an annual fair for Beverley to celebrate the birth of St John the Baptist, perhaps suggests that Beverley as a whole was growing as a result of the Minster's prestige.[66]

Cambridge has investigated and tried to interpret what the structure and lay-out of Beverley Minster must have been like through the ages. He discusses the possible dates at which the church acquired a crypt and, significantly, he identifies a major structural reorganisation that took place at some point between the late eleventh century and the late twelfth century, during which time the tomb of St John was moved from the east end of the church further westwards, to the east end of the nave. It seems that the building works carried out under Archbishop Ealdred were particularly formative as there is evidence to suggest that they replaced the original chancel of the Minster (which perhaps had been dedicated to St Peter) and it is from this moment onwards that the high altar in Ealdred's

Minster (*...and eac ofer þæm landum ðe Ealdred ærcebiscop hæfð siðþan begitan on minan dagan þider inn*).

63 Morris and Cambridge 1989, p. 13, where Cambridge points out that this passage about the ceiling only makes sense if we envisage that the presbytery and tower lay at opposite ends of the church and that the ceiling therefore took in the whole of the church in the intervening area.

64 See the *Chronicle of the Archbishops of York*, pp. 353–4. Ealdred evidently intended the Minster to be a place of some renown, for we are told that he had various fine paintings and sculptures made for the church, some of which were executed in imitation of German fashions (*opus Theutonicum*). Barrow 1994, p. 33, states that 'Ealdred's reforms were part of a wider trend visible in the English church in the middle decades of the eleventh century: the importation of manpower and ideas from the Empire, and more specifically from Lotharingia'. For Ealdred's ownership of Cotton Vitellius E.xii, a copy of a Romano-German Pontifical which he acquired from a trip to Germany, see Lapidge, *ALL* 2, pp. 453–67.

65 Folcard had no real connection with Beverley and it was only at the request of Ealdred, as Folcard explains at the beginning of his work, that he undertook to write this *Life*. Folcard had previously written some *Responsoria* about John for his feast day, again at the request of Ealdred; see Raine, *HCY* I, p. liii and p. 242. For Folcard's possible authorship of a set of royal acclamations (*laudes regiae*), see Lapidge, *ALL* 2, pp. 459–60.

66 Raine, *HCY* II, p. 354. The right to this fair was later confirmed in King Stephen's 1136 charter; Farrer, *EYC*, no. 99.

new presbytery was certainly dedicated to St John the Evangelist and 'this was probably the origin of the later medieval dedication of the church to that saint'.[67]

Beverley may have been spared devastation during the 'harrying of the north' by William the Conqueror in 1069, as the collection of miracles of St John drawn up by the Beverley clerk William Ketell narrates that it was the only place in Yorkshire left as a safe haven: '...praeter illos qui ad ecclesiam Beati Joannis, Beuerlacum, quasi ad azylum, confugerant'.[68] GDB states that Beverley's value to the archbishop (of York) had dropped by £10 over the period from TRE to TRW; but its value to the canons remained the same at £20, perhaps suggesting that there is some truth behind the statement in the collection of miracles that Beverley was one of the few places in Yorkshire to escape destruction at the hands of William the Conqueror. In 1086 the berewicks of Skidby and Bishop Burton were attached to the Beverley manor itself.[69]

It is therefore possible that the Conquest did not cause major disruption for Beverley Minster which, in the twelfth century, received various royal grants and confirmations allowing the right to: acquittance of geld; to have tithes as it did in the time of King Edward the Confessor and William the Conqueror; to increase the length of the Beverley fair from three to five days; and to have its thraves in the demesne manors of the East Riding of Yorkshire and its customs as in the time of William I and II.[70] But Beverley Minster's prosperity was interrupted later on in the twelfth century and again at the beginning of the thirteenth century and

[67] See Morris and Cambridge 1989, pp. 16–20 (quotation at p. 18). For the notion that Beverley Minster was originally dedicated to St Peter and only later dedicated to St John, see above, p. 175. Cambridge also suggests what Beverley may have looked like in the eleventh century (see Morris and Cambridge 1989, pp. 19–20, especially p. 20, where Cambridge talks about the special role Archbishop Ealdred played in bringing various architectural styles to the north of England). For a briefer account of the architecture of Beverley Minster in the eleventh and twelfth centuries, see Palliser 2000, pp. 30–2.

[68] '...except those who fled to the church of St John, Beverley, as if to asylum'; see Raine, *HCY* I, p. 266 and also Palliser 2000, p. 30. This collection of miracles is thought to have been composed by William Ketell in the first half of the twelfth century. Other accounts of the miracles of St John have survived and have been named *Alia Miracula A*, *Alia Miracula B* and *Alia Miracula C*; the first collection dates from *c.* 1180 and the others are undatable, although the latest event mentioned in *Alia Miracula C* is dated 1213. For this information, see Morris and Cambridge 1989, p. 29, n. 53. It may be that the harrying carried out by William was not as severe as has been traditionally thought; see Palliser 1993.

[69] For all of this information, see GDB, f. 304r, which also states that the Beverley church had possessions in South Dalton, Flotmanby, Lockington, Etton, Raventhorpe, Cherry Burton, Molescroft, Kelleythorpe, Kipling, Middleton-on-the-wolds, Great Kelk, Garton-on-the-wolds, Lowthorpe and Bentley. The same folio of GDB gives details about the berewicks in Beverley and Holderness that belonged to the archbishop. See Palliser 2000, p. 29, for more about GDB's record concerning Beverley.

[70] For all of these grants and confirmations, see Farrer, *EYC*, nos. 90, 91, 92, 94 and 97.

these events, and their potential effects on the Beverley archive, will be dealt with in the next section.

2. THE HISTORY OF THE BEVERLEY ARCHIVE

a. *The Pre-Conquest Beverley Archive*

Were it not for **13** and **14**, the Beverley archive would be wholly devoid of any genuine Anglo-Saxon documents. **12**, a charter cast in the name of King Æthelstan, is written in rhyming Middle English of the fourteenth century and is clearly a forgery. Various momentous historical events, such as the arrival of vikings in the mid-ninth century or later of the Normans in the 1060s, may have led to the almost wholesale destruction of Beverley's Anglo-Saxon muniments. Post-Conquest Beverley traditions themselves lay great stress on the destruction of the Minster and its books and possessions by vikings.[71] There is a section of the late fourteenth-century Beverley Cartulary,[72] unprinted in a modern edition, which discusses just this event. It is entitled *Pro fabrica* and reads:

> ...ecclesie beati iohannis Beuerlaci que prius combusta fuit cum libris uestimentis campanis et aliis ornamentis tempore quo dani inuaserunt Angliam, cum principibus duobus...Hyguar...et Wbba qui sanctum Edmundum regem occiderunt et maximam partem Anglie deuastauerunt. Proth dolor non remansit in ecclesia Beuerlaci temporibus illis uas aureum neque argenteum ubi posset corpus Christi reponi. Postea uero reparata fuit dicta ecclesia Beuerlac tempore Gregorii et iterum fortuito igne inuadente combusta. Et tunc iterum reperata fuit cum magna ruina media nocte cum lignis et lapidibus ad yma prosternebatur sed modo reparata. Unde eam oportet in ipsa reparacione per elemosinas fidelium sustentarus et cum indiguerit sumptuosis facultatibus et expensis una cum maximis artificis laboribus renouari.[73]

[71] It is a common topos to find the arrival of vikings as an event blamed for the destruction of charters; for this period in Beverley's history, see above, pp. 179–81.

[72] For the Beverley Cartulary, see below, pp. 199–200.

[73] See the Beverley Cartulary, BL Additional 61901, f. 82r. It may be translated as follows: '...of the church of Blessed John of Beverley which was first burned along with its books, vestments, "campanis", and other ornaments at the time when the Danes invaded England with their two chiefs Hygnar [Ivar] and Wbba [Ubba] who killed holy King Edmund and devastated the greatest part of England. Ah, the grief! There did not remain in the Beverley church in those times a golden or silver vessel in which the body of Christ could repose. But afterwards the said church of Beverley was repaired in the time of Gregory and again burned when attacked by an accidental fire. And then it was again repaired when with a great collapse in the middle of the night with wood and stone it was flattened to its base <even though> but recently repaired (?). Hence during its actual reparation it needed to be supported by the alms of the faithful and, though/since it lacked sumptuous facilities (?) and expenses, to be renovated with the greatest artistic (?) efforts'. The part of this quoted text which

'Hyguar' and 'Wbba', here described as responsible both for the death of King Edmund and for the destruction of a large part of England, are most probably to be identified with the two viking leaders of the 860s campaigns in England, 'Ivar' and 'Ubba'.[74] It became an established topos in post-Conquest historiography to blame Ivar and Ubba for the destruction of archives and muniments belonging to various religious houses and so this statement in the Beverley Cartulary should not be taken seriously.[75] Whilst the arrival of vikings certainly caused disruption and upheaval for many northern religious communities, it is difficult to estimate just how destructive a force they were; it may be that in this instance the Beverley community wished to stress this devastation so that it could explain its later change from being a monastic establishment to a church staffed by seven secular clerks.[76]

Whatever the case, Beverley's repository of Anglo-Saxon charters is meagre. Nevertheless, we can be sure that the Beverley Archive at one stage did hold more Anglo-Saxon documents than it has today. **6**, in the York archive, talks about those lands bought by Archbishop Oscytel of York. And so we find that 'he (i.e. Oscytel) bought Skidby for 20 pounds, and three hides at Bracken he bought from King Edgar, and he granted it to him by charter (*gebocode*) for St John's'. This is obviously a reference to a charter for Beverley and it is unfortunate that it does not still survive. In a similar fashion, **13** notes that Archbishop Ealdred has the right to draw up a *priuilegium* for those lands in Beverley belonging to the Minster, a *priuilegium* which does not exist today.[77] In the section of Domesday Book which deals with the West Riding of Yorkshire, there is record of a dispute between Drogo and the men of Beverley Minster over the possession of various lands. Domesday notes that Beverley was confirmed in its rights to these lands as they have the 'seal' (*sigillum*), presumably a sealed writ, of King Edward and of King William.[78] It may be that this is a reference to **13** and to the writ of William the Conqueror mentioned above. But it might also be referring to writs which

talks about an event in 'the middle of the night' (*media nocte*) seems to refer to the collapse of the crossing tower at Beverley Minster *c.* 1213 (for which see further below).

74 The death of Edmund is recorded very plainly in the *ASC C*, s.a. 871 (*recte* 870) in the following terms: '...and the Danes had the victory, and killed the king (i.e. Edmund) and conquered all the land'.

75 Professor Robert Bartlett recently discussed this in a conference paper, 'The Viking Hiatus in the Cult of Saints as seen in the Twelfth Century', which is to be published in the forthcoming volume, *The Long Twelfth-Century View of the Anglo-Saxon Past*, ed. M. Brett and D.A. Woodman.

76 See above, pp. 179–80.

77 A later writ of William the Conqueror also gave Ealdred permission to draw up a *priuilegium* for lands belonging to Beverley. This may represent a second *priuilegium* drawn up by Ealdred or it may be that Ealdred was simply having a previous right granted by Edward confirmed by the new king, William. See Bates, *RRAN: William I*, no. 32, which is addressed to Earls Morcar and Gamel son of Osbern and all William's barons in Yorkshire (it is also printed in Farrer, *EYC*, no. 88).

78 See GDB, f. 374r. It is recorded by Sawyer as S 1873 and by Harmer, *Writs*, p. 544.

Beverley owned and which have since been lost. Unfortunately we can say no more about the possible pre-Conquest contents of the Beverley archive.[79]

13 and **14** are the only two genuine Anglo-Saxon documents in the Beverley archive. The earliest Old English copy of **13** is to be found in an Inspeximus charter preserved in a Charter Roll dated 7 September, 1310, the fourth year of Edward II's reign (Manuscript C). The edited text of **13** is made from this Inspeximus charter. Various other charters in favour of the church of St John of Beverley were enrolled at this same moment, including one of William the Conqueror (also in Old English, on which see further below),[80] of Henry I, of Stephen (dated at York, 1135), of Henry II and one of John (dated 1202).[81] The fact that a copy of **13** was made at the Chancery in 1310 suggests the likelihood that a single-sheet version was still available by the early fourteenth century.

The next occurrence of **13** is in the Charter Roll of the fourth year of Edward III's reign, 1330 (Manuscript F), itself an Inspeximus of Manuscript C. This Inspeximus charter was made explicitly in favour of Nicholas de Hugate, provost of Beverley, the very same man whom we see in Beverley's *Chapter Act Book* as entrusted with the duty of taking charters to Westminster to prove Beverley's rights. It may have been at this point in Beverley's history, when the canons were aware of the importance of documentation proving ancient ownership, that they fabricated **12** in its current form in addition to having **13** confirmed.[82] All of the later confirmations of **13**, preserved in Patent and Confirmation Rolls up until the third and fourth years of Philip and Mary's reign in 1555–6, are simply confirmations of earlier Inspeximus charters and are not independent witnesses to **13**. They are all listed in the edited text of **13**. The entry in Sawyer's *Anglo-Saxon Charters* for **13** (number 1067) states that the Patent Roll of the sixth year of Henry VI's reign and the two Confirmation Rolls (of Henry VIII and of Philip and Mary) contain Latin versions of **13** when in fact all of these rolls preserve copies of the Old English text (with various degrees of corruption over time).[83]

[79] GDB's entry for Beverley on f. 304r gives information about various berewicks and manors (or parts of manors) owned by Beverley Minster in the late eleventh century. Some of these possessions would have been acquired in Anglo-Saxon times and one can imagine that at one stage the Beverley community had Anglo-Saxon documentation to prove their ownership of these estates. One estate, Cherry Burton, which is associated with an early gift by the *gesith* Addi (see above, p. 177), is named in GDB as a berewick belonging to Beverley, as is Skidby, which is mentioned in connection with Beverley in **6**.

[80] This is edited in Bates, *RRAN: William I*, no. 31.

[81] See *Calendar of the Charter Rolls Preserved in the Public Record Office*, vol. III, *Edward I, Edward II. A. D. 1300–1326* (London, 1908), pp. 140–2.

[82] For 1330–1 being the most likely date for the fabrication of **12** in its current form, see the commentary to **12**.

[83] For information about later copies of **13** made by antiquaries, see below, pp. 202–3.

Alongside these official Chancery copies of **13**, the Beverley community itself preserved a copy of **13** in the Beverley Cartulary, BL Additional 61901 (and also copies of **12** and **14**).[84] The cartulary is set out in double columns, using good quality membrane leaves and is decorated with illuminated initials. It contains *inter alia* a copy of Folcard's *Life of Saint John* (on ff. 1r–10v),[85] to which are appended accounts of miracles performed by John (ff. 10v–60v).[86] The remainder of the cartulary contains records of privileges of various types and date belonging to Beverley Minster (ff. 60v–90v) down to 1380, some of which are discussed below.[87] Some missing folios at the end of the manuscript mean that it is impossible to date it more narrowly than to the end of the fourteenth century.[88] It has a medieval binding of bevelled boards covered with white skin and on the back board there are the remains at the bottom of two nails. It is probable, as Doyle notes, that these were used to connect the volume to a strap which, in turn, was chained to a desk.[89] Its contents as a whole suggest that this de luxe manuscript was intended to be an up-to-date statement of Beverley Minster's history and privileges.[90] It may well have been on display in the Minster, which perhaps meant that it had to be fastened down so that it could not be easily removed.

[84] Davis, *Cartularies* (rev. edn), no. 49. These copies of **12**, **13** and **14** in the Beverley cartulary are discussed below.

[85] This is edited in Raine, *HCY* I, pp. 239–60.

[86] These miracles of St John are interrupted on ff. 22r–25r by a passage describing a miracle of Æthelstan: 'De Adelstano benedicto rege Anglorum qui et cognomento niger dicitur qui dedit libertates trauas et omnes liberas consuetudines ecclesie beati Iohannis Beu'laci' (edited in Raine, *HCY* I, pp. 294–8). A collection of miracles of St John was composed in the first half of the twelfth century by William Ketell (Raine, *HCY* I, pp. 261–91). This collection was later added to by an author who expresses surprise that only William Ketell has recorded John's miracles: it is referred to by scholars as *Alia Miracula A*, compiled *c.* 1180 and given in Raine, *HCY* I, pp. 293–320. Two further collections of miracles, *Alia Miracula B* (Raine, *HCY* I, pp. 321–5) and *Alia Miracula C* (Raine, *HCY* I, pp. 327–47) exist. *Alia Miracula B* are undatable and *Alia Miracula C* seem to belong to the early thirteenth century. For the naming of these miracle collections and their dates and the complicated manuscript tradition, see Morris and Cambridge 1989, p. 13 and p. 29, n. 53.

[87] A run of royal privileges from Edward the Confessor to an Inspeximus of Edward II (dated 1311) can be found on ff. 69v–78r; papal privileges from the time of Honorius II (1124–30) to Alexander III (1159–81) can be found on ff. 78r–82r. The cartulary concludes with a copy of an Inspeximus charter dated 10 February, 1 Richard II (1378) on ff. 87v–90v, an Inspeximus which contains an Old English copy of **13**.

[88] For a detailed description of the Beverley Cartulary, see the first appendix written by I. Doyle in Morris and Cambridge 1989, pp. 20–1, where there is an account of the handsome decoration on display in the cartulary (at p. 21); a useful summary of its contents, together with a list of modern editions of some of the Beverley material, is made in the second appendix (pp. 22–7) by E. Cambridge. For the possibility that the Beverley Cartulary was compiled in response to an attack on the community by Archbishop Neville, see Woodman 2012.

[89] See I. Doyle in Morris and Cambridge 1989, p. 20.

[90] See below, p. 196.

On folio 60v of the Beverley Cartulary occurs a wonderfully decorative page which marks the transition in the cartulary from a series of miracles performed by St John (occupying ff. 10v–60r) to an account of the liberties and privileges belonging to Beverley Minster. We are told that these passages had been translated into Latin from English by Master 'Alueredus sacrista'.[91] Some of the first passages to occur here describe the antiquity of Beverley Minster and delineate its customs and liberties.[92] As a whole these passages, occupying ff. 60v–69r, are of great interest and may, in places, rely on Anglo-Saxon documentation.[93]

On folio 69rv is a copy of **12** (for which see further below), followed on 69v–70r by a Latin copy of **13**.[94] A rubric introducing this copy of **13** describes the very great difficulty the copyist had had when making his translation from Old English. Later on in the Beverley Cartulary (on f. 87v–88r) is preserved a copy of an Old English version of **13** and the level of corruption in this text would seem to justify the translator's warning in his rubric. But this Old English copy was not made from an independent, early version of **13** but rather from an Inspeximus confirmation made in 1378, the first year of Richard II's reign (given as Manuscript G in the edition of **13**). Since this is not an independent copy, I have not supplied any of the readings of the Beverley Cartulary in my edition of **13**. I have given the Latin version of **13** alongside the Old English in the edited text.[95]

Folio 70r of the Beverley Cartulary contains our earliest, Latin copy of **14**; no Old English version survives.[96] This is followed by Latin versions of two writs of William the Conqueror on folios 70r–71r, one of which survives in Old English in the same Charter Roll that contains our earliest extant Old English copy of **13**.[97] There are some striking parallels between the two pre-Conquest Beverley writs and the two post-Conquest writs. **13** grants Ealdred the right to draw up a

[91] BL Additional 61901, f. 60v: 'Libertates ecclesie sancti iohannis de beverlik cum priuilegiis apostolicis et episcopalibus quas magister alueredus sacrista eiusdem ecclesie de anglico in latinum transtulit'. For Alfred of Beverley's work, see Sharpe, *Handlist*, p. 54.

[92] Examples of these are: on f. 61rv, entitled 'De antiquitate ecclesie Beuerlacensis'; on 61v–62r a passage entitled 'Quomodo rex Adelstanus eam exaltauerit' and on f. 62r a passage 'De pace ecclesie sancti Iohannis'.

[93] For these passages, see Raine, *SDSB*, pp. 97–108, where the text is edited from BL Harley 560, rather than from the earlier Beverley Cartulary (BL Additional 61901).

[94] On the mistaken entry in Sawyer's *Anglo-Saxon Charters*, which describes some of the Patent and Confirmation Rolls as containing Latin versions of **13**, see above.

[95] For the later copies of this Latin version of **13** by antiquaries, see below, pp. 202–3.

[96] Harmer, *Writs*, no. 119, incorrectly lists this as a York writ.

[97] These writs are edited in Bates, *RRAN: William I*, nos. 31–2; an Old English version of no. 31 exists in its earliest form in the same Charter Roll of Edward II that contains our earliest copy of **13**; no Old English version of no. 32 survives.

priuilegium for the lands belonging to the church of St John of Beverley and this right is what we also see granted in one of the post-Conquest writs addressed to Earl Morcar and Gamel son of Osbern.[98] **14** grants Ealdred judicial and financial rights over his men within the king's own soke and one of the post-Conquest writs addressed to the French and English thegns in Yorkshire states that Beverley, rather than Ealdred this time, was to have judicial and financial rights over its lands.[99] The terms of **14** are not exactly the same as those of this second post-Conquest writ because **14** refers specifically to rights within the king's soke and is a concession to Ealdred rather than the Minster itself; but since the writ of William I states that Beverley was to have sake and soke over all the lands that it was given in King Edward's day and also over those lands that Archbishop Ealdred had acquired in William I's day, and that these rights were to be free specifically in relation to the king, then this more general notice has the force of confirming the earlier grant in **14**.

It is important to remember that the writ, unlike the solemn charter, was not considered to be a perpetual record: when a king died, the grant was deemed to have lapsed. Sharpe has shown that this is why in the Bury St Edmund's archive we find so many documents issued for the same beneficiary, granting the same rights, but in the name of different kings. And, by looking at the twelfth-century situation, Sharpe demonstrates that it was the beneficiary who was likely to have requested such a document from the king and who would have paid a fee to have such a document made.[100]

Because the terms of writs were void once a king had died many archives simply removed older versions from their holdings and it is therefore rare to find a sequence of writs across the reigns of different kings for the same beneficiary, granting the same rights, as we do at Bury.[101] But it is possible that with these four writs at Beverley we are encountering the same phenomenon, although admittedly with much less evidence.[102] Upon the death of Edward the Confessor, and following the brief reign of King Harold, Archbishop Ealdred evidently took

[98] See Bates, *RRAN: William I*, no. 32.

[99] Bates, *RRAN: William I*, no. 31.

[100] See Sharpe 2003, pp. 252–3.

[101] Sharpe 2003, p. 262 and p. 271, stresses that the Conquest itself was not the event which triggered the reissuing and reconfirming of various documents but rather it was the change of king that was the catalyst. Thus in Bury we find the reconfirmation of charters of Edward the Confessor and William the Conqueror in the reigns of Henry I and Stephen I.

[102] Other useful parallels can be drawn between the Bury archive and the Beverley archive. Not only do they both preserve a sequence of writs restating various rights (as we have seen), but Bury is one of the only other places to have harnessed the idea of converting its charters into the medium of rhyming Middle English; see A. Hiatt, *The Making of Medieval Forgeries: False Documents in Fifteenth-Century England* (London, 2004), pp. 57–60, where a certain John Lydgate is credited with

measures to have two writs and their details reconfirmed and regranted in the name of William the Conqueror; and today we are fortunate to have preserved copies of all four.[103]

In 1310, as noted above, Old English versions of **13** and of the post-Conquest writ notifying French and English thegns in Yorkshire about financial and judicial rights granted to Beverley Minster in Edward's day (Bates, *RRAN: William I*, no. 31) were presented to the Chancery and subsequently enrolled on Charter Roll, 4 Edward II (on membrane 20, number 52); this roll is our earliest extant manuscript witness for both writs. It is noticeable that copies of **14** and of the charter of William granting Ealdred the right to draw up a *priuilegium* (Bates, *RRAN: William I*, no. 32) were not produced at this time and so Old English versions have not been preserved. Those men in charge of Beverley's archive and rights may have felt there was no point in taking two versions of documents which basically granted the same rights and so seem to have chosen those two which represented the fullest account of rights granted, rather than simply the two most recent versions. Or it may be the case that by 1310, single-sheet Old English copies of **14** and of the William I writ (Bates, *RRAN: William I*, no. 32) no longer survived, perhaps because of some previous pruning of the Beverley archive.

One of the earliest copies of **12** is BL Cotton Charter iv. 18, a single-sheet dated to the early or mid-fourteenth century.[104] Very recently, a further copy of about the same date has been identified in the Schøyen Collection, MS 33.[105] The Beverley Cartulary (BL Additional 61901) contains a third copy of **12** made in the late fourteenth century. Both the Schøyen and the Beverley Cartulary copies have six more lines than in the single-sheet version and it seems likely that there were, at various stages in the late thirteenth and fourteenth centuries, several different copies of **12** in circulation.[106]

---

turning four eleventh-century charters into Middle English verse. I am very grateful to Dr J. Crick for this reference.

103 The address of each of the four documents reflects the correct context for the date at which they were purportedly granted. For the importance of the address, see Sharpe 2003, pp. 251–2.

104 As previously mentioned, it was in the early fourteenth century that various documents granting rights to Beverley, including **13**, were taken to the Chancery to be confirmed and it may be as part of this programme that this single-sheet version of **12** was produced.

105 For this Schøyen manuscript, see Griffiths 1995, pp. 37–8, where the copy of **12** is not noted.

106 The extra lines in the Beverley Cartulary copy begin at line 11 and end at line 16; in the margin next to line 11, *va* has been written and in the margin next to line 16, *cat* has been inserted, by a late fourteenth- or early fifteenth-century hand. This demonstrates that someone was comparing the cartulary version with a shorter version (perhaps the single-sheet, although it is clear that the cartulary version is not a direct copy of the single-sheet) and marking that these lines were missing (*vacat*) from the single-sheet. For later copies of **12** by antiquaries, see below, pp. 202–3.

b. *The Later Beverley Archive*

As will be seen from the above summary, the Beverley archive contains only two genuine Anglo-Saxon documents. By contrast **12** was perhaps fabricated in the name of King Æthelstan as part of an attempt to explain the origin of Beverley's privileges (and by this means also to create a link with one of the most celebrated of Anglo-Saxon kings).[107] It is impossible to pinpoint when exactly the Beverley archive lost most of its Anglo-Saxon documents. It may be that there was already a deficiency in the time of Edward the Confessor. In **13** Edward grants the right to Archbishop Ealdred to draw up his own *priuilegium* to cover all of those lands belonging to Beverley Minster. Although this does not survive, it may have been designed as an early form of *pancarte*, a document intended to guarantee not just one privilege or possession but the Minster's entire endowment, perhaps therefore suggesting that there were gaps in the Minster's documentation even by this stage.[108]

The arrival of the Normans triggered uncertainty throughout Anglo-Saxon England and its institutions. Thus in the late eleventh and early twelfth centuries many religious establishments undertook the copying and indeed the forging of charters and other historical documents in order to prove status, rights and privileges. Just such a reaction is evident at York and at Durham. Some activity can be seen at Beverley, since the Beverley Cartulary preserves copies of a series of documents in the name of William I (d. 1087), Henry I (d. 1135) and Stephen (d. 1154).[109] And by the mid-twelfth century Alfred the Sacrist was copying and writing passages which he considered demonstrable of the ancient privileges owned by the Minster.[110]

In the early twelfth century, as we have seen,[111] the town of Beverley began to thrive and we can imagine that the Minster too profited from this period of

[107] It also seems likely that **12** was composed to confirm Beverley's rights to thraves; for more, see the commentary to **12**. The purported link to Æthlestan was evidently important to the Beverley community, to the extent that his name is invoked in the community's *Chapter Act Book* and the *Provost's Book* (for these manuscripts, see below, p. 197); see also above, p. 182, n. 51.

[108] See further the commentary to **13**. This is necessarily speculative, however, as *pancarte* can also be found in archives which have relatively full records.

[109] For the copies of documents in the name of William I, Henry I and Stephen preserved in the Beverley Cartulary, see the list in Morris and Cambridge 1989, pp. 25–6 (nos. 94–107). There are two writs in the name of William I which seem to restate rights already granted in **13** and **14** (discussed above), for which see Bates, *RRAN: William I*, nos. 31–2. There are seven documents in the name of Henry I, for which see *Regesta II*, p. 37 (no. 669), p. 88 (no. 923), p. 129 (no. 1112), p. 130 (no. 1113), p. 157 (no. 1257), p. 199 (no. 1454) and p. 261 (no. 1756). There are three documents issued by Stephen; see *Regesta III*, p. 36 (no. 99), p. 36 (no. 100) and p. 37 (no. 102).

[110] For Alfred, see above, p. 191 and Sharpe, *Handlist*, p. 54.

[111] See above, pp. 186–7.

prosperity. But any growth was soon checked by two major, successive incidents. First, in September 1188, a fire recorded both in chronicles such as that by Roger of Howden,[112] and also in inscriptions which are now lost but which were copied down in the sixteenth and seventeenth centuries, did damage to the town of Beverley and to the Minster.[113] The extent of the damage done by the fire is unknown but that it was a major event for the Minster seems to be corroborated by its mention in both these inscriptions and also chronicles. Whether or not it caused losses to the Minster's archives must also remain uncertain.

The second disaster to occur at the Minster involved the collapse of its crossing tower *c.* 1213, an event which led to the construction of the Minster as it is today. In one of the collections of posthumous miracles of St John, known as *Alia Miracula C*,[114] there is a lengthy chapter devoted to a description of the tower and its collapse.[115] We are told that the old tower had been large and beautiful and made entirely of stone. But it was too heavy for its supports and various cracks began to appear. Eventually the situation became so dire that stones fell on the clergy during services, so much so that they retreated first to the altar and later to the nave. It then collapsed but fortunately when nobody was in the church, a miracle accredited to intercession by St John. The tower itself is described as being at the very centre of the church (*in medio crucis ipsius basilicae*), an

112 See *Chronica magistri Rogeri de Houeden*, ed. W. Stubbs, RS (London, 1869), vol. II, p. 354: 'Eodem anno xii. kalendas Octobris, feria tertia, in uigilia Sancti Mathaei apostoli et euangelistae, tota fere uilla de Beuerlaco, cum nobili ecclesia Beati Johannis Archiepiscopi, combusta est'.

113 Leland, *Collectanea* IV, p. 102, made this record of the inscription: 'Haec scriptura inuenta postea in theca reliquiarum S. Joannis. "Anno D. 1188, mense Septembr: combusta fuit eccl: S. Joannis in sequenti nocte post festum Mathei apostolic." Translata sunt eodem tempore ossa S. Brithuni, abbatis Beuerlac:', quoted in Leach, *Memorials* II, p. 350. In the next century Dugdale also discovered this inscription and made a note of it; he describes how 'in *anno* 1664, upon taking up of a large and thick marble stone, lying in the midst of the Church of BEVERLEY, neare the entrance into the Quire', he found a vault in which a sheet of lead bore the following inscription: 'Anno ab incarnatione Domini Millesimo Centesimo Octagesimo VIII combusta fuit hec ecclesia in mense septembri in sequenti nocte post festum sancti Mathei apostoli [21/2 Se[tember], et in anno Millesimo Centesimo XCVIII VI idus Martii [10 March] facta fuit inquisitio Reliquiarum Beati Johannis in hoc loco et inuenta sunt hec ossa in orientali parte sepulchri et hic recondita et puluis cemento mixto ibidem inuentus est et reconditus'; quoted in *The Visitation of the County of Yorke, begun in Anno Domini MDCLXV and finished Anno Domini MDCLXVI by William Dugdale, ESQ, Norray King of Armes*, ed. R. Davies, SS xxxvi (Durham and London, 1859), p. 22 and by Morris and Cambridge 1989, p. 30, n. 61. Morris and Cambridge also suggest that there were two separate inscriptions recording the same fire in 1188 since Leland notes his source as being *scriptura* whilst Dugdale notes his as being on the *sepulchrum* (at p. 15).

114 See above, p. 190, n. 86.

115 *Alia Miracula C*, ed. Raine, *HCY* I, pp. 345–7.

indication that this was a major disaster for the structural integrity of the building. Clearly, therefore, this was an economic setback for the Minster.[116]

Copies of **12**, **13** and **14** can be found in the Beverley Cartulary (BL Additional 61901), made at some point in the late fourteenth century. It was in the spring of 1381 that a remarkable feud erupted between Alexander Neville, archbishop of York (1374–88), and the Beverley chapter, and it may be that one function of the Beverley Cartulary was to ward off that archbishop's intrusion.[117] Two further cartularies were produced at Beverley in the late fifteenth century, Oxford, University College 82 and Washington DC, Library of Congress, Sir Thomas Phillipps Papers, mm 78076737.[118] While the first of these contains an incomplete copy of the forged **12**,[119] neither have any copies of genuine Anglo-Saxon documents.[120]

Beverley suffered greatly during and after the Reformation in the mid-sixteenth century. After a 1547 act of Parliament, the Minster was suppressed along with a dozen chantries and any surviving religious guilds. The majority of the Minster's assets were seized and the Minster itself and its associated buildings were granted to Sir Michael Stanhope, governor of Hull, and John Bellow, the Crown surveyor. It was only thanks to a group of wealthy citizens that the necessary £100 was raised to save the Minster.[121] But the damage was nevertheless substantial and Beverley was transformed from one of the major northern churches, once staffed by seventy-four clergy, to a church dependent on the town's corporation, staffed by only two people.[122] The loss of its substantial endowments meant that the Minster fell into a pitiful state of disrepair.[123]

[116] Funds began to be raised for the rebuilding of the Minster as early as 1221 and construction started at the east end and moved westwards. In later times potential donors were encouraged by the offer of an indulgence in return for their payments, which was granted by the archbishop of York; see R. Horrox, 'The Later Medieval Minster', p. 37 in Horrox, *Beverley*.

[117] See Woodman 2012.

[118] See Davis, *Cartularies* (rev. edn), nos. 47–8.

[119] See below, pp. 201–2.

[120] The Beverley *Chapter Act Book* gives some detail about the organisation of the Minster's archives since there are various references to the making of copies of charters and bulls and their subsequent storage in a box (*cophinus* or *pixidus*) under the correct year. See, for example, Leach, *Memorials* I, pp. 141, 184, 254 and 308; there is an interesting example on p. 219 of a letter of Archbishop Greenfield dated 1308 which is described as being 'in quadam pixide inter cartas de Foston et Hothum'.

[121] For all of this, see D.J. Lamburn, 'The Minster and the Reformation', in Horrox, *Beverley*, pp. 51–63.

[122] D.J. Lamburn *ibid.*, p. 51.

[123] From 1716 to the early 1730s the Minster underwent some much needed restoration. One remarkable event involved the use of a wooden scaffold to return the leaning façade of the north transept back to its original vertical position. See Miller *et al.*, *Beverley*, p. 11.

It is impossible to be precise about the consequences of the Reformation for Beverley's archive and what documents may have been destroyed and lost. Apart from the three Beverley cartularies already mentioned,[124] three other ancient books survive from Beverley: the *Chapter Act Book* (London, Society of Antiquaries, MS 81, recording events dated 1286–1347);[125] the *Provost's Book* (compiled in 1416/17, of which extracts survive in Bodleian, Dodsworth 26);[126] and the *Sanctuary Book* (a register of those taking sanctuary in Beverley Minster from 1478 to 1540, now BL, Harley 4292),[127] all of which give fascinating information about the workings of the medieval minster.[128]

At three points in the Beverley Cartulary there are indications that soon after the Reformation, the manuscript was owned by a person called William Wray of Ripon. On folios 1r and 61r is the inscription, 'Ego sum liber Willelmi Wray de Rippon. 1586.'; and on folio 69r there is the monogram 'WW', presumably referring to the same man. Doyle notes that he is only one of several book collectors from Ripon who were called William Wray.[129] Since we know there to have been a connection between Beverley and Ripon, as exemplified by the rhyming charters **12** and **16**,[130] it may well be more than coincidence that someone from Ripon, perhaps an official who had duties at both religious establishments, came into possession of the cartulary.[131]

The Beverley Cartulary went on sale at Sotheby's on 6 February, 1861, where it is listed and described as lot 61. It had been one of the manuscripts in the collection amassed by Sir John Savile the Elder (1545–1607) and his brother Sir Henry Savile (1549–1622). After performing an 'unworthy trick', Sir Thomas Phillipps bought the manuscript; it was not numbered during his lifetime but was given the number 23875 afterwards.[132] It later came into the possession of Harry Lawrence

124 See above, p. 196.

125 Davis, *Cartularies* (rev. edn), no. 50, edited in Leach, *Memorials* I and II (pp. 1–136).

126 Davis, *Cartularies* (rev. edn), no. 51, edited in Leach, *Memorials* II, pp. 305–39.

127 Davis, *ibid.*, no. 52, edited in Raine, *SDSB*, pp. 109–211.

128 Leach, *Memorials* I, pp. lxxxiv–lxxxv, suggests that the Beverley community took good care of its documents and that 'loss of the Beverley documents is comparatively recent, and due not to the spoliation of Reformers or Puritans under Tudors and Stewarts, but to the neglect and carelessness of times which professed to be interested in ancient things' (at p. lxxxv).

129 See I. Doyle, in Morris and Cambridge 1989, p. 32, n. 116.

130 For more about the connection between these documents, see the commentaries to **12** and **16**.

131 This point is also made by I. Doyle, in Morris and Cambridge 1989, p. 21.

132 It appears that Sir Thomas Phillipps' behaviour was not beyond reproach on this occasion. A certain man named Boone acted not only in the interests of Phillipps but also in those of the British Museum's Manuscripts Department, a situation that angered the then Keeper of Manuscripts, Sir Frederic Madden (1801–73). During this sale Phillipps made only small bids in his own name (as communicated to Madden by Boone), thus leading the British Museum to believe that it would be able to bid for the more desirable manuscripts. But at the same time Phillipps made much larger

Bradfer-Lawrence, who collected a wide range of important manuscripts, and who died in 1965; it was purchased by the British Library in 1981.[133]

3. THE MANUSCRIPTS

a. *TNA: PRO Ch. R., 4 Edw. II, m. 20, no. 52* [C]

The earliest copy of **13** is in an Inspeximus charter preserved in C, a Charter Roll dated 7 September, 1310. Other, post-Conquest charters in favour of the Beverley church were enrolled at the same moment.[134] This Inspeximus charter itself formed the basis for further confirmations of **13** which were made into various Charter Rolls, Patent Rolls and Confirmation Rolls and which are listed below as manuscripts F, G, H, I, J, K, L and N and O.

b. *Olim Oslo and London, The Schøyen Collection, MS 33* [D]

This manuscript, at the moment numbered 33 in the Schøyen collection,[135] is an English manuscript which contains a mixture of historical and scientific works. It is written mainly in Latin but also contains texts in Middle English, French and Gascon. Until very recently, it was not known that D also has an early to mid-fourteenth century copy of **12**.[136] The manuscript has 185 leaves, with five leaves left blank. It is written in a fourteenth-century book hand with a continuation and various extra material added in later hands. Rubrics are written in red, while initials can be in blue decorated with red detail and yellow wash. There are thirteen portraits of English kings and various miniatures (including an interesting depiction of a classroom scene and of the White Ship showing the drowning of the sons of Henry I). The style of these miniatures has suggested links with Cambridge in the 1340s and London in the 1390s, but the ultimate

---

bids using various pseudonyms and so was able to purchase many of the best items for himself. Sir Frederic Madden later described this as an 'unworthy trick' in his journal. For all of this information, see A.N.L. Munby, *The Formation of the Phillipps Library From 1841 to 1872* (Cambridge, 1956), pp. 76–7.

133 P.M. Giles, 'A Handlist of the Bradfer–Lawrence Manuscripts Deposited on Loan at the Fitzwilliam Museum', *Transactions of the Cambridge Bibliographical Society* vi, ii (1973), pp. 86–99, where the Beverley Cartulary is listed as item number three.

134 For details about which charters were enrolled on 7 September, 1310, see above, p. 189

135 At the time of writing, this manuscript was being sold from the Schøyen collection.

136 I am most grateful to Peter Kidd for bringing this to my attention and to Dr T. Webber for advising me on the date of the script of this copy.

origin of D remains unknown.[137] It has an early eighteenth century binding, labelled 'Chronicles of England, London, Fourteenth Century'.

Two marks of ownership on f. 79v suggest that D later travelled to Scotland. The first, in a seventeenth-century hand, states: 'Joannes Neper de Merchistoun'; the second, also in a seventeenth-century hand, states: 'Deinde venit David comes Huntingdon'. The first of these people is John Napier (1550–1617), the eighth lord of Merchiston, Edinburgh, while the other is David I, earl of Huntingdon.[138] In the nineteenth century, D was owned by R. Graham of Grahamstown, South Africa, whose name can be found on the front pastedown and whose initials occur on f. 71r. In the summer of 1986, D went on sale at Christie's and in November 1987 it was bought by H.P. Kraus rare book dealers in New York, from where it came into the Schøyen collection.[139] It contains a range of texts such as Geoffrey of Monmouth's *Historia Regum Britanniae* (with the *Propheta Merlini*), a Latin metrical chronicle of the kings of England from 1087 to 1377, copies of letters by King John (1199–1216), a Latin chronicle of Bordeaux, a Latin computistical treatise attributed to John of Garland (*c.* 1195–*c.* 1272), a Latin verse copy of the *Carmen de Algorismo* by Alexander de Villa Dei, a Latin prose copy of the *Tractatus de Sphera* by Johannes de Sacro Bosco and so on.[140] A copy of **12** occurs on f. 47rv amidst a continuation of the *Historia Regum Britanniae* in Latin prose extending to the year 1217.

c. *BL Additional 61901 (the Beverley Cartulary)* [E]

E is a very beautiful cartulary dating to the end of the fourteenth century.[141] It is written on good-quality membrane leaves and set out in two columns per page.[142] It has a medieval binding of boards with white skin; the remains of leather straps

[137] For much of this information, and the stylistic links with London and Cambridge, see the online entry for this manuscript: <http://www.schoyencollection.com/historyMedieval.html#033> (accessed 7 November 2010). Other descriptions of D can be found in: the Christie's catalogue for 25 June, 1986, lot 208; a summary drawn up by the rare book dealers H.P. Kraus, based in New York; and in a very detailed description made by J. Griffiths in 1990, presumably on behalf of the Schøyen collection. The descriptions from H.P. Kraus and J. Griffiths were made available to me by Peter Kidd; the current discussion of D is greatly indebted to them. See also Griffiths 1995, pp. 37–8.

[138] For the difficulties involved in trying to identify this David, earl of Huntingdon, see pp. 8–9 in the description by J. Griffiths.

[139] See above, n. 137.

[140] For a much more detailed description of the contents, see the description by Griffiths (cited above, n. 137) and also Griffiths 1995.

[141] See I. Doyle in Morris and Cambridge 1989, pp. 20–1. For the Beverley cartulary, see Davis, *Cartularies* (rev. edn.), no. 49.

[142] There is a very full description and list of contents of the Beverley cartulary by Doyle and Cambridge in Morris and Cambridge 1989, pp. 20–7, to which this analysis is indebted.

and also of nails on the back board suggest the likelihood that the volume was at one stage strapped to a desk or altar.[143] The text of E is illuminated with decorative initials, which have been described by Doyle.[144] E opens with a copy of Folcard's *Life of St John*, together with accounts of miracles performed by that saint; this hagiographical material is followed by copies of charters and privileges of Beverley Minster which extend to 1380. Its general contents can be summarised as follows:

1. ff. 1–10v: Folcard's *Life of Saint John*.
2. ff. 10v–60v: accounts of miracles performed by John:
   ff. 22r–25r contain a passage which tells of rights and privileges that King Æthelstan supposedly gave to the Minster.
   ff. 53r–58v contain extracts about St John from Bede's *HE*.
3. ff. 60v–90v: details of privileges (royal, papal and episcopal) given to Beverley Minster, including copies of various charters and writs, which run to 1380:
   f. 60v: the beginning of this section detailing the Minster's rights is signalled by a decorative page which states that the passages cited had been translated into Latin from their original English by Master 'Alueredus sacrista'.[145]

All of the charters edited in this volume are found in the last section of the cartulary, item 3 in the list above. **12**, the rhyming Middle English charter that was so important to the Beverley community, is copied first on ff. 69rv; it is followed on ff. 69v–70r by a Latin copy of **13**. An Old English version of **13** can be found towards the very end of the cartulary on ff. 87v–88r, which was copied from the Inspeximus version made in 1378, manuscript G below. On f. 70r, straight after the Latin copy of **13**, is a Latin copy of the writ, **14**.[146]

In the sixteenth century, E was owned by a certain William Wray of Ripon and then, in the sixteenth and early seventeenth centuries, by Sir John Savile the Elder and his brother Sir Henry Savile; it later came into the possession of Sir Thomas Phillips (d. 1872) and then H.L. Brafder-Lawrence (d. 1965).[147]

[143] See Doyle in Morris and Cambridge, *ibid*., p. 20.
[144] Doyle in Morris and Cambridge, *ibid*., p. 21.
[145] See above, p. 191.
[146] This writ had been incorrectly listed as a York writ by Harmer; see above, p. 191, n. 96.
[147] For these details, see above, pp. 197–8 and Davis, *Cartularies* (rev. edn), no. 49.

d. *Enrolments* [F, G, H, I, J, K, L]

In 1310 a copy of **13**, together with other (post-Conquest) charters, was made into an Inspeximus charter in the name of Edward II, manuscript C above. This Old English version of **13** formed the basis for further enrolled confirmations of the same document in these Charter and Patent Rolls:

1. TNA: PRO Ch.R. 4 Edw. III, m. 13, no. 25 (MS F, 30 November, 1330).
2. TNA: PRO Pat. R. 1 Ric. II, pt. 3, m. 8 (MS G, 10 February, 1378).
3. TNA: PRO Pat. R. 5 Ric. II, pt. 2, m. 13 (MS H, 26 April, 1382).
4. TNA: PRO Pat. R. 2 Hen. IV, pt. 2, m. 6 (MS I, 1 March, 1401).
5. TNA: PRO Ch. R. 1 Hen. V, pt. 1, m. 11, no. 5 (MS J, 25 November, 1413).
6. TNA: PRO Ch. R. 3–4 Hen. V, m. 24, no. 15 (MS K, 20 June, 1415).
7. TNA: PRO Pat. R. 6 Hen. VI, pt. 2, m. 6 (MS L, 13 March, 1428).

Manuscripts N and O below constitute more enrolments of **13**.

e. *Bodleian, University College, 82* [M]

M dates to the second half of the fifteenth century, sometime after 1462;[148] it has a fifteenth-century fitting of horn and metal attached to seventeenth-century boards. It is a cartulary of the Beverley Vicars Choral, which contains:[149]

1. pp. 1–5: statutes.
2. p. 6: a table.
3. pp. 7–24: general charters of liberties, including an extract from **12** on p. 7.
4. pp. 25–32: blank.
5. pp. 33–56: *obitus et compositiones*.
6. pp. 57–134: charters arranged by places.

An extract from **12** can be found on p. 7 of M, a highly decorative page. In the top left, within an enlarged letter 'C', is a copy of the famous portrait of King Æthelstan handing over a sealed charter to Bishop John. It is followed by a summary of **12** in decorative capitals: 'Carta Adelstani Rex ... facta beato Johanni Beverlaci in hec verba: Als hert may make or egh may see'. Additional information about Æthelstan is squeezed into the right margin and below the decorative script in a hand which is smaller and less formal. The following pages contain information derived from the work of Alfred of Beverley about the 'libertates' that Beverley

[148] See Davis, *Cartularies* (rev. edn.), no. 47.

[149] This list of contents is taken from Davis, *Cartularies* (rev. edn), no. 47.

Minster possessed. This makes it clear that the scribe of M was here copying the Beverley cartulary, manuscript E.

f. *Further enrolments* [N, O]

As was noted above in section d, the Old English version of **13** was enrolled again in these two Confirmation Rolls:

1. TNA: PRO Conf. R. 26, 1 Hen. VIII, pt. 2, no. 13 (MS N, 1509).
2. TNA: PRO Conf. R. 75, 3+4 Phil. and Mary, pt. 1, no. 15 (MS O).

g. *Copies by Antiquaries* [P, Q, R, S, T, U, V, W]

i. *BL Cotton Otho C. xvi* (P): s. xvi^{ex}. This manuscript was badly burnt in the 1731 Cotton fire. P contains copies of all of the Beverley charters: **12** is copied on ff. 78v–81r; the Latin version of **13** occurs on f. 81v, whilst the Old English version can be found on f. 98rv; **14** is copied on ff. 81v–82r. All of these copies seem to have been made by reference to the Beverley cartulary, manuscript E above.

ii. *BL Harley 560* (Q): s. xvii^{in}. This manuscript, a copy of P, has copies of all of the Beverley charters; **12** can be found on ff. 21r–22v; the Latin version of **13** occurs on f. 23r, whilst a copy of the Old English version of **13** is on f. 40rv; finally a copy of **14** is also to be found on f. 23r.

iii. *BL Lansdowne 269* (R): s. xvii. This is a volume from John Philipott of Somerset's collections. A copy of **12** can be found on f. 97rv; this is made from the single-sheet Cotton charter, siglum B in the edited text.

iv. *Bodleian, Dodsworth 9* (S): s. xvii. This Dodsworth manuscript has an incomplete copy of **12** on f. 22r. On f. 23v is the heading 'Carta Adelstani facta sancto Wilfrido Ryponensi' with nothing afterwards, which must be a reference to **16** (or possibly **15**) in the Ripon archive. It also has copies of **1**, **3**, **4**, **5** and **8** from the York archive and **17** from the Durham archive.

v. *Bodleian, Dodsworth 10* (T): s. xvii. This manuscript has a copy of **12** on ff. 43v–44v; this copy omits the six extra lines found both in the Schøyen manuscript and the Beverley cartulary copies of **12** and so it was made either directly from the single-sheet copy of **12** (Cotton Charter iv. 18) or from some version of that single-sheet. It also has copies of **1** from the York archive and **17** from the Durham archive.

vi. *Bodleian, Dodsworth 95* (U): s. xvii. A copy of **12** occurs on ff. 32v–33r;[150] textual features suggest this copy was made either directly from the single-sheet copy of **12** (Cotton Charter iv. 18) or from some version of that single-sheet; see also Manuscripts T and V.

vii. *Bodleian, Dodsworth 116* (V): s. xvii. A copy of **12** can be found on ff. 116r–117v,[151] made from some version of the single-sheet, Cotton Charter iv. 18 or even directly from the single-sheet; see also Manuscripts T and U above.

vi. *BL Lansdowne 446* (W): s. xviii. This manuscript constitutes a collection of miscellaneous copies of single-sheet documents, owned by John Strype (1643–1737). A copy of the Old English **13** occurs on f. 89, just after a copy of S 433 (BCS 722). At the top of this copy of **13** is a note which states that it was made using manuscript C, the Charter Roll of the fourth year of Edward II's reign. On f. 90 of W, following the transcription of **13**, is a copy of William the Conqueror's writ for Beverley,[152] on the reverse of which is a note suggesting that these were the only two copies made of Beverley charters. John Strype was an eminent historian of the seventeenth and eighteenth centuries, interested in particular about London.[153]

150 *Summ. Cat.*, no. 5036.

151 *Summ. Cat.*, no. 5057.

152 Bates, *RRAN: William I*, no. 31.

153 See the entry on Strype by G.H. Martin and A. McDonnell in *ODNB*.

SIGLA

Note. The siglum A is reserved for original documents and the siglum B for non-contemporary copies on single-sheets.

a. *Principal manuscript sources*

B. BL Cotton Ch. iv. 18 (s. xiv$^{\text{in-med}}$)
C. TNA: PRO Ch. R. 4 Edw. II, m. 20, no. 52 (7 September, 1310)
D. *Olim* Oslo and London, The Schøyen Collection, MS 33 (s. xiv$^{\text{in-med}}$)
E. BL Additional 61901 (s. xiv^{ex})

b. *Other manuscript sources*

F. TNA: PRO Ch.R. 4 Edw. III, m. 13, no. 25 (30 November, 1330)
G. TNA: PRO Pat. R. 1 Ric. II, pt. 3, m. 8 (10 February, 1378)
H. TNA: PRO Pat. R. 5 Ric. II, pt. 2, m. 13 (26 April, 1382)
I. TNA: PRO Pat. R. 2 Hen. IV, pt. 2, m. 6 (1 March, 1401)
J. TNA: PRO Ch. R. 1 Hen. V, pt. 1, m. 11, no. 5 (25 November, 1413)
K. TNA: PRO Ch. R. 3–4 Hen. V, m. 24, no. 15 (20 June, 1415)
L. TNA: PRO Pat. R. 6 Hen. VI, pt. 2, m. 6 (13 March, 1428)
M. Oxford, University College, 82 (s. xv^{ex})
N. TNA: PRO Conf. R. 26, 1 Hen. VIII, pt. 2, no. 13 (1509)
O. TNA: PRO Conf. R. 75, 3+4 Phil. and Mary, pt. 1, no. 15
P. BL Cotton Otho C. xvi (s. xvi^{ex})
Q. BL Harley 560 (s. xvii^{in})
R. BL Lansdowne 269 (s. xvii)
S. Bodleian Dodsworth 9 (s. xvii)
T. Bodleian Dodsworth 10 (s. xvii)
U. Bodleian Dodsworth 95 (s. xvii)
V. Bodleian Dodsworth 116 (s. xvii)
W. BL Lansdowne 446 (s. xviii)

NOTE ON THE METHOD OF EDITING

12 is a Middle English rhyming charter. Since the three main copies of this charter, in B, D and E, were made by scribes who were native speakers of Middle English, it has seemed most sensible to print a transcription of the earlier text, B, whilst giving the variant readings from D and E in the critical apparatus. In B, D and E, **y** is commonly written by the copyists where thorn is intended; this is an obvious corruption and in the following text of **12**, **th** has been used instead of **y** (see the note in Leach, *Memorials* II, p. 280, for more explanation and also J.A. Burrow and T. Turville-Petre, *A Book of Middle English* (Oxford, 2nd edn, 1996) p. 13). The apparatus for **12** has been compiled in a line-by-line manner so that the large number of variants is easy to follow. Proper nouns have been capitalised and punctuation is editorial and follows modern practice. **13** and **14** offer no particular editorial complications.

THE CHARTERS OF BEVERLEY

12

King Æthelstan grants privileges to St John's, Beverley. [A.D. 927 × 939]

B. BL Cotton Ch. iv. 18: s. xiv$^{\text{in-med}}$, 267 × 167mm
Endorsement: Carta Adelstani facta sancto Johanni Beuerl'
D. *Olim* Oslo and London, The Schøyen Collection, MS 33, 47rv: copy, s. xiv$^{\text{in-med}}$
E. BL Additional 61901, 69rv: copy, s. xiv^{ex}
Rubric: Carta Adelstani regis benedicti quam dedit et concessit in perpetuum beato Iohanni Beuerlaci
M. Oxford, University College, 82, p. 7: copy of E, s. xv^{ex} [extract]
P. BL Cotton Otho C. xvi, 78v–81r: copy of E, s. xvi^{ex}
Q. BL Harley 560, 21r–22v: copy of P, s. xvii^{in}
R. BL Lansdowne 269, 97rv: copy of B, s. xvii
S. Bodleian, Dodsworth 9, 22r: copy, s. xvii [incomplete]
T. Bodleian, Dodsworth 10, 43v–44v: copy (of B?), s. xvii
U. Bodleian, Dodsworth 95, 32v–33r: copy (of B?), s. xvii
V. Bodleian, Dodsworth 116, 116r–117v: copy (of B?), s. xvii
Ed.: a. *Mon. Angl.*, i, pp. 171–2, from B
b. Dugdale, *St Paul's*, p. 54, from *Mon. Angl.*
c. *Mon. Angl.* (rev. edn.), ii, pp. 129–30 (no. 3)
d. Oliver, *Beverley*, pp. 543–4, from R
e. Poulson, *Beverlac* I, pp. 37–9, from *Mon. Angl.* (rev. edn)
f. Kemble 359, from *Mon. Angl.* (rev. edn)
g. Thorpe, *Diplomatarium*, pp. 180–2, from Kemble
h. Birch 644, from R
i. Birch 645, from *Mon. Angl.* (rev. edn)
j. Birch 1339, from B
k. Earle, *Hand-Book*, pp. 435–7, from Kemble
l. Leach, *Memorials* II, pp. 280–7, from B
m. Witty 1921, pp. 36–44, from B
Translated: Leach, *Memorials* II, pp. 280–7
Listed: Sawyer 451; Hart, *ECNE*, no. 120a
Edited from Manuscript B with variants from D and E

That witen alle that euer been,
That this chartre heren and seen,
That I, the kinge Adelstan,
Has yaten and giuen to seint John,
Of Beuerlik, that sai I yow,

1 witen] wite *D*; euer] euere *D*; been] ben *DE*
2 this...and seen] tis chartir her an sen *E*; seen] sen *D*
3 kinge] kyng *DE*
4 Has] haues *D*; yaten] yath *D*, yiaten *E*; to...John] til saint Johan *D*
5 Beuerlik] beuerle *E*; sai...yow] saẏ I yu *D*, sei hi yiou *E*

Tol and theam, that wit ye now,
Sok and sake ouer al that land,
That es giuen into his hand,
On euer ilk kinges dai,
Be it al fre ay and ay;
[And on that land eke bẏ mi red,
That than ercebẏscop Aluered
Haves geten in his daẏes
With gifte outher with other saẏes,
With gifte other with cheping,
That saẏ I you bi heuen kyng].
Be it almousend, be al fre,
Wit ilke man and eek wit me;
That wil I (be him that me scop)
Bot til an Ercebiscop,
And til the seuen minstre prestes,
That serues god thar Seint John restes.
That giue I god and seint John,
Her befor you euerilkan;
All my hest corn iueldeel
To uphald his minstre weel;

6 theam] tem *D*; wit ye] wite ye *D*, wite yie *E*; now] nu *D*
7 sake] sak *E*; al] alle *D*
9 euer…dai] Eluerede kẏnges daẏ *D*; dai] day *E*
10 al] alle *E*; ay] anḍ, y *supra lineam B*, aẏ *D*; ay] aẏ *D*
11 And] *has* va *in margin next to it E*
11–16 And on…heuen kyng] *omitted B*
11 on] in *E*; eke] *omitted* E; bẏ] bi *E*; red] rede *E*
12 than ercebẏscop] ane ercebiscop *E*; Aluered] Aldrede *E*
13 daẏes] dawes *E*
14 gifte] giftes *E*; outher] hor *E*; saẏes] sawes *E*
15 gifte] giftes *E*; other] hor *E*; cheping] cheeping *E*
16 That] *has* cat *in margin next to it E*; saẏ] seie *E*; I you] hi yiou *E*; kyng] king *E*
17 almousend…fre] almusned be it fre *D*, almound be it al fre *E*
18 Wit] With *DE*; eek wit] eke with *D*, ek with *E*
19 I be] I bẏ *D*, hi bi *E*; him] hẏm *D*; scop] schop *E*
20 Bot] but *D*; an Ercebiscop] than Ercebiscop *D*, ane ercebishop *E*
21 seuen minstre] seuene minister *D*
22 serues] seruen *E*; thar] ther *E*; Seint John restes] saint Johan ristes *D*
23 That…I] thet gif I *D*, thit gif hi *E*; seint John] saint Johan *D*
24 befor…euerilkan] bẏforen euerilkan *D*, bifor yiou euerilcon *E*
25 All] al *D*; my] mẏn *D*, mi *E*; iueldeel] yueldel *D*, ildel *E*, *for ?* iuerel deel
26 uphald his] uphalde this *D*; minstre weel] minister wel *D*, minster wel *E*

Ya, four threue (be heuen kinge),
Of ilk a plowgh of Estriding'.
If it swa betid or swa gaas,
That ani man her again taas,
Be he baron, be he erle,
Clerk, prest, person or cherel,
Na be he, na that ilk Gome,
I wil forsaye that he come,
That wit ye weel or and or,
Til saint John minstre dor,
And thar I wil (swo Crist me red);
That he bet his misded;
Or he be cursed son on on,
Wit al that seruis saint John.
Yif hit swa betid and swa es,
That the man in mansing es,
I sai yow ouer fourti daghes,
Swilk than be sain John laghes,
That the chapitel of Beuerlik'
Til ye schirref of Euerwik',
send thair writ son on an,
That this mansedman be tan;

27 Ya…kinge] ya foure threue bẏ heuen kẏng *D*, yia forne thraue bi heuen king *E*
28 ilk a] ilke aẏ *D*; plowgh] plou *DE*; Estriding'] Estriẏng *D*, Estreding *E*
29 If…gaas] Ya bot if it swa bẏ tide ouyer swa gas *D*, Yia bot if it so bi tide other so gas *E*
30 ani] anẏ *D*; her] ther *D*; again taas] ogaẏn mẏs tas *D*, ageyn tas *E*
31 baron] baronn *D*; erle] herel *D*
32 Clerk…cherel] Prest, clerk, persone oyer cherel *D*
33 Na be] Ne be *DE*; na that] ne that *DE*; ilk] ilke *D*; Gome] Gume *D for ?* Come
34 wil] wile *D*; forsaye] forso`o´ye *B*, forsoye *D*, for soothe *E*; come] cume *D*
35 wit…or] wite ye wel hure and hure *D*, wite ye wel hore and hore *E*
36 Til] To *D*, Tul *E*; saint] sein *E*; John] Johan *D*; minstre dor] ministre dure *D*, minster dore *E*
37 thar] thare *D*, that *E*; wil] wile *D*; swo] so *DE*; red] rede *DE*
38 bet] bete *DE*; misded] mẏsdede *D*, misdede *E*
39 Or] Outher *D*; cursed] kursed *E*; son] sone *D*; on on] on an *D*, anon *E*
40 Wit] With *DE*; seruis saint John] serue saint Johan *D*, seruen sein Ioh' *E*
41 Yif hit] Bot if it *D*, If it *E*; betid] bi tide *D*, bitid *E*; es] is *E*
42 the] this *DE*; es] lyes *D*, is *E*
43 sai] saye *D*, sei *E*; yow] *omitted in D*, yiou *E*; fourti] fourtẏ *D*; daghes] daẏes *D*, dawes *E*
44 Swilk] Swilke *D*; sain...laghes] saint Johan lawes *D*, sein Iohan lawes *E*
45 chapitel] chapitil *E*; Beuerlik'] Beuerlike *E*
46 ye] ẏe *D*; schirref] schiref *D*, shirreue *E*; Euerwik'] euerwike *E*
47 send thair writ] with thar writte send *D*, with ther writ send *E*; son on an] sone on ane *D*
48 be tan] betan *B*, be tane *D*, bitan *E*

The schirref than, say i the,
Wit outen ani writ oue me,
Sal nimen him (swo crist me red)
And in to mi prison lede,
And hald him, that es mi wilt,
Til he bet his misgilt;
If men reises newe laghes
In ani other kinges daghes,
Be thay fromed, be thai yemed,
Wit thham of the minstre demed;
The mercy of the misded,
Gif i saint John, (swo Crist me red).
Yif man be cald of limes or lif,
Or men chalenges land in strif,
Wit mi bodlaik, wit writ of right,
Y wil saint Johan haue the might,
That man thar for noght fight in feeld,
Now`th´er wit staf, no wit sheeld;
Bot twelue men wil i that it telle;
Swo sal it be, swo heer ibelle.
And he that him swo wer ne may,

49 schirref] shirreue *E*; say] saẏ *D*, sei *E*
50 Wit outen ani] with outen other *D*, with outen oither *E*; oue] of *D*
51 Sal] *omitted D*, shal *E*; nimen him] nime hẏm *D*; swo] so *DE*; red] rede *DE*
52 And…lede] And un to mẏ prisonn thu hẏm lede *D*
53 him, that es] hẏm thar, that is *D*, him, thar is *E*; mi wilt] mẏ willd] *D*
54 Til] tul *E*; he bet] he haue beted *D*, haue bec *E*; misgilt] mẏsgilt *D*
55 reises] raẏses *D*; newe laghes] newe lawes *D*; neu lawes *E*
56 ani] anẏ *D*; kinges daghes] kẏnges dawes *D*, kinges dawes *E*
57 Be thay fromed] In thi fredom *D*, Be thei fremed *E*
58 Wit thham] With thaẏm *D*, With tham *E*; the] thi *D*; minstre] minister *D*, minster *E*
59 mercy] mercẏ *D*; misded] misdede *DE*
60 Gif...red] Gif i saint Johan so Crist me rede *D*, Giue i sein Ioh' so Crist me rede *E*
61 Yif] Yif *altered from* Yaf *D*, If *E*; or] and of *D*, of *E*
62 Or] Outher *D*, Other *E*; chalenges] kalanges *D*, calanges *E*
63 Wit mi] With mẏ *D*, Wid mi *E*; bodlaik] bodlayke *D*; wit...right] with writ of rith *D*, wid writ of rith *E*
64 Y] I *DE*; wil] wile *D*, wile that *E*; saint Johan] sein Joh' *E*; might] mith *DE*
65 for] fore *D*; noght...feeld] noth fith te in felde *D*, nouth fith in feld *E*
66 Now`th´er...sheeld] Nouther with staf ne with schelde *D*, Nother wid staf no with scheld *E*
67 twelue...that] tuelue men with hath *D*, tuelmen with atthe *E*; it telle] it bi telle *D*
68 Swo sal] Swa sal *D*, Sua sal *E*; swo...ibelle] sa herẏ belle *D*, sua here `i´belle *E*, *for ?* swo bere i belle
69 him] hẏm *D*; swo] swa *D*, suo *E*; wer] were *D*; may] maẏ *D*

Ouercomen be he euer and ay,
Als he in feld war ouercomen;
The Crauantise of him be nomen,
That yat i god and saint Johan;
Her befor iow euer ilkon.
Yif man be fonden slan, dronkend,
Sterued on sain Johan rike,
His aghen men, wit outen swike,
His aghen bailiffs make the sight;
Nan other Coroner haue the might;
Swa mikel fredom giue i the,
Swo hert may think or eghe see;
That haue I thought and forbiseen,
I wil that thar <may> euer been,
Samening and minstre lif
Last follik' wit outen strif;
God help alle thas ilke men,
That helpes to the thowen.

70 Ouercomen] 'co' *in* ouercomen *concealed by red stain B*; euer] aẏ *D*; ay] aẏ *D*, ay *followed by empty space on line E*
71 Als] Al *E*; feld...ouercomen] felde were ouercomen *D*, fed wore ouercommen *E*
72 The] There *D*; Crauantise] creauntise *D*, cuantise *E*; of...nomen] be of hẏm numen *D*
73 That] Thet *D*; yat] hete *D*, yiate *E*; i] hẏ *D*, *omitted E*; saint Johan] seint iohan *E*
74 Her...ilkon] Here bẏfor yu euer ilkan *D*, Here bifor yiou euerilkcon *E*
75 Yif] If anẏ *D*, If *E*; fonden] funden *D*; slan] sclan *D*; dronkend] Drunkned *D*, dronken *E*
76 Sterued] stormed *D*, sterued *on previous line E*; on...rike] on his rike *D*, upon sein Iohannis rik *E*
77 aghen] agen *D*, haughen *E*; men] men *supra lineam B*; wit] with *DE*
77–8 swike...aghen] *written over fold B*
78 aghen] agen *D*, haghen *E*; bailiffs...sight] balifs maken the sith te *D*, bailis thei mak the sith *E*
79 Nan other] Na nothir *E*; Coroner] coronnere *D*; might] micte *D*, mith *E*
80 mikel...i] mikel fredam gif I *D*, mikil fredam gif hi *E*
81 Swo] Swa *D*, Sua *E*; hert] herte *D*; may] maẏ *D*; think] thenke *D*, thenk *E*; or] and *D*; eghe] ege *D*; see] se *DE*
82 That...forbiseen] Thet haue I thouth and forsen *D*, Thit i haue thouth and for sen *E*
83 wil] wille *D*; euer been] aẏ mare ben *D*, euerben *E*
84 Samening] Samenyng *D*; minstre] minister *D*, minster *E*
85 Last follik'] *obscured by red stain B*, last fullike *D*, last fullic *E*; wit outen] with outen *D*, widouten *E*
86 thas] thase *D*
87 helpes] filsenen *D*, filsen *E*; to] the *supra lineam E*; thowen] id est uilla *supra lineam B*, stowe. Amen. *D*, couen *E*

Translation[a]

This know all men, whoever they be,
Who hear and see this charter,
That I, Athelstan the king,
Have granted and given to St John
Of Beverley — so I say to you —
Toll and team, that know now ye,
(And) sok and sac over all the land
That is given into his (St John's) hand
In every king's day.
Be it wholly free, for ever and aye,
[And in that land also, by my advice,
Which one Archbishop 'Aluered' (Aldred)
Has acquired in his days
Either with gifts or with sayings
With gifts or with purchase
That I say to you by the King of Heaven]
Be it in frankalmoign, be all free,
As regards every man and even as regards myself;
Thus I decree, by Him that made me!
Except as regards one archbishop
And as regards the seven minster-priests
That serve God where St John rests.
This give I to God and St John
Here, before you every one,
All my daintiest corn, every bit of it,
To uphold his minster well,
Yea! four thraves, by the King of heaven,
From every plough in the East Riding.
If it so betide, or so happens
That any man takes (part) here-against,
Be he baron or be he earl,
Clerk or priest, parson or churl,
(Unless the same be wholly a stranger) —
I desire to announce that he must come.
So know ye well, before and beforehand,
To St John's minster-door;
And there I desire — so Christ advise me —
That he make amends for his misdeed;

Or he shall be cursed, soon anon,
By all that serve St John.
If it so betide, and so is,
That the man is excommunicate,
I tell you, beyond forty days,
Let such then be St John's laws,
That the chapter of Beverley
Unto the sheriff of York
Must send their writ, soon anon,
That this excommunicate man be taken;
The sheriff then, so I tell thee,
Without any writ from me,
Shall arrest him — so Christ advise me!
And lead him into my prison,
And keep him, that is my will,
Until he make amends for his misguilt.
If men propose new laws
In any other king's days,
If they be good, let them be observed,
(And) administered by those of the minster.
The amercement for the misdeed
I give to St John, so Christ advise me!
If one be summoned regarding limbs or life,
Or (if) men claim land in opposition
Against my decree, by a writ of right,
I desire that St John have the authority
That no one shall fight for it in the field
Either with staff, or with shield;
But I desire that twelve men shall decide it;
So shall it be — so may I bear the bell!
And as for him that may refuse for him (to do) so,
Away from men let him be, for ever and aye;
(Just) as if he were overcome in the field,
Let his confession of defeat be taken.
This grant I to God and St John
Here before you, every one;
If one be found slain, or drowned,
Or dead within St John's precinct,
Let his own men, without deceit,

His own bailiffs, namely, hold the view (of him);
Let no other coroner have the power.
So much freedom I give thee
As heart may think of or eye may see.
Thus have I thought and provided for.
I desire that there [may] ever be
A congregation and minster life
Lasting here, without strife.
God help all those same men
That give their help to the town.

[a] *Translation taken from Leach,* Memorials II, *pp. 280–7 (except lines 11–16)*

12 bears no resemblance to any other genuine Anglo-Saxon charter and is clearly spurious. Its form and language are very similar to **16** (**16** is an expanded, Middle English version of the Latin **15**) in the Ripon archive and the two require joint consideration (see further below).

There are three principal manuscript witnesses to **12**, given as manuscripts B, D and E above; the Schøyen manuscript (D) has only very recently been identified as having a copy of **12** in it. The single-sheet Cotton Charter iv.18 (B) was dated by Witty to the beginning of the fourteenth century but most recently by I. Doyle to the middle of the fourteenth century (Witty 1921, p. 37 and I. Doyle in Morris and Cambridge 1989, p. 20). This manuscript measures 26.7 cm along the top and 16.7 cm along its side. The charter is written across the page in continuous prose as if in the guise of an official diploma. There are comma stops throughout the single-sheet document which mark out its metre (Witty 1921, p. 41). It is endorsed on the bottom right corner of its verso by a fifteenth-century hand ('carta adelstani facta sancto johanni Beuerl'). It is cast in the name of King Æthelstan and written in rhyming couplets. It is listed in Brown *et al.*, *Index*, no. 3300 and, in a more accurate entry, in Boffey and Edwards, *Index*, no. 3300. McIntosh *et al.*, *Linguistic Atlas* I, p. 105, state that it is written in a dialect of the East Riding of Yorkshire (see also Earle, *Hand-Book*, p. 437; and Witty 1921, p. 36, who notes that it is 'certainly by a South Northumbrian or a North Mercian scribe').

The Schøyen manuscript (D) is an English production (which may display links with London and Cambridge; see above, pp. 198–9) and the part that contains a copy of **12** has been dated to the early or mid-fourteenth century (for the origin and dating criteria regarding D, see above, *ibid.*; for its contents, see Griffiths 1995, pp. 37–8, where the copy of **12** is not noted). A later version of **12** is preserved in the Beverley Cartulary (BL, Additional 61901), a manuscript of the late fourteenth century, here given as manuscript E. This is also listed in McIntosh *et al.*, *Linguistic Atlas* I, p. 103, where it is described as being written in a dialect of northern Middle English. The copy of the charter itself is introduced by a rubric written in red which states: 'Carta adelstani regis benedicti quam dedit et concessit in perpetuum beato Iohanni Beuerlaci'.

There is reason to believe that multiple versions of this charter may have existed. As we shall see below, **12** in its current form has been dated to the early 1330s, at a time when the issue of Beverley's rights to thraves, that is a render of grain, was in debate. But a letter from an earlier period, dated 9 April 1289, preserved in the register of John le Romeyn, archbishop of York from 1285 to 1296, from the archbishop himself to a certain James, Cardinal Deacon of S. Maria in Via Lata, demonstrates that the archbishop had, in 1289, seen an earlier version of the rhyming charter (for the letter, see Leach, *Memorials* II, pp. 156–7; for further discussion, see Woodman 2012). It may be that this version referred to by Archbishop Romeyn did not justify Beverley's rights to thraves and so it was later updated, in the 1330s, into the form represented by **12**.

It is difficult to know whether the single-sheet Cotton Charter iv.18 (B) or whether the Schøyen manuscript (D) preserves the earliest copy of **12**. For the moment it seems most sensible to accept that they are of roughly contemporary date. Analysis of the textual variations preserved in these copies, suggests that the Schøyen manuscript (D) and the Beverley Cartulary (E) have been copied from a similar version of **12**. This is most clear in the textual variations for lines 29, 47 and 87, although D has *stowe* in line 87 where E has *couen*, which perhaps we would not expect. It is also clear in the fact that D and E both preserve six lines not found at all in the single-sheet version (B), given in the edited text as lines 11–16. (These extra lines are marked out in the margins of the Beverley Cartulary by *va* at the beginning and *cat* at the end in a marginal hand dated to the late fourteenth- or early fifteenth-century; see I. Doyle, in Morris and Cambridge 1989, p. 20.) The single-sheet Cotton Charter iv.18 (B) may therefore have been copied from a different version of **12** and since there is evidence to suggest that there were multiple, earlier versions of this charter made (see above), this is not a difficult conclusion to accept.

Apart from variations in spelling, the six extra lines in D and E are the main difference between these copies and the single-sheet version, B. Since Middle English would have been the native language of the scribes of B, D and E, it has seemed inappropriate to interfere too much with the edited text. In the vast majority of cases I have therefore followed the reading of B and supplied all the variants given by D and E, in order to demonstrate the dialectal differences between the three versions. Since manuscripts M and P are direct copies of E, I have chosen not to list their variants in the critical apparatus.

As already mentioned, both B and E preserve indications that they were written by northern scribes. Typical northern characteristics include: use of *-es* in the third person singular instead of *-eth* (*serues*, line 22); *swa* instead of southern *swo* on line 29; *gaas* and *taas* instead of *goas* and *toas* on lines 29 to 30; *na…na*, using a northern *a*, on line 33; *thair*, a northern form, influenced by Scandinavian usage on line 47; *sal*, another northern form, on line 51 and *thar*, a northern *a* instead of *e* on line 83. There are numerous other examples. The fact that both scribes use *swo* as well as the northern form *swa* may indicate that they were comfortable with southern forms or that they were working in a border area. (I am very grateful to Dr R. Dance, Dr J. Wade and Dr J. Weiss for advice on the language of **12**.) The copy of **12** found in D also preserves some of these northern linguistic features (such as the use of *-es* in the third person singular or *swa* instead of *swo*), which are likely to be representative of the copyist's exemplar. I. Doyle considered the cartulary copy (E) to be inferior to the single-sheet copy (B), perhaps resulting from the scribe's 'incomprehension of the language he was trying to preserve or a very difficult exemplar' (I. Doyle in Morris and Cambridge 1989, p. 32, n. 113).

12 purports to grant toll and team and sake and soke (lines 6–7); *almousend* (lines 11–17; in Old French 'Almosner' = 'to give as alms' and therefore this should be thought of as a grant of 'frankalmoign'; see Leach, *Memorials* II, p. 281, n.); four thraves of corn from every plough in the East Riding of Yorkshire (lines 23–54; a thrave consists of two stooks of corn, each containing twelve sheaves; a plough is presumably a reference to the division of Yorkshire land into 'ploughlands', for which see earlier documents in the York archive, such as **7**); a writ *de excommunicando capiendo* (lines 42–54); the right to 'trial by battle' and 'trial by jury' (lines 61–72); the office of coroner (lines 73–9); and finally that there always be Minster life (*minstre lif*) there (lines 83–5).

Some of the rights and concessions being granted here could conceivably have a basis in Anglo-Saxon times, despite the fact that most of the document describes a situation which clearly belongs to a much later period. Toll and team and sake and soke are regularly granted in Anglo-Saxon documents (there are various examples in documents in the York archive; see **14** for an explanation of toll and team and **2** for an explanation of sake and soke) and it may be the case that the Beverley composer of **12** took the Beverley writ below, **14**, as his example as it grants all of these rights to Archbishop Ealdred, a York metropolitan who took great interest in the fortunes of Beverley Minster (see above, pp. 184–7). There are other hints that **12** may have been compiled by reference to extant Anglo-Saxon documents, for example the mention of seven Minster priests (*seuen minstre Prestes*), which was an aspect of Beverley's ancient constitution (for more on this see above, p. 181, n. 44). **12** ends by stating Æthelstan's wish that there always be Minster life at Beverley (*I wil that thar <may> ever been, Samening and minstre lif*), which bears resemblance to this statement in **13** in the Beverley archive: *7 ic wille ꝥ þær æfre beo mynsterlif 7 samnung þa hwile þe ænig mann leofað*. Whilst it is important to recognise that **12** may be relying on older documents, perhaps Anglo-Saxon documents still in the Beverley archive in the early fourteenth century, it is also entirely possible that notions of toll and team and sake and soke and so on, were so commonly established that the forger of **12** simply inserted them on the basis of his own knowledge. Indeed it is noticeable that none of the rights conveyed, which could perhaps belong to an Anglo-Saxon context, are particularly specific.

Lines 67–8 refer to twelve men who were to decide the outcome of any dispute (*Bot twelve men wil i that it telle, Swo sal it be swo heer ibelle*). Whilst law-codes of Æthelred clearly refer to such a judicial system involving twelve leading men from each wapentake in an Anglo-Saxon context (see III Æthlered 3.1, from the code issued at Wantage; see also GDB, f. 336r, the Lincolnshire survey, and its reference to 'twelve lawmen'; for the theory that the origins of the jury system were to be found after the 1166 Assize of Clarendon, see N.D. Hurnard, 'The Jury of Presentment and the Assize of Clarendon', *EHR* lvi [1941], pp. 374–410), here, in **12**, this method of trial is referred to alongside so-called 'trial by battle', which firmly dates it from beyond the Anglo-Saxon period (see Leach, *Memorials* II, p. 285, n; twelve 'governors of Beverley' can be found in *idem*, *Memorials* I, p. 384). Trial by battle involved two litigants settling their dispute in a duel. Quarterstaffs were used as were rectangular shields and these are referred to in **12**: *Nowther wit staf, no wit sheeld*.

Another clearly post-Conquest office referred to in **12** is that of the coroner (in line 79). Various historians have argued that the office of coroner could perhaps have originated before the Conquest but Hunnisett has shown that it actually originated in the articles of the September 1194 eyre; chapter twenty makes the following provision: 'praeterea in quolibet comitatu eligantur tres milites et unus clericus custodes placitorum coronae'; see W. Stubbs, ed., *Select Charters and other Illustrations of English Constitutional History* *from the Earliest Times to the Reign of Edward the First*, 9th edn, revised by H.W.C. Davis (Oxford, 1913), p. 254; see also R.F. Hunnisett, 'The Origins of the Office of Coroner', *Transactions of the Royal Historical Society*, 5th series, viii (1958), pp. 85–104, at p. 95, for the theory that the twelfth-century serjeant may have previously performed many of the duties of the coroner; for more on the coroner, see R.F. Hunnisett, *The Medieval Coroner* (Cambridge, 1961). Coroners were men of high status and power, often wealthy landowners. They had manifold administrative and inquisitorial duties and were introduced at a time when Richard I needed to keep tight rein on his finances raised through crown pleas in order to pay for various ransoms and wars. Some duties were specific to the coroner, for example the holding of inquests on dead bodies, the receiving of abjurations of the realm following a sanctuary case (therefore an office particularly pertinent to Beverley's needs), 'confessions of felons and appeals of approvers, and attending and sometimes organizing exactions and outlawries promulgated in the county court' (R.F. Hunnisett, *The Medieval Coroner*, p. 1). The law dictated that a coroner was to be amerced for any failure to record the details of his duties and so it is that the coroners' rolls today are some of the most useful medieval records for historians (see R.F. Hunnisett, 'The Origins of the Office of Coroner', p. 98, n. 3).

Line seventeen of **12** defines the grant as being 'almousend'. Leach, *Memorials* II, p. 281, n., suggests that this is a reference to the tenure of frankalmoign. This is a tenure by which religious houses held their lands and was common after the beginning of the twelfth century. A grant of frankalmoign is indicated by use of the Latin 'in elemosinam' (thus we have the related 'almousend' in **12**), followed by one, or a combination of, the adjectives 'libera', 'pura' and 'perpetua'. It was defined more specifically in 1219 when a distinction was made between two types of frankalmoign: that held in free alms and that held in pure alms. In theory land given as free alms still owed some form of service to the lord, whilst that given in pure and perpetual alms was quit from service. But this seems to have been the view of legal theorists like Bracton; in reality, charters indicate that lands given in frankalmoign tenure, whether they were in 'free alms' or 'pure alms', could always have a service attached and there are many examples where religious houses are made to do service to the grantor of frankalmoign lands; for all of this information, see E.G. Kimball, 'Tenure in Frank Almoign and Secular Services', *EHR* xliii (1928), pp. 341–53; for the judicial aspects of frankalmoign lands, see E.G. Kimball, 'The Judicial Aspects of Frank Almoign Tenure', *EHR* clxxxv (1932), pp. 1–11 and A.W. Douglas, 'Frankalmoin and Jurisdictional Immunity: Maitland Revisited', *Speculum* liii (1978), pp. 26–48. But the main difference between land granted as frankalmoign to a religious establishment, and land granted as socage to a secular person or institution, was that, since the grant was made primarily to God, the religious frankalmoign tenant was expected to deliver indefinite spiritual service in the form of prayers for the grantor (see E.G. Kimball, 'Tenure in Frank Almoign', p. 353; the issue of frankalmoign and secular burdens became particularly acute in 1258 with the petition of the barons at Oxford and the resultant documents relating to the provisions of Oxford; see W. Stubbs, *Select Charters*, pp. 369–89).

One of the most remarkable claims of **12** is contained in lines 35–48, where it is stated that the Beverley community has the right to send a writ directly to the sheriff of Yorkshire to request the arrest of certain excommunicated men and that this writ does not have to be confirmed by the king. Leach, *Memorials* II, p. 287, describes this as a writ *de excommunicato capiendo* and notes that this is an exceptional privilege which most more prestigious religious institutions, such as Winchester, did not have the right to. The Beverley *Chapter Act Book* seems to indicate how this process worked. First the Beverley provost and chapter had the right to excommunicate those who withheld thraves from them; in this particular instance we learn about the case of William of Briggham. Second, there is a letter dated 1318 sent by the king to the sheriff of York, which details that the Beverley community could have people arrested without having to wait for permission from a royal writ: *...etiam non expectato alio mandato secundum consuetudinem regni nostri, a Vicecomite Eboracensi et Ballivis nostris de Eboracsira capiantur et teneantur...* (for William of Briggham's excommunication and for the 1318 royal letter, see Leach, *Memorials* I, pp. 365–6). If we can accept these details as true, then Beverley Minster was a power to be reckoned with and this accords well with lines 49–52, which hint at the Minster's role in administering law in the locality (but only on the Minster's own terms).

It may be that the composition of **12** as it is preserved today can be dated more narrowly, to about 1330–1. It was at this time that the parochial clergy of the East Riding of Yorkshire actively complained and withheld payment of thraves to Beverley Minster. The right to thraves was crucially important to Beverley Minster and it is no coincidence that many of the entries in their *Chapter Act Book* are concerned with this privilege. Since a very large proportion of **12** is devoted to the issue of thraves and Beverley's rights to them, Leach and Witty both thought that **12** must have been composed at this time (see Leach, *Memorials* II, p. lviii and Witty 1921, p. 36 respectively). In an attempt to assert their rights, the Beverley clergy appointed one from their own number, Nicholas of Hugate, to represent their claims at Parliament. Hugate can be found taking copies of various charters with him and it may have been as a result of Hugate's actions that an exemplar of **12** was available in London to be copied into the Schøyen manuscript (for Hugate as recipient of an Inspeximus charter, see above, p. 189). On 7 October 1334 the matter was addressed in a letter from King Edward III. It seems as if Nicholas of Hugate must have succeeded in championing Beverley's case at Parliament for this letter states that warnings have been given to the parochial churches of the East Riding that they should recognise Beverley's rights to collect thraves; in particular the rectors of the churches of Harthill seem to have been a problem and the letter commands them not to obstruct the collection of thraves (Leach, *Memorials* II, pp. 109–10). Towards its close, the letter states famously that people 'should not insert their scythes into another's crop' (*...falcesque suas in messem non immittere alienam*).

It seems very likely that **12** was concocted to fill the lacuna in Beverley's documentary evidence from the Anglo-Saxon period (for the practical importance of **12**, which was quoted in *Quo Warranto* proceedings of 1338, see Woodman 2012). It was designed to explain and justify the manifold rights the Minster owned, in particular thraves, and as such it takes on the form of a *pancarte*. Whilst it is an obvious forgery, many of the rights it claims may indeed have belonged to the Minster (Leach, *Memorials* I, p. xxviii, describes it as an 'excellent summary of real charters'). In making its point it called on the name of the first king of a united Anglo-Saxon England, one known to have been generous to northern churches. This fabricated tradition was designed to guarantee the extent and authority of the rights claimed.

The connection with Æthelstan provided by **12** was evidently important to the Beverley community and Æthelstan is thus commemorated in various monuments and images built in to the very fabric of the Minster today (for the notion that **12**'s view of Æthelstan as founder became important for the canons of Beverley Minster so as to combat the intrusion of Archbishop Neville in the early 1380s, see Woodman 2012). So we find a fourteenth-century corbel in the north choir aisle in which King Æthelstan is depicted handing over a sealed charter (presumably a reference to **12**) to Bishop John. And this tradition continued to thrive. In the late eighteenth century, in front of the decorative choir screen, William Collins built two statues, one of Æthelstan and one of St John (see Horrox, *Beverley*, plate vii and p. 101, for the corbel and for the statues, respectively).

Perhaps more interesting still, there exists today a fifteenth-century wall panel in Beverley Minster which depicts King Æthelstan giving a sealed charter to Bishop John and which has the words *Als fre make I the, as hert may thynke, or eghe may see* written on it (see Horrox, *Beverley*, plate ix). Again this is reference to the famous lines 80–1 of **12**: *Swa mikel fredom giue I the, Swo hert may think or eghe see* (the same sentiments are expressed in **16** in the Ripon archive, *And in all thyngges be als free, As herte may thynk or egh may se*, which shows the close connection between these rhyming documents in the name of Æthelstan). From the evidence of **1** in the York archive, we saw the very great and real strides Æthelstan made in trying to incorporate Northumbria into his rule. It is fitting that Beverley and Ripon, two archiepiscopal minsters, when creating accounts of their origins and privileges, thought it entirely appropriate to cast two forgeries, **12** and **16**, in the name of Æthelstan. Written in Middle English, they were easily accessible and memorable (for the possibility that **12** and **16** were by the same author, see I. Doyle in Morris and Cambridge 1989, p. 20; for more detail about the connections between these two documents, see the commentary to **16**). And the continued importance and interest of **12** is shown by Leland's visit to Beverley Minster in the sixteenth century and his record of: 'charta ibidem Æthelstani regis de immunitate et libertate, denique asylo terrarum S. Joannis, Saxonice scripta' (see Leach, *Memorials* II, p. 350).

13

King Edward declares that Archbishop Ealdred has his permission to draw up a priuilegium *for all the lands pertaining to St John's Minster at Beverley; and that the Minster and its property shall be as free as any other minster.*

[A.D. 1060 × 1065]

Old English:
C. TNA: PRO Ch.R. 4 Edw. II, m. 20, no. 52: Inspeximus, 7 September, 1310
E. BL Additional 61901, 87v–88r: copy of G, s. xiv^{ex}
F. TNA: PRO Ch.R. 4 Edw. III, m. 13, no. 25: Inspeximus, 30 November, 1330
G. TNA: PRO Pat. R. 1 Ric. II, pt. 3, m. 8: Inspeximus, 10 February, 1378
H. TNA: PRO Pat. R. 5 Ric. II, pt. 2, m. 13: Inspeximus, 26 April, 1382
I. TNA: PRO Pat. R. 2 Hen. IV, pt. 2, m. 6: Inspeximus, 1 March, 1401
J. TNA: PRO Ch. R. 1 Hen. V, pt. 1, m. 11, no. 5: Inspeximus, 25 November, 1413
K. TNA: PRO Ch. R. 3–4 Hen. V, m. 24, no. 15: Inspeximus, 20 June, 1415
L. TNA: PRO Pat. R. 6 Hen. VI, pt. 2, m. 6: Inspeximus, 13 March, 1428
N. TNA: PRO Conf. R. 26, 1 Hen. VIII, pt. 2, no. 13: Inspeximus, 1509
O. TNA: PRO Confr. R. 75, 3+4 Phil. and Mary, pt. 1, no. 15: Inspeximus, 1556–7
P. BL Cotton Otho C. xvi, 98rv: copy of E, s. xvi^{ex}
Q. BL MS Harley 560, 40rv: copy of P, s. xvii^{in}
W. BL Lansdowne 446, 89: copy of C, s. xviii

Latin:
E. BL Additional 61901, 69v–70r: copy, s. xiv^{ex}
P. BL Cotton Otho C. xvi, 81v: copy of E, s. xvi^{ex}
Q. BL Harley 560, 23r: copy of P, s. xvii^{in}
Ed.: a. Poulson, *Beverlac* I, p. 42, from W
b. Kemble 1343
c. Thorpe, *Diplomatarium*, p. 391
d. Farrer, *EYC*, no. 87, from C
e. Harmer, *Writs*, no. 7, from C
f. *Councils and Synods*, no. 81, from C
Translated: Harmer, *Writs*, pp. 137–8
Listed: Sawyer 1067; Hart, *ECNE*, no. 137
Edited from Manuscript C

+ Eadƿeard cyngc gret Tostig eorl ⁊ ealle mine þegenas on Eoferƿicscire freondlice. ⁊ ic cyðe eoƿ ꝥ hit is min unna ⁊ min fulle leafe ꝥ Ealdred arcebisceop ꝥ he dihte priuilegium to þam landan þe licgað[a] innto Sancte Iohannes mynstre æt Beferlicc. ⁊ ic ƿille ꝥ ꝥ mynster ⁊ seo are þe þider innto hirð. ꝥ hit beo sƿa freols sƿa ænig oþer mynster is æt eallan þingan. ⁊ loc hƿilc bisceop þær ofer byð ꝥ hit beo him underþeod. ⁊ ꝥ he beo þær to geheald ⁊ mund under me. ꝥ þær nan[b] mann nan þing on ne teo butan he. ⁊ ꝥ he na geþafige ꝥ man þanon ut do ænig þæra þinga. þæs þe þær mid rihte to gebyrað. sƿa sƿa he ƿille beon ƿið Godd geborgen ⁊ Sanctus[c] Iohannes. ⁊ eallra þæra halgena þe seo halige stoƿ is fore gehalgod. ⁊ ic ƿille ꝥ þær æfre beo mynsterlif ⁊ samnung þa hƿile þe ænig mann leofað.

[a] ligead C [b] *obscured by black stain* C [c] *For* sancte

Translation[a]

+ King Edward sends friendly greetings to Earl Tostig and all my thegns in Yorkshire. And I inform you that Archbishop Ealdred has my consent and full permission to draw up a *priuilegium* for the lands that belong to St John's minster at Beverley. And my will is that the minster and the property belonging thereto shall be as free as any other minster is in all things: and, look you, whatever bishop shall be over it, that it be subject to him, and that he be its protector and guardian under me, so that no one but he shall take anything from it and so that he shall not permit to be alienated any of the things that lawfully pertain thereto, in so far as he wishes to be secure from [incurring the anger of] God and St John and all the saints in whose honour the holy foundation is consecrated. And my will is that minster-life and assembly shall be always maintained there as long as any man shall live.

[a] *Translation taken from Harmer,* Writs, *pp. 137–8 (with one slight modification)*

Latin Version (from Manuscript E):

Edwardus rex Tosti comiti et omnibus baronibus suis in Euerwiksyra salutem. Notum uobis facio quod hec est mea uoluntas et mea plena licencia quod Aldredus archiepiscopus dictet priuilegium ad omnes illas terras que adiacent ad ecclesiam sancti iohanis apud Beuerlacum. Et volo ut ecclesia illa et elemosina que illic seruit, sit ita libera sicut aliqua alia ecclesia est in omnibus rebus. Et uideat quicumque episcopus ibi fuerit, quod ecclesia illa sit ei obediens, et quod ipse sit ibi eius manutentor et protector sub me, ne aliquis aliquam ibi potestatem exerceat preter ipsum, et ne paciatur aliquem alienare ab illa ecclesia quicquam quod ad illam iuste pertineat; sicut ipse uult saluari a deo et sancto iohanne et omnibus sanctis pro quibus sanctus ille locus sanctificatus est. Et ego uolo ut ibi semper sit ecclesiastica uita et congregacio, quamdiu aliquis uixerit.

The earliest copy of **13** survives as an enrolled Inspeximus charter in a Charter Roll dated 7 September, 1310, the fourth year of Edward II's reign; it is this Inspeximus that forms the basis of the edited text of **13** (the Old English copy of **13** in the Beverley Cartulary was made from the Inspeximus charter in the first year of Richard II's reign, manuscript G, and is therefore not an independent witness). There seems to be no good reason to doubt the fundamental authenticity of **13** a document which, as we shall see, throws light on the possible circumstances in which an Anglo-Saxon charter might be produced.

13 is addressed to Earl Tostig (1055–65) and his Yorkshire thegns and it declares that Archbishop Ealdred (1060–9) has the right to draw up his own *priuilegium* for those lands belonging to St John's Minster at Beverley. The *Chronicle of the Archbishops of York*, a mid-twelfth century compilation, states that Ealdred, an influential man in political as well as ecclesiastical spheres, did more than many of his archiepiscopal predecessors when it came to supporting the houses of secular canons in York and he seems to have tried to consolidate a *vita communis* for the Beverley community (for Ealdred, see above, pp. 65–8 and 184–7). Having such a powerful figure as archbishop of York would have been a significant advantage for a minster in York's diocese, and in Ealdred's control, like Beverley.

Perhaps the most notable aspect of **13** is that it seems to delegate the production of a royal diploma not to royal scribes but to an ecclesiastical and local scriptorium. **13** therefore affords important evidence for how permission might be granted to some person, presumably a trusted individual, to draw up his own diploma without consulting the chancery (**21** is an interesting example in this connection of a late eleventh century writ granting various rights to a certain beneficiary, that was seemingly drawn up without acknowledgement of the king, in the north-west of the country; see further the commentary to this document). Since Ealdred had acted as a diplomat more than once for King Edward (above, pp. 67–8), it seems plausible that Edward could also trust the archbishop to draw up his own *priuilegium* for Beverley Minster. Together with two writs from the York archive, **9** and **10**, **13** demonstrates that Ealdred was permitted to operate with a good deal of freedom in the north of England.

Harmer has highlighted three other extant Anglo-Saxon writs which seem to delegate the production of charters to interested ecclesiastics (Harmer, *Writs*, pp. 38–41): one in the Christ Church, Canterbury archive, S 985, in which King Cnut declares that Archbishop

Lyfing has permission to draw up a charter of freedom; another in the St Denis archive in the name of King Edward (S 1105), granting Bishop Wulfwig permission to draw up a charter; and the last from the Wells archive is again granted by King Edward but this time to Bishop Giso, who is given permission to draw up a *priuilegium*, S 1115 (*Wells* 37). Keynes has demonstrated that King Edward quite often delegated the composition of charters to Giso, for lands in which Giso had an interest (Keynes 1988, esp. pp. 203–4; Keynes 1997, esp. pp. 227–39). Keynes further suggests that S 1042 (*Wells* 40), a general confirmation of lands and privileges for the Wells bishopric made in 1065, was a kind of *pancarte* composed by Giso himself on behalf of Wells (Keynes 1988, pp. 203–4; Keynes 1997, pp. 231–9; but see also the discussion by Kelly, *Bath and Wells*, pp. 241–7, esp. pp. 242–5, who suggests that, while it is difficult to be sure about the authenticity of this particular document, it is perhaps more likely to be a fabrication made after its supposed date of issue in 1065).

It is in the context of Giso's relationship with King Edward, that **13** becomes all the more interesting. It demonstrates a similar understanding between the Confessor and Archbishop Ealdred. Whilst we do not have the resultant *priuilegium* drawn up by Ealdred, **13** does envisage that the *priuilegium* will cover 'the lands that belong to St John's Minster at Beverley', suggesting that Beverley may once have possessed a form of *pancarte*, similar to S 1042 (*Wells* 40) produced by Giso (but see also the remarks of Kelly, *Bath and Wells*, pp. 242–5, on the perhaps dubious authenticity of this charter). (For the notion that the existence of **13** perhaps inspired the forging of **11**, see the commentary to **11**.) It may be possible to gain a better impression of what Ealdred's charter might have granted if we look at the evidence of Domesday Book and later writs (see Harmer, *Writs*, p. 432, for more detail on what follows). Domesday Book declares that in all the land of St John (i.e. Beverley Minster) 'neither the king, nor the earl, nor anyone else, had any customary dues there' (GDB, f. 298v). It also states that 'St John's carucate was always free from the king's geld' (GDB, f. 304r) and Harmer points out that a writ in the name of Henry I suggests that some of Beverley's lands had been free from the payment of geld in the time of both Edward and William (Harmer, *Writs*, p. 432; for other examples of communities exempted from geld, and further discussion, see Giandrea, *Episcopal Culture*, pp. 153–4). A writ issued by William the Conqueror in the period 1067 × 1069 again allows Archbishop Ealdred to draw up a second *priuilegium*, specifically for the lands belonging to the church of St John of Beverley and stipulating also that these same lands be free from the demands of the king, his reeves and all his men (Bates, *RRAN: William I*, no. 32). Another writ in the name of William the Conqueror (dated 1066 × September 1069) grants sake and soke to Beverley over all those lands given to it in the time of King Edward, and also over those lands subsequently acquired by Ealdred in William's reign, and finally it states that these are to be free in relation to the king and all men (Bates, *RRAN: William I*, no. 31). We can speculate, as Harmer does, that Ealdred's *priuilegium* may have covered all, or at least a combination, of these rights and lands described (Harmer, *Writs*, p. 432).

14

King Edward declares that he has granted to Archbishop Ealdred judicial and financial rights over his men within the king's own soke as fully and as completely as the archbishop has them in his own lands. [A.D. 1060 × 1065]

E. BL Additional 61901, 70r: copy, s. xiv[ex]
Rubric: De eodem. Aliud priuilegium dedit idem rex Edwardus archiepisco[po] Aldredo. Quod tale est.
P. BL Cotton Otho C. xvi, 81v–82r: copy of E, s. xvi[ex]
Q. BL Harley 560, 23r: copy of P, s. xvii[in]
Ed.: a. Farrer, *EYC*, no. 11, from Q
b. Harmer, *Writs*, no. 119, from Q
Listed: Sawyer 1160; Hart, *ECNE*, no. 118
Edited from Manuscript E

Edwardus rex Tosti comiti et omnibus baronibus suis[a] in Eboracensisyra[b] et in Nottinghamsyra salutem. Sciatis quod ego concessi Aldredo archiepiscopo ut ipse habeat sacam et socam[c] et toll et team super suos homines infra meam sacam et socam ita plenarie et principaliter sicut ipse habet in sua propria loca,[d] et nolo[e] ut aliquis ei auferat quod ego ei concessi.

[a] ? *For* meis [b] –ra *over erasure* E [c] so- *over erasure* E [d] lo- *over erasure* E [e] volo E

14 has survived only in Latin. Farrer, *EYC*, p. 29, questioned the authenticity of this writ as he could not understand why the thegns of Earl Tostig in Nottinghamshire, an area where Tostig had only a small amount of territory, would be addressed (*Tosti comiti et omnibus baronibus suis in Eboracensisyra et in Nottinghamsyra*). But reference to **13** might help: there Edward addresses both Tostig and *ealle mine þegenas*—i.e. the king's own thegns. If we are permitted to suggest a small textual emendation in **14** of *suis* to *meis* then this removes Farrer's objection and perhaps makes better sense (Farrer, *EYC*, p. 29, himself wonders 'perhaps also *suis* should be *meis*'); it would then follow that the thegns of Nottinghamshire were being addressed because that was one area where the church of York owned a significant amount of land (for this, see Harmer, *Writs*, pp. 413–14). Thus **14** can be accepted as a post-Conquest translation of an authentic Old English writ (use of the Latin *baro* to mean 'thegn' demonstrates that this translation was made after the Norman Conquest; see Harmer, *Writs*, pp. 414 and 428; see also S 1078, S 1092 [*St Aug's* 39] and S 1100). In many ways, **14** is almost a confirmation of those rights granted previously by **9**: we again learn that King Edward has granted to Ealdred 'sake and soke' and 'toll and team' over his men. But **14** goes further than **9** by stating that Ealdred was to have these rights even when those men were resident within the king's own jurisdiction (*infra meam sacam et socam*; on which see further below). Ealdred is to hold these rights as fully as if on lands that were his own.

The protocol of **14** is clearly a Latin rendering of the standard Old English salutation seen at the beginning of most Anglo-Saxon writs. It is useful in this regard to compare **14** to S 1068 from the Bury St Edmund's archive, a writ which survives both in its original Old English and in a translated Latin version; and there the Latin is very close to that in

14. A similar comparison can be made for the declaration in **14**. At first sight the Latin *Sciatis quod* seems to be rather different from the usual Old English declaration of *ic cyðe eow þæt*, as the Latin removes the first person singular. But there are various Latin versions of writs which show that this is how the Old English could be translated. Thus S 1091 (*St Aug's* 35) has *Sciatis me dedisse*, S 1106 has the similar *notum vobis sit quod*; see also S 1068, S 1072, S 1100, S 1111 (*Wells* 33), S 1112 (*Wells* 34) and S 1113 (*Wells* 35). The rights being conveyed in **14** (i.e. of 'sake and soke' and 'toll and team') are readily paralleled, as is the phrase *ita plenarie et principaliter*, whose Old English equivalent is *swa ful ond swa forð*; sometimes this is rendered in Latin translations of Old English writs as *tam plene et tam plane*; see S 1101 and S 1102. A slightly unusual concession in **14** is that which grants these rights to Ealdred not only over his own men but also over those men who live on the king's own land. As Harmer, *Writs*, p. 413, points out, an Ely writ contains a similar condition, which allows Abbot Wulfric toll and team 'wherever his man may dwell, whatever he may do'. Harmer, *Writs*, p. 414, also suggests that where **14** has *infra meam sacam et socam* we would really expect simply *infra meam socam*. But by reference to a later York writ in the name of William I (see Bates, *RRAN: William I*, no. 351), Harmer shows that the translator of **14** almost certainly had an Old English passage in front of him which read *on mine socne*. **14** ends with a Latin rendering of a standard Old English prohibition clause; similar Latin renderings can be found in S 1065 (*Abing* 148), S 1100 and S 1111 (*Wells* 33).

On the beneficiary of **14**, Archbishop Ealdred, see above pp. 65–8 and 184–7, and also the commentary to **9** and **13**.

RIPON

INTRODUCTION

1. THE HISTORY AND ENDOWMENT OF RIPON MINSTER

Not a single genuine Anglo-Saxon charter survives in the archives of Ripon. **15** and **16**, both cast in the name of King Æthelstan, are clearly forgeries. Nevertheless, Ripon may have housed charters at various stages in its existence. The extensive landed possessions of perhaps its most famous member, Wilfrid, meant that he developed a keen interest in the acquisition of charters which confirmed his rights, to the extent that some scholars have suggested he was influential in the development and diffusion of diplomatic practice in Anglo-Saxon England. The *Life* of Wilfrid has a celebrated passage which describes the dedication of the Ripon church in terms which make it very likely that Stephanus, the author, was using a charter as his source.[1] It may be that this was some form of foundation charter, issued at the public dedication of St Peter's church, Ripon, and authenticated by its placing on the church altar. There is a strong probability that in the years following Wilfrid's death, various kings would have favoured Ripon Minster with charters granting lands and rights; that local men of high rank may have deposited copies of charters in the Minster for safe-keeping; that archbishops of York may have accumulated wealth and landed endowment on behalf of Ripon, which later became an archiepiscopal minster, the records of which Ripon would have stored.[2] But unfortunately these charters no longer exist and it may well be that events in the Anglo-Saxon period itself led to the wholesale destruction of the Minster's records. Certainly by the early thirteenth century there seems to be no trace of any genuine Anglo-Saxon documents preserved at Ripon.[3] But study of the endowment and history of Ripon Minster, although scantily and disproportionately recorded, allows at least an appreciation of the church's fortunes throughout the Anglo-Saxon period.[4]

[1] The relevant passage is *VW*, c. XVII; for discussion, see below, pp. 234–6. On Stephanus' authorship of the *Vita Wilfridi*, see Kirby 1983.

[2] Of course charters did not constitute the only means of recording land ownership and the Ripon church may also have developed other methods of documenting its assets; see above, pp. 6–9.

[3] See below, pp. 250–2.

[4] For historical details about Ripon Minster, see Gent, *Rippon*; Fowler, *MCPW*; Hall (R.A.) 1987; Hall (R.A.) 1995; Hall and Whyman 1996; and Jones 2000.

a. *The Pre-Wilfridian Ripon Site*

Ripon is situated roughly thirty miles to the north-west of York. The glacial origins of the site have created a naturally enclosed area, surrounded by the Kirkgate ridge to the west, the River Ure to the north and the River Skell to the south, features which may have been attractive to later monastic settlers.[5] But there was certainly settlement there before the seventh century since the place-name 'Ripon' is thought to derive from the Old English *Hrype*, the name of an Anglian people.[6] It is likely that their territory stretched as far southwards as Ripley, a place-name which means, 'the forest-glade or clearing of the folk called the *Hrype*' and which has *Hrype* and *leah* as its constituent elements.[7] Excavations at Ailcy Hill, a prominent mound which lies 200 metres to the east of the present-day Minster, have revealed many strata of burials. Radio-carbon dating of this site has yielded a date range of 560–660 for the earliest stratum, which makes it very likely that the cemetery was in use before the establishment of the minster at Ripon and thus by this Anglian people.[8]

We are singularly fortunate to possess a *Life* of Wilfrid written by a monk of Ripon called Stephanus, an account which affords a relatively substantial amount of information about the early Ripon community. But in its description of the minster set up at Ripon by Wilfrid, Stephanus fails, perhaps deliberately, to mention that Wilfrid was not the first to build a minster there.[9] Bede, in his *VCP*, provides more information: he states that Alhfrith, sub-king of Deira (*c.*

[5] See Hall and Whyman 1996, pp. 137–40. Hall and Whyman also suggest that the visible archaeological legacy left in the area from the Neolithic and Bronze Ages may have influenced the choice of Ripon as the location of a minster (at p. 63). For more on the geology of the area, see G.K. Lott in Coatsworth, *Corpus*, pp. 23–34.

[6] For Ripon, see *PN YorksWR* Part V, pp. 77–8 and 164–5; see also Hall (R.A.) 1995, p. 12. On the basis of wells dedicated to St Helen in the Ripon area, Jones suggests that there may well have been a '*locus sanctus* of the Britons in the Ripon district during the post-Roman period'; Jones 2000, p. 21. For the difficulties involved in using such evidence, see Blair, *Church*, pp. 379–80; for the significance of the term '*locus sanctus*', see below, pp. 235–6.

[7] For the suggestion about the extent of the territory of the *Hrype* people, see *PN YorksWR* Part V, p. 165; for Ripley, see *ibid.*, p. 101. For further discussion of the *Hrype* element and of Repton, see A. Rumble, ''Hrepingas' Reconsidered' in *Mercian Studies*, ed. A. Dornier (Leicester, 1977), pp. 169–72.

[8] See Hall (R.A.) 1987, p. 22, for the notion that Ailcy Hill was a 'late pagan, Anglian-conversion period cemetery'. Hall and Whyman 1996, p. 122, note that although no archaeological remnants of a structure have been found on Ailcy Hill, the evidence of large-scale quarrying on the summit perhaps suggests that there may at least have been room for a small building, perhaps a chapel. They also suggest that the use of this prominent land-feature by the Anglian people was designed to demonstrate their claim to the surrounding territory (at p. 120).

[9] Any details about Eata's foundation would have detracted from Stephanus' account of Wilfrid. In a similar fashion, Stephanus ignores the fact that Tuda was the first to be elected bishop in Colman's place after the council of Whitby in 664, preferring instead to imply that Wilfrid immediately took over; for the information about Tuda, see Bede, *HE*, iii.26.

655–64) and son of the powerful King Oswiu (who acceded to Bernicia in 642 and took control of Deira in 651; he died in 670), gave Eata, abbot of Melrose, 'for the redemption of his soul', a certain place called Ripon so that he could build a minster (*monasterium*) there as a dependency of Melrose.[10] Upon the creation of the new minster, Eata installed some of the Melrose brethren at Ripon, including Cuthbert himself who was appointed guestmaster. Eata is also said to have imposed the same, Irish, rule of discipline as practised at Melrose.[11]

b. *Wilfrid and Ripon: a 'Great Blast of Trial'?*

Bede implies that Eata's minster did not last long; he states that Eata and his brethren, when asked whether they would adhere to Roman customs, would not abandon their Irish ways and instead preferred to renounce the monastic site.[12] As a result of this abandonment, King Alhfrith was able to grant Ripon to Wilfrid.[13] This was possibly a politically charged gesture as King Oswiu, Alhfrith's father, had been baptised and brought up in the Irish tradition; meanwhile Alhfrith had come under the influence of Wilfrid, one of the foremost exponents of Roman customs.

From this moment, Ripon's fortunes were intimately connected to Wilfrid's career.[14] An extremely controversial character, he was at times exiled from Northumbria, and can be frequently found seeking political refuge in other kingdoms and indeed abroad.[15] Whilst this may have had a negative effect on the Ripon church, his high-standing and ability to acquire landed estates would have inevitably brought periods of prosperity too.[16] Stephanus states that around the year 660, Wilfrid received just such an acquistion: 'Alhfrith first gave St Wilfrid the confessor an estate of ten hides at *Stanforda*, and shortly afterwards, for the good of his own soul, he granted him the monastery at Ripon together with thirty

[10] Bede, *VCP*, c. VII; for Ripon as a monastic dependency on Melrose, see Charles-Edwards, *Ireland*, p. 319 and Blair, *Church*, pp. 185–6.

[11] Bede, *VCP*, c. VII. At some point after the departure of Cuthbert from Ripon (perhaps in the period 661–9), the plague came to Gilling and its inhabitants were forced to move to Ripon; for which see Plummer, *Bede* I, p. 389 and II, p. 372. For the possibility that Eata's minster had been an entirely separate building, constructed at a different location to Wilfrid's later minster (perhaps on the site known as 'Scott's Monument Yard'), see Hall and Whyman 1996, pp. 140–1.

[12] Bede, *HE*, iii.25. For the ejection of Eata and his monks, see Charles-Edwards, *Ireland*, p. 319; for a summary of Eata's career, see the entry by Lapidge in *Blackwell*, p. 157.

[13] See Bede, *HE*, iii.25; see also Bede, *VCP*, c. VIII.

[14] In many ways, York had a similar experience under Wilfrid; see above, pp. 29–32.

[15] For a useful overview, see Charles-Edwards, *Ireland*, pp. 339–43.

[16] Roper 1974, pp. 61–3, conveniently divides Wilfrid's career as a landholder into six phases, which coincide with his ecclesiastical career.

hides of land, and he was ordained abbot'.[17] *Stanforda* has most recently been identified as modern-day Stamford on the River Derwent in the East Riding of Yorkshire.[18] The manner in which Stephanus describes these gifts of land to Wilfrid suggests that Stamford, although roughly thirty-five miles to the south-east of Ripon, was originally intended as part of the early Ripon estate.[19]

Wilfrid's crucial role in the council of Whitby in 664, and the subsequent retirement of Bishop Colman, saw his promotion to bishop.[20] But his prolonged absence whilst on a journey to the Continent to be consecrated in Gaul resulted in Chad being raised up to the episcopal see of Northumbria in his place.[21] In the same chapter which describes Wilfrid's return to Ripon (but now in the demoted role of abbot), Stephanus describes how King Wulfhere of Mercia (658–74/5) allowed Wilfrid to perform 'various episcopal duties' in Mercia itself; and also granted Wilfrid 'many pieces of land', some of which was used for the purpose of founding minsters.

When Stephanus says that Wulfhere's generosity was motivated by 'sincere affection' (*cum vera dilectione*) for Wilfrid,[22] the historical likelihood is that Wilfrid, marginalised from Northumbria, was seeking to foster good relations with Mercian powers. Nevertheless the results for Ripon may ultimately have been positive. The individual head of their church was now powerful enough to acquire land and minsters in Mercia. And a later chapter of Stephanus' work, describing a meeting of the Ripon community with Wilfrid as convener, seemingly alludes to the fact that the Mercian monks installed in Wilfridian minsters were in many ways thought of as belonging to the Ripon community.[23] It would only

[17] *VW*, c. VIII; see also Bede, *HE*, v.19. Hall and Whyman 1996, p. 65, suggest a possible re-dating here; that it was only following the council of Whitby in 664, and with it the blow to Irish ecclesiastical customs, that Eata was forced to leave Ripon, meaning that Wilfrid could take over.

[18] See Jones 1995, p. 28. Previous scholars had suggested an equation with the Lincolnshire Stamford but Jones warns against this. Jones suggests that the ten hides at *Stanforda* 'had been severed from an older and much larger royal estate centred at Catton' (at p. 28) but the evidence he cites from Domesday Book seems inconclusive. For the later structure of the Ripon estate, see GDB, f. 303v; for suggestions about the early structure of the Ripon estate, see Jones 1995, p. 26 (at p. 27 for a map).

[19] There is a discrepancy in the details of this land grant to Ripon as recorded by Bede; in *HE*, iii.25, the grant is of 40 hides at Ripon itself, whereas in *HE*, v.19, it is of 30 hides at Ripon and 10 hides at Stamford. This may imply that Bede thought of the 10 hides at Stamford as belonging to the early Ripon estate. Jones 1995, p. 29, suggests that Stamford later became part of the York church's assets.

[20] *VW*, cc. X–XI and Bede, *HE*, iii.25.

[21] Chad's consecration in Wilfrid's place seems to have been sponsored by King Oswiu, presumably a reaction to the earlier political machinations of his son, King Alhfrith; see above, p. 231 and *VW*, c. XIV, which is explicit in saying that this consecration contravenes canon law; and also Bede, *HE*, iii.28, who describes Oswiu in this instance as *imitatus industriam filii*.

[22] *VW*, c. XIV.

[23] *VW*, c. LXIV.

be natural for a Wilfridian foundation in Mercia to look to not only Wilfrid, but also Wilfrid's main church, Ripon, for guidance and leadership.[24] And Wilfrid's influence extended yet further; following an invitation from Ecgberht, king of Kent (664–673), he was able to ordain various priests and deacons of Kent, many of whom may therefore have regarded Wilfrid, and thus Ripon, as their spiritual leaders.[25] In short, as Wilfrid's 'ecclesiastical kingdom' grew, so too must have Ripon's.[26]

Wilfrid's connections with the Continent are well known: it was to Gaul that he had travelled to be consecrated, and he was to make several trips to Rome. His journeys exposed him to continental religious practice and Stephanus tells us that Wilfrid brought back the Rule of Benedict to Northumbria, a significant development.[27] It is likely that Wilfrid's adoption of the Rule reveals something about Ripon's own constitution at this time.[28]

[24] Many minsters seem to have been involved in hierarchical relationships, the details of which are now unknown, owed either to a larger, more influential minster, or to a powerful individual, such as Wilfrid. For these issues, see Blair, *Church*, p. 83, where the example of Wilfrid and Mercia is discussed (also p. 83, n. 25 for important information and pp. 138–40, for more about Mercian foundations looking to Wilfrid's Ripon).

[25] *VW*, c. XIV; the importance of such ordinations is made clear in chapter XXI: 'almost all the abbots and abbesses of the monasteries dedicated their substance to him by vow, either keeping it themselves in his name or intending him to be their heir after their death'. Blair, *Church*, p. 95, wonders whether Wilfrid's influence on King Ecgberht led to the transformation of Reculver from Roman fort to a minster in 669. For Wilfrid's claims regarding his spiritual authority, see Charles-Edwards, *Ireland*, pp. 429–38.

[26] Stephanus is explicit in describing Wilfrid's acquisitions as constituting a *regnum ecclesiarum*; see, for example, *VW*, cc. XXI, XXIV. (For more on the idea of Wilfrid's lands being his own, personal possessions, see Roper 1974, p. 63.) These were the beginnings of an extensive monastic network set up by Wilfrid. Blair, *Church*, p. 97, emphasises the significant ability of Wilfrid to attract endowments from rival kings for the purpose of establishing minsters; and similarly his cosmopolitan outlook. On Wilfrid's monastic network, see Foot, *Monastic Life*, pp. 258–65.

[27] *VW*, c. XIV. For the role of Wilfrid and also of Benedict Biscop in bringing the Benedictine Rule to Northumbria, see, for example, Knowles, *Monastic Order*, p. 22.

[28] As Blair, *Church*, pp. 80–1 warns, we cannot label ecclesiastical houses as simply being 'Roman' or 'Irish'. In fact many strands of influence dictated the constitution of minsters. Indeed the very behaviour of Wilfrid himself at times seems far from that expected of a Benedictine and so should act as a deterrent against such a generalisation. Wilfrid's epitaph (recorded by Bede, *HE*, v.19) notes how Wilfrid brought monks to Ripon: 'Within these walls a swarm of monks he hived…'. It is perhaps worth noting that the Benedictine Rule takes it for granted that minsters will be given land with which to support themselves. Given that Wilfrid is renowned for his extensive landed possessions, there may be some hidden implications behind his introduction of the Rule into England; Roper 1974, pp. 63 and 67. See also P. Sims-Williams, *Religion and Literature in Western England, 600–800*, Cambridge Studies in Anglo-Saxon England 3 (Cambridge, 1990), pp. 117–18 and Charles-Edwards, *Ireland*, p. 325 (and p. 330, for the possible role of Wilfrid as patron of a copy of the Rule written in uncial extant as Oxford, Bodleian, Hatton MS 48).

The year 669 marked a turning point in Wilfrid's career: Chad was deposed by Archbishop Theodore and Wilfrid reclaimed the Northumbrian episcopal see. At this moment he was the undisputed bishop of Northumbria and he was able to turn his attention to the fabric of the Northumbrian church. He found the stone church at York, begun under Paulinus, in a parlous state and set about having it repaired and endowed with an appropriate amount of land.[29] He then began the building of a new church at Ripon, which was apparently of 'dressed stone, supported by various columns and side aisles'.[30]

Once the Ripon church was finished,[31] Wilfrid had the inside richly decorated and, during a solemn occasion in the presence of various important dignitaries, notably Kings Ecgfrith (670–85) and Ælfwine (*c.* 670–9), he dedicated it to St Peter. In a remarkable passage which owes much to charter diplomatic, Stephanus describes how Wilfrid stood in front of the altar and read out the names of those places and regions to be given to Ripon. Just like the witness-list of a charter, Stephanus details the status of the men present, beginning with those of highest rank, 'the two most Christian kings and brothers, Ecgfrith and Ælfwini,' and descending to 'the abbots, the reeves and the sub-kings; dignitaries of every kind gathered together... they consecrated the house and dedicated it to the Lord in honour of St Peter'. Stephanus then recounts the ceremony that took place whereby 'Wilfrid the bishop stood in front of the altar, and, turning to the people, in the presence of the kings, read out clearly a list of the lands which the kings, for the good of their souls, had previously, and on that very day as well, presented to him'. The placing of a charter on an altar was meant to endow it with authority and prove its contents to be

[29] For Wilfrid's dealings with York Minster, see *VW*, c. XVI and above, pp. 29–30.

[30] *VW*, c. XVII. For the survival of a possibly seventh-century drum from the Ripon church, which may have been an impost block from one of these 'columns' described by Stephanus, see Coatsworth, *Corpus*, pp. 67 and 240–1 (and illustration 676); see Coatsworth, *ibid*., pp. 67–8 and 238–9, for the earliest surviving piece of Anglo-Saxon church furniture from Ripon, which some commentators have previously thought to be Roman. For Wilfrid's implementation of church architecture that was deliberately Roman in style and also his adoption of uncial script, a script inherited from Rome, see Charles-Edwards, *Ireland*, pp. 324 and 334. Another pre-Conquest church in close proximity to Ripon Minster, perhaps built in the late eighth century, was the Ladykirk, for which see below, pp. 240–1. Hall and Whyman 1996, pp. 142–3, point to four sites in the immediate environs of Ripon Minster (Ailcy Hill, Scott's Monument Yard, All Hallows Hill and the Ladykirk) which all preserve pre-Conquest artefacts and signs of occupation. They tentatively suggest that these are interesting in the context of other accounts of early monastic communities that had scattered foci within their boundaries – and in other words formed polyfocal monastic precincts.

[31] It has been suggested (Jones 2000, pp. 20–1) that material from old Roman sites (nearby Aldborough?) would have been used in the building of Wilfrid's new church. In fact, remains of what is thought to be a Roman pavement have been found near the Ladykirk, possibly indicating the presence of a Roman villa there.

binding.[32] Then Stephanus informs the reader that the chief men and all the bishops gave their signatures to the document, *cum consensu et subscriptione*. Stephanus seems to have selected these words carefully to recall the formula with which witnesses to charters often attested, *consensi et subscripsi*. Finally the names of the regions which had been given to Wilfrid and Ripon are detailed, which reminds one of the dispositive clause of a charter founding a minster.[33]

Those places named as gifts to Ripon were: 'round *Rippel* and *Ingaedyne* and the region of *Dunutinga* and *Incaetlaeuum* and other places', which Chadwick identified as Ribble, Yeadon, Dent and Catlow respectively.[34] Stephanus also states that Wilfrid had gained lands previously in the hands of British clergy: 'and also a list of the consecrated places (*loca sancta*) in various parts which the British clergy had deserted when fleeing from the hostile sword wielded by the warriors of our own nation'.[35] Ripon itself had been inhabited before the arrival of Eata or Wilfrid as a British *locus sanctus*,[36] and so the choice of Ripon for

32 Chaplais 1965, p. 33 and Kelly 1990, p. 44.

33 Stenton, *Preparatory to ASE*, pp. 181–4, suggested that the documents read out by Wilfrid would perhaps have been less formal than standard charters and more like S 1803–5 (*Pet* 4), the composite memoranda in the Peterborough archive. This passage of Stephanus' *VW* makes it likely that Wilfrid was closely involved with charters and one scholar has suggested that it was Wilfrid who was responsible for introducing the convention whereby charters are dated from the birth of Christ (so-called 'incarnational' dating); another has noted the possibility that Wilfrid brought various charter conventions to Sussex during a period of his exile; see respectively Sims-Williams 1988 and Kelly, *Selsey*, pp. xlvi–xlviii; for more about Wilfrid and Sussex, see below, p. 236.

34 *VW*, c. XVII; for the identifications made by Chadwick, see Colgrave, *Life of Wilfrid*, p. 164. Chadwick's suggestions have not been uniformly accepted in modern scholarship. Sims-Williams 1988, pp. 180–3, proposed that the *Rippel* could equally well refer to the 'Ripple' in Worcestershire as to the 'Ribble' in the Amounderness district (see also Foot, *Monastic Life*, p. 260, n. 35). On Yeadon, see *CamDEPN*, p. 710, *PN YorksWR* IV, pp. 155–7, Wood 1987, pp. 21–4 and Jones 1995, pp. 30–6. On Dent, see *CamDEPN*, p. 184 and Jones 1995, pp. 29–30. Chadwick's identification of *Incaetlaeuum* as 'Catlow', remains uncertain: see *CamDEPN*, p. 120. For a useful recent summary of all of this material, see Coatsworth, *Corpus*, p. 15. Another part of Wilfrid's gift was a handsomely decorated manuscript which was housed in a suitably ornate, golden case. At roughly the same time (672–8), Wilfrid was given Hexham by Queen Æthilthryth where he built another church, whose crypt displays architectural links to that at Ripon; see *VW*, c. XXII. The two crypts share very similar dimensions and have been shown to rely on a unit of measurement known as the 'northern rod', which measures sixteen and a half feet. One suggestion for the function of the crypts of Ripon and Hexham is that they are designed to invoke the catacombs of Rome, despite the fact that the catacombs are not a crypt. This is plausible given Wilfrid's adherence to Roman ways and his several visits to the Vatican. For the similar dimensions of the crypts, see Bailey 1991, pp. 6–7; for the reference to the catacombs at Rome and a similar comparison with the late seventh- and early eighth-century burial chamber at Hypogée des Dunes, Poitiers, see R. Gem, 'Towards an Iconography of Anglo-Saxon Architecture', *Journal of the Warburg and Courtault Institutes* xlvi (1983), pp. 1–18.

35 *VW*, c. XVII.

36 Above, pp. 230–1 and Hall and Whyman 1996, p. 143, who state that nearby Ailcy Hill had been used for burials before Eata arrived in Ripon. One of the earliest recorded name-forms for Ailcy Hill,

Wilfrid's church may have been pointed since it allowed him to take control of an old British *locus sanctus* and perhaps also its estates.[37]

Perhaps as a consequence of Wilfrid's success and his accumulated landed possessions, the year 678 saw an allegiance between Archbishop Theodore and King Ecgfrith, both of whom sought to limit his power.[38] These two figures had three new bishops consecrated so that Wilfrid's diocese could be partitioned.[39] Objecting to such measures, Wilfrid departed for Rome and later received papal blessing for his cause from Agatho.[40] But Ecgfrith dismissed this out of hand and Wilfrid was exiled from Northumbria. We can only guess what the consequences of this exile were for Ripon. With Wilfrid out of the way, there was opportunity to encroach on his possessions and rights – which perhaps included Ripon.

One consequence of Wilfrid's exile was a new allegiance with King Æthelwalh of Sussex (674–82), whom Wilfrid had managed to convert to Christianity. Stephanus states that as a result of this partnership, Æthelwalh gave his very own estate over to Wilfrid so that it could be an episcopal see; he further added a gift of eighty-seven hides in Selsey and Wilfrid set about preaching to the pagan South Saxons.[41] In her discussion of South Saxon diplomatic, Kelly has noted that one primary influence on charters produced in Sussex came from Northumbria.[42] A striking feature of South Saxon diplomatic is the use of incarnational dating; since it has been suggested that Wilfred himself was responsible for promoting this method of dating in charters,[43] it may be the case that it was during this period of exile from Northumbria that he brought Northumbrian priests and their diplomatic conventions to Sussex.[44]

---

from the early thirteenth century, is *Elveshov*, meaning 'the elf's mound'; see *PN YorksWR* Part V, p. 168. Blair, *Church*, p. 187, notes that the 'perpetuation of a pre-monastic and possibly pre-Christian cemetery (i.e. on Ailcy Hill) is remarkable'. For more about Ailcy Hill, see below, p. 240.

[37] See Blair, *ibid.*, pp. 186–7. Jones 1995, pp. 29–36, in his identification of various land grants made to Wilfrid, provides further evidence for Wilfrid's occupation of previous British ecclesiastical sites.

[38] *VW*, cc. XXIV and XXV; in chapter XXIV, Stephanus presents Queen Iurminburg as the person who persuaded her husband, Ecgfrith, against Wilfrid.

[39] As a result of Ecgfrith's recent conquest of Lindsey, Eadhæd was consecrated bishop there. Later, when Ecgfrith lost control of Lindsey, Eadhæd returned to Northumbria and was made bishop of Ripon in Wilfrid's place; see Bede, *HE*, iii.28 and iv.12.

[40] *VW*, c. XXXII.

[41] *VW*, c. XLI. For references to charters now lost, but which apparently contained details of grants of land by King Centwine of Wessex (676–85) to Wilfrid, see Finberg, *ECW*, nos. 362–3; and no. 366 for a supposed grant by Wilfrid to Beorhwald, abbot of Glastonbury.

[42] Kelly, *Selsey*, p. xlvii, suggests that the models for the first South Saxon charter-scribes came from Northumbria.

[43] Harrison 1973 and Sims-Williams 1988.

[44] Kelly, *Selsey*, pp. xlvi–xlviii; Kelly points out that there are also possible links between South Saxon charters and charters from the kingdom of the Hwicce. *VW*, c. XLII, notes how Cædwalla, king

In 686/7, there was a degree of reconciliation between Theodore and Wilfrid.[45] More particularly, after the death of King Ecgfrith at the Battle of Nechtanesmere in 685,[46] and the arrival of the new king of Northumbria, Aldfrith (686–705), Wilfrid was restored first to Hexham, but subsequently also to York and Ripon – and he once more received the revenues owed to each place.[47] But differences of opinion remained, with the result that in 691–2 Wilfrid was once more banished. Stephanus lists three of Wilfrid's principal grievances at this moment. They are worth close scrutiny not least because, although biased, they are written by Stephanus and so represent the house view of Ripon in the generation after Wilfrid's death.

In the first instance, the dispute is described as being of ancient origin, 'because the church dedicated to St Peter was unjustly (*iniuste*) deprived of its territories and possessions'.[48] We have already seen that Wilfrid himself was at times removed from positions of authority and also stripped of various landed possessions throughout his extensive 'ecclesiastical kingdom'. Secondly, Stephanus complains that 'the aforesaid monastery which was granted to us as our own property was changed into an episcopal see, thus losing the liberty which St Agatho and five kings had definitely established and firmly fixed'.[49] It was just such a situation that Bede complained about in his *Letter to Ecgbert*, where minsters were immune from worldly intrusion and could indeed be set up simply to avoid taxation on an area of land.[50] It may also display a concern on behalf of Stephanus that if Ripon were turned into an episcopal see, a bishop, who might not be from Ripon, could be placed over the Ripon community and threaten its

of Wessex (685–8), had summoned Wilfrid to his presence and subsequently gave him 'innumerable pieces of land'.

45 In this chapter (*VW*, c. XLIII), Stephanus makes Archbishop Theodore confess, in a passage of direct speech, to allowing kings to rob Wilfrid of his property.

46 Ecgfrith was killed by the Picts; see Bede, *HE*, iv.26.

47 *VW*, c. XLIV. It is said that King Æthelred of the Mercians (674/5–704) acted similarly, returning minsters and lands to Wilfrid (*VW*, c. XLIII).

48 It is absolutely clear from the context that the church referred to here is Ripon, rather than York, which was also dedicated to St Peter.

49 All of this information occurs in *VW*, c. XLV.

50 See chapters 10–12 of the *Letter to Ecgbert* in Plummer, *Bede* I, pp. 413–16. Blair, *Church*, p. 99, notes that it was normal procedure to locate the see of a new diocese in an existing minster. On monastic exemptions in general at this time, see P. Wormald, 'Bede and Benedict Biscop', in *Famulus Christi: Essays in Commemoration of the Thirteenth Centenary of the Birth of the Venerable Bede*, ed. G. Bonner (London, 1976), pp. 141–69, reprinted in *The Times of Bede. Studies in Early English Christian Society and its Historian*, ed. S. Baxter (Blackwell, 2006), pp. 3–29 (at pp. 7–9; he notes that 'monasteries were normally protected from tampering with their property, from interference in their elections, and from large-scale ceremonial in their churches' (at p. 8). See also Wood, *Proprietary Church*, p. 198.

property.[51] Stephanus states that Wilfrid's last grievance involved the injunction to obey Archbishop Theodore. And, as a result of this latest disagreement, Wilfrid sought refuge in Mercia where he lived 'amid profound respect of that bishopric which…Bishop Sexwulf had formerly ruled'.[52]

Wilfrid's situation worsened. At first, after the council of *Ouestraefelda c.* 703, he was stripped of all of his possessions both in Northumbria and Mercia. But the terms were softened later on and, as a slight concession, he was allowed to keep Ripon and all that belonged to it. But he could only do so on condition that he stayed there quietly, did not leave without the king's permission and did not exercise episcopal jurisdiction.[53]

Clearly such terms were unacceptable to Wilfrid, and he journeyed once more to Rome to lodge a complaint. Having received the support of Pope John, who Stephanus suggests wrote in person to King Æthelred of Mercia and King Aldfrith of Northumbria,[54] Wilfrid made a tour of continental holy shrines, where he was able to collect relics and also to buy expensive materials (such as purple vestments and silk) with which to decorate his church.[55] It has been suggested that a niche in the east wall of the main chamber of the crypt may have been built to house just such an important relic brought back to Ripon by Wilfrid.[56] The Ripon Jewel dates from the mid- to late seventh century, an object which has a unique combination of garnet and amber cloisonné, and which is further testimony to the environment of the early Ripon site.[57]

[51] There was good reason to be fearful of this possibility. Wilfrid himself was able to take over the Lindisfarne see and perhaps even threatened its continued existence; see below, pp. 277–8. Just such a concern was expressed at the synod of Hertford in 673: 'That no bishop shall in any way interfere with any monasteries dedicated to God nor take away forcibly any part of their property' (Bede, *HE*, iv.5).

[52] *VW*, c. XLV. S 45 (*Sel* 2), together with the addition to this document of S 1172 (*Sel* 2), represent a grant of land by Nothhelm (Nunna), king of Sussex (692–714), to his sister, Nothgyth, in 692 of thirty-three hides in order to found a minster. In the witness-list, Nothgyth declares her intent to hand over the land to Wilfrid. For more, see Kelly, *Selsey*, pp. 13–22. S 230 (BCS 50) and S 232 (*Sel* 1), which purport to be grants by King Cædwalla (685–8) directly to Wilfrid, are clearly interdependent forgeries and cannot be used as information about early land transactions in Sussex.

[53] For all of these details, see *VW*, cc. XLVI–XLVII; for discussion, see Cubitt 1989.

[54] *VW*, c. LIV.

[55] *VW*, c. LV.

[56] Bailey 1991, p. 10 (with a picture of the niche in the crypt on p. 24).

[57] R. A. Hall, E. Paterson and C. Mortimer, with N. Whitfield, 'The Ripon Jewel', in *Northumbria's Golden Age*, ed. J. Hawkes and S. Mills (Sutton, 1999), pp. 268–80, at p. 277, suggest that the find of the jewel near the centre of the monastic precinct and its cruciform motif make it possible that it was made at Ripon for an ecclesiastical purpose. They conclude: 'The Ripon Jewel could thus be considered a small but significant relic of the milieu which Wilfrid fostered in his monastery at Ripon' (at p. 280).

After another council *c*. 706, a more final decision was reached and Wilfrid was allowed to keep both Hexham and Ripon, together with their attendant revenues.[58] Towards the end of his account, Stephanus depicts a scene where Wilfrid, aware of his impending death, summons his treasurer to open his treasury at Ripon so that he could divide up his belongings and make future provision for his communities.[59] One part he bequeathed to the 'heads of the two oft-mentioned abbeys [to] divide among themselves so that they may be able to purchase the friendship of kings and bishops'.[60] Here is a measure of the instability of the times but also of the legacy Wilfrid's career had left for Ripon to deal with.[61] Having made one last journey to Mercia, he died at Oundle in 709,[62] and his body was then brought back and buried close to the altar on the south side in Ripon Minster.[63] Bede records the inscribed epitaph that was written over his resting-place, with lines that are appropriate for summarising what he brought to Ripon:

> Here lie great Wilfrid's bones. In loving zeal
> He built this church, and gave it Peter's name,
> Who bears the keys by gift of Christ the King;
> Clothed it in gold and purple, and set high
> In gleaming ore the trophy of the Cross;
> Golden the Gospels four he made for it,
> Lodged in a shrine of gold, as is their due.[64]

[58] *VW*, c. LX.

[59] R. Abels, 'What has Weland to do with Christ? The Franks Casket and the Acculturation of Christianity in Early Anglo-Saxon England', *Speculum* lxxxiv (2009), pp. 549–81, at p. 564, has recently suggested that the Franks Casket may have been designed to hold a gift of treasure such as is mentioned in this passage by Stephanus (at p. 565, n. 49, for the tentative suggestion that Wilfrid was the donor of the Casket). There is a significant amount of secondary literature about the Franks Casket. See, for example, I. N. Wood, 'Ripon, Francia and the Franks Casket in the Early Middle Ages', *NH* xxvi (1990), pp. 1–19.

[60] *VW*, c. LXIII.

[61] For Wilfrid's last gifts and so-called 'final gifts' in general, see Wood 2010, pp. 110–11. It was also at this moment that Wilfrid declared Tatberht the priest, and his kinsman, should be the next head (*praepositus*) of Ripon. In *VW*, c. LXIV, a certain Caelin (*Celinus*) is described as having been *praepositus* of the community in recent times and therefore perhaps had the role of abbot. For Wilfrid's designation of his heirs, see Wood, *Proprietary Church*, p. 128. It may be significant that Wilfrid appointed his kinsman as his successor; for a recent discussion of early Northumbrian minsters as potential family minsters, see Wood 2010, pp. 96–8 (for the example of Wearmouth).

[62] *VW*, c. LXV; Wilfrid proclaimed that his follower, Acca, should be his heir at Hexham.

[63] See also *ASC D*, s.a. 709.

[64] The epitaph goes on to describe Wilfrid's role in the fixing of the date for the celebration of Easter, his introduction of monks to Ripon and his periods of stay abroad; Bede, *HE*, v.19.

c. *Into the Gloom: the Post-Wilfridian Minster to the Early Tenth Century*

The relative abundance of source material for the early times at Ripon means that a good deal can be said about its fortunes in that period. But from then onwards relatively little can be inferred about the history of Ripon; and what can be found is often only incidentally mentioned.

Hall and Whyman have been able to discern three distinct phases of use of Ailcy Hill as a cemetery, which are worth summarising here. The first was as a prominent cemetery of the seventh, possibly even the sixth century; at this stage, the cemetery was used to bury people from a wide range of society, whose bodies were laid out in a disordered fashion. The second phase saw bodies being buried in the eighth and ninth centuries which had been aligned on a west–east axis.[65] Some of these were interred in wooden coffins held together with iron fastenings and all of the excavated examples were male; so it may well be that this second phase in particular is to be associated with the nearby Minster. In the last phase of the ninth and possibly tenth centuries, Hall and Whyman suggest that there may already have been a period of abandonment, after which only certain members of society were buried on Ailcy Hill, none of whom can be linked directly to the Minster.[66]

The late eighth century may have seen further building at the Ripon site. Commenting in the sixteenth century, John Leland witnessed an ancient church, the Ladykirk, which stood to the north-east of the Minster itself. He described:

> The old abbay of Ripon stoode wher now is a chapelle of our Lady in a botom one close distant by…from the new minstre. One Marmaduke [Huby]…abbate of Fountaines, a man familiar with Salvage Archebisshop of York, obteinid this chapelle of hym…and pullid down the est end of it, a pece of exceeding auncient wark…leving the weste ende of very old werk stonding…One thing I much notid, that was 3. crossis standing in a row at the est ende of the chapelle garth. They were thinges *antiquissimi operis*.[67]

Excavations of 1955 and 1974 proved the existence of the Ladykirk and an associated cemetery; whilst this church was certainly *in situ* by the early eleventh century, it may even have been present in the late eighth century.[68] Interestingly,

[65] This second phase caused largescale disturbance to the first phase of burials.

[66] Hall and Whyman 1996, p. 124 and Blair, *Church*, p. 314, n. 123, who points out that there is continued evidence for burial into the eleventh century, in a subsidiary chapel at Ripon (for which see Hall and Whyman 1996, pp. 129–30).

[67] *The Itinerary of John Leland in or about the Years 1535–1543, Parts I to III*, ed. L.T. Smith (London, 1907), pp. 80–1; this same extract is quoted in Hall and Whyman 1996, p. 124. For more about these three crosses mentioned by Leland, see W. MacKay, 'The Development of Medieval Ripon', *YAJ* liv (1982), pp. 73–80, at p. 77.

[68] See Hall and Whyman 1996, pp. 124–30 (at p. 130 for the date).

fragments of sculpture from the site can be dated to the eighth and ninth centuries and display cultural links with Hexham and York.[69]

The Chartres manuscript of the *Historia Brittonum* provides incidental evidence for life at Ripon in the eighth century: it has an addition which describes how Abbot Sléibíne of Iona (754–67) found and obtained the date of the Saxons' arrival in Britain from the 'city of Ripon'.[70] And it may be that the Ripon community was successful in promoting Wilfrid's cult at this time since a mid-ninth century calendar from Germany records the date of Wilfrid's *depositio* as being 24 April, as does the ninth-century calendar from the north of England in Oxford, Digby MS 63.[71] Beyond such details, there is only a minimum of documentary record relating to Ripon. The *Anglo-Saxon Chronicle* and the *Historia regum* together supply the bare dates and names of a few abbots of Ripon.[72] So we learn that in 786 Abbot Botwine died and was replaced by Abbot Ealdberht, who himself died in 787 and was replaced by Abbot Sigered.[73] Botwine can be found in correspondence with Bishop Lull.[74] Byrhtferth, in his *VSO*, records how Oswald found the remains of Wilfrid, together with those of the abbots already mentioned but also a certain Wilthegn (*Vilden*) about whom there is no more information.[75] In one of the extant Anglo-Saxon episcopal lists, CCCC 140, dated *c.* 1100 and localised to Bath Abbey, there is a brief list of bishops of Ripon on folio 115r,

69 Three fragments are discussed by D. Tweddle in Hall and Whyman 1996, pp. 128–9. The first two fragments show interesting links with Acca's cross from Hexham and date to the eighth and ninth centuries; the last is from the end of the Anglo-Saxon period.

70 This is referred to by Jones 2000, p. 22. The addition reads: 'Et in tempore Guorthigirni Regis Britanie Saxones pervenerunt in Britanniam, id est in anno incarnacionis Christi, sicut Libine abasiae inripum civitate invenit vel reperit, ab incarnatione Domini anni D usque a Kl. jan. in XII luna, ut aunt (*sic*) alii intis (*sic*) CCC annis a quo tenerunt Saxones Britanniam usque ad annum supradictum'; the text is given in F. Lot, *Nennius et l'Historia Brittonum*, Bibliothèque de l'École des Hautes Études, fourth section (Paris, 1934), p. 172, n. 2 and also p. 228.

71 The *Anglo-Saxon Martyrology* also gives 24 April as the date of Wilfrid's death. This evidence is conveniently summarised in B.J. Muir and A.J. Turner, *Vita Sancti Wilfridi Auctore Edmero: The Life of St Wilfrid by Edmer* (Exeter, 1998), pp. xxi–xxii. For the entry about Wilfrid in Oxford, Digby MS 63, see F. Wormald, *English Kalendars Before A.D. 1100*, Henry Bradshaw Society lxxii (Boydell, 1934), p. 5.

72 The annal for 790 (but relating to events of 791) in the *Historia regum* is more interesting: it tells of the execution of Ealdorman Eardwulf just outside the gate of the Ripon minster: *HR*(4), p. 52 (s.a. 790).

73 See *ASC D*, s.a. 787 and *HR* (4), pp. 50–1 (s.a. 786 and s.a. 787). The subscription of Abbot Ealdberht can be found in a letter of Bishop George to Pope Hadrian regarding the papal legates' mission to England in 786; see Story, *Carolingian Connections*, pp. 65–6.

74 One letter survives in which Botwine thanks Lull for his previous note and in which Botwine makes a gift of six cloaks to Lull; see M. Tangl, *Die Briefe des Heiligen Bonifatius und Lullum*, MGH, *Epistolae Selectae*, vol. 1 (Berlin, 1916), no. 131.

75 See Byrhtferth, *VSO*, v. 9, where the other abbots said to have been found alongside Wilfrid are named as Tatberht, Botwine, Ealdberht and Sigered.

column five, where the names of Wilfrid, Ecgberht, Coena (i.e. Æthelberht), Eanbald and Wulfsige are given.[76] In the other extant Anglo-Saxon episcopal lists these names are placed as (arch)bishops of York, demonstrating that the list in CCCC 140 has been misclassified as a list of bishops of Ripon.

Not much more can be said about the history of Ripon from the mid-eighth century to the late ninth century.[77] Whilst it is impossible to be precise about the effects of viking settlements in Northumbria in the years following 867,[78] disruption must have been caused and it is likely that Ripon's assets were diminished as a result.[79] The deposition of various coin hoards in the mid-ninth century (which contained coins of the mid-eighth to the mid-ninth centuries) is indicative of the uncertainty of the times.[80] There is evidence to suggest that Archbishop Wulfhere engineered the survival of the York church by siding with the Scandinavian incomers.[81] King Eadred's punitive raid against Ripon Minster in the 940s (which itself implies that some sort of ecclesiastical community at

[76] For the date and edition of this episcopal list, see R. I. Page, 'Anglo-Saxon Episcopal Lists, Part III', *Nottingham Mediaeval Studies* x (1966), pp. 2–24, at pp. 17–20; for discussion of all extant Anglo-Saxon episcopal lists, see R. I. Page, 'Anglo-Saxon Episcopal Lists, Parts I and II', *Nottingham Mediaeval Studies* ix (1965), pp. 71–95; no room was left for further additions to this Ripon list (at p. 78, n. 30).

[77] Ripon tradition links the Ripon Horn as a gift belonging to the time of King Alfred. But the horn comes from a type of longhorn cattle not found in England before the post-medieval period. See N. Crummy, J. Cherry and P. Northover, 'The Winchester Moot Horn', *Medieval Archaeology*, lii (2008), pp. 211–29 (at p. 227). Gent's 1733 history of Ripon states: 'Here I must remark, from an antient Manuscript, That *Rippon* was first incorporated in the Fourteenth Year of the Ever-memorable King ALFRED, *Anno Domini* 886' (see Gent, *Rippon*, p. 101; the same page discusses the Ripon horn).

[78] *ASC C*, s.a. 868 (*recte* 867).

[79] Ecclesiastical lands in the north of England seem to have been particularly exploited by vikings; see Fleming 1985, p. 250 and Dumville, *Wessex and England*, p. 37. For discussion of the York church's endowment during this time, see above, pp. 42–55; for the situation with St Cuthbert's community, which preserves at least some documentary evidence for how, and under what circumstances, lands passed into viking control, see below, pp. 289–95.

[80] The difficulty with Northumbrian coin hoards of this period is understanding whether they are symptomatic of viking pressure or of unrest between native Northumbrian factions; see N.P. Brooks and J.A. Graham-Campbell, 'Reflections on the Viking-Age Silver Hoard from Croydon, Surrey', *Anglo-Saxon Monetary History: Essays in Memory of Michael Dolley*, ed. M.A.S. Blackburn (Leicester, 1986), pp. 91–110, repr. in N. Brooks, *Communities and Warfare, 700–1400* (London and Rio Grande, 2000), pp. 69–92 (at p. 87). In 1695 a coin hoard was found by Ralph Thoresby near Ailcy Hill; see E. J. E. Pirie, 'The Ripon Hoard, 1695: Contemporary and Current Interest', *BNJ* lii (1982), pp. 84–103. For the possible number of styca hoards found at Ripon, see D. M. Metcalf, 'Some Finds of Medieval Coins from Scotland and the North of England', *BNJ* xxx (1960), pp. 88–123, at p. 99, where he states that Ripon 'was a centre of monetary affairs in the Northumbria kingdom'; but Hall (R.A.) 1995, p. 26, urges contextualisation. Although monastic burial on Ailcy Hill may have ceased *c*. 850, burial at the Ladykirk site has been recorded for the period from the late ninth century to the early eleventh century; see Hall and Whyman 1996, pp. 124 and 129–30.

[81] See above, pp. 47–8.

Ripon had survived the Scandinavian settlement) may suggest that Ripon had done similarly.[82]

York had had to be pragmatic: at one moment it looked to vikings for support, at another it can be seen seeking an alliance with the West Saxons. It seems entirely likely that Ripon would have been faced with a similar dilemma and may even have followed York's example. In 1974, masons working on the vault beneath the Markenfield Chapel in the present-day Ripon Cathedral discovered part of a pre-Conquest cross-head which had been used as filling. The scene depicted on the cross-head has been identified as that of the Germanic hero, Sigurd, and the dragon Fafnir.[83] Such a motif was popular in tenth-century Northumbrian sculpture, and means that the cross-head was clearly produced in the Anglo-Scandinavian period.[84] It would be interesting to know who commissioned such an item.

d. *Kings of Anglo-Saxon England in the North: from Æthelstan to the Norman Conquest*

In 927 King Æthelstan drove out the viking king, Guthfrith, from his stronghold in York. He was the first English king able to exert some form of control over Northumbria. **1** in the York archive bears witness to this situation. Written in ostentatious Latin prose, it heralds Æthelstan's success whilst simultaneously seeking to garner the support of the York archbishopric (and its notoriously

[82] For the continued ecclesiastical presence at Ripon after the Scandinavian settlement, see Hadley, *Northern*, pp. 235–6. For King Eadred and Ripon, see below, pp. 245–6.

[83] See J. T. Lang, 'Sigurd and Weland in Pre-Conquest Carving from Northern England', *YAJ*, xlviii (1976), pp. 83–94 and J. T. Lang, 'An Anglo-Scandinavian Cross-Head from Ripon Cathedral', in R. A. Hall, 'Rescue Excavations in the Crypt of Ripon Cathedral', *YAJ*, xlix (1977), p. 63. For recent discussion, see Coatsworth, *Corpus*, p. 236 (Ripon 4).

[84] Hall (R.A.) 1995, p. 26. This cross-head may be related to another piece of Ripon sculpture which was once housed in the crypt but is no longer in the Cathedral; it is now preserved in St Wilfrid's Church, Blackpool. The two may even be by the same carver (J. T. Lang, 'An Anglo-Scandinavian Cross-Head', p. 63). For the other Ripon example, see, for example, W. G. Collingwood, 'Anglian and Anglo-Danish Sculpture in the West Riding', *YAJ* xxiii (1914), pp. 129–299 (at pp. 234–5) and Coatsworth, *Corpus*, pp. 235–6 (Ripon 3); in the same volume (at pp. 65 and 75), Coatsworth notes both that these Ripon examples employing Scandinavian themes appear on monuments with Christian forms or motifs and also that these late ninth century, or early tenth century, Ripon stones do not match the 'quality of the early period, here perhaps implying a change of status for the site, although it seems to have continued as an archiepiscopal estate' (at p. 75). For further discussion of Ripon sculpture, and the sculpture of the West Riding of Yorkshire in general, see E. Coatsworth, 'The Cross in the West Riding of Yorkshire', *The Place of the Cross in Anglo-Saxon England*, ed. C.E. Karkov, S.L. Keefer and K.L. Jolly, Publications of the Manchester Centre for Anglo-Saxon Studies Volume 4 (Woodbridge, 2006), pp. 14–28 (esp. pp. 17–24).

rebellious archbishop, Wulfstan) by making it a significant grant of land.[85] **15** and **16** both credit Æthelstan as confirming various rights and lands belonging to Ripon. They are quoted side-by-side in a fifteenth-century manuscript within the body of a record of a lengthy trial held in the Ripon chapter in 1228.[86] They are very clearly forgeries.

Although the memory of a genuine gift or association between Æthelstan and Ripon may underlie **15** and **16**,[87] it is impossible to accept that the specific rights being granted were gifts ultimately from Æthelstan. The reality is that Ripon in later times sought to connect many of its rights with the first king who had united Anglo-Saxon England and so concocted **15** and **16**.[88] Furthermore, the interdependence of **16** and **12**, another rhyming Middle English charter from the Beverley archive, raises the possibility that Ripon may simply have inherited this tradition regarding Æthelstan from Beverley Minster.[89]

One privilege, said in **16** to have been granted by Æthelstan to Ripon, is the right to a circular sanctuary zone which extended for a mile on each side of the Minster, known as a banleuca.[90] Although it is not possible to demonstrate that this was a gift from Æthelstan himself, there is nonetheless evidence that this privilege had its origins in the Anglo-Saxon period. **7 (c)**, from the York archive, implies that this liberty existed in the 1020s since it too describes a privileged zone extending for a mile around Ripon.[91] And another document of the early eleventh century,

[85] For more on the nature and context of this grant, see the commentary to **1**.

[86] For the text of this trial, see Fowler, *MCPW* I, pp. 51–63.

[87] Since there is genuine documentation to the effect that both York (above, pp. 51–2) and St Cuthbert's community (then at Chester-le-Street; below, pp. 299–302) were beneficiaries of Æthelstan's generosity, it may be that this generosity extended to other major northern ecclesiastical communities, such as Ripon. Since Æthelstan was making initial forays into Northumbria, it would have been to his benefit to gain the support of major institutions like Ripon.

[88] For other institutions that similarly invoked the name of Æthelstan as donor of various rights, see Foot, *Æthelstan*, p. 125.

[89] **12** is written in Middle English of a kind that is contemporary to **16** and the two documents seem clearly to be interrelated (for the relationship between these two forgeries, see the commentaries to **12** and **16**). Beverley Minster relied heavily on its perceived grants from Æthelstan (see above, pp. 181–2) and Ripon evidently took care to preserve the memory of Æthelstan in later times also: see the Chapter Act which calls for services to be done for Æthelstan; Fowler, *MCPW* IV, pp. 144 and 282; at p. 283, for the town crier who was expected to ring his bell for the memory of Æthelstan.

[90] **16** makes Æthelstan grant: 'Thar pees at Rypon, On ilke side the kyrke amyle'. The privileged area extending for a mile around Ripon was known as 'St Wilfrid's League' (*leuca*); it is recorded as such in GDB, for which see below, pp. 248–9. For a thorough discussion of Ripon and Beverley's sanctuary rights, see Lambert 2009; Lambert suggests (at pp. 136–40) that the banleuca at Ripon and Beverley evolved over time from offering initially personal protection to an individual claiming sanctuary, to becoming an area of general spatial protection and finally to becoming a formalised zone of protection which possessed privileged jurisdictional rights (these stages are summarised on p. 138).

[91] **7 (c)** opens with the statement: 'Æt Rypum ærest mile gemet on ælce healfe' ('At Ripon first the space of one mile on each side'), clearly a reference to this same sanctuary privilege.

Norðymbra ciricgrið, suggests that by this stage St Peter's in York, St Wilfrid's in Ripon and St John's in Beverley all possessed similar privileges of sanctuary, privileges which *Norðymbra ciricgrið* regarded to be greater than those granted to other churches.[92] It therefore seems likely that the banleuca at Ripon (and also at Beverley) had been granted in the Anglo-Saxon period but it is still unclear if Æthelstan had any involvement in the donation of this liberty.[93]

Whether or not Ripon benefited from King Æthelstan's munificence, a subsequent southern king, Eadred, was not so generous. For the years 947–8, the *ASC* preserves details of how the Northumbrians, led by Archbishop Wulfstan, broke an allegiance made with Eadred at Tanshelf and instead took Eric Bloodaxe as their king.[94] As part of a punitive raid into Northumbria, the 'glorious minster at Ripon, which St Wilfrid had built, was burnt down'.[95] The Anglo-Scandinavian sculpture found in Ripon Minster (discussed above) may imply that that church had allied itself to the viking cause, or at least that it had Scandinavian sympathies, which perhaps meant that it was targeted by Eadred.[96] Alternatively, it may be that the burning of Ripon Minster served as a warning to Archbishop Wulfstan both

[92] See Liebermann, *Gesetze* I, p. 473. In the mid-twelfth century the sacrist of Beverley, Alfred, defined the zones of protection on offer to those seeking sanctuary at Beverley Minster (see Raine, *SDSB*, pp. 97–108). Alfred states that the closer one came to the 'frithstool', the safer one became; the 'frithstool' still exists today at Beverley. Although no such Anglo-Saxon 'frithstool' exists at Ripon, **16** does indeed refer to a *Grythstole*. Another Anglo-Saxon 'frithstool' survives at Wilfrid's other foundation, Hexham. It is interesting that similar sanctuary zones are found with minsters in Cornwall, zones which are also described as having been created by Æthelstan; Blair, *Church*, p. 224, states that, 'Æthelstan's involvement with both groups suggests an anxiety to consolidate a reputation for good lordship on the fringes of his power, and hence to foster an esoteric and inherited anomaly rather than suppress it'.

[93] Blair, *Church*, pp. 223–4, suggests that these circular sanctuary zones found in the north of England could have been of seventh-century origin, influenced by Irish practice; in the case of Beverley and Ripon, Lambert traces the privilege back to at least the late tenth century: Lambert 2009, pp. 128–31. The record of the 1228 trial, within which **15** and **16** are quoted, notes that the bounds of Ripon's sanctuary were delineated by the 'crosses of Æthelstan', some of which still exist today (similar 'crosses of Æthelstan' exist also at Beverley). In the thirteenth century it was possible to locate eight of these crosses but by the mid-eighteenth century only the Sharow Cross, to the north-east of the Minster and beyond the River Ure, the Kangel Cross, to the south-east of the Minster and Æthelstan's Cross on Hutton Moor could be identified. Jones 2000, pp. 16–18 concludes, on the basis of topography and old township boundaries, that there would have been mile-crosses on every old road emanating from the Minster (see also *PN YorksWR* Part V, p. 169, for the Æthelstan crosses). Jones, *ibid*., p. 16, n. 15, also notes that St Wilfrid's League would have covered an area of some 4.25 square miles.

[94] *ASC D*, s.a. 947 and 948. Downham, *Viking Kings*, pp. 115–20, questions the identification of this Eric as Eric Bloodaxe; see further Woolf, *Pictland*, pp. 187–8 and above, p. 46, n. 145.

[95] *ASC D*, s.a. 948. This annal seems clearly to imply that Eadred's army was responsible for burning down Ripon Minster; see Plummer, *Chronicles* II, p. 148 and Stenton, *ASE*, pp. 360–1.

[96] This suggestion is necessarily speculative; see above, p. 243, for the Anglo-Scandinavian sculpture found at Ripon.

that treachery would not be tolerated and that even celebrated churches were not beyond punishment.

Whatever the motivation, Eadred's raid was disastrous for Ripon.[97] It may have been in the aftermath of this event that the Canterbury church was able to assert that it possessed Wilfrid's relics, claiming to have seized them and taken them to Canterbury.[98] As part of his rebuilding of Canterbury Cathedral, Archbishop Oda (941–58) had an altar built specifically for the purpose of housing Wilfrid's relics. Such a deed would have sharpened Eadred's message to the treacherous Northumbrians. As Brooks puts it, 'In an age when the cult of saints was very closely allied to local patriotism, there could be no more striking demonstration of Eadred's power'.[99] Canterbury went even further in its claim to Wilfrid and commissioned a new *Vita* to be written by Frithegod, the *Breuiloquium uitae beati Wilfridi*.[100] The preface to this work (written in the name of Archbishop Oda, but with a style closely resembling Frithegod's) states that Wilfrid's remains had been shamefully neglected at Ripon and that his crypt was entirely overgrown.[101] Canterbury's claim to possess Wilfrid's relics was part of a much wider issue of its supremacy over the Northumbrian Church.[102] It is therefore impossible to accept such statements about the decay of Ripon at face value; but previous

[97] Hall (R.A.) 1995, p. 27, notes the irony of the fact that a silver penny of Eadred discovered at Ripon is one of the few indications of continuing life there.

[98] D.W. Rollason, 'Relic-cults as an Instrument of Royal Policy *c*. 900–*c*. 1050', *ASE* xv (1986), pp. 91–103, suggests that Eadred's raid was made for the purpose of acquiring Wilfrid's relics (at p. 96).

[99] Brooks, *Church of Canterbury*, p. 228 (and pp. 227–31, for a full account).

[100] This work adds no new information about Wilfrid and is merely a new rendering of the earlier account by Stephanus. It is edited by A. Campbell, *Frithegodi Monachi Breuiloquium Uitae Beati Wilfredi* (Zurich, 1950). I.N. Wood, 'Ripon, Francia and the Franks Casket', pp. 5 and 17, has suggested the possibility that it was Frithegod who took the Franks Casket to the church of Brioude.

[101] Brooks, *Church of Canterbury*, p. 230, notes that those men responsible for taking Wilfrid's relics from Ripon may also have brought a copy of Wilfrid's *Life* by Stephanus with them since Frithegod's spelling of personal names reflects a Northumbrian exemplar.

[102] Canterbury's ownership of Wilfrid's relics became a hot topic. Towards the end of the eleventh century, Eadmer of Canterbury produced yet another *Life* of Wilfrid which was 'deeply concerned with establishing Canterbury's ownership of Wilfrid's relics'; B.J. Muir and A.J. Turner, *Vita Sancti Wilfridi Auctore Edmero*, p. xxx (and p. xxv, for the notion that this *Vita* was designed to demonstrate Christ Church's 'suzerainty over the Northumbrian church'). It is interesting to find that MS D of Eadmer's work (Ballarat, Fine Art Gallery, MS Crouch 10) omits reference to Wilfrid's relics being taken to Canterbury, which strongly suggests this was originally a northern version (see Muir and Turner, *ibid*., p. xliii and pp. lxvi–lxvii). Although Canterbury's possession of Wilfrid's relics may have supported its claim to supremacy over the northern church, it was not the only southern church to have northern relics; for the relics of Aidan and Hild, and other northern figures, claimed by Glastonbury in the eleventh century, see J.P. Carley, *Glastonbury Abbey: The Holy House at the Head of the Moors Adventurous* (Woodbridge, 1988), pp. 127–8.

events, and later documentation,[103] mean there may have been an element of truth about them. York would later reassert Ripon's possession of Wilfrid's remains and relics.[104]

When Oswald succeeded to the York archbishopric, he conducted a survey of those estates taken from the York church; it is preserved today as **6** and is interesting for two reasons. First, it seems to suggest that by the late tenth century Ripon was considered to be an archiepiscopal minster. This may be a new development, since, as Wood points out, no support from York is envisaged in Stephanus' account of Wilfrid's provision for Ripon following his death.[105] It may be that Ripon's existence had been made precarious by the ninth-century viking settlement in Northumbria, so much so that York was able to take steps to incorporate it within its jurisdiction. If such a sequence of events can be believed, one can imagine York boosting their claim by reference to Wilfrid's position as Bishop of York and also of Ripon.[106]

Certainly Ripon seems to have been left vulnerable. **6**, in addition to describing Ripon's relationship to York, secondly gives an impression of its bad fortune at this moment:

> These townships have been taken from Ripon: the first is Hewick, the second Hewick,[107] the third *Ansætleh*,[108] the fourth one hide at Stainley, the fifth Helperby, the sixth at Myton. Two hides from Poppleton.

The *VSO* by Byrhtferth reinforces this impression, describing as it does Oswald's visit to Ripon where he found the Minster to be entirely dilapidated.[109] It is in the

103 See below, p. 248.

104 As we will see, Byrhtferth, in his *VSO*, talks of the discovery of Wilfrid's remains at Ripon. Oswald may well have laid claim to the relics of early abbots of Ripon since he was responsible for bringing some relics of Wilfrid and Tatberht to Peterborough in 963; see A. Thacker, 'Cults at Canterbury: Relics and Reform Under Dunstan and his Successors', in *St Dunstan, His Life, Times and Cult*, ed. N. Ramsay, M. Sparks and T. Tatton-Brown (Boydell, 1992), pp. 221–45, at p. 234, n. 91. In the later tenth century some calendars start to record a new date for the feast of Wilfrid (12 October) and B.J. Muir and A.J. Turner, *Vita Sancti Wilfridi Auctore Edmero*, p. xxiii, suggest the possibility that this date refers to the translation of Wilfrid's remains by Oda.

105 Wood 1987, p. 22 and *VW*, c. LXIII.

106 This is also the opinion of Wood 1987, p. 22.

107 Whitelock, *EHD*, p. 521, n. 2, identifies these as Copt and Bridge Hewick.

108 The place-name *Ansætleh* may contain the element *ansetl*, 'a hermitage'; for further discussion, see *The Vocabulary of English Place-Names (Á-BOX)*, ed. D.N. Parsons and T. Styles, with C. Hough (Nottingham, 1997), s.v. 'ansetl' and above, p. 136.

109 This is also the occasion when Wilfrid's relics are said to have been found at Ripon. Ripon is described as *tunc dirutum erat*; see Byrhtferth, *VSO*, v.9. Some relics of Wilfrid, his successor Tatberht, and other early Ripon saints were perhaps moved by Oswald to Peterborough: A. Thacker, 'Æthelwold and Abingdon', in *Bishop Æthelwold: His Career and Influence*, ed. B. Yorke (Boydell, 1988), pp. 43–64 (at p. 62).

same passage of the *VSO* that Byrhtferth seems to imply that Oswald introduced monks to Ripon.[110] If this particular reading of the *VSO* can be accepted, then the combined evidence of **6** and Byrthferth's *VSO* may suggest that Oswald was first investigating the state of Ripon's resources and way of life and then trying to effect positive changes for the enhancement of religious life there. Whether or not this would have involved an associated campaign to rebuild Ripon's endowment as, for example, Bishop Æthelwold did for Peterborough, is a good question.[111] It would certainly be instructive to know what St Cuthbert's community found when they stayed there in 995.[112]

7 (c), an estate survey of those places owned by the York see carried out in the early eleventh century, gives further evidence for what happened to Ripon and for the structure of the estate there. **7 (c)** is divided into four sections, the second of which states that there were areas of Ripon considered to be 'waste': Sawley, Grantley, Eavestone, Wilshill and half of Knaresford. Despite these waste areas, **7 (c)** describes various amounts of land and privilege which the Ripon estate owned (and in turn owed to the York archbishopric) in the early eleventh century: thirty-seven and a half hides of sokeland in eleven different towns, nine hides of 'priests' land' in six different towns and sixteen hides of *agenland* in nine different towns. Of those seven villages noted as lost from Ripon in **6**, three were recovered and listed in **7 (c)**: the two Hewicks and Stainley. Helperby, Myton and Poppleton and *Ansætleh* remained lost.[113] But the location of these villages to the south and east of the Ripon estate proper, means that their loss may have been part of a move to consolidate Ripon's holdings.[114] Perhaps **7 (c)** contains signs that the Ripon estate was being rejuvenated.

Whether or not **7 (c)** does indicate improvement in Ripon's prosperity, Domesday Book's record of the Archbishop of York's holdings at Ripon in 1086

[110] There is some confusion about the details of this passage. The entry by N. Brooks on Oswald in *ODNB* suggests that it demonstrates Oswald's introduction of monks to Ripon (as does Raine, *HCY* I, p. 462); Whitelock 1959, p. 76, n. 3, points out that this could refer to York or to Ripon. Lapidge in Byrhtferth, *VSO*, p. 172, n. 101, thinks this describes Oswald's introduction of monks to Worcester.

[111] For Æthelwold and Peterborough see, for example, Kelly, *Peterborough*, pp. 41–51.

[112] Symeon of Durham, *LDE*, iii.1; Hall (R.A.) 1995, p. 27. Aird suggests that St Cuthbert's community perhaps moved to Ripon because of Cuthbert's earlier role as guestmaster there (Aird, *St Cuthbert*, p. 45, n. 131).

[113] For a more detailed discussion, which notes also the interesting structure of the Ripon estate, see the commentary to **7 (c)**.

[114] Keynes 1986, pp. 90–1. As already noted, **7 (c)** mentions Ripon's ownership of 'the space of one mile on each side', reference to a privileged area. Domesday Book also notes that Ripon possessed this liberty, which was free of geld, and calls it 'St Wilfrid's League'. Ripon claims Æthelstan as the supposed grantor of this liberty in **15** and **16**. See also GDB, f. 303v and f. 380r.

gives the impression of an estate in decay.[115] The Archbishop of York's Ripon estate owned fourteen outlying berewicks, an area which amounted to forty-three carucates to the geld and the ability to have thirty ploughs. But the Domesday survey describes most of this as being waste, so much so that only nine ploughs were in use, in only three of the berewicks. Ripon also owned two bovates in the township of Aldfield, these too being waste. A similar scene is found in Ripon's sokeland belonging to the archbishop. Although the sokeland had the capability of fifteen ploughs, it actually only had three in operation in 1086.[116] **6**, **7** **(c)** and Domesday Book provide evidence of fluctuating fortunes at Ripon and one is left to wonder what effect punitive expeditions such as that of 948 by Eadred and that of 1069 by William the Conqueror may have had on the area.

2. THE HISTORY OF THE RIPON ARCHIVE

a. *The Pre-Conquest Archive*

Unfortunately, no genuine Anglo-Saxon documents survive from the Ripon archive. Wilfrid's role as an extensive landowner and his part in the development of charter diplomatic make it very likely that Ripon would have housed Anglo-Saxon charters in its earliest days. And it may be that Stephanus, in his famous passage about the dedication of Ripon Minster, was actually using a charter as the basis of his account.[117] Perhaps the treasurer (*clauicularius*), called upon by Wilfrid to open the treasury (*gazofilacium*) and to divide the proceeds into four parts, was also entrusted with the keeping of charters.[118]

15 and **16**, although cast in the name of King Æthelstan, are clearly forgeries. But Æthelstan's actions in the north and his gifts to York (**1**) and to St Cuthbert's community at Chester-le-Street (noted in the *HSC*) at least make it possible that he made some form of gift to Ripon, the exact details of which will never be recovered. **12**, **15** and **16** are forgeries naming Æthelstan as the grantor of rights

115 For all of the subsequent information, see GDB, f. 303v; for a more detailed discussion of this Domesday evidence, see Jones 2000, pp. 16–18.

116 See further Jones 2000, p. 18.

117 *VW*, c. XVII and above, pp. 234–6.

118 *VW*, c. LXIII. There is evidence that, later in the Anglo-Saxon period, those men responsible for keeping the king's treasures (including relics) were the very same men responsible for keeping charters; and so there was an association between the royal treasures and the royal archives. See Keynes, *Diplomas*, pp. 148–9, at p. 149, for the suggestion that charters gained in authority for being kept with the holy relics. A *gazophylacium* can have the meaning of 'muniment-room'; a *clauicularius* is literally a 'keeper of keys'; see *DMLBS*, under the relevant entries.

and privileges to northern religious communities, and it is unclear whether any substance underlay such claims. These houses may have invented an association with Æthelstan, the first king of Anglo-Saxon England, as the source of their principal rights. One house, Beverley, may even have taken the initiative in this matter and have then been imitated by Ripon.[119]

It may be that events in the Anglo-Saxon period itself led to the loss of documents from the Ripon archive. The 948 destruction of the Minster, carried out by King Eadred, was so traumatic that Archbishop Oswald found the Minster in a sorry state in the late tenth century.[120] Events after the Conquest may not have helped. It is noticeable that the value of the Ripon estate dropped dramatically from 1066 to 1086, perhaps suggesting that William the Conqueror's 'harrying of the north' was particularly damaging for Ripon.[121]

b. *The Later Ripon Archive*

In the early twelfth century, King Stephen issued a confirmatory charter declaring that Ripon Minster was to have its peace within St Wilfrid's League,[122] a fair at Ripon for five days and other privileges and immunities, as had been granted by King Edward and King William.[123] This suggests the possibility that Ripon had once possessed charters granted by Edward the Confessor. Since we still have such documents granted in the name of Edward for York (**9** and **10**) and for Beverley (**13** and **14**),[124] it is possible that Ripon had also benefited as a result of this king's generosity.[125] It is interesting that this confirmation charter of Stephen does not refer to any grants previous to the time of Edward and so no mention of **15** and **16**, or of Æthelstan, is made. Perhaps therefore, if the details of Stephen's charter are to be believed,[126] the fabrication of **15** and **16** postdates 1139.

[119] See below, p. 264.
[120] See **6** and Byrhtferth, *VSO*, v. 9.
[121] See above, pp. 248–9.
[122] St Wilfrid's League was an area of privilege given to Ripon Minster, for which see above, pp. 244–5.
[123] See Farrer, *EYC*, no. 117, dated 1136–9. The manuscript copy of this charter has been lost; Farrer prints his version from Fowler, *MCPW* I, pp. 95–6; see also the comments in *Regesta III*, pp. 263–4 (no. 717). Farrer notes (p. 110), 'The terms in which it is expressed are unusual' and it may be a cause for concern that a Beverley confirmation charter also in the name of King Stephen (Farrer, *EYC*, no. 99) is written in almost identical terms; nevertheless, Farrer seems to accept it as genuine.
[124] **11** is a forgery in the name of Edward the Confessor in the York archive.
[125] In Edward the Confessor's reign, Ripon belonged to the archbishop of York and so any writ for Ripon is likely to have been addressed to Archbishop Ealdred.
[126] For the problems in accepting Stephen's charter as authentic see above, n. 123, where a possible link to an almost identical charter of Stephen in the Beverley archive is hypothesised. If there is any

It was in the mid- to late twelfth century that the town of Ripon itself grew in prosperity; and it is likely that the fortunes of the Minster increased similarly. Various documents of this period testify to Archbishop Thurstan's role in this process.[127] But it seems to have been during the archiepiscopate of Roger de Pont l'Evêque (1154–81) that things began to change more dramatically at Ripon. It was under his supervision that a new Minster was commissioned, which either suggests that the Minster was in need of an overhaul or that Wilfrid's cult had outgrown its previous home.[128] Roger himself granted £1000 for the rebuilding of the church.[129] Progress seems to have been intermittent and an indulgence was issued for the rebuilding of the church.[130]

It is unclear what the consequences of this rebuilding were for any archives at the Minster. But it is likely that any Anglo-Saxon documents held at Ripon had long since disappeared or been destroyed. The record of the 1228 trial at the Ripon chapter house was designed to demonstrate all of the rights belonging to the Minster. In the process of enumerating such rights, the Ripon chapter was not able to quote or refer to any Anglo-Saxon charters other than the forged **15** and **16** in the name of Æthelstan, which they included verbatim in the transcript of the trial now held in the Duchy of Lancaster archives.[131] It seems probable that **15** and **16** were forged so that the Ripon chapter could bolster their defence at the 1228 trial.

From the fourteenth to the sixteenth centuries, there are frequent references to decay and damage at the Minster.[132] A raid by the Scots in 1318 seems to have been particularly disastrous.[133] There are also references to those people who had been charged with collecting alms for the church fabric but who in fact could not be trusted; and to those who saw fit to carry off charters or even steal rolls of charters.[134] The Register of Archbishop Christopher Bainbridge (1508–14) notes an indulgence conceded to the Ripon church on 1 June 1512,

suspicious connection, it is interesting that whereas the Beverley version does refer to grants made by Æthelstan, the Ripon version has no such detail.

127 Thurstan was archbishop of York from 1114 to 1140. For Thurstan's role at Ripon see, for example, Farrer, *EYC*, nos. 115–16.

128 For more, see W. MacKay, 'The Development of Medieval Ripon', *YAJ* liv (1982), pp. 73–80. Roger's death seems to have left problems for Ripon; see S. Harrison and P. Barker, 'Ripon Minster: An Archaeological Analysis and Reconstruction of the Twelfth-Century Church', *Journal of the British Archaeological Association* clii (1999), pp. 49–78, at p. 51.

129 Fowler, *MCPW* I, p. 97.

130 Fowler, *MCPW* I, p. 98.

131 For more about this trial, see the commentary to **16**; for the Duchy of Lancaster archives, see below, p. 252. For a complete text of the trial, see Fowler, *MCPW* I, pp. 51–63.

132 See, for example, Fowler, *MCPW* II, pp. 26, 109, 152, 155

133 Fowler, *MCPW* I, pp. 78–9 and Jones 2000, p. 28.

134 See Fowler, *MCPW* II, pp. 37, 142 and 143.

which tells of great decay.[135] And in 1538 the Register of Archbishop Edward Lee (1531–44) states that the building was in such a bad state that it might fall down.[136]

Whatever the veracity of such accounts,[137] national events of the sixteenth century were to be still more serious for Ripon. In 1547, the Dissolution meant that chantries were the first to disappear; later, collegiate churches were included in this, which meant that Ripon was particularly vulnerable. Accordingly, all of Ripon's possessions were annexed to the Duchy of Lancaster and it may have been at this moment that the record of the 1228 trial held at the Ripon chapter house, which today exists in a fifteenth-century copy within which **15** and **16** are quoted, came to be in the Duchy of Lancaster archives.[138]

3. THE MANUSCRIPTS

a. *TNA: PRO DL 41/270* [C]

C is an early fifteenth-century Plea roll from the Duchy of Lancaster archives, preserved today in the National Archives. The roll itself is a transcript of a 1228 trial held at the Ripon chapter house before the king's judges, within which copies of **15** and **16** in the name of King Æthelstan have been made.[139]

b. *Copies by Antiquaries* [D, E]

i. *Bodleian, Dodsworth 160* (D): s. xvii. A copy of **15** can be found in this Dodsworth manuscript on f. 250v and a copy of **16** on f. 250r.[140] A marginal note states that Dodsworth made this copy 'Att Rippon 6 Sept. 1620'.

135 Fowler, *MCPW* II, pp. 165–6.
136 Fowler, *MCPW* II, p. 179; the chapter-house was in a similar state of decay.
137 Fowler, *MCPW* III, p. xxii.
138 This roll is now catalogued DL 41/270 in the National Archives. The Duchy of Lancaster was turned into a palatinate in 1351. Transcripts of various cases seem to have been made and stored so that precedents could be consulted for cases in the palatinate later on – it may be that this roll, on which we find **15** and **16**, was transcribed for this reason (I am very grateful to Prof. C. Carpenter for help with this aspect of the Lancaster records). For an account of the Duchy of Lancaster records, see *The Thirtieth Annual Report of the Deputy Keeper of the Public Records* (London, 1869), pp. i–viii.
139 For a full text of this 1228 trial, see Fowler, *MCPW* I, pp. 51-63. For more information, see above, p. 251.
140 *Summ. Cat.*, no. 5101.

ii. *Cambridge, Trinity College, O.3.2* (E): s. xvii. E is a collection of miscellaneous papers. A copy of both **15** and **16** can be found on f. 51r among material collected by Sir Thomas Herbert (d. 1682) for a history of the Ripon church. There are also impressive drawings of the steeple at Ripon and of various Ripon seals.

SIGLA

Note. The siglum A is reserved for original documents and the siglum B for non-contemporary copies on single-sheets.

a. *Principal manuscript source*

C. TNA: PRO DL 41/270 (s. xv^{in})

b. *Other manuscript sources*

D. Bodleian Dodsworth 160 (s. xvii)
E. Cambridge, Trinity College, O.3.2 (s. xvii)

NOTE ON THE METHOD OF EDITING

15 and **16** both survive in one principal manuscript witness, a Plea roll from the Duchy of Lancaster archives preserved today in the National Archives: manuscript C. The roll itself is the copy of a trial held in 1228 at the Ripon chapter house. As part of an attempt to define their rights, the Ripon chapter produce and cite **15** and **16**. The readings from D and E are not given since they are printed in full in Fowler, *MCPW* I, pp. 91–3. In C's copy of **16**, **y** is often written where **th** is intended; since this is an obvious corruption of thorn, **th** has been used in the text of **16** (for the same approach, see **12** in the Beverley archive and also Leach, *Memorials* II, p. 280).

THE CHARTERS OF RIPON

15

King Æthelstan confirms the Ripon Church and Chapter's rights to its peace, all its liberties and rights, a court in which to hear quarrels, its judgment through frodmortele *and that all its lands and men are to be believed* per suum ya et per suum na. [A.D. 927 × 939]

C. TNA: PRO, DL 41/270: copy, s. xv[in]
D. Bodleian, Dodsworth 160, 250v: copy, s. xvii
E. Cambridge, Trinity College, O.3.2, 51r: copy, s. xvii
Ed.: a. *Mon. Angl.* i, p. 173
b. Dugdale, *St Paul's*, p. 38, from *Mon. Angl.*
c. *Mon. Angl.* (rev. edn.), ii, p. 133 (no. 6)
d. Kemble 358, from *Mon. Angl.* (rev. edn)
e. Thorpe, *Diplomatarium*, p. 179, from *Mon. Angl.* (rev. edn)
f. Fowler, *MCPW* I, pp. 89–90, from C
g. Birch 646, from *Mon. Angl.* (rev. edn)
h. Birch 858, from C
i. Earle, *Hand-Book*, p. 438, from *Mon. Angl.* (rev. edn)
j. Harmer, *Writs*, Appendix I, p. 537, from Fowler, *MCPW* I
Listed: Sawyer 456
Translated: Gent, *Rippon*, p. 100
Edited from Manuscript C

In nomine sanctae et indiuiduae trinitatis, Atelstanus rex dei gratia rex Angliae omnibus hominibus suis de Eboratura per totam Angliam, salutem. Sciatis quod ego confirmo ecclesiae et capitulo Rypon' pacem suam, et omnes libertates et consuetudines suas, et concedo eis curiam suam de omnibus querelis et in[a] omnibus curiis de hominibus Sancti Wilfridi, ipsis et hominibus suis uel contra ipsos uel intra se ad inuicem, vel que fieri possunt, et iudicium suum per frodmortele, et quod homines sui sint credendi per suum ya et per suum na, et omnes terras habitas et habendas, et homines suos, ita liberos quod nec rex Angliae nec ministri eius nec archiepiscopus Eborum, nec ministri eius aliquod faciant uel habeant quod est ad terras suas uel ad sokam capituli. Testibus T. archiepiscopo Ebor., et P. praeposito Beuerlaci.

[a] *supra lineam* C

The earliest copies of **15** and **16** are quoted verbatim as part of the proceedings of a trial which is said to have taken place in 1228 in the chapter house at Ripon before the king's judges; the record of this event is preserved on an early fifteenth-century Plea roll in the Duchy of Lancaster holdings in the National Archives (it was after 1547 that various muniments from Ripon were transferred into the keeping of the Duchy of Lancaster, see above, p. 252). This record of a 1228 trial is lengthy and internally repetitive (for more about this document, see the commentary to **16**). In basic terms, it describes how 'Philippus de Ascelles', the sheriff of York, and 'Willelmus de Wychcombe', the bailiff of Walter de Gray, archbishop of York (1215–55), invaded Ripon's franchise and threatened the church's rights (for a full text of this document, see Fowler, *MCPW* I, pp. 51–63). According to this record, the church and chapter first called upon one of their own members, Geoffrey de Lardare, to enumerate Ripon's rights and immunities. As part of the proof of Ripon's rights, **15** and **16** are produced and they are quoted in their entirety in the text. In many ways **16** is a Middle English version of **15**, but it does add slightly more detail and elaboration.

15 is very clearly a forgery. It is in the form of a royal writ of King Æthelstan and is in Latin, even though no writ earlier than the reign of King Cnut survives and all authentic pre-Conquest writs are in Old English. It begins with a verbal invocation, something not found in pre-Conquest writs. In general, most of its terminology belongs more appropriately after 1066. The supposed witnesses, 'T. archiepiscopo' and 'P. praeposito Beuerlaci', themselves reveal that **15** is a post-Conquest composition. No archbishops of York before the Conquest have a name which begins with 'T'; the archbishops in the time of Æthelstan were Hrothweard (904 × 928–931) and Wulfstan I (931–56). This leaves the possibility that 'T.' here refers to Thomas I (1070–1100), Thomas II (1108–14) or Thurstan (1114–40). The record of the 1228 trial in which **15** is quoted describes how charters in the name of Henry and Stephen were produced to show to the king's justices, which ratified and confirmed all the liberties, customs and lands of the Ripon chapter (Fowler, *MCPW* I, p. 55). It may be that one of these documents formed the model on which **15** was based, but which does not now survive.

15, in the name of Æthelstan, purports to grant many extensive rights to Ripon: its peace (i.e. the peace of St Wilfrid as described in Domesday Book), all its liberties and rights, a court in which to hear quarrels, its judgement through *frodmortele* (Fowler, *MCPW* I, p. 90, n. 1, notes that this is a reference to 'Freomortel', 'an immunity for committing manslaughter'), all its lands and men and that its men are to be believed 'per suum ya et per suum na' (an expression which seems to imply that Wilfrid's men should be believed without the confirmation of an oath; see Fowler, *MCPW* I, p. 90, n. 2). **15**'s prohibition clause suggests that the Ripon chapter possesses these rights so freely that no king of England or any of his ministers, nor any archbishop of York or any of his ministers, may do anything to, or have any of, Ripon's lands or jurisdiction. The specific reference here to the king's ministers and to the archbishop of York and his ministers is telling since the 1228 trial (in which **15** is quoted) was a reaction to the invasion of Ripon's franchise by the sheriff of York and the archbishop's bailiff. There is the distinct possibility that **15** was concocted so that it could be used as part of this 1228 trial. Indeed all of the individual rights granted by **15** are mentioned at various points in the narrative record of the 1228 trial, adding to the suspicion that **15** was fabricated to help the case.

As with **12** in the Beverley archive, it is Æthelstan in particular who is credited as being the grantor of various rights and liberties to Beverley and Ripon. Since he is known to have made gifts to other northern religious communities (see **1** in the York archive and below, pp. 299–302), it is possible that he also had some genuine association with Ripon. But it may be that Ripon fabricated this connection at some later date (see further the commentary to **16**).

16

King Æthelstan grants privileges to the Church and Chapter of Ripon.
[A.D. 927 × 939]

C. TNA: PRO, DL 41/270: copy, s. xv^{in}
D. Oxford, Bodleian Library, Dodsworth 160, 250r: copy, s. xvii
E. Cambridge, Trinity College, O.3.2, 51r: copy, s. xvii
Rubric: Alia Charta Regis Adelstani
Ed.: a. *Mon. Angl.* i, pp. 172–3, 'Ex antiquo Registro penes…Lindale sub-decanum Ecclesiae Ripponensis 1630'
b. Dugdale, *St Paul's*, p. 38, from *Mon. Angl.*
c. *Mon. Angl.* (rev. ed.), ii, p. 133 (no. 5)
d. Kemble 360, from *Mon. Angl.* (rev. edn)
e. Thorpe, *Diplomatarium*, pp. 182–3, from *Mon. Angl.* (rev. edn)
f. Fowler, *MCPW* I, pp. 90–3, from C (with transcriptions of D and E)
g. Birch 647, from *Mon. Angl.* (rev. edn)
h. Birch 859, from C
i. Earle, *Hand-Book*, pp. 438–9, from *Mon. Angl.* (rev. edn)
j. Farrer, *EYC* I, no. 114, from C
k. Witty 1921, p. 39, from Earle
Listed: Sawyer 457
Edited from C

Wittyn' al that is and is gan,
That ich kynge Attelstane,
Has gyuen' as frelich as ich may,
To kyrke and Chaptel of Seynt Wylfray,
Of my fre deuocon',
Thar pees at Rypon',
On ilke syde the kyrke amyle,
For al ille dedes and ilke Gyle;
And wyth ine thayr kyrke yate,
Atte the stane that Grythstole hatte,
w^{t} Inne the kyrke dore And the quere
Thay have thayr pese for lesse an mare.
Ilkan of this stedes shal haue pees
Of frod mortel, and ilke dede;
That with heuten hit don' is,
Tol, Tem, Soke et Sake w^{t} yryn' and with water
deme and do wrak.
And atte the land of Seint Wilfray
Of ilkyn' Geld fre shal ben' ay,
That ẏ ne haue nan that langes me to
In thar wharshape shal haue at do.

And for ich will that thay ben' saue,
I wyll that thay alkyn' fredom haue,
And in all thyngges be als free
As herte may thynk or eghe may se.
Atte powar of a kynge
Mast may make fre any thing
And my sele haue I set her to,
For I will that naman this gyft undo.

Translation

Know all that is and all that has been,
That I, King Æthelstan,
Have given as freely as I may,
To Church and Chapter of St Wilfrid,
Out of my generous affection,
The peace at Ripon,
On each side of the church a mile,
For all ill deeds and also Guile;
And within the church gate,
At the stone that is called "Grythstole",
Within the church door and the choir
They have their peace for less or more.
Every one of these places shall have peace
From 'frod mortel' (i.e. manslaughter) and similar deed
That is done outside of it,
Toll, team, soke and sake, with iron and water,
  shall judge and punish.
And in the land of St Wilfrid,
Of every geld it shall be free forever,
Such that I have nothing that belongs to me
That in their discretion (*or possibly* lordship) shall have at their disposal.
And because I desire that they be unharmed,
I wish that they have every freedom,
And in all things be as free
As heart may think or eye may see.
At the power of a king,
Must make free any thing,
And I have attached my seal hereto,
For I will that no man this gift undo.

20–1 *These lines are obscure and the syntax is incomplete; the translation is not literal, in an attempt to make sense of the text.*

16 is copied directly above **15** as part of the record of a 1228 trial held in the Ripon chapter house. The earliest manuscript copy is that preserved in the Duchy of Lancaster archives as an early fifteenth-century transcript (Manuscript C); it subsequently attracted the attention of Dodsworth, in whose Manuscript 160 there is a copy (Manuscript D) and of Sir Thomas Herbert who made a copy of it (together with one of **15** and of charters of Henry I and Stephen and of drawings of St Wilfrid's steeple and of the old chapter seals) in the manuscript which is now Cambridge, Trinity College, O.3.2 (Manuscript E). **16** is edited from Manuscript C.

It is listed in Brown *et al.*, *Index*, as number 4183 and, most recently, in Boffey and Edwards, *Index*, also as no. 4183. It is also indexed in McIntosh *et al.*, *Linguistic Atlas* I, p. 126, where it is described as being in a dialect belonging either to Lancashire or North-West Yorkshire. In Fowler's edition, he notes the possibility that it was originally written in Northumbrian versified English but then copied by a scribe who introduced Midland forms (see Fowler, *MCPW* I, p. 91, n. 6, with a facsimile facing p. 91). Doyle suggests that the language of **16** belongs to the fourteenth century; see I. Doyle in Morris and Cambridge 1989, p. 20.

16 purports to grant to Ripon its peace on each side of the Minster for the space of a mile, the liberty known as St Wilfrid's League (for which see above, pp. 244–5); its right to sanctuary which involved the *Grythstole* and allowed a man to be immune from committing manslaughter (*frod mortel*); its right to toll and team, sake and soke; to the ordeal by hot iron and water (later accounts of Ripon Minster make reference to 'St Wilfrid's burning iron', something that gained the church revenue up until the Reformation; see Fowler, *MCPW* II, p. 167 and p. 192, for it being discontinued); and that it should be free from geld. Finally Æthelstan, the notional donor, is made to say that he has affixed his seal to the document so that no one could undo its terms. Many of these rights can also be found in **15**.

In lines 15–17 (beginning, *That with heuten*...) the copy of **16** seems to be corrupt. The rhyming couplets are interrupted with text that is both too long and does not rhyme. This text may well have been inserted at a late stage as an attempt to justify Ripon's rights to toll and team, sake and soke and judgement by iron and water; it reads very awkwardly. **16** in its original form perhaps would have moved from the line *Of frod mortel and ilke dede* to *And atte the land of Seint Wilfray*. It may be that **16** was designed as a kind of *pancarte* to cover all of Ripon's rights and privileges and, if so, could be updated as necessary. Just such an updating seems to explain the six extra lines found in both the Schøyen and Beverley cartulary copies of **12** (for more, see the commentary to **12**). Birch, in a footnote to his edited version of **16**, charter 859, suggests a possible textual emendation of: 'And do Wrak and ilke dede[s], Yat with heuten hit don, Sak 7 Sak To [7] Tem, W[t] Yrn and with water deme'.

The meaning of lines 20–1 is obscure. Fowler, *MCPW* I, p. 91, n. 5, suggests a possible translation of, 'That I have none that belong to me, (who) in there (sc. in the Liberty) warship (military service) shall have to do'. Farrer, *EYC*, p. 108, n. 1, suggests that *wharshape*, which is rendered by Dodsworth as *Harpfac* (manuscript D) and by Herbert as *Harshape* (manuscript E), might be a reference to 'the obsolete "hership", evidently meaning in this instance "lordship"'. Dr J. Wade has recommended a different translation to me, which has been used above.

The very idea that a charter of Æthelstan could be written in the form of rhyming Middle English marks **16** as unusual and it seems likely that it should be thought of as being linked somehow to **12** in the Beverley archive. It would be difficult to believe that two such idiosyncratic documents could emerge from the same area of the country, in the name of the same king, without there being some collusion. Ripon and Beverley, as archiepiscopal minsters, enjoyed a similar status and so it may have seemed appropriate that such a similarity was celebrated by these idiosyncratic rhyming charters.

There is some difficulty, however, in determining whether or not **12** and **16** were originally both composed at roughly the same time. In its current form, **12** seems most properly to belong to the early 1330s at a time when Beverley sought to justify its claims to collect thraves (see above, p. 219). But study of other documents in the Beverley archive suggests that earlier versions of **12**, dating at least to 1289, existed. It seemed probable, as mentioned previously (see **12**), that **12** was a document that could be updated by the Beverley community as and when it accumulated new rights or needed to demonstrate new privileges; the fact that it is written in Middle English makes this all the more likely. Any decision about the initial date at which **12** was composed is therefore very difficult but we should not rule out the possibility that it is older than 1289.

Two lines of **16** (*And in all thyngges be als free, As herte may thynk or eghe may se*) confirm the connection with **12**, which has similarly: *Swa mikel fredom giue i the, Swo hert may think or eghe see*. The problem with this connection is that **16** is preserved as part of the proceedings of the 1228 trial held in the Ripon chapter house, in other words from a much earlier time than the date given for **12**. Matters are made more complicated by the fact that **16** does not survive as an early thirteenth-century contemporary manuscript but as an early fifteenth-century transcript, with Middle English that belongs to the fourteenth century.

The questions that therefore remain are whether **16** could be seen to belong to the context of a trial dated as early as 1228 and whether **12** and **16** should be thought of as being composed at a similar date. Some comment should first of all be made about the whole text of the 1228 trial itself (for which see Fowler, *MCPW* I, pp. 51–63). There seems no good reason to doubt the authenticity of this record. In 1227 the young Henry III was finally able to rule without the intervention of regents and it was at this moment that a renewal of all claims to royal privileges was required. Thus to have the record of a 1228 trial at Ripon designed to investigate Ripon's rights is not unusual. Of the four king's justices named at the beginning of the document, and before whom the trial took place, William de Stuteuill, Richard de Percy and Robert de Lexyngton can all be easily found acting elsewhere as justices in the Close Rolls for 1227–31. Therefore such justices may well have held a special session at Ripon outside the normal context of the meeting of an eyre (I am very grateful indeed to Prof. M. Clanchy for his invaluable help with this document; it is his opinion that this record is what we would expect for an exceptional case of this kind in an eyre roll). In fact the only really suspicious element of the whole record, is the insertion of **16** itself into the text.

Doyle deemed **16** to be written in Middle English which belongs to the fourteenth century (see above). It is therefore clear that this part of the 1228 trial cannot belong to the early thirteenth century. Since there is every reason to believe that the rest of the text of the 1228 trial is genuine, there are various possibilities for how **16** came to be included in this record. It may be that the later copyist of the early fifteenth century version of the 1228 trial simply decided to insert **16** when no such document had formed part of the original 1228 proceedings. If we are to imagine such a scenario, we may wish to believe that this copyist was prompted to make such an addition by his knowledge of **12** in the Beverley archive.

Perhaps a more likely situation involves the copyist of the fifteenth century updating whatever vernacular record he found as part of the 1228 trial he was transcribing, into more current Middle English. It is clear that **12** was very important to the Beverley community and we can imagine that **16** was equally important to Ripon. It is presumably cast in rhyming Middle English so that it could be read out publicly and easily remembered; in such a situation it would need to be written in a form of Middle English that was understandable to contemporaries. Various manicules in the margins of **16**, which point to the parts of the trial in which Æthelstan's grants figure, suggest that these were indeed the important portions which needed to be quickly located so that they could be read out. Claims to liberties like those of Ripon and Beverley were challenged in the *Quo Warranto* proceedings of Edward I, held from 1278 to 1294. In the aftermath of these proceedings, those religious houses that kept their liberties often reinforced and updated their documentary position. Since various versions of **12** might belong to the late thirteenth century and to the early fourteenth century, it is perhaps logical to envisage a similar undertaking at Ripon and at the same time, with **16**.

In the end it is frustratingly difficult to pin down an exact moment when Beverley and Ripon may have colluded in their fabrication of **12** and **16**. It is also possible that these forgeries were not made contemporaneously: one religious house may have decided at a later point that the example set by the other was one worth following. But a document preserved in the Southwell *Liber Albus* may provide evidence for the inspiration, or indeed the collusion, behind **12**, **15** and **16**. It takes the form of a letter in the name of the York chapter concerning the liberties and customs of York Minster, which seems to have been written to assist Southwell Minster in its response to *Quo Warranto* proceedings of the years 1330–3, in which the Southwell chapter was obliged to substantiate its various privileges (Rollason *et al.*, *Sources*, pp. 30–1; for useful comments about the Southwell *Liber Albus*, see R. Sharpe, 'Peoples and Languages in Eleventh- and Twelfth-Century Britain and Ireland: Reading the Charter Evidence', forthcoming in *The Reality behind Charter Diplomatic in Anglo-Norman Britain. Studies by Dauvit Broun, John Reuben Davies, Richard Sharpe and Alice Taylor*, ed. D. Broun, p. 15, n. 40; I am most grateful to Professor Sharpe for showing me a copy of his work in advance of publication). In an attempt to do just this, the York chapter quote the rights of the York church as had been established at an earlier inquest of 1106, the implication being that Southwell, as an archiepiscopal minster, possessed many of the same rights (not all of this letter can be accepted as authentic; see Lambert 2009, pp. 128–30). It is crucial to find in this letter that the rights, customs and liberties of the York church were all thought to have been anciently given by King Æthelstan. It also states that Beverley and Ripon had almost identical liberties and many of the rights mentioned as belonging to these two churches in this letter can also be found granted in **12** and **16**. Leach drew attention to the importance of this letter as 'one of the most ancient records of the Chapter of York, showing the ancient privileges of the Archbishop and Canons dating from pre-Norman times'. Here is evidence that the rights known to belong to York were thought also to apply to its dependent churches. Leach even suggested that this letter 'became a model for the…sister churches of Beverley, Southwell and Ripon' (for an edited text of this letter, see Leach, *Visitations*, pp. 190–96, at p. 190, n. a, for the quotations). It is therefore of great interest that a section of the early fifteenth-century copy of the 1228 trial held at Ripon, in which **16** is quoted verbatim, also refers back to this inquest of 1106 (Fowler, *MCPW* I, p. 58) in an attempt to justify the antiquity of Ripon's rights.

The connections between the Beverley and Ripon archives, embodied in **12** and **16**, provide evidence for the relative standing of all these northern churches with regards to the York archbishopric. The letter composed to assist Southwell in its claim to various liberties was written in the early 1330s, as also was **12** in its current form. **16** may be of an earlier date but what is clear is that Southwell, Beverley and Ripon all believed that their liberties came from the time of Æthelstan, just as did York's. And in so doing, Beverley and Ripon concocted two of the most idiosyncratic forgeries of Anglo-Saxon charters known to exist.

DURHAM

INTRODUCTION

1. THE HISTORY AND ENDOWMENT OF ST CUTHBERT'S COMMUNITY

The religious community which was founded and established at Lindisfarne, an island off the north-east coast of England, in 635, and which evolved to become known as the community of St Cuthbert, did not remain in that location for the duration of the Anglo-Saxon period. In fact, it underwent two subsequent physical dislocations, first *c*. 875 when it set out on a period of seven years' wandering (eventually to find a new home at Chester-le-Street in about 883) and then, in 995, it settled, for the final time, at Durham.[1] Throughout these times the Cuthbertine community built up a landed endowment which made it, by the end of the Anglo-Saxon period, one of the most wealthy and influential institutions in Northumbria. But what is even more remarkable is that the Cuthbertines managed to accumulate these estates without the use of standard Anglo-Saxon charters; instead they seem to have operated outside the diplomatic mainstream which was in use further south in Anglo-Saxon England and to have relied on notes entered into the community's precious manuscripts as justification for their possessions. Extant records show that anyone wishing to grant land to the community had to deal with St Cuthbert himself; it was not sufficient to address a grant of land to the bishop of the community. Unfortunately only a few of these manuscript notes still exist;[2] but an early narrative source, the *Historia de Sancto Cuthberto*, which is probably to be dated to the mid-eleventh century, complements these notes.[3] It gives details of the endowment of the community from its foundation to the time of King Cnut.[4]

[1] For the difficulties in establishing these dates exactly, see below, p. 293, n. 144.

[2] The few notes which testify to this process are edited and explained below as **18**, **19** and **20**.

[3] For the date of composition of the *HSC*, see below, pp. 324–6. The seminal study of the *HSC*, and the land grants it describes, is that of Craster 1954. The most recent edition, with an accompanying commentary, is that of Johnson South, *HSC*; see also the unpublished Oxford DPhil. dissertation of Hall (D.) 1984.

[4] The *HSC* is one of the principal sources for the pre-Conquest history of St Cuthbert's community. More information comes from a variety of texts, including primarily: the *Cronica monasterii Dunelmensis* (*CMD*) a text written between 1072 and 1083 and closely related to the *HSC* (it was originally written into a gospel book that served also as a kind of register or cartulary; it is reconstructed and explained in Craster 1925*a*); the *De Obsessione Dunelmi et de probitate Uchtredi comitis, et de comitibus qui ei*

It is not the intention of this section to give an exhaustive history of St Cuthbert's community or of its accumulation of properties. Both of these subjects have already been thoroughly discussed.[5] But it is necessary to offer some outline of the primary events and the primary estate acquisitions of the Anglo-Saxon period. Such an exercise helps to explain why it was that St Cuthbert's community came to use its own, idiosyncratic approach to the documentation of its landed estates.[6]

a. *The Foundation of the Community at Lindisfarne and its Irish Roots (635–664)*

The Lindisfarne community had its roots in a deeply troubled and divided Northumbria of the early 630s. By 633 King Edwin had been in power for approximately seventeen years, but it was in October of this year that the King of the Britons, Cadwallon, defeated him in a fierce encounter at Hatfield.[7] The consequences of this defeat seem to have been severe: not only was Edwin himself killed, along with the majority of his army, but Cadwallon, together with his heathen Mercian ally Penda, was able to make hostile advances into Northumbria.[8] Many now found Northumbria an inhospitable place and chose to flee in order to secure their own safety.[9]

In 634, however, Oswald of Bernicia defeated Cadwallon at a place called *Hefenfelth*.[10] At the same time, Oswald united the Northumbrian royal houses of

successerunt (a kind of aide-memoire which documents, among other things, the history of six vills originally granted by Bishop Aldhun to Earl Uhtred as part of a dowry on the occasion of Uhtred's marriage to Aldhun's daughter; for discussion, see Morris (C.J.), *Marriage*); the *Historia regum*, a notoriously complicated historical compilation, surviving in only one manuscript (CCCC 139) whose rubrics declare it to be the work of Symeon of Durham but which in fact was made in various distinct stages using various different sources (one stage seems to represent the editorial work of Byrhtferth of Ramsey); for discussion, see especially Blair (P.H.) 1963, Offler, *North of the Tees*, pp. 3–26, Lapidge, *ALL* 2, pp. 317–42, Story, *Carolingian Connections*, pp. 116–26 and, for the historiographical context, see the collection of essays, Rollason, *Symeon: Historian*; and finally, the *Libellus de exordio atque procursu istius hoc est Dunhelmensis ecclesie*, which is more certainly the work of Symeon of Durham and which was written at some point between 1104–7 and 1115 (see Rollason, *Symeon: Libellus*, p. xliii).

[5] See, for example, Kapelle, *Norman*; Rollason, *Cuthbert*; Bonner 1989; Rollason 1989; Simpson 1989; Thacker 1989; Rollason 1992; Rollason 1995; Kirby 1995; and the two collections of essays, *St Cuthbert* and *AND*. In particular, Aird, *St Cuthbert*, pp. 9–59, discusses the history and endowment of St Cuthbert's community in depth, from which this section has greatly benefited.

[6] See above, pp. 9–16.

[7] Bede, *HE*, ii.20. Rollason, *Northumbria*, pp. 99–101, describes the hostility that existed between the British and English in Northumbria at this time.

[8] Bede, *HE*, ii.20. For Edwin and the York church, see above, pp. 25–7.

[9] Paulinus took Edwin's widow, Queen Ethelberga, his daughter, Eanfled and his son, Wuscfrea, with him to Kent and the safety of the regime of King Eadbald.

[10] See Bede, *HE*, iii.2. The location of this field was to the north of Hadrian's wall and eight miles to the north east of Hexham (see Colgrave and Mynors, *Bede's Ecclesiastical History*, p. 217, n. 2).

Bernicia and Deira under his rule, thus creating a period of relative stability and permitting him the opportunity of introducing Christianity into Northumbria.[11] When seeking instruction as to how to accomplish this goal, Oswald looked to Iona,[12] and Bishop Aidan was sent to Northumbria to offer guidance. 'On Aidan's arrival, the king appointed the island of Lindisfarne to be his see at his own request';[13] thus the religious community at Lindisfarne was established;[14] and its very location at Lindisfarne, only two miles from Oswald's 'royal city' of Bamburgh, the heart of the Bernician kingdom, perhaps indicates the close ties between secular and religious powers at this time.[15]

[11] Bede's *HE* and the anonymous *Life of Gregory the Great* state that King Edwin had, previously, been baptised by the Roman missionary Paulinus (in 627). There exists a tradition in British sources (in the *Historia Brittonum* of Nennius and the *Welsh Annals*) which credits Edwin's baptism to Rhun, son of Urien, but this does not seem likely. See N.K. Chadwick, 'The Conversion of Northumbria: a Comparison of Sources', in *Celt and Saxon: Studies in the Early British Border*, ed. N.K. Chadwick (Cambridge, 1963), pp. 138–66 and Rollason, *Northumbria*, pp. 120–1.

[12] Just prior to his accession to the Northumbrian kingdom, Oswald had spent a period of exile in Ireland and had received baptism there. For relations between England and Ireland at this time, see Hughes 1971; for the Ionan mission to Northumbria (and to Anglo-Saxon England in general), see Charles-Edwards, *Ireland*, pp. 308–26.

[13] Bede, *HE*, iii.3. It is very likely that Aidan thought Lindisfarne a good location because of its physical similarity and situation to Iona where he had received his training; the spiritual connotations of being cast out into the solitude of the wilderness would also presumably have been important; see O'Sullivan 2001, pp. 34 and 36–7 (at p. 37, for the importance of the tides to the symbolism of the Lindisfarne site). Nevertheless, many journeys would have been made by sea at this time and Lindisfarne's coastal location would have meant that it occupied an important position in this network of sea transport; see Blair, *Church*, p. 194. For the similarities between Lindisfarne and an Irish religious life, see Stancliffe 1989 and M. Herity, 'Early Irish Hermitages in the Light of the *Lives* of Cuthbert', in *St Cuthbert*, pp. 45–63.

[14] Lindisfarne was established in 635. This date is not given by Bede but it is found in later Durham tradition (Symeon, *LDE*, i.2) and also in the relevant annalistic entries in the *ASC*, the *Annales Lindisfarnensis* and in John of Worcester's *Chronicon*. In 635 Cuthbert was, in all probability, still a very young child (Colgrave, *Two Lives*, p. 5, suggests that Cuthbert's birth must have been within a year or so of 634). The precise arrangements for the various inhabitants of the early community at Lindisfarne are difficult to determine. Initially Aidan controlled the diocese whilst an abbot looked after the community. However, these arrangements appear to have been flexible as when Eata became bishop in 678 the roles of bishop and abbot were combined. Then, in Cuthbert's time, these functions were again separated as Herefrith became abbot of the community. For archaeological information about Lindisfarne at this time, see D. O'Sullivan, 'The Plan of the Early Christian Monastery on Lindisfarne: a Fresh Look at the Evidence', in *St Cuthbert*, pp. 125–42 and Blair 1991. For evidence of pre-viking sculptured stones, see Peers, 'The Inscribed and Sculptured Stones of Lindisfarne', *Archaeologia* lxxiv (1925 for 1924), pp. 255–70 and Cramp, *Corpus*, pp. 194–208 and plates 189–203.

[15] Bede, *HE*, iii.3, makes this relationship explicit, 'The king (i.e. Oswald) always listened humbly and readily to Aidan's advice and diligently set himself to establish and extend the Church of Christ throughout his kingdom'. Bamburgh is described three times by Bede as a 'royal city'; see Bede, *HE*, iii.6, iii.12 and iii.16. In Bede, *HE*, iii.12, we are told that, after Oswald's death, Oswiu placed his head in the church of Lindisfarne and his hands and arms in 'his own royal city of Bamburgh', which perhaps indicates that the Lindisfarne community was thought just as important as its secular counterpart.

Although we can be sure that Lindisfarne would have benefited from Oswald's favour and that it would have been provided with a grant of land, it is unfortunate that no early source gives any details about the extent or location of such a grant. Instead we have to rely on sources of a much later date to provide this information. Thus the *Historia de Sancto Cuthberto* sets out the boundaries of Lindisfarne territory; it describes a swathe of land primarily in modern-day Northumberland but also extending northwards, beyond the River Tweed, into the Lothian region.[16] The entry for 854 in the *Historia regum* also contains a list of Lindisfarne's possessions; although this takes much of its information from the account given in the *Historia de Sancto Cuthberto*, it adds 'Melrose and *Tigbrethingham* and Abercorn to the west of Edinburgh and Pefferham and Aldham and Tyningham and Coldingham and Tillmouth and Norham'.[17] Since these sources are of a later period, the details they contain should be used with caution. Whilst it seems reasonable to suggest that Lindisfarne, in the early seventh century, possessed territory in its immediate surroundings, it is perhaps less probable that such a recent foundation would be able to control lands which were in Lothian and thus far removed from Lindisfarne itself.[18] And Aird shows that there are certain chronological difficulties in some of these passages in the *Historia de Sancto Cuthberto* and the *Historia regum*.[19] Perhaps the most that can be said is that the *Historia de Sancto Cuthberto*, as a production by St Cuthbert's community, represents eleventh-century house traditions concerning the early endowment.[20]

[16] The southern part of this territory is described in the *HSC*, c. 4, as being 'from the river Tweed as far as the mouth of Warren Beck, and from there upwards as far as the place where Warren Beck rises next to Hepburn Hill, and from that hill as far as the river that is called Breamish, and from there as far as the river that is called Till, and all the land that lies on both sides of the same river Breamish up to the place where it rises'. The northern portion, situated beyond the Tweed, is described as extending 'from the place where the river Blackadder rises in the north as far as the place where it flows into the Tweed, and all the land that lies between that river Blackadder and another that is called the Leader towards the west, all the land that lies on the east side of that water that is called the Leader as far as the place where it flows into the Tweed toward the south, and all the land that pertains to the monastery of St Balthere, which is called Tynningham, from the Lammermuir Hills as far as the mouth of the Esk'. Rollason, *Northumbria*, pp. 44–5, describes this chapter of the *HSC* as being a 'free-standing document'.

[17] *HR* (8), pp. 101–2 (s.a. 854); see also Aird, *St Cuthbert*, pp. 13–15, where the same section of the *HR* is quoted (at p. 15). Blair, *Church*, p. 83, n. 26, suggests that this particular annal in the *Historia regum* could be evidence for a kind of monastic confederation. As Blair, *ibid.*, notes, minsters were often involved in hierarchical relationships whose details remain largely unknown (see also Craster 1954, pp. 178–9 and Rollason, *Northumbria*, p. 133). For minsters that owed obedience to Wilfrid, see Foot, *Monastic Life*, pp. 258–65; Rollason, *Northumbria*, pp. 133–4 and above, pp. 232–3.

[18] Aird, *St Cuthbert*, p. 15.

[19] Aird, *ibid.*, pp. 16–17.

[20] Craster 1954, p. 178, estimated that Oswald's foundation grant would have included Holy Island itself, the nearby Farne Islands and Islandshire. For a more recent appraisal of Lindisfarne's early possessions, see Johnson South in *HSC*, pp. 79–80.

These are the circumstances in which Lindisfarne was created.[21] Bede, our main source for these events, suggests that the Lindisfarne community had been intended to be the spiritual hub of the north. As the primary seat of Bishop Aidan, Lindisfarne became the centre of the Irish mission to the English and it is generally assumed that it also took on the role of 'mother church' in Northumbria.[22] Bede describes the general spread of the Christian faith at this time, a phenomenon influenced by the Irish.[23] Not only was Northumbria targeted but other kingdoms, such as that of the East Angles, were guided by Irishmen.[24] Lindisfarne became a natural focal point for many of these missions. Cedd, for example, was appointed by Finan, bishop of Lindisfarne (651–61), to travel to the province of the East Saxons in order to convert them.[25] Such processes inevitably led to Lindisfarne's becoming an influential ecclesiastical community. Finan enhanced the status of the Lindisfarne community further by building a church which was worthy of an episcopal see.[26] The very fabric of the church demonstrated an Irish influence as it was made of oak rather than stone and roofed with reeds.[27]

[21] *HSC*, c. 3, suggests that Lindisfarne may have owned other territories such as the Bowmont valley. For problems in accepting the authenticity of this grant of Bowmont, see Johnson South in *HSC*, pp. 73–4.

[22] In many ways Lindisfarne did fulfill this role of 'mother church' and of spiritual guide. In Bede, *HE*, iii.23, we learn that after Cynebill (the brother of Cedd) had built the monastery at Lastingham (near Whitby), he 'established there the observance of the usages of Lindisfarne where he had been trained'. Nevertheless, Blair, *Church*, pp. 44–5, demonstrates that Bede's narrative gives unusual prominence to Lindisfarne and points out both that the Irish mission itself was much wider yet (taking in other areas of England and places like Luxeuil), and also that the Irish influence was only one of a 'web of influences between the insular peoples and their neighbours' (at p. 44).

[23] So pervasive is the Irish influence in early Northumbrian monasticism that Campbell 1989, p. 4, urges us to think of Northumbria as not only being influenced by Ireland but as being a 'continuum' with it. Until 664, Iona itself appointed the bishops of Northumbria (see, for example, Bede, *HE*, iii.25). In its records of various gifts of lands and privileges to St Cuthbert's community, the *HSC* preserves the unusual detail that these gifts were made to the founding saint of the community, Cuthbert, which may be evocative of the 'Celtic' tradition of charter writing; for this suggestion, see Wormald, *Bede and the Conversion*, p. 17. For further discussion of Northumbrian diplomatic, see above, pp. 9–16.

[24] In 633 the Irishman Fursey established a monastery for the East Angles; see Bede, *HE*, iii.19. For a useful summary of the complicated subject of what the Irish contributed to the development of the English Church, see Blair, *Church*, pp. 43–9.

[25] Bede, *HE*, iii.22.

[26] There is reason to believe that there was more than one church on Lindisfarne in the time of Bede. For this, see Blair 1991, p. 47 (but note also the comments of O'Sullivan 2001, p. 40, about the alignment of these churches). Some founders of early Anglo-Saxon monastic complexes seem to have followed the Frankish pattern of providing two churches for the minster. See the comparable situation at Malmesbury (Kelly, *Malmesbury*, p. 8) and, for an overview, Blair 1992.

[27] Archbishop Theodore (668–90) later dedicated the church to St Peter. Eadberht, a later bishop of Lindisfarne (688–98), took down the reeds and covered both roof and walls with lead; see Bede, *HE*, iii.25. Very little physical evidence has survived relating to the early monastic site: O'Sullivan 2001,

b. *The Council of Whitby (664) and a Time of Competing Sees*

After more than two decades of relative stability, the 660s witnessed a growing disharmony in Northumbrian ecclesiastical ideology. The central issue around which this disagreement revolved was the correct method for calculating the date of Easter.[28] Religious communities were divided on how to calculate the defining holy day of the church. The council at Whitby was designed to resolve all the related issues and to establish a fixed date for Easter upon which religious men could agree, promoting the notion and existence of a united Anglo-Saxon church. The two main protagonists at the council were Colman, bishop of Lindisfarne, who spoke first and defended the Irish method of calculating Easter (which was rejected by Rome), and Wilfrid the priest, who championed the Roman observance.[29] Wilfrid's argument proved more persuasive and King Oswiu, who presided over the council, pronounced in his favour.[30] Colman could not reconcile himself to the new Roman method and, together with the Irish clergy who would not conform, left.[31] However, King Oswiu's judgement at Whitby had far greater implications yet; it rocked the ecclesiastical composition of Northumbria and allowed many different religious communities to compete for episcopal status. Although Bede depicts Whitby as an event which aided the unification of the Anglo-Saxon church,[32] it also provided a most public display of the rivalry between the Lindisfarne religious community, which had represented Irish customs, and those which represented the Roman cause, as championed by Wilfrid.[33]

Initially, Tuda, a man originally trained in Ireland but who had agreed to conform to Roman conventions, was selected by Oswiu as an ideal choice to replace Colman as bishop of Lindisfarne.[34] But Tuda's death the same year allowed Oswiu's son

---

p. 41. For Anglo-Saxon churches built of wood after the Irish fashion (including Lindisfarne), see Foot, *Monastic Life*, pp. 110–17 (at pp. 112–14 for Lindisfarne).

[28] Kirby 1974, p. 8; Cubitt, *Councils*, pp. 316–17; Rollason, *Northumbria*, pp. 123, 130 and 141–2; and Blair, *Church*, p. 79. Of course the council of Whitby had political significance also; see R. Abels, 'The Council of Whitby: a Study in Early Anglo-Saxon Politics', *The Journal of British Studies* xxiii (1983), pp. 1–25.

[29] Rollason, *Northumbria*, p. 130, stresses that it is important not to think of this council as a simplistic contest between 'Roman' and 'Celtic' and he points to the vast range of influences on early Northumbrian Christianity.

[30] Kirby 1974, pp. 8–9. For some of the consequences of the decision made at Whitby, see Stancliffe 1989, p. 21 and Stancliffe, *Bede, Wilfrid and the Irish*, pp. 5–6.

[31] *VW*, c. X and Bede, *HE*, iii.25.

[32] Bede, *HE*, iii.25. The importance of this event for Bede is suggested both by the detail in which he describes it and by the placement of the relevant chapter towards the centre of his *Historia ecclesiastica*.

[33] For the complex Northumbrian attitudes, especially those of Bede and Wilfrid, towards the Irish, see Stancliffe, *Bede, Wilfrid and the Irish*.

[34] Bede, *HE*, iii.26.

Aldfrith (king of Northumbria from 686 to 705) to support the election of Wilfrid, star of Whitby, as bishop of Northumbria. This was a moment of grave crisis for the Lindisfarne community: Wilfrid relocated the Northumbrian episcopal see to York, which meant that Lindisfarne temporarily ceased to be a bishopric at all;[35] accordingly, from 664 to 678, there is no record of a bishop at Lindisfarne.[36] From 669, when Wilfrid was confirmed as bishop of York, until 678, when he quarrelled with King Ecgfrith of Norhumbria (670–85), Wilfrid dominated the Northumbrian church and, at the height of his success, his authority and status must have rivaled that of King Ecgfrith and Archbishop Theodore.[37]

The year 678 represented a turning point in the fortunes of the Lindisfarne community as Wilfrid's ecclesiastical monopoly was broken: he was sent into exile from Northumbria, and, although he made several trips to Rome to plead that he had been unjustly treated, he never recovered his previous levels of power.[38] His vast episcopal diocese was divided into various smaller dioceses. Eata became bishop of the Bernician kingdom and had his see at Hexham. Later he transferred his seat to Lindisfarne, simultaneously becoming its abbot. At the same time Bosa was appointed as bishop for Deira, with his see at York,[39] and Eadhæd became bishop of Lindsey, which had been recently seized from the Mercian King Wulfhere by King Ecgfrith of Northumbria. Further restructuring occurred in 681 when Lindisfarne and Ripon became separate sees and Abercorn, with Trumwine at its head, was founded as a bishopric for the Picts.[40]

c. *A 'Great Blast of Trial' in the Lindisfarne Community and Consequent Cult Promotion*

Our later sources suggest that, initially, the 680s were a more prosperous time for the Lindisfarne community. A significant event was the 685 election of

[35] This was in accordance with Pope Gregory's initial plan; see Cubitt 1989, pp. 18–19 and above, pp. 31–2. For the notion that the move of the see to York was already intended in the time of Bishop Tuda, see John 1970, pp. 42 ff. (esp. p. 49); but see also the comments of Wallace-Hadrill (J.M.), *Bede*, p. 129.

[36] See Thacker 1989, p. 115.

[37] Theodore was archbishop of Canterbury from 668 to 690. On Wilfrid's high standing, see Cubitt 1989, p. 19.

[38] For Wilfrid's career, see above, pp. 28–32 and pp. 231–9

[39] For Bosa and the uncertainties of his tenure of the York church, see above, pp. 31–2.

[40] For more detail, see, for example, Kirby 1974, p. 9 and Rollason, *Northumbria*, pp. 44–5. As Blair, *Church*, p. 30, notes, Abercorn kept its British name, *Aebbercurning*, which may suggest some degree of continuity after it had been transferred into English control. For Wilfrid's deliberate acquisition of British *loca sancta* in territories recently taken from British control, see Blair, *ibid.*, pp. 30–1 and above, pp. 235–6.

Cuthbert, who was then a hermit on one of the Farne islands, to the bishopric of Lindisfarne.[41] Archbishop Theodore and King Ecgfrith had decisive roles in Cuthbert's promotion and the *Historia de Sancto Cuthberto* credits these two men in particular with the subsequent granting of estates to the religious community. Lindisfarne is supposed to have received land in York itself, the vill of Crayke, and also Carlisle, Cartmel, Gilling and Carham.[42] There is difficulty in establishing when exactly Lindisfarne could first claim possession of these areas. Aird suggests that the details supplied by the *Historia de Sancto Cuthberto* regarding these estates have suffered from the anonymous author's desire to associate every grant with Cuthbert himself. Aird notes that the pre-existence of a nunnery at Carlisle before the time of Cuthbert may cause us to doubt the information in the *Historia de Sancto Cuthberto* that Cuthbert himself established a congregation of nuns there.[43] And there may be similar problems in assigning Lindisfarne's acquisition of Crayke to such an early period as the reign of Ecgfrith. For, if the subject of the poem known as the *De Abbatibus* by Æthelwulf is indeed Crayke, then Crayke's establishment would have to be dated to a later time, that of King Osred (706–16).[44] It is even more problematic to know whether or not the Lindisfarne community possessed Cartmel and Gilling in the west, and Carham near the River Tweed, at this time as no other early sources links these estates to Lindisfarne.[45]

Although it is difficult to be sure how far these details can be taken at face value, it may be inferred that some of the estates mentioned had definite associations with the early Lindisfarne community; for example, Cuthbert visited Carlisle in 685.[46] And Crayke is intimately connected to the later history of the Lindisfarne community;[47] it was to be at Crayke, in North Yorkshire, that the community rested during its period of wandering,[48] and a later note in the Durham *Liber Vitae* (**18**) states that Crayke, having been stolen from the Cuthbertines by Ælle, was

[41] Bede, *HE*, iv.28, states that it was initially intended that Cuthbert should have his episcopal seat at Hexham rather than at Lindisfarne but Cuthbert himself seems to have been displeased with this suggestion.

[42] See *HSC*, cc. 5, 6 and 7; for the grant of land in York, see above, p. 31, n. 36.

[43] See *HSC*, c. 5 and Aird, *St Cuthbert*, pp. 18–19.

[44] Scholars are divided as to the identity of the subject of Æthelwulf's poem, which means that the early association of Crayke with Lindisfarne cannot be ruled out. Lapidge, *ALL* I, pp. 394–8, favours a Crayke identification; D. Howlett, 'The Provenance, Date and Structure of the *De Abbatibus*', *AA*[5] iii (1973), pp. 121–30, suggests Bywell as a more likely location.

[45] See Johnson South in *HSC*, pp. 81–2.

[46] See Bede, *VCP*, c. XXVII; it was on this occasion that Cuthbert had a premonition of King Ecgfrith's defeat at the battle of *Nechtansmere*. *VCA*, IV.8 and Bede, *HE*, iv.29, also associate Cuthbert with Carlisle; see also Blair, *Church*, p. 152.

[47] Both Carlisle and Crayke are estates supposedly granted by King Ecgfrith in the spurious charter, **17**.

[48] For Crayke as a *mansio* for the bishop of Lindisfarne, see Cambridge 1989, p. 380 and Aird, *St Cuthbert*, p. 19.

restored to the community in the 970s.[49] Cuthbert's community still laid claim to Crayke in the late eleventh century as it is noted in Domesday Book as belonging to the bishop of Durham, who had a church and a priest there.[50]

No definitive resolution is possible concerning the exact period when these estates came into Lindisfarne's ownership. But we should remember that it was Ecgfrith who provided the endowment for the foundation of both Monkwearmouth and Jarrow, a fact which demonstrates that he was a king who took care to enrich religious institutions in Northumbria.[51] It had also been Ecgfrith and Theodore who managed to convince Cuthbert to accept the episcopal see. There are therefore suggestions that Ecgfrith had taken a special interest in the welfare of the Lindisfarne community.[52]

King Ecgfrith's purported gifts of land and his role in the election of Cuthbert to the episcopacy suggest that the Lindisfarne community benefited from this king's support and favour. And Eata, who had been bishop of Lindisfarne, simultaneously took up the episcopal see of Hexham in place of the recently deposed Tunberht.[53] This meant that, early in 685, there had been Lindisfarne appointments to two Northumbrian episcopal sees. And these appointments represented direct attacks on the ecclesiastical monopoly previously enjoyed by Wilfrid, of whom Tunberht had been a staunch supporter.[54]

But King Ecgfrith died later in 685, and in 686 Eata died and left the see of Hexham vacant. But the most worrying event for the Lindisfarne community was the return to Northumbria of Wilfrid himself. In 686 Archbishop Theodore had persuaded King Aldfrith of Northumbria to restore Wilfrid to his former ecclesiastical positions.[55] Thus Wilfrid once again took charge of Hexham, Ripon, and also of York, and regained a good deal of his previous stature in the Northumbrian church.[56]

The death of Cuthbert himself in 687 meant that the Lindisfarne community was in a vulnerable position. Most seriously, it allowed Wilfrid to take control of the Lindisfarne see and thus to add it to his growing ecclesiastical jurisdiction.

49 For more detail about Ælle's theft of Cuthbertine estates, see below, pp. 287–9.

50 GDB, f. 304v and f. 381r.

51 There is a stone inscription in the chancel at Jarrow which credits Ecgfrith as being its founder; see Cramp, *Corpus*, plate 98. See also *HE*, iv.18–19 and Rollason, *Northumbria*, p. 165.

52 Aird, *St Cuthbert*, p. 21.

53 See Bede, *HE*, iv.27.

54 For an overview of the tensions that existed in the early Northumbrian church, see W.A. Goffart, *The Narrators of Barbarian History (A.D. 550–800)* (Princeton, 1988), pp. 235–328, esp. pp. 278–83, for the competition between Cuthbert's and Wilfrid's followers.

55 Aldfrith had come under the influence of Agilberht and Wilfrid; they persuaded Aldfrith of the validity of the Roman form of Christianity; see Colgrave, *Two Lives*, pp. 6–7.

56 For greater detail about these events, see Kirby 1995, p. 395 and above, pp. 237–9.

Although Bede, in his *Historia Ecclesiastica*, notes simply that 'the venerable Bishop Wilfrid held the see for a year until a successor could be appointed',[57] the reality was that Wilfrid's presence was a direct threat to the very existence of the Lindisfarne community; Wilfrid was a churchman who did not agree with the division of the Northumbrian diocese into smaller bishoprics and it is possible that he did not desire the re-establishment of Lindisfarne's episcopal status.[58] Certainly the Lindisfarne community was aware of the challenge posed by Wilfrid. Bede, in his prose *Vita* of St Cuthbert, refers to the period when '… after the man of God (i.e. Cuthbert) was buried, so great a blast of trial beat upon that church'. It is impossible not to link this statement about a 'blast of trial' to exactly that year when Wilfrid was in charge of the Lindisfarne see.[59] So serious was the situation that many of the brethren 'chose to depart from the place rather than be in the midst of such dangers'.[60]

That Lindisfarne managed not only to survive this crisis but also then to become one of the principal religious houses in Northumbria was due both to chance and to exceptional methods of self-promotion. As it happened, Wilfrid did not retain his levels of ecclesiastical power. In 687 John of Beverley was consecrated to Hexham, thus removing Wilfrid from that see. This perhaps lessened the pressure on the Lindisfarne community as it weakened Wilfrid's monopoly and diverted his immediate attention elsewhere. Wilfrid's position deteriorated more dramatically when he was exiled for a second time in 691 and he did not return until 705. Thus the period from 691 until 705 was one of relative security for the Lindisfarne community, which thus had the freedom to concentrate on methods to help ensure its future survival. Their principal strategy involved the promotion of Cuthbert and his cult, to an extent not seen before in the Insular world.

Lindisfarne, having had its very existence repeatedly undermined (especially by Wilfrid and his followers), recognised the need for an event which would propel it to the forefront of peoples' minds as a religious house of special sanctity and religious worth. The anonymous author of the prose *Vita* of Cuthbert records how,

[57] Bede, *HE*, iv.29.

[58] Any division into smaller bishoprics would have meant that Wilfrid was unable to build up an ecclesiastical franchise in Northumbria. Kirby 1995, p. 395, notes that Wilfrid was not in favour of the re-establishment of Ripon as an episcopal see and he stresses that it is likely that Wilfrid would have had a similar opinion regarding Lindisfarne's survival. Bede fundamentally disagreed with Wilfrid on this matter. In his *Epistola ad Ecgbertum*, Bede describes his desire for the Northumbrian diocese to be broken down into smaller areas to be managed by a greater number of bishops. For more about this, see above, p. 34, n. 59.

[59] Colgrave, *Two Lives*, p. 9.

[60] Bede, *VCP*, c. XL.

after a council of the elders of Lindisfarne had been convened, Bishop Eadberht (688–98) gave his permission for the opening of Cuthbert's tomb:

> Invenerunt itaque...quod dictu mirum est totum corpus tam integrum, quam ante annos xi deposuerunt. Non enim marcescente et senescente cute et arescentibus nervis strennue corpus erectum et rigidum est, sed membra plena vivaciter in articulis motabilia requiescebant...[61]

The discovery that Cuthbert's body was incorrupt was a miracle of central importance for the growth of Cuthbert's cult.[62] The Lindisfarne brethren, wishing to put the fact of Cuthbert's incorruptibility and sanctity to good effect, did not replace all of the goods that had originally been buried with Cuthbert's body: his shoes and his chasuble were kept and exhibited in the Lindisfarne church and later became wonder-working relics in their own right.[63] In fact most of those items and places with which Cuthbert was most closely associated in life received promotion at the hands of the Lindisfarne community at this time.[64]

The importance of the cult promotion undertaken by the Lindisfarne community can only be properly understood if one recognises that, in an Insular context, these measures were almost entirely unique.[65] In their dissemination of Cuthbert's cult, the Lindisfarne community drew on examples which were external to the Insular mainstream; many of the methods used to promote Cuthbert took their inspiration from contemporary continental cults.[66] Such measures are evocative

61 *VCA*, IV.XIV: 'And...they found a thing marvellous to relate, namely that the whole body was as undecayed as when they had buried it eleven years before. The skin had not decayed nor grown old, nor the sinews become dry, making the whole body tautly stretched and stiff; but the limbs lay at rest with all the appearance of life and were still moveable at the joints...' (trans. Colgrave).

62 For a more detailed analysis of this event, see D.W. Rollason, *Saints and Relics in Anglo-Saxon England* (Oxford, 1989), pp. 35–7 and also Thacker 1989, p. 106.

63 For those of Cuthbert's possessions which were not put back into his tomb, see *VCA*, IV.XIV and Bede, *VCP*, c. XLII. For the miracles wrought by these relics see, for example, *VCA*, IV.XVI and Bede, *VCP*, c. XLV. For information about Cuthbert's grave goods, see Battiscombe, *Relics*. Cuthbert's body was covered with magnificent garments: a white dalmatic (see H. Granger-Taylor, 'The Weft-patterned Silks and their Braid: The Remains of an Anglo-Saxon Dalmatic of *c.* 800?', in *St Cuthbert*, pp. 303–27), a chasuble made from silk *purpura* and an alb embroidered with golden thread (for the importance of silk in Anglo-Saxon England, and its many uses, see R. Fleming, 'Acquiring, Flaunting and Destroying Silk in Late Anglo-Saxon England', *Early Medieval Europe* xv (2007), pp. 127–58, at p. 152, for the shrouding of Cuthbert's body in silk). Perhaps the most famous of the grave goods is the gold and garnet pectoral cross (for which see R. Bruce-Mitford, 'Pectoral Cross', in Battiscombe, *Relics*, pp. 308–25).

64 For the promotion of Cuthbert's cult at this time, see D.W. Rollason, 'Why was St Cuthbert so Popular?' in Rollason, *Cuthbert*, pp. 9–22 and Thacker 1989.

65 See Thacker 1989, pp. 106–8, where he notes that Æthelthryth, the abbess of Ely, was the only other holy figure to have received similar cult attention. Thacker also shows that Iona, the mother house of Lindisfarne, did not foster or promote the image of its saint, Columba.

66 Thacker 1989, pp. 106–7, shows that the physical aspects of Cuthbert's cult were promoted according to contemporary continental fashions. Thus the shape of the wooden tomb in which Cuthbert was

of a community with high aspirations and a desire to promote itself above and beyond contemporary Northumbrian religious communities.

It is entirely in keeping with this outlook that, some time between 699 and 704, the Lindisfarne community produced a prose *Vita* to commemorate and publicise the life of Cuthbert.[67] No such work had yet been composed in Anglo-Saxon England, making the anonymous Lindisfarne author exceptional for being the first to produce a saint's *Vita* in its developed form.[68] The anonymous *Vita* of Cuthbert's life is significant in another regard: it enables us to recognise that one continental cult in particular had an influence on the development of Cuthbert's cult. Although the anonymous author's prologue borrows from four different authors including the Evagrian *Vita Antonii*,[69] the *Actus Silvestri*, and a letter drawn up *c.* 450 introducing the paschal cycle by Victorius of Aquitaine and addressed to Hilarus who was elected pope in 461,[70] its most substantial debt is to the *Vita Martini* by Sulpicius Severus, a late fourth-century work.[71]

The cult of St Martin was one of the most celebrated episcopal cults on the Continent. It is important to realise that the *Vita Martini* by Sulpicius was launched at a time of great ecclesiastical dissension; in this atmosphere, Sulpicius' work was designed as a kind of propaganda which championed the ascetic cause and thus as an indirect attack on those worldly bishops of Gaul.[72] The period just prior to the writing of the anonymous *VCA* had witnessed similar ecclesiastical dissension and uncertainty in the Northumbrian church: it was particularly apparent that Wilfrid, a worldly bishop, constituted a direct threat to Lindisfarne. By advertising that Cuthbert was a saint in the Martinian mould the Lindisfarne community aimed to transcend these divisions and to uphold Cuthbert, like Martin, as the most successful holy man, and bishop, of the time.

---

buried bears resemblance to Merovingian stone sarcophagi and, more precisely, the archangels which appear on the tomb recall those carved on a slab in Abbot Mellebaudis's funerary chapel at Poitiers.

[67] For the date at which this *Vita* was written, see Colgrave, *Two Lives*, p. 13. For the context surrounding the production of this *Vita*, see Colgrave 1958.

[68] Traces of the roots of the hagiographic genre can be detected in various texts; see M. Lapidge and R. Love, 'The Latin Hagiography of England and Wales (600–1550)', *Hagiographies: histoire internationale de la literature hagiographique latine et vernaculaire en Occident des origines à 1550*, Corpus Christianorum, vol. iii (2001), pp. 203–325, at pp. 208–13.

[69] Evagrius had made a translation of the original *Vita Antonii* by Athanasius.

[70] Colgrave 1958, pp. 42–4 and Colgrave, *Two Lives*, pp. 60–5 and pp. 310–11, describes this remarkable opening to the anonymous Lindisfarne *Life*.

[71] Thacker 1989, pp. 110–11, notes how Cuthbert's missionary activities, his techniques in performing miracles, his relations with angels and his dislike of spectators all take their inspiration from the *Vita Martini*. C. Stancliffe, *St Martin and his Hagiographer: History and Miracle in Sulpicius Severus* (Oxford, 1983), pp. 71–2, states that the *Vita Martini* was completed by the date of Martin's death in 397, but that it may even have been completed earlier, in the summer of 396.

[72] See Stancliffe, *St Martin and his Hagiographer*, pp. 71–86.

But Wilfrid remained a problem. In 703 King Aldfrith had to convene a council at *Ouestraefelda* to determine how to deal with Wilfrid; this led to the excommunication of Wilfrid and his followers.[73] But in 705 King Aldfrith died, which meant that one of Wilfrid's most powerful opponents had been eliminated. Then John of Beverley, who, in 687, had been elected as bishop of Hexham, left Hexham to become bishop of York (to replace Bosa who had just died).[74] This meant that the see of Hexham was vacant and Wilfrid was able to return for a second time. He was restored as bishop of Hexham, and this thrust him, once again, to some sort of ecclesiastical power in Northumbria.[75] Wilfrid even managed to extend his influence further by gaining the support of Aldfrith's sister, Ælfflæd, abbess of Whitby (who had previously been in favour of Cuthbert) and by becoming the adoptive father of the new king of Northumbria, Osred.

Despite Wilfrid's death in 710, there was no immediate eclipse of the Wilfridian faction; in fact his death provided the occasion for the creation of a new, Wilfridian cult, a cult which received promotion, *c.* 720, through the medium of its own *Vita*.[76] And Acca, his disciple and follower, replaced him as bishop of Hexham which must have caused continued anxiety for the Lindisfarne community.[77] In addition, between 721 and 724 there was a break in the sequence of Lindisfarne bishops, from which it may be inferred that Lindisfarne's continued existence as an episcopal see was being questioned.[78]

It is almost certain that the crisis being felt at Lindisfarne had been caused by Wilfrid's cult. The *Vita Wilfridi* was followed very closely by the production, *c.* 721, of another prose *Vita Cuthberti*, this time written by Bede.[79] Such a proliferation of written material was quite extraordinary for the time, especially since there was a paucity of hagiography in this early period and since the Lindisfarne community already possessed a recently finished (699 × 704) prose *Vita* of Cuthbert. Although Bede's *Vita* includes material not found in the anonymous *Vita*,[80] it cannot have been the case that the extant anonymous *Vita* was simply out-dated. It seems rather that this burst of hagiographical material points to a period of exceptional ecclesiastical tension and competition when the

73 *VW*, cc. XLV–XLVII and above, p. 238.

74 Bede, *HE*, v.3; these events took place in 706; see above, pp. 32–3.

75 *VW*, c. LX and Bede, *HE*, v.3.

76 The *Vita* of Wilfrid was written by Stephanus; see Kirby 1983.

77 Acca was closely associated with Wilfrid. Earlier on in his career he had received training at Wilfrid's hands and had accompanied him to Rome; see Bede, *HE*, v.20 and also Kirby 1995, p. 396.

78 For this suggestion, and for details about the break in episcopal succession, see Kirby 1995, p. 396.

79 By this stage Bede had already produced a metrical *Vita Cuthberti* which was finished in the period 704 × 716 but probably nearer 704, and possibly revised at a later stage (see Lapidge 1989, pp. 84–5).

80 This material came from conversations with abbot Herefrith; see, for example, Bede, *VCP*, c. VIII.

followers of Cuthbert and of Wilfrid were vying for superiority and influence within the Northumbrian church.[81] The Bedan *Vita* looked to sharpen the image of Cuthbert in direct response to the literary challenge offered by Wilfrid's cult.[82] Indeed Wilfrid's cult was such a threat to Lindisfarne at the time when Bede was writing that this would seem to be the reason for Bede's concentration on the crisis of 687–8, the 'great blast of trial', which had been initiated by the period of Wilfrid's tenure of Lindisfarne. Bede also included allegedly autoptic testimony to the effect that the dying Cuthbert urged the community to depart from Lindisfarne with his bones rather than place themselves under the control of schismatics; a clear indication that Lindisfarne felt that its position was being threatened.[83]

d. *Post-Bedan Lindisfarne: 735–875*

The Lindisfarne community was closely involved in politics of the day. In 731 we find King Ceolwulf of Northumbria (729–37) being temporarily deposed, retreating to Lindisfarne, and then, later in the same year, being restored to power.[84] It is of considerable interest that the *Anglo-Saxon Chronicle* notes, for the same year, that Acca, bishop of Hexham, had been 'driven from his bishopric'.[85] If it is correct to assume that Ceolwulf had retreated to Lindisfarne earlier on in 731 and thus before Acca had been driven from his see at Hexham,[86] then it is perhaps possible to conjecture about the political situation. That Ceolwulf chose to retreat to Lindisfarne, the community with traditional links to the ancient Bernician royal house situated at Bamburgh, was no coincidence. Ceolwulf, who was of the Bernician line,[87] reckoned that Lindisfarne, with its associated connections, would be supportive of his cause. Acca had been a staunch Wilfridian and it is entirely likely that his expulsion from Hexham in 731, whether engineered by Cuthbert's community or not, allowed for, or was the result of, the return to power of Ceolwulf, who was, at the least, closely associated with Cuthbert's

[81] Kirby 1995, p. 397, suggests that the period from 715 to 723/4 was one which witnessed increasing pressure on the conservatism practised at Lindisfarne (manifested by Lindisfarne's stance on the dating of Easter at Whitby) and he argues further that Acca and other Wilfridians of the time were challenging Lindisfarne's episcopal status.

[82] It was also at this time, during the episcopate of Eadfrith, that the relics of Cuthbert were brought to the fore and publicised by the Cuthbertine community; see Thacker 1989, p. 119.

[83] Bede, *VCP*, c. XXXIX.

[84] Bede, *HE*, v.23 'Both the outset and course of Ceolwulf's reign were filled by so many grave disturbances that it is quite impossible to know what to write about them or what the outcome will be'. For comments about this period, see Kirby 1974, pp. 20–1.

[85] *ASC DE*, s.a. 733 (*recte* 731).

[86] This is the order of events suggested by the relevant entry in *HR* (4), p. 30 (s.a. 732).

[87] Kirby 1974, p. 21.

community. These are the indications that the struggle which had been initiated, after the council of Whitby (664), between Cuthbert's community and Wilfridians (who were now dispersed across the various sees over which Wilfrid had had jurisdiction) was continuing into the eighth century.

In 737 Ceolwulf was forced to retire permanently to the religious community of Lindisfarne and this retirement involved him granting the vill of Warkworth with its dependencies to St Cuthbert's community.[88] Ceolwulf's successor to the throne in Northumbria was Eadberht (737–58), who clearly had a different power base from Ceolwulf. Eadberht's brother was Archbishop Ecgberht of York; Ecgberht had assumed his archiepiscopal position before his brother acceded to the throne and it seems likely that Ecgberht, following his elevation to metropolitan status, aided Eadberht in his accession to the throne.[89] Thus Eadberht's supporters would have been drawn from a more southerly centre, a centre which perhaps revolved, at this time, around York. York had once been the see of the kingdom of Deira and had also been, at intervals, in the possession of Wilfrid.[90]

It seems, therefore, that Eadberht had been promoted to the throne by those powers that were in direct opposition to Ceolwulf and his Lindisfarne allies. Subsequent events in our sources, which involve Eadberht, are more explicit about such divisions. In 750 Eadberht can be found chasing Offa, the son of a previous Northumbrian king, Aldfrith (686–705), who was forced to take sanctuary with the Cuthbertine community in order to escape Eadberht. Offa's seeking of aid at Lindisfarne would again seem to indicate that he thought it likely that this old centre of the Bernician kingdom would lend him support. Eadberht was affronted by the aid and sanctuary that Lindisfarne had offered to Offa. As a consequence, Eadberht imprisoned Cynewulf (d. 782/3), who was then bishop of Lindisfarne, at Bamburgh, and laid siege to the Lindisfarne community itself, in order to extricate Offa from his sanctuary.[91] Symeon adds a significant detail to this event when, on the imprisonment of Cynewulf, he notes that 'Frithuberht, bishop of Hexham, administered the see of Lindisfarne until the king was placated and Cynewulf,

[88] See *HSC*, c. 8. Ceolwulf perhaps remained an influential figure even after his retirement since his death is recorded in *HR* (4), p. 42 (s.a. 764). For Ceolwulf's gifts of land, see also the entry common to the *Cronica monasterii Dunelmensis* (hereafter *CMD*, for which, see below, p. 326), p. 523 and Symeon, *LDE*, ii.1. For the genuineness of these grants, see Craster 1954, p. 185 and Johnson South in *HSC*, pp. 82–3 and 85–6.

[89] Ecgberht became bishop of York in 732 and archbishop in 735. For suggestions about the special power of archbishops at this time, see Campbell 1989, p. 16. For the combined rule of Ecgberht and Eadberht, see above, pp. 33–6.

[90] On the general political context, see Rollason 1996.

[91] See *HR* (4), pp. 39–40 (s.a. 750). On this event, see also Hall (D.) 1989, p. 432 and Rollason, *Northumbria*, pp. 193–5.

who was then released from his captivity, returned to his own church'.[92] That Eadberht punished Lindisfarne by having a bishop of Hexham assume control of the community suggests that Lindisfarne was still in competition with Hexham.[93] The old division between those who supported Cuthbert's cult, and were thus representative of the ancient Bernician kingdom, and those who supported Wilfrid's cult, and were representative of the ancient Deiran kingdom, endured.[94]

It should not be thought of as surprising that the Northumbrian religious communities were heavily involved in, and able to influence, the secular political scene. Most of the bishops of Lindisfarne are described as being from noble background.[95] Indeed a religious community's ability to influence certain secular factions perhaps provided the most certain means for its security. Some of the political events which are given only scanty attention in our extant sources perhaps display the influence of a religious community.[96] The entry for 788 in the *Anglo-Saxon Chronicle* notes that 'Ælfwald, king of the Northumbrians, was killed by Sicga on 23 September...and he (Ælfwald) was buried inside the church at Hexham'.[97] It can be inferred from Ælfwald's burial at Hexham that he had affiliations with that see.[98] No other detail about Sicga is given at this point. The entry for 793 in the *Anglo-Saxon Chronicle* famously describes the sacking of the Lindisfarne church at the hands of vikings. Added to the end of this entry is the detail that 'Sicga died on 22 February'.[99] In the very same moment as describing the miserable fate of the Lindisfarne community, the *Anglo-Saxon Chronicle* has seen fit to include information about Sicga, a figure otherwise known only for his slaying of Ælfwald. It may be pushing the evidence too far, but it is possible that the chronicler knew, or simply thought of, Sicga as having Lindisfarne affiliations. And this receives corroboration from the entry for 793 in the *Historia*

[92] Symeon, *LDE*, ii.2.

[93] There are persistent suggestions that Hexham and Lindisfarne were in direct competition with one another during this early period. For the cessation of the Hexham see later in the ninth century, see below, pp. 289–94.

[94] For further discussion, see Aird, *St Cuthbert*, pp. 22–3.

[95] See Aird, *St Cuthbert*, p. 23. Archaeological investigations at Northumbrian monastic sites such as Hartlepool and Whitby have revealed how difficult it is to distinguish religious sites from aristocratic ones; see Rollason, *Northumbria*, p. 183.

[96] It is striking how many of the eighth-century Northumbrian kings' reigns end in a king receiving the tonsure and retiring into a religious community. See, for example, *ASC DE*, s.a. 757 (*recte* 758), where Eadberht is tonsured and his son, Oswulf, succeeds.

[97] See *ASC DE*, s.a. 789 (*recte* 788).

[98] *HR* (4), p. 52 (s.a. 788), notes just how closely Ælfwald was affiliated with Hexham and the Wilfridian cult. The subsequent entry in the same source for 791, *HR* (4), p. 53 (s.a. 791), describes how Ælfwald's sons had found refuge at York which supports the notion that this family had a power base which was closely related to Deira. For the murder of Ælfwald's sons, see above, p. 39.

[99] See *ASC DE*, s.a. 793.

regum which notes that Sicga was later buried at Lindisfarne.[100] It may be that the Lindisfarne community was somehow involved in the elimination of a king who was unsympathetic to its cause.[101]

The Lindisfarne community, feeling the pressure of encroaching factions, perhaps had no choice but to involve itself in politics of the day in order to safeguard its land and wealth.[102] But an altogether more shocking event occurred at the end of the eighth century, with the arrival of vikings at Lindisfarne in 793.[103] Alcuin regarded the viking raid on Lindisfarne in 793 as a divine manifestation prompted by the lax morals of the community and wrote accordingly to Bishop Higbald (780/1–803).[104] Later Durham historical traditions, by various methods, depict this attack as leading to the church of Lindisfarne being 'destroyed almost to the point of extermination by a most lamentable devastation, abounding in blood and rapine'.[105]

The arrival of vikings led to a period of uncertainty for the Lindisfarne community, with the result that Bishop Ecgred (830–45) oversaw a certain amount of reorganisation, perhaps as part of an initiative designed to protect the community from future viking incursions. The *Historia de Sancto Cuthberto* states that Cuthbert's body was translated from Lindisfarne to Norham-on-Tweed. Although the later Durham chronicler, Symeon, makes no mention of this translation, other sources seem to confirm that it did take place.[106] We are

100 See *HR* (4), p. 54 (s.a. 793): 'Ipso quoque anno Sicga dux, qui interemit Elfwaldum regem, interiit propria nece, cuius corpus ad insulam Lindisfarnensem perlatum est ix. Kal. Maii.'. The slaying of Ælfwald took place in the very north of the kingdom of Northumbria, on Hadrian's wall, and thus very close to the centre of Lindisfarne's power; *HR* (4), p. 52 (s.a. 788).

101 Rollason, *Symeon: Libellus*, p. 86, n. 20, notes that it is odd that Symeon, given his interest in Cuthbert, does not mention the church of St Oswald and St Cuthbert which was built on the site of King Ælfwald's death. If Lindisfarne had been in some way implicated in the murder of this king then this could be the reason for Symeon's silence. Story, *Carolingian Connections*, p. 92, likewise suspects that Sicga's burial at Lindisfarne 'implies that the community of St Cuthbert was deeply involved in the secular political intrigues of the day'.

102 Note the comments of Aird, *St Cuthbert*, pp. 22–3.

103 See Woolf, *Pictland*, pp. 43–7 (at p. 43, for the possibility that there had been Scandinavian attacks on Shetland before 793).

104 For the famous letter addressed to Bishop Higbald and the Lindisfarne community, see Allott, *Alcuin* 26. Alcuin thought that this attack presaged things to come and so sent a letter to nearby Monkwearmouth-Jarrow in order to warn inhabitants there against immoral behaviour (see Allott, *Alcuin* 29). Higbald had been consecrated bishop at Sockburn, County Durham: *ASC DE*, s.a. 780.

105 Symeon, *LDE*, ii.5. Symeon had a particular agenda when depicting these early viking raids as being disastrous for the continued existence of the Lindisfarne community (see, for example, Johnson South in *HSC*, p. 99). See also the account in *HR* (4), pp. 54–5 (s.a. 793), where vikings 'laid all waste with dreadful havoc, trod with unhallowed feet the holy places, dug up the altars, and carried off all the treasures of the holy church' (at p. 55).

106 The first source to mention this translation is the eleventh-century list of the burial places of English saints known as *Secgan be þam Godes sanctum þe on Engla lande ærost reston* (on which,

told that the religious community took down the church originally built by Aidan at Lindisfarne and then reconstructed it at the new site at Norham; the relocation also involved the transportation of Cuthbert's and Ceolwulf's relics.[107]

Although it is impossible to be certain, it is likely that the community's move to Norham was a temporary measure designed to alleviate the threat of viking raids.[108] Norham is located slightly inland and to the north-west of Lindisfarne and, as such, was out of the immediate path of vikings. And Bishop Ecgred tried to consolidate the community's position; not only did he add more land to their jurisdiction in the vicinity of Norham,[109] but he also furthered the community's landed interests in a more southerly direction as he granted to St Cuthbert the vill of Gainford which is situated on the River Tees and also the vills of Cliffe, Wycliffe and Billingham in Hartness which lay south beyond the Tees.[110]

---

see Rollason 1978). It states that Cuthbert's body rested at *Ubbanford*: Rollason 1978, p. 87. The annal for 854 in the *Historia regum* explains that *Ubbanford* was an ancient version of the place-name Norham: *HR* (8), p. 101 (s.a. 854); see also Craster 1954, p. 188 and Aird, *St Cuthbert*, p. 24. William of Malmesbury (in his *GP*, iii.129.2) also notes this translation. For explanation of these events, see Johnson South in *HSC*, pp. 84–5. Although the present church of Norham is of post-Conquest date, the survival of pre-Conquest sculpture there suggests that it originated in the Anglo-Saxon period: see Craster 1954, p. 187 and below, p. 289, n. 125.

107 *HSC*, c. 9.

108 See also Aird, *St Cuthbert*, p. 25. Woolf, *Pictland*, pp. 80–3, makes the interesting suggestion that in the period following the removal of the Lindisfarne see to Norham, a single Bernician see was consolidated at Carlisle, thus removing Norham from that role. This may help to explain why we later find Abbot Eadred of Carlisle acting as the head of Cuthbert's community (for Eadred, see further below, p. 289, n. 125).

109 *HSC*, c. 9, notes that Ecgred 'gave the vill itself [i.e. Norham] to the holy confessor with two other vills, Jedburgh and Old Jeddart and whatever pertains to them, from Dunion Hill as far as Jedmouth, and from there to Wilton, and from there beyond the hill [Dunion?] towards the south'. For more about these estates, see Johnson South, *HSC*, pp. 83–4. Rollason 1989, p. 417, n. 17, suggests that this translation to Norham did not occur.

110 See *HSC*, c. 9, where it is also stated that Ecgred built the churches of Billingham and Gainford. But the existence of Anglian sculpture of an earlier date from both places indicates that these churches had already been founded by the time of Ecgred's pontificate: Craster 1954, p. 187; see Cramp, *Corpus*, pp. 48–53 (plates 15–18) and pp. 80–90 (plates 57–75), for sculptural remains at Billingham and Gainford respectively. Chapter 11 of the *HSC* also notes that Ecgred and King Ceolwulf together gave the vills of Woodhorn, Whittingham, Edlingham and Eglingham to St Cuthbert's community. It is clearly not possible that Ceolwulf (who abdicated his throne in 737) could make a grant alongside Bishop Ecgred (830–45). Aird, *St Cuthbert*, p. 26, suggests either that this entry in the *HSC* represents the occasion of Ecgred's 'reconsecration' of these churches which were originally granted by King Ceolwulf or that Ecgred won back estates that had previously been granted by King Ceolwulf and then lost from the patrimony of Cuthbert's community in the eighth century. For a map of all the estates given to St Cuthbert's community in the *HSC*, see Johnson South in *HSC*, between pp. 118 and 119. For the great importance of wealthy bishops like Ecgred for the survival of episcopal sees, see Giandrea, *Episcopal Culture*, pp. 147–50 (at p. 147, n. 132, for Ecgred himself).

Of course the *Historia de Sancto Cuthberto*, a text produced by the Cuthbertine community itself, had every reason to fabricate, and in the process augment, details of land given to the Cuthbertine community.[111] This being the case, it is essential to consider its details with care.[112] But what is absolutely certain is that Lindisfarne managed to survive this tumultuous period in Northumbrian history better than many of its counterparts, Monkwearmouth and Jarrow being examples of celebrated pre-viking Northumbrian monastic houses that disappear from view after the mid-ninth century.[113] Perhaps, then, the most valuable use of the *Historia de Sancto Cuthberto* lies in the hints it delivers as to how Lindisfarne engineered its survival. Events such as the translation of Cuthbert's body and his relics to Norham echo that earlier period of Lindisfarne history when the community practised shrewd cult management and augmented Cuthbert's image in the face of threats from Wilfridians.

The 860s saw the renewal of internal conflict within the kingdom of Northumbria and these tensions seem to have had a direct and negative effect on the Lindisfarne community. The *Anglo-Saxon Chronicle* notes, for the year 867, that 'there was great civil strife going on in that people (i.e. the Northumbrians), and they had deposed their king Osberht and taken a king with no hereditary right, Ælle'.[114] The *Anglo-Saxon Chronicle* suggests that Osberht (848/9, expelled 862/3; restored 867, died 867) had a claim to be the rightful king. Whether or not this is the case, the *Historia de Sancto Cuthberto* preserves the tradition that neither king was well inclined towards Lindisfarne, Osberht having stolen the vills of Warkworth and Tillmouth from the community and Ælle (862/3–867)

[111] Chapters 1 to 9 of the *HSC*, which cover the period from Lindisfarne's foundation to the mid-ninth century, suggest that the community had acquired estates in the north around the River Tweed (e.g. Norham and Carham), in the west near the River Teviot (e.g. Carlisle, Holm Cultram and Jedburgh); also a group of estates (e.g. Eglingham, Whittingham, Edlingham, Warkworth, Brinkburn and Hauxley) which lay between the Rivers Aln and Coquet; and also a group of estates on the east coast (e.g. Easington, Little Eden, Horden, Castle Eden, Monk Hesleden, Hutton Henry, Hartlepool, Billingham, Gainford) between the Rivers Tyne and Tees.

[112] For an assessment of the details supplied in the *HSC*, see Craster 1954 (at pp. 180 and 186, for those lands said to have been given by Bishop Ecgred), Aird, *St Cuthbert*, pp. 9–59 and the commentary of Johnson South in *HSC*.

[113] See the comments in Blair, *Church*, pp. 312–13. For the fate of Monkwearmouth and Jarrow in the mid-ninth century, see, for example, R. Cramp, 'Monastic Sites', *The Archaeology of Anglo-Saxon England*, ed. D. Wilson (Cambridge, 1976), pp. 201–52, at pp. 229–41 and R. Cramp, 'Monkwearmouth (or Wearmouth) and Jarrow', in *Blackwell*. R. Cramp, *Wearmouth and Jarrow Monastic Sites*, Volume 1 (Swindon, 2005), pp. 34–5, emphasises that there were many destructive episodes which could have led to the abandonment of Monkwearmouth and Jarrow and also that 'the process of their depopulation may have been slow or fast' (at p. 34).

[114] *ASC C*, s.a. 868 (*recte* 867).

having stolen Billingham, Cliffe, Wycliffe and Crayke.[115] Ælle is also depicted as being based at Crayke, a vill traditionally associated with Cuthbert's community, and being able to raise an army from there.[116]

Despite the fact that Ælle, once in power, seems to have acted quite to the detriment of the Lindisfarne community, it may be the case that it was the Lindisfarne community which had enabled his rise to the throne in the first place. The estates stolen by Osberht lay in the old kingdom of Bernicia whilst those taken by Ælle lay in Deiran territory. Aird therefore suggests that Osberht's support came primarily from Bernicia and that Ælle's support came from Deira. Aird then highlights the potential significance of the following statement in the *Historia de Sancto Cuthberto* which refers to the actions of Ælle with regard to St Cuthbert's community: 'who (i.e. Ælle) made good promises to the holy confessor but acted badly'. It is possible that the *Historia de Sancto Cuthberto* here reveals the existence of an arrangement whereby Ælle, before he became king, promised to treat the Lindisfarne community favourably. Aird proposed as one possibility that 'Osberht's fall and replacement by Ælle may have involved the complicity or perhaps active agency of the Cuthbertine community'.[117]

If Aird is correct,[118] then this is once again evidence of Lindisfarne's involvement in politics of the day. It is the trace of an event which is distinctly reminiscent to that found with regard to the murder of King Ælfwald by Sicga.[119] Lindisfarne's political pragmatism led it to abandon its traditional, Bernician allies, in the form of Osberht, and to look instead to Deira, and to Ælle, for support. Lindisfarne perhaps recognised that, with the arrival of a greater number of vikings in the south and around York, it was in danger of being isolated. For once, however, its pragmatism failed as the Deiran Ælle did not meet the Cuthbertine community's demands. The relevant chapter in the *Historia de Sancto Cuthberto* ends its

[115] Osberht's actions deprived the community of estates previously given by King Ceolwulf, while Ælle's thefts undid the good work recently done by Bishop Ecgred. For more about Osberht and Ælle and their dealings with St Cuthbert's community, see Aird, *St Cuthbert*, pp. 28–9.

[116] *HSC*, c. 10. It may have been this protracted stay of Ælle at Crayke which led to Crayke being one of the venues for Cuthbert's community when they embarked on their period of seven years' wandering, for which see below, pp. 289–94.

[117] See *HSC*, c. 10 and Aird, *St Cuthbert*, p. 28, n. 71, where he makes several suggestions about the Cuthbertine community's dealings with Osberht and Ælle.

[118] It is possible to view the allegiances of Osberht and Ælle in a different light. Since we find Osberht stealing Bernician lands it could be argued that he was, in origin, a Deiran man who wished to limit the power of his Bernician rival. The same approach to the evidence could be applied to those estates stolen by Ælle and this would mean that we would view Ælle as a Bernician man seeking to limit the power of the Deiran Osberht. However, the strength of the phrase in the *HSC* that Ælle had 'made good promises...but acted badly' (*HSC*, c. 10) suggests that Aird's interpretation of events is correct.

[119] See above, pp. 284–5.

description of these events with this note: 'therefore let kings and princes beware lest they lie and lest they take anything from St Cuthbert'.[120] This statement seems to betray a bitterness towards Ælle which had not been forgotten by the time the *Historia de Sancto Cuthberto* was written in the mid-eleventh century.

It appears that leading Northumbrians managed to persuade Osberht and Ælle to forget their differences in order to counteract the very real threat posed by the Scandinavian annexation of York in 867.[121] But despite the mustering of a large army, both Osberht and Ælle were killed in the battle; and those Northumbrians who did survive made peace with the vikings. From this moment onwards, especially from 875 and the rule of Halfdan, the Scandinavian kings at York were a major threat to the existence and status of Cuthbert's community.[122]

e. c. *875–c. 883: The Arrival of vikings, the Seven Years' Wandering and the Cessation of the Hexham See*

In 875 the Great Army of vikings divided itself into three, one part of which journeyed northwards under Halfdan.[123] Previous viking incursions of the late eighth century had been conducted with the aim of recovering wealth and booty. But by the 870s, viking armies were bent on conquest and settlement.[124] Symeon, who provides the principal account for northern events in this period, suggests that the Cuthbertine community was so weakened by the arrival of vikings that not only did most of its members flee, but Bishop Eardwulf (854–99) and Abbot Eadred (of Carlisle) felt it necessary to elevate the body of Cuthbert from its resting place at Lindisfarne and 'wandered with it through the land, carrying it from place to place for seven years'.[125] At first they transported the body,

[120] *HSC*, c. 10.

[121] *ASC C*, s.a. 868 (*recte* 867), *HR* (5), pp. 74–5 (s.a. 867) and *HR* (8), pp. 105–6 (s.a. 867); see also above, p. 42.

[122] For these events, the sequence of Scandinavian kings at York and the effects of the Scandinavian settlement on the York church, see above, pp. 42–55.

[123] *ASC C*, s.a. 876 (*recte* 875).

[124] See Keynes 1999*a*, pp. 54–5.

[125] No information is given in our sources about when the community's stay at Norham may have ended. All we know is that *c.* 875 the community set out on a period of wandering from Lindisfarne which shows that it was by this date that the Cuthbertines had returned to Lindisfarne from Norham. For the seven years' wandering, see *HSC*, c. 20 and Symeon, *LDE*, ii.12; for the difficulties in accepting the traditional date of 875 for the beginning of the community's wandering, see below, p. 293, n. 144. The role of Eadred, abbot of Carlisle, is unclear. It may be that he had been forced to flee the north west after Scandinavian settlement there (see Aird, *St Cuthbert*, p. 38) or that he joined the wandering religious community after it had already departed Lindisfarne (see the commentary of Johnson South in *HSC*, p. 95, n. 74). Another possibility is that a single Bernician episcopal see had been created at Carlisle in the period following the earlier withdrawal of Cuthbert's community from Lindisfarne to

together with the community, to the mouth of the River Derwent in order to cross over to Ireland but, having been dissuaded from crossing by a storm at sea, the community went to Crayke and, after a stay of four months there, the Cuthbertine community finally came to rest at Chester-le-Street.[126] The entry for 876 in the *Anglo-Saxon Chronicle* suggests that the situation may have worsened since Halfdan is described as being able to share 'out the land of the Northumbrians, and they (i.e. vikings) proceeded to plough and to support themselves';[127] this led to the creation of the area which was to become known as the Danelaw.[128]

Despite the fact that Symeon has evidently exaggerated his account of the devastation caused by vikings,[129] we can be sure that any event which caused St Cuthbert's community to remove itself from its traditional home on Lindisfarne Island was a severe one. Nevertheless, it is striking that whilst other Northumbrian religious communities were having their power and resources severely curtailed,[130] the Cuthbertine community seems to have lost little of its standing. In fact, viking influence and settlement north of the River Tees seems to have been much less dramatic and the community of St Cuthbert remained a major land owner between the Tees and the Tyne.[131]

Norham during Ecgred's episcopate, which may help to explain Eadred's later association with the Cuthbertine community (for this, see Woolf, *Pictland*, pp. 81–3 and above, p. 286, n. 108). As Blair, *Church*, p. 312, points out, even after Cuthbert's community had moved on both from Lindisfarne and Norham, the practice of marking burials with sculpture continued in both places; Blair suggests that this is an indication that groups of priests must have continued to exist at Lindisfarne and Norham, who were perhaps dependent on the main Cuthbertine community; see also Hadley, *Vikings*, pp. 198–9. For Lindisfarne sculpture, see above, p. 271, n. 14; for Norham, see Cramp, *Corpus*, pp. 208–14, where the extant sculptural evidence dates from between the second quarter of the ninth century and the last half of the tenth century.

126 *HSC*, c. 20.

127 *ASC C*, s.a. 877 (*recte* 876). Halfdan managed to enter Cuthbertine territory; he can be found sailing down the River Tyne, as far as a place called *Wircesforde*, at which point, we are told, the intervention of St Cuthbert caused him to be driven across the sea, never to be seen again: *HSC*, c. 12.

128 Keynes 1999*a*, p. 63 and Abrams 2000, p. 136, n. 2. For the Danelaw, see above, p. 57, n. 207.

129 Symeon has engineered a certain 'tweaking' of his text in order to emphasise the impression that the community was hard-pressed: in his *LDE* Symeon has juxtaposed the description of the first attack of vikings on Lindisfarne in 793 to his description of the second attack, dated by him to 875 (Book two, chapters 5 and 6). This creates the feeling of a community constantly beset by marauding vikings when in fact there was a gap of eighty-two years between the two attacks. This aspect of Symeon's work is likewise highlighted by Johnson South in *HSC*, pp. 98–9.

130 See above, pp. 42–55, 178–83 and 240–3, for York, Beverley and Ripon during the viking period; for the demise of Monkwearmouth and Jarrow, see above, p. 287.

131 A gauge for levels of Scandinavian influence is provided by place-names and sculpture. Scandinavian place-names are found in abundance south of the Tees as is Scandinavian sculpture (see Aird, *St Cuthbert*, p. 32, n. 86 and Rollason, *Northumbria*, p. 244), whereas such influences north of the Tees are sporadic (for the evidence of place-names, see V.E. Watts, 'Northumberland and Durham: the Place-Name Evidence', *Scandinavian Settlement in Northern Britain: Thirteen Studies of Place-Names in their Historical Context*, ed. B.E. Crawford, Studies in the Early History of Britain

The *Historia de Sancto Cuthberto* affords an impression of the means employed by St Cuthbert's community in order to maintain its status in the face of viking settlement and expansion south of the Tees. It describes how, after Halfdan had been repelled, Cuthbert's community was instrumental in the election of one of the kings of the vikings, Guthred: Cuthbert, having appeared in a dream to Eadred, abbot of Carlisle, ordered him to go to the army of 'Danes' (*Danorum*) and to tell them that if they wanted to be obedient to him (i.e. Cuthbert), they should show Eadred a man called Guthred, a slave of a widow. Having purchased Guthred's freedom, Cuthbert says that the man is to be led to the hill called *Oswigesdune* where a 'golden armlet' (*armillam auream*) is to be placed on his right arm and he shall then be pronounced king. The *Historia de Sancto Cuthberto* narrates that Eadred did just as Cuthbert had told him and that as a result of Guthred being made king in this manner, Cuthbert's community is supposed to have received all the land between the River Tyne and the River Wear and also rights of sanctuary. Finally, Bishop Eardwulf brought the body of St Cuthbert to the army of vikings on the hill, over which Guthred himself swore an oath of peace.[132]

It is extremely difficult to interpret this event: there is much that is evident fabrication and exaggeration.[133] But if one discards the miraculous detail, there are elements present which support the notion that St Cuthbert's community had something to do with the election of a viking king. It is first of all important to recognise that a king by the name of Guthred did exist. Northumbrian sources acknowledge the presence of a King Guthred in the 880s but, as Johnson South notes, these could well depend on the *Historia de Sancto Cuthberto* for their information.[134] It is therefore encouraging that a source independent to the *Historia de Sancto Cuthberto*, the *Chronicon Æthelweardi*, states, 'When the course of one year was at an end, Guthfrid, king of the Northumbrians, died…and his body is entombed in the city of York in the high church'.[135] It is then significant that some of the procedures described in Guthred's election can be paralleled in contemporary practice. Cuthbert, in his appearance to Abbot Eadred, tells him to

(London and New York, 1995), pp. 206–13). Hogback monuments, which reflect Anglo-Scandinavian integration, are mainly grouped to the south of the River Tees (although there are some examples on the north bank of the Tees); see, for example, R.N. Bailey, *Viking Age Sculpture in Northern England* (London, 1980), pp. 85–100, at p. 91 (with a useful distribution map on p. 93).

132 For all of this, see *HSC*, c. 13.

133 See Dumville 2004, pp. 87–8 and above, pp. 48–9. For discussion of Guthred's relations with Cuthbert's community, see Aird, *St Cuthbert*, pp. 29–32, Rollason, *Northumbria*, pp. 244–6 and Hadley, *Vikings*, pp. 37–41.

134 See Johnson South in *HSC*, pp. 87–8.

135 *Chronicon Æthelweardi*, IV.3, relating to the year 895. It is likely that the 'Guthfrith' of this entry in the *Chronicon Æthelweardi* is one and the same as the 'Guthred' of the *HSC*; see Rollason, *Northumbria*, p. 216. For Guthred and York, see above, pp. 48–9.

place on Guthred's right arm a 'golden armlet' so that the multitude of vikings would recognise him as their new king. King Alfred had made similar recourse to Scandinavian ritual when enacting a peace treaty with vikings.[136] The description of the sanctuary afforded by Cuthbert's body may also contain some element of truth,[137] since these rights seem to have been recognised by Bede already in the early eighth century.[138]

In their involvement in the elevation of Guthred as king, it seems that Cuthbert's community had reached some kind of agreement and settlement with viking incomers. The presence of the 'golden armlet' as an indication of status points to Scandinavian practice whilst the swearing on Cuthbert's relics was a concession to the Cuthbertine community: the use of these two rituals in this context represents the agreement which had been reached by both parties.[139] There is also some suggestion that this agreement was particularly beneficial for the religious community. Craster notes that one manuscript version of the *Historia de Sancto Cuthberto* credits King Guthred with the confirmation of the rights which belonged to Cuthbert's community between the Tyne and the Tees. Craster suggests that this affirmation had the effect of creating a special form of 'franchise' for the Cuthbertine community.[140] It is perhaps, then, to this period in particular that we should look for the origins of the unique privileges enjoyed by Cuthbert's followers; what came to be known as the 'liberty' of St Cuthbert's community.[141]

[136] See *ASC C*, s.a. 877 (*recte* 876): 'and then the king made peace with the enemy and they gave him hostages, who were the most important men next to their king in the army, and swore oaths to him on the holy ring'; see also Rollason, *Northumbria*, p. 246. I am most grateful here to Dr L. Abrams who has suggested to me that the 'armlet' of the Cuthbert episode is unlikely to be the same as the 'holy ring' used by Alfred. For the failure of such rituals in pacifying vikings, see R. Abels, 'Paying the Danegeld: Anglo-Saxon peacemaking with vikings', *War and Peace in Ancient Medieval History*, ed. P. de Souza and J. France (Cambridge, 2008), pp. 173–92, at pp. 180–1.

[137] Aird, *St Cuthbert*, pp. 30–2 and Rollason, *Northumbria*, pp. 245–6, similarly draw attention to these elements in the description of Guthred's election as king.

[138] Bede, *VCP*, c. XL. For discussion of Northumbrian sanctuary in general, see Hall 1989 and Lambert 2009.

[139] See also Aird, *St Cuthbert*, pp. 31–2 and p. 37 and Rollason, *Northumbria*, pp. 245–6. On the mutual benefit of the agreement, see Abrams 2001, p. 37 and Hadley, *Vikings*, p. 40.

[140] Craster 1954, p. 198, where he points out that the *Cronica monasterii Dunelmensis* confirms this interpretation of the privileges enjoyed by Cuthbert's community (*CMD*, p. 524); an extended version of this liberty is given in Symeon, *LDE*, ii.13. However Johnson South in *HSC*, pp. 117–18, urges for caution: '...there seems in fact to be no way to substantiate whether Oswiu, Guthred, Alfred or any other Anglo-Saxon king actually gave to the community of St Cuthbert the sort of formal royal immunity over its holdings...' (at p. 118).

[141] Rollason, *Northumbria*, pp. 245–6, also seems to suggest that it was this event in particular which led to the creation of the 'liberty' of St Cuthbert between the Tyne and the Tees; see also Hadley, *Vikings*, pp. 39–40. It is important to notice the significance attached to St Cuthbert's body in the

Although, *c.* 875, vikings had proved a serious enough threat that the Cuthbertine community chose to leave Lindisfarne, the community subsequently engineered both its survival and also co-operation with its Scandinavian neighbours south of the River Tees.[142] Part of the community's success came from its ability to be pragmatic in the face of adversity. Thus, as Rollason has shown, Cuthbert's followers made use of this period of uncertainty and wandering by visiting their various landed estates in the north of England:[143] Bishop Eardwulf and Abbot Eadred bore Cuthbert's body first to the mouth of the River Derwent, then to Crayke and finally, in about 883, to Chester-le-Street.[144] These are all places which, before the wandering began *c.* 875, Cuthbert's community laid claim to. Rollason suggests, therefore, that these peregrinations were partly the result of the community's desire to strengthen its ties with its outlying estates.[145]

In an attempt to guarantee their ownership of these estates, Cuthbert's followers transported the body of Cuthbert, together with those relics of the principal early Northumbrian luminaries, with them as they went.[146] This was the most effective method they possessed for carrying out such a confirmation of ties.[147] One can imagine that, at each port of call, the religious community conducted a ceremony whereby the outlying estate in question affirmed its allegiance to Cuthbert by swearing on his body and his relics. Just such a ceremony was used when dealing with the Scandinavian king, Guthred, and it seems possible that the notes in the Durham *Liber Vitae* which form **18**, **19**, and **20** could be the result of similar occasions.[148]

enactment of this deal; this helps to explain the style of the notes **18**, **19**, and **20** which are contained in the *LVD* and which are made over directly to Cuthbert himself. For more about such matters, see above, pp. 9–16.

142 For the York church's co-operation with Scandinavians, see above, pp. 42–55. Rollason 1987, p. 50, notes that the lands which must have formed the core of Lindisfarne's earlier endowment still belonged to the later bishops of Durham. He therefore proposes that these estates were not lost from Cuthbert's community during this period of wandering. Nevertheless, the rapidity with which land could change hands in this period (demonstrated by **6** and **7**), suggests that we should be wary of making such conclusions. Aird, *St Cuthbert*, p. 29, suggests that Cuthbert's community was significantly increasing its endowment during these early years of Scandinavian settlement. Hadley, *Vikings*, p. 41, is more cautious.

143 Rollason 1987, pp. 50–1.

144 *HSC*, c. 20. The traditional dating for the abandonment of Lindisfarne (875) and the arrival at Chester-le-Street (883) has recently been questioned by Woolf, *Pictland*, pp. 82–3, who suggests that the period of wandering may have begun in 873 and concludes, 'all we can really say is that the see was established at Chester-le-Street during Guðfrið's reign (c. 880–95)' (at p. 83). Johnson South in *HSC*, pp. 97–8, also questions these traditional dates.

145 Rollason 1987, p. 50 and Blair, *Church*, p. 312.

146 Rollason, *Northumbria*, p. 247.

147 Aird, *St Cuthbert*, p. 34, states: 'Cuthbert's body was the corporeal title deed to estates granted to him and his church'.

148 See further above, pp. 9–16.

But the movements further southwards during these seven years perhaps had a more defined purpose yet. From its very beginnings at Lindisfarne, St Cuthbert's community had struggled for status and influence with other Northumbrian religious communities; and this was particularly the case with Hexham.[149] The see of Hexham had, rather mysteriously, ceased to exist earlier in the ninth century.[150] It has therefore been suggested that it was not only the arrival of vikings which caused the Lindisfarne community to set out on its wanderings: perhaps it was also the disappearance of Hexham which prompted Cuthbert's community to relocate.[151] The eventual settlement of the community at Chester-le-Street *c.* 883 may represent the final act in the downfall of Hexham. When the *Historia regum* details the arrival of the Cuthbertine community at Chester-le-Street *c.* 883 it makes the following two statements:

> Est autem locus ille inter Dunelmum et Extoldesam, sex millibus passuum distans a Dunelmo...Iam enim multo ante defecerat episcopatus Hagustaldensis ecclesiae.[152]

The information given about Hexham would seem to be an odd addition to an annal whose primary interest lay in the description of the relocation of the Cuthbertine community; although it may be the result of a later interpolation made by someone with an interest in Hexham's history,[153] it nevertheless suggests that in the mind of the author (or interpolator) of this part of the *Historia regum*, the movement of the Cuthbertine community to Chester-le-Street was intimately connected to the cessation of the Hexham see.[154]

[149] See above, pp. 275–84.

[150] The last known bishop of Hexham was Tidferth who died in 821. For the succession of bishops at Hexham in the early ninth century, see H.S. Offler, 'A Note on the Last Medieval Bishops of Hexham', *AA*[4] xl (1962), pp. 163–9, repr. in Offler, *North of the Tees*, no. II.

[151] See Rollason, *Northumbria*, p. 247, 'We may well suspect that the two things were related to the extent that the Community of St Cuthbert's southward move was designed to take advantage of Hexham's demise'. Cuthbert's community also seems to have gained control over the old community of Monkwearmouth-Jarrow which they held until the late eleventh century: see Aird, *St Cuthbert*, p. 36, n. 99, where he also notes the possibility that the Cuthbertine community was directly attacking Hexham and seeking its removal.

[152] *HR* (8), p. 114 (s.a. 883): 'This is a place (i.e. Chester-le-Street) between Durham and Hexham, six miles distant from Durham...Long before this the bishopric of the church of Hexham had ceased to exist'.

[153] For twelfth-century Hexham interpolations in the *Historia regum*, see Blair (P.H.) 1963, pp. 87–90 and H.S. Offler, 'Hexham and the *Historia Regum*', *Transactions of the Architectural and Archaeological Society of Durham and Northumberland*, new series ii (1970), pp. 51–62, repr. in Offler, *North of the Tees*, no. X.

[154] See also Rollason 1995, pp. 27–8.

f. c. 883– c. 920: *St Cuthbert's Community Arrives at Chester-le-Street*

In about 883 St Cuthbert's community settled at Chester-le-Street.[155] Later sources suggest that this time should be thought of as a slump in the Cuthbertine community's history. Symeon's account in particular creates this impression: his *Libellus de exordio* devotes only twelve chapters out of its sixty-nine to a description of the Chester-le-Street years, thus heightening the sense that the community was weak and struggling.[156] But such a view is perhaps too extreme an interpretation.

Although it is inevitable that these were difficult times, Cuthbert's community not only survived, but it also took measures to guarantee its elevated standing in Northumbria. As we have already seen, the period of seven years' wandering was perhaps an ordered relocation which sought simultaneously to strengthen ties with outlying estates and also, by its final move to Chester-le-Street, to fill the gap in ecclesiastical jurisdiction left by the disappearance of the Hexham see. And it seems likely that Lindisfarne bishops of old had prior connections with Chester-le-Street, perhaps using it as a type of *mansio* at which to rest on their way to and from York.[157] It may be that this move, although necessitated by the threat of viking attack on Lindisfarne, had been designed simultaneously to move the Cuthbertine community towards the centre of their landed possessions and closer to the major southern political powers.[158]

The arrival and settlement of vikings at York in the late-ninth century led to those areas and communities situated to the north of the River Tees becoming steadily more isolated. Thus Cuthbert's community was operating within an English-controlled territory which was no longer part of any kingdom. It is for this reason that the land grants noted in the *Historia de Sancto Cuthberto* take on a new aspect in this period. Whereas practically all of the grants recorded

155 See above, p. 293, n. 144, for Woolf's suggestion that the arrival at Chester-le-Street cannot be dated so narrowly.

156 Bonner 1989, p. 387.

157 Cambridge 1989 and Aird, *St Cuthbert*, p. 36.

158 See also Aird, *ibid*., p. 36. Chester-le-Street was a good choice for a new settlement site. Not only was it ideally located so that communication with the south would be easier than it had been on the remote Lindisfarne Island, but it also brought the Cuthbertines closer to the wealth that was on offer in the Tyne Valley. The community took up residence within the confines of the ruined Roman fort in Chester-le-Street. The church itself seems to have been situated in exactly the same position as today's parish church (Cambridge 1989, pp. 367–7). Given the abundance of stone available (from the Roman ruins), it seems odd that the church at Chester-le-Street was made of wood. But Cambridge 1984, suggests that wood was the material for the building of contemporary important, non-monastic sites. Later in the community's history, when it had relocated to Durham, Bishop Æthelric (1041–56) replaced the wooden church at Chester-le-Street with a stone one (Symeon, *LDE*, iii.9).

for Lindisfarne were made by kings,[159] those for the time at Chester-le-Street are mainly by lesser figures or constitute purchases by the bishops themselves. Bishop Cutheard seems to have been particularly successful in augmenting the landed assets of the Cuthbertine community,[160] as he added the vills of Sedgefield 'and whatever pertains to it' and of Bedlington 'with its dependencies'.[161] Such was the prestige of the Chester-le-Street church at this time that certain people can be found trying to buy favour with, and entrance into, Cuthbert's community: '... Bernard the priest gave his township named *Twilingatun* to St Cuthbert so that he might be a brother in his monastery'.[162]

Although the *Historia de Sancto Cuthberto* suggests that the community, owing to figures such as Bishop Cutheard, was able to manufacture its own survival during the early years of its time at Chester-le-Street, there are indications that viking movements on the western coast of Anglo-Saxon England were beginning to apply new pressures on St Cuthbert's community: 'Elfred son of Brihtwulf, fleeing pirates (*piratas*), came over the mountains in the west and sought the mercy of St Cuthbert and Bishop Cutheard so that they might present him with some lands'.[163] Although the Cuthbertine community was in such a position as to be able to lease the townships of Easington, Monk Hesleden, Little Thorp, Horden Hall, Yoden, the two Shottons, Castle Eden, Hulam, Hutton Henry, *Twilingatun*, Billingham (with its dependencies) and Sheraton to Elfred, it is nonetheless apparent that the Scandinavian presence had been such as to force Elfred to flee

[159] This picture of the early endowment of Lindisfarne being entirely funded by royal donations must nonetheless be a simplified account since the early bishops presumably also had a role in the acquisition of land; see Aird, *St Cuthbert*, p. 28.

[160] Johnson South in *HSC*, p. 101, suggests that Cutheard's episcopate was from 901 to 915. Woolf, *Pictland*, p. 83 (and n. 24) prefers the dates *c*. 904–18; on the difficulties in calculating the chronology of Cutheard's episcopate, see also the comments of Rollason, *Symeon: Libellus*, p. 132, n. 96.

[161] *HSC*, c. 21. Not all of the Sedgefield vill was acquired outright by Cutheard, since three men, Aculf, Æthelbriht and Frithlaf continued to keep their own land there. Nevertheless, the *HSC* describes how Cutheard and the community of St Cuthbert possessed jurisdictional rights ('sake and soke') over the land of these three men.

[162] *HSC*, c. 21; the same section of the *HSC* tells how Tilred, abbot of Heversham, had bought Castle Eden and given half of it to the Cuthbertine community in an attempt to become a brother there. For all of these estate acquisitions, see Craster 1954, pp. 189–90 (at p. 190, for the possible identification of *Twilingatun* with Willington near Wallsend). *Twilingatun* had previously been bought by Abbot Eadred from King Guthred: *HSC*, c. 19.

[163] *HSC*, c. 22. For vikings settled in the north west, see, for example, Ekwall, *Scandinavians*; F.T. Wainwright, 'Ingimund's Invasion', *EHR* lxiii (1948), pp. 145–69; G. Fellows-Jensen, 'Scandinavian Place-Names of the Irish Sea Province', *Viking Treasure from the North-West: the Cuerdale Hoard in its Context*, ed. J. Graham-Campbell (Liverpool, 1992), pp. 31–42; Rollason, *Northumbria*, pp. 249–55; D. Griffiths, 'Settlement and Acculturation in the Irish Sea Region', in Hines *et al.*, *Land, Sea and Home*, pp. 126–38 and Hadley, *Vikings*, pp. 61–3.

over the Pennines and into the jurisdiction of St Cuthbert's community.[164] And it is the same chapter of the *Historia de Sancto Cuthberto* which describes the arrival of King Rægnald with a fleet of ships and his subsequent occupation of the territory of Ealdred, son of Eadwulf of Bamburgh. Ealdred, having found support from King Constantine in Scotland, drew Rægnald into battle at Corbridge.[165]

There is some confusion surrounding the number of battles that took place at Corbridge,[166] but there can be no doubt as to the severity of the threat posed by King Rægnald.[167] Although a formidable alliance, which comprised Constantine (king of the Scots), Ealdred (the son of Earl Eadwulf) and Elfred, was formed to combat Rægnald, the Scandinavian man was still victorious.[168] Constantine and Ealdred represented two of the most powerful authorities in the region, the Scots and the House of Bamburgh respectively. The third person, Elfred, was the very same man to whom, having fled across the mountains from the western coast, the Cuthbertine community had leased a group of estates. It is possible, therefore, as Aird notes, that upon the arrival of Rægnald the religious community called in a favour, and urged Elfred to take up their cause in alliance with Constantine and Ealdred.[169]

In its recording of a second encounter with King Rægnald,[170] the *Historia de Sancto Cuthberto* states that a certain Eadred, son of Ricsige, a man who had been in the protection of the Cuthbertine community following his murder of Eardwulf, and who for three years cultivated lands given to him by Bishop Cutheard, was killed at Corbridge by the Scandinavian king.[171] The pattern here is exactly the same as the one seen in the first meeting with Rægnald whereby a man indebted to St Cuthbert's community is employed in that community's defence.[172] Thus the leases

164 For more about these leases, see Morris 1981, pp. 223–4. After 902, those vikings expelled from Ireland were relocating on the west coast of Anglo-Saxon England; see Woolf, *Pictland*, pp. 131–3. Aird, *St Cuthbert*, p. 37, notes that the situation was made worse by the simultaneous movement southwards of the Strathclyde Britons.

165 *HSC*, c. 22. For Rægnald, see above, p. 45.

166 Some scholars suspect that there were, in fact, two battles at Corbridge, one in 914 and one in 918; see Wainwright 1975, pp. 163–9 and Smyth, *Scandinavian* I, pp. 97–9. For the probability that there was only one battle in 918, see Craster 1954, p. 191, n. 1, Johnson South in *HSC*, pp. 105–6, Downham, *Viking Kings*, pp. 92–3, Woolf, *Pictland*, p. 144 (where the date of the battle of Corbridge is discussed in conjunction with the difficulties in establishing the dates of Cutheard's episcopacy) and above, p. 45, n. 127.

167 See the comments of Woolf, *Pictland*, p. 138.

168 *HSC*, c. 22.

169 Aird, *St Cuthbert*, pp. 38–9.

170 This used to be thought of as a reference to the second of the two Corbridge battles, but it is more likely that there was only one battle at Corbridge in 918; see above, n. 166.

171 *HSC*, c. 24.

172 Aird, *St Cuthbert*, p. 40, has noted a further dimension implied by the community's alliance with Eadred. Eadred's father is named by the *HSC* as being Ricsige and this is probably the same figure as that Ricsige who was elevated by the Danes to rule the area north of the River Tyne in the period 873

undertaken by the religious community represented shrewd tactics: the lessee could be called upon at any stage to repay his debt and to defend Cuthbert's patrimony.[173]

In the aftermath of his 918 victory at Corbridge, Rægnald was in the ascendancy. That he was disinclined to reach a political settlement with the Cuthbertine community, in the way that previous Scandinavian leaders had done (such as Guthred), is indicated by the fact that he divided some of the community's estates between two of his followers, Scula and Onlafbald, as noted by the *Historia de Sancto Cuthberto* itself.[174] The *Historia de Sancto Cuthberto* ends its description of the depredations suffered at the hands of King Rægnald with the statement: 'and of the things that he (i.e. Rægnald) had stolen from St Cuthbert he took away with him nothing except [his] sin', which suggests that Cuthbert's followers, after Rægnald had died, somehow recovered all of the land which had been taken from them.[175] Yet it seems likely that the *Historia de Sancto Cuthberto* is here oversimplifying events, as some of the community's estates perhaps remained lost after Rægnald's death, Staindrop being an example.[176]

to 876 (see above, pp. 47–8). Eadred's brother, Egbert II, who had taken over from Ricsige as ruler north of the Tyne, was later replaced by Eardwulf and it seems plausible that it was this Eardwulf whom we find Eadred murdering (*HSC*, c. 24). Thus the Cuthbertine community, by aligning itself with Eadred, seems to have been taking sides against its traditional ally, the House of Bamburgh. As Aird suggests, the uncertainty promoted by the arrival of figures such as Rægnald, quite possibly led to the religious community exploring every possible avenue of survival and self-promotion. What has become clear is that, throughout its history, the Cuthbertine community was ruthlessly pragmatic; and such changing of allies has been seen before. An even greater change was to come in the community's dealings with English kings from the south.

173 For more about the Cuthbertine community's renting-out of land, see Morris 1977, p. 93. Although Rægnald killed Eadred at Corbridge, he nevertheless granted lands to Eadred's sons, Esbrid (perhaps 'Egbrid'; see Craster 1954, p. 191, n. 2) and Earl Ælstan (*HSC*, c. 24). Scholars have frequently suggested that this Ælstan should be identified as being the father of a certain Scott who is said to have given *Aclea* (Aycliffe?) to St Cuthbert's community in one place in the Durham *Liber Vitae* (see Craster 1954, p. 191, Hart, *ECNE*, p. 142, Morris 1978, pp. 98–9, Morris 1984, pp. 6 and 8, Aird, *St Cuthbert*, p. 40, n. 114 and Hadley, *Vikings*, p. 44). But they all fail to mention that this record of a gift by Scott occurs in the midst of a forged charter of Bishop William of St Calais (d. 1096) inserted into the Durham *Liber Vitae* which takes Symeon's *LDE* as its model. In no way can it be trusted as the 'rehabilitation' of a 'tenth century donation' (Morris 1978, p. 99). See also the comments of Offler, *Durham Episcopal*, p. 10.

174 *HSC*, c. 23; see also Aird, *St Cuthbert*, pp. 40–1. The lands taken over by Scula and Onlafbald seem to have covered areas previously leased out to Elfred and Eadred: Morris 1981, pp. 224–5. For Rægnald's provision of land for his own followers, but also for local men like Esbrid and Ælstan, see Hadley, *Vikings*, pp. 41–4 (esp. p. 42).

175 *HSC*, c. 24.

176 Some of the land seized by Rægnald included 'Gainford and whatever pertains to it' (*HSC*, c. 24); Johnson South in *HSC*, p. 115, notes that this territory would have covered the Staindrop estate as well. Since the *HSC* states that Staindrop was later given by Cnut to the Cuthbertine community (*HSC*, c. 32), it is possible that it had remained alienated following Rægnald's depredations in the early tenth century; see further the comments of Johnson South in *HSC*, pp. 107–8.

Meanwhile the royal West Saxon house was enjoying and exercising ever increasing levels of power and influence both south of the Humber and north of it. And this house had already, and most spectacularly, under King Alfred, demonstrated its ability to withstand a viking onslaught.[177] It is at this point in the Cuthbertine community's history, in the wake of the losses inflicted by Rægnald, that it looked, for the first time ever, further than the borders of Northumbria, and towards English kings from the south, for aid.[178]

g. *St Cuthbert's Community and the Cultivation of Ties with Kings of Anglo-Saxon England: from* c. *934 to 995*

Several West Saxon kings, perhaps beginning with King Egbert,[179] had had occasion to claim overlordship of the Northumbrians. But it is only with the accession of Æthelstan to the kingdom of Northumbria in 927 that a concerted and realistic attempt at the incorporation of that northern region within southern hegemony was made.[180] Various forms of evidence testify to the extent to which Æthelstan tried to forge new bonds with the Cuthbertine community in particular.[181] And the *Historia de Sancto Cuthberto* contains a chapter which describes a special visit by Æthelstan to St Cuthbert's shrine in 934, an event which was accompanied by that king's donation of gifts to the saint.[182]

177 Alfred proved himself in particular in the encounter against Guthrum and his men at the battle of Edington in 878, for which see *ASC C*, s.a. 879 (*recte* 878). But this victory alone did not secure Wessex and Alfred put in place a series of more permanent defensive measures for which see, for example, R. Abels, 'King Alfred's Peace-Making Strategies with the Vikings', *Haskins Society Journal* iii (1991), pp. 23–34 and *idem*, *Alfred the Great: War, Kingship and Culture in Anglo-Saxon England* (London and New York, 1998), pp. 194–218.

178 See also Aird, *St Cuthbert*, p. 41.

179 See *ASC C*, s.a. 827 (*recte* 829).

180 Initial contact between the community of St Cuthbert and southern kings was perhaps made during the reign of Edward the Elder (899–924); see *HSC*, cc. 14, 18, 19, 21, 24 and 25, and the comments of Aird, *St Cuthbert*, pp. 41–2; and see Simpson 1989, for the significance in this regard of the substantial sections concerning King Alfred in *HSC*, cc. 14–19. For Edward the Elder's dealings with Northumbria, see, for example, R. Hall, 'A Kingdom too far: York in the Early Tenth Century', *Edward the Elder 899–924*, ed. N.J. Higham and D.H. Hill (London and New York, 2001), pp. 188–99 and M.R. Davidson, 'The (Non)Submission of the Northern Kings in 920', in *ibid*., pp. 200–11. For Æthelstan's conquest of Northumbria, see *ASC D*, s.a. 926 (*recte* 927). Æthelstan employed various means of propaganda to announce that he considered himself to have united the various kingdoms, which comprised Anglo-Saxon England, into one. His charters display a unique awareness of this success, especially those composed by the draftsman known as 'Æthelstan A'. The style of Latin in which they are written is designed to broadcast Æthelstan's success: see Woodman, forthcoming. The earliest document preserved in the York archive is an 'Æthelstan A' charter and is printed above as **1**.

181 For Æthelstan's dealings with St Cuthbert's community, see further, Foot, *Æthelstan*, pp. 208–11.

182 See *HSC*, c. 26. Indicative of Æthelstan's favour for St Cuthbert's community are the gold-embroidered maniple and stole made on the order of Queen Ælfflæd for Bishop Frithestan of

The *Anglo-Saxon Chronicle* records Æthelstan's journey northwards in 934 in order to conduct a military campaign in Scotland;[183] he seems to have broken his journey at various points on his way north,[184] one of which was at Chester-le-Street.[185] Æthelstan's interest and role in the patronage of religious communities and in the collection and dissemination of relics is well attested, even on the Continent.[186] The *Historia de Sancto Cuthberto* includes a chapter which corroborates the impression of Æthelstan as patron as it describes that king's gifts both of valuable and symbolic objects (including a prose and metrical *Life* of St Cuthbert which is generally assumed to be the manuscript that is now CCCC 183) and of the vill of Bishop Wearmouth with its dependencies.[187]

Perhaps the most important of Æthelstan's gifts for Chester-le-Street was that of land: from this the community gained security and material prosperity. Indeed the gift of the vill of Bishop Wearmouth and its dependencies comprised an area which had recently been removed from the Cuthbertine community's hold and given to one of Rægnald's chief followers, Onlafbald. Æthelstan's gift therefore seems to represent the success of that king in recovering lands originally

Winchester but in fact given by King Æthelstan to St Cuthbert's community at Chester-le-Street and preserved in the coffin of St Cuthbert. Both the stole and maniple bear the inscription: 'ÆLFFLÆD FIERI PRECEPIT' and 'PIO EPISCOPO FRIÐESTANO'; see E. Plenderleith, 'The Stole and Maniples; (a) The Technique', pp. 375–96, C. Hohler, 'The Stole and Maniples; (b) The Iconography', pp. 396–408 and R. Freyhan, 'The Stole and Maniples; (c) The Place of the Stole and Maniple in Anglo-Saxon Art of the Tenth Century', pp. 409–32, all in Battiscombe, *Relics*. For a more recent discussion of these embroideries, which places them in a wider European context, see E. Coatsworth, 'The Embroideries from the Tomb of St Cuthbert', in *Edward the Elder 899–924*, ed. N.J. Higham and D.H. Hill (London and New York, 2001), pp. 292–306, at p. 296, for the uneasy relationship between Frithestan and the royal family, which perhaps led to the embroideries being sent northwards. For the importance of silk in general in Anglo-Saxon England (with reference also to the Cuthbert silks), see R. Fleming, 'Acquiring, Flaunting and Destroying Silk in Late Anglo-Saxon England', cited above, p. 279, n. 63. See also M. Gretsch, *The Intellectual Foundations of the English Benedictine Reform*, Cambridge Studies in Anglo-Saxon England 25, (Cambridge, 1999), pp. 325–31, for more about Frithestan and his opposition to Æthelstan.

183 *ASC C*, s.a. 934. For possible reasons why Æthelstan marched north at this moment, see Woolf, *Pictland*, pp. 160–5.

184 Æthelstan had made a stop at Nottingham and the document **1**, which is a land grant in favour of the York archiepiscopal see, is the result of a meeting of the king's council at Nottingham on 7 June, 934.

185 A certain Wigred (*c*. 925–?942) was bishop of Chester-le-Street at this time, having taken over from Tilred (*c*. 912 × 915–*c*. 925); for these bishops, see Symeon, *LDE*, ii.17–18, where Tilred is noted for his good deeds.

186 See, for example, a letter written to Æthelstan by Prior Radbod of St Samson's at Dol in *c*. 927 which says '...And now I send to you relics, which we know to be dearer to you than all earthly substance, namely bones of St Senator, and of St Paternus...' (see Whitelock, *EHD*, p. 892); for more, see Keynes 1985.

187 For all of these details, see *HSC*, c. 26; for CCCC 183, see Keynes 1985, pp. 180–5, Rollason 1989 and below, p. 320.

appropriated by Rægnald and also in restoring Cuthbert's followers to previous levels of regional primacy.[188]

Æthelstan seems to have been an important patron for Cuthbert's community.[189] A fitting tribute to Æthelstan's role in the preservation and expansion of the status of the Cuthbertine house at Chester-le-Street is found in a manuscript which would have been displayed on one of the church's altars. The Durham *Liber Vitae* contains, among other things, a list of royal and noble benefactors compiled in chronological order.[190] Æthelstan's name should thus have appeared, just like any other, in its proper sequence among those kings of the early tenth century. However, a tenth-century scribe has elevated Æthelstan's name to the very top of the list so that it occurs immediately after the heading *nomina regum vel ducum* and thus before the names of the earliest kings of seventh-century Northumbria, such as Edwin and Oswald.[191]

It was the religious community's custom to enter notes of land transactions into their treasured books.[192] The notes edited below as **18**, **19** and **20** are just such items. The conveyance of Anglo-Saxon charters in general quite possibly involved some kind of ceremony whereby the charter itself, or perhaps a sod of earth, was symbolically placed on the altar of the church: such a practice both involved the enactment of the handing over of the charter and simultaneously endowed the document in question with divine authority.[193] Therefore one can imagine that these notes, which were copied directly into gospel books (and here the Durham *Liber Vitae*), were the result of some similar ceremony which marked the original occasion of the grant. It must remain as speculation, but perhaps Æthelstan had stood as witness to a ceremony which had ultimately involved his name being inserted in a prominent place in the Durham *Liber Vitae*; whilst this insertion of Æthelstan's name at the forefront of the list of Northumbrian kings served to elevate and praise Æthelstan as a king of the same standing as such ancient Northumbrian luminaries as King Edwin and King Oswald, it was thus also designed to implicate Æthelstan in a form of contract with the Cuthbertine

188 Aird, *St Cuthbert*, pp. 42–3; see also the comments of Johnson South in *HSC*, pp. 109–10.

189 The establishment of a relationship between English kings from the south and the Cuthbertine community was a situation from which both parties could profit: whilst the English kings gained an ally in the often rebellious Northumbrian kingdom, Cuthbert's community stood to gain from gifts of land, money and precious objects.

190 For the Durham *Liber Vitae* in general, see Rollason *et al.*, *The Durham* and the new edition in *LVD*.

191 The words *aeðelstan rex* are written after the title *nomina regum uel ducum* on f. 15r of the *LVD*.

192 For this practice, see below, pp. 316–23.

193 See Chaplais 1965, p. 33, Kelly 1990, p. 44 and Angenendt 2004.

religious establishment.[194] We have already seen something of the mentality of Cuthbert's community at Chester-le-Street in its granting of leases to powerful individuals, so that these men could later be employed in a moment of crisis.[195] This note of Æthelstan's name made that king aware of the contract he had effected with Cuthbert's community.[196]

Æthelstan's brother, Edmund, succeeded to the throne of Anglo-Saxon England in 939 and he too seems to have cultivated relations with Cuthbert's community. The *Anglo-Saxon Chronicle* states that in 944 Edmund came north and 'reduced all Northumbria under his rule, and drove out two kings, Olaf, Sihtric's son, and Rægnald, Guthfrith's son'.[197] It was probably this expedition which provided the opportunity for Edmund to make a stop at Chester-le-Street and to grant to St Cuthbert, 'two golden armlets and two Greek palls upon the holy body, [and he] granted peace and law better than any it ever had to the whole territory of St Cuthbert'.[198]

Following the assassination of Edmund in 946, his brother, Eadred, became king of the English and immediately tried to bring Northumbria within his control.[199] Despite the fact that Wulfstan, archbishop of York at the time, and 'all

[194] It is interesting to note that scholars have identified this insertion of Æthelstan's name as being written in Anglo-Saxon Square Minuscule script. The origins and growth of this script are intimately connected to the royal court and to Æthelstan's reign in particular: D.N. Dumville, 'English Square Minuscule Script: the Background and Earliest Phases', *ASE* xvi (1987), pp. 147–79 and *idem*, 'English Square Minuscule Script: the Mid-Century Phases', *ASE* xxiii (1994), pp. 133–64. It is just possible, then, that a representative of Æthelstan's court, as recognition of its part in the ceremony and in the contract with the Chester-le-Street community, inserted Æthelstan's name at the head of folio 15.

[195] See above, pp. 296–8.

[196] Gerchow 2004, p. 52, suggests a different interpretation, that this note commemorates Æthelstan's role as donor of the *Liber Vitae* to St Cuthbert's community, a manuscript that Gerchow suggests was perhaps originally compiled at Monkwearmouth-Jarrow. For the suggestion that Lindisfarne was actually the scriptorium responsible for the Durham *Liber Vitae*, see below, p. 318, n. 294. Æthelstan not only rewarded the Cuthbertine community in a tangible and physical manner with grants of land, but he was also involved in the promotion of Cuthbert's image and cult. Two manuscripts which are closely associated with Æthelstan and with St Cuthbert's community bear witness to this process: BL Cotton Otho B. ix and CCCC 183. Keynes 1985, pp. 170–85, suggests that these manuscripts were gifts to St Cuthbert's community. Rollason 1989, suggests that CCCC 183 was not a gift from Æthelstan but instead had remained in the king's possession in Wessex and therefore is an example of the king's personal devotion to St Cuthbert.

[197] *ASC C*, s.a. 944. For viking kings at York at this moment, see above, pp. 46–7.

[198] *HSC*, c. 28. The bishop of Chester-le-Street at this time was a certain Uhtred who was consecrated *c.* 942 but whose date of death is unknown (Symeon, *LDE*, ii.18–19). Uhtred's successor, Seaxhelm, tried to appropriate some of the community's possessions and so, with the help of St Cuthbert, he was driven from his see within only a few months: Symeon, *LDE*, ii.19. For the problems in dating the episcopates of Uhtred and Seaxhelm, see Rollason, *Symeon: Libellus*, p. 141, n. 110.

[199] *ASC ABCD*, s.a. 946.

the councillors of the Northumbrians', swore an oath of fidelity to Eadred,[200] the Northumbrians were ultimately treacherous and took Eric Bloodaxe as their king at York instead.[201] One consequence of this duplicity was that, in 948, Eadred marched northwards and ravaged Northumbria; as part of this raid, the minster at Ripon was burnt down which may have been intended as a warning for Archbishop Wulfstan that even celebrated churches were not beyond punishment.[202] Whether or not Eadred, in an attempt to secure Northumbria for the English kingdom,[203] felt that he had to deal in a similarly severe manner with St Cuthbert's community is difficult to tell. But Symeon's statement that Eadred, 'a man of piety and a lover of justice' (*vir pietatis cultor et iustitie*), brought 'royal gifts' (*regalibus donariis*) to the community, suggests that whatever contact there was with this English king, was remembered positively.[204]

Since Æthelstan, Edmund and perhaps Eadred sought to foster ties with Cuthbert's community, it is rather surprising to find that the *Historia de Sancto Cuthberto* and Symeon's *LDE* make no further mention of contact with any subsequent king of Anglo-Saxon England until the reign of Cnut (1016–35).[205] After the removal of Eric Bloodaxe, the last Scandinavian king of York, in 954,[206] Northumbria was at least nominally part of the kingdom of Anglo-Saxon England.[207] It was during this period that a series of earls can be found governing southern and northern Northumbria.[208] This encouraged the community of St Cuthbert to strengthen ties with the earls of northern Northumbria who were drawn from the House of Bamburgh and it is perhaps for this reason, with the community's attention turned northwards rather than south of the Humber, that

200 *ASC D*, s.a. 947.

201 A remarkable sequence of annals in the *ASC* for the years 946–54 detail the behaviour of the Northumbrians with King Eadred. Archbishop Wulfstan seems to have been instrumental in the political manoeuvrings of this period; see Keynes 1999*b*, Downham, *Vikings Kings*, pp. 110–15 and above, pp. 53–5.

202 For the burning of Ripon Minster and the possible motivations for this deed, see above, pp. 245–6.

203 The political situation in Northumbria at this moment was very complicated, with the presence of two Scandinavian rulers, Olaf Sihtricson and Eric Bloodaxe; for an overview, see above, pp. 45–7.

204 Symeon, *LDE*, ii.20; *CMD*, p. 526 (ll. 109–115) also describes Eadred's gifts to St Cuthbert's community but adds no new information. The *HSC* has no record of a visit, or of gifts, made by Eadred.

205 Brief reference is made to King Æthelred (978–1016) in *HSC*, c. 29 and in Symeon, *LDE*, iii.4, but only in the context of a gift of land by Styr, son of Ulf; Craster 1954, p. 193. The *CMD*, p. 526 (ll. 116–126), has a passage which gives a very brief summary of the reigns of Eadwig and Edgar but which does not state that they had any particular dealings with the Cuthbertines. For Cnut and Cuthbert's community, see below, pp. 310–11.

206 *ASC DE*, s.a. 954. See also Craster 1954, p. 192. On the identity of Eric, see above, p. 46, n. 145.

207 Aird, *St Cuthbert*, pp. 43–4. For the independence of Northumbria at this stage, see Rollason, *Northumbria*, pp. 265–8.

208 For more details about these earls, see Whitelock 1959, p. 77 and Rollason, *Northumbria*, pp. 266–7.

less mention is now made of kings of England in the *Historia de Sancto Cuthberto* and Symeon's *LDE*.[209]

The lack of detail in our narrative sources of any further contact between St Cuthbert's community and a king of Anglo-Saxon England during the second half of the tenth century has been taken by some as a sign that this religious house had regained its 'corporate strength' and could therefore afford to relax its relationship with southern powers.[210] But evidence that the two parties continued to have at least some form of communication is suggested by the manuscript Durham, Cathedral Library MS A.IV.19, otherwise known as the Durham Collectar.[211] Aldred, priest and provost of the community at Chester-le-Street,[212] made additions into this manuscript which state, among other details, that the Durham Collectar was acquired by Bishop Ælfsige (? 968–? 990) on 10 August 970, at Oakley Down, to the south of Woodyates in Dorset.[213] And a charter of 970, preserved in the Ely archive, confirms Ælfsige's presence at a southern council convened by Edgar.[214]

Witness-lists to charters of Edgar (king of Anglo-Saxon England from 959 to 975) suggest that the presence of a Chester-le-Street bishop in the south was a rarity. Bishop Ealdred (? before 946–? 968) had been witness to three charters of Edgar in 958–9,[215] but these were all issued while Edgar was king only in the north following the 957 division of the kingdom.[216] After the re-unification of the kingdom following Eadwig's death on 1 October 959, Bishop Ælfsige's

[209] The extent to which the earls of Bamburgh were reliant on the kings of Anglo-Saxon England for their position is a difficult question: see Rollason, *ibid.*, pp. 267–8.

[210] Aird, *St Cuthbert*, p. 43.

[211] For more about this manuscript, see A. Corrêa, *The Durham Collectar*, Henry Bradshaw Society cvii (London, 1992) and A.H. Thompson and U. Lindelöf, *Rituale ecclesie Dunelmensis: The Durham Collectar*, SS cxl (Durham and London, 1927).

[212] For Aldred, see N.R. Ker, 'Aldred the Scribe', *Essays and Studies by Members of the English Association* xxviii (1942), pp. 7–12.

[213] For these details, see Bonner 1989, p. 393, where he also notes that the manuscript was written in Anglo-Saxon minuscule of the early tenth century but that the text is of a 'collectar of the community of Augustinian canons of St Quentin in Vermandois, in northern France'. For Bishop Ælfsige, see Symeon, *LDE*, ii.20.

[214] S 781 (BCS 1269).

[215] For the problems in dating Ealdred's episcopate, see Rollason, *Symeon: Libellus*, p. 141, n. 110.

[216] Two charters are from 958: **3** and S 675 (BCS 1042); one is from 959: S 681 (*Pet* 14). Kelly, *Peterborough*, p. 244, suggests that Bishop Ealdred attested this 959 Peterborough document, which is a grant of land at Howden and Old Drax, because St Cuthbert's community had a pre-existing interest in the Howden estate. For a summary of the attestations of bishops during King Edgar's reign, see Keynes, *Atlas*, table LIV. The presence of bishops from the Cuthbertine community at councils conducted by kings of the West Saxon line seems to have reached its climax in the reign of Æthelstan (see Keynes, *Atlas*, table XXXVII), where Bishop Wigred can be found attesting several 'Æthelstan A' charters.

attestation of 970 stands alone. Ælfsige's arrival in the south also coincides with the famous council of Winchester, which produced the *Regularis Concordia*, an attempt to provide a *Rule* for all Benedictine houses to follow. Bonner suggests the possibility that Bishop Ælfsige and his provost Aldred were present in the south in order to advise on religious matters and that the subsequent acquisition of the Durham Collectar by Ælfsige and Aldred, a manuscript which contained material unknown to the Cuthbertine community, indicated a desire on the part of these two ecclesiastics to bring Chester-le-Street into line with liturgical developments in the south.[217] Whether or not these propositions go too far, the presence of these Chester-le-Street men in the south at this time displays continuing contact with southern circles of power.

One of the last notices we have concerning the community's time at Chester-le-Street takes the form of a note in the Durham *Liber Vitae*, and printed below as **18**. This records that a certain Earl Thored gave land at Smeaton, Crayke and Sutton to St Cuthbert's church.[218] Thored was a powerful man; he may have been King Æthelred's father-in-law and he was entrusted, at the end of his career, with the leadership of a fleet of ships to combat Scandinavians.[219] His accession as earl may have been at the direct expense of the previous earl, Oslac,[220] and it resulted in Thored's depriving the York see of some of its estates.[221] The group of lands granted by Thored to St Cuthbert's community in **18** were all situated in the heart of the territory which belonged to the York see. Thus **18** would seem to constitute a direct attack by Thored on that 'faction' which had supported his predecessor, Earl Oslac, and which presumably had had its base in the York area. The combined evidence of **6** and **18** suggests that Thored had deprived the York see of various lands and entrusted those lands to one of its major rivals, the Cuthbertine community. **18** is therefore indicative of the readiness of the Cuthbertine community to involve itself once more in politics of the day, always with a view to enhancing its position.

[217] Bonner 1989, pp. 393–5.

[218] Earl Thored was politically active from *c.* 975 to 992 at which point he disappears from our records: these dates thus provide the time frame within which **18** was composed.

[219] *ASC CDE*, s.a. 992. On the possibility of Thored being King Æthelred's father-in-law, see Whitelock 1959, p. 80.

[220] Whitelock 1959, p. 79 and above, pp. 60–1; for a grant of land by Edgar to *Æslac* (probably Oslac), see **4**.

[221] This detail can be found in the *Memorandum* composed by Archbishop Oswald, **6**, although Thored's name occurs in a part of **6** that is difficult to read (see the commentary to **6** for further discussion). See also **18** for more about Thored.

h. *995: The Move to Durham and the House of Bamburgh*

In 995 Cuthbert's community moved, for the last time in its history, to the peninsula in Durham.[222] Given the magnificence of the cathedral that stands today in Durham, and which is a visible indication of the success and stature that Cuthbert's community achieved, it is striking that very few of our northern sources document this last relocation. If we accept that the *Historia de Sancto Cuthberto* is a source which belongs to the mid-eleventh century, and which is thus the closest we have to contemporary evidence, then it seems particularly odd that it makes no mention of what must have been a recent and momentous event. Indeed the *Historia de Sancto Cuthberto*, as we have seen, is primarily concerned with documenting the landed possessions accumulated by the Cuthbertines. Now one would expect that the removal to Durham would have involved some form of accompanying land grant and that a record of this grant would find its place in the *Historia de Sancto Cuthberto*. Even if, as seems likely, the community already owned the land in question or in the vicinity, one would still anticipate that the community would celebrate or, at the least, justify its move.[223]

In fact it is again Symeon who provides the details of the move to Durham.[224] He describes how the saint's body was first moved to Ripon and then, after a stay of three or four months there, it was being returned to its original resting place at Chester-le-Street when, as the result of heavenly intervention, the community stopped at Durham. There is much in this account which is based on hagiographical topoi, in particular the crediting of St Cuthbert with a major role in the relocation. But it is also difficult to know what to make of the detail that the community went first to Ripon, not least because Ripon was directly associated with the York church, the ecclesiastical rival to Cuthbert's community in the north.[225] There may be some reason to suppose that vikings were again a realistic threat. An independent source, the *Anglo-Saxon Chronicle*, records, for the year 993, that '...Bamburgh was sacked and much booty was captured there, and after that the army came to the mouth of the Humber and did great damage there, both in Lindsey and in Northumbria'.[226] Perhaps, then, Ripon,

[222] For the possibility that this date is incorrect and that the move was made earlier in 992, see Cooper 1968, pp. 133–4.

[223] The foundation, or re-foundation, of other religious houses was often a magnificent affair; see, for example, the extraordinary charter commissioned by Edgar for the New Minster, Winchester, on the occasion of its refoundation in 966, S 745 (*WinchNM* 23); for comments on this document, see Miller, *New Minster, Winchester*, pp. 105–111.

[224] Symeon, *LDE*, iii.1. See also the *Historia regum*, which states plainly and curtly, 'Bishop Aldhun translated the body of St Cuthbert from Chester to Durham': *HR* (8), p. 136 (s.a. 995).

[225] For Ripon and York, see, for example, the details supplied in **6** and **7**.

[226] *ASC CDE*, s.a. 993.

which was located a little further inland, provided a safer haven for the religious community.[227]

Symeon affords a little more information and explanation for the subsequent move to Durham; he describes how the location in Durham, while not easily habitable, did possess natural defences. Another important detail provided by Symeon is that the religious community was closely allied to the political power in the region and had been aided in the cultivation of the Durham site by that power, Earl Uhtred.[228] More information about this alliance is provided by the *De obsessione Dunelmi et de probitate Uchtredi comitis, et de comitibus qui ei successerunt* (hereafter the *De Obsessione*), which was probably composed by a member of the Durham community at an uncertain date between 1070 and 1120.[229] This tract is a form of aide-memoire.[230] Its primary purpose is to provide a context for, and to chart the subsequent history of, six estates. But in doing so, it contains invaluable information about the interplay between the church and secular powers, and also amongst differing noble families, in Northumbria. At the outset, it states that 'Bishop Aldhun had given his daughter, Ecgfrida, as a wife to Waltheof's son, Uhtred: a young man of great energy and very skilled in war. Aldhun gave with her these vills of the Church of St Cuthbert...that he (Uhtred) retain them for as long as he always lived honourably in marriage with his daughter'.[231] At the time of this union Uhtred was son of the then elderly Earl of Bamburgh, Waltheof. It is therefore apparent that the bishop of Cuthbert's community was the father-in-law to the heir apparent of the House of Bamburgh; this was the confirmation of a bond which had manifested itself as early as the 630s between two of the leading powers, secular and spiritual, of northern Northumbria. The *De Obsessione* goes on to describe how Uhtred was successful in the repulsion of a siege initiated by the Scottish king, Malcolm.

The recognition of this alliance and of the role of Uhtred in repelling the Scots leads to a re-consideration of two of Symeon's statements: first that Durham was to be commended for its easily defensible location and second that it was the very

[227] There may be a parallel for this tactic in the community's previous move to Norham (see above, pp. 285–6). See also Aird, *St Cuthbert*, p. 45, n. 131: he suspects that not all of the religious community made the move to Ripon but rather only 'the immediate minster community'. For Ripon in the late tenth century, see above, pp. 243–9.

[228] For all of this, see Symeon, *LDE*, iii.2.

[229] It is edited and discussed by Morris (C.J.), *Marriage*, pp. 1–31 (at pp. 7 and 10, for the possible date and p. 9 for its being composed at Durham). Meehan 1976, pp. 18–19, suggests a more precise date of composition, in the years 1073–6. Sharpe 1998, p. 219, explores the possibility that Symeon was the author of this text (at p. 219, n. 22, for the dating of the text).

[230] Morris (C.J.), *Marriage*, p. 10. For its place in the proliferation of historiographical material produced at Durham in the twelfth century, see below, pp. 324–8.

[231] See *De Obsessione* in Morris (C.J.), *Marriage*, p. 2.

same Uhtred who so assiduously aided Cuthbert's community to cultivate the site. As Aird suggests, the move to Durham may have been politically motivated with the implication that Durham perhaps had its origins as a fortress from which Uhtred was able to combat a Scottish siege.[232]

Having been appointed as earl of Northumbria, Uhtred, at first sight, seems to have abandoned the support he had received from Cuthbert's community. The *De Obsessione* records how, on his return from King Æthelred's court, he 'dismissed the daughter of Bishop Aldhun' and, as a result of this, Bishop Aldhun took back the lands given to Uhtred on his marriage to Ecgfrida. Uhtred then married a certain Sige, the daughter of Styr, son of Ulf, a wealthy man. This second marriage was only concluded on the condition that Uhtred would kill Styr's leading enemy, Thurbrand.[233] But far from Styr's being an enemy of the Cuthbertine community, he can be found, in the *Historia de Sancto Cuthberto*, making them a gift of land.[234] Styr, we learn from the *De Obsessione*, was an influential character at York; the *Historia de Sancto Cuthberto* adds the detail that he may have been a member of the southern court of King Æthelred and the witness-lists to charters for that king's reign would seem to corroborate this.[235] There is the possibility, then, that the religious community, allied to Earl Uhtred, were exploiting their connections to King Æthelred and trying to gain some kind of political influence at York.[236]

Bishop Aldhun was evidently prepared to ally himself, and thus Cuthbert's community, to any potentially significant secular figure of the day, even if it

[232] Aird, *St Cuthbert*, pp. 46–7. The *De Obsessione* (in Morris (C.J.), *Marriage*, p. 2), records that, upon his successful repulsion of a Scottish siege, Uhtred displayed the heads of the dead Scots in the Durham market place. He was rewarded for his success by King Æthelred with the position of earl of all of Northumbria. Rollason, *Northumbria*, pp. 268–9, shows that it is very likely that the move to Durham was made because of an alliance to Uhtred.

[233] The conditions of this marriage led to a remarkable and celebrated feud which spanned generations. For an account of the feud, see Fletcher, *Bloodfeud*. For more about the feud, and about Northumbrian politics at this time, see Bolton, *Cnut*, pp. 119–23.

[234] *HSC*, c. 29; Styr gave the vill of Darlington, four carucates of land at High Coniscliffe, and four at Cockerton, and four at Haughton-le-Skerne, and four at *Northmannabi*, and two at Ketton, and two at Great Lumley, to St Cuthbert's community. See also *CMD*, p. 526 and Symeon, *LDE*, iii.4.

[235] *HSC*, c. 29. Styr attests S 877 (*WinchNM* 31), S 906 (*Burt* 28) and S 922 (*Burt* 32) of Æthelred's reign.

[236] See also Aird, *St Cuthbert*, pp. 47–8, who describes these events in more detail. Earlier in the tenth century, the Earls of Bamburgh looked to Scotland for help in their encounters against the Scandinavian, King Rægnald (see above, pp. 296–7), and it may be the case that they acknowledged the Scottish kings as their overlords (see Morris, *Marriage*, p. 10). It is striking that at this point in the early eleventh century, at just the moment when Cuthbert's community was shifting itself and its ambitions southwards, so too were the Earls of Bamburgh; see Rollason 1995, p. 31.

meant the dissolving of his daughter's marriage.[237] It is in this light that we should view the record in the *Historia de Sancto Cuthberto* of leases made by him 'to these three, Earl Ethred, Earl Northman and Earl Uhtred',[238] leases which were probably contracted in order to bind the earls to Cuthbert's community.[239] There is, however, the possibility that Aldhun's policy of leasing these vills backfired, as they seem to have been alienated from the community until the time of Cnut.[240] But not all of the vills were lost, and **19**, a note made into the Durham *Liber Vitae*, is an entry which records the return of Escomb by Earl Northman to the community.[241]

As we have seen, Aldhun and the Cuthbertine community may have been in alliance with Uhtred in his marriage to Sige, the daughter of a prominent York citizen. But, as at so many previous junctures in the community's history, its political manoeuvrings were to come unstuck. In due course Earl Uhtred repudiated his marriage to Sige and married Ælfgifu, daughter of King Æthelred.[242] But his most recent marriage was only to Uhtred's brief advantage for, in 1013, the arrival of viking Swein in Anglo-Saxon England caused Æthelred to flee for safety to Normandy and to the court of Duke Richard. Swein died in 1014, which allowed Æthelred to return; but this too proved to be momentary as, in 1015–16, a huge viking force arrived under the leadership of Cnut and Æthelred was to die soon afterwards. So the unfolding of events had led to the political isolation of Uhtred. The *De Obsessione* describes how Cnut had previously sought help from Uhtred in order to overcome Æthelred but Uhtred is supposed to have refused and is made to say: '"No reward could persuade me to do what I ought not to. I will serve the king as long as he lives"'.[243] This refusal led ultimately to Uhtred's death

237 Aldhun was remembered in favourable terms by Cuthbert's community; Barlow, *English Church*, p. 171, n. 5, draws attention to the following words written at the end of the Durham Ritual in commemoration of Aldhun: 'Dominus salvet, honoret, amet Aldhunum antistitem'.

238 *HSC*, c. 31. The lands leased were, 'Gainford, Whorlton, Sledwich, Barforth, Startforth, Lartington, Marwood Green, Stainton, Streatlam, Cleatlam, Langton, Morton Tinmouth, Piercebridge, Bishop Auckland and West Auckland, Copeland, *Weardseatle*, Binchester, St Andrew Aucklad, Thickley, Escombe, Witton-le-Wear, Hunwick, Newton Cap, Helme Park'.

239 Leases were made for just this purpose in the dealings of Cuthbert's community with the men Elfred and Eadred (and perhaps with the recording of Æthelstan's name in the *LVD*); see above, pp. 296–8. For a slightly different interpretation, which stresses that the leases were made by Aldhun out of necessity, see Bolton, *Cnut*, p. 112, n. 28.

240 See Symeon, *LDE*, iii.4: '...but the violence of the earls who succeeded them resulted in virtually all of them being alienated from the dominion of the church'.

241 Bolton, *Cnut*, p. 135, suggests that Earl Northman had been forced by Cnut to return this estate to the religious community.

242 For details, see *De Obsessione* (in Morris (C.J.), *Marriage*, p. 2), where the 'greater and greater military success' of Uhtred is the reason given for his marriage to King Æthelred's daughter.

243 See the *De Obsessione* in Morris (C.J.), *Marriage*, p. 3.

as Cnut enticed him to a meeting (at a place called *Wiheal*) with a promise of safe passage which proved to be false.[244]

The removal of Uhtred left Cuthbert's community in a precarious situation. He had been their principal ally, and their very move to Durham may have been inspired by his need for a fortress situated in a readily defensible area. Although Uhtred's brother, Eadwulf Cudel,[245] succeeded at Bamburgh, the Bamburgh family was naturally removed from its role of supplying earls to Northumbria and instead one of Cnut's followers, Eric of Hlathir, assumed the position.[246] It is clearly likely that the Cuthbertine community's association with Uhtred prompted Cnut to view them with suspicion.

i. *St Cuthbert's Community and Extraneous Influence*

It is perhaps the case that Cnut, unlike previous Anglo-Saxon kings, managed to exert some form of control over the Cuthbertine community. Upon the death of Bishop Aldhun, either in 1016 or 1018,[247] there was a vacancy in the line of bishops at Durham which lasted for a period of three years.[248] The members of the religious community appear to have found this a troublesome time until eventually a priest from amongst their number, Edmund (*c.* 1020–*c.* 1040), was elected as Aldhun's successor. In his account of Edmund's election, Symeon describes how Edmund was escorted to Cnut, who then commended his appointment; Symeon also notes that the consecration itself took part in the heart of West Saxon territory, at Winchester.[249] The symbolism of such a ceremony

[244] Cnut had promised to discuss terms of peace at this meeting but in the event soldiers emerged from behind a curtain and 'slaughtered the earl and forty of his chief men who had entered with him' (*De Obsessione* in Morris (C.J.), *Marriage*, p. 3). Uhtred's murderer was the very same Thurbrand whom Uhtred had promised to murder as part of a marriage contract with Sige, the daughter of Styr, son of Ulf. For the meeting at *Wiheal*, see Fletcher, *Bloodfeud*, pp. 1–12.

[245] This name may mean Eadwulf 'Cuttlefish', from Old English, *cudele*; see also Woolf, *Pictland*, p. 236.

[246] *ASC C*, s.a. 1017. For more about Uhtred's execution and his replacement with Eric, see Bolton, *Cnut*, p. 118. The historiographical traditions concerning Eadwulf suggest that he was a 'lazy and cowardly man' (see, for example, *De Obsessione*, in Morris (C.J.), *Marriage*, p. 3); it would appear, therefore, that the House of Bamburgh lacked a man with the potential to return it to a position of authority. Nevertheless, northern Northumbria may have continued to be in the control of the House of Bamburgh, perhaps in subordination to Eric; see Whitelock 1959, pp. 82–3 and Meehan 1976, p. 17, where he suggests that 'Eadwulf Cudel's local position was probably strong enough to withstand Eiric' and therefore goes against the testimony regarding Eadwulf in *De Obsessione*.

[247] See Cooper 1968, p. 133, where she prefers 1016 rather than 1018 as the date for the Battle of Carham and Aldhun's death. But, for 1018 as more likely for both events, see Meehan 1976, p. 14, n. 1 and p. 15.

[248] Symeon, *LDE*, iii.6.

[249] Symeon, *LDE*, iii.6.

would not have been lost on Edmund and these details may suggest that the episcopal vacancy had been caused by some intervention on Cnut's part.[250] Certainly he would have had good reason to intrude upon the everyday life of the Cuthbertine community, the very community that had been so heavily and recently involved in secular politics.

An interesting feature of the confirmation of Edmund's position is his stopping off at Peterborough in order to pick up the monk, Æthelric, who became bishop of Durham later, in 1041.[251] It may have been a condition of Edmund's election that a man drawn from a more southerly religious house would succeed him. Perhaps some form of compromise had been reached between Cuthbert's community and Cnut whereby the community was initially permitted to appoint a man from their own number (but one whom Cnut approved of) but then had to accept an outsider. Such an agreement would have made perfect sense to Cnut who was only too aware of the Cuthbertine community's natural tendency to side with the Earls of Bamburgh. It was perhaps as a result of this understanding that Cnut, following a barefoot pilgrimage of five miles from Garmondsway to Cuthbert's shrine, gave the vill of Staindrop with its dependencies and also that of Brompton, in Yorkshire, to St Cuthbert.[252] In the promotion of a man to the Durham bishopric whose natural orientation was to the south rather than to the north, Cnut perhaps sought to break the possibility of a subsequent alliance.[253]

It has already been noted that the community's move to Durham may have been instigated by Earl Uhtred who perhaps thought of the location as an ideal one from which to defend against the Scots. We can therefore postulate that the Scots

250 On the role of Cnut, see Barlow, *English Church*, pp. 105 and 111, n. 4; see also Aird, *St Cuthbert*, pp. 49–51 (at p. 51, for Cnut's restoration of lands previously lost to St Cuthbert's community during Aldhun's pontificate) and Rollason, *Northumbria*, p. 272. Bolton, *Cnut*, pp. 125–6, suggests that the evidence does not uphold the proposition that a candidate was being favoured by Cnut. But this seems to underestimate the significance of the fact that this is the first time in Symeon's *LDE* that a bishop of the Cuthbertine community is described as having to receive confirmation at the hands of a southern king, a fact which strongly suggests that Cnut was successful in gaining some influence with the community. Edmund himself can be found attesting only one, wholly spurious, charter from Cnut's reign, S 995 in the Bury St Edmund's archive, where he is styled *Lyndisfarnensis episcopus*. The anachronistic style, 'bishop of Lindisfarne', in this forged charter is interesting since Aldhun, the first bishop of Durham, was given the same title in *HSC*, c. 29.

251 This detail is given in the same passage of Symeon, *LDE*, iii.6. For Æthelric's assumption of the bishopric, see *ASC CD*, s.a. 1041.

252 *HSC*, c. 32; *CMD*, pp. 527–8 and Symeon, *LDE*, iii.8.

253 This was just the same policy of Anglo-Saxon kings of the tenth century when dealing with the archbishopric of York; see Whitelock 1959 and above, pp. 55–9; Aird, *St Cuthbert*, p. 52, likewise compares this action by Cnut to the earlier tenth-century situation at York. The most telling evidence that Æthelric was considered an outsider (*extraneus*) and not someone loyal to the north, is that he was regarded as foreign and an intruder by the Durham community: see below, pp. 313–14.

had become a threat by the period immediately prior to 995.[254] Perhaps the most formal acknowledgement of an increase in Scottish power came with the cession of the area of Lothian by the Northumbrians. Unfortunately it is difficult to know when exactly this territorial loss took place.[255] The twelfth-century text *De primo adventu Saxonum* suggests that King Edgar relinquished Lothian to Kenneth II, king of the Scots, in the late tenth century.[256] But the *De Obsessione* suggests that the ineffectiveness of Earl Uhtred's brother, Eadwulf Cudel, led to the loss of Lothian in the period after Uhtred's death.[257] Another possibility is that Lothian was lost after the Battle of Carham, dated by Symeon to 1018.[258] Unlike previous occasions when the men of Northumbria managed to resist Scottish incursions, this battle seems to have been a crushing defeat, so much so that 'almost all perished, including even their old folk'.[259] In the end, it is difficult to know exactly when the formal cession of Lothian took place and it may be, as Rollason suggests, that a date earlier in the tenth century is more likely, since the king of Scotland had been willing to intervene in a battle against viking Rægnald as far south as Corbridge.[260]

Symeon tells of another attack in the year 1040 in which Duncan, king of the Scots, laid siege to Durham.[261] The Scots were unsuccessful, and on their return to Scotland King Duncan was killed by Macbeth.[262] Following the murder of Duncan, Symeon describes how, on the death of Bishop Edmund *c.* 1040,[263] a certain Eadred, who had been second in rank to Edmund,[264] took a large amount

[254] Woolf, *Pictland*, pp. 232–40, discusses Scottish aggression at this time and suggests that the Scots were taking advantage of the political turmoil in England *c.* 1000.

[255] The rest of this paragraph is indebted to Rollason, *Northumbria*, pp. 275–6.

[256] *De primo adventu Saxonum*, ed. Arnold, *Sym. Op.* II, pp. 366–84: 'Qui (i.e. Kenneth), cum illi fecisset hominium, dedit ei rex Eadgarus Lodoneium, et multo cum honore remisit ad propria' (at p. 382). Kenneth had been led to Edgar's court by the earl of York and Northumbria and by Bishop Ælfsige. For more comment on this account, see Woolf, *Pictland*, p. 211.

[257] *De Obsessione*, in Morris (C.J.), *Marriage*, p. 3.

[258] Rollason 1995, p. 33.

[259] Symeon, *LDE*, iii.5. Woolf, *Pictland*, p. 240, suggests that the period following Uhtred's assassination provides the most likely context for the cession of lands north of the Tweed by Cnut to Malcolm, in return for Malcolm's submission.

[260] Rollason, *Northumbria*, p. 276; see also Meehan 1976 (esp. p. 17) and A.A.M. Duncan, 'The Battle of Carham, 1018', *Scottish Historical Review* lv (1976), pp. 20–8. For the 918 battle of Corbridge, see above, pp. 297–8.

[261] Symeon, *LDE*, iii.9.

[262] See Woolf, *Pictland*, pp. 254–5.

[263] Rollason, *Symeon: Libellus*, p. 170, n. 41, using the evidence of Symeon's *LDE*, prefers 1042 for Edmund's death; see also Aird, *St Cuthbert*, p. 52, who suggests 1040. The matter is complicated by the notice in the *ASC* of the election as bishop of one of Edmund's successors, Æthelric, already in 1041; see above, p. 311, n. 251.

[264] Barlow, *English Church*, p. 230, n. 11, suggests Eadred was dean of the Durham community at this stage.

of the Durham church's treasure and used it to buy the bishopric from King Harthacnut (1040–2).[265] Even if this might have been an attempt by St Cuthbert's community to recover some of its former independence,[266] it was nevertheless short-lived as Eadred died having been bishop for only ten months. Not long afterwards, probably in the year 1041, Siward, a Scandinavian from York (d. 1055), murdered Earl Eadwulf of the House of Bamburgh and thus took control of the whole of the Northumbrian earldom.[267] There is some suggestion that King Harthacnut, the son of King Cnut, had a role to play in the killing of Eadwulf. The *Anglo-Saxon Chronicle* states in its annal for 1041: 'And in this year also Harthacnut betrayed Earl Eadwulf under his safe-conduct and he was then a pledge-breaker. [And in this year Æthelric was consecrated bishop in York on 11 January]'.[268] A combination of the details provided by Symeon and by the *Anglo-Saxon Chronicle* suggests that King Harthacnut and Siward had allied in order to remove the threat posed by the Bamburgh earls; they then had Æthelric, a southern man, installed as bishop of Cuthbert's community.

In a double sweep powers from the south neutralised those two most troublesome elements of the Northumbrian kingdom: the Bamburgh earls and the Cuthbertine community.[269] Members of the religious community were not pleased with their new bishop and a faction emerged which *c.* 1045 managed to oust Æthelric from the scene. But Æthelric was able to rely on Siward for help, as the earl is remembered in Symeon's *Libellus de exordio* as been intimately involved in the reinstallation of Æthelric as bishop.[270] It is in the same passage of the *Libellus de exordio* that Symeon accuses Æthelric and his brother Æthelwine, who was at that time managing the bishopric under Æthelric, of defrauding the church of Cuthbert. It is striking that Æthelric is described as an 'outsider' (*extraneus*) and it is therefore plausible to connect the unfavourable reputation of

[265] Symeon, *LDE*, iii.9.

[266] Another possibility is simply that Eadred was seeking personal gain. For all of this, see Aird, *St Cuthbert*, pp. 52–3.

[267] Symeon, *LDE*, iii.9. Aird, *St Cuthbert*, p. 53, notes that Siward further consolidated his position by marrying Ælfflæda, the daughter of Earl Ealdred of the House of Bamburgh.

[268] *ASC CD*, s.a. 1041. It may be significant that the part in square brackets is only found in the 'D' manuscript, that is the northern recension, of the *ASC*. Perhaps the northern author thought of the accession of Æthelric to the bishopric of Durham as inextricably linked to the betrayal of Earl Eadwulf by King Harthacnut.

[269] The situation in general seems to have worsened for Cuthbert's community. One of Siward's first acts was to claim that he was the rightful heir (through his wife Ælfflæda who was of the House of Bamburgh) to those estates granted to Uhtred by Bishop Aldhun as a dowry: Aird, *St Cuthbert*, p. 53.

[270] See Symeon, *LDE*, iii.9. Despite the description given here of Siward, there is evidence to suggest that the religious community grew to appreciate his period of tenure as earl for the peace and stability it brought to the kingdom: see Aird, *St Cuthbert*, p. 54.

both Æthelric and Æthelwine with the fact that they were not drawn from brethren of the Cuthbertine community itself.[271]

In 1055 Earl Siward died and was buried in his minster of St Olaf at Bootham Bar in York.[272] He was replaced by Tostig, who was the first man from south of the Humber to become Earl of Northumbria.[273] In 1056 Bishop Æthelric left his see under what would appear to be rather dubious circumstances. Symeon narrates that whilst the demolition of the wooden church at Chester-le-Street was taking place, those involved in the work came upon a huge treasure which had been hidden at the site.[274] Symeon describes how Æthelric took up the treasure, sent it on to Peterborough and 'firmly resolved to follow it there himself';[275] Symeon therefore accuses Æthelric of stealing from the Cuthbertine community.[276]

But other sources for the event are not so negatively charged. The *Historia regum*, relying on John of Worcester, states plainly that Æthelric voluntarily gave up his see and retired to Peterborough;[277] no mention is made of Æthelric's supposed stealing. Evidently there is a separate, more neutral, tradition, which finds confirmation in the account of the same event in the *Cronica monasterii Dunelmensis* (hereafter *CMD*), a source compiled in the late eleventh century.[278]

The description in the *CMD* would seem to suggest that Æthelric's actions were praiseworthy; he chose to accept a personal loss rather than inflict one upon the Durham see. It may be that Æthelric's chief crime, and the cause of his bad

[271] One of Æthelric's episcopal predecessors, Edmund, had been a resident of the Cuthbertine community before his elevation to the role of bishop and he is thus remembered in favourable terms: see Symeon, *LDE*, iii.6. For the community's reaction to outside influence, see Meehan 1975 (esp. p. 46).

[272] *ASC CDE*, s.a. 1055.

[273] See also Aird, *St Cuthbert*, p. 54. Siward, though also an outsider, was a Dane acceptable to the Anglo-Danish aristocracy of Yorkshire and he had shrewdly sought to placate the traditional powers in Northumbria by marrying into the ruling family of Bernicia. Tostig was the brother of Earl Harold of Wessex, both of whom were members of the powerful Godwine family.

[274] It had apparently been hidden by the sacristan and a few others on account of the tyranny of Seaxhelm (on whom, see above, p. 302, n. 198).

[275] Symeon, *LDE*, iii.9.

[276] For the Peterborough view of these events, see Kelly, *Peterborough*, pp. 56–7, and p. 244, for the suggestion that the connection between Peterborough and Durham perhaps led to Howden, a place granted in S 681 (*Pet* 14) to Quen *matrona*, being transferred from Cuthbert's community to Peterborough. It was in the possession of the bishop of Durham again in the late eleventh century: GDB, f. 304v.

[277] *HR* (8), p. 173 (s.a. 1056) and *John of Worcester II*, s.a. 1056. See the comments of Meehan 1975, pp. 51–2.

[278] For the date of composition of the *CMD*, see below, p. 326. For the description of Æthelric's departure, see *CMD*, p. 528: 'Seeing that he (i.e. Æthelric) had no help from anywhere else, and that by himself he was unable to resist the violence with which malevolent men were attacking and weakening the freedom of the church, he preferred to leave the bishopric than to ruin the freedom and tranquility of the church through his own weakness, and he returned to his own monastery and ended his life without a bishopric'.

reputation, was that he was an *extraneus*; Symeon, writing in the early twelfth century, found it necessary to create a more serious reason for the vilification of this intruder and so invented this tale of theft.[279] After Æthelric had departed for Peterborough, his brother, Æthelwine (1056–71), succeeded to the bishopric, supported by Earl Tostig.[280] This continued the close relationship between earl and bishop seen earlier with Siward and Æthelric. But Æthelwine too, like his brother before him, was considered an *extraneus* by the Durham church and is remembered as being 'to a greater extent than his brother before him intent on removing from it ornaments and other things'.[281]

On his acquisition of the earldom, Tostig found himself in a unique position. Unlike every previous earl of Northumbria, Tostig, as a newcomer to the region, could not rely on the backing of any local faction. It is possible that this was to Tostig's advantage as it also meant that he lacked local enemies. His neutrality may have allowed him to govern Northumbria more effectively and he is certainly remembered as an efficient enforcer of the law.[282] Tostig later involved himself with the Cuthbertine community, not only aiding in the election of Æthelwine as bishop, but also adorning the Durham church with gifts. And his wife, Judith, is also celebrated as having been a generous donor.[283]

The late 1050s saw Tostig's position undermined by external factors as the Scots become a major threat to Northumbria.[284] In 1059 the growing power of Malcolm III was perhaps checked since we find him being escorted to a meeting with King Edward the Confessor by Cynesige, archbishop of York, Æthelwine, bishop of Durham and Tostig, earl of York, in what seems to have been an act of submission.[285] However, in 1061 Malcolm, taking advantage of Tostig's

[279] Meehan 1975, esp. pp. 50–3, suggested as the reason for the discrepancy in our sources that Symeon, writing in the aftermath of the Conquest, expected the worst of an *extraneus*. Symeon states that the money sent by Æthelric to Peterborough was used to construct roads and churches in the Fens; and so it may be that Symeon's bad impression of Æthelric stemmed from the fact that this money had not been spent on the fabric of the Durham church (see Aird, *St Cuthbert*, p. 55, n. 169).

[280] Symeon, *LDE*, iii.9. For Tostig's support of Æthelwine, see Kapelle, *Norman*, p. 90 and Fletcher, *Bloodfeud*, p. 156.

[281] Symeon, *LDE*, iii.11.

[282] See Kapelle, *Norman*, p. 89 and Aird, *St Cuthbert*, p. 56.

[283] Symeon, *LDE*, iii.11. Judith is said to 'have loved St Cuthbert even more than did her husband, [and] also gave various ornaments to the saint's church; and she promised to give more still together with many landed possessions'. The extent of the gifts made by Tostig and his wife led to their commemoration in the *LVD*: their names are entered (in gold lettering in Tostig's case) on f. 15v (Tostig) and f. 48v (Judith); see *LVD*, pp. 92 and 144, respectively.

[284] For more about St Cuthbert's community and the Scots, see W.M. Aird, 'St Cuthbert, the Scots and the Normans', *Anglo-Norman Studies* xvi (1993), pp. 1–20 and Aird, *St Cuthbert*, pp. 227–67.

[285] *HR* (8), p. 174 (s.a. 1059) and Woolf, *Pictland*, p. 270. Aird, *St Cuthbert*, p. 232, notes that it may have been a traditional duty for the bishop of Cuthbert's community to be involved in meetings with the

prolonged absence whilst on pilgrimage with Judith in Rome, 'furiously ravaged the earldom of his sworn brother earl Tostig, and violated the peace of St Cuthbert in the island of Lindisfarne'.[286] It may be that these raids by Malcolm led to him recapturing parts of Cumbria from Northumbrian control.[287] Whatever the case, Tostig's absence and his inability to broker peace with the Scottish king would have done nothing to advance his own position in Northumbria.

The men of Northumbria were so disenchanted with Tostig that in 1065 'all the thegns in Yorkshire and in Northumberland came together and outlawed their Earl Tostig and killed his bodyguard...and they sent for Morcar, son of Earl Ælfgar, and chose him as their earl...and the king granted this and sent Harold back to them at Northampton...and he (i.e. Harold) proclaimed this to them and gave them surety for it, and he renewed there the law of King Cnut'.[288] In the end Tostig's failure ensured that all powers in Northumbria, whether from the House of Bamburgh, or from York, were against him.[289] Thus, by the end of the Anglo-Saxon period, it was clear that anyone who did not have a Northumbrian heritage, but who was appointed to a leading role within Northumbria, would experience opposition. This was a valuable lesson for the next monarch, William the Conqueror.

2. THE HISTORY OF THE DURHAM ARCHIVE

a. *The Pre-Conquest Documents in the Durham Archive*

By the end of the Anglo-Saxon period, St Cuthbert's community had accumulated a large amount of territory which spanned the region between the River Tweed in the north and the River Tees in the south. In the process of acquiring this

Scots. As we have seen (above, p. 312, n. 256), in the period 971 × 975, Kenneth II of Scotland was led to King Edgar's court by the earls of York and Northumbria and by Ælfsige, bishop of Chester-le-Street.

286 *HR* (8), pp. 174–5 (s.a. 1061). For continuing religious life at Lindisfarne following the departure *c.* 875 of Cuthbert's community, see above, p. 289, n. 125.

287 By 1070 Cumbria had clearly passed into Malcolm's hands since Earl Gospatric ravaged the area as a reprisal for Malcolm's actions in Northumbria: *HR* (8), p. 191. It is perhaps as a result of Malcolm's actions in the period 1066–70 that the kingdom of Strathclyde/Cumbria came to an end: see below, pp. 361–2 and Woolf, *Pictland*, pp. 270–1.

288 *ASC DE*, s.a. 1065.

289 Kapelle, *Norman*, pp. 95–8, suggests that two factors in particular led to Tostig's downfall: first that he had tried to reduce the power of the House of Bamburgh in Northumbria by murdering some of its leading figures; second that St Cuthbert's community deliberately incited rebellion against the unpopular earl; see esp. Kapelle, *ibid.*, p. 98, for Alfred Westou's supposed role in the rebellion. However, Aird, *St Cuthbert*, pp. 57–8, shows that it was unlikely that Cuthbert's community were implicated in this way.

land, the Cuthbertines would have required written documentation which proved their ownership of various estates. One could speculate that this would have led inevitably to the possession of Anglo-Saxon charters, issued in the name of a king and displaying the normal diplomatic elements such as a verbal invocation, a royal superscription, a dispositive section, a dating-clause, a sanction and a witness-list. But in fact the evidence for this is slender at best: two groups of names entered into the Durham *Liber Vitae* in the twelfth century may represent some of those councillors present at meetings of Æthelstan's royal assemblies in 927 and 934, which perhaps suggests that two of that king's charters were available at Durham in the post-Conquest period, there to be copied;[290] and two sections of the *Historia de Sancto Cuthberto* show at least an appreciation of charter diplomatic, although it is difficult to know what provided the inspiration for these passages and one in particular can be shown to have been made on the basis of information from a gospel book rather than any pre-existing charter.[291] While it could be the case that charters belonging to St Cuthbert's community have been lost or destroyed, the surviving evidence seems rather to suggest that the Cuthbertines deliberately eschewed the use of such documents. Instead, it seems to have been their practice to enter details of landed transactions into their precious books. Keynes has identified four high-grade manuscripts which were used by the community for this purpose.[292] Of these, two are still extant: the Durham *Liber Vitae* and Cambridge, Corpus Christi College, MS 183 (a manuscript commissioned by King Æthelstan as a gift for St Cuthbert's community). We also have references to, and fragments of, one manuscript which

[290] However, it is also possible that the second group of names, reflecting a meeting of 934, was taken from a list of names in a gospel book rather than a charter; for this suggestion, and for discussion of both of these groups of names, see Barker 1977 and also below, p. 320

[291] *HSC*, c. 29, has formulae resembling a verbal invocation and a sanction; it also has what may be a reference to a witness-list. It is probably significant that this transaction is explicitly said to have taken place at York, at a moment when Cuthbert's community was trying to gain political influence south of the River Tees (see above, p. 308). If a charter somehow underlies this extract in the *HSC*, this southwards orientation may be the reason why. *HSC*, c. 26, which constitutes the famous *testamentum* placed at the head of Cuthbert's shrine by King Æthelstan, likewise has recognisable diplomatic elements including a verbal invocation, royal superscription and sanction. But as Keynes 1985, pp. 177–8 demonstrates, it seems unlikely that this *testamentum* ever had any separate existence as a single-sheet document and it is more probable that it was based on information recorded in a gospel book, perhaps Cotton Otho B. ix (for which see below, pp. 321–2); see also the comments of J.A. Robinson, *The Times of Saint Dunstan*, The Ford Lectures Delivered in the University of Oxford in the Michaelmas Term, 1922 (Oxford, 1923), pp. 52–3.

[292] I am very grateful to Prof. Keynes who, at the beginning of my research on the northern archives, provided me with a copy of his profile of the Durham archive. Although I do not cite this work (which Prof. Keynes informs me he is not intending to publish), this section is indebted to its insights. See also the comments of Johnson South in *HSC*, pp. 6–8.

has been destroyed but which used to contain notes of a similar form (Cotton Otho B. ix); and to a manuscript which is now lost but which evidently fulfilled the same function (the *Cronica Monasterii Dunelmensis* which was kept on the high altar at Durham).

(a) **British Library, Cotton Domitian A. vii** is better known as the Durham *Liber Vitae* (hereafter *LVD*).[293] The *LVD* is an impressively adorned manuscript which is concerned primarily with the recording of people's names but into which other miscellaneous material was also inserted. It is helpful to envisage three periods in the use of the *LVD*: (i) The original core of the manuscript was composed sometime in the period *c*. 800 × *c*. 840 in the north of Anglo-Saxon England (probably at Lindisfarne) and consists of lists of names of those persons who, from the early 600s onwards, had some special association with St Cuthbert's church.[294] (ii) There was a break in the use of the *LVD* from the 830s to the time of the episcopate of Bishop William of St Calais (1081–96), during which only a few names and items were inserted.[295] (iii) After Bishop William of St Calais had reformed the community of secular canons at Durham as Benedictine monks in 1083, use of the *LVD* again took off and was added to in a more regular fashion.[296]

As Gerchow points out, the compilation of *Libri Vitae*, in general, involved the re-organisation of information which already existed in the form of complete manuscripts or, alternatively, of lists on individual folios.[297] Such a process often led to the resultant *Liber Vitae* being disordered and unruly in form. But the original core of the *LVD* has the appearance of a de luxe manuscript. It maintains a good deal of its original format as lists of names are not obstructed or crowded by later insertions. One or two scribes were responsible for the original core of the manuscript and they inserted names in alternating gold and silver lettering. No

[293] It is listed in Ker, *Catalogue*, no. 147 and Davis, *Cartularies* (rev. edn), no. 349; see also Mynors, *Durham Cathedral*, pp. 24–5 (no. 13). A facsimile version is available in Thompson, *Lib. Vit.*; a printed version is given in Stevenson, *Lib. Vit.*. For discussion of the Durham *Liver Vitae*, see Rollason *et al*., *The Durham* (especially Gerchow 2004 and Briggs 2004). A new three-volume edition with extensive commentary and discussion is *LVD*.

[294] For the date of the original core of the *Liber Vitae*, see L. Rollason, 'Periods of Use and Disuse' in *LVD*, pp. 23–4; see also L. Rollason, 'Historical Background', in *ibid*., pp. 31–3, for Lindisfarne as the scriptorium most likely to have produced the manuscript (relying on Briggs 2004). Gerchow 2004, pp. 47–57, proposes Monkwearmouth-Jarrow as an alternative origin for the Durham *Liber Vitae*.

[295] For these additions, see L. Rollason, 'Periods of Use and Disuse', in *LVD*, p. 24.

[296] Gerchow 2004, p. 48. For a more detailed view of the periods of use of the *Liber Vitae*, see L. Rollason, 'Periods of Use and Disuse', in *LVD*, pp. 23–9.

[297] Gerchow 2004, p. 46. For this process with regards to the Durham *Liber Vitae*, see S. Keynes, *The Liber Vitae of the New Minster and Hyde Abbey, Winchester, British Library Stowe 944*, Early English Manuscripts in Facsimile xxvi (Copenhagen, 1996), p. 57.

other contemporary *Libri Vitae* can be found aiming at such effects and, although the manuscript itself is not large, its overall aspect suggests that it was once considered a precious item.[298] The sixteenth-century *Rites of Durham* confirm that the *LVD* was thought of as an important manuscript at Durham as they state that it was kept on the high altar there.[299] The *LVD* therefore formed the perfect medium into which to insert records of land transactions which were of benefit to the religious community and thus to be remembered.

From the mid-ninth century until *c.* 1083, relatively less material was inserted into the *LVD*. But we do find some Anglo-Saxon entries: in the late tenth century, the verso of f. 47 was used to record a gift of land in Yorkshire by Earl Thored to the community (**18**).[300] Later on, in the early eleventh century, the remainder of this folio was used to insert details of grants of land in County Durham: one by Earl Northman (**19**) and the other by Ulfketel, son of Osulf (**20**).[301] Other Anglo-Saxon additions can be found. The recto of f. 47 was used to record the only known Northumbrian example of a manumission whereby 'Geatflæd has given freedom, for love of God...to Ecceard Smith, and Ælstan and his wife...'.[302] Twenty-five Anglo-Saxon names were added during this second period of use.[303] The most famous example is that of 'Aeðelstan rex', which occurs directly after the list which is headed 'Nomina regum vel ducum' on f. 15r. A group of another four names, two of which, Wulfstan and Æthelstan, occur on the recto of f. 24, and two deacons Eadhelm and Ealhhelm whose names are found on f. 26r, may have been made by the same scribe who entered King Æthelstan's name; Keynes

298 Gerchow 2004, pp. 45–6: 'It must have been an experienced *scriptorium* with extensive resources of materials which produced it' (at p. 46).

299 See Fowler, *Rites*, pp. 16–17: 'There did lye on the high altar an excellent fine booke verye richly covered with gold and silver conteining the names of all the benefactors towards St Cuthberts church from the first originall foundation thereof, the verye letters for the most part beinge all gilded as is apparent in the said booke till this day the layinge that booke on the high altar did show how highly they esteemed their founders and benefactors, and the dayly and quotidian remembrance they had of them in the time of masse and divine service did argue not onely their gratitude, but also a most divine and charitable affection to the soles of theire benefactors as well dead as living, which booke is as yet extant declaringe the sd use in the inscription thereof'.

300 It is listed as S 1660 and edited in Robertson, *Charters*, no. LX. Earl Thored can also be found making a gift of land to the Christ Church community in S 1222 (KCD 958); a record of this grant has been entered into one of the three fragmentary Pontificals contained in Cotton MS. Claudius A. iii (on f. 6r); it is printed in Robertson, *Charters*, no. LXXXVIII. See also D.H. Turner, ed., *The Claudius Pontificals: From Cotton Claudius A. iii in the British Museum*, Henry Bradshaw Society xcvii (Chichester, 1971), p. v, n. 3.

301 They are listed as S 1659 and 1661 respectively; and edited as one document in Robertson, *Charters*, no. LXVIII.

302 It is printed as Birch 1254; it is discussed in Craster 1925*b* and by D.A.E. Pelteret, 'The Manumissions in the Durham *Liber Vitae*', in *LVD*, pp. 66–72.

303 For a summary of these, see Gerchow 2004, p. 48.

has postulated that these four ecclesiastics may therefore have been in attendance on the king.[304]

From *c.* 1083 use of the *LVD* increased dramatically. Details of confraternities were entered into it: one of the most celebrated is that between the Cuthbertine community and King Malcolm of Scotland on f. 52v.[305] Ff. 53–4 contain a forged charter in the name of Bishop William of St Calais and ff. 54v–55r contain charters of King William I.[306] Of course the *Liber Vitae* was also used for its primary purpose: to record names for commemoration. Among some of the names added in the twelfth century are two interesting groups, inserted on f. 15v and f. 46v, which may ultimately depend on the witness-lists of two now lost charters of King Æthelstan (although the second group of names is perhaps more likely to derive from a record made into a gospel book).[307]

(b) **Cambridge, Corpus Christi College, MS 183** (hereafter CCCC 183) is an early tenth-century manuscript containing a remarkable collection of texts relating to St Cuthbert (Bede's prose and verse *Lives*, a glossary of difficult words from the latter, extracts about the saint from *HE*, and a liturgical section comprising a hymn, a proper mass and a rhyming office for the saint). A Latin sequence with musical notation and an inventory of church goods has been added to f. 96v of this manuscript.[308] The inventory directly precedes the record of a vernacular lease inserted in the later eleventh century of land in County Durham by Bishop Walcher (1071–80) and Cuthbert's community to a certain Ealdgyth.[309] It was prefaced by an illumination showing the king and the saint and seems to have been commissioned by King Æthelstan and then later given by him to St Cuthbert's community.[310]

[304] See Keynes, *The Liber Vitae of the New Minster*, p. 58, n. 67; see also Gerchow 2004, pp. 48–50 and L. Rollason, 'Periods of Use and Disuse', in *LVD*, p. 24.

[305] There are details of other confraternities on f. 52rv.

[306] See Offler, *Durham Episcopal*, no. 3 and above, p. 298, n. 173, for the mistaken belief that this charter of Bishop William of St Calais contains a genuine Anglo-Saxon land grant.

[307] See Barker 1977, who suggests that the group of names on f. 15v was taken from a charter made after a meeting of the *witan* in 927 and that the group of names on f. 46v was taken from a record in a gospel book of a meeting of 934.

[308] The inventory is printed in Robertson, *Charters*, Appendix II, no. 4.

[309] This document is printed in Robertson, *Charters*, Appendix I, no. 2 and in Offler, *Durham Episcopal*, no. 1. The land leased consisted of the vills of Thornley and Wingate which are in the parish of Kelloe. For more comment, see Craster 1925*b*, pp. 193–4.

[310] It is listed in Ker, *Catalogue*, no. 42 and Mynors, *Durham Cathedral*, p. 26 (no. 16). Keynes 1985, pp. 180–5, suggests that this manuscript was intended as a gift from King Æthelstan. Rollason 1989, pp. 420–3, suggests that it may not have been a gift at all and was perhaps representative of Æthelstan's personal devotion to Cuthbert.

(c) **British Library, Cotton Otho B. ix** is a gospel book which was written in Brittany in the late ninth or early tenth century.[311] The codex was given by King Æthelstan to Cuthbert's community probably on the occasion of the king's expedition to Scotland in 934.[312] Tragically the fire which destroyed Sir Robert Cotton's library at Ashburnham House on 23 October 1731 also devastated Cotton Otho B. ix, leaving only twelve fragments which remain today. But Keynes, by using earlier accounts of the manuscript, early catalogues and antiquarian material, has been able to recreate much of the manuscript's contents.[313] As well as material expected in a gospel book, Cotton Otho B. ix contained a miniature portrait of some interest. It was found on the reverse side of a leaf which depicted St Matthew and it showed Æthelstan presenting a book to St Cuthbert. Above the portrait was an inscription which announced that the scene represented King Æthelstan offering a manuscript as a gift to St Cuthbert.[314] Although this portrait has been destroyed, Keynes suggests that it would have been similar to the one found in CCCC 183 which also depicts Æthelstan and Cuthbert.

It seems that this gospel book, like CCCC 183 and the *LVD*, was used as a sometime repository for other more temporal matters. A description of the contents of the manuscript was added, perhaps by one of the Cottonian librarians. It is now lost but was transcribed by a Durham antiquary on the occasion of a visit made to the Cotton library on 10 November 1715. It reads:

> Catalogus tractatuum in isto volumine. Evangelia quatuor quae Æthelstanus dedit ecclesiae Dunelmensi interseruntur privilegia et consuetudines aliquot ad ecclesiam...sunt et manumissionum antiquarum formae, et licentia nubendi....[315]

This summarises the type of compilation Cotton Otho B. ix must have been, suggesting that it was gospel book which had a subsidiary role as a cartulary.

By reference to copies of certain excerpts of the original manuscript made by Cotton's librarian, Richard James, it is possible to see that, as stated in the above summary, it was used to record details of Anglo-Saxon manumissions. On the folio which came directly before the beginning of the gospel of St Matthew are the names, written in Old English, of those persons who were freed by

311 Mynors, *Durham Cathedral*, pp. 25–6 (no. 15) and Ker, *Catalogue*, no. 176.

312 The expedition is recorded in *ASC C*, s.a. 934. For more about Æthelstan's dealings with St Cuthbert's community, see above, pp. 299–302.

313 Keynes 1985, pp. 171–9.

314 Keynes 1985, pp. 173–4; he recreates these details from descriptions made by the antiquaries Smith, Wanley and James.

315 It can be found in Mickleton and Spearman 36, p. 239 and can be translated: 'A catalogue of the tracts in that volume: the four gospels which Æthelstan gave to the Durham church; interleaved are some privileges and customs for the church; there are also forms of ancient manumissions and a licence for marrying...'. See also Keynes 1985, p. 172, n. 142 and p. 175, n. 158.

Mældorth. Similarly the last page of the gospel book was used to note three other manumissions, one of which saw a certain Ælfred 'Lareow' ('teacher/master') free seven men; Ælfred 'Lareow' can be identified with that famous Durham character of the mid-eleventh century, the relic-collector Ælfred son of Westou.[316] The ceremony which released these people from slavery was presumably carried out at the high altar in the Durham church and a record of the deed was subsequently entered into one of the community's high-grade manuscripts, and one usually kept on the altar; in this instance the gospel book, Cotton Otho B. ix.

Other insertions were made into Cotton Otho B. ix. In the tenth or eleventh century two Old English notes were written in a space which preceded the Gospel of St John. A copy of the first was made by Wanley in 1705; it formed another record (in addition to the inscription which accompanied the miniature portrait of Æthelstan and Cuthbert) of the gift of Cotton Otho B. ix by Æthelstan to Cuthbert's community. Keynes has shown that the interest of this note lies in the fact that it was written by someone who had a familiarity with the diplomatic formulae of mid-tenth-century Anglo-Saxon charters. Unfortunately Wanley did not make a copy of the second note, but Keynes suggests that the Latin *testamentum* in the *Historia de Sancto Cuthberto*, which records a list of gifts made by Æthelstan to the Cuthbertine community, is a conflation of these two Old English lists.[317]

(d) A **fourth text** which had been used as a repository for notes concerning landed transactions and historical events is that of a gospel book now lost. The first trace we have of this manuscript comes from incidental information supplied by the *Liber Ruber*, a codex which, for a long time, was itself thought to have been lost.[318] Craster has since shown that the *Liber Ruber* is not lost at all but exists as London, Lincoln's Inn, Hales MS 114.[319] Codicological study

[316] For the original texts of these manumissions, their translations and the identification of Ælfred Lareow, see Craster 1925*b*, pp. 190–2. For discussion of Durham manumissions in general, see D.A.E. Pelteret, *Slavery in Early Mediaeval England*, Studies in Anglo-Saxon History (Woodbridge, 1995), pp. 161–2 and *idem*, 'The Manumissions in the Durham *Liber Vitae*', in *LVD*, pp. 66–72. For Ælfred son of Westou, see Symeon, *LDE*, iii.7.

[317] Keynes 1985, pp. 175–78; for the *testamentum*, see *HSC*, c. 26.

[318] An extract from MS 23 of the collection of Mickleton and Spearman documents now kept in the Durham Cathedral Library talks of the finding of the *Liber Ruber* and the tradition surrounding its loss. Folio 18r has: '...I have respectively...found and sundry other things worthy remembrance collected out of the records of the church and the exchequer of Durham, the Tower of London, Sir Robert Cotton's library and elsewhere, a great part thereof collected and translated from that valuable and ancient record called "Liber Ruber" or the "Red Book of Durham", the grand repository of that county's records and church Evidenciaries – with which Bishop Kellow's Leger Book were lost in the civill warrs in the year 1642'.

[319] Craster 1925*a*, p. 504. This same Lincoln's Inn manuscript contains a copy of **17**, the forged charter in the name of King Ecgfrith, for which see below, pp. 339–40.

has shown that the *Liber Ruber* is made up of two manuscripts bound into one cover. The first manuscript contains a single work entitled the *Libellus de exordio et statu ecclesie cathedralis quondam Lindesfarnensis, post Conchestrensis, demum Dunelmensis, ac de gestis pontificum eiusdem*. The second manuscript is a conflation of seven tracts which are mostly hagiographical in character and with a focus on St Cuthbert.[320] Our primary interest lies with the first manuscript bound into the *Liber Ruber* and more immediately with the incidental references which it contains. The *Libellus* which constitutes part one of the *Liber Ruber* was written by Prior Wessington *c*. 1416. Wessington had made use of various texts in the Durham monastic library in order to compose his work.[321] His significant contribution comes from historical passages which he inserts and which are not known elsewhere. Against one of these passages Wessington made the note that it was excerpted 'Ex libro summi altaris ecclesie Dunelmensis'. Craster suggests that the manuscript from which Wessington drew his passages may be the very same as that described in a 1383 inventory of the relics kept at St Cuthbert's shrine: 'Item textus Evangeliorum ornatus auro cum crucifixo deaurato, cum multis evidenciis et monumentis'.[322] From this summary it would appear to have been a gospel book which served also as a kind of register or cartulary. Now the other manuscript known to have been kept on the high altar at Durham was, as we have seen, the *LVD*. But Craster shows that this cannot have been the manuscript from which Wessington drew his historical passages. Instead there seems to have been a separate de luxe manuscript which was kept on the Durham altar, into the margins of which were inserted records of deeds and historical events. It is recreated by Craster and named the *Cronica Monasterii Dunelmensis*.[323]

b. *The Later Durham Archive*

The arrival of the Normans may have left St Cuthbert's community feeling vulnerable to exploitation. Durham's response is without parallel. In the late eleventh and early twelfth centuries the community produced or sponsored a

320 Craster 1925*a*, pp. 505–6. All subsequent details about the *Liber Ruber*, unless otherwise stated, are taken from Craster's article.

321 For Prior Wessington and his work, see R.B. Dobson, *Durham Priory 1400–1450*, Cambridge Studies in Medieval Life and Thought, Third Series vi (Cambridge, 1973), pp. 378–86 (at pp. 379–81, for Wessington's *Libellus*). See also A.J. Piper, 'The Historical Interests of the Monks of Durham', in Rollason, *Symeon: Historian*, pp. 301–32, esp. pp. 322–4.

322 Fowler, *Extracts*, p. 432.

323 Craster 1925*a*, pp. 523-29. On the basis of codicological evidence, M.P. Brown, *The Lindisfarne Gospels: Society, Spirituality and the Scribe* (London, 2003), pp. 114–21 (at pp. 120–1), has recently suggested that this fourth manuscript used by St Cuthbert's community for recording details of its landed transactions, was actually the Lindisfarne Gospels themselves.

whole series of historiographical material by which it sought to justify its existence and to make the links with its ancient sees of Lindisfarne and Chester-le-Street more explicit. By creating an understandable framework for the history of their community, the Cuthbertines announced that it should not be considered odd that they laid claim to lands and possessions which had once belonged to Lindisfarne and Chester-le-Street. Four texts in particular are worth brief scrutiny, since they are all explicitly concerned, to varying degrees, with the documentation of landed estates.

The *Historia de sancto Cuthberto* (hereafter *HSC*) is a text which encapsulates the idiosyncratic approach to the documentation of landed transactions taken by the Cuthbertine community.[324] It mixes hagiographical elements and dream-visions with the more mundane details of gifts of land and jurisdiction. For Symeon, a twelfth-century Durham historian, it had the primary function of a 'cartula'.[325] It has a rather complicated manuscript tradition, one which has led to debate over the date of its original composition.[326] In his study of the first manuscript of two bound into the *Liber Ruber*,[327] Craster identified a more ancient manuscript copy of the *HSC* as being a source for Wessington's work, but one which has since disappeared. Although it is now lost, a marginal addition in BL Cotton Claudius D. iv, suggests that it was originally inserted at the end of a volume known as the 'Prior's Book': 'In fine libri prioris de vita sancti Cuthberti de manu valde antiqua'.[328] Leland saw this volume and, in his *Collectanea*, described it as 'Veteres libri monasterii Dunelmensis'.[329] For Craster this was a pre-Conquest narrative cartulary which contained 'old landbooks' of Durham; as an earlier version of the *HSC*, it would have been of great interest to the historian of Northumbrian diplomatic.[330]

The text of the *HSC* as we have it today comes down to us in three different manuscripts: the oldest dates to the end of the eleventh century and is catalogued as Oxford, Bodleian Library, 596; the second dates to the late twelfth century and is Cambridge, University Library, MS Ff.i.27; the final witness is of the early

[324] The following discussion of the *HSC* is indebted to the profile of the Durham archive given to me by Prof. S. Keynes; see above, p. 317, n. 292.
[325] Symeon, *LDE*, ii.18.
[326] For a full and detailed account of the surviving manuscript copies of the *HSC*, see Johnson South in *HSC*, pp. 14–36.
[327] For the contents of the *Liber Ruber*, see above, p. 323 and below, pp. 339–40.
[328] This occurs in Cotton Claudius D. iv, f. 23v. See Craster 1925*a*, p. 507 and below, p. 341, for the Cotton manuscript, which also contains a copy of **17**.
[329] Leland, *Collectanea* II, p. 369 (of both the 1770 and the 1774 edition), has the following description: 'Et, ut in veteres libri monasterii Dunelmensis scribitur, rex Ecfridus…'.
[330] For this identification, see Craster 1925*a*, p. 518; see also Johnson South in *HSC*, pp. 26–7.

fifteenth century and is London, Lincoln's Inn, Hales MS 114.[331] The *HSC* is made up of thirty-three paragraphs. The Cambridge manuscript differs from its Oxford counterpart in omitting the last six paragraphs (i.e. 29–34); it concludes, after chapter 28, with its account of the visit by King Edmund to Cuthbert's shrine in *c*. 945. Craster suggested that this Cambridge version, although composed after the Oxford manuscript, was based on an older copy of the *HSC* because it lacked the final paragraphs; this further led him to assign the date of the original composition to the mid-tenth century.[332]

Craster himself recognised a problem with his supposition. In paragraph 16 Cuthbert appears to King Alfred in a dream-vision and predicts that he will have a victory over the Danes at the hill of *Assandune*.[333] In fact this is an anachronistic reference by the author. King Alfred did have a victory but it occurred at *Ethandune*, which was the famous 878 battle of Edington when Alfred put the vikings to rout. But the author has referred to a 1016 battle in which King Cnut defeated Edmund Ironside at *Assandune* and which therefore is a chronological impossibility if the *HSC* is given a mid-tenth-century date. To overcome this difficulty of chronology, Craster conjectured that paragraph 16 was an interpolation into the text and one which could not have been made before the reign of Cnut.

More recent scholarly opinion has proposed that the Alfred episode should not be considered as a later interpolation (as Craster thought) but rather as integral to the text; this has the consequence that the *HSC* as a whole should be dated to the middle years of the eleventh century. L. Simpson shows that cross-references within the text indicate that the story of Alfred's dream had always been part of the main narrative and that, if removed, the remainder would make less sense.[334] Johnson South, the most recent editor, agrees with this assessment and assigns a mid- to late eleventh-century origin for the work.[335] If Johnson South's suggestion is correct, then the *HSC* may well be a post-Conquest text. Now the arrival of the Normans witnessed a period of great insecurity where religious houses felt their rights and possessions to be at risk. The general national reaction to this threat took the form of the production or fabrication of charters in order to prove ownership; it may be that the *HSC* took its cue from this trend and represented the Durham equivalent. The author of the *HSC* quite probably drew his information from oral house traditions and also from those notes he found in the community's

331 The Cambridge and Lincoln's Inn copies of *HSC* both have copies of **17** also, for which see below, pp. 335–7 and 339–40 respectively.

332 Craster 1954, pp. 177–8; see also Johnson South in *HSC*, pp. 27–32.

333 *HSC*, c. 16.

334 Simpson 1989.

335 Johnson South in *HSC*, p. 36.

treasured books such as the *LVD*, CCCC 183, Cotton Otho B. ix and others now lost. Although the proposal of a later date of composition might be seen to dent the credibility of the *HSC*, some of its details can be corroborated by other means, presumably because they were based on those entries found in the community's manuscripts.[336] However, not all of its information can be trusted and some will inevitably have suffered from a degree of embellishment.[337]

The *Cronica monasterii Dunelmensis* (hereafter *CMD*) was written between 1072 and 1083 (and later added to) and is closely related to the *HSC*: not only are many of its details based on the *HSC* but it too seeks to combine facts of land transactions within an historical narrative.[338] The *CMD* adds only a little to the material already found in the *HSC* but, when it does, it is mostly concerned with providing extended accounts of the punishments that people will suffer should they contravene any terms as set out by Cuthbert's community. It may therefore be the case that the *HSC* was not felt to be sufficient guarantee or threat to would-be defrauders and that the *CMD* represented a second attempt to ward off anyone wishing to misappropriate property from the Cuthbertines.

A fascinating Durham text of the late eleventh or early twelfth century is the *De Obsessione Dunelmi, et de probitate Uchtredi comitis, et de comitibus qui ei successerunt* (hereafter *De Obsessione*).[339] It takes the form of an aide-memoire; its principal concern is to document the history of six vills originally granted by Bishop Aldhun (the first bishop of Durham) to Earl Uhtred as part of a dowry on the occasion of Uhtred's marriage to Aldhun's daughter, Ecgfrida.[340] Uhtred later repudiated his first wife and both partners can be found to have remarried. The *De Obsessione* records what happened to the six vills through succeeding generations and into whose possession they passed. In its recounting of these estates' history the *De Obsessione* affords an insight into the often violent interactions of Northumbrian aristocratic families. In particular we learn of a remarkable feud between the family of Uhtred and Thurbrand Hold.[341]

The last text to be considered is Symeon's *Libellus de exordio atque procursu istius hoc est Dunhelmensis ecclesie* (hereafter *LDE*). Written at some point

[336] For the reliability of the *HSC*, see Craster 1954, Aird, *St Cuthbert*, pp. 9–59 and Johnson South's commentary in *HSC*.

[337] See the words of caution by Johnson South in *HSC*, pp. 7–8.

[338] The *CMD* no longer exists but has been recreated in Craster 1925*a*, pp. 523–9.

[339] A translation and commentary is provided by Morris (C.J.), *Marriage*, pp. 1–31. It is also discussed in Hart, *ECNE*, pp. 143–50.

[340] For the possibility that Symeon was the author of this text, see Sharpe 1998, p. 219. For more about the *De Obsessione* and Durham history, see above, pp. 307–10.

[341] See Fletcher, *Bloodfeud*.

between 1104–1107 and 1115,[342] it is a far more literary affair than anything hitherto published by the Durham community and, while it does contain some information about the Durham church's estates,[343] such details are not its priority.[344] Composed in part to justify the introduction of monks into Durham by Bishop William of St Calais in 1083,[345] it attempts to provide an over-arching account of the community's history from its origins at Lindisfarne. Rather surprisingly, given the early twelfth-century date at which it was produced, the *LDE* is the first of our texts which affords detail about the community's move to Durham in 995.[346]

These four texts are of immediate interest because they deal with issues of land ownership (although Symeon's *LDE* is less concerned with this).[347] But they have to be judged within the context of all of the material emanating from Durham in the late eleventh and early twelfth centuries,[348] which includes items like, the *De iniusta vexacione Willelmi episcopi primi*,[349] the *De miraculis et translationibus sancti Cuthberti*,[350] the *Annales Lindisfarnenses et Dunelmenses*,[351] and the *De primo Saxonum adventu*.[352] As a whole, these historical compilations demonstrate that the Durham community reacted to the arrival of the Normans in a most vigorous

342 Rollason, *Symeon: Libellus*, p. xlii.

343 See particularly, Symeon, *LDE*, ii.1, ii. 5, iii.8 and iii.14.

344 Rollason, *Symeon: Libellus*, p. lxxxvi, suggests that Symeon was more concerned with the division of estates between the bishop and the monks.

345 See Rollason, *ibid*., pp. lxxxi–lxxxii and, for a slightly different view, W.M. Aird, 'The Political Context of the *Libellus de Exordio*', in Rollason, *Symeon: Historian*, pp. 32–45.

346 For more about this peculiar silence regarding the move to Durham, see above, pp. 306–07.

347 An annal for 854 in section 8 of the *Historia regum* should be mentioned in this connection, since it contains details about the property of Lindisfarne which, although mostly derived from the *HSC*, does have some unique information whose source is unknown. See *HR* (8), pp. 101–2 (s.a. 854) and, for more discussion, above, p. 272 and Johnson South in *HSC*, pp. 10–11.

348 For useful overviews of all of this Durham historical material, see Offler, *Medieval Historians* (esp. pp. 6–12) and Rollason, *Symeon: Libellus*, pp. lxxi–lxxx.

349 For the text of this 1088 trial of Bishop William of St Calais, see Offler, *De Iniusta*; for discussion, see Offler 1951 (esp. pp. 334–5) but see the contrary view from Philpott 1994 (esp. pp. 131–2).

350 Colgrave 1950 and Aird 1992.

351 For an edition and discussion of these annals, see W. Levison, 'Die "Annales Lindisfarnenses et Dunelmenses" kritisch untersucht und neu herausgegeben', *Deutsches Archiv für Erforschung des Mittelalters* xvii (1961), pp. 447–506 (at pp. 478–506, for text and critical notes). For Symeon as the author and scribe of these annals, see M. Gullick, 'The Hand of Symeon of Durham: Further Observations on the Durham Martyrology Scribe' in Rollason, *Symeon: Historian*, pp. 14–31, at pp. 17–18, for the *Annales Lindisfarnenses et Dunelmenses* being a compilation written over an extended period of time and at p. 21, for the suggestion that the annals were written in the 1120s. For the importance of these annals in discerning Symeon's working methods (and his interest in the history of Francia), see Story 1998, pp. 207–8 and Story, *Carolingian Connections*, pp. 119–20.

352 For the *De primo Saxonum adventu*, see Arnold, *Sym. Op.* II, pp. 365–84 and, for discussion, Offler, *Medieval Historians*, pp. 11–12 and Rollason, *Symeon: Libellus*, p. lxxix.

fashion. Rather than fabricating charters to guarantee its pre-Conquest estates,[353] Cuthbert's followers promoted an explosion of historiography which resulted in the composition of wide-ranging genres of texts.[354] The *HSC* was the first text to be composed; its author perhaps gathered those details of land transactions that he could find inserted in the community's treasured books. A striking aspect of the material which followed this first community history is that, for the earliest events it describes, it cannot be shown to rely on any source older than the *HSC*. Does this suggest that, between the death of Bede and the compilation of the *HSC*, no other account of the community's history was composed? Perhaps the very absence of such a work was one feature which prompted an enlivened response at Durham; the community felt it necessary to possess tracts which justified and explained its status. And in the process it showed no knowledge of the existence of early charters, or even of memoranda of early charters, which were not already known to the *HSC*.[355]

The burst of historiographical activity in the late eleventh and early twelfth centuries was quickly followed by an equally energetic interest in the preservation of archival material. In charters and diplomas of the twelfth century, the Durham archive is enormously rich: its pre-Dissolution muniments number some forty thousand documents. So extraordinary is the collection amassed at Durham that it is comparable only to those two other large collections of Christ Church, Canterbury, and St. Peter's, Westminster.[356] From the second half of the twelfth century, the community developed a keen interest in methods of cataloguing and preserving muniments. Their first attempt involved the use of rolls, some beautifully written, which listed all of the grants conferred upon the Prior. The thirteenth century saw the advent of cartularies to Durham. These were less cumbersome than rolls and allowed for greater ease of classification.[357]

There were three sequences of cartularies used in Durham. The *Cartuarium vetus* came first,[358] which was largely compiled in the years 1220 to 1230 and contains, besides grants, documents which relate to litigation. A general cartulary

353 The exception to this is **17**.

354 For the place of the early twelfth-century poem *Durham* in this historiographical output, see H. Blurton, '*Reliquia*: Writing Relics in Anglo-Norman Durham', *Cultural Diversity in the British Middle Ages: Archipelago, Island and England*, ed. J.J. Cohen (Hampshire, 2008), pp. 39–56.

355 These same issues are raised and discussed by Johnson South in *HSC*, pp. 11–12.

356 Davies (J.C.) 1951–2, p. 78. An overview of the Durham library is given by D. Hughes, *A History of Durham Cathedral Library* (Durham, 1925).

357 For all of this, see Davies (J.C.) 1951–2.

358 Davis, *Cartularies* (rev. edn), no 326; it has additions from the thirteenth to the fifteenth centuries. Fragmentary remains of a cartulary of the 1220s are catalogued as Davis, *ibid.*, nos. 324–5.

was then begun in the late fourteenth century, resulting *c*. 1400 in three volumes, *Cartuarium I*, *Cartuarium II* and *Cartuarium III* (part ii, ff. 1–152).[359] Finally, between the fifteenth and early sixteenth centuries, another general cartulary was initiated, apparently as a review of the former attempt *c*. 1400, and again completed as three volumes, *Cartuarium III* (part ii, ff. 153–353), *Cartuarium IV* and *Cartuarium III* (part i, ff. 1–48).[360]

The Durham community also developed efficient methods of recording its muniments in the form of repertories. The first such document to appear was one of the fourteenth century entitled a *Catalogue of Muniments*; it was arranged into four main sections, those of *Papales*, *Regales*, *Pontificales* and *Generales*. The *Generales* section was further subdivided according to geographical areas of Northumberland (for example, Northumbria beyond the River Coquet).[361] Another catalogue was composed *c*. 1400, the *Parvum Repertorium*;[362] this classified its documents in exactly the same fashion except that the *Generales* were renamed *Speciales* and placed in a different order.[363]

But the *Magnum Repertorium*, in its efficiency and in its scope, superceded both previous repertories.[364] It comprises 159 folios and is prefaced by a contemporary alphabetical index of places on 56 folios. It was written in the time of Bishop Robert Neville, *c*. 1450, but it would seem that the impetus for the volume originally came from Prior Wessington.[365]

17 is the only document in the Durham archive which takes the form of an Anglo-Saxon diploma; but it is a forgery. One of the witnesses to this grant can be shown to be already dead by the time of its taking place (supposedly in 685) and some of **17**'s text is evidently taken from Bede's *VCP* and the *HSC*. Even if it does contain genuine diplomatic elements, as some have argued, these would have a bearing on the *HSC* rather than on **17**.[366] The earliest copy of **17** is in a manuscript of the late twelfth century, Cambridge, University Library, Ff. 1. 27, p. 186, col.

[359] See Davis, *ibid*., nos. 327–9 respectively.

[360] For these details, see Davis, *ibid*., nos. 330–2 respectively. *Cartuarium III* was dismembered and rebound to accommodate later additions, which created these different parts. More information about these Durham cartularies comes from a search-room typescript made by A.J. Piper, available online at this address: <http://reed.dur.ac.uk/xtf/view?docId=ead/dcd/dcdcvet.xml> (accessed 22 December, 2010), from which the present discussion has greatly benefited.

[361] See Davies (J.C.) 1951–2, p. 83.

[362] Davis, *Cartularies* (rev. edn), no. 341, where it is suggested that the compiler of this repertory may also have been responsible for the general cartulary that was begun in the late fourteenth century.

[363] See Davies (J.C.) 1951–2 and Davis, *Cartularies* (rev. edn), no. 341.

[364] Davis, *Cartularies* (rev. edn), no. 342.

[365] Davies (J.C.) 1951–2, p. 84. The *Magnum repertorium* classified just under six thousand documents in total; it has later additions and corrections throughout.

[366] See the commentary to **17** below.

2; here it fills a space between the end of a copy of Symeon's *LDE*, Book 4, and the beginning of the first Continuation. It is written in a hand which is different from, but contemporary with, that of the main text.[367] The late eleventh century provides a possible date for the original fabrication of this document, since this was a time when Carlisle, one of the estates claimed in **17**, was an area over which rival institutions claimed jurisdiction.[368]

It is interesting that there exists a late, single-sheet copy of **17**.[369] The main text of this copy is written in a hand of the late fourteenth century and on the reverse of the single sheet are two endorsements. One of the endorsements reads:

> Dominus Johannes de Kyngeston et dominus Ricardus de Castro Bernardi receperunt originale istius copie per indenturam de Rogero de Alverton per preceptum domini prioris.[370]

This states that the original document had been received by *Johannes de Kyngeston* and *Ricardus de Castro Bernardi*.[371] Since we are able to identify these people, it may be that we can date the time of composition of this single-sheet copy. John de Kyngeston was clerk to Thomas Hatfield, bishop of Durham, and we find him involved with the Durham cathedral chancery in the late fourteenth century.[372] Richard of Barnard Castle was also a member of the Durham cathedral chancery, having acted both as clerk and as chancellor. We find an example of Richard's hand, when he drafts an inspeximus-confirmation charter in the name of Thomas Hatfield, bishop of Durham,[373] and he is also the direct recipient of a grant by Bishop Hatfield.[374]

The second endorsement to this single-sheet document is a summary of its contents. Exactly the same summary is to be found in the margin of the Durham cartulary copy of **17**: this is given in an early sixteenth century section of

[367] For a description of the contents of this Cambridge manuscript, see below, pp. 335–7.

[368] For a more detailed discussion of the fabrication of this diploma, see **17**.

[369] It is classified in the Durham archives as 1.1.Pont.6.

[370] For an image of this single-sheet, see Plate 1.

[371] The same endorsement is reproduced below the text of **17** copied into *Registrum III*. For this manuscript, see below, pp. 340–1.

[372] We have preserved a number of charters written in the hand of John de Kyngeston. See, for example, 2.3. Pont.13, which is a grant by Thomas Hatfield to Richard of Barnard Castle and his heirs of free warren in Richard's demesne lands of Rilley near Durham (dated 20 April, 1368). For other late-fourteenth century charters for which John de Kyngeston is scribe, see 2.3.Pont.17 and 1.4.Reg.19.

[373] See 2.3.Pont.8.

[374] See 2.3.Pont.13. Richard of Barnard Castle, as chancellor, also oversaw chancery proceedings. See, for example, 1.6.Pont.5. It has been more difficult to find information about Roger of Alverton, but he is presumably synonymous with the Roger of Allerton who appears elsewhere in the Durham archives of the 1360s.

Cartuarium III, f. 274r.[375] This may allow us to see something of the methods of the Durham archivists of the early sixteenth century. Whoever was responsible for the cataloguing of the single-sheet copy of **17**, perhaps first made a summary of its salient details on the verso of the single-sheet, then copied the whole text into *Cartuarium III* and added the same summary (as the one used on the reverse of the single-sheet) in the margin next to the cartulary text. The single-sheet was also given a classmark, '1.1.Pont.6', and entered into the *Magnum Repertorium*. This wrongly classified the single-sheet copy of **17** as an episcopal deed rather than a royal deed.[376]

Later Durham historiography made use of **17**. As we have already seen, Prior Wessington composed a historical tract entitled *Libellus de exordio et statu ecclesie cathedralis Dunelmensis*, which he had bound into the volume known as the *Liber Ruber*. This historical tract exists in four manuscripts and it shows knowledge of **17**. Those manuscripts are: (i) Bodleian Library, MS Laud Misc. 748, (ii) Lincoln's Inn Library, Hales MS 114 (the *Liber ruber*), (iii) British Museum, Cotton MS Claudius D. iv and (iv) a manuscript known to Leland who made excerpts from it in his *Collectanea*.[377]

The Durham archive continued to be well looked after and maintained. Various assiduous individuals such as Prior Wessington or those who held the position of *Librarius* or *Cancellarius* ensured that charters and the like were preserved. Even the Dissolution of the Monasteries did little to affect the storage of muniments at Durham.[378] Indeed the dissolution of dependencies of Durham meant that the mother house acquired extra inhabitants and muniments: it is for this reason that the Durham archive is equipped with very full collections of charters relating to Finchale and Coldingham. And, when Durham itself was dissolved, continuity rather than disruption was the order of the day. Cuthbert Tunstall remained as bishop and Hugh Whitehead, the last Prior of Durham, became the first Dean of Durham.[379] And, as a most visible symbol of continuity with the pre-Dissolution days, the *LVD* was exhibited on the altar.

In the seventeenth century, the remarkable custodian of Durham's muniments was John Cosin. He undertook a comprehensive examination of the archive; if he found a document listed in the *Magnum Repertorium* to be missing, he marked the

375 For the sections of *Cartuarium III* and the dates at which they were produced, see above, pp. 328–9.

376 For the division of the *Magnum Repertorium* into *Papales*, *Regales*, *Pontificales* and *Generales*, see above, p. 329.

377 For Prior Wessington's historical tract, see Craster 1925*a*, pp. 507–19 (esp. p. 518).

378 It is, however, interesting to note that the list of papal deeds (i.e. *Papales*) has been removed from the repertory known as the *Parvum Repertorium*; see Davis, *Cartularies* (rev. edn), no. 341.

379 For these details, see Davies (J.C.) 1951–2, p. 81.

margin of the catalogue next to the relevant entry with the note *deest*.[380] The end of the seventeenth century witnessed the activity of Thomas Rud, who carefully catalogued both the Chapter Library and Cosin's Library; many a charter or roll can still be found imprinted with his monogram TR.[381]

The seventeenth and early eighteenth centuries were also a time when Durham antiquaries took an interest in the history and antiquities of the County Palatine. The collection of Mickleton and Spearman manuscripts was initiated by Christopher Mickleton (1613–1669), an attorney at law. His son, James Mickleton (1638–1693), a barrister, continued this work, as did the grandson of James Mickleton, also called James (1688–1719). Upon the death of the latter James Mickleton, the collection came into the possession of the Spearman family and continued to be added to. Eventually the evidence collected by the Spearmans formed the basis for their volume known as the *County Palatine of Durham*, published in 1729.[382]

These manuscripts are today stored in the Durham University Library and number some one hundred volumes. They contain extracts which show an interest in the origins of Cuthbert's community. Many of these are helpful in understanding those early methods used by the Cuthbertines in documenting their landed transactions. James Mickleton made a visit to the Cotton library in 1715 which, crucially, preceded the destruction of Ashburnham house by fire in 1731. It was on the occasion of this visit that he transcribed details concerning the gospel book known as Cotton Otho B. ix, details which, as we have seen, enable us to recreate the nature and form of that volume.[383]

James Mickleton was a lawyer by profession and the notes he made during this visit to Cotton's library indicate the kind of document he was interested in. We find a transcription of part of Cotton Domitian A. xv: 'Cod: membr: in Quarto ageris de Ecclesia Eliensi in quo…recitatur charta Eadgari Regis Latine et Saxonice…',[384] which is evidently a reference to a 970 grant of land by King Edgar to Ely Abbey written in both Old English and Latin (i.e. S 779). There is also a description of Cotton Nero D. iii: 'Registrum Cartarum et munimentorum Hospitalis Sci Leonardi Ebor a tempore Æthelstani Regis Anglosaxonum ad Edw:'.[385]

But there are some rather troubling references too, which are more difficult to understand. The manuscript known as Mickleton and Spearman 44 was compiled in the early eighteenth century, probably by George Spearman. The first six folios

[380] Davies (J.C.) 1951–2.
[381] Davies (J.C.) 1951–2, p. 80.
[382] For an overview of the Mickleton and Spearman collection, see Harding 1945–55. For a description of the formation of the collection, see Doyle 1992.
[383] See above, p. 321.
[384] Mickleton and Spearman 36, p. 232.
[385] Mickleton and Spearman 36, pp. 124–5.

list extracts from charters and concessions made to the bishopric of Durham from the time of King Oswald to that of King Edward the Confessor. Spearman, if he is indeed the author, gives his sources for these extracts as William Dugdale's *Monasticon Anglicanum*, William Camden's *Britannia* and Francis Godwin's *De Praesulibus Angliae Commentarius*, and the *Liber Ruber*; there is one more source, given as *L.C.*, which is difficult to identify. The title allotted to these extracts reads:

> Charte et concessiones regum et aliorum non solum episcopis Dunelmensibus sed et aliis concessis facetque, episcoporum etiam Dunelmi et aliorum Episcopatui Dunelm' Ac separales etiam aliorum Res notabiles tanges Episcopatum Dunelmi predictum.[386]

The title is promising in any search for early Northumbrian charters connected to St Cuthbert's community. But unfortunately most of the extracts then given by Spearman can be easily found in extant narrative sources such as the *HSC* or the *CMD* and therefore provide no new information.

One excerpt, however, concerns a grant made by King Ceolwulf (729–737) of the vill of Warkworth. Details of this donation can again be found in the *HSC* and the *CMD*. But Spearman provides a description of the transaction which might suggest that he is not relying on the *HSC* or on the *CMD* as his source. His summary states:

> Rex Ceolwulphus **per chartam suam** dedit Deo et Sancto Cuthberto villam de Werkemouth, ut ipsius ecclesiae possessio esset cum appendiciis suis.[387]

Spearman lists as his sources for this extract Dugdale's '*Monasticon Anglicanum*, fol. 39,' and '*L.C.* 31'. A similar description of this charter of Ceolwulf can be found elsewhere. Manuscript 10 of the Mickleton and Spearman collection contains another list of charter-extracts of kings and other personages to the bishopric of Durham from the time of Oswald to that of Henry VIII. This list is cancelled. Among its items we find:

> Rex Ceolwulphus **per chartam suam** dedit Deo et Sancto Cuthberto villam de Werkworth ut ipsius ecclesiam possessio esset cum appendiciis suis...[388]

The source for this extract is given as '*Monasticon Anglicanum* fol. 39b'; no mention is made, this time, of the '*L.C.*'.

The *HSC* tells of how Ceolwulf gave up his temporal kingdom and retired to the Lindisfarne monastery. Ceolwulf's entry into the Cuthbertine community was accompanied by the gift of Warkworth which is described in the following terms: '...et sancto Cuthberto villam nomine Werceworthe cum suis appendiciis dedit.

386 Mickleton and Spearman 44, f. 1r.

387 Mickleton and Spearman 44, ff. 3v–4r.

388 Mickleton and Spearman 10, f. 153v.

Et hii sunt termini istius villae…'.[389] The *CMD* affords similar information: 'Post hunc Ceuowlfus Rex thesauros regios et terras Breiesne et Wer[c]uutha cum suis appendiciis, et ecclesiam quam ipse ibi edicaverat…'.[390] One of the sources quoted in the extracts from the Mickleton and Spearman manuscripts is the *Monasticon Anglicanum* and, in volume one of that work, a recapitulation of Ceolwulf's grant is made in the following terms: '(Ceolwlfus) intravit autem Lindisfarnense monasterium Sancto Cuthberto secum conferens thesaurus regios et terras, id est, Brigesne et Werceword, cum suis appendiciis, simul et ecclesiam quam ibidem aedificaverat…'.[391] It is clear that the *HSC*, the *CMD* and *Monasticon Anglicanum* are all referring to the exact same grant as the one summarised in two places in the Mickleton and Spearman collection. But none of these mentions a 'charter' as being their ultimate source, making it possible that the Durham antiquaries knew of some other document which mentioned Ceolwulf's grant.[392]

Whether or not this could be a reference to an early charter of King Ceolwulf but now lost, it is clear that we are missing records of landed transactions relating to St Cuthbert's community. Unfortunately Domesday Book does not make a record of those estates north of the River Tees; we are therefore unable to conjecture what may be missing from the Durham archive. The most startling absence is of a notice of the community's move to Durham. But it may be that this is deliberate and a reflection of the shadowy political circumstances surrounding the relocation.[393] Similarly we have no record of the original grant of lands later leased out by Bishop Aldhun and one can only speculate when they may have come into the possession of the religious community and by whom they were granted.[394] A survey of the bishop's lands was conducted in 1183 and resulted in the compilation of 'Boldon Book'; and here too we find details of estates owned by the bishop of Durham for which we have no other documentation.[395] It would be fascinating to find out more about the circumstances of these early grants; one can even hope that a volume such as the 'Prior's Book', which evidently contained

[389] *HSC*, c. 8.

[390] *CMD*, p. 523 (ll. 7–10).

[391] See *Mon. Angl.* I, p. 39, second column.

[392] The observation in A.J. Piper, 'The Historical Interests of the Monks of Durham' in Rollason, *Symeon: Historian*, pp. 301–32, at p. 324, n. 124, might be of importance here. An alternative explanation is that the Durham antiquaries themselves, although using a narrative source such as the *HSC*, the *CMD* or *Mon. Angl.*, described what they were seeing as a 'chartam'.

[393] Above, pp. 306–8.

[394] The leases are found in *HSC*, c. 31.

[395] Boldon Book is of a different form to Domesday Book: it is a customal, a catalogue of those dues owed by custom to the Bishop by right of his temporal lordship over the estate. Domesday Book on the other hand is an assessment of the tax owed to the crown. See D. Austin, *Boldon Book: Northumberland and Durham* (Phillimore, 1982), pp. 6–9.

details of land transactions, may someday be discovered. But an assessment of the records we do possess suggests that Cuthbert's community had engineered their own, idiosyncratic methods for guaranteeing their possessions. And, to judge by the vast swathe of land they owned at the end of the Anglo-Saxon period, we may be fairly sure that these methods were effective.

3. THE MANUSCRIPTS

a. *BL Cotton Domitian A. vii (the Durham* Liber Vitae*)* [C]

C is the Durham *Liber Vitae*, a de luxe manuscript whose principal concern is the recording of individuals' names.[396] The original core of this manuscript was written at some point in the period *c*. 800 × *c*. 840.[397] Only a few additions were made to the *Liber Vitae* in the period following the mid-ninth century and before the late eleventh century.[398] But at the end of the tenth century, **18** was added to f. 47v and then at the beginning of the eleventh century **19** and **20** were also added to the same f. 47v.

b. *Cambridge, University Library, Ff.i.27* [D]

D is comprised of two originally separate manuscripts which have subsequently been bound together at a date in the sixteenth century to form a new whole.[399] One manuscript constitutes part of a fourteenth-century book from Bury St Edmunds.[400] The second manuscript in D was copied at the end of the twelfth century,[401] and contains this assortment of texts as listed by Rollason:[402]

396 Davis, *Cartularies* (rev. edn), no. 349.

397 See L. Rollason, 'Periods of Use and Disuse', in *LVD*, pp. 23–4. For a facsimile edition, see Thompson, *Lib. Vit.* and, for discussion, see Rollason *et al.*, *The Durham* and also the new edition, *LVD*.

398 For the additions made to the *Liber Vitae* in the period after the mid-ninth century, see L. Rollason, 'Periods of Use and Disuse', in *LVD*, p. 24. For more about the Durham *Liber Vitae* and the Cuthbertine community's practice of recording land grants, see above, pp. 316–23.

399 A detailed description of this manuscript can be found in C. Hardwick and H.R. Luard, *A Catalogue of Manuscripts preserved in the Library of the University of Cambridge*, 6 vols. (Cambridge, 1856–67), II, pp. 318–29 (no. 1160).

400 Rollason, *Symeon: Libellus*, p. xxiv, notes that the Bury manuscript is found between pp. 40 and 73 and after p. 252, in D.

401 A date in the early thirteenth century is proposed by D.N. Dumville, 'The Corpus Christi 'Nennius'', *The Bulletin of the Board of Celtic Studies* xxv, Part iv (1974), pp. 369–80 (at pp. 371 and 377), repr. in D.N. Dumville, *Histories and Pseudo-Histories of the Insular Middle Ages* (Aldershot, 1990), IX; but see also Meehan 1994, p. 442, n. 24, who reasserts a date in the late twelfth century, as does Norton 1998*a*.

402 This list is taken almost exactly from Rollason, *Symeon: Libellus*, pp. xxiv–xxvi, which is more detailed than the version given here.

1. pp. 1–14: Gildas, *De excidio Britanniae*.
2. pp. 14–40: *Historia Brittonum*, attributed here to Nennius.
3. pp. 73–120: Bede, *De temporum ratione*.
4. (i). p. 122: preface to Symeon of Durham's *LDE*.
   (ii). pp. 123–5: a summary of Symeon, *LDE*.
   (iii). pp. 125–8: list of chapter headings for Symeon, *LDE*.
   (iv). pp. 128–30: genealogy of King Æthelwulf together with a brief account about Northumbrian and English kings from Ida to Henry I and an account of the sees and shires of England.
   (v). pp. 131–86: main text of Symeon, *LDE*. On the last page of this section, p. 186, a scribe contemporary, but different to the scribe of the main text of the *LDE*, has made a copy of **17**.
5. pp. 187–94: a continuation of Symeon, *LDE*.
6. p. 194: list of Durham relics.
7. pp. 195–201: the *HSC*.
8. pp. 201–2: a list of gifts made by King Æthelstan to St Cuthbert's community, derived from the *HSC*; p. 202 also has a copy of the Old English poem, *De situ Dunelmi*.
9. pp. 203–20: Æthelwulf, *De abbatibus*.
10. pp. 221–36: Richard of Hexham, *De statu et episcopis Hagustaldensis ecclesie*.
11. pp. 237–52: Gilbert of Limerick, *De statu ecclesie*.

As it exists today, D may not be in its original form; in fact the late twelfth-century half of D used to be bound with another manuscript, extant today as CCCC 66. After the Dissolution of the Monasteries, this original manuscript (comprising the late twelfth-century part of D and CCCC 66) became the property of Archbishop Matthew Parker. He gave the two halves to Cambridge University Library and to Corpus Christi College respectively and it was at this moment that each half was bound together with two other halves of a fourteenth-century Bury historical manuscript.[403] An early modern foliation in D and in CCCC 66 suggests that they once formed a single manuscript and, if this can be accepted,[404] it also enables the original structure of this manuscript to be recreated.[405] It seems most likely that

[403] For this information, see Norton 1998*a*, p. 63.

[404] Meehan 1994, pp. 442–5, questions whether D and CCCC 66 do constitute two halves of one and the same manuscript; he suggests rather that the two manuscripts were 'conceived in sections which were combined at an early date into a single volume' (at p. 444).

[405] See D.N. Dumville, 'The Sixteenth-Century History of Two Cambridge Manuscripts from Sawley', *Transactions of the Cambridge Bibliographical Society* vii (1980), pp. 427–44 (esp. p. 434),

this original manuscript was a product of the Durham scriptorium and Norton has suggested that it was first made around the year 1188 as a gift for Bishop Hugh le Puiset.[406] F. 1v of CCCC 66 has a *Mappa mundi* image together with a Sawley *ex libris* at the top of the page, indicating that the original manuscript was later kept at Sawley Abbey. There are many interesting connections between this Sawley manuscript and CCCC 139, another Durham manuscript which contains our only extant copy of the *Historia regum*, and which has an erased Sawley *ex libris*.[407]

As is clear from the list of contents given above, D is of very great interest for the range and type of historical text it contains. At the end of the copy of Symeon's *LDE*, on p. 186, a scribe who was contemporary, but different to the scribe of the *LDE* text, has made a copy of **17**, the forged charter in the name of King Ecgfrith. Rollason suggests that the scribe of the copy of **17**, whom he considers to have been working at some point in the second half of the twelfth century, was also responsible for items 4 (i), 5, the corrections to the last seven lines of p. 36, column b, and also the rubrics for pp. 1–40 in the list of contents above.[408]

c. *Enrolments* [E, F, G]

At the beginning of the 1390s, a copy of **17** was made into an Inspeximus charter of Richard II's reign, TNA: PRO Ch.R. 15–17 Ric. II, m. 32, no. 29 (MS E, 1391–3). Further enrolments can be found in Charter Rolls of the reign of Henry IV and Henry V:

1. TNA: PRO Ch.R. 8 Hen. IV, no. 3 (MS F, 1407).
2. TNA: PRO Ch.R. 1 Hen. V, pt. 1, no. 15 (MS G, 1413).

Yet more enrolled copies of **17** were made in a Patent Roll of the fifteenth century and in a Confirmation Roll of the sixteenth century, manuscripts L and N below.

---

repr. in his *Histories*, VIII. For a useful table setting out the original contents, order and collation of the manuscript, see Norton 1998*a*, pp. 64–5.

406 See Norton 1998*a*, pp. 71–89, for the origin of the manuscript and pp. 99–101, for it being designed as a gift for Bishop Hugh le Puiset; an *explicit* on f. 50v of the *De primo Saxonum aduentu* gives an 1188 date for the year of writing of the manuscript, for which see Norton, *ibid*., pp. 71–2.

407 Much like CCCC 66 and D (which perhaps originally formed one manuscript), CCCC 139 also contains a fascinating range of historical texts. For more about the connections between these manuscripts, see Dumville, 'The Sixteenth-Century History', pp. 427–44; for CCCC 139, see Blair (P.H.) 1963, Dumville, 'The Corpus Christi "Nennius"', pp. 369–80 (repr. in his *Histories*, IX), D. Baker, 'Scissors and Paste: Corpus Christi, Cambridge, MS 139 Again' in *The Material Sources and Methods of Ecclesiastical History*, ed. D. Baker, Studies in Church History xi (Oxford, 1975), pp. 83–123 and Meehan 1994, pp. 440–2.

408 Rollason, *Symeon: Libellus*, p. xxvi.

d. *Bodleian, Laud Misc. 748* [H]

One of the historical treatises that H contains is the *Libellus de exordio et statu ecclesie cathedralis Dunelmensis* and it is on f. 8rv of this treatise that a copy of **17** has been made. This tract, which is a history of the sees of Lindisfarne, Chester-le-Street and Durham, was the work of John Wessington, prior of Durham from 1416 to 1446; in fact, Craster demonstrated that H was Wessington's own working copy of his history; London, Lincoln's Inn, Hales 114 and BL Cotton Claudius D.iv, manuscripts I and K below, are further, revised copies of this same history.[409]

H is made up of 94 paper folios and has four main parts which have been described by Craster:[410]

1. Part I, 48 leaves originally numbered 1–48, but now ff. 4–49 with two unnumbered. This part has two different types of paper and distinctive watermarks, which consist of a group of three acorns and also of a knot.[411] The *Libellus de exordio et statu ecclesie cathedralis Dunelmensis* commences on f. 6 and stops on f. 47r; a copy of **17** is made on f. 8rv.

2. Part II, 18 leaves, originally numbered 49–65 (with 52 repeated) and now numbered 50–67. Part II has various sheets of paper, some with the watermark T, others with the watermark A or with a crown or a unicorn's head. Craster proposed a dating range of 1385–1438 for these various watermarks.[412] The narrative begun in Part I is here continued without interruption and it ends on f. 67.

3. Part III, 14 leaves, now numbered 69–74, with eight leaves that are unnumbered. There is the same acorn watermark as found in Part I and also a mount watermark.[413]

4. Part IV consists of four unnumbered leaves which Craster suggests were probably intended as fly–leaves.[414]

On the basis of the manuscript's contents, and also its script and watermarks, Craster estimated that this manuscript most probably dates to the period *c.* 1405–15; he also suggested that Part II is a first draft of Wessington's history

[409] Craster discovered this work by Wessington when he identified London, Lincoln's Inn, Hales 114, as being the Durham *Liber Ruber*; see Craster 1925*a*, at pp. 515–19, for Wessington as author and for the character of the *Libellus de exordio et statu ecclesie cathedralis Dunelmensis*, which relies primarily on Symeon's *LDE* but also on sources like the *HSC*, Geoffrey of Coldingham and Robert of Greystanes.

[410] All of the following details are taken from Craster 1925*a*, pp. 508–10.

[411] For the watermarks, which Craster dates to *c.* 1420, see Craster 1925*a*, p. 508.

[412] Craster, *ibid.*, p. 508.

[413] Craster, *ibid.*, p. 508.

[414] Craster, *ibid.*, p. 508.

(the *Libellus de exordio*) while Part I is a revised draft.[415] H has a remarkable later history, having been owned at times by Leland, John Stow, John Dee and Archbishop Laud.[416]

e. *London, Lincoln's Inn, Hales 114 (the* Liber Ruber*)* [I]

I, the Durham *Liber Ruber*, is a small manuscript, written in various different hands dating to the first quarter of the fifteenth century. The Durham *Liber Ruber* was thought lost for many years but was identified in 1925 by Craster as being one and the same as this Hales manuscript.[417] As noted by Craster, it consists of 219 leaves in total, of which there are 156 vellum leaves (numbered 1 to 156), 51 paper leaves (the first 27 are numbered 157 to 183) and 12 unfoliated leaves.[418]

The *Liber Ruber* actually contains two manuscripts bound within one volume. The first manuscript contains a copy of one work only, Prior Wessington's *Libellus de exordio et statu ecclesie cathedralis Dunelmensis*;[419] Craster judged this to be a fair copy of the author's own draft of the same historical treatise in Bodleian, Laud Misc. 748, manuscript H above.[420] A copy of **17** can be found in this first manuscript on f. 5rv.

The second manuscript bound within the *Liber Ruber* consists of three gatherings of parchment leaves and four of paper leaves. It contains the following seven tracts:[421]

1. ff. 134–40: a metrical life of St Cuthbert.
2. ff. 141–5: poem about the island of Farne.
3. ff. 146–52: a second metrical life of St Cuthbert.
4. ff. 153–59r: the *HSC*.
4. ff. 159v–163r: a short chronicle of the see of Lindisfarne, from 625 to 847.
5. ff. 163v–168: 'notabilia de vita ac miraculis beati Oswaldi regis'.
6. ff. 169: the 'de nativitate sancti Cuthberti episcopi', otherwise known as 'de ortu sancti Cuthberti'.

415 Craster, *ibid.*, pp. 509–10.
416 Craster, *ibid.*, pp. 510–12.
417 Craster, *ibid.*, pp. 504–7.
418 Craster, *ibid.*, p. 504.
419 Craster, *ibid.*, p. 505, where he states that this first manuscript consists of seventeen numbered quires.
420 Craster, *ibid.*, pp. 512–13.
421 For a more detailed version of this list, see Craster, *ibid.*, pp. 506–7, from which the present list is derived.

Sir Matthew Hales's acquisition of the manuscript is noted on the inside of the front board: '4 Ap. 1657, bought of Mr Washington for 30s'.[422] On the flyleaves at the beginning of I are two catalogues of the bishops of Lindisfarne and Durham, from Aidan to Wolsey, in a hand which is that of Thomas Swalwell, chancellor of Durham cathedral in the years 1497–9.[423] A certain John Barnes, who has written his name on f. 1 of I, was chancellor of Durham cathedral in 1577.[424]

f. *Durham Cathedral Muniments,* Registrum III [J]

J is a register of Durham Priory business, compiled in the years 1401–44. It is distinct from a cartulary in that it preserves copies of outgoing documents, rather than documents received by the Durham church.[425] The contents of J are arranged in a broadly chronological framework, although occasionally documents of an earlier or later date are interspersed in the record.[426] J has copies of documents issued under the priory seal and also copies of episcopal documents which would have been of importance to the priory. It is written mainly in Latin, but does have passages in English, French and Scots. J is made up of 340 leaves; its contents are listed on the Durham University Library website where the following broad outline is given:[427]

1. ff. e–h: flyleaves (with modern foliation).
2. ff. ir–xiiv: copies of earlier documents (with modern foliation).
3. ff. xiiir–xxiv: index to ff. 1r–311v.
3. ff. 1r–51r: the Priory register for the years 1401–17, in chronological order but with the insertion of copies of some earlier documents.
4. ff. 51r–140r: the Priory register from the period of John Fishburn, chancellor of Durham monastery (1417–31), again with copies of some earlier documents; a copy of **17** occurs on f. 137r.
5. ff. 140v–240r: the Priory register from the period of William Dalton, chancellor of Durham monastery (1431–39), again with copies of some earlier documents.

[422] Craster, *ibid.*, p. 504, n. 2, suggests that this Washington is perhaps the same man as William Washington, a bookseller in St Dunstan's churchyard in 1627–9.

[423] Craster, *ibid.*, pp. 505 and 513.

[424] Craster, *ibid.*, pp. 504–5.

[425] For the definition of a *registrum* and its usual contents, see Pantin 1933, pp. 201–2 (at p. 215, for the Durham *Registrum III*).

[426] All of these details are taken from the catalogue entry for the *Registrum III* on the Durham University website, for which see: < http://reed.dur.ac.uk/xtf/view?docId=ead/dcd/dcdregr3.xml> (accessed 17 October, 2011).

[427] For the *Registrum III* and its contents, see the website address quoted above, from which this present list is derived.

6. ff. 240r–311v: the Priory register from the period of Robert Westmerland, chancellor of Durham monastery (1439–44), again with copies of some earlier documents.

A copy of the forged **17** in the name of King Ecgfrith is entered on f. 137r following a copy of a document dated 18 November 1430, in which Prior John and the chapter of Durham ask the archbishop of York to institute a certain Robert Beleby, priest, in the fourth vicarage of Hemingbrough collegiate church. This copy of **17** seems clearly to have been made by reference to some version of the text preserved in the single-sheet, 1.1.Pont.6.[428]

g. *BL Cotton Claudius D. iv* [K]

K is quite a handsome volume; its decorative first page bears three shields, two of which are of the see of Durham and Durham priory and the last of which is of the Wessington family, and more particularly John Wessington, prior of Durham from 1416 to 1446. Craster judged that K dates to Wessington's priorate in the first half of the fifteenth century.[429]

A copy of Wessington's historical treatise, the *Libellus de exordio et statu ecclesie cathedralis Dunelmensis*, can be found in the first 87 leaves of K.[430] On f. 88 is a single leaf from another manuscript containing part of Reginald of Durham's preface to his *De virtutibus et miraculis Cuthberti*. The rest of K, ff. 89–113, contains historical excerpts relating to Durham.[431] A copy of **17** has been made on ff. 8v–9r.

h. *Further enrolment* [L]

A copy of **17** was enrolled once more in a Patent Roll dated to 1423, TNA: PRO Pat. R. 11 Hen. VI, pt. 2, m. 22 (MS L). For earlier enrolments, see manuscripts E, F and G above.

428 Immediately following this copy of **17** in the *Registrum*, the scribe has also noted down the endorsement about 'Johannes de Kyngeston' and 'Ricardus de Castro Bernardi', which can be found on the back of the single-sheet copy of **17**, 1.1.Pont.6; for this endorsement, see above, p. 330.

429 Craster 1925*a*, p. 513.

430 Craster, *ibid*., p. 515, demonstrated that this copy is a considerably revised version of Wessington's work in which the introductory chapters especially have been expanded and reworked.

431 Craster, *ibid*., p. 514. For the importance of K in discerning that there used to be a fourth, now lost, copy of the *HSC*, see above, p. 324 and Johnson South in *HSC*, pp. 26–7.

i. *Durham Cathedral Muniments*, Cartuarium III [M]

M is a vast Durham cartulary of 401 folios, which is made up of three main sections:[432] the oldest section is ii. ff. 1–142v and 151–152v and can be dated to the beginning of the fifteenth century;[433] the second section, i. ff. 1–48, can be dated to the end of the fifteenth century or the beginning of the sixteenth century;[434] the last section, ii. ff. 153–357v, has a document of 1504 and may date to about that period.[435] The contents of M have been listed by the Durham University Library on their website and are here reproduced almost identically (the numbering in the following list is that used by the Durham Library):[436]

1. i. ff. 1r–4v: replies, by the prior of Durham, to complaints of the mayor and burgesses of Newcastle about their rights in the Tyne, among other things.
2. i. ff. 5v–9v: Index to ii ff. 1–52.
3. i. ff. 10r–15v: evidences for the prior's jurisdiction over Lazenby chapel and Yorkshire parish churches.
4. i. ff. 16–30: not present.
5. i. ff. 31r–48v: documents relating to Yorkshire.
6. ii. ff. 1r–145r: documents relating to property and churches outside Durham and Northumberland.
7. ii. ff. 145r–150v: acts of Durham prior and convent *sede vacante* 1406.
8. ii. ff. 151r–152v: documents concerning Howden.
9. ii. ff. 153r–204v: papal documents.
10. ii. f. 205: not present.
11. ii. ff. 206r–247v: royal documents.
12. ii. ff. 248r–272v: archiepiscopal documents.
13. ii. f. 273: not present.
14. ii. ff. 274r–357v: episcopal documents, including a copy of **17** on f. 274r.

[432] *Cartuarium III* and its three main sections are listed in Davis, *Cartularies* (rev. edn), nos. 329, 330 and 332. It is also catalogued in detail and described by the Durham University Library, here: <http://reed.dur.ac.uk/xtf/view?docId=ead/dcd/dcdcart3.xml#dcdcart3-11> (accessed 2 September, 2010), from which the present work has greatly benefited. A very useful overview of the Durham muniments and more particularly the Durham cartularies is provided by a search-room typescript written by Alan Piper entitled, *Durham Cathedral Priory: Thirteenth-Century Cartularies. A Preliminary Guide* (Durham, rev. edn, 1998), which can also be accessed on the Durham University Library website at: < http://reed.dur.ac.uk/xtf/view?docId=ead/dcd/dcdcvet.xml>. For the sequence of Durham cartularies, and the division of *Cartuarium III*, see also above, pp. 328–9.

[433] Davis, *Cartularies* (rev. edn), no. 329.

[434] Davis, *Cartularies* (rev. edn), no. 332.

[435] Davis, *Cartularies* (rev. edn), no. 330.

[436] See: <http://reed.dur.ac.uk/xtf/view?docId=ead/dcd/dcdcart3.xml#dcdcart3-11> (accessed 2 September, 2010).

The copy of **17**, a charter in the name of King Ecgfrith, was made into the early sixteenth-century section of M and wrongly included amongst episcopal documents; it is derived from a version of the single-sheet copy of **17**, 1.1.Pont.6.

j. *Further enrolment* [N]

Another copy of **17** was made into a Confirmation Roll of Elizabeth I's reign, TNA: PRO Conf. R. 6 Eliz., m. 1, no. 10 (MS N). For earlier enrolled copies of **17**, see manuscripts E, F, G and L above.

k. *Copies by Antiquaries* [O, P, Q, R]

i. *BL Harley 533* (O): s. xvii. This manuscript consists, among other things, of an antiquary's copy of Symeon's *LDE*. A copy of **17** can be found on f. 100r; it was probably made by reference to manuscript D above, which also has a copy of **17** inserted into a copy of Symeon's *LDE*.

ii. *Bodleian, Dodsworth 9* (P): s. xvii. This manuscript has a copy of **17** on f. 8rv;[437] it begins with the verbal invocation which manuscript D lacks. This same Dodsworth manuscript has copies of York charters (**1**, **3**, **4**, **5**, **8**) and of the Beverley rhyming charter, **12**.

iii. *Bodleian, Dodsworth 10* (Q): s. xvii. A copy of **17** can be found on f. 34v;[438] it has the verbal invocation which manuscript D lacks. Q also has copies of **1** and **12**, York and Beverley documents.

iv. *Bodleian, Dugdale 21* (R): s. xvii. A copy of **17** can be found on f. 97r.[439]

[437] *Summ. Cat.*, no. 4151.
[438] *Summ. Cat.*, no. 4152.
[439] *Summ. Cat.*, no. 6511. Craster 1925*a*, p. 511 (and n. 6), suggests that Sir William Dugdale was here copying from Bodleian Laud Misc. 748 (manuscript H above), Prior Wessington's own version of his *Libellus de exordio et statu ecclesie cathedralis Dunelmensis*.

SIGLA

a. *Principal Manuscripts of the Charters of Durham*

B. Durham Cathedral Muniments, 1.1.Pont.6 (late single-sheet, s. xiv^{ex})
C. BL Cotton Domitian, A. vii (s. ix^{in-med}, with Old English additions of s. x^{ex} and s. xi^{in})
D. Cambridge, University Library, Ff.i.27 (s. xii^{ex})

b. *Manuscripts of* **17**

E. TNA: PRO Ch.R. 15–17 Ric. II, m. 32, no. 29
F. TNA: PRO Ch.R. 8 Hen. IV, no. 3
G. TNA: PRO Ch.R. 1 Hen. V, pt. 1, no. 15
H. Bodleian, Laud Misc. 748 (s. xv^{in})
I. London, Lincoln's Inn, Hales 114 (s. xv^{in})
J. Durham Cathedral Muniments, *Registrum III* (s. xv^{in})
K. BL Cotton Claudius D. iv (s. xv^{in})
L. TNA: PRO Pat. R. 11 Hen. VI, pt. 2, m. 22
M. Durham Cathedral Muniments, *Cartuarium III* (s. xvi^{in})
N. TNA: PRO Conf. R. 6 Eliz., m. 1, no. 10
O. BL Harley 533 (s. xvii)
P. Bodleian, Dodsworth 9 (s. xvii)
Q. Bodleian, Dodsworth 10 (s. xvii)
R. Bodleian, Dugdale 21 (s. xvii)

NOTE ON THE METHOD OF EDITING

Those documents preserved in the Durham archive and printed here do not pose any difficult editorial decisions. The principal manuscript witnesses to **17** are (1) Durham Cathedral Muniments, 1.1.Pont.6 (Manuscript B) and (2) Cambridge, University Library, Ff.i.27 (Manuscript D). The version from Manuscript D has been used as the basis for the text, with significant variants supplied from Manuscript B. Manuscripts E–R all preserve later copies of **17** which do not diverge significantly in their readings from B or D and have therefore not been included in the critical apparatus. The notes about land transactions which are here given as **18–20** all exist in late tenth- or early eleventh-century form in British Library, Cotton Domitian A. vii (Manuscript C), better known as the Durham *Liber Vitae*. I have simply provided diplomatic copies of these notes.

THE CHARTERS OF DURHAM

17

*Ecgfrith, king of Northumbria, grants land at Crayke in North Yorkshire and at Carlisle (*Lugubalia*) to St Cuthbert.* A.D. 685

B. Durham Cathedral Muniments, 1.1.Pont.6; single sheet, s. xiv[ex], 154 × 171mm
Endorsements: (I) dominus Johannes de Kyngeston et dominus Ricardus de Castro Bernardi receperunt originale istius copie per indenturam de Rogero de Alverton per preceptum domini prioris (2) *in a hand of s. xvi[in] (?)*: donatio Regis Egfridi de Creake et Carleolle sancto Cuthberto…
D. Cambridge, University Library, Ff.i.27, p. 186: copy, s. xii[ex]
E. TNA: PRO Ch.R. 15–17 Ric. II, m. 32, no. 29
F. TNA: PRO Ch.R. 8 Hen. IV, no. 3
G. TNA: PRO Ch.R. 1 Hen. V, pt. 1, no. 15
H. Bodleian, Laud Misc. 748, 8rv: copy, s. xv[in]
I. London, Lincoln's Inn, Hales 114, 5rv: copy, s. xv[in]
J. Durham Cathedral Muniments, *Registrum III*, 137r: copy, s. xv[in]
K. BL Cotton Claudius D. iv, 8v–9r: copy, s. xv[in]
L. TNA: PRO Pat. R. 11 Hen. VI, pt. 2, m. 22
M. Durham Cathedral Muniments, *Cartuarium III*, 274r: copy, s. xvi[in]
N. TNA: PRO Conf. R. Eliz., m. 1, no. 10
O. BL Harley 533, f. 100r: copy, s. xvii
P. Bodleian, Dodsworth 9, 8rv: copy, s. xvii
Q. Bodleian, Dodsworth 10, 34v: copy, s. xvii
R. Bodleian, Dugdale 21, 97r: copy, s. xvii
Ed.: a. *Mon. Angl.*, i., p. 39, from H
b. *Mon. Angl.* (rev. edn), i. 234
c. Smith, *Bede*, p. 782, from J
d. Kemble 25
e. Birch 66, from P
Listed: Sawyer 66; Hart, *ECNE*, no. 146
Edited from Manuscript D with variants from B

[a]In nomine patris et filii et spiritus sancti. Amen.[a] Anno dominicae incarnationis .DC. octogesimo quinto congregato[b] sinodo iuxta fluuium Alne in loco qui dicitur Ættuiford[c] cui Teodorus archiepiscopus Doruernensis[d] praesidebat cum Cuthbertus multis legatariis ac literis ad se praemissis nequaquam sua insula posset erui tandem ego Ecgfridus[e] rex Northimbrorum[f] cum antistite Trumwine[g] et aliis religiosis uiris insulam nauigaui et inuitum ad sinodum[h] pertraxi ubi[i] omnium iussione episcopatus officium suscipere compellitur cui et omnibus successoribus eius consilio Theodori[j] archiepiscopi et Trumwini[k] et totius[l] consilii pro salute animae meae et successorum meorum donaui uillam quae uocatur Creic[m] et tria miliaria in circuitu ipsius uillae donaui etiam ciuitatem quae uocatur Lugubalia et in circuitu eius quindecim miliaria ut haec tam ipse quam successores eius[n] ad dei seruitium imperpetuum habeant ita sicut ego habui libera et quieta et [o]secundum uoluntatem suam[o] disponenda.

Ego Theodorius[p] archiepiscopus Doruuernensis subscripsi +
Ego Bosa episcopus subscripsi
Ego Cedd[q] orientalium[r] saxonum episcopus[s] subscripsi
Ego Sexulf[t] Merciorum episcopus subscripsi
Ego Eata Hagustaldensis[u] episcopus subscripsi
Ego Trumwine[v] Pictorum episcopus subscripsi
Ego Ceadda Licefeldensis[w] episcopus subscripsi
Ego Eadhet[x] Lindissi[y] episcopus subscripsi
Hec donatio [z]firmata est[z] tempore[a2] Agatonis pape anno etatis regis Egfridi .xl. regni vero eius .xv.

[a..a] In nomine patris...Amen *omitted in* D [b] congregatur B [c] Twyforth B [d] *For* Doruuernensis [e] Egfridus B [f] Norhumbrorum B [g] Trumwyne B [h] synodum B [i] ubi *(supra lineam)* B [j] Teodorii B [k] Trumwyni B [l] totis B [m] Crec B [n] sui B [o..o] secundum suam uoluntatem B [p] Teodorus B [q] Cedde B [r] orentalium B [s] episcopus *(supra lineam)* B [t] Sexulx B [u] Haugustaldensis B [v] Trumwyne B [w] Lychefeldensis B [x] Eadhed B [y] Lyndissi B [z..z] scripta est B [a2] tempore *(supra lineam)* B

The earliest copy of **17** is preserved in the late twelfth-century manuscript, Cambridge, University Library, Ff.i.27; it is written in at the end of a copy of Symeon's *LDE* and the beginning of the first Continuation to that work. This copy has been used as the basis for the edited text. It is interesting to find that a later, single-sheet version of **17** also exists: it measures 15.4 centimetres in height and is 17.1 centimetres wide. It is folded twice, once vertically and once horizontally; this has led to the destruction of some of those words which happen to coincide with these folds. The only significant difference in the text of the single sheet from that of the earlier copy is that the latter omits the verbal invocation with which the single sheet version begins. The single sheet is written in a hand of the late fourteenth century. One of the endorsements on the verso, which appears to be contemporary to the main text, tells us that the original document was in the possession of John de Kyngeston and Ricardus de Castro Bernardi. These people are readily identifiable: John de Kyngeston was clerk to Thomas Hatfield, bishop of Durham, and we find him involved with the Durham cathedral chancery in the late fourteenth century (see, for example, 2.3.Pont.13 which is written in the hand of John de Kyngeston; see also 2.3.Pont.17, dated 27 December 1368, and 1.4.Reg.19, dated 2 April 1364). Richard of Barnard Castle was also a member of the Durham cathedral chancery, having acted as both clerk and chancellor. We possess an example of an inspeximus-confirmation charter written in Richard's hand and also a charter which makes Richard the beneficiary of a grant by Bishop Hatfield (see 2.3.Pont.8, dated 10 May 1372, and 2.3.Pont.13 respectively). It seems likely, therefore, that we can associate the drawing-up of this late, single-sheet copy with these cathedral officials and that its composition can be dated quite narrowly to the late 1360s or early 1370s.

17 is a forgery. One of the most obvious problems with accepting the details given in **17** is that the transaction itself is dated to 685 in the main body of the charter and yet we find Eadhæd attesting as bishop of Lindsey, despite the fact that he had been expelled from that role in about 679, at which point he became bishop of Ripon (see Bede, *HE*, iii.28 and iv.12 and above, p. 236, n. 39); and likewise Cedd, bishop of the East Saxons, is listed as a witness even though he had already died of the plague in 664 (Bede, *HE*, iii.23). Another problem lies with the diplomatic formulae used in **17**: the part which describes how King Ecgfrith and Bishop Trumwine, along with other religious men, sailed to Farne island to try to persuade Cuthbert to reject his eremitical lifestyle in favour of the assumption of the bishopric is clearly borrowed from parts of Bede's *VCP* (c. XXIV), his *HE* (iv.28) and from the *HSC* (c. 5).

Since **17**, although spurious, relies on information given by Bede and later by the *HSC*, some of its details regarding estates acquired by the Cuthbertine community in the Anglo-Saxon period may be correct. For example, Carlisle was, according to Bede, closely associated with the Cuthbertine community in the late seventh and early eighth centuries. Whilst not all of Bede's information regarding Carlisle can be accurate, there is reason to accept that the Cuthbertine community may have had an estate in the environs of Carlisle and that this may be synonymous with the parish of St Cuthbert Without (Craster 1954, p. 181, Sharpe 1998, p. 216 and above, pp. 276–7). And this association seems to have endured since by the late ninth century we find a certain Eadred, abbot of Carlisle, acting as the head of the Cuthbertine church (see *HSC*, c. 13; Woolf, *Pictland*, pp. 81–3, in trying to understand Eadred's role, wonders whether a single Bernician see may have been consolidated at Carlisle at some point in the mid- to late ninth century following the removal of Cuthbert's community from Lindisfarne). Crayke also has a tradition of being associated with the Cuthbertine community; it was there that the community rested for four months before their relocation to Chester-le-Street (*HSC*, c. 20). Crayke was later the subject of a grant of land made by Earl Thored to the Cuthbertines at the close of the tenth century and preserved in the *LVD* (i.e. **18**; for more about Crayke, see Craster 1954, pp. 182–3).

Chaplais has noted that there may be a genuine diplomatic element in **17**. Towards the end of **17** the extent of the grant by King Ecgfrith is described in the words *...donavi villam...et tria miliaria in circuitu*. The expression *in circuitu* is quite an unusual one in an Anglo-Saxon diplomatic context; it is also similar to the phrase *...ab omni parte per in circuitu miliaria quattuor*, which occurs in early charters for the monastery of San Colombano founded at Bobbio in 614 by the Irishman Columbanus (Chaplais 1969, pp. 101–2). Although it is difficult to posit a direct influence of Bobbio on Northumbrian diplomatic traditions, Chaplais notes that Bobbio was an Irish foundation and that it is therefore possible that an Irish diplomatic tradition was the influence behind the Bobbio charters; perhaps the appearance of the expression *in circuitu* embodies the preservation of a genuine diplomatic formula common to both Irish and Northumbrian charter production. The physical situation of Crayke may further suggest that the *in circuitu* formula should be taken seriously since Crayke is located within a 'curvilinear parish where boundaries appear to preserve the trace of two concentric circuits' (see Blair, *Church*, pp. 222–3). It is unclear, as Blair points out, whether this original formula would simply have granted possession of an area around Crayke or whether it would have created a kind of protected circuit in the Irish fashion. (For the Irish practice of creating concentric zones around a holy core, see Blair, *Church*, pp. 221–2; it is interesting in this regard that, later in the Anglo-Saxon period, circular sanctuary zones of a mile's radius are recorded at York, Beverley and Ripon, for which see above, pp. 244–5.) But even if Chaplais is correct in his identification of a genuine diplomatic element in **17**, this cannot be used to comment on the form of **17** itself. Rather **17** is a forgery, and one which is compiled by reference

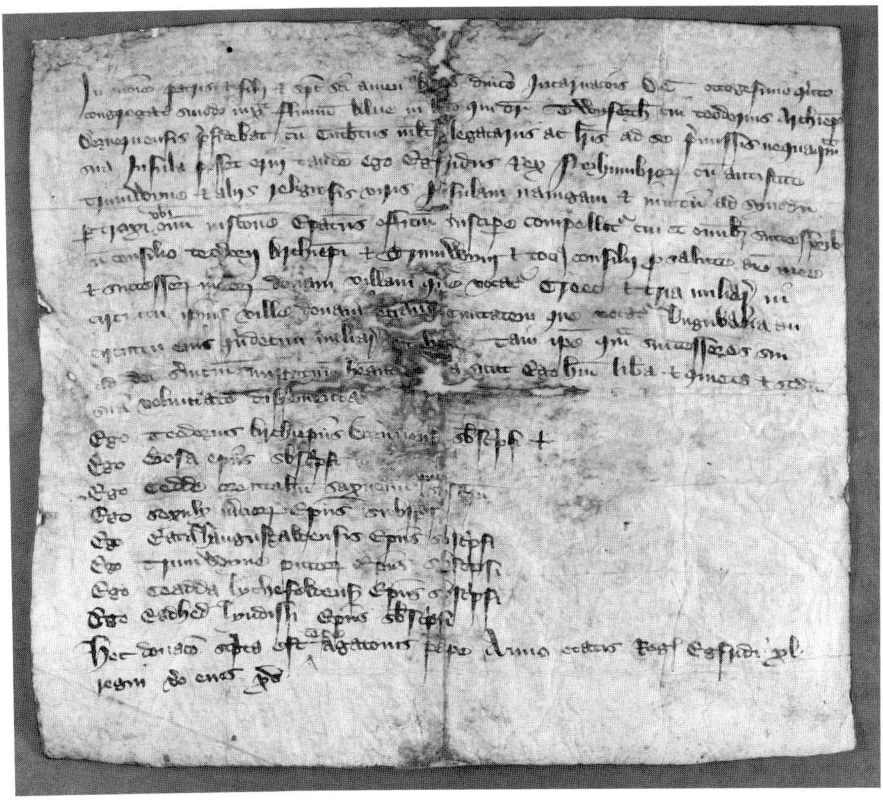

Plate I. Durham Cathedral Muniments, I.I.Pont.6: s. xiv^ex

and allusion to earlier sources; therefore any statement on the nature of its phrasing is one which actually concerns the *HSC*, the ultimate inspiration for **17**'s information (for another discussion of early Northumbrian charters, see Wormald, *Bede and the Conversion*, pp. 1–32, at pp. 19–20, for the existence of Northumbrian charters at Jarrow and Ripon).

It is impossible to be sure when, exactly, **17** was forged but the late eleventh century provides a possible context for its production; this was a time when Durham was involved in the composition of many historical works in order to justify its rights and lands. It was also during this period that Carlisle, one of the estates claimed in **17**, became an area over which rival institutions and peoples sought jurisdiction. In 1092 King William Rufus marched northwards, captured Carlisle, and drove out a certain Dolfin who had ruled the surrounding territory as Earl of Northumbria (*ASC E*, s.a. 1092). This briefly allowed Durham to claim spiritual jurisdiction over Carlisle which was initially recognised by William Rufus and Archbishop Thomas of York (two writs of King William Rufus, dated 1092 × 5 and 1096 × 9; in *Regesta I*, nos. 463 and 478 and one of Archbishop Thomas I of York confirm Durham's spiritual jurisdiction over Carlisle). But this claim did not go undisputed, as both Glasgow and York subsequently declared authority over Carlisle. It is perhaps as a result of running arguments with both Glasgow and York over the extent of their ecclesiastical jurisdiction that the Durham community felt the need to fabricate **17**. The Durham community may have thought that their authority over the district of Carlisle was best guaranteed by reference to that very old tradition which associated St Cuthbert with the area. And this was perhaps not their only attempt to secure their right to Carlisle by such a reference. In Symeon's *LDE* we are told that 'Luel (which is now called Carlisle) had not only been under the personal jurisdiction of St Cuthbert, but also from the time of King Ecgfrith it was always placed under the governance of his bishopric' (*LDE*, ii.5). At this point in the text, one of the manuscript copies of the *LDE* (Durham, University Library, Cosin V.II.6) is followed by an erasure of seventeen lines, which is perhaps suspicious. Not much of the original text can be deciphered but Rollason suggests that it would have elaborated on Durham's late-eleventh century claim to jurisdiction over Carlisle, a claim which was again being disputed by Glasgow and York (see Rollason, *Symeon: Libellus*, p. 95, n. 38; for this erasure, see Rollason 1998, pp. 148–50 and Sharpe 1998, pp. 217–18; Sharpe here identifies a pamphlet probably composed by Symeon to justify Durham's claims over Carlisle, although it is not clear that it was ever circulated). The first Continuation to Symeon's *LDE* states that Durham's rights over Carlisle were lost during the period of exile of Bishop Ranulf Flambard in 1101 (see Symeon, *LDE*, p. 275; for comments on these events, see Craster, 'A Contemporary Record of the Pontificate of Ranulf Flambard', *AA*^{4} vii (1930), pp. 33–56, at pp. 37–9). In 1133 Carlisle became a separate diocese which ended Durham's claims to jurisdiction (in fact this marked a threefold loss for Cuthbert's community in Carlisle: Sharpe 1998, p. 217).

Members of the Durham cathedral chancery later converted the fabricated **17** into the form of a single sheet document in the late 1360s or early 1370s; and they effected this transformation with some skill, as its lay-out represents what one would expect of a single-sheet Anglo-Saxon charter. As has already been seen, the men involved in the compilation of this document were closely associated with Bishop Hatfield. Hatfield was bishop of Durham from 1345 to 1381 and he commissioned a survey of the landed interests of the Durham church to be made along the lines of that survey represented by Boldon Book. The resultant book included two remarkable omissions: 'Bedlingtonshire, which had a full notice in Boldon Buke, is only very shortly referred to under Chester Ward…Norhamshire, also described at length in Boldon Buke, is entirely omitted in Hatfield's Survey. In common with Boldon Buke, the manor of Creyke in Yorkshire is wanting' (W. Greenwell, ed., *Bishop Hatfield's Survey*, SS xxxii [Durham, 1856], pp. ix–x). Here, then, is a possible reason for the fabrication of a second copy of **17**, the single-sheet version. Perhaps those men of the Durham chancery, recognising that Crayke was not represented in the new survey, sought to correct this omission and to create a deed which explicitly gave Durham jurisdiction. But we should also bear in mind the possibility that the forged **17** had become so useful in general that it was felt necessary to possess a single-sheet version. Certainly the large number of extant copies of **17**, particularly the copies enrolled at the chancery in London (Manuscripts E, F, G, L and N), suggest that this was an important document for the Durham community.

18

Note of a Grant of Land at Smeaton, Crayke and Sutton-on-the-Forest, Yorkshire, from Earl Thored to St Cuthbert's Community [late tenth century?]

C. BL Cotton Domitian A. vii, 47v: s. x^{ex}
Ed.: a. Stevenson, *Lib. Vit.*, p. 56, from C
b. Birch 1255, from C
c. Robertson, *Charters*, no. LX (pp. 124–5), with translation, from C
d. *LVD*, p. 140, from C
Facsimile: Thompson, *Lib. Vit.*, f. 47v
Listed: Sawyer 1660; Ker, *Catalogue*, no. 147b; Hart, *ECNE*, no. 126

Her is gemearcod hu manega hyda landes Ðureð eorl betæht hafað into sancte Cuðberht[es] stowe.[a] Nu is æryst on Smiþatune tƿa hyda landes · and on Creic tƿa hyda · and on Suþtune anre hyde · þæt he afað ðam halegan 'ƿere'[b] to lofe and to ƿeorðmynde gegyfen á to ecean life · and se þe þyses ofteo hæbbe hit ƿiþ Gód gemæne and ƿið ðone hal<e>gan[c] ƿer · ær oððe siþor.

[a] effoc *(supra lineam); an addition of s. xi/s. xii (see* LVD, *p. 140)* C
[b] ƿere *(supra lineam)* C [c] –e– *in* halegan *erased* C

Translation[a]

Here it is recorded how many hides of land Earl Thored has assigned to St Cuthbert's foundation. First of all he has given 2 hides of land at Smeaton and 2 hides at Crayke and 1 hide at Sutton, to the praise and honour of the holy saint for all time. He who withholds this shall have to account for it to God and to the holy saint, sooner or later.

[a] *Translation taken from Robertson,* Charters, *p. 125*

18 forms the first of three notes (the other two are **19** and **20**), on the same folio of the *LVD* (f. 47v), all of which record grants made to St Cuthbert's community. Although this folio is now separated from the so-called old 'original core' of the *LVD* (which occupies ff. 15–45), Gullick points out that its ruling pattern, which is the same as that of the 'original core', and the very quality of the parchment, which is of a thick Insular type, makes it very likely that it belongs originally to ff. 15–45 (see M. Gullick, 'The Make-Up of the Durham *Liber Vitae*', in *LVD*, pp. 43–57, at p. 45). The folio on which these grants are preserved is, in its general aspect, arranged in a rather haphazard way. Throughout the *LVD*, clusters of names have been added at various different stages of its existence. On this folio such groups of names are squeezed into the margins both to the left of the main text, above the main text and also below it (for a discussion of these later layers of names, see L. Rollason, 'The Late Medieval Non-Monastic Entries in the Durham *Liber Vitae*', in D. Rollason *et al.*, *The Durham*, pp. 127–37). However it seems that **18**, the note about land given by *Đureð eorl*, was always intended to be one of the principal records on the page. It is written in a script which mixes majuscule with minuscule letter-forms, a hand that has been identified as being one of the scribes responsible for the Durham Ritual (see Brown, *Durham Ritual*, pp. 34–5 and *LVD*, pp. 24 and 254). The beginning of the text starts with an enlarged initial 'H' which shows some of the pretensions of this entry. In other words, **18** seems to have been intended as a note of worth and substance; it was designed to be remembered. Up until this point in the *LVD*, the majority of the manuscript has been concerned to preserve names and names only. F. 48r, which directly follows the folio on which **18** is written, also diverges from the practice of listing names, containing as it does a charter of Bishop Ranulf of Durham (Ranulf Flambard was bishop of Durham from 1099 to 1128; for an overview of his career, see H.S. Offler, 'Ranulf Flambard as Bishop of Durham, 1099–1128', *Durham University Journal* lxiv [1971], pp. 14–25, repr. in his *North of the Tees*, no. VII). From here onwards, the manuscript is a more regular mixture of lists of names and longer notes about deeds such as confraternities and also charters.

Đureð eorl is no doubt the same man as Thored, Earl of Northumbria (Ailred of Rievaulx suggests that King Æthelred's first wife was the daughter of Earl Thored. For comment about this marriage, see Whitelock, *EHD*, p. 48 and Keynes, *Diplomas*, p. 187, n. 118). Thored took over as earl from Oslac (for Oslac see **4**; it is possible that Thored was the son of Oslac but Whitelock 1959, p. 79, suggests that it is more likely that he was Thored Gunner's son who ravaged Westmorland in 966; *ASC DEF*, s.a. 966). As we have seen when discussing the documents preserved in the York archive, Thored came to power as a result of the anti-monastic reaction which was led by Ealdorman Ælfhere of Mercia and which was triggered by the death of King Edgar in 975. One of Thored's first actions as earl was to deprive the York archbishopric of some of its estates, perhaps because York had been closely associated with his predecessor, Earl Oslac (for the depredations effected by Thored see **6**). **18** is therefore of significant interest because it demonstrates Thored's attempt to buy favour with St Cuthbert's community, a religious institution which was York's greatest rival in the north. And, in turn, it highlights the willingness of the Cuthbertine community to involve itself in a political movement which might increase its standing.

Thored may have been a trusted man at the southern court of King Æthelred. The evidence provided by the witness-lists to Æthelred's charters is problematic when used to investigate the careers of Northumbrians, because these men seem not to have been regularly present at Æthelred's councils. Thus Thored first attests a charter of 979, S 834

(*Pet* 18) but disappears from meetings of the *witan* in the period 980–2 and then again in 986–8. Because Northumbrian earls only sporadically attended the southern court during these years, it is impossible to speculate as to why Thored may have been absent from the king's council in these periods (for the formation of King Æthelred's council at this time, see Keynes, *Diplomas*, pp. 157–8 and p. 158, n. 11). Thored last attests a charter of King Æthelred in 989 (S 877 [*WinchNM* 31]) but this does not mean that it was at this point that he disappeared from the political scene. Reason to believe that Thored was a faithful member of Æthelred's entourage is provided by an event in 992 which saw an important military mission being allotted to Thored: he was one of four men to whom the king and his councillors entrusted a fleet of ships in order to prevent viking incursions (*ASC CDE*, s.a. 992; the other three men were Ealdorman Ælfric, Bishop Ælfstan and Bishop Æscwig; for more, see Keynes, *Diplomas*, p. 197 and Whitelock 1959, p. 80). The failure of this campaign quite probably led to Thored's downfall, as Whitelock points out that his successor, Ælfhelm, can be found attesting official documents already in 993 (Whitelock *ibid*., p. 80).

In **18** Thored grants 'two hides of land at Smeaton and two hides at Crayke and one hide at Sutton' to St Cuthbert's community. Smeaton is situated in Yorkshire (*DEPN*, p. 427). Domesday Book does not link Smeaton with Cuthbert's community. In the time of King Edward, Great Smeaton and Little Smeaton belonged to the manor of Northallerton which was itself held by Earl Edwin (GDB, f. 299r). After the Conquest, both the king himself and Count Alan had interests in Great Smeaton, which is described as being 'waste' (GDB, f. 299r and f. 309r); the king also had interests in Little Smeaton (GDB, f. 299r and f. 300v).

Creic is the town of Crayke which is situated just to the north of York (*DEPN*, p. 129). As we have already seen with regard to **17**, Crayke is thought of, at various stages in its history, as belonging to St Cuthbert's community. The *HSC* notes that the grant of 'Crayke and three miles in circumference around the same vill' was given to St Cuthbert himself when he was alive so that '[Cuthbert] might have a stopping-place there whenever he went to, or returned from, York. And St Cuthbert installed a congregation of monks there and ordained an abbot' (*HSC*, c. 5; the same details about this grant of Crayke are also found in Symeon, *LDE*, i.9, which relies on the *HSC* for its information). The *HSC* also preserves the tradition that King Ælle later, *c*. 867, stole Crayke from St Cuthbert (*HSC*, c. 10). However, it would appear that the community of monks which had been installed by Cuthbert at Crayke continued to exist; later, in the period *c*. 875–*c*. 883, Cuthbert's community was received by Abbot Geve and resided at Crayke for four months (*HSC*, c. 20; this took place when Cuthbert's community was forced to relocate and endure a period of 'seven years' wandering'). Domesday Book states that TRE Bishop Æthelwine of Durham (1056–71) held Crayke as one manor and the Durham church had a continued interest there TRW; at the time of the Domesday commission there was a church and a priest at Crayke (for all of these details, see GDB, f. 304v and f. 381r).

Suþtune is a very common placename meaning literally 'southern tun' ('Suþ-tun'; see the many examples in *DEPN*, p. 454). The *Suþtune* in **18** is probably to be identified as Sutton-on-the-Forest in Yorkshire (see Robertson, *Charters*, p. 368 and Thompson, *Lib. Vit*., p. xxv). None of the Durham narrative sources or Domesday Book records St Cuthbert's community possessing land at Sutton-on-the-Forest.

It is not possible to apply to **18** any form of diplomatic test which would illustrate whether or not it should be considered as genuine. But it is important to understand the 'tone' of **18**. It begins with the statement *Her is gemearcod*; this displays a self-conscious awareness of the importance of the fact that this has been written down. The recipient is named as *sancte Cuðberhtes stowe*, which is indicative of the sense of identity the community had in the late tenth century. It was around their patron saint that the religious community was gathered and held together, and gifts of land were made to Cuthbert rather than to a terrestrial figure such as the bishop. This was clearly a deliberate ploy: the religious community thought it to be the most appropriate method by which to guarantee that land given to it would not in future be taken away from it (donation of land to a saint rather than to a secular figure was not an uncommon methodology; for a similar situation in the Celtic world, see W. Davies, 'The Latin Charter-tradition in Western Britain, Brittany and Ireland', in *Ireland in Early Mediaeval Europe*, ed. D. Whitelock *et al.* [Cambridge, 1982], pp. 258–81 and also B. Rosenwein, *To be the Neighbour of Saint Peter: The Social Meaning of Cluny's Property, 909–1049* [Cornell, 1989], esp. pp. 75–7; see also above, pp. 9–16). Likewise at the end the quasi-sanction announces, …*se þe þyses ofteo hæbbe hit þiþ Gód gemæne and þið ðone hal[e]gan per ær oððe siþor*. The threat of having to account to God and also to Cuthbert himself for any depredation would have been a significant deterrent to would-be defrauders: it is perhaps notable here that Cuthbert's name itself is not invoked but rather he is left as *hal[e]gan*, the 'holy man'; his holiness is emphasised and brought out as a distinct threat. The implication is that the penalty for stealing land from the community is beyond imagination.

19

Note of a Grant of Land at Escomb, Durham, from Earl Northman to St Cuthbert's Community [early eleventh century]

C. BL Cotton Domitian A. vii, 47v: s. xi[in]
Ed.: a. Stevenson, *Lib. Vit.*, p. 57, from C
b. Kemble 925, from C
c. Birch 1255, from C
d. Robertson, *Charters*, no. LXVIII (pp. 140–1), with translation, from C
e. *LVD*, p. 140, from C
Facsimile: Thompson, *Lib. Vit.*, f. 47v
Listed: Sawyer 1659; Ker, *Catalogue*, no. 147c; Hart, *ECNE*, no. 127

Her syleð Norðman eorl into sancte Cuðberhte Ediscum ⁊ eall ꝥ ðær into hyreð · ⁊ ðone feorðan æcer æt Feregenne.

Translation[a]

Earl Northman here grants to St Cuthbert's Escomb and all that belongs to it, and the fourth acre at Ferryhill.

[a] *Translation taken from Robertson,* Charters, *p. 141*

19 follows directly on from **18** on the same folio of the *LVD*. It is very different in aspect from **18**, as it is written in a script which is both smaller and slighter but which is also made up entirely of minuscule letter-forms rather than of a mixture of majuscules and minuscules as we saw in **18**: even Cuthbert's name is written in minuscules (although some attempt has been made to imitate the enlarged initial 'h' of **18**). It is a little unclear whether or not we should regard **19** and **20** (below) as having been written at the same time and as constituting one record (Robertson, *Charters*, LXVIII, has kept **19** and **20** as one record. Sawyer has separated them and listed them as S 1659 and S 1661 respectively). It is possible that they are written in the same hand (compare the form of *cuðberhte* in each and the *e* in *Feregenne* (**19**) with the first *e* in *mete* (**20**); but note also the various forms of *s*), and the use of the expression 'And I, Ulfketel,...' at the beginning of **20** perhaps suggests that it is to be seen as a continuation of the previous grant. However, at the end of **19**, half a line has been left blank and a new line is then started for **20** (at the end of **19** four names, beginning with 'Ascelina...', have been inserted in the early twelfth century; see *LVD*, p. 141); this may be an indication that a separate and distinct record was felt to be necessary for **20**. Because these records preserve the details of land transactions involving two distinct individuals and two sets of territory, I have maintained the distinction between these two grants found in Sawyer's list.

Very little information survives concerning Earl Northman. The *HSC*, c. 31, preserves the tradition that Bishop Aldhun (990–1018) leased various territories (including Escomb) to three earls 'Ethred, Northman and Uhtred' and this Northman is probably to be equated with ours in **19** (for these leases, see above, pp. 308–9). As noted by Robertson, Earl Northman is perhaps found elsewhere attesting S 881 (KCD 687), a 994 charter of King Æthelred (granting land to St Mary's church, Wilton) alongside that other northern earl, Waltheof (Robertson, *Charters*, p. 383). Robertson and Whitelock make it clear that the Northman in **19** is not to be confused with the Northman who was the son of Earl Leofwine and who seems to have been firmly associated with the Worcestershire area (Robertson, *Charters*, p. 383, where she also notes others with the name of Northman; also Whitelock 1959, pp. 81–2, where, at p. 82 she suggests that the Northman in **19** is probably the very same as he who is described as attending, along with other northern figures, a meeting in London in 989/990). The fact that it is quite difficult to identify Earl Northman perhaps suggests that he could have been a subordinate earl, with rule over part of Northumbria only (such figures were common in Northumbria; see Whitelock 1959, p. 82, Craster 1954, p. 194, Hart, *ECNE*, p. 324 and Rollason, *Symeon: Libellus*, p. 154, n. 16).

Ediscum is Escomb which is situated near Bishop Auckland in County Durham. There is still, to this day, an Anglo-Saxon church at Escomb (Taylor and Taylor, *Anglo-Saxon Architecture* I, pp. 234–8). It is impossible to be precise about the date of the original church but there are some surviving late seventh- or early eighth-century church furnishings, for which see Cramp, *Corpus*, Part 1, p. 78. The church also boasts a remarkable sundial in the middle of the main south wall of the nave. The sundial dates to the eighth century and is thought to be the earliest extant in its original place in Britain; Taylor and Taylor, *Anglo-Saxon Architecture* I, p. 236 and Cramp, *Corpus*, Part 1, p. 79). Since Escomb is listed as one of those estates that had been leased out by Bishop Aldhun, it is possible that **19** represents a written record of the returning of that estate to St Cuthbert's community. *Feregenne* is Ferryhill which lies just to the south of Durham ('Ferryhill' literally means 'wooded hill'; *DEPN*, p. 178).

20

Note of a Grant of Land at Norton, County Durham, from Ulfketel, son of Osulf, to St Cuthbert's Community [early eleventh century?]

C. BL Cotton Domitian A. vii, 47v: s. xi[in]
Ed.: a. Stevenson, *Lib. Vit.*, p. 57, from C
b. Kemble 925, from C
c. Birch 1256, from C
d. Robertson, *Charters*, no. LXVIII (pp. 140–1), with translation, from C
e. *LVD*, p. 140, from C
Facsimile: Thompson, *Lib. Vit.*, f. 47v
Listed: Sawyer 1661; Hart, *ECNE*, no. 128

⁊ ic Ulfcytel Osulfes sunu sylle Norðtun mid mete ⁊ mid mannan into sancte Cuðberhte · ⁊ all ꝥ ðer into hyreð mið sace ⁊ mið socne ⁊ se ðe þis aꝑende sy he ascyred from Godes dæle ⁊ from eallum haligdome.

Translation[a]

And I, Ulfketel, Osulf's son, grant Norton to St Cuthbert's with its produce and its men and all that belongs to it and with rights of jurisdiction. He who alters this shall be cut off from any part in God and from all holy things.

[a] *Translation taken from Robertson,* Charters, *p. 141*

The fact that it is impossible to give a precise date for **20** makes it difficult to identify Ulfketel and Osulf with any certainty. A *minister* Ulfketel attests in two charters of King Edgar which have definite associations with the north and with Yorkshire in particular: the one because it is a grant of land in Yorkshire, S 681 (*Pet* 14), dated 959, and the other because it is a grant of land in Nottinghamshire, the charter of which is preserved in the York archive (**3** above, dated 958). The identification of the Ulfketel of **20** with this Ulfketel in King Edgar's charters has much to recommend it (see Robertson, *Charters*, pp. 383–4, who also draws attention to these two Edgar charters). The two charters in question were composed at a time when Edgar was king of Mercia and Northumbria only and not of the whole of Anglo-Saxon England. As such he would have had various court attendants (perhaps especially Scandinavian figures) who would later, on Edgar's assumption of the rule of all England, have remained in the north and would have ceased to attend Edgar's courts. This certainly seems to be the case with this Ulfketel *minister* as, after his attestation in S 681 (*Pet* 14), on the eve of Edgar's accession to the whole kingdom, he no longer appears as a witness at court. (Of course it was not necessarily the case that every individual at Edgar's Mercian court would cease to attend once Edgar had acceded to rule of the whole of the kingdom and figures such as Wulfgar and Wulfhelm continue to attest and to be present. The case of Wulfhelm is particularly interesting. When at Edgar's court in Mercia and Northumbria he can be found attesting in a rather elevated position, often as the second thegn to sign. He evidently became less important on Edgar's accession to the rule of England and is demoted to signing most often as the twelfth thegn. For a summary of these political standings, see Keynes, *Atlas*, table LVII. Here, Keynes also suggests the possibility that an attestor called 'Ufa' could be synonymous with our 'Ulfketel'. An Ulfketel can be found attesting later on in Edgar's reign in 970 (S 779 [KCD 563]) but this is in a diploma which is evidently spurious). Thus a figure like Ulfketel would have had some standing in the north and it is just such an individual that we would expect to be making a grant like that described in **20**.

Osulf is equally difficult to identify. Robertson, *Charters*, p. 384, suggested that he could be that Osulf mentioned in the Old English *Memorandum* (**6**) drawn up by Archbishop Oswald on the estates lost by the see of York. This states, '...He (i.e. Archbishop Oscytel) bought Everingham for 44 pounds from Osulf's father, when he was at the point of death...'. Another possibility is that the Osulf of **20** could be the very same person as Osulf (also spelled Oswulf), the high-reeve of Bamburgh (he attests *inter alia*, S 520 [BCS 815] of 946 as *Hæhgerefa* and S 544 [*Abing* 43] of 949 as *ad Bebb' hehgr* (perhaps an abbreviated form of *ad Bebbanbyrig hehgerefa*; see Kelly, *Abingdon* I, p. 177); on these attestations, see Whitelock 1959, p. 77, n. 1; for Osulf, see Rollason, *Northumbria*, pp. 266–7). Unfortunately, it is unclear whether Osulf had any sons other than Waltheof (fl. 975–1066); see Rollason, *Northumbria*, p. 268.

Norðtun is a very common place-name but this is perhaps to be equated with 'Norton' which is in County Durham (see Robertson, *Charters*, p. 384 and *DEPN*, pp. 344–5). **20** is the earliest record of the gift of Norton to St Cuthbert's community; the estate was still in Durham's possession at the time of the late twelfth-century Boldon Book and it is unclear whether the see had ever lost Norton in the intervening period (see Robertson, *Charters*, p. 384 and *Boldon Book: Northumberland and Durham*, ed. D. Austin [Phillimore, 1982], p. 27). Partial remains of two tenth-century cross-shafts have been built into the fabric of the Norton church (Cramp, *Corpus*, Part 1, p. 134; see also Craster 1954, p. 193 and Taylor and Taylor, *Anglo-Saxon Architecture* I, pp. 465–9).

mið sace ⁊ mið socne is an expression, used for example in the mid-tenth century in **2** in the York archive, which denotes the particular jurisdictional rights a lord had over an estate (the Southwell estate granted in **2** was so large that it became necessary, in the formal context of a charter, to specify that the new lord would possess the rights of justice over the whole of the property granted to him; see the commentary to **2**, Stenton, *Types*, pp. 78–81 and Hadley, *Northern*, pp. 167–72, on sake and soke; for another charter of the same period with the same phrase, see S 681 [*Pet* 14]). Robertson notes that the term *socn* can be used alone to have the same meaning and also that *mið* is a Northumbrian form (see Robertson, *Charters*, p. 384).

LOWTHER CASTLE

INTRODUCTION

1. HISTORICAL OVERVIEW OF THE NORTH WEST

The history of Cumbria, and of the north west in general, is poorly recorded for the Anglo-Saxon period.[1] In the pre-Viking era, we can discern a situation whereby Northumbria in the north west was bordered by a British kingdom centred on Dumbarton, a kingdom about which we know very little.[2] A serious viking raid of 870 seems to have marked the end of Dumbarton as the chief citadel of the kingdom and it is from about this time,[3] as highlighted by Alex Woolf, that we begin to see references to 'Strathclyde' and to the 'Strathclyde Welsh'; for Woolf, these new notices of Strathclyde represent 'the political reconfiguration of the northern Britons following the destruction of Dumbarton'.[4] Around the same time as Scandinavian intrusion in the area,[5] from at least the early tenth century, a sequence of British kings of Strathclyde emerges beginning with Dyfnwal (*Donéualdus*), who is mentioned only in the *Chronicle of the Kings of Alba* and who died at some point in the period 906–915.[6] The last extant reference to a king

[1] This opening section is intended as a necessarily brief introduction to the political situation in the north west. For accounts of Cumbrian history of this time, see, for example, Kirby 1962; N. Higham, *The Northern Counties to AD 1000* (London and New York, 1986), pp. 316–35; Phythian-Adams, *Land of the Cumbrians*; Rollason, *Northumbria*, pp. 249–55; Broun 2004, esp. pp. 125–30 and 136–40; Woolf, *Pictland*, esp. pp. 152–8; Edmonds 2009 and T. Clarkson, *The Men of the North: The Britons of Southern Scotland* (Edinburgh, 2010), pp. 169–93.

[2] Rollason, *Northumbria*, p. 32 and Woolf, *Pictland*, pp. 4–5, who notes that after the death of King Dyfnwal son of Teudebur in 760, Dumbarton is not heard of again for over a century.

[3] The *Annals of Ulster* record this 870 raid on Dumbarton; see *The Annals of Ulster to A.D. 1131*, ed. S. Mac Airt and G. Mac Niocaill (Dublin, 1983), pp. 326–7, s.a. 870.

[4] Woolf, *Pictland*, p. 110.

[5] For Scandinavian settlement in the north west, see above, pp. 51–2. I am most grateful to Dr F. Edmonds for allowing me access to an article she has forthcoming which deals with the issue of Brittonic and Scandinavian influence in the north west.

[6] It used to be thought that these kings of Strathclyde were Gaels rather than Britons; but see Broun 2004, pp. 125–30, who summarises previous scholarship on the matter and argues the case for these kings being Britons. The *Chronicle of the Kings of Alba* is preserved in a mid-fourteenth manuscript which itself is a copy of a late twelfth- or early thirteenth-century compilation of Scottish historical material. The ultimate exemplar of this copy seems to have been a near-contemporary chronicle covering the mid-ninth century to the late tenth century, compiled by a Gaelic-speaking person writing in Latin, to which later additions were made. For all of this information, see B.T. Hudson, 'The

of Strathclyde is to Owain 'the Bald' (*Eugenius Calvus*), who took part in the 1018 battle of Carham;[7] and it has been suggested that the Strathclyde royal line came to an end at about this time or slightly later in the mid-eleventh century.[8]

These Strathclyde kings are clearly of great importance in any consideration of the extent of English involvement, or of English overlordship, in north-western Northumbria from the tenth century onwards. The political situation is complex and obscure and this is made worse by one vexed problem of terminology: Anglo-Saxon sources refer both to 'Strathclyde' (*Stræcled*) and to 'the land of the Cumbrians' (*Cumbra land*).[9] In 1966, P.A. Wilson argued that these terms referred to the same kingdom.[10] Since then, scholarly opinion has been divided and there are those who have preferred to suggest that Cumbria and Strathclyde, already by the tenth century, denoted two separate political entities, Cumbria situated in modern England, Strathclyde situated in modern Scotland.[11] Nevertheless, more recent discussions uphold Wilson's interpretation of the synonymity of 'Stratchclyde' and 'the land of the Cumbrians' and Woolf has suggested that 'Cumbrian' was the term used by Northumbrians when referring to Strathclyde Britons.[12] From the tenth to mid-eleventh centuries, 'Strathclyde' and 'Cumbria' refer to a kingdom situated between Clydesdale and Cumberland.[13] By the end of the Anglo-Saxon period, 'Cumberland' had come to refer more specifically to the area surrounding Carlisle.[14]

Scottish Chronicle', *The Scottish Historical Review* lxxvii (1998), pp. 129–61, at pp. 150 and 157, for Dyfnwal, and pp. 130 and 133–8, for the preservation and composition of the chronicle; for more useful discussion of this chronicle, with further references, see Woolf, *Pictland*, pp. 88–93.

[7] *HR* (8), pp. 155–6 (s.a. 1018); see also Broun 2004, p. 128.

[8] Higham, *Northern Counties*, p. 321–2 and Broun 2004, pp. 127 and 136–40. In 1070, following a series of attacks on Northumbria by Malcolm, king of Scotland, the *Historia regum* states that Earl Gospatric ravaged Cumberland (*Cumbreland*) as a reprisal because it then belonged to Malcolm, who had violently subjugated it to his rule: *HR* (8), p. 191. There are two possible men who could be synonymous with the Gospatric who issued **21** and one of them is this very Gospatric who ravaged Cumberland. For further discussion, see below, pp. 363–4.

[9] For references to 'Strathclyde' (*Stræcled*), see *ASC C*, s.a. 875 and *ASC A*, s.a. 923 (*recte* 920); for references to 'the land of the Cumbrians' (*Cumbra land* or *Cumer*/*Cumber lande*), see *ASC ABCDEF*, s.a. 945 and *ASC CDE*, s.a. 1000. For discussion of this evidence, see Woolf, *Pictland*, pp. 153–4, where it is noted that Symeon of Durham and also entries in the *Historia regum* refer additionally to 'Cumbrians', when discussing events of the early tenth century.

[10] Wilson 1966.

[11] For useful overviews of all of this scholarly material, see Broun 2004, pp. 129–30 and Woolf, *Pictland*, pp. 153–4. Phythian-Adams, *Land of the Cumbrians*, pp. 110–12, has recently argued strongly for the view that 'Cumbria' and 'Strathclyde' were separate kingdoms.

[12] Woolf, *Pictland*, pp. 153–4; others who endorse this view include Broun 2004 and Edmonds 2009.

[13] Edmonds 2009, p. 44.

[14] Woolf, *Pictland*, p. 153.

2. THE DATE AND HISTORICAL SIGNIFICANCE OF GOSPATRIC'S WRIT (**21**)

The north west was therefore a politically, and ethnically, mixed area over which various different political forces, including the Gaelic-Scandinavians, the Strathclyde kings, the Scottish kings and the rulers of Northumbria, vied for control. Both because of the dearth of historical evidence to have survived from this part of Anglo-Saxon England, and because of the political complexity of the area, **21**, a writ issued by Gospatric, is of singular historical importance.[15]

But before **21** can be interpreted historically, it is important to try to date the document as narrowly as possible. The issue turns on the identity of Gospatric himself. There are two possible candidates: the first is Gospatric (d. 1064), son of Earl Uhtred (d. 1016) and Uhtred's second wife, Sigen. The second is Gospatric's nephew, Gospatric (Earl of Northumbria 1067–8 and 1070–2), son of Maldred.[16] H.W.C. Davis argued strongly in favour of the former identification, partly on the basis that Earl Siward is referred to in **21** as if still alive and partly also because he thought that Earl Siward would have had every reason to appease this older Gospatric, who was a member of the House of Bamburgh and yet had not become earl (Davis argues that Siward achieved this by giving Gospatric lands in Cumbria); and whose brothers, Ealdred (d. 1038) and Eadwulf (d. 1041), had both been in control of the Northumbrian earldom.[17]

Phythian-Adams has recently put forward a strong argument in favour of an identification with the younger Gospatric, son of Maldred; and, in doing so, he takes particular issue with the article by Davis and the edition by Harmer.[18] Phythian-Adams questions whether the writ implies that Siward was alive when the grant was made. He proposes that it has an alternative meaning, in that Siward had previously guaranteed the peace and now, after him, Gospatric was doing

[15] The importance of **21** was recognised as soon as it was discovered by Ragg in October 1902: see Ragg 1903, p. 244 and Ragg 1905, p. 73; other early twentieth-century discussions of **21** can be found in Liebermann 1903 and Wilson 1904.

[16] For the identification of Maldred's father, see G.W.S. Barrow, 'Some Problems in Twelfth- and Thirteenth-Century Scottish History – A Genealogical Approach', *The Scottish Genealogist* xxv (1978), pp. 97–112, at p. 98.

[17] For these arguments, see Davis 1905, pp. 62 and 64; others who endorse this view are Stenton, *Preparatory to ASE*, p. 217, n. 1 and B. Dickins in *PN Cumb. III*, p. xxx. Harmer, *Writs*, pp. 420 and 531, tentatively assigns **21** to the period after the murder of Earl Eadwulf in 1041 and possibly before 1055, when Siward died; but she notes that this rests on the unprovable suggestion that **21** implies that Siward was alive when it was issued.

[18] See especially, Phythian-Adams, *Land of the Cumbrians*, pp. 174–81; others who favour a similar identification include Wilson 1904, pp. 62–9 and A.O. Anderson, *Early Sources of Scottish History A.D. 500–1286* (Edinburgh, 1922), vol. II, pp. 36–9.

similarly and to the same extent.[19] Phythian-Adams furthers his argument for this particular Gospatric by reference to the foundation charter of Wetheral priory.[20] He suggests that those men listed in Gospatric's writ, or their immediate descendants, can also be found attesting the Wetheral charter which has been dated by Prescott to the period 1092–1112.[21] He therefore concludes that we should view **21** as a product of the late eleventh century and in the name of the younger Gospatric, son of Maldred.[22] But the edition of the Wetheral cartulary was made from transcripts rather than the original late-thirteenth-century manuscript and in the manuscript itself the charter appears as part of additional fifteenth-century material.[23] We should therefore be careful in any handling of the Wetheral charter.

All of these discussions mentioned are polarised in their views but, given the ambiguous nature of **21**, it seems impossible to be conclusive about Gospatric's exact identity.[24] But what we can say is that both possible identifications belong to the same family, the House of Bamburgh. And, as Edmonds has demonstrated, the name Gospatric is of great interest in the reconstruction of the House of Bamburgh's dealings in the north west. The first element of the name derives from Brittonic *Gwas-*, 'servant', and so it comes to mean 'servant of Patrick'. She argues that 'the interaction between the earls of Northumbria and the kingdom of Strathclyde in the early to mid-eleventh century explains the adoption of the name *Gwas-Patric* by the House of Bamburgh'. By using a Brittonic name (or perhaps epithet), the Northumbrian earls sought thereby to ingratiate themselves with those in Cumbria.[25] Another Gospatric (*Cwæspatrike*) is listed in the Durham *Liber Vitae* as part of a manumission in which an unidentified female frees the men whom she has received from *Cwæspatrike*.[26]

Despite the difficulties in dating **21** precisely, it is clear that the writ is of great historical significance, providing information about political authority in the area, its ethnic make-up and the type of administrative document in everyday use. It

[19] Phythian-Adams, *Land of the Cumbrians*, p. 175.

[20] For the Wetheral foundation charter, see J.E. Prescott, *The Register of the Priory of Wetherhal* (London, 1897), pp. 1–5.

[21] Prescott, *The Register of the Priory of Wetherhal*, p. 6, n. 15.

[22] Phythian-Adams, *Land of the Cumbrians*, pp. 174–81.

[23] The problem with the edition of the Wetheral cartulary is briefly alluded to by Phythian-Adams, *Land of the Cumbrians*, p. 177; for more see Sharpe, *Norman Rule*, pp. 22–3, p. 23, n. 52 and p. 47, n. 119, who talks about the very great problems involved in dating these documents and suggests a dating range of 1101–1112 and also Edmonds 2009, p. 55. I am also grateful to Dr Hugh Doherty for much helpful discussion on these matters.

[24] In the current edition, **21** is dated broadly to the mid- or late eleventh century, thus taking into account both possible identities of Gospatric.

[25] Edmonds 2009, pp. 51–5, 58 and 61, at p. 54, for the quotation.

[26] See BL Cotton Domitian A. VII, f. 47r; edited in *LVD*, p. 138.

begins by addressing people in the 'lands that were Cumbrian' (*on eallun þam landann þeo weoron Cōmbres*), suggesting that by the time **21** was issued, in the mid- or late eleventh century, the Strathclyde kingdom had ceased to exist.[27] Instead Northumbrians had come to dominate in Cumbria and in **21** Gospatric, from the House of Bamburgh, was able to grant Thorfynn mac Thore freedom 'in all things that are mine in Allerdale as any man may be'.[28] The name Thorfynn mac Thore, as pointed out by Harmer, combines two Scandinavian names with the Gaelic *mac*, demonstrating perfectly the ethnic mix of the north west,[29] as by this stage Cumbria consisted of English men, Scandinavians, Gaelicised Scandinavians, including people from Ireland, the Hebrides and the Isle of Man.[30]

21 also provides information about the levels of authority of certain individuals in Cumbria: it describes how Siward, earl of Northumbria (d. 1055), was able to grant the *gyrth*, 'peace', to Thorfynn in those Cumbrian lands to the south of the Solway;[31] it also describes how Gospatric, the main actor in **21**, was able to declare that those who were dwelling at Cardew and Cumdivock were to be exempt from the geld (*geyldfreo*), just as he himself was. While circumstances in this area of the country (recently ceded from the kingdom of Strathclyde) may have made the requirement of tax an unlikely expectation,[32] it is nevertheless clear that these are grants of significant privileges, made by men who had come to hold quasi-royal positions in Cumbria.[33]

21 therefore offers a view into the obscure and complex history of the north west of England, at a time just after the end of the kingdom of Strathclyde. It is of significant interest, as highlighted by Harmer, that Gospatric, in making this grant of rights such as sake and soke and toll and team, does so by using a document

[27] Broun 2004, pp. 139–40.

[28] As noted by Broun 2004, p. 138, a passage in Hugh the Chanter's *History*, which describes the consecration of two bishops of Glasgow by Archbishop Cynesige of York (1055–60), may imply that Strathclyde had been under Northumbrian control since at least the mid-eleventh century. For the relevant passage, see *Hugh the Chanter*, pp. 52–3 (at p. xlv, n. 2 and p. 53, n. 3, for the 'doubtful' connection of these two consecrated bishops with Glasgow).

[29] Harmer, *Writs*, p. 423.

[30] Harmer, *Writs*, pp. 419–20. *þorfinnr* was a popular name in the north of England and Scotland and so it is difficult to identify such people with precision; Edmonds 2009, p. 58. Allerdale (*Alnerdall*) is a Scandinavian word meaning 'Valley of the River Alen', which became the River Ellen; *PN Cumb. I*, p. 1. On the lordship of Allerdale, see Phythian-Adams, *Land of the Cumbrians*, pp. 38–41.

[31] The exact nature, and extent, of Siward's rule in Cumbria cannot be determined: J. Wilson 1904, pp. 63–4; for more detail about Siward and his power in the north west, see Woolf, *Pictland*, pp. 260–3 and Edmonds 2009, pp. 53–4. Siward can elsewhere be found waging war in Scotland and defeating the Scottish king, Macbeth: *ASC CD*, s.a. 1054.

[32] Harmer, *Writs*, p. 421.

[33] Exemption from payment of the land-tax, geld, was traditionally something only granted by the king himself; see Harmer, *Writs*, p. 376.

whose diplomatic formulation adheres in a general fashion to the mainstream of English royal writs.[34] But although **21** can broadly be classified as an English writ, many of its features, including its display of Gaelic, Brittonic, Scandinavian and English names, its use of Northumbrian linguistic forms and its intermingling of terms not appropriate for Anglo-Saxon writs, are less usual and have to be understood as adaptations made according to local usage.[35] In its idiosyncracies it is reminiscent of the ways in which other charters in the northern archives, such as **1** or **2**, conform to broad, contemporary English diplomatic trends, but also adapt their exemplars to suit the situation beyond the River Humber. It leaves one wondering just what kind of documents must have been in everyday use across the north of England and which unfortunately have not survived.

3. THE HISTORY OF THE LOWTHER ARCHIVE

21 forms part of the Lowther archive, a collection which was originally stored at Lowther Castle in the muniments room there. Already from the twelfth century, the Lowther family were established in Lowther, Westmorland, and by the fourteenth century they had increased their assets in the north west with additional estates in Cumberland.[36] Sir John Lowther (d. 1637), in the seventeenth century, acquired more estates for the family, including the manor of St Bees in Cumberland.[37] Since 1963, parts of the Lowther archive have been transferred to the Cumbria County Record Office, now known as the Cumbria Archive Centre, Carlisle, which is where **21** is now kept. The archive as a whole has over one thousand medieval deeds, mainly relating to Cumberland and Westmorland but including also twelfth- to nineteenth-century deeds about Yorkshire and

[34] Harmer, *Writs*, pp. 421–2, where she also demonstrates the use of the official West Saxon dialect in **21**: words such as *ealle*, *gret* (*greot*) and *weald*. For more detail about the diplomatic formulation, see the commentary to **21**.

[35] Northumbrian linguistic forms include *mið* for *mid* or *freals* for *freols*, although Harmer emphasises that we cannot be sure exactly when these forms were introduced into the writ and so it cannot be ruled out that they are not the work of a later copyist. Diplomatic formulae influenced by the local situation include the use of the Scandinavian 'with *bode* and witnessman', the Scandinavian reference to *dreng* and the Cumbric *wassenas*. For all of these forms, see Harmer, *Writs*, pp. 419–23.

[36] For this, and most of what follows, see *Principal Family and Estate Collections: Family Names L–W*, Guides to Sources for British History 11, The Royal Commission on Historical Manuscripts (London, 1999), pp. 11–13 (no. 63). For additional information, and for the picture of the single-sheet copy of **21**, I am indebted to Alison Day, the Lonsdale cataloguing archivist in the Cumbria Archive Centre, Carlisle.

[37] For a much more detailed overview of the Lowther family history, see *Principal Family and Estate Collections: Family Names L–W*, pp. 11–12.

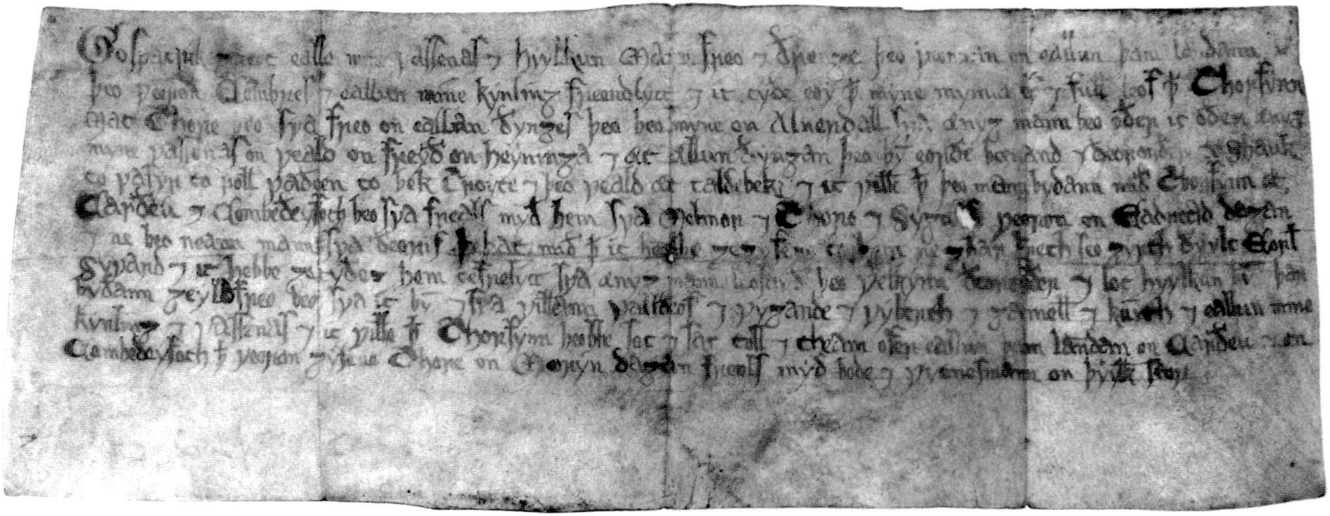

Plate 2. CACC, Lowther of Lowther, DLONSL/5/1/44/C1: s. xiii–s. xvii

twelfth- to sixteenth-century deeds of Northumberland.[38] The vast majority of deeds are of a date much later than the Anglo-Saxon period and **21** therefore seems to be a chance survival.[39]

On the face of it, **21** has potential importance as a rare example of an Anglo-Saxon charter that may have survived outside of the protection of a church archive. But the lack of any endorsement on the back of the single-sheet, coupled with an uncertainty of the evolution of the Lowther archive, makes it impossible to know for certain the date at which **21** came to belong to the Lowther family. There are many different possible scenarios in which the writ could have become part of Lowther's holdings, and the possibility that **21** once formed part of an ecclesiastical community's muniments should not be ruled out. For example, it may be that the writ came into the possession of the Lowther family following the major upheavals caused by the Reformation, a period when many such documents passed from ecclesiastical archives into lay hands. Another possibility is that the Lowther family, in expanding their landed possessions, came to acquire deeds which once belonged to an ecclesiastical establishment. It was in just such circumstances that Sir John Lowther, having taken ownership of the manor of St Bees in the seventeenth century, then also received the only known copy of the register of the Priory of St Bees, together with various of the Priory's original deeds.[40] In short, any comments regarding the preservation of **21** from the time of its issuing in the mid- or late eleventh century, until its discovery in the Lowther archive, are necessarily speculative and await a comprehensive study of the Lowther archive as a whole.

38 There are also later medieval deeds from Norfolk, Suffolk, Middlesex, Surrey and Rutland; for all of this, and other manuscripts from the Lowther archive, see *Principal Family and Estate Collections: Family Names L–W*, p. 12.

39 For those later deeds in the Lowther archive, see *Principal Family and Estate Collections: Family Names L–W*, pp. 12–13 and Historical Manuscripts Commission, *Thirteenth Report, Appendix, Part VII. The Manuscripts of the Earl of Lonsdale* (London, 1893).

40 Wilson, *St Bees*, pp. xxxvi–xxxvii.

SIGLUM

Note. The siglum A is reserved for original documents and the siglum B for non-contemporary copies on single-sheets.

B. CACC, Lowther of Lowther, DLONSL/5/1/44/C1 (s. xiii–s. xvii)

THE CHARTER OF LOWTHER CASTLE

21

Writ of Gospatric declaring that Thorfynn mac Thore be free with regards to all things that are Gospatric's in Allerdale; and that those men dwelling with Thorfynn at Cardew and Cumdivock be as free, along with him, as Melmor and Thore and Sigulf were; and Thorfynn is also to have jurisdictional rights over all the lands in Cardew and Cumdivock that were given to Thore in the days of Moryn, free from the obligation of providing messengers and witnesses. s. xi$^{\text{mid-ex}}$

B. CACC, Lowther of Lowther, DLONSL/5/1/44/C1: non-contemporary single-sheet, s. xiii–s. xvii, parchment, 254 × 95.25mm

Ed.: a. Liebermann 1903, pp. 276–7, with translation into German and facsimile facing p. 280
b. Ragg 1903, pp. 246–7, with translation
c. Wilson 1904, pp. 66–9, with translation
d. Greenwell 1904, pp. 25–6, with translation
e. Wilson in *VCH Cumb*. ii, pp. 232–3, with translation
f. Ragg 1905, pp. 71–3, with translation
g. Wilson, *St Bees*, pp. 526–7
h. Ragg 1917, pp. 207–9, with translation and facsimile facing p. 207
i. Hinckley 1935, pp. 211–12, with translation
j. B. Dickins in *PN Cumb. III*, pp. xxviii–xxix, with translation and facsimile facing p. xxvi
k. Harmer, *Writs*, no. 121, with translation
l. Phythian-Adams, *Land of the Cumbrians*, p. 173, translation only

Listed: Sawyer 1243; Hart, *ECNE*, no. 134

Gospatrik greot ealle mine ƿassenas ⁊ hƿylkun[a] mann freo ⁊ ðrenge þeo ƿoonnan on eallun þam landann þeo ƿeoron Cōmbres[b] ⁊ eallun mine kynling freondlyce.[c] ⁊ ic cyðe eoƿ[d] ꝥ myne mynna[e] is ⁊ full leof ꝥ Thorfynn Mac Thore beo sƿa freo on eallan ðynges þeo beo myne on Alnerdall sƿa ænyg mann beo, oðer ic oðer ænyg myne ƿassenas, on ƿeald, on freyð, on heyninga, ⁊ æt ællun ðyngan þeo byn eorðe bœnand[f] ⁊ ðeoronðer, to Shauk, to Ƿafyr, to poll Ƿaðœn, to bek Troyte ⁊ þeo ƿeald æt Caldebek. ⁊ ic ƿille ꝥ þeo mann <þe>[g] bydann mið Thorfynn æt Carðeú ⁊ Combeðeyfoch beo sƿa freals myð hem sƿa Melmor ⁊ Thore ⁊ Sygoolf[h] ƿeoron on Eadread dagan. ⁊ ne beo neann mann sƿa [i]ðeorif þehat[i] mið ꝥ ic heobbe gegyfene to hem [j]neghar brech[j] seo[k] gyrth ðyylc[l] Eorl Syƿard ⁊ ic hebbe getyðet hem [m]se frelycc[m] sƿa ænyg mann leofand þeo ƿelkynn ðeoronðer.[n] ⁊ loc hƿylkun[o] byn <þe>[p] þar bydann[q] geyldfreo beo sƿa ic byn ⁊ sƿa [r]Ƿillann <⁊>[r] Ƿallðeof ⁊ Ƿygande ⁊ Ƿyberth ⁊ Gamell ⁊ Kunyth ⁊ eallun mine kynling ⁊ ƿassenas. ⁊ ic ƿille ꝥ Thorfynn heobbe soc ⁊ sac, toll ⁊ theam, ofer eallun þam landan on Carðeu ⁊ on Combedeyfoch ꝥ ƿeoron gyfene Thore on Moryn dagan freols myð bode ⁊ ƿytnesmann on [s]þy ylk[s] stoƿ.

[a] hyylkun B [b] *Line over second letter of* Combres, 'o', *and over first two strokes of third letter,* 'm', *in* B [c] freondlycc B [d] eoẏ B [e] mynua B; *for* unna [f] *for* boouan *(*PN Cumb. III, *p. xxviii)* [g] *Suggested by Ragg 1917, p. 208* [h] *Last three letters of* Sygoolf *illegible owing to destruction of the parchment; reading supplied from previous editions: Liebermann 1903, p. 276 and Wilson 1904, p. 68* [i..i] ðeor of þeaht *(Ragg 1917, p. 212)* [j..j] *Perhaps for* nahwær brece *(see Ragg 1917, p. 214 and Harmer,* Writs, *p. 534)* [k] *For* þæt *(see Ragg 1917, p. 214 and Harmer,* Writs, *p. 534)* [l] *Perhaps a fusion of* þe *and* ilca *(Ragg 1917, p. 215)* [m..m] cefrelycc B [n] ðeorenðer B [o] hyylkun B [p] *Perhaps omitted in copying, for which see commentary* [q] byðann B [r..r] *See commentary for the suggestion that* Þillann *is a personal name and therefore that* ⁊ *has been mistakenly omitted during copying* [s..s] þyylk B

Translation

Gospatric greets all my *wassenas* (?retainers) and every free man and *dreng*, who dwell in all the lands that were Cumbrian and all my kindred in friendly fashion. And I inform you that I give my consent and full permission that Thorfynn mac Thore be as free in all things that are mine in Allerdale as any man may be, either I or any of my *wassenas* (?retainers), in forest, in heathland, in enclosed arable, and in respect of all things that are above the earth and under it, as far as Chalk Beck as the Waver as the Wampool as Wiza Beck and the plain at Caldbeck. And it is my will that the men dwelling with Thorfynn at Cardew and Cumdivock shall be as free, along with him, as Melmor and Thore and Sygoolf[a] were in the days of Eadread. And let no man be so bold that – with what I have given to him [?] – anywhere break the peace which [?] Earl Siward and I have granted him as freely as to any man living under the sky. And look whoever there is that dwells there let them be exempt from geld as I am, [b]and as (are) Willann [and] Waltheof and Wigand and Wiberht and Gamell and Kunyth and all my kindred and *wassenas* (?retainers).[b] And it is my will that Thorfynn shall have soke and sake, toll and team, over all the lands in Cardew and Cumdivock that were given to Thore in the days of Moryn, [c]free from the obligation of providing *bode* and witnessman,[c] in the same place.[d]

[a] *for* ?Sigulf [b..b] *or possibly* and as Waltheof and Wigand and Wiberht and Gamell and Kunyth may wish, and all my kindred and *wassenas* (?retainers); *for which see commentary* [c..c] *or possibly* freely, with the right to claim *bode* and witnessman; *for which see commentary* [d] *Translation based on that by Dickins in* PN Cumb III *and Harmer,* Writs

21 is of great importance both historically (see above, pp. 363–6) and linguistically, as it displays an intermingling of Gaelic, Norse and Brittonic elements which in turn reflect the ethnic composition of Cumbria in the eleventh century (this discussion of **21** is indebted especially to the work of Harmer, *Writs*, pp. 419–24 and 531–6). It is granted in the name of a certain Gospatric, who could either be synonymous with Gospatric (d. 1064), son of Earl Uhtred (d. 1016) or with Gospatric, earl of Northumbria (1067–8 and 1070–2), son of Maldred. Scholarly opinion has been divided on this matter and the wording of the writ makes it difficult to be conclusive; see above, pp. 363–4. **21** was issued at some point in the period from the mid- to the late eleventh century (depending on the identity of Gospatric), at a time when the north-western British kingdom of Strathclyde had recently come to an end. In it, Gospatric grants a range of rights, some of which are normally associated with royal prerogative. The diplomatic formulation of **21** is of great interest; while it broadly conforms to what we would expect of a mainstream English royal writ, it also has idiosyncratic elements which have been introduced on the basis of local, north-western conditions. Although **21** seems fundamentally to be authentic (see the discussion of its diplomatic formulation below), the corruption of various sections suggest the likelihood that it has suffered at least some later rewriting or updating and therefore that some of its terms may not belong to the original Anglo-Saxon writ.

Description of B

21 exists on a single, rectangular sheet of parchment measuring 254mm by 95.25mm, which has been folded three times vertically and once horizontally. The folding of the document has led to some destruction of the parchment and of parts of words that coincide with the folds. It is kept in the Cumbria Archive Centre, Carlisle, formerly the County Record Office. Various facsimiles exist, which have been listed above; the image in Plate 2 is reproduced with kind permission from the owner of the archive, Jim Lowther, and the Lowther Estate Trust. The script of B is very odd. It was dated palaeographically by Ragg and by Harmer to the thirteenth century (Ragg 1917, p. 204 and Harmer, *Writs*, p. 421) and there are certainly features which point to this date, including the presence of the diacritical mark on single **i**, elaborate forked ascenders and a large **a** with the top compartment looped or left open (on the ascenders and the form of **a**, see M.B. Parkes, *English Cursive Book Hands 1250–1500* (Oxford, 1969; repr. London, 1979), pp. xiv–xv). There are also various attempts to recreate Anglo-Saxon letter-forms (including **ð**, **þ**, **s** and long **r**; B also has **ƿ** but sometimes this is confused for **ẏ**; it is never confused where **ƿ** occurs at the beginning of words, only when it is used in the middle; for these forms, see Harmer, *Writs*, p. 531) and this led Harmer to suggest that the thirteenth-century scribe was copying an Anglo-Saxon exemplar which he was trying in part to imitate. But Dr J. Crick and Dr T. Webber have urged caution (pers. comm.). They have both pointed out to me that there are such numerous errors of execution and comprehension of thirteenth-century script (including the very strange ductus of **g**, variation in the form of standard letters like **a** and some badly executed forked ascenders) that it seems likely that this is a late- or post-medieval imitative copy of a thirteenth-century exemplar which itself was relying on an Anglo-Saxon document. For this reason, it seems safest to conclude that B could have been copied at any point between the thirteenth and seventeenth centuries (I am sincerely grateful to Dr J. Crick and Dr T. Webber for their generous advice and guidance).

Editorial Decisions/Conventions

At some point in the textual tradition of **21**, an Anglo-Saxon exemplar was used which a copyist (not necessarily the copyist of B) could not consistently understand or imitate. This has resulted in some obvious copying errors such as the writing of *hyylkun* or *eoy* where the copyist did not recognise the Anglo-Saxon wynn character (*hpylkun* and *eop*); such errors of transcription have been corrected in the edited text of **21** and the manuscript reading reported in the apparatus. Because the copyist struggled at times to interpret his exemplar, this has resulted in the corruption of various parts of the text. It may be that the later copyist, or possibly copiers of previous generations of versions now lost, when confronted with a passage that was difficult to understand or simply illegible, tried to rewrite it and make it comprehensible; but because the copyist's knowledge of Old English was imperfect, the result itself is flawed. This seems the most likely explanation for the highly corrupt sentence *ic heobbe gegyfene...welkynn ðeoronðer*, whose general meaning is clear but whose grammatical details are far from correct; it is discussed in detail by Harmer, *Writs*, p. 422 and pp. 534–4 and also further below. It has proved impossible to know exactly what underlies this sentence but various suggestions have been made either in the edited text itself or in the apparatus.

21 was, in part at least, originally written in a West Saxon dialect; Harmer demonstrates that the forms *ealle*, *peald*, *gret* (*greot*) and *gegyfen* are all typically West Saxon (Harmer, *Writs*, p. 422). It is unclear whether the Northumbrian forms found in **21**, such as *leof*, *freals*, or *mið*, belonged to the original version of **21** or whether they were added at a later stage of copying; Harmer, *ibid.*, p. 422. At some point in its later history, various words in **21** were spelled according to post-Conquest orthographical standards: one example of this is the use of *eo* where simply *e* would be expected in Old English; thus *greot* in the first line of **21** instead of *gret* (Harmer, *ibid.*, p. 422). In its original form **21** would have included Gaelic, Brittonic and Scandinavian words (for example the term *passenas*, which is based on a Brittonic word, and Gaelic *mac*, and Scandinavian *ðrenge* and *heyninga*). All of these idiosyncratic spellings and word-forms, which are valuable evidence for the linguistic historian of the north west of England, have been preserved in the edited text. Where corruption in the text has led to uncertainty, I have made appropriate suggestions in the critical apparatus, making use of pre-existing editions. Different interpretations of particular textual difficulties obviously result in different translations of particular passages; therefore possible alternative translations have been provided as footnotes to the translation and each one is discussed in the commentary to **21**.

Diplomatic Formulation

The overwhelming majority of extant Anglo-Saxon writs are royal grants addressed to a representative group such as a shire court; they can confer privileges or property. The few writs which are not royal grants are usually concerned with litigation or dispute; see, for example, S 1383 (*Sherb* 13). **21** does grant certain standard privileges typical of royal writs (such as sake and soke and toll and team) and employs diplomatic evocative of mainstream English documents. But it is clearly unusual both in the fact that it is in the name of Gospatric rather than the king and in its use of various idiosyncratic diplomatic formulae. As already mentioned, some of its formulae may have been rewritten at a later date during the process of copying. (I am particularly grateful to Dr S.E. Kelly for much helpful discussion of the diplomatic of **21**.)

The protocol of **21**, with the grantor addressing people in the third person *greot*, is entirely standard for an Anglo-Saxon writ (although it is spelt in an unusual way; see above). In **21** we are told that those people being addressed 'live in all the lands that were Cumbrian'; similar geographical descriptions are common in writs and **13** is an example of this. The notification, *ic cyðe eop*, is also standard formulation. What follows the notification in the manuscript is *þ myne mynna is ⁊ full leof þ*. Comparison with **13** in the Beverley archive, which has *hit is min unna 7 min fulle leafe þ*, suggests the likelihood that *mynna* is a misreading for *unna* in Gospatric's writ and this has been suggested in the critical apparatus (this conforms to one of Harmer's categories of writs according to their style of announcement: Harmer, *Writs*, p. 65 and also p. 424 for this instance in **21**).

A very common formula in writs is the use of *swa full ⁊ swa forð swa*, 'as fully and to the same extent as'; **21** has *spa freo…spa ænyg mann beo* which, although not identical, serves the same function (**13** has *spa freols spa ænig oþer mynster is*, which is closer to the form in **21**). **21** delineates that Thorfynn be as free in all things that are Gospatric's in Allerdale, *on peald, on freyð, on heyninga*. This technical expression is more normally given in Anglo-Saxon writs by some combination of *on wuda, on felda, on strande, on streame, on stræte*; see, for example, S 1088, S 1091 (*St Aug's* 35), S 1105, S 1141 and so its adaptation in our example is of importance in showing how these documents could be adjusted to particular local situations; see Harmer, *Writs*, p. 533. Gelling and Cole, *LPN*, p. 225, suggest that *on peald, on freyð, on heyninga* should be translated, 'in forest, in heathland, in enclosed arable'. Gospatric's writ also allows that those men dwelling with Thorfynn at Cardew and Cumdivock shall be 'as free, along with him, as Melmor and Thore and Sygoolf were in the days of Eadread'. This is another variation of the formula *swa freals swa*, and in this instance reference is made to these men having the same level of freedom as Melmor, Thore and Sygoolf had previously possessed. Other Anglo-Saxon writs make similar references to the rights of specific individuals, for example S 1064, S 1076, S 1078 and S 1084.

Most Anglo-Saxon writs contain some kind of prohibition clause and in **21** a slightly unusual variation can be found: *ne beo neann mann spa ðeorif þehat mið þ ic heobbe gegyfene to hem neghar brech seo gyrth*. The reference to *gyrth* is particularly interesting since various other extant writs mention the grant of *griðbrice* (as noted by Harmer, *Writs*, p. 420). This is usually granted alongside other rights such as *hamsocn*, *infangenþeof*, or *fyrdwite* (see, for example, S 1064, S 1065 [*Abing* 148], S 1084, S 1088, S 1091 [*St Aug's* 35]; for the first use of these legal terms, the so-called 'pleas of the crown', see Wormald, *Law I*, p. 310) and here, in Gospatric's writ, the grant seems again to have been adapted according to local usage. Harmer notes that *griðbrice* is a grant of the king's special peace or protection, either from the king himself or from his deputy; Harmer, *Writs*, p. 80. Another right granted by Gospatric is that of freedom from *geyld*, the national land tax paid by landowners to the king; this may be compared to an exemption from *heregeld* (S 1075) and from the payment of *gaful* (S 1131).

Gospatric also grants sake and soke (for which see **2**) and toll and team, which can be found regularly in Anglo-Saxon writs and charters. What is perhaps less common is the notion that Thorfynn was to have the lands in Cardew and Cumdivock, *freols myð bode ⁊ pytnesmann*. As noted in Harmer, *Writs*, p. 535, the phrase is ambiguous and is capable of two interpretations, either, 'free from the obligation of providing *bode* and witnessman' or, 'freely, with (the right to claim) *bode* and witnessman'; the two possibilities are given in my translation. The term '*bode* and witnessman' appears in northern records from Lancashire, Westmorland, Cumberland and Durham in the thirteenth and fourteenth centuries, where it is a service expected of land-holders. By reference to these later contexts, Harmer concludes that in **21** '*bode* and witnessman' 'stands for the duty of providing men to carry messages and to act as witnesses', where 'witnessman' derives from the Old Norse, *uitnismaðr*, and *bode* would stand for the Old English *boda* or the Old Norse *boði*, 'announcer, messenger' (Harmer, *Writs*, p. 535; see also Ragg 1917, pp. 216–17, for the official known as a 'witnessman').

Linguistic Features

The text displays linguistic features unusual for normal Old English grammar, some of which seem to have belonged to the original document. These are discussed fully by Ragg 1917, pp. 209–17, by Harmer, *Writs*, pp. 532–36 and by Breeze 1992; particularly distinctive characteristics are noted here, using the work of these scholars.

The use of the term *wassenas* at three points in the writ demonstrates something of the ethnic context within which the writ was produced. *Wassenas* derives from the Brittonic language spoken in North Britain, Cumbric. Breeze notes that the first element is 'cognate with Cornish *guas*, Old Breton *guos*, Old Irish *foss* 'man-servant, attendant', and Gaulish *–uassos*' (Breeze 1992, p. 272). The same element appears in the beginning of Gospatric's name (for which see above, p. 364). Where Harmer, *Writs*, p. 532, thought that the *—en—* element in *wassenas* was related to the Welsh diminutive suffix, Breeze disagrees and wonders whether here we see a so-called double plural, a mixture of a Cumbric and an English plural form (Breeze 1992, pp. 272–3). The *wassenas* addressed in the writ seem to have been of a similar status to the *dreng* also addressed and, by comparing its use to that of *gweision* in Welsh legal texts and indeed in other contexts, Breeze concludes that *wassenas* must have been an early borrowing by Northumbrian from Cumbric to mean most probably 'retainers' (*ibid.*, pp. 273–4). The word *dreng* is of Old Norse origin and points to Scandinavian influence; Stenton regards the *dreng* as the Scandinavian equivalent of the English *cniht*, a man who held his land by military service (Stenton, *Feudalism*, pp. 146–7; Harmer, *Writs*, p. 532; despite Stenton's simplified analogy, there are perhaps differences between the way the term *dreng* was used in Scandinavia and England, for which see Sharpe, *Norman Rule*, pp. 10–11, n. 10 and references cited therein). Another group of people addressed by Gospatric are described as the *kynling*, a very rare word derived from Old English *cynn*, 'kindred', and presumably with the same meaning (Harmer, *Writs*, p. 533). Thorfynn is here granted freedom in Allerdale and *on peald, on freyð, on heyninga*. For the meanings of these terms and a translation, which has been adopted above in my translation, see M. Gelling, *Place-Names in the Landscape* (London, 1984), p. 223 and Gelling and Cole, *LPN*, p. 225.

On two occasions in **21** we find *hyylkun*; what is probably intended is *hpylk*, the Anglo-Saxon 'wyn' having been miscopied as a *y* (Harmer, *Writs*, p. 532, speculates that *hyylkun* could stand for an 'earlier *gehwylcne*, 'every', with northern omission of *ge-*'). We also see *mann* where the more usual *man* or *men* would be expected. As Ragg points out, *eallum* is rendered *eallun* in the writ as in *eallun þam landan*, which he concludes must be a local dialectal custom (Ragg 1917, pp. 209–10). The unusual *þeo* which occurs several times must be for the pronoun, *se*; Ragg 1917, p. 209.

The phrase *æt ællun ðyngan þeo byn eorðe bænand ⁊ ðeoronðer* is, as Harmer points out, corrupt. She wonders whether there may have been several stages of misreading of this part of the text. She notes that there is no Old English word *bænand* which can be used here but she suggests that it has the meaning 'of all things that are above the earth and under it', where the reference to things under the earth is presumably to some form of mining or quarrying; Harmer, *Writs*, pp. 533–4.

The phrase *⁊ ne beo neann mann spa ðeorif þehat mið þæt ic heobbe gegyfene to hem neghar brech seo gyrth ðyylc Eorl Sypard ⁊ ic hebbe getyðet hem se frelycc spa ænyg mann leofand þeo pelkynn ðeoronðer* offers equally difficult questions of interpretation. It is analysed in detail by Harmer, who ultimately concludes that something may well have been omitted from this part of the text at an early stage and that subsequent copyists may have tried to rewrite it, although doing so with an imperfect understanding of Old English; see Harmer, *Writs*, pp. 534–5. F. W. Ragg also investigates this part of the text in detail. He too notes that something must have been omitted from the text and suggests that a *þæt he* should be inserted after *gegyfene* since the *Spa ðeorif* needs to be balanced; Ragg 1917, pp. 211–13, for a much more detailed explanation.

The *neghar brech* part of the phrase quoted above shows that at some stage after its original issue, a later copyist was not fully comfortable with his Old English exemplar. It seems clear that it represents Old English *nahwær*, 'nowhere', and Ragg's suggestion that *brech* should be the subjunctive form *brece* leads him to believe that the original writer of **21** only knew Old English as an acquired language (Ragg 1917, p. 214 and Harmer, *Writs*, p. 534). *seo gyrth* is also ungrammatical; *gyrth* evidently stands for Old English *grið* (*gryð*). Since *grið* is neuter we would expect the definite article to be the accusative singular form, *þæt*, but what we have is the feminine nominative singular, *seo* (for all of this, see Harmer, *Writs*, p. 534). Further on in the same phrase, reference is made to the grant having been given by Earl Siward and Gospatric 'as freely as to any man living under the sky', where the text of the extant charter reads *cefrelycc spa ænyg mann leofand þeo pelkynn ðeorenðer*. The phrase 'as freely as' in the context of delineating rights is one often used in Anglo-Saxon writs and is normally rendered by the use of *swa...swa*. But a perhaps more logical emendation from *cefrelycc* is to *se frelycc*, since this is closer to what is given in the manuscript and *se* can have the same meaning as *swa* of 'so, as', in Old English; see Harmer, *Writs*, p. 534. (See Ragg 1917, p. 215, for the interesting suggestion that the termination of the verb *getyðet*, which would more normally be *getyðed*, is reminiscent of Scottish practice.) *pelkynn* appears to be a Middle English word, whose Old English equivalent is *wolcnu*, 'sky, heavens'; it was presumably introduced at a later stage of copying: Harmer, *Writs*, p. 534.

The penultimate sentence, *⁊ loc hpylkun byn <þe> þar bydann geyldfreo beo spa ic byn ⁊ spa Þillann, Þallðeof ⁊ Þygande ⁊ Þyberth ⁊ Gamell ⁊ Kunyth ⁊ eallun mine kynling ⁊ passenas* ('and look whoever there is that dwells there let them be exempt from geld as I am, and as (are) Willann, Waltheof, and Wigand and Wiberht and Gamell and Kunyth and all my kindred and *wassenas* (?retainers)'), offers a few complications. Again there is the unusual suffix *–un* in *hpylc*. A more startling reading is *byn þar* and it seems likely that something has been omitted here. The easiest solution is to suggest that the relative pronoun *þe* ('who/which') should be inserted after *byn*. This solves the sense and would be an easily explicable oversight on the part of the copyist (I am very grateful to Dr R. Dance for discussion about this sentence). This emendation has been suggested in angled brackets in my text.

Another problem occurs with the word *pillann*. This could either be taken as a rare personal name, Willann, or as the subjunctive plural of the Old English verb, *willan*, 'to be willing, wish, desire'. Editors have been divided in their opinion (Harmer, *Writs*, p. 424, prefers the personal name; B. Dickins, *PN Cumb. III*, p. xxviii, prefers the verb, *willan*). It may be that the absence of the Tironian sign between Willann and Waltheof should be taken to imply that Willann should not be seen as a name among those other names listed in this clause. If this were the case, the sentence would mean: 'and look whoever there is that dwells there let them be exempt from geld as I am, and as Waltheof and Wigand and Wiberht and Gamell and Kunyth may wish, and all my kindred and *wassenas* (?retainers)'. But it seems to me that this would make less sense in the context. The writ is given in the name of Gospatric and is a grant by him to Thorfynn mac Thore, which is clearly addressed to his subjects. If we were to take *pillann* as a verb, it would serve to elevate Waltheof, Wigand, Wiberht, Gamell and Kunyth to the same status as Gospatric and would detract from the overall point of the writ. It is common practice in Anglo-Saxon writs to find rights being granted and referred to as having been held 'just as X does'. It is distinctly less common to find a grantor donating a right which is only valid if it is confirmed by other magnates in the region. It is quite possible that in the copying process a Tironian sign has been omitted between Willann and Waltheof, especially since there is a queue of them in this line of the manuscript and the copyist's eye could easily have been drawn. The insertion of this Tironian sign has been suggested in angled brackets in my text. To make it clear that *pillann* could also be a verb, I have offered an alternative translation in the critical apparatus to my translation (but see Phythian-Adams, *Land of the Cumbrians*, p. 173, for an alternative view).

Groups of People named in **21**

At one stage in the writ, Gospatric declares that it is his will that the 'men dwelling with Thorfynn at Cardew and Cumdivock shall be as free, along with him, as Melmor (*Melmor*) and Thore (*Thore*) and Sigulf (*Sygoolf*) were in the days of Eadread (*Eadread*)'. Melmor derives from Gaelic (*Máel-Muire*; on the possibility that Melmor gave his name to Melmerby, see Phythian-Adams, *Land of the Cumbrians*, p. 142). Thore is a common Scandinavian name. It occurs three times in **21**, the first as the father of Thorfynn, the second in connection with Melmor and Sigulf and the third as an owner of lands in Cardew and Cumdivock. The popularity of the name makes it difficult to assert with confidence that all three of those people named in the writ are the same person and I agree with Harmer in this (Harmer, *Writs*, p. 574; but see Phythian-Adams, *Land of the Cumbrians*, pp. 176–7, who strongly disagrees; Phythian-Adams also makes the interesting suggestion that Thursby, which lies to the west of Cardew and Cumdivock, may have been one of those places granted to Thore in Moryn's day, at pp. 141 and 177; and at p. 150, for the identification of various settlement names ending in *–by* around Carlisle which may date to Siward's rule of the area and which may represent his attempt to introduce a new ruling elite into the area). The Eadred (*Eadread*) mentioned in **21** has been much discussed. Davis accepted Ragg's suggestion that the later copyist had incorrectly transcribed *Eadread* from *Ealdred*, which they both thought was a reference to Ealdred, the son of Uhtred, and earl of Northumbria from 1019 to 1038 (see Davis 1905, p. 63). But Eadred is a common name in its own right and, given the difficulties in dating **21**, there seems no reason to fasten on an identification with Ealdred (see also Harmer, *Writs*, p. 559 and Phythian-Adams, *Land of the Cumbrians*, p. 176). **21** seems to suggest that Eadred was Thorfynn's predecessor at Cardew and Cumdivock.

In another part of **21**, Gospatric allows that 'whoever there is that dwells there let them be exempt from geld as I am, and as (are) Willann (*Ƿillann*) [and] Waltheof (*Ƿallðeof*) and Wigand (*Þygande*) and Wiberht (*Þyberth*) and Gamell (*Gamell*) and Kunyth (*Kunyth*) and all my kindred and *wassenas* (?retainers)'. Of these, Wigand is an Old German name, Wiberht is Old English (*Wigbeorht*; or possibly Old German *Wigbert*), Gamell is a very common Scandinavian loan-name and Kunyth seems to be derived from Old Welsh, *Cennydd* (all of this information is taken from the relevant entries in Harmer, *Writs*, Part IV, pp. 546 ff.). If we are correct to suggest that Willann is a personal name rather than a verb (see above), then it may be that his name is a replacement for an earlier version, *Weland*; see Harmer, *Writs*, p. 577. This list of names is another reminder of the mix of ethnicities in the north west.

Boundaries and places named in **21**

21 tells us that the bounds of freedom granted to Thorfynn were in Allerdale, whose northern and eastern limits are described as extending 'as far as Chalk Beck (*Shauk*) as the Waver (*Wafyr*) as the Wampool (*poll Waðœn*) as Wiza Beck (*bek Troyte*) and the plain at Caldbeck (*Caldebek*)'. *Shauk* is derived from the Old British *Scawāco-*, 'abounding in elders'; it joins the River Wampool near Thursby (Harmer, *Writs*, p. 533). The River Waver connects with the sea at Solway Firth; its name in the writ, *Wafyr*, may derive from the Old English *Wæfre*, reflecting the 'wandering' nature of its course. The Wampool also flows into the Solway Firth but to the north of the River Waver (Harmer, *Writs*, p. 533). The *poll* element of this name means 'pool, stream' (it could derive from Old Irish *poll*, Welsh *pwll* or Old English *pōl*) while the remaining element is uncertain (*PN Cumb. I*, p. 30, point out that Ekwall's equation of this uncertain element with Old Norse *uaðill*, 'ford', is unsustainable; see also *CamDEPN*, p. 649); the order of the place-name elements as *poll Waðœn* is inverted in the Celtic manner. *bek Troyte* (Wiza Beck) is similarly inverted; it is probably formed of Old Norse *bekkr* and the personal name *Troyte*. It flows into the River Wampool near Wigton (Harmer, *Writs*, p. 533). Caldbeck (*Caldebek*) is the most southerly of the rivers in **21** (Harmer, *Writs*, p. 533). It means 'cold stream' and derives from the Old Norse *kaldr* and *bekkr* (for all of these derivations, and for the locations of the bounds, see the relevant entries in *PN Cumb. I–III* and *CamDEPN* and also Harmer, *Writs*, p. 533).

Gospatric also desired that those men living with Thorfynn 'at Cardew (*Carðeú*) and Cumdivock (*Combeðeyfoch*) shall be as free, along with him, as Melmor and Thore and Sygoolf were in the days of Eadread'. Cardew and Cumdivock are two towns in the parish of Dalston, south of Carlisle and near the Chalk Beck (Harmer, *Writs*, p. 534; for more about these towns, see Phythian-Adams, *Land of the Cumbrians*, pp. 147–9). *Carðeú* may be derived from *caer-ddu*, 'the black caer' and *Combeðeyfoch* might be from the British **cumbā*, 'valley', combined with the personal name, **Dubācos* (see *PN Cumb. I*, pp. 131–2; Cardew belonged to the later barony of Dalston for which, see Ragg 1917, pp. 198–218).

APPENDIX I

Inventory of Church Treasures at Sherburn-in-Elmet. s. xi[med]

D. York, Minster Library, Add. 1, 161r: Old English Addition, s. xi[med]
Ed.: a. Raine, *Fabric Rolls*, p. 142
b. Birch 1324
c. Stevenson 1912, p. 9
d. Robertson, *Charters*, Appendix II, no. 2
Listed: Ker, *Catalogue*, no. 402d

Þis syndon þa cyrican madmas on Scirburnan · ꝥ synd tƿa Xp̄es[a] bec · 7 II. rodan · 7 I. aspiciens · 7 I. adteleuaui · 7 II. pistolbec · 7 I. mæsseboc · 7 I. ymener · 7 I. salter · 7 .I. calic · 7 .I. disc · 7 tƿa mæssereaf · 7 III. mæssehakelan · 7 II. ƿeouedsceatas · 7 II. ouerbrædels · 7 IIII. handbellan · 7 VI. hangendebellan.

[a] *Abbreviation for* Cristes

Translation[a]

These are the church treasures at Sherburn: namely, two gospel books, and two crosses, and one *Aspiciens*, and one *Ad te leuaui*, and two epistolaries, and one sacramentary, and one hymnal, and one psalter, and one chalice, and one paten, and two mass vestments, and three chasubles and two altar cloths and two altar covers, and four hand-bells and six hanging bells.

[a] Translation taken from Keynes 1986, p. 97

This list of church furniture, vestments and liturgical books belonging to Sherburn-in-Elmet can be dated palaeographically to the mid-eleventh century (Ker, *Catalogue*, no. 402d). It may be compared to a similar inventory surviving in the Durham manuscript, CCCC 183, on f. 96v, for which see Robertson, *Charters*, pp. 250–1. The *Aspiciens* was an antiphonary and the *Ad te leuaui* was a gradual (see Lapidge 1985, pp. 56–7; Gneuss 1985, p. 117 and p. 103, respectively and Keynes 1986, pp. 96–7; for what this antiphonary implies about the singing of the Office in smaller communities of secular clerks, see Giandrea, *Episcopal Culture*, p. 78).

As discussed by Keynes, the preservation of this inventory in the York Gospels, may imply that the manuscript had once resided at Sherburn. But, as Keynes points out, Wulfstan's role in the insertion of **7** into the Gospels must mean that the manuscript was at York during his lifetime and it was certainly kept there during the later medieval period (see Keynes 1986, p. 97).

APPENDIX 2

The List of Ælfric's Festermen. s. xi^med

D. York, Minster Library, Add. 1, f. 161v: copy, s. xi^ex
Ed.: a. Stevenson 1912, pp. 12–13
b. Farrer, *EYC*, no. 9
Listed: Ker, *Catalogue*, no. 402f

Ðis sindan þa festermen Elfricas: Ulfcetel · cyninges réue · 7 Merlespuain · Ƿulstain · Ulf · Ligolf · Barað · Farðain greua · [a]\7 Ascetel/[a] · Ósulf 7 Ƿulfeh · Folcric 7 Elfric · Ƿegga 7 Áldsceorl · Gamal pres<byter>[b] · Grim 7 Grimcetel · Asmund roš[c] · Grimcetel in Barnabi · Godƿina · Folč[d] · Berhðor · Bretecol 7 Árðolf · 7 Forna · Menning 7 Ƿulger · Þór in Cǎ[e] 7 Arcetel · Siuerð · Rauan · Arň[f] · Colbrand[g] cě[h] · Blíh · Elfƿine uel[i] · Snel · Godƿine · Lef̌ · Eðastan · Ulf̌ · Elnoð · Frě · Roscetel 7 Edric · Grimcetel Háp̌ · Ascetel · Grím in Ciř[j] · Cetel pres<byter>[b] · Gunner · Alfcetel[k] in Hǎ[l] · Ioluarð in Burhtun · Ulfcetel pres<byter>[b] · Alfcetel 7 Asmund · Leofnoð in Broðortun · Þorcetel Unbainas<una>[m] · Ulf pres<byter>[b] · Þirne beorn · 7 Áilaf in Braiþatun · Ƿúlfric[n] 7 Iustan · Rót in Hillum · . . . orfana[o] 7 Gr<im>cetel[p] hís mah · Raganald Asbeornnas suna · Órd ru[q] . . . proh[r] in Bærnabi · Hálpærð Sæfugalasuna 7 Arðor[s] . . . ldolf[t] pres<byter>[b] · Auðcetel pres<byter>.[b]

[a...a] *Interlineated above* Farðain greua *in* D [b] D *has* pš *where the mark of suspension implies an abbreviated form of* pres; -byter *has been supplied in the edited text* [c] roš *is either a nickname of* Asmund *or a shortened form of a separate name; the symbol* ˇ *is used throughout the text as a mark of abbreviation by suspension* [d] *This is either a shortened form of some compound name in* Folc- *or a nickname of* Godƿina [e] Cǎ *is probably for* Ca<wuda> [f] *This is probably a shortened form of some compound name in* Arn- [g] *The initial* C *in* Colbrand *has been altered from* G *by erasure in* D [h] *The meaning here is obscure*
[i] D *has* uł *which is a standard abbreviation for* uel*; but the lack of a point before it in* D *might suggest that the Latin conjunction is not the correct reading; Farrer,* EYC*, no. 9 suggests the possible reading* Ule [j] *Perhaps for* Cir<cebi>*; see Stevenson 1912, p. 13, n. 54*
[k] *The* t *in* Alfcetel *is faded* D [l] *Perhaps for some form of the place-name 'Hambleton'; see commentary and Keynes 1986, p. 98* [m] *The* s *in* Unbainas *is faded* D*; the termination* -una *is suggested by Stevenson 1912, p. 13* [n] *Part of the* r *in* Ƿúlfric *is faded* D [o] *The manuscript is damaged here which has meant that the initial capital letter of this word has been obscured; the letter* r *in* ...orfana *is uncertain and the* n *could also be a* r *whose descender has been removed because of damage to the manuscript; Farrer,* EYC*, p. 28, n.1, suggests this could read* þor fara*; see also Stevenson 1912, p. 13, n. 59* [p] *The* -im- *in* Gr<im>cetel *are missing because of damage to the manuscript* [q] *There is a space of about five or six letters after* ru

which occurs at the end of the line, perhaps because the copyist could not decipher his exemplar. The beginning of the next line, for the space of about fourteen or fifteen letters, is missing owing to damage in the manuscript; see also Stevenson 1912, p. 13, n. 61 [r] *The* r *in* proh *could be the upper part of an* f *or* r*; Stevenson 1912, p. 13, n. 62* [s] *A space at the end of the line of about five or six letters follows* Arðor D [t] *A space of about twenty-two letters has been omitted at the beginning of this line because of damage to the manuscript; the lower parts of the* l *and* d *in* ldolf *have also been lost* D*; see Stevenson 1912, p. 13, n. 64*

This list of *festermen* was added to the York Gospels at some point in the late eleventh century (Ker, *Catalogue*, no. 402f); it is a copy of a document which itself was compiled before the Norman Conquest (Stevenson 1912, pp. 11–12); for a thorough discussion of this list, see Keynes 1986, pp. 98–9, to which this present analysis is indebted. It is impossible to know exactly how many individuals are represented in the list since it is unclear whether certain entries are nicknames or surnames of persons already mentioned or whether they might represent different individuals; damage to the end of the list has also resulted in the loss of some names. But it is evident that between seventy and eighty people are listed. The word *festerman* is of Scandinavian origin and means 'a man who stands bail or surety'; the *festermen* here were most likely standing as surety for Ælfric in some kind of land transaction (see Cooper 1969, p. 331 and Keynes 1986, p. 99; for more about the term *festerman*, its use in Northumbria and the reasons why these men would have been standing as sureties for Ælfric, see above, pp. 6–8).

Since Ælfric himself is not given a title, scholars have disagreed on the question of his identity. Farrer, *EYC*, p. 28, and Cooper 1969, p. 332, were both reluctant to accept that this Ælfric was one and the same as Ælfric 'Puttoc', archbishop of York from 1023 to 1051. For Cooper, it was unlikely that a man of archiepiscopal status would need men to stand as surety either for his reliability or as guarantors of a land transaction. She thought it more likely that this Ælfric was a prominent Yorkshire landowner, a man who probably had roots near Sherburn-in-Elmet, given that nine of the *festermen* themselves came from this area (for these nine *festermen*, see further below). But the preservation of the list in the York Gospels—among a series of other Old English additions, one of which (**7**) concerns land that belongs to the York archbishopric—suggests that the identification of Ælfric as archbishop is the most logical explanation. He was perhaps not given his title because it was considered clear to whom the record referred, and the fact that nine of the *festermen* came from the vicinity of Sherburn-in-Elmet may simply be reflective of the York church's long-standing influence in that area (for this identification, see Stevenson 1912, p. 11 and Keynes 1986, p. 99; for the York church's involvement in the Sherburn-in-Elmet area see, for example, **6** and **7**).

The list begins with Ulfcetel who is described as being the 'king's reeve' (*cyninges réue*); six other men, 'Gamal' (ON Gamall; for this, and all of the following ON derivations, see the relevant entries in Fellows-Jensen, *SPNLY*), 'Cetel' (ON Ketill), 'Ulfcetel' (ON Ulfketill), 'Ulf' (ON Ulfr), '...ldolf' and 'Auðcetel' (ON Auðketill), are given the title of priest (*presbyter*). But these are the only men in the whole list to be allotted any kind of title. The other men listed were probably landholders in Yorkshire and the high level of Scandinavian names, as one would expect of the Danelaw, would seem to corroborate this (Keynes 1986, p. 98). For nine of the men a place of origin is given, presumably, as Keynes notes, to differentiate them from other men with the same name (see Keynes 1986, p. 98): 'Grimcetel in Barnabi' (ON Grímketill) and '...proh in Bærnabi' probably came from Barmby-on-the-Marsh; 'Þór in Cā ' (ON Þórr) probably came from Cawood; 'Grím in Cir̄ ' (ON Grímr) probably came from Kirkby-Wharfe; 'Alfcetel in Hā ' (ON Alfketill) probably came from Hambleton; 'Ioluarð in Burhtun' (ON Jólvarðr) probably came from Burton Hall in Brayton (*PN YorksWR* IV, pp. 27 and 40; but Farrer, *EYC*, p. 28, prefers an identification of Burton Salmon); 'Leofnoð in Broðortun' probably came from Brotherton; 'Áilaf in Braiþatun' probably came from Brayton and 'Rót in Hillum' probably came from Hillam. As Farrer, *EYC*, p. 28, and Keynes 1986, p. 98, point out, all of these places are situated very close to the archiepiscopal estate of Sherburn-in-Elmet; and in fact Cawood, Brayton, Brotherton, Hillam and Burton are all listed in **7 (a)** as part of the soke belonging to Sherburn.

As pointed out by Keynes 1986, p. 99, positive identification of these *festermen* is hindered by the lack of extant comparative documentation. Various names among the *festermen*, 'Ulfcetel' (ON Ulfketill), 'Farðain' (ON Farþegn), 'Forna' (ON Forni) and 'Rauan' (ON Rafn), appear also in the witness-list of **8**, a charter of King Cnut granting land at Patrington to Archbishop Ælfric, and so there is at least the possibility that these were the same people (see also above, p. 8, n. 34). The name of the first *festerman*, Ulfcetel the king's reeve, can be found (as some derivation of 'Ulchil') listed among the 1066 landholders in GDB (Fellows-Jensen, *SPNLY*, p. 326 and Keynes 1986, p. 99); and, while it is possible that this is a reference to the same Ulfcetel, it is impossible to know to how many different individuals the instances in GDB refer. 'Merleswuain' (ON Merlesveinn), the second *festerman* listed, seems to be one and the same as the 'Merlesuen' of GDB, who was sheriff of Lincoln (Fellows-Jensen, *SPNLY*, p. 196 and Keynes 1986, p. 99). Many of the names of the other *festermen* can also be found listed in GDB; but until the evidence for landholding in GDB has been properly investigated, it cannot be said with certainty whether any of these instances refer to the same individual (Farrer, *EYC*, p. 28, nonetheless attempts such identifications; the new project based at King's College, London, 'Domesday Book: Profile of a Doomed Elite', will do much to help such investigations). Because some of the *festermen* are described as coming from the vicinity of Sherburn-in-Elmet (see above), it may be that we should expect many of the other *festermen* listed as coming from the same area (Keynes 1986, p. 99).

INDEXES

In these indexes ƿ of the MSS is replaced with **w** and **uu** is alphabetised as **w**. Except in Index 3, **ð** and **þ** have been replaced by **th**. Charters are referred to by their numbers, in bold type; other numbers refer to the pages of the introduction or the commentaries.

1. INDEX OF PERSONAL NAMES

The forms of name have mostly been normalised and the various textual readings are provided in accompanying parentheses. Where so-called 'original' forms of name are unclear, I have always followed the form of name given in the text. This is an index of names and titles rather than of individuals. Therefore no attempt is made to distinguish individuals with the same name or who held more than one office. Where two or more bishops of a see had the same name, they are distinguished by the numbers that have conventionally been assigned to them. The majority of names in Ælfric's list of *festermen* (edited as Appendix 2) have not been included in this index.

2. INDEX OF PLACE-NAMES

3. WORDS AND PERSONAL NAMES IN BOUNDARY CLAUSES

dile, 'dill'. *þere dil halle* **2**(ii)
dreng, 'warrior'. *to dreng haga* **2**(iii)
dun, 'a hill, an expanse of open hill-country'. *to cpeorn dune, of cpeorn dune* **2**(iv)

eald, 'old'. *se ealda stream* **2**(i), *on þa ealdarn treot* **2**(ii), *⁊lang þare ealdan strat* **2**(iii); *on þa ealdan dic* **5**
earn, 'eagle'. *to earearnes hoh, to earnes hoh* **8**
east, 'east'. *East* **4**; *east onan* **5**; *to þaes dices east and* **8**
efes, 'eaves, an edge or border (esp. of a wood)'. *be suðan ðam esete* **2**(i) (see commentary)
eg, 'island'. ? *da cy* **4** (see commentary)
ende, 'end'. *to þaes dices east and* **8**

feld, 'open country, cleared land'. *þone felð* **3**(i); *on felda* **4**
fen, 'fen, marsh'. *þaes fennes* **8**
fleot, 'small stream'. *fule fleot, ⁊lang fleotes* **2**(iii); *Brodan fleote* **3**(ii); *Pateringatune fleotes muðan, andlang þaes fleotes up to cros fleotes, mid þam fleote* **8**
ford, 'ford'. *of ðam forda, on þone ford* **2**(i); *on hasele forð, of ðam forda* **2**(iv); *of langan forda dic, on langan forð* **3**(i), *of fulan forda, on langan forð, eft on fulan forð* **3**(ii)
ful, 'foul'. *fule fleot* **2**(iii); *on þone fulan broc* **3**(i); *of fulan forda, on langan forð, eft on fulan forð* **3**(ii)

gerihte, 'directly, straight'. *on gerihte* **2**(i)
graf, 'coppiced wood'. *þane graf* **2**(i); *to þam grafe, mid þone graf* **3**(ii)
grene, 'green'. *grene peges* **5**

hæsel, 'hazel'. *on hasele forð* **2**(iv)
haga, 'enclosure, hedge'. *andlang þas hagan* **2**(ii); *to dreng haga* **2**(iii)
haugr (ON), 'hill, tumulus, mound'. *þing hougum* **5**
heafod, 'head, headland, projecting piece of land'. *be þan heafdan* **2**(i); *a be þan heafidan* **2**(ii)
healh, 'small hollow, dip, nook, corner'. *þere dil halle* **2** (ii)
hege, 'hedge'. *þan on hise, a be þare hicse* **2**(ii)
herepæð, 'highway'. *on ðone herepoð* **4**
hid, 'hide, measure of land'. *hida, healfe hide on Hibaldes tofte, ⁊ ane hide on Fryþetune, ⁊ on Stiuetune ⁊ on Miclanfelda ii hyda landes ⁊ eal Luttringtun butan anre hide ⁊ oder healf hyde on Fentune ⁊ oðre healf hyde on Kapuda* **4**
hlæw, 'burial mound, tumulus'. *to Saxferdes lape, of Saxferdes lapa, to brugun lapa, of rugun lapa, to fif lapan* **5**
hlinc, 'ridge, bank, strip-linchet, cultivation terrace'. *⁊lang broces ꝥ up be þan hlince* **2**(i)
hocer, 'a hump, a rounded hill'. *Hocerpuda* **2**(iii)
hoh, 'hill-spur'. *to earearnes hoh, to earnes hoh* **8**
hol, 'hollow'. *on holan broc* **2**(i); *on hole dic* **8**
holmr, 'an isle, a small island, a water-meadow'. *besuðan sunninsale holme* **2**(i); *to bradan holm* **8**

igil, 'hedgehog', *ylemere (*for ? *igil + mere)* **5** (see commentary)

lang, 'long'. *of langan forda dic, on langan forð* **3**(i); *on langan forð* **3**(ii)
land-gemære, 'boundary, estate-boundary'. *landgemare* **2**(i); *longemaere* **2**(ii); *landgemare* **2**(iii); *landgemare* **2**(iv); *landgemara* **3**(i); *landgemarei* **3**(ii); *Landgemara* **4**; l*andgemaera* **5**; *landgemare* **8**
leah, 'clearing, wood'. *on bradan lege* **2**(i); *beo lege, beo leage* **3**(i)

(ge)mære, 'boundary'. *gemaere* **5**
mearc, 'boundary'. *yrd merce* **8**
mere, 'mere, pond'. *ylemere (*for ? *igil + mere)* **5** (see commentary); *þon meare, to sealtan meare (*see commentary and **mersc***)* **8**
mersc, 'marsh'. *to sealtan meare (*see commentary and **mere***), Sumeres mersc* **8**
micel, 'big, great'. *miclan beorh* **2**(iii); *miclan dic, miclan strat* **3**(i)
middeweard, 'the middle part of'. *middepeardne* **3**(ii); *middenpeard* **8**
mor, 'moor, marsh, wasteland'. *ofer þaene mor, inon þaene mor* **2**(iii)
muða, 'mouth [of a river]'. *Pateringatune fleotes muðan* **8**

niwe, 'new'. *durħ nipa tunes broc* **2**(i); *on nipan tunes broc* **2**(iv)
norþ, 'north'. *on þone norðran þorn* **2**(i); *norð ut þone felð* **3**(i); *norð* **4**; *norð, norð to ylemere, norð on þa dic* **5**
norðweard, 'to the north of, to the north part of, on the north side of'. *norðepeardan* **2**(iii)

oxangang, 'oxgang; an eighth of a "plough-land", hide'. *tpegra oxenagang, on Lundby tpegra Oxenagang* **4**

pytt, 'pit'. *on pit, to pitte* **8**

ruh, 'rough, shaggy, uncultivated'. *to brugun lapa, of rugun lapa* **5**

Saxferth (pers. n.). *to Saxferdes lape, of Saxferdes lapa* **5**
scearp, 'sharp, pointed', perhaps also 'steep'. *scearpan brycge* **4**
scela, 'a temporary hut'. *to scelle toft* **8** [or **stell**]
scypen, 'cow-shed'. *to scare scypne* **8**
sealt, 'salt'. *to sealtan meare* **8**
sic, 'small stream' (Old Norse: 'a ditch, a trench'). *on þene sic, ⁊lang sices* **5**; *mid þam sice* **8**
Skroppa (pers. n.) ? *Scroppenþorpe* **3**(i)
slæd, 'slade, valley, especially wet, flat-bottomed valley'. *⁊lang sledes* **4**
stan, 'stone'. *to þan stane* **8**
stell, 'enclosure'. *to scelle toft* **8** [or **scela**]
stræt, 'road, often Roman road'. *of cottan andlang stræte* **2**(i); *on þa ealdarn treot, ⁊lang straet* **2**(ii); *⁊lang þare ealdan strat, of þære strat* **2**(iii); *streot* **2**(iv); *miclan strat, ⁊lang strat* **3**(i); *⁊lang stret* **3**(ii); *serirtre (*for ? *stræt*; see commentary*), on þa strete, of þere strete, ꝥ eft to saerirtre (*for ? *stræt*; see commentary*)* **5**
stream, 'stream, water-course'. *se ealda stream* **2**(i)

suð, 'south'. *suð ⁊lang peges, suð andlang denes* **5**
suðeweard, 'to the south of, the south part of'. *suðepearde* **3**(i); *suðepeardan* **4**; *suðpeard* **5**

toft, 'homestead, site of a house'. *Hibaldes tofte* **4**; *scelle toft* **8**
tun, 'farm, village'. *ðurħ nipa tunes broc* **2**(i), *on nipan tunes broc* **2**(iv)

þing, 'assembly, council'. *þing hougum* **5**
þorn, 'thorn tree'. *on þone norðran þorn, of þam þorne on Greotan* **2**(i); *anes þornes* **5**
þorp, 'farm, village'. *bepestan þorp* **8**
Þurir (ON Þorir) (pers. n.). *Þuresby* **3**(i)

(ge)wæd, 'a ford'. *gepeade* **3**(i)
wæter, 'water'. *on pæter* **4**
weg, 'way'. *⁊lang peges, on ðone peg* **4**; *peg, þes grene peges, up to þan pege, andlang peges, ⁊lang peges* **5**
well, 'spring'. *earnes hoh pelle* **8**
west, 'west'. *pest* **4**; *pest, pest to þan dice* **5**
westweard, 'westward, in the west'. *peastepearde* **2**(i)
wold, spelling of **weald**, 'forest, wood'. *up one palde* **5**
wudu, 'wood'. *Hocerpuda* **2**(iii); *on puda* **4**

yrð, 'earth'. *yrð merce* **8**

4. LATIN GLOSSARY

The following abbreviations are used: n. = noun; v. = verb; adj. = adjective; p.p. = past participle; sp. = spelling.

agius (adj., from Greek ἅγιος) [**4**]: holy
altitronus (adj.) [**5**]: high-throned (epithet of the Deity)
anathema (n.) [**11**]: curse, anathema
Angligena (n.) [**4, 8**]: English-born man or woman
antistes (n.) [**17**]: bishop
apex (n.) [**1, 3**]: letter, character
archipresul (n.) [**11**]: archbishop
astipulatio (n.) [**4**]: confirmation, support

baratrum (n., from Greek βάραθρον) [**5**]: Hell
basileus, basilius (n., from Greek βασιλεύς) [**5**]: king, ruler

carta (n.) [**8**]: charter
cartula (n.) [**4**]: charter
cas(s)atus (n.) [**3, 4, 5, 8**]: a measure of land, a hide
cleronomus (n., from Greek κληρονόμος) [**5**]: heir
cliuippa (n.) [**1**]: some form of musical instrument
constipulator (n.) [**1**]: supporter, witness
cosmus (n., from Greek κόσμος) [**5**]: world

debacchari, ~are (v.) [**1**]: to rage, vent fury (on)
deificus (adj.) [**3**]: divine, godly (w. *contemplatio*) beatific vision

eiulandus (gerundive) [**1**]: to be bewailed

fellitus (adj.) [**1**]: steeped in gall

gabulus (n.) [**4**]: gallows, *hence* cross
gnosticus (n., from Greek *γνωστικός*) [**5**]: learned man, one who knows
grammula (n.) [**1**]: letter, character

ierarchia (n., sp. for *hierarchia*, from Greek *ἱεραρχία)* [**1**]: (holy) rule, hierarchy
immarcessibilis (adj., sp. for *immarcescibilis*) [**1**]: unfading
impertio (v.) [**4**]: to give, grant
indiculum (n.) [**1**]: charter

karisma (n., from Greek *χάρισμα)* [**4**]: gift

mansa (n.) [**2**]: a measure of land, a hide
metropolis (n., from Greek *μητρόπολις*) [**11**]: see of a metropolitan archbishop, cathedral church in which the throne of a metropolitan archbishop is sited
metropolitanus (n.) [**11**]: metropolitan, archbishop

omnicreans (adj.) [**4**]: the all-creator, God
omnipatrans (adj.) [**1**]: all-accomplishing, almighty

poliandrium (n., sp. for *polyandrium*, from Greek *πολυανδρειον*) [**1**]: cemetery, common burial place
priuilegium (n.) [**11**]: privilege, charter

sartago (n.) [**3, 8**]: frying-pan, instrument of torture
satago (v.) [**3, 8**]: to endeavour
scedula (n.) [**1, 8**]: written document, charter
sigillum (n.; see also *sygillum*) [**4, 11**]: sign, seal
signaculum (n.) [**4**]: sign, mark
sinodus (n., sp. for *synodus*) [**17**]: ecclesiastical gathering, synod
soma (n., from Greek *σωμα*) [**1**]: body
sophia (n., from Greek *σοφία*) [**5**]: wisdom
spiramen (n.) [**4**]: breath
sygillum (n.; see also *sigillum*) [**2**]: sign, seal

teter (adj., for *taeter*) [**1, 3, 8**]: foul, noisome, offensive
tanaliter (adv., perhaps from Grecism *thanataliter*) [**1**]: mortally

5. DIPLOMATIC INDEX

1. Verbal invocations and proems

(a) *Invocations*

(b) *Proems*

2. Dispositive words

(a) *Present tense*

(b) *Perfect tense*

3. *Royal styles*

	(A) *Dispositive section*	(B) *Subscription*
Ecgfrith, **17**	rex Northimbrorum	
Æthelstan, **1**	rex Anglorum per omnipatrantis dexteram, que Christus est, totius Britannie regni solio sublimatus	rex
Eadwig, **2**	rex Anglorum	rex
Edgar, **3**	industrius Anglorum rex ceterarumque gentium persistentium gubernator et rector	rex Anglorum
Edgar, **4**	omnicreantis disponente clementia Angligenarum omniumque gentium undique secus habitantium rex	gratia Dei totius Britannie telluris dominus
Edgar, **5**	totius Britannie basilius	rex Anglorum
Cnut, **8**	omnipotentis Dei disponente clementia Angligenarum omniumque gentium undique secus habitantium rex	rex Anglorum
Edward, **11**	rex Anglorum	Anglorum rex